CHARLES DICKENS

THE PUBLIC READINGS

REGISTERED AT THE GENERAL POST OFFICE FOR TRANSMISSION ABROAD.

No. 442.   LONDON, SATURDAY, MARCH 19, 1870.   Vol. XVIII.

MR. CHARLES DICKENS'S FAREWELL READING AT ST. JAMES'S HALL, ON TUESDAY NIGHT.—SEE NEXT PAGE

The Final Farewell Reading, St. James' Hall, London, 15 March 1870. From the *Penny Illustrated Paper*, 19 March 1870

CHARLES DICKENS

The Public Readings

edited by

PHILIP COLLINS

CLARENDON PRESS · OXFORD
1975

Oxford University Press, Ely House, London W.1

GLASGOW NEW YORK TORONTO MELBOURNE WELLINGTON
CAPE TOWN IBADAN NAIROBI DAR ES SALAAM LUSAKA ADDIS ABABA
DELHI BOMBAY CALCUTTA MADRAS KARACHI LAHORE DACCA
KUALA LUMPUR SINGAPORE HONG KONG TOKYO

ISBN 0 19 812501 1

*Printed in Great Britain
by William Clowes & Sons, Limited, London, Beccles and Colchester*

PREFACE

THIS is the first complete edition of Dickens's public-reading texts. Of the twenty-one items, ten have never been published before and one (the famous *Sikes and Nancy*) has appeared only in a limited edition of 275 copies. Only two items have hitherto been published with editorial or textual commentary: *Mrs. Gamp* and *A Christmas Carol*, recently produced in facsimile by the New York Public Library.

The texts are printed from Dickens's own copies, all but four of which contain his manuscript emendations, performance-signs, and other marginalia. In some cases more than one Dickens copy has survived; in a few others it is evident that an earlier or later version existed, which either has not survived or has not come to this editor's attention. Dickens kept revising and abbreviating his reading-texts while they remained in repertoire; the versions printed in this edition are, so far as can be established, his final ones. The headnote to each item contains an account of the circumstances of its composition and the development of its text, and particulars about how he performed these items, drawn from various contemporary accounts, published and manuscript. His underlining of passages, for special effect or emphasis, is represented by italics, and his marginal stage-directions are given in the footnotes. The conventions of italicization, etc., are explained in the final section of the Introduction. It is hoped that, without deploying an inordinate amount and complexity of annotation, the edition presents both a readable text and a tolerably full picture of how Dickens evolved and read these items and how audiences responded in Britain, France, and America during the years (1853 to 1870) of his platform appearances as a solo reciter.

University of Leicester   P.A.W.C.
July 1973

CONTENTS

LIST OF PLATES ix

ACKNOWLEDGEMENTS xi

REFERENCES AND ABBREVIATIONS xv

INTRODUCTION xvii

1. The History of the Readings xvii
2. Number of Performances, and other Figures xxv
3. The Preparation of the Texts xxx
4. The Prompt-copies: their Later History xxxvi
5. The Published Editions xlii
6. The Victorian Soloist Tradition xlvi
7. The Performer and the Novelist liii
8. The Present Edition: Aims, Procedures, and Conventions lxvi

A CHRISTMAS CAROL 1

THE CRICKET ON THE HEARTH 35

THE CHIMES 75

THE HAUNTED MAN 103

THE STORY OF LITTLE DOMBEY 125

THE POOR TRAVELLER 153

BOOTS AT THE HOLLY-TREE INN 167

MRS. GAMP 181

BARDELL AND PICKWICK 195

DAVID COPPERFIELD 214

NICHOLAS NICKLEBY AT THE YORKSHIRE SCHOOL 249

THE BASTILLE PRISONER 279

MR. CHOPS, THE DWARF 295

GREAT EXPECTATIONS   305

MR. BOB SAWYER'S PARTY   365

DOCTOR MARIGOLD   379

MRS. LIRRIPER'S LODGINGS   401

BARBOX BROTHERS   421

THE BOY AT MUGBY   445

THE SIGNALMAN   453

SIKES AND NANCY   465

LIST OF PLATES

The Final Farewell Reading, St. James' Hall, London, 15 March 1870. From the *Penny Illustrated Paper*, 19 March 1870

frontispiece

I and II From the *Sikes and Nancy* prompt-copy (*Berg*). Henry W. and Albert A. Berg Collection, The New York Public Library. Astor, Lenox and Tilden Foundations

between pp 474–75

ACKNOWLEDGEMENTS

My thanks must go first to the senior descendant of Charles Dickens, Mr. Christopher C. Dickens, for his permission to use unpublished material, and secondly to the possessors and curators of the prompt-copies of the Readings here printed or cited, from all of whom I have had kindly co-operation and, when visiting their collections, generous hospitality and assistance: the Trustees of the Henry W. and Albert A. Berg Collection in the New York Public Library (and its Curator, Mrs. Lola L. Szladits, and her colleagues); the Suzannet Collection at the Dickens House, 48 Doughty Street, London (and its Custodian, Miss Marjorie E. Pillers); the Gimbel Collection in the Beinecke Library, Yale University (and particularly Dr. John Podeschi of its staff); the William M. Elkins Collection in the Free Library of Philadelphia (and its Bibliographer, Dr. Howell J. Heaney); and Mr. Kenyon Law Starling, of Drayton, Ohio. During the earlier stages of my working on this project, some of the prompt-copies and other unpublished material were owned by the Comtesse de Suzannet and the late Colonel Richard Gimbel, who kindly allowed me access to, or gave me information about, their possessions. I am also obliged to the Tennyson Research Centre (Lincoln Public Library), the New York Public Library, the Henry E. Huntington Library, San Marino, California, the J. Pierpont Morgan Library, New York, and Dickens House for permission to cite unpublished letters, etc.

Mr. John Greaves, Honorary Secretary of the Dickens Fellowship and for years past a student of Dickens's public readings, has been most generous in placing at my disposal a copy of his press-cuttings book about performances in the provinces. Dr. Podeschi, similarly, has provided me with a photocopy of a fine collection of New York newspaper cuttings about American performances, now in the Beinecke Library at Yale. Dr. Michael Slater, Editor of the *Dickensian*, has kindly drawn my attention to unpublished information, notably the Hill notes on the *Carol* reading. Mr. Simon Nowell-Smith has given me particulars of the Boston printing (1867–8) of some of these items. Mrs. Madeline House, co-editor of the Pilgrim Edition of Dickens's letters, has answered questions about unpublished correspondence, and Professor Robert L. Patten has allowed me to draw upon his unpublished researches into Dickens and his publishers. Several former colleagues and students have kindly drawn my attention to relevant items about Victorian readings, or have checked bibliographical details for me: Dr. J. L. Madden,

Dr. P. G. Scott, Dr. Eric Trudgill, Dr. William Oddie, Miss Diana Dixon, and Mr. Mick Rodger.

Many Librarians, and members of their staffs, have gone to great trouble to answer my questions about Dickens's performances in their cities, or about people associated with him, and have sent me transcripts or photocopies of reviews from local newspapers. I warmly thank the staffs of the following civic, and other, libraries: in the British Isles—Ashford, Birmingham, Bristol, Carlisle, Cheltenham, Coventry, Croydon, Dorset County, Dover, Dublin, Folkestone, Glasgow, Greenwich, Harrogate, Hull, Kent County, Leeds, Leicester, Lincoln, Liverpool, Manchester, Northampton, Norwich, Oxford, Scarborough, Sheffield, and Torquay. And in North America—Albany, N.Y.; Halifax, Nova Scotia; Hartford, Conn.; New Bedford, Mass.; New Haven, Conn.; New York Public Library; Portland, Maine; Providence, R.I.; Springfield, Mass.; Worcester, Mass.; and Yale University. Some of the British libraries had already helped Mr. John Greaves in the compilation of his press-cuttings book, but I take this opportunity to thank, on his behalf and with his assent, other Librarians and their staffs who, by providing him with materials which he has allowed me to use, have greatly enriched my knowledge of Dickens's performances: those of Aberdeen, Bath, Belfast, Berwick-upon-Tweed, Blackburn, Bolton, Bradford, Brighton, Cambridge, Chester, Colchester, Derby, Dundee, Durham, Edinburgh, Exeter, Halifax, Hastings, Hereford, Huddersfield, Ipswich, Lancaster, Leamington, Limerick, Newcastle-upon-Tyne, Newport (Mon.), Nottingham, Peterborough, Plymouth, Portsmouth, Preston, Reading, Shrewsbury, Southampton, Stoke-on-Trent, Sunderland, Swansea, Wakefield, Warrington, Wolverhampton, Worcester, and York. This list is some mark of Mr. Greaves's energy, and of how considerable my debt to him is.

I also thank members of the following firms, who have answered my enquiries: Chappell & Co. Ltd., William Clowes & Sons, Limited, House of El Dieff Inc., Charles Sawyer & Co. Ltd., and Henry Sotheran & Co. I am delighted that, by happy accident, the present edition is printed by William Clowes & Sons, Ltd., the firm which Dickens engaged to produce most of the privately-printed prompt-copies upon which it is based: a felicitous reunion, more than a century later.

I have published essays on various aspects of the Readings and, though I rarely reproduce below phrases or passages from these earlier studies, I necessarily draw upon materials and ideas which have appeared in them. So I thank the Editors of the following journals for the hospitality of their pages and for permission to draw upon articles which they published: *Bulletin of the New York Public Library, Dickens Studies Annual, Dickensian, Listener, Studies in the Novel, Times Literary Supplement*, and *Yale University Library Gazette*.

It is a pleasure and a duty to salute my predecessors. After the accounts by Dickens's contemporaries (Kate Field, Charles Kent, and George Dolby), no serious work was done on the Readings until the early 1920s, when John Harrison Stonehouse published a useful bibliography. In the early 1940s, Walter Dexter wrote a long series of factual surveys, published in the *Dickensian*. In the mid-1950s, John D. Gordan produced a distinguished catalogue and the first edited text of a Reading (*Mrs. Gamp*). The early files of the *Dickensian* were rich in recollections of the Readings, and reprints of reviews of performances. My researches and thinking were greatly eased, and saved from some likely shortcomings, by these bibliographical and editorial efforts.

I must again record my very great debt to the Leighton-Straker Bookbinding Co., Ltd., the binders of the *Nonesuch Dickens*, who have generously granted me a permanent loan of a set of the *Letters* in that edition, without which all my work on Dickens, including the present edition, would have been seriously impeded.

I have received much help from the staff of the Clarendon Press, and useful cautions from the Press's learned advisers. My text has been typed with splendid accuracy by Mrs. Sylvia Garfield, Mrs. Win Abell, and Miss Anne Sowter, to whom I am deeply grateful.

My wife Joyce has helped me in the preparation and checking of the text, and has borne with my long silent absences from the family hearth, as I tussled with editorial problems. I dedicate the result to our elder son Simon, who, by manifesting an enthusiasm for such aspects of Dickens as are most likely to excite the attention of a seven-year-old, both cheers me on my way and helps to keep me in touch with a basic Dickens which the academic student of his works is tempted to forget or undervalue.

REFERENCES AND ABBREVIATIONS

(Place of publication London, unless otherwise noted)

1. TEXTS OF THE READINGS

Berg
Elkins
Gimbel   Dickens's own copies, specified by the names of the collec-
Starling   tions in which they are now located (see Acknowledge-
Suzannet   ments, above)

T & F   *The Readings of Mr. Charles Dickens as Condensed by Himself* (Boston, Ticknor & Fields, 1868)

2. OTHER BOOKS AND MANUSCRIPTS

Coutts   *Letters from Charles Dickens to Angela Burdett-Coutts 1841–1865*, ed. Edgar Johnson (1953)

Dolby   George Dolby, *Charles Dickens as I knew him: the Story of the Reading Tours 1866–1870* (1885). Photographic reprint (New York, 1970)

Field   Kate Field, *Pen Photographs of Charles Dickens's Readings* (1871)

Gordan   John D. Gordan, *Reading for Profit: the Other Career of Charles Dickens. An Exhibition from the Berg Collection* (New York, 1958)

Hill   Rowland Hill, typescript 'Notes on Charles Dickens's *Christmas Carol*' [1930], in the Suzannet Collection, The Dickens House, London

Kent   Charles Kent, *Charles Dickens as a Reader* (1872). Photographic reprint, introd. Philip Collins (1971)

Life   John Forster, *The Life of Charles Dickens*, ed. J. W. T. Ley (1928)

N   *The Letters of Charles Dickens* [Nonesuch edition], ed. Walter Dexter (3 vols., 1938)

Speeches   *The Speeches of Charles Dickens*, ed. K. J. Fielding (Oxford, 1960)

Wright   Marginalia by W. M. Wright in his copy of Dickens's *Readings* (*T & F*, bound into 2 vols.), in the Dickens House, London

INTRODUCTION

I. THE HISTORY OF THE READINGS

'I do not know if I have ever told you seriously,' Dickens wrote to John Forster in 1845, 'but I have often thought, that I should certainly have been as successful on the boards as I have been between them.'[1] This letter was occasioned by some plans for amateur theatricals: but a few months earlier Dickens had unwittingly begun to discover what was to be his true platform career, for it was in December 1844 that he had given, to small but illustrious audiences of friends, the private readings of *The Chimes* in which Forster was subsequently to recognize 'the germ of those readings to large audiences by which, *as much as by his books*, the world knew him in his later life'.[2] In his letter of 1845, Dickens went on to tell Forster how he had nearly become a professional actor at the age of twenty, and how around that time he had gone 'to some theatre every night, with a very few exceptions, for at least three years; really studying the bills first, and going to where there was the best acting: and always to see Charles Mathews whenever he played'. This predilection for Charles Mathews provides a bridge, indeed, between Dickens's early ambition to become a professional actor and his eventually becoming a great soloist, for Mathews was a performer of ostentatious versatility. In one evening he would assume a dozen characters; Dickens, as a public reader, would in one evening both be narrator and take on the voice and visage of as many as twenty characters in an item (and his programme generally consisted of two, and sometimes three, items). Inevitably, critics of his Readings were reminded of Mathews (1776–1835) and his son Charles James Mathews (1803–78), who took over this family tradition—and not to Dickens's disadvantage. 'The elder Mathews in his palmy days could not have shadowed forth a scene more characteristic of one of the many phases of London life' than Dickens's presentation of the Mould family in *Mrs. Gamp*, wrote a critic in 1858. Another, referring to Mathews the younger, reported that Dickens was 'as clever a comedian' as him, but 'with a power of pathos to which even that most versatile of players has not the slightest pretension. Hence his reading is not only as good as a play, but far better than most plays, for it is all in the best style of acting': and an American newspaper noted that, compared with Dickens, Mathews *fils* was 'cold, stiff, and conventional'.[3]

[1] *Life*, p. 380.　　[2] *Life*, p. 363; my italics.
[3] *Glasgow Herald*, 11 October 1858; *Scotsman*, 28 November 1861; *New York Herald*, 10 December 1867. It is noteworthy that Dickens chose a Mathews item for his audition-

By 1845, when Dickens confided to Forster his long preoccupation with the stage, he had written some plays, with some commercial but little artistic success, and had begun his series of occasional amateur theatrical productions. He starred in the latter as well as directing them, and they continued until within a year of his becoming a paid reader, culminating in his celebrated performances as Aaron Gurnock and Richard Wardour in Wilkie Collins's dramas *The Lighthouse* (1855) and *The Frozen Deep* (1857). After one of his amateur performances he wrote to Bulwer-Lytton, assuring him, as he had assured Forster, that he felt 'seriously' about his passion for the theatre:

I can most seriously say, that all the sights of the earth turned pale in my eyes, before the sight of three thousand people with one heart among them, and no capacity in them, in spite of all their efforts, of sufficiently testifying to you how they believe you to be right, and feel that they cannot do enough to cheer you on.[1]

Small wonder that Dickens's eldest son Charley felt that 'if ever a man seemed to have been born for one particular pursuit it was my father in connection with'—and Charley specified, not the novel, but—'the stage. He was, indeed, a born actor.'[2] Dickens himself, indeed, greatly relished such tributes to his histrionic powers, particularly when actors and actresses, having seen him in plays or heard his Readings, told him that they regretted that writing had prevented his joining their profession. Of his delight in the footlights there is no doubt, nor can one doubt that he was at least competent both in ensemble playing and as a soloist. Many good judges regarded him as much better than competent; Professor Adolphus Ward, for instance, wrote that he possessed 'an almost equal genius for rendering and for producing life-like creations of human character'.[3]

Apart from the amateur acting in which he had shown such conspicuous skill before turning professional reader, he had often given to his family or friends private readings of his latest story or instalment. His reading *The Chimes* in 1844 has already been mentioned: a notable occasion, for he had travelled to London largely for this purpose and had got Forster to assemble various distinguished friends and fellow artists to hear, and be mightily impressed by, him. He may be forgiven some boastfulness about realizing 'what a thing it is to have power' when he had thus reduced the leader of the English stage, Macready, to 'un-

---

piece in 1832, when seeking to go on the stage, and that his acting-style resembled Mathews's (*Life*, p. 60; *Dickensian*, xxxviii (1943), 74). See also Ana Laura Zambrano, 'Dickens and Charles Mathews', *Moderna Språke*, lxvi (1972), 235–42.

[1] *N*, ii. 377.

[2] 'Glimpses of Charles Dickens', *North American Review*, clx (1895), 530.

[3] *Manchester Guardian*, 4 February 1867. Internal evidence shows this critique to be by Ward; cf. his *Charles Dickens* (1882), pp. 152–3.

disguisedly sobbing and crying on the sofa as I read'.[1] Most of his readings of his recently-finished works were more informal affairs than his *Chimes* event of 1844, though he made a fairly regular practice of specially inviting friends, in early December, to hear his latest Christmas book or story. Angela Burdett Coutts was often invited to such previews, or he would read at her house (as, for instance, he read her his part of the 1854 Christmas Number of *Household Words*—and she heard the opening numbers of *Bleak House* and *Hard Times* too). Other friends who were present on several such occasions were the Honourable Mr. and Mrs. Richard Watson. Dickens became acquainted with them in Switzerland in 1846, and soon invited them, together with a good number of other friends, to 'A Soirée . . . to hear him read the first number of his new work *Dombey and Son*' (as Richard Watson recorded in his diary, adding that 'He reads exceedingly well'). Two months later Dickens was reading them 'his new Christmas Book called *The Battle of Life* . . . with wonderful charm and spirit'. The Watsons heard further instalments of *Dombey* as they were completed, and the next time Dickens was writing a Christmas Book he offered, several months in advance, to 'come down [to their seat, Rockingham Castle] and read you that book before it's published. Shall it be a bargain?' Instead, as it happened, they came to London, where they heard him read *The Haunted Man* 'with his usual energy and spirit. . . . Mr. Forster, Stanfield, Mr. Chapman and Miss Coutts present.'[2] Significantly, a number of the pieces, such as *Dombey* and several of the Christmas Books and stories, which he had thus read with some aplomb and to the admiration of his guests, appeared in his early programme or plans as a public reader. It is noteworthy too that, after his reading career had ended, he continued to read to Forster the latest instalment of his final novel *Edwin Drood*: also, as a reminder of some connections between his written and his histrionic arts, that he used to summon the illustrator of *Drood* down to Gad's Hill and 'would act the scenes he wanted illustrating'.[3]

It was his private reading of the opening Number of *Dombey and Son*, in Lausanne on 12 September 1846, that first suggested to Dickens the notion of giving public readings for pay. 'It was a great pleasure to read it,' he told Forster, and the event had been 'an unrelateable success'; and soon he was reflecting that '. . . in these days of lecturings and readings, a great deal of money might possibly be made (if it were not infra dig) by one's having Readings of one's own books. It would be an *odd* thing.

[1] *N*, i. 647–8; and see K. J. Fielding, 'Two Sketches by Maclise: the Dickens Children and *The Chimes* Reading', *Dickens Studies*, ii (1966), 7–17. For Macready's great admiration for Dickens's professional readings, see below, pp. lvii, 216, and 469.

[2] Richard Watson's diary, quoted in *Dickensian*, xlvii (1951), 18–20, 63; *N*, ii. 111, 127. See below, p. 34, for a reading in Italy in 1845.

[3] *Edwin Drood*, ed. Margaret Cardwell (Clarendon edn., 1972), pp. xxiii, xxiv, 239.

I think it would take immensely. What do you say?'[1] Forster made a joke of it at the time, though later, when Dickens became serious in such proposals, he never ceased to advise that the project was indeed 'infra dig' and objectionable on other grounds too. It may be more than coincidental that this notion of 1846 and Dickens's more determined and conclusive return to the idea in 1857–8 occurred at times when he was feeling unsettled. The letters which immediately precede those provoked by the *Dombey* reading contain his anguished complaints about the difficulty of writing in Switzerland without crowded streets around him ('*My* figures seemed disposed to stagnate without crowds about them . . .', 'It is quite a little mental phenomenon').[2] The anguish of 1857–8 was of course caused by the crisis in his marriage, which in fact broke up within a fortnight of his embarking upon his career as a paid reader: and, as will be seen, he then manifestly found great comfort in thus having 'crowds about' him.

Before turning professional in 1858, he had for over four years been giving much-acclaimed public readings for charitable purposes. These 'charity readings' had begun in Birmingham, just after the Christmas of 1853, when he gave two performances of *A Christmas Carol* and one of *The Cricket on the Hearth*.[3] Within two days of this début, the idea of turning professional had been revived. His friend and aide-de-camp W. H. Wills wrote from Birmingham on 30 December 1853: 'If Dickens does turn Reader he will make another fortune. He will never offer to do so, of course. But if they *will* have him he will do it, he told me today.'[4] Evidently he was not reluctant to be, or to feel himself, impelled towards professional status—'if they *will* have him'. During the next few years he gave another dozen or so performances for charity, always of the *Carol* and generally around Christmas, and the temptation to turn professional recurred. Indeed, as he kept telling the hostile John Forster, many of the institutions and organizers plaguing him with invitations assumed that he was already a professional, and asked him to name his fee. He was tempted, in 1854, to accept an offer of £100 for two performances, from one such institute, but (as Forster records) he decided

---

[1] *Life*, pp. 424–5; 'one's having . . .' [*sic*]—a misprint for 'giving'?

[2] *Life*, pp. 423–4.

[3] Other towns than Birmingham have been credited with being the place of 'Dickens's Very First Public Reading' (the title of an article in *The Free Lance*, 22 December 1900, pp. 279–80, which claims the honour for Chatham). Peterborough is the claimant in 'The First Public Reading, by One who heard it', appended to Dickens's *Speeches, Literary and Social* (1870), pp. 342–6. His first readings in Chatham and Peterborough were in fact given in 1857 and 1855 respectively. The *Yorkshire Herald* claimed that the first public reading was given in Leeds in 1847 (quoted by J. B. Van Amerongen, *The Actor in Dickens* (New York, 1927), p. 31, in a well-informed and intelligent chapter on 'The Reader').

[4] Lady Priestley, *The Story of a Lifetime* (2nd edn., 1908), p. 215.

'with some reluctance' not to do so, 'upon the argument that to become publicly a reader must alter without improving his position publicly as a writer, and that it was a change to be justified only when the higher calling should have failed of the old success'.[1]

Things came to a head late in 1857. As a novelist, he was (at least in one important sense) not 'failing of the old success', for he boasted in the Preface to *Little Dorrit* (May 1857) that he had never had so many readers. It is possible, however, that his confidence and spirit as an author had been jolted by the hostile reviews which that novel had received. Moreover, as Forster notes of this unhappy period of the mid-1850s, he was finding writing more difficult than before ('the old, unstinted, irrepressible flow of fancy had received temporary check') and less compulsive and satisfying ('his books had lost for the time the importance they formerly had over every other consideration in his life'). An excuse for embarking on this new career came in the autumn of 1857, when he had depleted his finances by purchasing Gad's Hill. 'What do you think of my paying for this place', he wrote to Forster, that September, 'by reviving that idea of some Readings from my books? I am very strongly tempted. Think of it.' Forster reiterated his various objections, but Dickens found other trusted friends who would give him more congenial advice, and in March 1858 he told Forster what was certainly the proximate determining reason for his embarking on this enterprise. Referring to his marital unhappiness, he wrote: 'I must do *something*, or I shall wear my heart away. I can see no better thing to do that is half so hopeful in itself, or half so well suited to my restless state.'[2] Curiously, he had, in jest more than earnest, anticipated this recourse a decade earlier when in 'a mad-cap mood' at a party after one of his amateur company's performances in the provinces. Wild with excitement, he had then exclaimed: 'Blow Domestic Hearth! I would like to go on all over the kingdom, . . . acting everywhere. There's nothing in the world equal to seeing the house rise at you, one sea of delightful faces, one hurrah of applause!'[3]

By 1858 it was a case of 'Blow Domestic Hearth!' indeed, and public readings manifestly seemed a welcome diversion of energy and an escape from home, while that 'sea of delightful faces' might provide him with

---

[1] *Life*, p. 572. He gave the institute (at Bradford) a gratuitous performance.

[2] *Life*, pp. 624, 641, 646. Gad's Hill cost him £1,790 (*N*, ii. 701, 751), though he spent further money on improving it. As will be seen, he quickly recouped this sum during his first paid season. During that season, he wrote to Wilkie Collins, referring to his 'restless state': 'I miss the thoughtfulness of my quiet room and desk. But perhaps it is best for me not to have it just now [August 1858], and to wear and toss my storm away . . . in this restless manner' (*N*, iii. 38).

[3] Mary Cowden Clarke, *Recollections of Writers* (1878), p. 324. She was perhaps remembering, or embroidering upon, Dickens's letter to her of 24 July 1848: 'I loathe domestic hearths. I yearn to be a vagabond . . .' (*N*, ii. 110).

some of the emotional nourishment which he could not now find in his marriage. When trying to justify the project to Forster, and to demonstrate that it could not fail, he referred pointedly to 'that particular relation (personally affectionate and like no other man's) which subsists between me and the public',[1] and his letters, particularly during his first provincial tour, harp on the daily demonstrations of affection which had indeed proved both remarkable and deeply gratifying. Not only was it 'a great sensation to have a large audience in one's hand' but also

> ... the manner in which the people have everywhere delighted to express that they have a personal affection for me and the interest of tender friends in me, is (especially at this time) high and above all other considerations [of financial profit]. I consider it a remarkable instance of good fortune that it should have fallen out that I should, in this autumn [1858] of all others, have come face to face with so many multitudes.

Nor was he deceiving himself in these reports about his audiences. At the close of his performance, wrote one observer, 'it was not mere applause that followed, but a passionate outburst of love for the man'.[2] It may be remarked too that it was characteristic of Dickens, and of his feelings about his art and his relationship with his society, that at a time of personal misery he did not take refuge in reclusion or misanthropy, but sought comfort (and could so unfailingly find it) in seeing and amusing his public. As he told his friend Miss Coutts, two years later, 'As to my art, I have as great a delight in it as the most enthusiastic of my readers; and the sense of my trust and responsibility in that wise, is always upon me when I take pen in hand. If *I* were soured, I should still try to sweeten the lives and fancies of others . . .'[3] His turning to public Readings may have been, as Forster urged, an act of irresponsibility towards his vocation as a novelist, and certainly in its immediate origins in 1858 it was the product of desperation and self-indulgence: but, in a fashion, this Readings career was one of Dickens's ways (his journalistic and editorial work was another) of fulfilling his 'trust and responsibility . . . to sweeten the lives and fancies of others'.

It was on 29 April 1858, in St. Martin's Hall, London, that he began his paid Readings. Within a fortnight, his marriage had broken up: and, as has been seen, his embarking upon this enterprise was closely connected with the tensions surrounding this event. It is indeed possible that the break-up of his marriage (inevitable some-time though it doubtless was, with Dickens in such a state of mind) occurred just when it did partly

[1] *Life*, p. 646. This formulation, as well as the experience it describes, held a special meaning for Dickens, for he repeated it (evidently expecting Forster to have remembered it) three years later, in a letter about the 1861 Readings tour: 'everywhere I have found that peculiar personal relation between my audience and myself on which I counted most when I entered on this enterprise' (*Life*, p. 689). It appears also in a letter to his publishers, 16 March 1858 (*N*, iii. 11).

[2] *Coutts*, pp. 360, 364; Moncure D. Conway, *Autobiography* (1904), ii. 7.

[3] *Coutts*, p. 370.

because this was the right time of the year to embark upon a course of Readings in London, and because Readings had by then become his private distress-signal, 'Blow Domestic Hearth!' The spring and early summer were the traditional season for many kinds of platform events (including of course the famous 'May-meetings' of religious and philanthropic bodies). The point is well made by Thomas Carlyle, whose own annual series of lectures in London, from 1837 to 1840, had all been given in May, on one occasion stretching into June. When he was advising Emerson about his projected visit to England in 1847, Carlyle wrote that 'the time for lecturing to the London West-End, I was given everywhere to understand, is *from the latter end of April* (or say April altogether) *to the end of May*: this is a fixed statistical fact, all men told me.'[1] As will be seen below, Dickens gave spring series of Readings in London in four later years—more, indeed, than he gave series at the Christmas season with which he had such a special association.

Over the first three months of his career as a paid reader, Dickens performed in London once or twice a week, and then he embarked on an extended and strenuous provincial tour, so that by mid-November, when he stopped, he had given a hundred performances. His initial plans had been much more modest, in terms of both the number of performances and of the extent of his repertoire. At the end of March 1858, his idea had been simply to read the *Carol* on four or six occasions in London, and then undertake a provincial tour of about forty performances, after which he would return to the more lucrative of the provincial towns, and to London, 'to read a new Christmas story written for that purpose'— beyond which he had glimpsed the possibility of earning ten thousand pounds in America 'if I could resolve to go there'. A few days later his ideas for the programme had changed: he would read in London three of the other Christmas Books—*The Cricket on the Hearth*, *The Chimes*, and *The Haunted Man*.[2] The programme which was in fact announced consisted of successive readings of *The Cricket*, *The Chimes*, and the *Carol*; the *Haunted Man* text was prepared, but never delivered. Soon, too, his idea of keeping to the Christmas Books was modified, for he devised and rehearsed two other programmes, so quickly that he was able to give the first, *The Story of Little Dombey*, on 10 June 1858, just six weeks after his London début, and the second a week later (a triple-bill consisting of items from two of his *Household Words* Christmas stories, *The Poor Traveller* and *Boots at the Holly-Tree Inn*, and one from another novel, *Mrs. Gamp*). His initial repertoire was now complete and, ten days after concluding in London, he set off on his provincial tour. This lasted from the beginning of August until mid-November,

---

[1] *The Correspondence of Emerson and Carlyle*, ed. Joseph Slater (New York and London, 1964), p. 419; Carlyle's emphasis.
[2] *Life*, p. 647n; *N*, iii. 17.

and was followed by a short London season over Christmas and the New Year. One new item had meanwhile been added to the repertoire: *Bardell and Pickwick* (more often known as *The Trial from 'Pickwick'*). With selections from the same repertoire, Dickens undertook a short provincial tour in October 1859 and short London seasons at Christmas 1859 and in March–April 1861. He was heavily engaged at this period in establishing his new weekly magazine *All the Year Round*, to which he contributed *A Tale of Two Cities* (30 April to 26 November 1859) and *Great Expectations* (1 December 1860 to 3 August 1861), and he always avoided substantial Reading commitments while he was writing a novel.

With *Great Expectations* completed, he felt able and inclined to contemplate a big new series of Readings, and for this purpose he devised during the summer of 1861 a number of new scripts—*David Copperfield* and *Nicholas Nickleby at the Yorkshire School* (which opened his provincial tour that October), *Mr. Chops, the Dwarf* (deferred until later), *The Bastille Prisoner* and, almost certainly at this time, *Great Expectations* (neither of which was ever performed). Another item, which proved to be one of his most popular, was probably also prepared at this time: *Mr. Bob Sawyer's Party*. With this refurbished repertoire Dickens made a long provincial tour over the autumn and winter of 1861–2, and he repeated some of these items in short London seasons in the springs of 1862 and 1863 and in a brilliant short visit (for charity) to Paris in January 1863. Then the composition of a novel again prevented his undertaking more Reading commitments—*Our Mutual Friend*, serialized from May 1864 to November 1865.

Soon after completing this novel he began to feel the itch to start reading again, and, his initial tour-manager Arthur Smith having died in 1861 and Smith's successor Thomas Headland having proved unsatisfactory, he began negotiations with several firms of impresarios. In February 1866 he concluded an agreement with Chappells (who were to remain his British agents for the rest of his platform career) for thirty performances at £50 a night. George Dolby, the tour-manager appointed by Chappells, soon became a close and trusted associate and later wrote a very informative book about these tours, *Charles Dickens as I knew him* (1885). For his first Chappell tour, Dickens devised an extremely popular reading from his most recent Christmas story, *Doctor Marigold*. He had never written new stories specifically for the Readings, as he had projected in his early 1858 plans, but it is likely that, when writing Christmas stories for his magazines during this period, he sometimes did so with half an eye, at least, towards producing a text which could be adapted for performance. The *Mrs. Lirriper* stories (1863–4) and *Doctor Marigold* (1865) are probably examples of this, and the 1866 Christmas Number too, *Mugby Junction*, was immediately adapted into three Readings—*Barbox Brothers*, *The Boy at Mugby*, and *The Signalman*—the first two of which opened Dickens's next season for Chappells, in January 1867. *The Signalman* was never performed, nor was a *Mrs. Lirriper* Reading which he devised.

After his second Chappell season, which ended in May 1867, Dickens at last undertook the prolonged American tour which he had long been contemplating. His repertoire for this was unadventurous; indeed, he decided to open in every city with his most tried successful programme (*A Christmas Carol* and *The Trial*), and in many smaller cities this constituted his only performance. The other items, given in cities where he stayed longer, were the most popular from his repertoire. By now, half a dozen of his performed items had proved relative failures, and these were not taken to America. As will be seen below, the American repertoire was important in that it was these items, published in Boston in 1867–8 and later reprinted in Britain, which have hitherto constituted the only collected edition of the Readings.

Only one further item was added to the repertoire—the horrific *Sikes and Nancy*, which Dickens devised under the justification (or excuse?) that the financial terms for his Farewell Season of 1868–9 had been so generous that it was his duty to provide a compelling new attraction which would ensure that Chappells would not lose on the deal. In fact, for reasons given in the *Sikes and Nancy* headnote, this item was not introduced into the repertoire until the series was nearly half completed (and was clearly a financial success): but anyway the series was abandoned prematurely when Dickens's health broke down in April 1869. His doctors, probably ill-advisedly, allowed him to give a short Farewell series in London, in January–March 1870. In these London Farewells, *Sikes and Nancy* shared the honours, for most frequent performance, with *Boots at the Holly-Tree Inn*—the latter surprisingly, for few readers of Dickens now remember or particularly admire that story. The other items most performed in the 1870 series were *The Trial* and *Mr. Bob Sawyer's Party*, but for the final performance, at which he made the lapidary statement, '. . . from these garish lights I vanish now for evermore', [1] he chose as the main item the one with which he had started in 1853, and which had remained the quintessential Dickens Reading— as it has been, ever since, the greatest of platform pieces from his works— *A Christmas Carol*.

2. NUMBER OF PERFORMANCES, AND OTHER FIGURES

Altogether, Dickens gave about 472 public readings, of which 27 were 'charity' ones. This is a slightly higher figure than appears in previous accounts, which have mostly been based on Charles Kent and George

---

[1] *Speeches*, p. 413. These words were inscribed on the funeral card distributed at Westminster Abbey, less than three months later.

Dolby, who concur in stating that he gave 423 paid readings.[1] I make it 445, but any figure must be somewhat approximate. Occasionally a performance was advertised but for some reason cancelled, and I may have failed to note some cancellations; on the other hand, I have discovered, sometimes quite by accident, odd performances which seem not to have been previously recorded. For the great majority of the performances I have press accounts, mentions in Dickens's letters, or other such firm evidence, and my total of 472 is at least, I am sure, closer to the truth than previous estimates.

The numbers of performances in his various series is, by my reckoning, as follows:

Charity readings: 1853–8 (before turning professional)	18
1858–65 (after turning professional)	9
First London season (29 April to 22 July 1858)	17
First provincial tour (2 August to 13 November 1858)	83
London, Christmas 1858 (24 December 1858 to 8 February 1859)	8
Second provincial tour (10 to 27 October 1859)	14
London, Christmas 1859 (24 December 1859 to 2 January 1860)	3
London, Spring 1861 (14 March to 18 April)	6
Second series, provincial tour (28 October 1861 to 30 January 1862)	46
London, Spring 1862 (13 March to 27 June)	11
London, Spring 1863 (2 March to 13 June)	13
First Chappell season (10 April to 12 June 1866)	30
Second Chappell season (15 January to 13 May 1867)	52
American tour (2 December 1867 to 20 April 1868)	75
Farewell tour (6 October 1868 to 20 April 1869)	72
London Farewells (11 January to 15 March 1870)	12
Miscellaneous	3
Total	472

His pattern of work changed little over his professional years except that later he generally gave fewer performances in a week. When giving seasons in London, usually around Christmas or Easter, he would read once or twice weekly over successive weeks. On tour, he worked harder. During his first provincial tour (1858), indeed, he read as many as eight times a week, including two 'morning' performances (usually given at 3.0 p.m.); but he disliked matinées, partly because they attracted a less heterogeneous audience, and later he gave them rarely except that, on provincial tours, he sometimes read on Saturday afternoons so that he could travel home for the weekend. He often took a long weekend off, and after 1858 never attempted as many as eight performances a week; his maximum was usually five and later (on the American and Farewell tours) four. Under the Chappell management he did no continuous

---

[1] Kent, pp. 56–7; Dolby, pp. 450–1. Kent was doubtless using Dolby's records, as Dickens had promised that he might do (N, iii. 768).

London seasons, except the 1870 Farewells when his doctors had forbidden him to travel. Instead, Dolby generally booked his London performances for a Monday or Tuesday after a weekend at Gad's Hill.

The constitution of a programme changed during his first season, but thereafter remained constant. His opening repertoire, it will be recalled, consisted entirely of Christmas Books, all of which occupied the whole of the two hours scheduled for his performances. *Little Dombey*, his first break from this practice, was another two-hour item, performed by itself. But the triple bill which soon followed gave Dickens the chance to experiment with shorter items, and soon he changed his policy. Henceforth nearly all his programmes consisted of one long item (about seventy to eighty minutes) and one short item (about thirty to forty minutes). The shorter item was usually comic, and had something of the effect of a theatrical 'afterpiece'. The longer one tended to be more inclusive, emotionally; though it might be predominantly comic, it generally found a place for other effects, pathetic or dramatic. Some variants on the two-item programme will be mentioned below but it was, from the autumn of 1858, much his frequent pattern.

How popular the various items were cannot be indicated solely from the number of performances given of each. Some were in repertoire from 1853 until 1870, others were devised only in the mid-1860s or later. Also the more popular short items stood more chance of frequent performance, for they could be paired with several of the longer ones, which might nevertheless be the main attraction in the programme. Something, however, may be learned from such figures as can be given. (I have been unable to ascertain the programmes of 14 of the 472 performances known to me, but it is unlikely that the general picture would be much different if these further particulars were discovered.) The number of performances of the various items is as follows, in descending order of magnitude. The longer items are asterisked.

Item (*short title*)	First public performance	Number of performances
The Trial from Pickwick	19 October 1858	164
A Christmas Carol *	27 December 1853	127
Boots at the Holly-Tree Inn	17 June 1858	81
Doctor Marigold *	10 April 1866	74
David Copperfield *	28 October 1861	71
Mr. Bob Sawyer's Party	30 December 1861	64
Mrs. Gamp	17 June 1858	60
Nicholas Nickleby *	29 October 1861	54
Little Dombey *	10 June 1858	48
The Poor Traveller	17 June 1858	30
Sikes and Nancy	5 January 1869	28
The Chimes *	6 May 1858	10
The Boy at Mugby	15 January 1867	8

Barbox Brothers *	15 January 1867	5
Mr. Chops, the Dwarf	28 October 1868	5
The Cricket on the Hearth *	29 December 1853	4

There were also of course the five items, prepared but never performed: *The Haunted Man* *, *The Bastille Prisoner* *, *Great Expectations* *, *Mrs. Lirriper's Lodgings* *, and *The Signalman*. The significance of the figures given above will be discussed in a later section.

One other kind of figure may be noted here: the financial returns for this enterprise. During his first week of touring (2–6 August 1858) nearly £400 was taken at the box-office; by the end of that month, the profits, with all expenses paid, amounted to a thousand guineas. 'The work is very hard, sometimes overpowering,' he reported a week later, and he felt 'not at all disposed to go away again'. But 'the intelligence and warmth of the audiences are an immense sustainment, and one that always sets me up.'[1] As has been seen, he often went back for more, partly because the financial inducement was so considerable—a steady, and increasing, income, and one which was much less dependent upon inspiration than was novel-writing. As he wrote during a period of depression: 'I can force myself to do at that reading-desk what I have done a hundred times; but whether, with all this unsettled fluctuating distress in my mind, I could force an original book out of it, is another question.'[2] And not only was reading easier, in this sense, than writing: also he soon discovered, like Thackeray before him, that he could earn much more from platform appearances than from the hard tussle of creating a novel. That first month on tour, over which he had been so jubilant, had netted him a thousand guineas for twenty-five performances—over £40 a performance. This was very high pay, by theatrical standards; it was more than Macready could command at the peak of his career.[3] A thousand guineas a month compared very well, too, with Dickens's literary earning capacity, which averaged less than £3,000 a year.[4] Moreover, the receipts from his Readings increased later, though the price range of tickets did not change much. He always insisted that some seats should be available at one shilling, for his poorer admirers; the top

---

[1] *N*, iii. 36, 65, 49, 50, 52, 50.

[2] Letter to Forster, October 1862, *Life*, pp. 693–4. This remark occurs in a letter about a project which attracted Dickens in the latter half of 1862: an Australian readings tour. He had been offered £10,000 for eight months, but reckoned that, employing his own manager, he could net £12,000 in six months, and maybe visit India and Tasmania too (see *N*, iii. 298, 312–20, 328). Nothing came of this scheme, but several years later he was still hoping to undertake such a tour.

[3] In 1845, Macready was demanding £100 a week for three performances: in 1849, £40 a night for the first three nights of a week and £30 a night for any performance beyond that (*Diaries of W.C. Macready*, ed. William Toynbee (1912), ii. 299, 431).

[4] Robert L. Patten, Appendix to *Dickens: the Critical Heritage*, ed. Philip Collins (1971), p. 620.

price was generally four shillings until 1863, five shillings thereafter, but seven shillings for the Farewells. Chappells agreed to pay him £50 a performance for his first engagement with them (1866), £2,500 for 42 performances for his second (1867), and £80 a performance for his Farewells (1868–9, 1870). All the travelling and hotel expenses, etc., for Dickens and his staff were paid by Chappells.

Meanwhile he had made a fortune in America, where his average nightly profit was nearly three times as much as even his Farewells brought him in Britain. With better management, or greater ruthlessness, he could indeed have made far more in America. His takings could have been greater: he charged $2.00 a seat throughout the house, which many thought rather steep, but as the black-market price for tickets rose to $26.00 he might well have set a higher top price. 'Why doesn't Mr. Dickens charge five dollars a seat,' remarked the *New York Tribune* (13 December 1867), 'and have no reserved seats and no sales until the hall opens? If the money is to be paid to him, no one will murmur. It goes to speculators, however, who probably make more out of Mr. Dickens than he does himself.' He lost some profit through the malversations of one of his staff and the cancellation of a few performances when a political fever swept the country and emptied its theatres. But his biggest loss occurred through his insistence on changing dollars into gold, since he (mistakenly) had no faith in the stability of the post-Bellum American economy. He thus dropped nearly 40 per cent on the face value of his dollar profits (nearly £38,000, on his enormous box-office takings of nearly a quarter of a million dollars at 75 performances). Even so, when all expenses and commission were paid, he banked nearly £19,000 in England.[1] Again, a theatrical comparison is telling. Henry Irving, performing in Boston in 1888, was said to have broken all American theatre box-office records by taking $4,582; twenty years earlier, Dickens had broken his own box-office record by taking, also in Boston, and for his final performance there, $3,456.[2] But as Irving had the whole cast of *Faust*, and ancillary staff, to pay, and Dickens had only a staff of half-a-dozen, it is obvious who profited the more.

Altogether the Readings earned Dickens about £45,000—nearly half of the estate which he left in 1870 (£93,000). His manager George Dolby, who provides much of the financial evidence, rightly commented that, on the one hand, these handsome results 'were purchased at the dear

[1] Dolby, pp. 331–2.

[2] Bram Stoker, *Personal Reminiscences of Henry Irving* (1906), i. 183; Dolby, p. 301. Probably the only performer before Dickens to exceed his American profits was the legendary Jenny Lind. In 1850 she contracted with P. T. Barnum to sing 150 times for $150,000. Her success was so phenomenal that Barnum renegotiated the contract. She ended her connection with him after 95 performances, for which she received $176,675 (*Barnum's Own Story*, ed. Waldo R. Browne (New York, 1961), pp. 240–1; Irving Wallace, *The Fabulous Showman* (1960), pp. 110–32.)

cost of the sacrifice of his health', but also that, on the other, 'setting aside his pecuniary profits, the pleasure he derived from [this career] is not to be told in words'.[1]

3. THE PREPARATION OF THE TEXTS

Dickens's first public Reading—the *Carol*, on 27 December 1853—took over three hours, though he had made some cuts in the 1843 text. During the next few years he reduced its length further until, in the first paid season (1858), it took the advertised time then for his performances: two hours, including one interval of ten minutes or two of five. To prepare a Reading version of one of the Christmas Books, which constituted the whole of his initial repertoire, was relatively simple: mainly a matter of abbreviation, writing in an occasional summary or bridge-passage where a cut had been made, and altering a word or phrase here and there, generally for the sake of simplicity or euphony or to bring to the end of a sentence the punch-line of a joke. Words or passages were underlined for emphasis or to indicate that some special vocal effect was required, and in the margins Dickens wrote some 'stage-directions' to remind himself about a tone of voice or a gesture ('Low', 'Cheerful Narrative', 'Mystery', 'Action', etc.). Neither in these early scripts nor later did he introduce any substantial new material, nor did he often change the order in which episodes had occurred in the original novel or story.

So he found it quite convenient to use an ordinary printed copy of the *Carol* and other Christmas Books, though to give himself more marginal space for manuscript interpolations or revisions, and for the stage-directions, he had pages (foolscap octavo) from such a copy inlaid into a larger (octavo) page, after which the enlarged copy was handsomely bound. (One exception to this practice, the *Elkins* copy of *The Cricket*, is discussed in the headnote to that item.) Where a lengthy deletion was made, Dickens often stuck the unwanted passages together with wafers or stamp-edging; in one case he laced them together with tape. Another way of quickly indicating to his eye where a cut of, say, a paragraph had been made was to paint the deletion out with red wash, though this, like several other fads, was confined to one phase of his Readings career.

Generally he seems to have used the same 'prompt-copy'[2] of an item for the whole time that it remained in repertoire. There are certainly at least two exceptions: of *The Chimes*, only a version dating from 1868 has apparently survived, and of *The Trial* only one dating from three years after he began performing the item. Sometimes he experimented,

[1] Dolby, p. 451.
[2] I follow John D. Gordan in using this term to refer to Dickens's own Reading-copies, amended or annotated in his autograph (see Gordan, pp. 3–4).

during rehearsal or later, with making a new version in a second or third copy (*Little Dombey* is an example), and I would guess that other preliminary attempts were discarded at the time: or he would use, for a while, an alternative prompt-copy (*Mrs. Gamp* and *Nicholas Nickleby* are examples of this). It is surprising, however, how often he continued to use a much-altered and heavily cut prompt-copy instead of making a new fair copy. Probably he felt the trouble and expense unnecessary because, when performing such long-established items, he hardly needed to consult the text anyway. How irrelevant the prompt-copy could become appears in a letter from America, in 1868, about the *Carol* (for which a single prompt-copy seems to have served from 1853, and certainly served from 1859 to 1870): 'I have got to know the Carol so well that I can't remember it, and occasionally go dodging about in the wildest manner to pick up lost pieces.'[1]

When he departed from the Christmas Books during his first season he needed to adopt a different procedure in preparing his prompt-copy. The first two readings from the novels (*Little Dombey* and *Mrs. Gamp*) were much-abridged extracts, and to use a copy of the novel would have been impracticable. Moreover, the typeface in the existing editions was too small, and the page too crowded, to be convenient for platform reading: and this was even more the case with the *Household Words* Christmas stories (*The Poor Traveller* and *Boots*) which entered the repertoire at this time, for these were printed in small type on a double-column page. So henceforth all the Readings were privately printed in an easily legible type, being set up from an emended copy of the original story or a scissors-and-paste version of extracts from the novel, with manuscript alterations or insertions. (Scraps of the printers' copy for *Little Dombey* and *Mrs. Gamp* survive; these are mentioned in the appropriate headnotes.) Dickens was indeed using his printer as later authors would use a typist, to secure a legible fair copy. Of these privately printed items, some seem to have survived in a unique copy, and I know of none which exists in more than three copies, so presumably very few copies were printed. Dickens relics being prized as they have been and are, surely more Reading-copies would have survived if their printings had been at all large.[2] Only a very few copies, given to friends or relations, seem to have passed through the sale rooms; of these, only the 'Billington'

---

[1] *N*, iii. 627. As a glance at the facsimile (1971) of the *Carol* prompt-copy will show, there are many passages so altered by deletions and verbal substitutions or additions that they could certainly not have been sight-read at performance speed.

[2] Messrs. William Clowes & Sons, Limited, who printed most of Dickens's Reading-copies, lost their records during the Blitz, so cannot give any information about his print-orders. The firm of C. Whiting, which printed *Sikes and Nancy*, is defunct. The surviving records of Messrs. Bradbury & Evans (now in the Victoria & Albert Museum), the firm which printed the 1858 copies, contain no separate figures about these items (information from Professor Robert L. Patten).

copy of *Sikes and Nancy* seems to be important for scholarly or biblio-graphical purposes.

Having got his privately printed version from the printers, Dickens would then set to work. Rehearsing was a formidable business: he claimed to have rehearsed *Doctor Marigold* over two hundred times, and he told an American friend in 1867-8 that he reckoned it took three months' hard labour to get up a new item.[1] During rehearsals, or after a private 'trial reading' to selected friends, he sometimes decided that the text was so inadequate or incomplete that a revised or expanded version had to be printed; this was the case, in various ways, with *Little Dombey*, *David Copperfield*, and *Sikes and Nancy*.

Apart from the addition of underlinings, stage-directions, and minor rewordings, the main textual concern was abbreviation. The tendency always was for scripts to become shorter, and this process generally continued long after the rehearsal stage. A particularly trenchant phase of abbreviation must have taken place around October 1858 when, as was noted above, Dickens began to perform two items in a programme instead of one, while adhering to his two-hour schedule. The two-hour items still in repertoire (the *Carol* and *Little Dombey*) had therefore to be reduced by about thirty minutes to accommodate an afterpiece (generally, at that stage, *Boots* or *The Trial*). In the 1861 tour, another two-hour script was introduced, *David Copperfield*, but after a while this too was abbreviated so that another short item (generally *Bob Sawyer*) could be included in the same programme. Sometimes, at first, one of these longer items might still, after abbreviation, be given occasional performances by itself, especially at matinées, which were then sometimes advertised as lasting 'about an hour and a half', or even, for one Saturday when Dickens wanted to get home from Edinburgh, 'within an Hour and a Quarter'. Very occasionally a normal double-bill was advertised as lasting two hours and twenty minutes. But the great majority of performances were advertised as lasting, or to be 'comprised within', two hours. In his final tours, the performance quite often ended inside an hour and three-quarters. Maybe Dickens was speaking faster; more

---

[1] Kent, p. 204; J. T. Fields, *Yesterdays with Authors* (1872), p. 241. An American journalist learned 'on the best authority' (presumably an interview with Dickens) that 'he never attempts a new part in public until he has spent at least two months over it in study . . . extend[ing] not merely to the analysis of the text, to the discrimination of character, to the minutest points of elocution, . . . but [also to] the facial expression, the tone of the voice, the gesture, the attitude, . . . of the actor' (*New York Tribune*, 3 December 1867). It is worth noting that all these remarks about prolonged rehearsal come from late in Dickens's career (1866 onwards): he seems to have become increasingly exacting and conscientious. Thus, in 1867, feeling that, 'as their reputation widened, [the Readings] should be better than at first, I have *learnt them all*, . . . made the humorous parts much more humorous; corrected my utterance of certain words; . . . and made myself master of the situation' (*N*, iii. 527; cf. iii. 620).

likely he was omitting more, because he was artistically more selective or simply tired and bored. Certainly the prompt-copies show a continual process of deletion, even after the American tour of 1867–8 when the prompt-copies of items in that repertoire were used as printers' copy for the Boston (*T & F*) edition; several of the prompt-copies contain deletions of passages which that edition had included. Sometimes, however, Dickens changed his mind, and *stetted* a deletion. Also he had, in some prompt-copies, signs indicating optional cuts, though often these options were later excluded and the cut made final.

Most of the abbreviations, and indeed of the other emendations of the original published text, are (it must be acknowledged) not specially revealing about Dickens's art or craftsmanship. Rather, they are very much what any competent and painstaking recitalist would do, if preparing a reading version of these pieces. Thus, indications of who was speaking, and how, were generally deleted; the context, and the reader's voice, would indicate this. Similarly many descriptions of facial expression, gesture, movement, and demeanour were superfluous in a performance. Another obvious category of deletions is irrelevant matter: particularly when a Reading was extracted from a novel, there were many passages in the selected chapters which referred to characters or plot-developments which had no place in the Reading-narrative, and these were cut. In the interests of brevity or clarity, two minor characters might be conflated, or an omitted character's entry and speeches were given to someone else. Dickens, it has been noted, rarely wrote any substantial new passages, but he did extemporize new jokes or amplify existing ones. Some of these became a regular part of the performance, though they were very seldom written down in the prompt-copy; examples of this will be found in Serjeant Buzfuz's speech, and Mr. Squeers's 'practical mode of teaching', and Bob Sawyer's reproach to Jack Hopkins for 'chorusing'. Often plums from parts of a novel not used in a Reading narrative would be extracted and interpolated into the script; thus, *Martin Chuzzlewit* and *David Copperfield* were raided for Gampisms and Micawberisms, which appear in new contexts in the scripts drawn from those novels.

The *David Copperfield* Reading may be used to illustrate these techniques of abbreviation and rearrangement, for it is one of Dickens's most ambitious efforts, and was also both his favourite and his longest item. Originally it consisted of five chapters, but then Dickens must have decided that it began too abruptly, so he added a long new opening chapter. The main plot (Chapters I, II, IV, and VI) concerns David's introducing Steerforth to the Peggotty group, Emily's elopement, Mr. Peggotty's search for and eventual recovery of her, and the deaths of Ham and Steerforth in the great storm. Chapters III and V are light relief—David's courtship of Dora and their early married life, and his

bachelor dinner for the Micawbers and Traddles.[1] The Peggotty–
Steerforth episodes proved easiest to adapt. There are the usual kinds
of abbreviation—descriptions of people and places are reduced or omitted,
indications about speakers are jettisoned or made more economically (so
that 'he stammered' replaces 'he said, with much faltering and great
difficulty'), bystanders and other irrelevant characters are written out.
Thus, Martha Endell disappears from both the occasions where she had
been present in the corresponding passages in the novel, Mr. Peggotty
taking over her lines and actions where necessary; 'my dear old nurse,
Mr. Peggotty's sister' was eventually eliminated from the scene of
Emily's elopement; Betsey Trotwood is not present to applaud Mr.
Peggotty's long narrative. Similarly, in the David scenes, the disastrous
dinner ruined by Mrs. Crupp is not taken over by Littimer (he is given
no entrance). The episodes about the Micawbers and Dora are very
cleverly selected. Several of the best Micawber and Mrs. Micawber jokes
are transferred from other chapters, and Chapter V of the Reading, about
David's courtship and marriage, brings together many of the most
amusing passages from six chapters of the novel. In all these mechanical
tasks, Dickens is as skilful, resourceful, and industrious as one would
expect, though his skill is sometimes baffled when he has to make drastic
cuts. Thus, Chapter VI opens with Mr. Peggotty's exultant cry that he
had found Emily; there followed, in the prompt-copy, eight pages about
how she had reached England and been rescued; but eventually all this
went, so David's ludicrously over-abrupt response to this triumphant
cry is a cool 'You have made up your mind as to the future, good friend?'
Dickens was anxious, by this point, to get on to the great climax of the
storm scene.

The *Copperfield* prompt-copy, as it happens, is not very rich in stage-
directions; Dickens's practice in this varied greatly, and sometimes he
has many, sometimes no, marginalia. Nor has it many newly written
phrases: a happy one, though, for Mrs. Crupp who, explaining how she
knows that David is in love, adds to her iterated axiom, 'Mr. Copperfull,
I'm a mother myself', the perceptive 'Your boots and your waist is
equally too small.' An interesting (and characteristic) example of Dickens's
frugality appears in a phrase of Mr. Peggotty's. The printed Reading
text has, in one of his speeches: '[this is] the brightest night of my life,
and a reg'lar merry-go-rounder.' The words after 'my life' had been
transferred, slightly emended, from ch. 7 to this new context in ch. 21.
This speech was then deleted, but Dickens, unwilling to lose 'merry-go-
rounder', inserted it in another Peggotty speech, a page or so earlier,
when the printed exclamation 'such a thing . . . !' is emended, by hand,
to the more interestingly idiosyncratic 'such a merry-go-rounder . . . !'

---

[1] The next few paragraphs are largely derived from my essay 'Dickens's Public
Readings: Texts and Performances', *Dickens Studies Annual*, iii (1974), 182–97.

Dickens's revision of the privately printed text was indeed painstaking, and the final text is much less than half the length of the corresponding passages in the novel. Even the *pièce de résistance*, the storm scene, had been reduced from 5,500 to 3,400 words before the Reading-text was printed, and then lost a further 1,500 words in rehearsals and playing.

Other characteristic changes in the *Copperfield* text are that Mr. Peggotty is given more dialect phrasings (Dickens often thickened-up a speaker's idiom), and that local references which might puzzle provincial or American audiences, or which simply impeded the narrative, are omitted. Thus 'Kentish Town' becomes 'the neighbourhood' and 'Bow Street' becomes 'the Police Office'. In other Readings, outdated topicalities are omitted or details about manners are updated: so 'is' becomes 'was then' in reference to customary attire. Perhaps it is for this reason that, in *Mr. Bob Sawyer's Party*, 'punch' becomes 'bottles' (of spirits), and that, in *Mrs. Gamp*, the weakness of Mr. Gamp's wooden leg is attributed to 'its constancy of walking into public-'ouses' instead of into the 'wine-vaults' specified in the novel. Another minor variety of emendation: possibly offensive, or incomprehensible, phrases were removed. Either or both of these reasons could account for 'the scorbutic youth' in *Bob Sawyer* becoming something less distinctive.

Another frequent kind of alteration is the pointing-up of jokes. In *Bob Sawyer*, for instance, Mr. Pickwick puts his foot instead of his hat (as in the novel) into the tray of glasses, and in the maudlin speeches of reconciliation after the tipsy quarrel in that Reading, the novel's 'Mr. Gunter replied that, upon the whole, he rather preferred Mr. Noddy to his own brother' becomes—Mr. Gunter's role having been coalesced with that of Jack Hopkins—'Mr. Hopkins replied that he infinitely preferred [*later revised to* replied that on the whole he preferred] Mr. Noddy to his own mother.' Or new jokes are made: when Mr. Winkle gives his name, in *The Trial*, the novel's '"What's your Christian name, sir?" angrily inquired the little judge' becomes 'COURT.—"Have you any Christian name, sir?"' Or jokes are thwacked home: for instance, in the story of *Mr. Chops, the Dwarf*, Magsman says, 'The gentlemen was at their wine arter dinner, and Mr. Chops's eyes was more fixed in that Ed of his than I thought good for him. There was three of 'em (in company, I mean) . . .' but, when revising his script, Dickens helped the hard-of-hearing by inserting 'not his eyes—in company, I mean'. Or hard cases are made harder: Trotty Veck, 'over sixty' in the story, becomes 'over sixty-eight' in the *Chimes* reading; books at Dotheboys Hall averaged 'about one to eight learners', until Dickens rounded it up to 'a dozen' in the Reading. Similarly, the Miss Fezziwigs' admirers, in the *Carol*, were increased from six to ten, and the number of couples at the Fezziwig ball from 'three or four and twenty' to 'seven or eight and thirty', according to one reporter.[1]

One other kind of deletion should be mentioned—passages of social criticism. The Readings which were performed were, it will be noted, not drawn from the later and more socially critical novels. Indeed, over half of them were taken, not from the novels, but from the Christmas books and stories (a fact discussed below). But even from the Christmas books, the more significant passages of this kind—Scrooge's vision of the terrible children Ignorance and Want, and Will Fern's big social-protest speeches, for instance—were eventually omitted in the Readings, though critics had been greatly impressed by Dickens's rendering of these two passages when, at an earlier stage, they had been included in his scripts.

The Readings texts never reached a definitive condition. So long as they remained in repertoire, they were subject to further abbreviation, rephrasings, and extempore improvements, while the mode of perform-ance too remained surprisingly fresh and spontaneous, as many critics noted. Even such a well-tried favourite as the *Carol* was not allowed to ossify: Dickens told a friend that he thought he had greatly improved his presentation of it while in America, and an ardent English admirer who often heard him perform this item in his final years recorded many phrasings which do not appear in the prompt-copy and noted, too, how both text and presentation varied from performance to performance, not only in details of wording but also in the inclusion or omission of lengthy passages.[2]

4. THE PROMPT-COPIES: THEIR LATER HISTORY

With a few exceptions, Dickens retained in his possession all his prompt-copies, even of items which he had ceased performing and was unlikely to revive. Sometimes, it seems likely, he discarded a prompt-copy when he had a fair copy or a new version privately printed. He gave a friend one of his *Mrs. Gamp* prompt-copies, and somehow one of his copies of *The Cricket* left his possession during his lifetime. But in March 1870, just after retiring from the platform, he could offer to lend 'the books from which I read' to his friend Charles Kent, who wanted to write a book about the Readings (which appeared eventually in 1872). Promising Kent this and other help, Dickens added that these reading-copies were 'afterwards going into Forster's collection'.[3] Within three months he was dead, but none of the Reading-copies went to Forster. The terms of

---

[1] Rowland Hill, cited in my edition of *A Christmas Carol: the Public Reading Version* (New York, 1971), p. 190.

[2] James T. Fields, *Yesterdays with Authors* (1872), p. 241; Rowland Hill, typescript 'Notes' (see previous footnote).

[3] *N*, iii. 768.

Dickens's Will were that Forster should have 'such manuscripts of my published works as may be in my possession at the time of my decease', but that his eldest son Charles should have 'my library of printed books'. The Reading-copies were of intermediate status—printed books with many manuscript emendations and marginalia. Reasonably, his executors (Forster was one of them) must have decided that they were part of the library; maybe they did not know that Dickens had wanted Forster to have them. Charley did not retain them for long, however. In poor health and financial difficulties, he sold Gad's Hill and its library in 1878, the latter being bought entire by the London booksellers, Henry Sotheran. It was thus that, regrettably, the Reading books became dispersed among various purchasers until, in recent decades, most of them were reassembled in two collections, the Berg and the Suzannet (described more fully below).

Sotheran's notebook, listing the contents of the Gad's Hill library, with a valuation of them (in letter-code), survives in the possession of the firm, where, through the courtesy of its staff, I have consulted it. The list includes:

1 David Copperfield Reading Copy.   Priv Printed
1 Christmas Carol   D°   with Engagements
1 Haunted Man   mounted
1 Nicholas Nickleby   Notes
                  Readg Copy   Priv Printed
1 Mrs Gamp   D?   Boston 1868

—and so on. Many of these items were more fully described when they were put on sale later that year (*Sotheran's Prices Current of Literature*, New Series, nos. clxxiv–v, 30 November and 31 December 1878). Under the heading 'Charles Dickens's Public-Reading Books: the Identical Copies read from by the Author . . .' this catalogue offered seven volumes, at the prices here given in brackets.[1] These were—to identify them by their present ownership—the *Berg* copies of the *Carol* (£25), *Cricket* (£25), the triple item *Barbox Brothers: The Boy at Mugby: and The Signalman* (£12. 12s.), *Marigold* (£12. 12s.) and *Mrs. Lirriper* (£1. 10s.); the *Suzannet* copy of *Nickleby* (£21); and a copy, the identity of which is discussed below, of *Mrs. Gamp* (£10). The valuation notebook lists further items, not offered for sale in the 1878 catalogue, such as the *David Copperfield* Reading-copy heading my transcription above. The descriptions of these

[1] Reprinted in *Catalogues of the Libraries of Charles Dickens and William Makepeace Thackeray*, ed. John Harrison Stonehouse (1935), pp. 28–30. A page of Sotheran's 1878 notebook is reproduced in this reprint (facing p. 5); this page contains all the Readings items listed, except those transcribed above (from *David Copperfield* to *Mrs. Gamp*) and *The Cricket on the Hearth* (amply described in Sotheran's 1878 catalogue, though the notebook listing of it is inexplicit).

items are (as the transcription shows) terse, so that one cannot always be absolutely certain about their identity, but there is little doubt as to what they were. To give two examples: the 'Haunted Man   mounted' is not described as a Reading copy, but it appears in the page and a half devoted wholly to Reading copies, and the (unique) *Suzannet* prompt-copy of *The Haunted Man* was indeed 'mounted', as described above. Another item listed is '1 Chimes D° D° *Not Published*'; the 'dittos' refer to the preceding items, described as 'Notes . . . Reading Copy . . . Priv. Printed'. This item must be the *Berg* prompt-copy of *The Chimes*, which has on its title-page the words 'Not Published' included in the Sotheran notebook entry. This prompt-copy is bound, and continuously paginated, with *Sikes and Nancy*—an item conspicuously missing from the Sotheran notebook and catalogue. Thus it would appear that, in 1878, the Gad's Hill library did not contain two prompt-copies which, as I argue below, must have existed once but which seem never to have been seen: an earlier one of *The Chimes*, and a later one of *Sikes and Nancy*, than the *Berg* copy. One can go through the Sotheran notebook list thus, and with similar confidence identify other items briefly described.

The upshot of such a scrutiny of the notebook is reassuring to the present editor, for the list appears to contain all the prompt-copies presently known, with the following exceptions: the *Elkins* copy of *The Cricket* and the *Starling* copy of *Mrs. Gamp*, both of which (as noted above) left Dickens's possession during his lifetime; two of Dickens's three copies of *Little Dombey* (doubtless the two less authoritative ones, now in the Berg and Gimbel collections); and the *Gimbel* copy of *Nicholas Nickleby* (Dickens's association with which is very uncertain). Thus the Sotheran notebook adds considerable weight to the opinion I have formed, that it is highly unlikely that any further prompt-copies are extant—with the possible exception of the *Mrs. Gamp* copy, in the Boston 1868 edition, which is listed.

This copy of *Mrs. Gamp* cannot be either the *Starling* one (which Dickens had presented to a friend in 1868) or the *Berg* one (which was included in the volume described in Sotheran's notebook as 'Boots at the Holly Tree &c / Reading Copy   Curious   1858'). Unfortunately, the 1878 catalogue, which contains some description of Dickens's holograph alterations to the other Reading books offered for sale, says nothing about this *Mrs. Gamp*, except that it was in the Boston 1868 edition. It is possible that it was simply a virgin copy of that edition—but unlikely, for three reasons. First, it was catalogued under 'Charles Dickens's Public-Reading Books . . .'; secondly, its price (£10) was in line with the price of other prompt-copies, but would have been far too high for a virgin copy of an ordinary trade edition; thirdly, Charles Kent in 1872 did remark that the Gad's Hill library contained two prompt-copies of *Mrs. Gamp*. So maybe this *Mrs. Gamp* prompt-copy, catalogued in 1878,

will come to light some time: but, as Kent notes that the two prompt-
copies which he examined were textually 'all but identical',[1] it is unlikely
to be of very great significance for any future editor of the Readings. It
may be added that this *Mrs. Gamp* is the only prompt-copy mentioned,
described, or cited by Kent which is not known to the present editor.

The above account seems to conflict (it should be acknowledged) with
Dickens family tradition and with a statement by one of his sons, Henry.
It has been said, by his descendants, that until well into the twentieth
century the revered prompt-copies were brought out at Christmas for
a family reading around the fire. Henry Fielding Dickens reports, moreover, that during the 1914–18 War he gave public readings in aid of the
Red Cross, using his father's copies of the *Carol, Cricket, Chimes, Copperfield, Marigold, Boots*, and *Mr. Chops*.[2] But as several of these were on
sale in 1878 and others were sold not long afterwards, he (and family
tradition) must have been mistaken in their belief or memory—unless,
of course, it was Henry or other members of the family who bought the
prompt-copies from Sotheran, or from their later owners, or unless he
borrowed them for these occasions. Or possibly Charley retained some
or all of the prompt-copies listed by Sotheran in 1878 but not offered
for sale in November–December of that year.

No prompt-copies remain in the family's possession now, I am assured,
and all that are known to me eventually came on to the market. In 1913,
all the items offered for sale in 1878, except *Doctor Marigold*, were included in a Dickens Exhibition mounted by the Grolier Club of New
York, and so were most of the others—*The Chimes, Little Dombey* (the
Suzannet copy), the triple-item *The Poor Traveller/Boots/Mrs. Gamp,
David Copperfield, The Bastille Prisoner*, and *Sikes and Nancy*.[3] By then
all the remaining items seem to have passed through the sale-rooms,
and in 1921 John Harrison Stonehouse was able to give an almost complete
listing in his 'First Bibliography of the Reading Editions'.[4]

All but one of the prompt-copies known to me are now in institutional
libraries. Most are in the Berg Collection at the New York Public Library,

[1] Kent, p. 141. It is possible that the copy of *Mrs. Gamp* (Boston, 1868) sold in
1878 was the proof-copy, with corrections by Dickens, now in the Berg Collection;
it is described below, in section 5 of the Introduction.

[2] H. F. Dickens, *Recollections* (1934), pp. 301–2.

[3] *Catalogue of an Exhibition of the Works of Charles Dickens*, with an Introduction
by Royal Cortissoz (New York, The Grolier Club, 1913), pp. 187–90. The Catalogue
does not identify the owners or lenders of these items.

[4] Appended (pp. 49–57) to his facsimile reprint of *Sikes and Nancy* (1921). Stonehouse
fails to list a few second or third copies of items, and does list (as have other biblio-
graphers) one item which is not Dickens's—what is now the *Huntington* copy of *Doctor
Marigold*. One other blemish in Stonehouse's useful Bibliography is his wrongly
surmising 1866 as the date of many of the private printings. This he does, apparently
on the authority of a statement in Maggs Brothers' *Catalogue of Rare Books*, April–
May 1913: but there is no good reason to accept it.

which possesses eleven Readings volumes, three of which contain more than one item—sixteen items altogether, all but three of which (*Little Dombey*, *Mrs. Gamp*, and *Sikes and Nancy*) provide the copy-texts for the present edition. The thirteen *Berg* texts here printed are: the *Carol*, *The Cricket*, *The Chimes*, *The Poor Traveller*, *Boots*, *Copperfield*, *Nickleby*, *Great Expectations*, *Doctor Marigold*, *Mrs. Lirriper*, *Barbox Brothers*, *The Boy at Mugby*, and *The Signalman*. The other substantial collection of Readings texts was assembled by the late Comte Alain de Suzannet; in 1971 his widow donated it to The Dickens House, London, with the exception of one item. This, the version of *Mrs. Gamp* devised in 1867–8 (in a copy which Dickens presented to a friend in 1868), was sold at Sotheby's on 22 November 1971 and is now in the collection of Mr. Kenyon Law Starling; as the latest extant version, it is used as the copy-text in the present edition. Of the *Suzannet* copies in Dickens House, all except *Nicholas Nickleby* are used as copy-texts: *The Haunted Man*, *Little Dombey*, *The Trial*, *Bob Sawyer*, *The Bastille Prisoner*, *Mr. Chops*, and *Sikes and Nancy* (the 'Billington' copy). The *Suzannet* copy of *Nickleby* is the 'short-time' version, treated as a separate item in *T & F* but not in the present edition.

Two other libraries contain Reading-copies, of minor interest. The Elkins Collection in the Free Library of Philadelphia has a prompt-copy of *The Cricket* (but in the headnote to that item it is argued that the *Berg* copy should be regarded as the later and therefore, by the policy of this edition, the preferable version). The Gimbel Collection in the Beinecke Library, Yale University, contains three items: a preliminary prompt-copy of *Little Dombey*, a copy of the *Great Expectations* reading which (like the only other one known to this editor) contains no manuscript deletions, emendations, or annotations by Dickens, and a puzzling and probably non-Dickensian version of *Nickleby*. In the Henry E. Huntington Library, San Marino, California, there is an apparently unique copy of a reading-version of *Doctor Marigold* which is attributed to Dickens in various bibliographies (but not in the Huntington's own catalogue) though, as is argued in the headnote to that item, it was not prepared or owned by him.[1]

These collections contain all of Dickens's own copies which are listed or mentioned by Kent (1872), Sotheran (1878), the Grolier Club (1913),

[1] Further particulars of these collections may be found in John D. Gordan, *Reading for Profit: the Other Career of Charles Dickens: an Exhibition from the Berg Collection* (New York Public Library, 1958); Michael Slater, *Catalogue of Treasures from the Collection formed by the late Comte Alain de Suzannet* (London, Dickens House, 1970); Philip Collins, 'The Texts of Dickens' Readings', *Bulletin of the New York Public Library*, lxxiv (1970), 360–80, 'The Dickens Reading-copies in Dickens House' and 'A Dubious Dickens Item [the Huntington copy of *Doctor Marigold*]', *Dickensian* xviii (1972), 173–9, and forthcoming, and 'Dickens Reading-copies in the Beinecke Library', *Yale University Library Gazette*, xlvi (1972), 153–8.

Stonehouse (1921), and such other catalogues of auctions and exhibitions as I have examined (except the 1868 *Mrs. Gamp* listed by Sotheran in 1878). There must have existed at some time earlier prompt-copies of some items than are known to me (*The Chimes* and *The Trial*) and a later prompt-copy of *Sikes and Nancy* than the *Berg* one. Similarly, true prompt-copies of items which at present survive only in virgin copies with no writing in them by Dickens may appear some time (*The Trial*, *Great Expectations*, *Mrs. Lirriper*, and *The Signalman*): but, as no such copies seem ever to have been recorded, the probability of their appearing is not great.

One other kind of manuscript source, analogous to the prompt-copies, may be mentioned here: spectators' point-by-point records of how Dickens performed various items. Two examples (both in the Dickens House collection, London) are known to me, and have proved most valuable, and it is possible that other such annotated copies of the Readings survive; if so, it is to be hoped that they will come to light. The first is a 32-page typescript by Rowland Hill, 'Notes on Charles Dickens' "Christmas Carol"', almost incredibly dated (in the text, p. 28) 1930. Hill, a Bedford journalist and ardent Dickensian, had as a young man attended a number of Dickens's performances of this item between 1868 and 1870, and, with book on knee, had noted in great detail his textual cuts and variants and his vocal and gestural effects. The other such source is a set of *T & F* booklets, bound into two volumes. The owner's name is inscribed: 'W. M. Wright, May, 1868' (or the initials might possibly be N.M.). On p. 2 of the *Little Dombey* text, Wright remarks: 'The notes in the margin explain the gestures of Dickens, and the tones of his voice in the Readings. Most of the abbreviations have been made by W.M.W.' Unfortunately the binders trimmed the pages, and some of the marginalia have thus been lost. I have not been able to discover Wright's identity, but doubtless he was a resident of Canada or the U.S.A., for he refers to giving Dickens readings himself in Yarmouth, Nova Scotia (hence his 'abbreviations') and to seeing Dickens perform in Boston (see also p. 212, below).

Both Hill and Wright were accurate and perceptive observers, as is apparent when their notes are compared with the prompt-copies containing Dickens's own textual revisions and stage-directions. Hill's achievement in re-creating the *Carol* performance sixty years after Dickens's death is astonishing (and Hill survived until 1945, intellectually active and alert to the end). His account, confined to one item, is much fuller than Wright's, and more sensitive too. Wright had a special fondness for Dickens's hammier gestures (such as 'Both hands supplicatingly'), and one suspects that his own performances lovingly reproduced, and maybe amplified, them. Both accounts add considerably, in detail, to our knowledge of Dickens's gestures, emphases, tones of voice, etc., in his most popular items.

5. THE PUBLISHED EDITIONS

During Dickens's first professional season in 1858, copies of the texts of the items in his initial repertoire were on sale—little green-covered paperbacks, published by Bradbury & Evans and sold at one shilling. The 'Reading Edition' of the three Christmas Book items, however, consisted simply of reprints of the complete original texts, and so bore no relation to the versions which Dickens was actually reading. The other two volumes published in this series were reprints of his privately printed versions, with some printing errors corrected but with passages retained which Dickens had deleted before he presented the items in public. These volumes were *The Story of Little Dombey* and the triple-item *The Poor Traveller: Boots at the Holly-Tree Inn: and Mrs. Gamp.*

Dickens's letters at this time mention the popularity of these booklets with his audiences. For instance,

> The men with the reading books were sold out, for about the twentieth time, at Manchester. Eleven dozen of the Poor Traveller, Boots, and Gamp being sold in about ten minutes, they had no more left; and Manchester became green with the little tracts, in every bookshop, outside every omnibus, and passing along every street. The sale of them, apart from us, must be very great.[1]

His own staff were, he said, selling from six to twelve dozen of these booklets every night.[2] Chapman & Hall, the publishers to whom Dickens transferred soon after this, kept these booklets in print, but they published no further items from his latest repertoire. The reason seems to be that the venture had proved unprofitable. Professor Robert L. Patten, of Rice University, who is researching into Dickens's relations with his publishers, tells me that his impression is that the selling price of one shilling barely covered costs and that reprintings often resulted in a loss. Copies of these items, it may be mentioned, are now not easy to find. Like most paperbacks, they easily fell to pieces, and, having no great bibliographical value, they have not been carefully collected and preserved.

By 1861 Dickens was, in effect, repudiating the texts of this series, for he told a friend:

> There are no printed abridgements of the Carol, Dombey, &c., as I read them, or nearly as I read them. Nor is there any such abridgement in existence, save in my own copies; and there it is made, in part physically, and in part mentally, and no human being but I myself could hope to follow it.[3]

---

[1] *N*, iii. 70.

[2] *Coutts*, p. 363. The sales were not, in fact, enormous. Thus, Bradbury & Evans printed 7,500 copies of *Little Dombey* and 8,000 of the *Poor Traveller* (etc.) booklet between June and October 1858, and there were still unsold stocks of both items to be transferred, on 31 May 1861, to Chapman & Hall. (Information from Professor Robert L. Patten.)

[3] *N*, iii. 217.

He was exaggerating—but under-statement was never his foible—the difficulty of 'following' his prompt-copies, for in 1867 they were used as printer's copy for the edition published in Boston by Ticknor & Fields (his American publishers, and his Readings agents in Boston). George Dolby gives an account of this edition:

> Before the announcement of the Readings in Boston, an intimation had reached me that the 'pirates' had decided on sending shorthand writers to the Readings to 'take them down' as they progressed, with a view to their reproduction and sale—an intimation which was conveyed to Messrs. Ticknor and Fields; and they promptly anticipated such a proceeding by at once issuing the Readings (taken from Mr. Dickens's own reading books) in small volumes, and selling them at their store at such a price as made it impossible for the 'pirates' to get anything out of their publication.[1]

The 'intimation' must have reached Dolby during his exploratory visit to Boston in August–September 1867, to assess the prospects of an American tour. He reported favourably to Dickens and sailed back to Boston, as his advance-guard, on 12 October. The Ticknor & Fields edition carries Dickens's letter of authentication, dated from Gad's Hill, 10 October 1867; doubtless this letter, and the precious prompt-copies, were carried to Boston by Dolby when he sailed two days later.

Certainly this edition was, as Dolby says, set up from the prompt-copies: some uncorrected errors or anomalies in it are manifestly caused by the compositor's misunderstanding, or following too closely, a prompt-copy text.[2] There are, however, a number of minor differences between the *T & F* text and that of the prompt-copies. Most of these are details of punctuation or paragraphing, some of which can be accounted for as the house-style of the American printers. Where there is a difference in wording, however, it is generally safe to assume the Dickens was responsible for it. His letters (including, as Mrs. Madeline House assures me, his unpublished ones) say nothing about his reading the proofs of this edition: but evidence has come to light recently that he proof-read at least one item in the series, *Mrs. Gamp*. In 1972, proof-sheets of this Reading, corrected by Dickens, came on to the market, and were bought by the Berg Collection.

The extent of Dickens's emendation of the prompt-copy text, as set up in these *T & F* proof-sheets, may be judged from the following figures. He made nine alterations to the punctuation, three re-paragraphings, and twenty-five verbal alterations. Almost all of the latter are very minor: the transposition of two successive words, the deletion of one or two words, or the substitution of one word for another. The most extensive alteration consists of four words. He corrected ten printer's errors. The printer's reader had already corrected a few errors—but eventually two of Dickens's corrections to the punctuation were not adopted. The

---

[1] Dolby, p. 177.   [2] E.g., see below, p. 9, note 2.

Ticknor & Fields house-style accounts for a number of minor differences between *T & F* and the prompt-copy (e.g., 'is n't' is substituted for 'isn't'), and some re-paragraphing has taken place, unwarranted by the prompt-copy but not challenged by Dickens.

His making twenty-five verbal alterations in the *Mrs. Gamp* text represents a considerably higher degree of activity than is apparent in most of the *T & F* items, which generally contain few verbal divergencies from the prompt-copy texts. My text of *Mrs. Gamp* is based upon a copy of *T & F* which Dickens used as a prompt-copy, so his proof-reading alterations of 1867 are incorporated into it. In cases, however, where an item is printed from a prompt-copy anterior to *T & F*, significant verbal differences between it and *T & F* are given in my footnotes (for Dickens, when emending the *T & F* proof-sheets, did not bother to transcribe the new wording into the corresponding prompt-copy). Some of these differences, however, are (as was mentioned above) the result of his further revising his prompt-copy texts after *T & F* was printed. The *Mrs. Gamp* corrected proof-sheets—apparently a unique survival from this 1867-8 edition—certainly make one the more inclined to believe that Dickens read all the *T & F* items in proof (as one would have expected). He had time to do so. Many of these items were on sale in December 1867, though the series is dated 1868: but Dickens had arrived in Boston on 19 November, and had nearly a fortnight clear before he began performing on 2 December.

Every item in *T & F* was set up and paginated separately, with an illustration by Sol Eytinge, Junior (an illustrator whom Dickens highly commended). For every item there was a separate title-page in this style: *Mrs. Gamp./by/Charles Dickens./As Condensed by Himself, for His/ Readings*. Items were then bound into twos, corresponding to the various double-bill programmes which Dickens was presenting in America, such as the *Carol* with *The Trial*, or *David Copperfield* with *Bob Sawyer*. These fascicules containing two items were sold at 25 cents. In March 1868 Ticknor & Fields published a collected edition, *Readings by Mr. Charles Dickens*. This was a binding-together of copies of the original printing, so individual texts remained separately paginated. The contents were *A Christmas Carol, The Trial, Copperfield, Bob Sawyer, Little Dombey, Nickleby* (in four chapters), *Boots, Marigold, Nickleby* (in three chapters), and *Mrs. Gamp*. The inclusion of the three-chapter version of *Nickleby* is puzzling, for Dickens seems not to have read this 'short-time' version during his American tour; presumably he had expected to do so.

The ten-in-one collected *Readings*, with Eytinge's engravings, were reprinted in 1877 by Lee & Shepard of Boston, in association with Charles T. Dillingham of New York, and some (maybe all) of the individual items were also reprinted in 1877-9 by one or both of these firms.

Dickens's English publishers, too, belatedly produced *The Readings of Charles Dickens as Arranged and Read by Himself* (London, Chapman & Hall, 1883). This was a simple reprint of the 1868 Boston collection, with no additional items. It was again reprinted by Chapman & Hall in 1907 (*Readings from the Works of Charles Dickens as Arranged and Read by Himself*). The 1907 reprint carried, as Introduction, an essay 'Charles Dickens as a Reader' by John Hollingshead, 'written in 1864' (as a footnote claims), though in fact it was published in *The Critic*, 4 September 1858, and reprinted by Hollingshead, with a few omissions, in 1864: so its account is confined to the initial repertoire.

Since 1907 there has been no further reprinting of the collected Readings, but six individual items have been published. Henry Sotheran & Co. published small limited editions of *Sikes and Nancy* (1921) and the five-chapter version of *David Copperfield* (1922). These were fac-similes of Dickens's privately printed editions—virgin copies, not his prompt-copies. More recently the New York Public Library has published facsimiles of two prompt-copies in its Berg Collection: *Mrs. Gamp*, edited by John D. Gordan (1956), and *A Christmas Carol*, edited by Philip Collins (1971). *Mr. Bob Sawyer's Party* was reprinted, from the *T & F* text, in Edgar and Eleanor Johnson's anthology *The Dickens Theatrical Reader* (London, Gollancz, 1964). A facsimile of the Suzannet copy of *Nicholas Nickleby* was published in 1973 by the Ilkley (Yorkshire) Literature Festival Committee.

Ten items have not hitherto been published. These comprise the five Readings which Dickens prepared but never performed (*The Haunted Man*, *The Bastille Prisoner*, *Great Expectations*, *Mrs. Lirriper's Lodgings*, and *The Signalman*) and the five less popular performed items which were not taken to America and were thus not included in the Boston edition (*The Cricket*, *The Chimes*,[1] *Mr. Chops, the Dwarf*, *Barbox Brothers*, and *The Boy at Mugby*). All but three of these are now published from the prompt-copies, the three exceptions being *Great Expectations*, *Mrs. Lirriper*, and *The Signalman*. The only copies of these—and of *The Trial from Pickwick*—known to me are virgin copies of the privately printed editions, with no writing or deletions by Dickens in them.

A number of items in the present edition have been virtually set from the prompt-copies, like the Ticknor & Fields edition of 1867–8 (but even more accurately, I hope). Photocopies of the prompt-copies have often been clear enough—manuscript marginalia, as well as printed text—to send to the printers, and it is a matter of sentimental gratification, at least to the editor, that, perhaps for the first time since Forster's *Life* was sent to the printers with Dickens's letters pasted into Forster's text, compositors have been setting from unpublished Dickens manuscripts.

[1] The 'Reading Editions' of *The Cricket* and *The Chimes* published in 1858 were, it will be recalled, reprints of the original stories, not of the Readings texts.

6. THE VICTORIAN SOLOIST TRADITION

'Mr. Dickens has invented a new medium for amusing an English audience, and merits the gratitude of an intelligent public,' wrote a London critic during his first season, and provincial journalists repeated the description and the praise during his first tour ('This is a novelty in literature and in the annals of "entertainment"').[1] A decade later, the Farewells provoked other such remarks: 'In taking leave then of Mr. Dickens as a public reader or reciter, we need only reiterate the universally expressed opinion that in their kind these entertainments have been unique.'[2] What, then, was their 'kind', and how unique were Dickens's performances in their conception and execution?

In many ways, the Readings justified the claim of their official chronicler, Charles Kent, that they constituted 'a wholly unexampled incident in the history of literature'.[3] Few, if any, of his literary predecessors could rival Dickens in the prestige and affection, international and relatively classless, which he had enjoyed for over twenty years before he turned professional reader. None of his conceivable rivals, in these respects, had possessed the histrionic talents and the zest for an audience which (as many good judges said) could have taken Dickens to the top of the theatrical profession. His leading contemporary rival in English prose fiction, Thackeray, had so much admired his acting in what proved to be his last performance in a play (*The Frozen Deep*, 1857) as to exclaim: 'If that man would now go upon the stage he would make his £20,000 a-year.'[4] The combination of such supreme literary eminence with such an accomplished stage presence was indeed unique: but Dickens could not have conceived of, nor have succeeded in, his Readings career without some precedents and models, and some auspicious cultural factors, and it is illuminating, I think, to see him (more fully than has been done before) in these contexts.

Several of the analogies to his Readings, as well as the distinctions between him and his predecessors, are indicated by an enthusiastic but perceptive critic during his Farewell tour:

Hear Dickens, and die; you will never live to hear anything of its kind so good. There has been nothing so perfect, in their way, as those readings ever offered to an English audience. Great actors and actresses—Mrs. Siddons herself among them—have read Shakespeare to us; smaller actors, like the Mathews, elder and younger, John Parry, and others, have given 'entertainments' of a half-literary, half-histrionic order; eminent authors, like Coleridge, and Hazlitt, and Sydney Smith, and Thackeray, have read

---

[1] *Illustrated London News*, 31 July 1858, p. 100; *Liverpool Daily Post*, 17 August 1858.

[2] *Clifton Chronicle*, 27 January 1869.

[3] Kent, p. 36. Kent has some further interesting observations on this, pp. 36–8. See also Mark Twain (below, p. lxii, note 1).

[4] Thackeray reported by William Howitt, 15 January 1857, in Carl Ray Woodring, *Victorian Samplers: William and Mary Howitt* (Lawrence, Kansas, 1952), p. 184.

lectures—and many living authors lecture still—but all those appearances, or performances, or whatever else they may be called, are very different from Mr. Dickens' appearances and performances as a reader. He is a story-teller; a prose *improvisatore*; he recites rather than reads; acts rather than lectures. His powers of vocal and facial expression are very great; he has given them conscientious culture; and he applies them heartily and zealously to the due presentment of the creations of his own matchless genius. It has been said that an author is generally either greater or less than his works— that is, that in the works we see the best of a man, or that in the man there is better stuff than he is able to put into his works. In Mr. Dickens, as a reader, each is equal to the other. His works could have no more perfect illustrator; and they are worthy of his best efforts as an artist.[1]

Of the several traditions mentioned here, only one has been mentioned already: the virtuoso performance initiated by Charles Mathews the elder, whom Dickens as a young man so warmly admired.[2] Mathews in his 'At Homes', and his imitators and successors, were sometimes accompanied by a small group of actors, but more often by a single partner and perhaps also by a pianist and vocalist. (Hence the quip by Andrew Arcedeckne, teasing Thackeray after his début as a lecturer: 'Ah, Thac my boy! you ought to ha' 'ad a pianner.')[3] Notable exemplars in this kind of entertainment included Frederick Yates, W. S. Woodin, John Parry with his 'Mrs. Roseleaf's Evening Party', and Mr. and Mrs. German Reed in their perennial 'Evening Gatherings'. The object of all these 'monopolylogues', as they were sometimes called, was to enable the star performer to assume a dazzling range and number of characters in one evening, the formula of an 'At Home' or 'party' or 'gathering' being a simple way of providing such opportunities.

Similar, though pointing more directly towards Dickens's author-recitals, were Albert Smith's one-man shows—comico-dramatic travel-ogues with narrative, songs, and impersonations—the most famous of which, his *Ascent of Mont Blanc*, ran intermittently from 1852 to 1858 and became one of the institutions of London.[4] Smith was a journalist and miscellaneous writer, not an actor, and was thus writing his own scripts and exploiting on the platform his reputation as an author. His great popularity and success (*Mont Blanc* alone earned him £30,000)

[1] *Scotsman*, 8 December 1868.

[2] See above, p. xvii. On several of the matters which follow, I have written more fully in *Reading Aloud: a Victorian Métier* (Lincoln, the Tennyson Society, 1972), 'The Reverend John Chippendale Montesquieu Bellew', *Listener*, 25 November 1971, pp. 716–18, and 'Agglomerating Dollars with Prodigious Rapidity' (on American lecture-tours, etc.), forthcoming.

[3] Quoted in *The Letters and Private Papers of William Makepeace Thackeray*, ed. Gordon N. Ray (1945), ii. 777 n.

[4] See Raymund Fitzsimons, *The Baron of Piccadilly: the Travels and Entertainments of Albert Smith* (1967), which contains (pp. 97–104) a useful account of the 'monopolylogue' tradition. It was significant that Dickens engaged Albert Smith's brother Arthur as his first Readings manager. Bayle Bernard, *Life of Samuel Lover* (1874), i. 242–7, is also very informative about recitals and monopolylogues.

led others to try to exploit this vein, and he was often blamed for, or credited with, this new phenomenon of the personal appearance:

Albert Smith has much to answer for in drawing out of the retirement of their studies our popular authors to gratify the curiosity of their readers and admirers, with the sight of the man with whom they are familiar only as a writer. . . . This shewing of one's-self, however, seems to pay, . . . and as long as they keep each other in counten-ance we may expect occasionally to see Charles Dickens, Thackeray, and a host of the small fry of literature advertizing themselves and their works in the country by reading samples in all the Town Halls where an audience can be collected.[1]

The platform successes of the two leading novelists of the day—Thackeray as a lecturer from 1851 onwards, and Dickens as a paid reader from 1858—certainly gave a fillip to the business (and Dickens, initially uncertain whether Readings might be 'infra dig', must have felt 'kept in counten-ance' when Thackeray, more indisputably a gentleman than himself, had preceded him in lucrative platform appearances). 'All our literati seem inclined to become "oral instructors,"' commented the *Illustrated London News* in 1858, referring to this rush to the platform; four years later the *Saturday Review*, in a penetrating article on 'Readings', deplored the host of 'literary gentlemen, who, without oratorical gifts, seem merely to make an exhibition of their own faces'—though it acknowledged that Dickens was indeed 'endowed with histrionic talent of no common order'.[2] Authors who had lately taken to the boards included Edmund Yates, George Augustus Sala and 'Arthur Sketchley' (the Reverend George Rose); Henry Mayhew had tried it, very briefly; Mark Lemon, the editor of *Punch*, was soon to join in as a professional. Clearly the platform band at this time were—with the conspicuous exceptions of Dickens and Thackeray—the second- or third-raters of literature. The other major literary figures were disqualified by lack of platform talent, or by holding full-time posts or avocations (thus, Disraeli had another kind of platform), or by belonging to the more retiring sex (one can hardly imagine Mrs. Gaskell or George Eliot entertaining a large audience), or they felt scruples against such an occupation (Tennyson, who could certainly have triumphed in it, refused a munificent offer for an American tour).[3]

Dickens's position as author-recitalist was the more unchallengeable, with the most eminent of his literary contemporaries out of the competi-tion, except for Thackeray, who confined himself to the less spectacular

---

[1] *Exeter Flying Post*, 15 January 1862.
[2] *Illustrated London News*, 15 May 1858, p. 487; *Saturday Review*, 4 October 1862, p. 411.
[3] J. B. Pond, the American lecture-agent, offered him $50,000 (=£10,000) for fifty readings: see his letter to Tennyson, 1 October 1885 (Tennyson Research Centre, Lincoln Public Library), and Hallam Tennyson, *Tennyson and his Friends* (1911), p. 489.

genre of the lecture. Nevertheless, his success owed much to the vogue for readings and virtuoso displays. Thus, in the spring of 1863, when he was giving a short season of Readings at the Hanover Square Rooms, Londoners could also see the German Reeds (with John Parry) at the Gallery of Illustration, Arthur Sketchley's 'Mrs. Brown' recital at the St. James's Hall (often Dickens's London place of performance), Edmund Yates's 'Invitations to Evening Parties' (with Harold Power, vocalist) at the Egyptian Hall, Fanny Kemble's Shakespearean Readings at the Dudley Gallery, or Mark Lemon's dramatic readings in aid of charity. There were many of the 'small fry of literature' at work in the business too, who never got nearer than Islington Town Hall to the fashionable metropolitan halls, and never received the tempting offers from the American lecture agencies which, from around 1870, began to attract across the Atlantic increasing numbers of authors, recitalists, public men, and notorieties, all hopeful of 'agglomerating dollars with prodigious rapidity' (to use Thackeray's exultant phrase during his first American tour, which was a conspicuous early demonstration of the cash potential of that lecture-avid country).[1]

Albert Smith had indeed a good deal to answer for, though he had been preceded by a few author-recitalists who had performed with less éclat. *The Times*, in an interesting retrospect on public readings (7 October 1868), named the dramatist T. J. Serle as the first author of the period to read his works in public. Sheridan Knowles, another dramatist who, like Serle, had been a professional actor, also tried giving recitals of his own plays. Other authors, notably from Coleridge onwards, had given occasional series of lectures, mostly in London, and some of the smaller fry, such as Charles Cowden Clarke, had made a practice of travelling further afield, though, of the more eminent, Thackeray seems to have given the lead in touring both the provinces and America (intermittently from 1851 to 1858). But the idea of 'readings', whether by author, actor, or professional recitalist, was relatively new when Dickens began his charity performances in 1853. The *Times* critic cited above dated it from the day when 'Charles Kemble first read *Cymbeline* in public, and the notion that a multitude could be attracted by hearing another man do what nine-tenths of the assembly would fancy they could do as well for themselves was deemed almost presumptuous'. That was in 1844; and in the same year the Irish novelist and poet Samuel Lover began giving recitals from his works (he met with considerable success, both in Britain and in America). Two years later, it will be recalled, Dickens was wondering whether he might exploit 'these days of lecturings and readings'; two years earlier, indeed, in 1842, another senior actor, Macready, had been reflecting 'how popular one might make readings, by good selection'

[1] Letter of [2?] January 1853, *Letters and Private Papers*, iii. 166.

(and he sketched out a programme).[1] Another Kemble, the great Mrs. Siddons, had indeed given a few readings back in 1812 but that was an illustrious flash in the pan: and a third Kemble, Charles's daughter Fanny, impatiently awaited her father's retirement in 1847 before beginning her long career in this line, giving memorable Shakespearean recitals during the next few decades all over Britain and America. Suddenly the idea caught on, and many leading actors and actresses gave such readings, either occasionally and gratuitously for charitable or educational purposes (like Macready), or between ordinary theatre engagements (like Irving), or in a few eminent cases such as Fanny Kemble or Miss Glyn (Mrs. E. S. Dallas) virtually abandoning stage-plays for recitals. They were joined by professional recitalists such as the Reverend J. C. M. Bellew, who were neither actors nor authors.

By 1868 that *Times* reviewer could remark that '"Readers" are abundant; there is not a literary institution that does not in the course of a year publish a programme of entertainment in which some plays or poems to be "read" by some person of celebrity, general or local, do not hold a prominent place'—though, he added, 'amid all the variety of "readings" those of Mr. Charles Dickens stand alone'.[2] The 'literary institutions' mentioned here were conspicuous in promoting such events, and were a major cause of the vogue for readings. Fittingly, indeed, Dickens's first public readings, in 1853, had been given to aid the funds of just such a venture, the Birmingham and Midland Institute: and most of his other charity readings were given for other such adult-educational bodies. He had been preceded by enough humbler recitalists for J. W. Hudson, surveying British adult education in 1851, to complain that Shakespearean readings and other such items were creating an 'unhealthy excitement' and directing students' energies into 'a wrong channel'. As a recent historian has remarked, 'lectures' at Mechanics' Institutes increasingly became 'programmes of excerpts from favourite authors, sometimes interlarded with appreciative comments. The most popular professional lecturers were elocutionists who offered "A Night with Swift (or Defoe, Dr. Johnson, Thomas Hood, Sydney Smith, Spenser, Carlyle, Burns, etc.)." Platform artists who read plays aloud were in particular demand.'[3] Dickens's platform career seems indeed to have coincided with the peak of the vogue for public readings, both in such establishments and in the commercial West End venues. One indication of this occurs in the centenary history of the Newcastle Literary and Philosophical Society, one of the most flourishing and

[1] *Diaries*, ii. 176.

[2] *The Times*, 7 October 1868.

[3] Richard D. Altick, *The English Common Reader 1800–1900* (Chicago, 1957), pp. 202–203, quoting Hudson on p. 202. For a fuller account of Dickens's involvement with the movement, see Philip Collins, *Dickens and Adult Education* (Leicester, 1962).

enterprising of those provincial 'Lit. and Phil.'s which, like the Athen-
aeums, Literary Institutions, Mechanics' Institutes, and Lyceums, were
often the local centres for such events. The Newcastle book lists all
the Society's activities between 1803 and 1896. During the twelve years
of Dickens's professional Readings career, the Society heard twenty-five
readings, but in the previous fifty-odd years only four, and in the next
quarter-century only a further thirteen.[1] Another indication of the wide-
spread interest in such entertainments, at a very different social level,
was the Penny Readings movement, which began, under clerical auspices,
in 1859 (again, a date close to Dickens's début): and within a few years
most conscientious parish priests were running weekly events of this
kind.[2] Penny Readings, though considered old-fashioned by the 1880s,
survived into the twentieth century in many parishes; they were an important feature of D. H. Lawrence's boyhood, and Dickens (still the
favourite topic) thus became his favourite novelist.[3]

Dickens, then, was inheriting several traditions: that of the versatile
show-off monopolyloguist, that of the actor or elocutionist giving Shakespearean or other literary selections, and that of the author giving lectures
or readings from his own work. Most of these developments stemmed
from the 1840s and 1850s, when they were favoured by several circumstances. Firstly, there was the establishment, mostly from the late 1820s
onwards, of those 'literary institutions', which greatly welcomed such
entertainments, since they were respectable on both moral and intellectual
grounds and had the further advantage of being cheap and easy to stage.
Secondly, some relaxation was occurring in the Nonconformist conscience; the respectable now wanted something like the pleasures of the
drama, though (as George R. Sims recalled, of the 1860s and 1870s)
there was still 'a very considerable portion of the public who would not
enter a theatre . . . And so there was always a plentiful supply of entertainment arranged in such a way as to ease the scruples of the conscientious objector.'[4] Hence such bizarre moral compromises as the Reverend
Bellew's reciting the whole of a Shakespeare play, while a company of
mute actors mimed the action on a stage above him: this performance,
staged in a hall and not a theatre, counted as a recital (and therefore
respectable) and not as a play. Thirdly, developments in transport had

[1] Robert Spence Watson, *The History of the Literary and Philosophical Society of
Newcastle-upon-Tyne (1793–1896)* (1897), pp. 339–61.
[2] See H. P. Smith, *Literature and Adult Education a Century Ago: Pantopragmatics
and Penny Readings* (Oxford, 1960).
[3] Harry T. Moore, *The Intelligent Heart: the Story of D. H. Lawrence* (1955),
pp. 12, 55.
[4] Sims, *My Life* (1911), p. 310. On this, see also 'Readings', *Saturday Review*,
4 October 1862, pp. 411–12. Newspaper reports on Dickens's Readings often commented upon the fact that clergymen, and their families, were present.

made touring in such one-night-stand entertainments easy and comfort-able—the expansion of the railway system in the 1840s and of trans-atlantic steam-shipping from that decade onwards. Thackeray, on tour in 1857, thanked God for 'the railroad that whisks me about to get this money ... You see without railroads I couldn't have made this little fortune w[hic]h is dropping into us, Sheffield, York to Newcastle w[oul]d have been 40 hours journey instead of $5\frac{1}{2}$ without any fatigue.'[1] Finally, there was (as was maintained at the time) a new cult of literary personality which made the public eager to see as well as read their favourite authors. Thus, a newspaper noticing Dickens's first readings-tour, and alluding to his recent marital difficulties, saw the publicity about such episodes as a sign of the times:

... nowadays the public must know all about your domestic relations, your personal appearance, your age, the number of your children, the colour of your eyes and hair—must peep into the arcana of your social existence ... A photography likeness sells a book; how much more likely that it would sell when the living author stands before you.[2]

There were, then, precedents for Dickens's taking to the platform in this way—but none so close, or with authors so illustrious or beloved or so talented in this line, as much to subtract from the uniqueness asserted by the critics quoted at the beginning of this section. After his first public reading, *The Times*, in a long review, stressed the novelty of this enterprise by 'the most admired fiction-writer of his time':

It is an unprecedented thing now-a-days to hear authors reading their own works in public. The simple fashion of bardic times is past, and the fastidiousness of modern ideas finds or fancies something egotistical in such displays. ... There is probably no author in this country, except Mr. Dickens, who would have ventured to do so.

The critic then noted how well his texts lent themselves to such rendering, and how skilful a reader he was; so, he concluded, was it surprising that, 'bringing these personal advantages to bear upon such a work as the *Christmas Carol*, ... Mr. Dickens ... should have achieved a triumphant success?'[3]

When arguing the case for the Readings, against Forster's opposition, Dickens (it will be recalled) referred more than once to 'that particular relation (personally affectionate and like no other man's) which subsists between me and the public'.[4] This special quality of feeling about him, beyond the general admiration for his literary and histrionic abilities,

[1] *Letters and Private Papers*, iv. 22.

[2] *Saunders's News-Letter* [Dublin], 26 August 1858. Both Dickens and Thackeray noted that their 'personal appearances' increased the sales, or copyright value, of their books.

[3] *Times*, 2 January 1854.

[4] *Life*, p. 646. See above, p. xxii.

indeed elevated the Readings to a class of their own. 'No one thinks first of Mr. Dickens as a writer. He is at once, through his books, a friend,' wrote the great American scholar Charles Eliot Norton, during the Readings tour of the States.[1] When Dickens was there, in the flesh, reading from those familiar and much-loved books, the emotional (as well as artistic) impact was potent. At the end of his Farewell performances in Dublin, 'the people stood up and cheered him lustily. It is not that the world knows Mr. Dickens to be merely a great man; but we all know him to be a good man. And, therefore, his reading is not looked upon as a performance, but as a friendly meeting longed for by people to whom he has been kind.'[2] Many reviews made this point; one more may be cited, from an account of a notable occasion in his Readings career, his New York début. Everyone in 'that vast assembly', wrote a reviewer, was united in wanting to do homage to

... a man of true and beneficent genius. To see and feel this was to be deeply and inexpressibly thrilled—was to realize, with gladness and gratitude, the profound devotion of true-hearted men and women to a great natural guide and leader. An immense chord of feeling has been touched and sounded by Charles Dickens. In thirty years of literary life ... he has created immortal works of art ... and has won in equal measure the homage and the love of his generation. Something of this affectionate feeling was heartily expressed by his audience last night; nor in all that great throng was there a single mind unconscious of the privilege it enjoyed in being able, even so partially, to thank Charles Dickens for all the happiness he has given to the world. It is a better world because of him.

In this, and a follow-up review next day, this critic discussed the technical skill of these performances and how adequately Dickens's selections represented his literary achievement. One other general point is worth quoting: '... what he is doing now is only the natural outgrowth of what he has been doing all the days of his life. To have heard these readings is to have witnessed the spontaneous expression of a great nature in the maturity of its genius.'[3] With which one might compare an anticipation of the Readings, in *David Copperfield*: Agnes Wickfield tells David how his 'old friends ... read my book as if they heard me speaking its contents'.[4] In the Readings, Dickens's hundreds of thousands of 'friends' had the opportunity to hear him do just that: and for most of them it was an overwhelming experience.

7. THE PERFORMER AND THE NOVELIST

'His reading', wrote that Dublin critic, 'is not looked upon as a performance, but as a friendly meeting longed for by people to whom he has

---

[1] 'Charles Dickens', *North American Review*, April 1868, cited (with similar material) in *Dickens: the Critical Heritage*, ed. Philip Collins (1971), p. 1.

[2] *Freeman's Journal*, 12 January 1869.

[3] *New York Tribune*, 10 and 11 December 1867.

[4] *David Copperfield*, ch. 48 (Oxford Illustrated edition, p. 698).

been kind': but affection, however intense, could no more be relied upon
to fill large halls, night after night, than the sale of his books could be
sustained by readers' thinking of him (in Charles Eliot Norton's phrase)
as a friend rather than a writer. Happily the Dublin critic, awestruck by
Sikes and Nancy two days later, reminded his readers that Dickens,
besides being a great and good man, was an outstanding author and performer too, and he put it handsomely: 'It can honestly be said that Mr.
Dickens is the greatest reader of the greatest writer of the age.'[1] But, a
year before, a magnificently impudent advertisement had appeared in a
New York newspaper while he was performing there:

ELOCUTION.—ALL of 'DICKENS'S READINGS' taught by an accomplished
Instructor so as to enable the pupil to make each character perfectly discriminated in
quality of voice and manner from all others, and to personate the same with a vivacity,
spirit and naturalness far superior to the style of the great novelist. To all possessing
average reading abilities, he guarantees perfect success, together with the skill to fill
the largest hall with the greatest ease to reader and listener. Charges in advance, $5.[2]

Where between these extremes—granted that the 'accomplished Instructor' in New York was not altogether disinterested—might a just estimate
of Dickens's platform skills lie? How, and how well, did he read? and
what relation does his career as a reader bear to his work as a novelist?

Clearly—as many accounts already quoted have averred—he was
talented. Nor are the box-office statistics irrelevant. A curiosity to see
the great man, a desire to do homage to a respected and beloved author,
could account for a first-time success, but not for continuous, repeated,
and undiminished successes when he returned to such major cities as
London, Edinburgh, Dublin, and New York. He had a good voice, able
to command auditoria holding three or four thousand people, though it was
not especially powerful and some desirable vocal effects were beyond him.
As for his histrionic skills: when applying for an audition at Covent
Garden in 1832, he had claimed to have 'a strong perception of character
and oddity, and a natural power of reproducing in my own person what
I [have] observed in others'.[3] Accounts of his acting confirm that he was
indeed a clever character-actor (there was less unanimity about his
narrative or pathetic powers)—and the Readings manifestly provided
many opportunities for 'character and oddity'. Carlyle, a man little given
to easy enthusiasm, wrote after a Reading: 'Dickens does it capitally . . .;
acts better than any Macready in the world; a whole tragic, comic, heroic
theatre visible, performing under one *hat*, and keeping us laughing . . .
the whole night' (though Carlyle had remembered to be properly sour
too in those ellipses, for the first is 'such as *it* is', and the second 'in a

---

[1] *Freeman's Journal*, 14 January 1869.
[2] *New York Tribune*, 23 December 1867.
[3] *Life*, p. 59.

sorry way, some of us thought').[1] On another occasion Carlyle remarked: 'I had no conception, before hearing Dickens read, of what capacities lie in the human face and voice. No theatre-stage could have had more players than seemed to flit about his face, and all tones were present.'[2] Many reports refer to the mobility and expressiveness of his face, and to his effective, though generally restrained and sparing, use of gesture. 'What Dickens *does* is frequently infinitely better than anything he says, or the way he says it,' wrote one observer (who admired the words too): and another, 'In his ever-active hand an unlimited power of illustration resides. Frequently a mere motion of the hand shed a hitherto undreamt-of meaning upon a whole passage.'[3] It was through such practised skills, and his authorial intimacy with the text, that he enhanced his audience's previous apprehension of the texts 'a thousand-fold' (as the more enthusiastic put it). To hear him read, instead of reading the book oneself, was like meeting someone instead of getting a letter from him— or like seeing a stereoscopic instead of a two-dimensional photograph, or a great painting instead of an engraving of it—or it was to experience 'surprises and new thoughts that come like revelations of suddenly discovered facts in the lives of old acquaintances'.[4]

Inevitably, not all accounts were as favourable. Not only did critics differ in perceptiveness and standards, and in sympathy for Dickens and for this kind of performance, but also his performances differed markedly, both over the years, and from night to night, and from audi-torium to auditorium (for their shape, feeling, and acoustic qualities greatly affected his mode and success). His closest friends and associates noted how successive performances of the same item would vary con-siderably, according to his health and spirits and the degree of his rapport with his audience. Also, to avoid a tedious sense of routine, he would bring out now this, and now that, range of possibilities in a text. As any actor will say, no audience is the same as last night's, and no performance can be, either. A soloist, upon whom everything depends, is all the more likely to be affected by the subjective and objective exigencies of the

[1] J. A. Froude, *Thomas Carlyle: a History of his Life in London* (1884), ii. 270.

[2] D.A. Wilson, *Carlyle to Threescore-and-Ten, 1853–1865* (1929), p. 505.

[3] Field, p. 33 (see below, *A Christmas Carol*, p. 21, n. 3); *Belfast News-Letter*, 9 January 1869. In earlier seasons, there might be instead 'an expressive . . . wave of the paper-knife which he held in his hand' (*Huddersfield Chronicle*, 11 September 1858). This paper-knife—seen in various photographs of him at his reading-desk—was later not used. I do not know when he stopped using it, nor why he ever started doing so. Maybe it was a reminiscence of Albert Smith's pointer? Wilkie Collins, praising his own readings in America (1874), sneered at this (and other?) aspects of Dickens's: 'My readings have succeeded by surprising the audiences, . . . because I don't flourish a paper knife and stamp about the platform, and thump the reading desk' (R.C. Lehmann, *Memories of Half a Century* (1908), p. 66).

[4] *Preston Guardian*, 14 December 1861; *Yorkshire Post*, 1 February 1867; *Birmingham Gazette*, 1 January 1862; *New York Herald*, 13 December 1867.

moment.[1] 'He depended, as I remember,' wrote one of his admirers, 'in a most extraordinary degree upon the temper of his audience. I have heard him read downright flatly and badly to an unresponsive house, and I have seen him vivified and quickened to the most extraordinary display of genius by an audience of the opposite kind.'[2] Nor, of course, are reviewers immune to such variability, even captiousness. A striking instance occurs in the *New York Times*, reporting his début in that city (and the echoing of phrases from day to day suggests that one man wrote all these reviews). On 16 December 1867, after Dickens's first week at the Steinway Hall, the critic recorded 'a feeling of keen disappointment' even among Dickens's loyallest admirers. 'Enthusiasm for the man has to a certain degree covered it up, but it has on many occasions found tolerably loud expression.' Far from his being 'without an elocutionary rival', there were a dozen actors in New York who could read his works better than he could. He was good in humorous character and narration but 'in everything else he fails'. But a week earlier, on 10 December, for the same critic, the readings 'fully proved the truth of what has often been said: that he is one of the best of living actors', and 'we never have had, and . . . never shall have, any entertainments more charming'. The next day, Dickens's second programme was judged 'even a greater triumph', and of one (non-humorous) moment the critic wrote: 'Acting more impressive than this we have never witnessed.'[3] On 14 December, his final performance of the week was reported 'in every way delightful'. And in the two days succeeding its report that audiences were 'keenly disappointed', the *New York Times* noted that his popularity 'exhibits no sign of diminution'—indeed, 'The longer Mr. Dickens reads here the better people like to hear him' (17 and 18 December). He might well, it suggested, stay in America, reading nightly, for the rest of his life. All of which is a reminder both that a a critic can be intemperate or injudicious in his phrasing, and that random dippings into accounts of the Readings can be misleading.

Enjoying the benefit of previous students' work on this topic and the generous help of the many individuals and institutions thanked in my Acknowledgements, I have probably read more press reports, and other

---

[1] I write here from some experience of this kind, having myself performed six of Dickens's items (*Mrs. Gamp*, *Boots*, *Little Dombey*, *The Trial*, *Bob Sawyer*, and *Sikes and Nancy*) and episodes from four of the others, besides extracts from his work which he never read. I hope that, without succumbing to the danger which besets Dickensian commentators—confusing themselves with him—I have thus gained some insight both into the technical problems which a soloist faces when committed to holding a large audience's attention for two hours, and into the ways in which any proficient reader can make his hearers aware of features of the text which are easily overlooked in a silent reading: insight also into the aural qualities of this prose

[2] David Christie Murray, *Recollections* (1908), p. 50.

[3] See below, *David Copperfield*, p. 248, note 4.

records and reminiscences, of the Readings than anyone since Dickens and his tour managers: and it is not, I feel sure, my partiality for him (which I admit to) that makes me say that reports were overwhelmingly favourable, with many more running to the superlative and ecstatic end of the scale than to the dismissive or severely critical. 'Acts better than any Macready in the world,' Carlyle said: and Macready himself— a severe judge of actors, as his diaries show—thought very highly of Dickens. 'He reads as well as an experienced actor would—he is a surprising man,' he noted as early as 1838, when Dickens read him the manuscript of his *Lamplighter* farce. Six years later he was 'undisguisedly sobbing and crying' at the private reading of *The Chimes*—the first of a number of exultant reports, in Dickens's letters, of the effect which he could produce upon the great actor.[1] Macready's diary for 1862 shows that he did indeed greatly admire Dickens's skills: 'His reading [of *Nickleby*] was very artistic, giving point and force to every prominent passage. It was a very interesting and satisfactory evening's entertainment.' *Copperfield*, the next night, was read 'admirably. The humour was delightful, and the pathos of various passages gave me a choking sensation, whilst the account of Emily's flight brought the tears to my eyes. The reading of the story was altogether a truly artistic performance.'[2] During his Farewell series, Dickens gave, by special request, two daytime performances so that members of the theatrical profession could attend: and he triumphed with that critical audience too. 'We all seemed spellbound under his varying powers,' wrote the Bancrofts, and Dickens wept at 'the wonderful reception' the actors gave him.[3]

Comparisons between his platform skills and those of professional actors were indeed generally more favourable than the *New York Times* remark quoted above. This Introduction began by quoting the critics who thought him more than the equal of the versatile Charles Mathews (father or son); the headnote to *Bardell and Pickwick* (below) quotes critics who found his impersonations of characters in that much-dramatized episode superior to those familiar on the stage; in a comparison between him and the most esteemed professional recitalist of the period, the *New York Tribune* (10 January 1868) remarked that it was futile to ask 'whether he or Mrs. [Fanny] Kemble is the more artistic reader. Both are wonderful in their line. Both have the magical power to enchain an audience spellbound from the first word to the last.' Many other such comparisons could be quoted, few of them to his discredit.

[1] *Diaries of William Charles Macready 1833–1851*, ed. William Toynbee (1912), i. 480. For Dickens's letters about Macready as an audience, see above, p. xix, and below, pp. 216, 469.

[2] Quoted in Sir Nevil Macready, *Annals of an Active Life* [1924], i. 20. Macready's grand-daughter, Mrs. Lisa Puckle, tells me that he always said that Dickens was the only amateur actor who was equal to a professional.

[3] *Mr. and Mrs. Bancroft on and off the Stage*, by Themselves (6th edn., 1889), p. 138.

Another suggestive comparison is Turgenev's, between him and another major novelist of that period who was renowned for reading from his own works, Nikolai Gogol, 'the Russian Dickens'. Turgenev, who heard them both, wrote:

Dickens could be said to give a public performance of his novels; his reading was dramatic, almost theatrical: there were several first-class actors in his face alone who made you laugh and cry. Gogol, on the other hand, struck me by the extraordinary simplicity and restraint of his manner, by a sort of grace and at the same time naive simplicity; he did not seem to care whether there were any listeners or what they were thinking of. It seemed as though all Gogol was concerned about was how to convey his own impression more convincingly. The effect was quite remarkable. . . .[1]

The difference between the two novelists' readings was partly due to circumstances: Gogol read only to private literary gatherings, Dickens in auditoria where it would have been both implausible and impracticable for the reader to behave as if he did not 'care whether there were any listeners or what they were thinking of'. Perhaps, however, Dickens was too evidently conscious of his audience. Edward Dowden, for instance, remarked that his eye 'kept roving throughout his audience from face to face, as if seeking for some expression of the effect he was creating'; and another intelligent critic, R. H. Hutton, discussing the Readings with some distaste, and relating them to his writings, remarked that Dickens 'had *too much* eye to the effect to be produced by all he did. . . . He makes you feel that it is not the intrinsic insight that delights him half so much as the power it gives him of moving the world. The visible word of command must go forth from himself in connection with all his creations.'[2]

This is an aspect of his fiction which need not be judged adversely, as Robert Garis well argues in his book *The Dickens Theatre*. Dickens the novelist, he remarks, is strongly 'present before us . . . as a performer, as a maker and doer. . . . Our response to Dickens's presence in his prose takes the form of an impulse to applaud. The performer is "there" in the sense that he is displaying his skill.'[3] The fiction is theatrical in

---

[1] I owe this comparison, and this quotation from Turgenev's *Literary Reminiscences*, to Mr. M. Beresford, commenting in a letter to the *Listener* (22 January 1970) on a broadcast talk of mine about Dickens's readings (*Listener*, 25 December 1969). Further information about Turgenev's opinion of the Readings appears in Patrick Waddington, 'Dickens, Pauline Viardot and Turgenev', *New Zealand Slavonic Journal*, No. 1 (1974), 55–73.

[2] Dowden quoted in *Dickensian*, v (1909), 66; Hutton, reviewing Forster's *Life* in *Spectator*, 7 February 1874, pp. 175–6 (reprinted in *Dickens, the Critical Heritage*, pp. 585–6). Cf. John Ruskin in a letter of 1870, reprinted ibid., p. 444: as a novelist, Dickens 'was essentially a stage manager, and used everything for effect on the pit'. Of Ruskin's more famous remark, in his appreciation of *Hard Times* (reprinted ibid., p. 314), that Dickens 'chooses to speak in a circle of stage fire', Forster pertinently comments that this has a 'wider application to this part of Dickens's life [the 1850s] than its inventor supposed' (*Life*, p. 566).

[3] *The Dickens Theatre* (Oxford, 1965), p. 9.

another respect too, which helps to account both for its lending itself so admirably to public reading and for some of Dickens's platform techniques: much of the action is conceived dramatically (in terms of speech, gesture, and tableau), it is full of 'character-parts', and the narrative prose is highly aural in quality. Indeed, in reading his works aloud Dickens was re-enacting in public an important stage of his creative process, which took place before he set pen to paper. I refer here to his daughter Mamie's famous account of how she was once allowed to sit in his study while he was composing: he would rush to a mirror, make 'extraordinary facial contortions' in front of it, at the same time 'talking rapidly in a low voice', and then go to his desk and write. It was, as it were, a private 'reading' as an immediate preliminary to writing. And this anecdote belongs to Dickens's maturity: he was performing *Hard Times* in front of that mirror.[1] Maybe it was such curious practices, and not only the general nature of his imagination, that led Forster to remark on his 'power of projecting himself into shapes and suggestions of his fancy. . . . What he desired to express he became.' And, discussing Dickens's early ambition to go on the stage, he comments that no one need regret 'how great an actor was in Dickens lost. He took to a higher calling, but it included the lower.'[2] That is, his fiction partook—in no pejorative sense—of the theatrical; and in giving Readings from that fiction ('a substitution of lower for higher aims', as Forster regarded it),[3] he was both adopting a variant of that 'lower calling' to which he had been so drawn, and also demonstrating his long-standing debt, as a writer, to it.

'He does not only *read* his story; he *acts* it,' wrote one reviewer. 'Each character . . . is as completely assumed and individualised . . . as though he was personating it in costume on the stage.' Only in the pathetic passages, wrote another reviewer of the same performance, were his dramatic efforts 'too effective—too *stagey*, in fact'.[4] How tasteful and appropriate was his compromise between acting and reading? His solution varied from item to item; thus, in *Sikes and Nancy* he abandoned (triumphantly, as most critics thought) the convention of the reader, conscious of his audience, and became an actor immersed in his roles. Generally he was reported as having found a happy compromise, and as having narrated and impersonated with restraint (though two interesting dissentients will be quoted below). An American reviewer wrote: 'Simplicity, delicacy, reality—these are the chief elements of Mr. Dickens's

[1] Mamie Dickens, *My Father as I recall him* [1897], p. 47. She does not specify the novel, but states that this episode took place at Tavistock House (where Dickens lived from 1851 to 1860) and while she was recovering from a serious illness (which was in 1854).
[2] *Life*, pp. 380, 381.
[3] *Life*, p. 641.
[4] *Courant* (Edinburgh) and *Scotsman*, both 28 November 1861.

method . . . directed and governed by the instinct of taste.'[1] He 'carefully avoids making his dramatic faculty too prominent in his reading', noted another reviewer: 'He does not, except on very rare occasions, act thoroughly *out*; he suggests, and suggests very forcibly; but he leaves to his hearers to supply what he does not feel it necessary to delineate . . . This is just what the very best reading—that is, reading, and not acting—ought to be.' Many reviews praised him for being thus 'careful not to confound the actor and the reader', and distinguished him from his noisier rivals in the platform trade, who indulged also in 'distressing physical exercises, which make some elocutionists objects of pity rather than of admiration'.[2]

'Be not too tame neither,' Hamlet told the Players, in his advice about how 'to hold, as 'twere, the mirror up to nature.' Dickens, as accounts already quoted have suggested, was far from tame: but how 'natural' did he appear? Accounts differ, of course, and the question must be considered in relation to the prevalent histrionic and elocutionary conventions. Wonderful, but undeniably 'stagey', was G. A. Sala's verdict: Dickens often over-acted.[3] But this was not the general opinion. It is notable how many reviews, in sophisticated journals, of Dickens's final appearance in a play—as Wardour in *The Frozen Deep*—praised him for subtlety and restraint in a role which offered much temptation to saw the air and tear a passion to tatters. 'His acting is quiet, strong, natural, and effective,' reported the *Saturday Review* (rarely one of his warmest admirers). 'Where an ordinary artist would look for "points" of effect he looks for "points" of truth,' wrote *The Times* critic. If professionals would learn from him, it 'might open a new era for the stage', the *Leader* went so far as to suggest.[4] So he was certainly capable of what, by contemporary standards and conventions, was very 'natural' acting: and many reports of the Readings credit him with this kind of ease—an absence of affectation, exaggeration, or strain. Doubtless he sometimes fell short of his intention to strike this note. A solo performer is subject to grosser temptations than is a member of an acting company. He is in a show-off situation, and can easily lose control and go too far; he has no on-stage colleagues, and no director, to correct his level or to look askance on any crudities or amplifications in which he indulges

[1] *New York Tribune*, 11 December 1867.

[2] *Northern Whig* (Belfast), 21 March 1867; *Brighton Gazette*, 22 October 1868. There is a perceptive account of how, in a huge auditorium, Dickens managed to stay close in spirit to 'the gentlemanly drawing-room, with its limiting conventionalities', in *Nation* (New York), 12 December 1867, p. 482.

[3] George Augustus Sala, *Charles Dickens* [1870], pp. 91-2.

[4] Quoted by Robert Louis Brannan in his *Under the Management of Mr. Charles Dickens: his Production of 'The Frozen Deep'* (Ithaca, N.Y., 1966), pp. 80, 82, 74. On acting and elocutionary techniques of the age, see Theresa Murphy, 'Interpretation in the Dickens period', *Quarterly Journal of Speech*, xli (1955), 243-9.

himself. Faced with an unresponsive audience, or playing in an un-congenial auditorium, he may over-exert himself to warm things up. (Forster noted 'a certain loss of refinement' after his return from America, where auditoria were generally much larger; but 'the old delicacy . . . and a subdued tone' returned for the Farewells.)[1] And Dickens, repeating his more popular items scores of times, must have varied his performance, to avoid monotony—and must sometimes have taken the level up, and sometimes played it down. ('Je suis payé pour le savoir.')

Two further contemporary comments may be quoted, to end this part of my discussion. Both came from well-informed reviewers who greatly admired the Readings, but they concur in criticizing (with some justice, I suspect) the intensity with which Dickens impersonated his characters. It is not exactly over-acting that they charge him with, but rather a distinctness of characterization that was not always appropriate in a solo reading. The first is by Professor Adolphus W. Ward:

Now the art of reading, even in the case of dramatic works, has its own laws, which even the most brilliant readers cannot neglect except at their peril. A proper pitch has to be found in the first instance, before the exceptional passages can be, as it were, marked off from it; and the absence of this groundtone sometimes interfered with the total effect of a reading by Dickens. On the other hand, the exceptional passages were, if not uniformly, at least generally excellent; nor am I at all disposed to agree with Forster in preferring, as a rule, the humorous to the pathetic. At the same time, there was notice-able in these readings a certain hardness which competent critics likewise discerned in Dickens' acting, and which could not, at least in the former case, be regarded as an ordinary characteristic of dilettanteism. The truth is that he isolated his parts too sharply—a frequent fault of English acting, and one more detrimental to the total effect of a reading than even to that of an acted play.[2]

The other quotation comes from a long critique in an American magazine, which includes comparisons between Dickens and other recitalists. Fanny Kemble, it noted, in her Shakespearean readings,

. . . changes utterly at every change of person; but she changes only by the wonderful modulation of her matchless voice. There is no gesture—no movement of figure or face. Mr. Dickens is the perfect opposite. He regularly acts the character he personates . . . This . . . is the weak point of his effort. He is an admirable actor—an almost perfect mime. But no human face can attempt to represent in rapid succession a bloated old visage, a pinched, dry set of features, and the tender devotion of young womanhood—and fail to degenerate into ineffective grimace.[3]

Dickens's intention—and he seems generally to have succeeded—was to present a relatively relaxed, dignified, gentlemanly performance. 'With-out resort to artifice or clap-trap', as an American newspaper remarked,

[1] *Life*, p. 847.

[2] A. W. Ward, *Charles Dickens* (1882), pp. 153–4. Ward reviewed many of the Readings in the *Manchester Guardian*, and is quoted in the annotation to several items. 'Hard' is Henry James's adjective too: 'the hard charmless readings (or *à peu près*)' (*Notebooks*, ed. F. E. Matthiessen and Kenneth B. Murdock (New York, 1947), p. 319).

[3] 'Mr. Dickens' Readings', *The Land we Love*, March 1868, p. 430.

he concentrated the audience's attention upon the texts and not upon himself.[1] His avoidance of obvious opportunities for clap-traps was manifested, too, by his mode of beginning and ending his performances. He would stride rapidly on to the platform, and go straight into his text, without any commentary or reminders that the reader was also the illustrious author. After a bow to his audience, he would say: 'I am to have the pleasure of reading to you first tonight . . .' and then, with the title, he would be into the opening sentence.[2] At the end of the evening, he would bow and retire, but only on the most exceptional occasions would he return to take a further curtain-call. There was indeed, as R. H. Hutton remarked, reviewing Forster's *Life* and noting Dickens's 'unbounded triumph' in the size and enthusiasm of his audiences, 'something a little ignoble in this extravagant relish of a man of genius for the evidence of the popularity of his own writings. Dickens must have known that theatrical effects are by no means the best gauge of the highest literary fame.'[3] It is a judgement on this phase of Dickens's career which must carry some weight: and the Victorian science of phrenology may almost seem to have been vindicated by one distinguished practitioner's observation that Dickens's most developed organs among the Feelings were Acquisitiveness and Love of Approbation, and 'he literally killed himself in their gratification' (through the Readings).[4] Nevertheless, he apparently denied himself many of the ploys which could easily have moved his audiences to manifest even more ecstatically their Approbation of his performance, his writings, and his presence. Given the immensity of his opportunities and temptations in this kind—and when has a larger and more demotic literary giant gone on circuit?—he seems to have been artistically self-disciplined to a commendable degree. As even the *Saturday Review* acknowledged, anyone who argued that there was 'something slightly undignified about this method of turning one's reputation into cash' had to recognize that no other writer had Dickens's singular and manifold advantages.[5]

He must have known, though, to requote R. H. Hutton, that 'theatrical effects are by no means the best gauge of the highest literary fame'. Some discussion of his selection of items for performance, and of their

---

[1] *New York Tribune*, 21 December 1867.

[2] During the 'Charity' readings, and his first professional season, he generally gave a little speech stating that there would be an interval of ten minutes, and urging the audience to laugh and cry as much as they liked, for it would please and not distract him (for samples, see *Speeches*, pp. 169, 246). Also, occasionally, he remarked briefly on the circumstances of the writing of the Readings texts (see headnote to *The Chimes*). These practices, never very felicitous, were soon abandoned.

[3] *Spectator*, 7 February 1874, p. 175 (reprinted in *Dickens: the Critical Heritage*, p. 585).

[4] Charles Bray, *Phases of Opinion and Experience* [1884], p. 28.

[5] *Saturday Review*, 9 May 1868, p. 612.

adequacy as a representation of his literary achievement, must conclude this section of the Introduction. Whatever Dickens 'knew' or judged about these matters, however, he kept to himself. The letters—garrulous about his audiences, and about the satisfactions, the strains, and the financial results of the Readings—contain practically nothing about why he chose these items, nor about the technical problems of devising and performing a script, nor about what one might call the 'philosophy' of the art of public reading. A short chapter in Mark Twain's autobiography, about his experiences in this kind, and about (for instance) how the spoken word differs from the written, offers more analysis than can be found in all of Dickens's available letters and conversations.[1]

His Readings, wrote a reviewer, might be better described as 'illustrations, ... running critical commentaries upon his own works',[2] and many accounts have already been quoted which show that he gave his audiences that enriched sense of the power and subtlety of a text which a critical commentary attempts to convey by analysis and argument. But to what extent does Dickens's choice and arrangement of scripts also reflect his critical judgement of his writings? Surely only in a very modified degree, though at least one important indication does arise from his repertoire—that he presumably would not choose to repeat in public samples of his fiction which he disliked or felt critically ashamed of. (Thus, to mention one of the worst of the Readings, he may be presumed to have approved of *The Poor Traveller*.) It would, however, be foolish to assume that his choice of items represented what he judged to be the masterpieces of his art. Obviously readings in a two-hour programme must be of anecdotal, short-story, or at best *nouvelle* length; this was rarely a length in which Dickens's art as a writer most fully manifested itself. Episodes could of course be extracted from the novels, and some fine and characteristic achievements (such as the character of Mrs. Gamp) could thus be represented—but inevitably some violence and injustice is done to his art when a more or less detachable part is removed from its context. (Dickens eased his technical problem, it may be noted, by assuming that his audiences knew these contexts: thus, he does not bother to explain why Jonas Chuzzlewit acts in a guilty fashion, or who Mr. Pickwick or Mr. Micawber is or what his relations to the other characters are.)

One obvious feature of Dickens's choice of items is its heavy concentration

[1] *The Autobiography of Mark Twain*, ed. Charles Neider (New York, 1959), ch. 35; see also chs. 32–3. Twain saw Dickens as the pioneer: 'What is called a "reading". as a public platform entertainment, was first essayed by Charles Dickens, I think. . . . [He] set a fashion which others tried to follow' (p. 190).

[2] John Hollingshead, 'Mr. Charles Dickens as a Reader', *Critic*, 4 September 1858, p. 537, reprinted in his *Today* (1865), his *Miscellanies* (1874), and as an Introduction to the *Readings* (1907 edn.).

on the Christmas Books and Christmas Stories. These—which comprised almost all the shorter narratives that he wrote, for he was not much attracted to the short-story form—were manifestly easier to adapt into coherent and self-contained scripts of performable length than were the novels. Also of course, he was much associated with, and attached to, the Christmas spirit, though of the Christmas writings which remained for long in his Readings repertoire only the *Carol* had much to do with Christmas itself. Of the twenty-one items that were prepared, only nine indeed came from the novels (and two of these were never performed); of the rest, four came from the Christmas Books and eight from the Christmas Stories—and these included some of his most popular items. Thus, of the six most frequently-performed items (see the table in Section 2, above) two were from *Pickwick Papers* (*The Trial* and *Bob Sawyer*), one was the *Carol*, two were from the Christmas Stories (*Boots* and *Marigold*), and the other was *David Copperfield*. In the six next items, to be sure, the novels are more fully represented (*Mrs. Gamp*, *Nickleby*, *Little Dombey*, and *Sikes and Nancy*), with *The Poor Traveller* and *The Chimes* coming from the Christmas writings. Also it should be noted that the four least-often performed items did not come from the novels (*The Boy at Mugby*, *Barbox Brothers*, *Mr. Chops*, and *The Cricket*). Or, to aggregate the figures given in that table: in the performances surveyed, he read items from the novels 491 times, from the Christmas Books 141, and from the Christmas Stories 203. All three categories are represented among the Readings prepared but never performed— *The Bastille Prisoner* and *Great Expectations*; *The Haunted Man*; and *Mrs. Lirriper's Lodgings* and *The Signalman*.

So, though he prepared more scripts from the Christmas writings than from the novels, he gave more performances from the novels. Still, it is conspicuous that, though his most often performed item was *The Trial from Pickwick*, the next three were the *Carol*, *Boots*, and *Marigold*. The *Carol* was an inevitable choice: but who except Dickens specialists now remember those other two Christmas stories?[1] *Boots* and *Marigold*, it may be noted, have several features in common: both are character-monologues, narrated by wryly witty Cockneys; both blend humour and pathos; both give prominence to children; and both contain situations, centring on these children, which were generally found moving at the time but which are now likely to be found sentimental. Both are indeed characteristic of Dickens's talent, but neither is a prime example of his genius—nor, fond though he evidently was of these two Readings, can one imagine that he valued them, as pieces of writing, among his highest achievements. Here then, certainly, is an instance of the Readings' repre-

---

[1] Pop-fans will however be familiar with the title, at least, of one of them, for a pop-group was recently formed, taking the name 'Doctor Marigold's Prescriptions': an esoteric allusion, indeed.

senting the writings at their second-best—effective scripts filled out by Dickens's histrionic abilities, and making a special appeal to the laughter-and-tears predilection of his audiences.

Besides the prominence of the Christmas writings, the other most striking feature of the repertoire is that it over-represents the earlier fiction. The novels represented in the repertoire were *Pickwick, Oliver Twist, Nickleby, Chuzzlewit, Dombey,* and *Copperfield.* Indeed, of the novels up to *Copperfield,* only *The Old Curiosity Shop* and *Barnaby Rudge* did not furnish Readings; from those after *Copperfield,* only two Readings were devised (*The Bastille Prisoner* and *Great Expectations*), but both remained unperformed.[1] It will be recalled that the repertoire was mainly devised in 1853, 1858, 1861, 1866, and 1868: years when, eventually, he had behind him the great series of social novels from *Bleak House* to *Our Mutual Friend* (the novels upon which his critical reputation now most depends)—and he performed nothing from them. Was he, then, in selecting his Readings from the earlier novels, implying a greater respect, or a greater private affection, for them? or did he find it easier to extract performable scripts of the right length from them than from their successors? or did he make these selections in the belief that his public would most enjoy hearing episodes from the good old favourites, some of them familiar for over twenty years before he began performing them?

He made no pronouncements which offer even tentative answers to these questions. Two points may, however, be made. First, as was noted above (p. xxxvi), he evidently judged that public readings were not the occasion for social criticism. Passages such as Scrooge's vision of Ignorance and Want were deleted in the Reading texts: and this may be one reason why the later and 'darker' novels struck him as less appropriate for Reading purposes. He may be imagined as making a distinction between his fiction and his Readings similar to that which Mr. Graham Greene used to make between his novels and his 'Entertainments': the Readings were conscientiously prepared and presented, were fully professional and defensible manifestations of his art, but were 'entertainments' from which some graver notes and larger pretensions had to be excluded. As an analogy to this hypothesis about his Readings policy,

---

[1] But he did jot down, as possibilities, some items from *Bleak House.* In his 'Memoranda' book (MS Berg) he wrote:

Subjects for Readings

Mr. Bob Sawyer's Party

Mrs. Jellyby and Mr. Turveydrop

———— or Mrs. Pardiggle

Chesney Wold.

As is argued in its headnote, *Bob Sawyer* was devised in 1861, so this entry (apparently all written at once) belongs to that year, or earlier. Nothing further is known of the *Bleak House* notions.

one might note that he avoided ending his programmes with the items which had a 'tragic' conclusion (*Little Dombey*, *Copperfield*, and *Sikes and Nancy*); a cheering comic 'afterpiece' restored his audience's good humour. It can hardly be maintained, on the existing evidence, that Dickens undervalued the later novels,[1] or regarded the social concerns of his fiction as a peripheral or merely topical or journalistic element in it. So this cannot be the reason why he gave no Readings from the later novels.

My second point is that the novels from which he gave Readings (and indeed those from which he prepared Readings which were never performed, *A Tale of Two Cities* and *Great Expectations*) were, as they still are, the essential 'popular' Dickens. During his lifetime, the earlier novels were also more esteemed, as well as more loved. Obituary assessments in 1870 mostly named as his masterpieces *Pickwick* and *Copperfield*, together with the *Carol* and maybe *Chuzzlewit*.[2] So in confining his Readings to the earlier novels, as in relying so heavily upon the *Carol*, Dickens was—whether to please them, or himself, or both—giving his public what he rightly guessed they would most want. 'It is a difficult thing for a man to speak of himself or of his works,' he said, on what has been described as his first triumph in public speaking (in Edinburgh, 1841). 'But', he continued, 'perhaps on this occasion I may, without impropriety, venture to say a word on the spirit in which mine were conceived.' The word he then spoke was modest, and cannot be taken as an adequate comment on what, over the next three decades, he was to create. But it pointed to something central in that achievement, and was a more fitting comment upon the Readings: 'I felt an earnest and humble desire, and shall do till I die, to increase the stock of harmless cheerfulness.'[3]

8. THE PRESENT EDITION: AIMS, PROCEDURES, AND CONVENTIONS

As has already been stated, the aim of this edition is to present the texts of the Readings in—so far as can be established—their latest form, and to indicate, both typographically in the text and by annotation, how Dickens performed the items (sixteen of the twenty-one) which went into his repertoire. All but four of the Readings have been printed from his prompt-copies, so these texts incorporate his verbal revisions and additions, marginalia, underlining, etc.; also they omit passages which he deleted. When more than one prompt-copy survives, the later has

---

[1] I have attempted a fuller discussion of this in 'Dickens's Self-Estimate: some new Evidence', in *Dickens the Craftsman*, ed. Robert B. Partlow (Carbondale, Ill., 1970), pp. 21–43.

[2] See *Dickens: the Critical Heritage*, pp. 182, 503, and *passim*.

[3] *Speeches*, pp. 9, 14.

been taken as copy-text, and the headnote to the item offers the evidence for believing it to be the later. The other four items (*The Trial from Pickwick*, *Great Expectations*, *Mrs. Lirriper*, and *The Signalman*) have been printed from copies of Dickens's privately printed editions; but no prompt-copy containing his underlining, revisions, etc., seems to have survived.

Many of these texts underwent considerable revision and abbreviation (some were in repertoire for over a decade), and it seemed best to publish them in their latest state. By an extensive textual apparatus, all the stages through which the text was evolved could have been detailed, but this has not been attempted. How bulky and complex the apparatus would have needed to be may be discerned if the reader consults the facsimile editions of *Mrs. Gamp* (1956), *A Christmas Carol* (1971), and *Nicholas Nickleby* (1973). The Readings are not, as I think, literary documents of such prime importance as to merit a textual apparatus on such a scale. Instead, my text contains indications of major deletions, and the footnotes draw attention to some particularly significant revisions or rewordings.

As was noted in section 5, some items at least in *T & F* (1868) were proof-read by Dickens, and incorporate his corrections and revisions. It might therefore be argued that *T & F* should be taken as the copy-text for the nine items printed in that edition. I have not done so, for the following reasons. (1) The extent of Dickens's proof-reading of *T & F* remains uncertain. (2) At least some of the differences between *T & F* and the prompt-copies were introduced by the printers, not by Dickens. (3) He further revised a number of the prompt-copies after *T & F* had been set up from them, so in these cases the prompt-copy remains the latest text. (4) To use *T & F* for some items, and prompt-copies, etc., for the others, would have created some anomalies (e.g., either the underlinings would have had to be excluded from the *T & F*-derived texts, or they would have had to be superimposed on a text which did not in fact contain them). (5) Anyway, the new readings arguably introduced into *T & F* by Dickens are few and minor, and, where significant, can be (as they have been) mentioned in the annotation.

Items are printed in the order in which Dickens devised them, so far as this can be established. The headnotes contain information about the dates, both of the original devising and of any substantial revisions later.

The text has been silently corrected and regularized in the following respects:

(1) Printing-errors in the prompt-copies, etc., have been corrected.
(2) When Dickens made deletions and wrote in manuscript insertions, he was generally efficient in providing any requisite new terminal

punctuation, contingent changes from upper- to lower-case letters, etc., and in indicating whether, after a deletion, the text should run on or whether a new paragraph should begin. When he has failed, I have silently corrected the error, or adopted a common-sense solution, unless the matter is so doubtful or so significant as to justify a footnote.

(3) Chapter-headings have been regularized to the style CHAPTER I (etc.), whether or not Dickens used Roman numerals or wrote the word 'Chapter'. (In the *Carol* and *Cricket*, however, the original STAVE and CHIRP have been retained: and where Dickens preferred PART to CHAPTER, this too has been retained.) In the editorial matter, the style 'Chapter I' refers to parts of the Readings texts; the style 'ch. I' refers to the original novel or story. Page-references to the novels and stories refer to the Oxford Illustrated edition (1947–58).

The following conventions have been used in printing the text:

(1) Words underlined by Dickens in his prompt-copies are printed in *italic*. When he has underlined words doubly, or trebly or more, this is recorded in the footnotes.[1] Words printed in italic in the prompt-copies, or privately printed copies, are also printed in italic, but all these occasions are mentioned in the footnotes.

(2) Dickens's marginal stage-directions ('Low', 'Action', 'Cheerful narrative', etc.—almost always underlined, often doubly) are recorded in the footnotes, in *italic*.

(3) To help the reader to compare the final Readings text with the novel or story from which it was derived, and to know at what point in the evolution of the text some of the major abbreviations were made, two devices have been used:

* an asterisk signifies that a long deletion (of about 100 words or more) had been made *before* the privately printed edition went to press.

† a dagger signifies that a long deletion (of about 100 words or more) was made, by pen or ink, in the prompt-copy.

'A man can't write his eye (at least *I* don't know how to), nor yet can a man write his voice, nor the rate of his talk, nor the quickness of his action, nor his general spicy way.' A dramatic critic noticing a performance of *Doctor Marigold* aptly quoted this sentence from that story, to suggest the difference between reading Dickens oneself and

---

[1] Dickens's conventions for (and quantities of) underlining varied considerably, and in some prompt-copies he made plentiful use of double interrupted underlining. This is similar to the conventional printer's correction sign indicating small capitals: but when he used this device prodigally he evidently did not mean it to carry that special degree of emphasis, so I have then silently treated it as the equivalent to single underlining. This, I realize, is a questionable decision. In defence of it, I can only posit my conviction—which may be a delusion, but I hope not—that, after frequenting the prompt-copies for several years, I can recognize the signs of Dickens's degrees of urgency and intensity.

hearing him give a public reading: also to suggest any critic's feelings of inadequacy in registering or analysing 'his general spicy way'.[1] An editor a century later, while necessarily feeling such frustration even more acutely, may however draw encouragement from Marigold's next sentence: 'But he can write his turns of speech, when he is a public speaker.' Dickens's performances were so widely reported and lovingly remembered that many of them can be reconstructed in some detail. Many contemporary accounts have therefore been quoted in the head-notes and footnotes: for these texts are of interest, not as competent abbreviated versions of Dickens, but as indications of how their author regarded and interpreted them. Reconstructing the performance, when this can be done, has been regarded as no less important than establishing a correct text.

[1] *Scotsman*, 19 April 1866; 'Doctor Marigold's Prescriptions', *Christmas Stories* (Oxford Illustrated edn.), p. 452. This sentence does not appear in the Reading text.

A CHRISTMAS CAROL

A Christmas Carol, the first public Reading that Dickens ever gave, remained in repertoire throughout his career and was the main item in his final Farewell performance in 1870. This was indeed the quintessential Dickens Reading—as the story which it told has been, ever since its publication in 1843, both one of the most central and beloved of his achievements, and also one of the great popular classics of world literature. The first and far the best of the Christmas Books, it is also the most dramatic. In Dickens's day, and ever since, it has been a perennial favourite both for recitalists and in adaptations for stage, screen, radio, and television. Eminently through the *Carol*, Dickens had identified himself with the Christmas spirit—an identification clearly signalled by his choosing late December for what proved to be the initiation of his public readings career, the three performances in aid of the funds of the Birmingham and Midland Institute. The *Carol* was the obvious choice, and it was given on 27 and 30 December 1853 in the Birmingham Town Hall; on an intervening night, *The Cricket on the Hearth* was performed. Not only had they a seasonal appropriateness, but also (like the two other Christmas Books which, a few years later, were his next Readings adaptations) they had the technical advantage of being short self-contained narratives, which could without much difficulty be reduced to the length of an evening's entertainment.

Most of the charity performances which Dickens gave between 1853 and 1858 took place around Christmas, and (except for the single performance of *The Cricket* in Birmingham) the programme always consisted of the *Carol*. His attachment to the Christmas spirit appeared further when he was planning his first professional season. Since this began in April 1858, Christmas writings had no seasonal relevance; nevertheless, his original plan was to read nothing that season except Christmas Books. After six weeks, however, he began to perform items drawn from other areas of his work, and soon the *Carol* was the only Christmas Book retained in the repertoire. Over the years, it was included in well over a quarter of his performances. The only item given more often was *The Trial from Pickwick* (a short 'afterpiece'); these two were considerably more popular than any of his other items, and together they constituted what he clearly (and with good reason) regarded as his safest and most endearing programme. Significantly, he chose this combination of the *Carol* and *Trial* for his opening performance in every American city, during his tour of 1867–8, and for other such notable occasions at his final performances in Paris, New York, and London.

He had estimated that his original Birmingham performance of the *Carol* would take about two hours, with a ten-minute interval half-way through: but in fact it took three hours. By 1857, when it was first performed in London (for the Douglas Jerrold Fund), it took two and a half hours; by May 1858, it had been further reduced to the standard two-hour length of the professional Readings. By the end of that year, it was abbreviated by a further thirty minutes or so, to accommodate *The Trial* inside a two-hour programme. Thereafter the text underwent no substantial revisions, though Dickens often inserted new effects or phrasings when stimulated by his own or his audience's high spirits, and some of these extempore improvements became a standard part of the text (without ever being written down in the prompt-copy). In later years he was so familiar with this item that he scarcely needed to glance at the text. With many past improvisations as well as the basic script in his memory, and with various optional cuts marked in the prompt-copy or kept in his mind, his text varied considerably from night to night, as many observers noted. This puzzled audiences in America, who could try to follow him in the Boston edition of the Readings, set up though these were from the prompt-copies—but Dickens himself was often lost or surprised, too (see above, Introduction, p. xxxi). After a triumphant performance in Paris he wrote: 'You have no idea what [the audience] made of me. I got things out of the old Carol—effects I mean—so entirely new and so very strong, that I quite amazed myself and wondered where I was going next' (*N*, iii, 340).

The only surviving prompt-copy is in the Berg Collection. Like other early prompt-copies of Readings from the Christmas Books, it is an ordinary copy of the story (12th edn., 1849) inlaid into large octavo pages, to give Dickens more space for marginal jottings and rephrasings, and handsomely bound in three-quarters red morocco. This copy was certainly in use in 1859 (Dickens wrote a list of engagements for that October in the front fly-leaf), and it was still the current prompt-copy in 1867, when the Boston trade edition was set up from it (see p. 9, note 2, below). Probably indeed, this copy was in use from the start, in 1853; certainly no other prompt-copy has ever been recorded. The possibility that an earlier prompt-copy than *Berg* may have existed, which was later lost or destroyed, is discussed in the headnote to *The Cricket on the Hearth*.

Berg is much amended, in brown and blue inks and in pencil, and at eight places a sequence of pages has been stuck or fastened together so that a long cut could be more easily handled. While it is often easy to deduce the order of priority of minor cuts, it is generally difficult or impossible to be certain which sequence of cuts was made in early 1858 and which in late 1858, at both of which periods the length of the Reading was reduced by about thirty minutes. The text is heavily cut throughout; the only episode which, conspicuously, is left almost entire is the Cratchits' Christmas dinner. The beginnings and endings of most of the Staves are much cut, and the fourth and fifth are run into a single Stave. In Stave II, Scrooge's schooldays are omitted, as is much of the episode concerning his fiancée. In Stave III, the long descriptions of Christmas Day in the London streets and among the miners and mariners are deleted, and the jollifications at Scrooge's nephew's house are much abbreviated. The deathbeds of Scrooge and of Tiny Tim in Stave IV are virtually eliminated, and the re-entry in Stave V of the portly gentleman collecting for charity is omitted.

A particularly interesting omission occurs at the end of Stave III—the whole of the vision of the terrible waifs, Ignorance and Want (a passage which had, however, provoked great applause during the 1853 Birmingham performance). This is the only episode in the *Carol* carrying strong overt social criticism. As was noted in the Introduction, the Readings as a whole greatly under-represented the elements of social and political reference in Dickens's work. Some of the other cuts in the *Carol* reduced the element of pathos (Tiny Tim's deathbed, for instance). A reviewer of the first London performance noted that 'With his pathetic scenes he is more cautious than with his mirth. He would evidently avoid all imputation of maudlin sentimentality and where he would elicit the tears of his audience he trusts to a manly, unaffected tone in the description of sorrow' (*The Times*, 1 July 1857). The pathos was generally found very moving, though some critics thought he overdid it in the scene of lamentation over the death of Tiny Tim.

After his first Birmingham performance, Dickens reported (or boasted) to a friend: 'the success was most wonderful and prodigious—perfectly overwhelming and astounding altogether' (*N*, ii, 536). And the following Christmas, at Bradford, he had an audience of 3,700—'And yet but for the noise of their laughing and cheering they "went" like one man' (*N*, ii, 615). Triumphs, attested by others than the performer himself, followed so regularly, during these charity readings, that he had gained a 'gigantic', but wholly deserved, reputation before turning professional, remarked *The Times* (16 April 1858). A reviewer of his first London performance, in 1857, wrote:

We have rarely witnessed or shared an evening of such genuine enjoyment, and never before remember to have seen a crowded assembly of three thousand people hanging for upwards of two hours on the lips of a single reader . . . with an excited and even passionate interest that it was impossible to repress. . . . The reports of Mr. Dickens's success in the provinces as a reader, which at the time seemed exaggerated, scarcely did justice to his peculiar power; his oral interpretation of the story, from first to last, being admirable. In the first place, Mr. Dickens's voice, naturally powerful and expressive, and specially rich in its lower tones, is completely under his control, and he modulates it with the practised ease of one accustomed to address the public from the platform rather than through the pen. In the second place, his reading is thoroughly dramatic throughout; and it is the more important to insist on this point, as certain critics, through some strange oversight, failed to recognize it. Every fragment of the dialogue was treated dramatically—the rendering of each character being equally successful . . . The narrative part and reflections Mr. Dickens of course read in his natural voice,—so effectively that, at one point, a philanthropic legislator, carried away by his feelings, gave forth a vigorous 'Hear, hear!' that echoed through the hall. At the close there was an outburst, not so much of applause as of downright hurrahing, from every part—the stalls even being startled from their propriety into the waving of hats and handkerchiefs, and joining heartily in the contagious cheer. (*Leader*, 4 July 1857, p. 640)

To quote one other tribute about these early performances: 'Never did we see or hear a man throw himself so entirely into the spirit of a book' (*Bristol Times*, 23 January 1858).

With a score of characters, Dickens had ample chance here to show his histrionic powers, and most critics were delighted by his versatility. Scrooge and Bob Cratchit were the greatest successes, but many of the minor figures (such as the fat man yawning over Scrooge's death, or the boy sent to buy the turkey) became memorably distinctive. And somehow Dickens contrived to prevent this skill from becoming too ostentatious: 'Above all, though each person in the drama retained throughout his proper voice, and we might almost say features, Mr. Dickens never in his imitations allowed himself to overstep the line which separates imitation from caricature, nor by violent gesture or declamation brought back the minds of his hearers from the story to its reader' (*Bury and*

Norwich Post, 18 October 1859). The great moments were the Cratchits' dinner, culminating in the pudding; Scrooge's nephew's party, culminating in 'It's your Uncle Scro-o-o-o-oge!'; Scrooge's dialogue with the boy about the turkey; and '. . . to Tiny Tim, who did NOT die . . .'

Dickens's narration was generally regarded as only less fine than his assumption of the various characters; in either respect, 'those who have not heard the author read the work have never half enjoyed it. Undiscovered pieces of humour are presented at every page. The pathos of all that is pathetic becomes doubly affecting' (*Belfast Newsletter*, 28 August 1858). Moreover, the Christmas sentiment of the piece, and Dickens's association with this and other wholesome beliefs, predisposed hearers of this item in particular to credit him with moral as well as technical virtues. Reporters often asserted, too, that audiences left the hall, after hearing the *Carol*, better moral beings; unlike the other Readings, there was about this one an element of a rite, a religious affirmation.

One other account of his performance may be quoted, to illustrate the importance of Dickens's visual effects in this piece (as in others). This reporter had been criticizing his elocution, and in particular a certain monotony in his narrative voice:

But it is his dramatic genius that overcomes these defects. His power of facial expression is wonderful; it is as much what he does as what he says that constitutes the charm of his performance. He gives a distinct voice to each character, and to an extraordinary extent assumes the personality of each. At one moment he is savage old Scrooge, at the next, his jolly nephew, and in the twinkling of an eye little timid, lisping Bob Cratchit appears. All this is effected by the play of features as well as the varying tones of voice. It is the comical or the savage twist of the mouth—the former to the right, the latter to the left— the elongation of the face, the roll or twinkle of the eyes, and above all the wonderful lift of the eyebrows, that produce such surprising and delightful effects. And then he not only personates his characters, he performs their actions. This he does by means of wonderfully flexible fingers, which he converts at pleasure into a company of dancers, and makes to act and speak in a hundred ways. He rubs and pats his hands, he flourishes all his fingers, he shakes them, he points them, he makes them equal to a whole stage company in the performance of the parts. But then the man himself is also there. Dickens, the author, comes in at intervals to enjoy his own fun; you see him in the twinkle of the eye and the curve of the mouth. When the audience laughs he beams all over with radiant appreciation of the fun. (*Portland [Maine] Transcript*, 4 February 1868)

The annotation below will detail some of these visual and vocal effects. For fuller particulars of these, and of the textual development of this Reading, see my Introduction and Notes to the facsimile of *Berg* (published by the New York Public Library, 1971). My annotation there depends heavily on the remarkable page-by-page account of how the *Carol* was performed, written sixty years after Dickens's death by a Bedford journalist, Rowland Hill. Since preparing the New York facsimile, I have discovered W. M. Wright's similar, though less extensive, notes on the Readings (see above, p. xli); the *Carol* is one of the items he describes. Some of Hill's and Wright's notes will be quoted below. The prompt-copy contains many marginal stage-directions, such as 'Tone to Mystery' and 'Cheerful Narrative', but much less underlining than was Dickens's usual practice later.

A Christmas Carol

In Four Staves

STAVE ONE

Marley's Ghost

MARLEY was dead: to begin with. There is no doubt whatever about that. The register of his burial was signed by the clergyman, the clerk, the undertaker, and the chief mourner. *Scrooge*[1] signed it: and Scrooge's name was good upon 'Change, for anything he chose to put his hand to. Old Marley was as dead as a door-nail.

Scrooge knew he was dead? Of course he did. How could it be otherwise? Scrooge and he were partners for I don't know how many years. Scrooge was his sole executor, his sole administrator, his sole assign, his sole residuary legatee, his sole friend, his sole mourner. †

Scrooge never painted out old Marley's name, however. There it yet stood, years afterwards, above the warehouse door: Scrooge and Marley. The firm was known as Scrooge and Marley. Sometimes people new to the business called Scrooge Scrooge, and sometimes Marley. He answered to both names. It was all the same to him.

Oh![2] But he was a tight-fisted hand at the grindstone, was Scrooge! a squeezing, wrenching, grasping, scraping, clutching, covetous old sinner![3]†

Nobody ever stopped him in the street to say, with gladsome looks, 'My dear Scrooge, how are you? when will you come to see me?' No beggars implored him to bestow a trifle, no children asked him what it was o'clock, no man or woman ever once in all his life inquired the way to such and such a place, of Scrooge. Even the blindmen's dogs appeared to know him; and when they saw him coming on, would tug their owners into doorways and up courts; and then would wag their tails as though they said, 'no eye at all is better than an evil eye, dark master!'

But what did Scrooge care!

---

[1] *Scrooge* here, and in the next paragraph, doubly underlined. Dickens's way of saying his name instantly and vividly conjured up 'Scrooge in the flesh' (Kent, p. 95). 'Old Marley . . . ' was spoken 'Low' (Wright).

[2] 'The *Oh*! was drawn out for some seconds, 3 or 4 perhaps' (Hill).

[3] The ensuing description of Scrooge (in *1843*) was deleted because, in performance, 'we saw and heard it without any necessity for its being explained' (Kent, p. 95). but *T & F* prints the paragraph beginning 'External heat and cold . . . ', which was subsequently deleted. But Kate Field and Hill describe how he read that paragraph, so it was sometimes restored.

[1]Once upon a time—of all the good days in the year, upon a Christmas Eve—old Scrooge sat busy in his counting house. It was cold, bleak, biting, foggy weather, and the city clocks had only just gone three, but it was quite dark already. The door of Scrooge's counting-house was open that he might keep his eye upon his *clerk*,[2] who in a dismal little cell beyond—a sort of tank—was copying letters. Scrooge had a very small fire, but the clerk's fire was so very much smaller that it looked like one coal. But he couldn't replenish it, for Scrooge kept the coal-box in his own room; and so surely as the clerk came in with the shovel, the master predicted that it would be necessary for them to part. Wherefore the clerk put on his white comforter, and tried to warm himself at the candle; in which effort, not being a man of a strong imagination, he failed.[3]

[4]'A merry Christmas, uncle! God save you!' cried a cheerful voice. It was the voice of Scrooge's nephew, who came upon him so quickly that this was the first intimation Scrooge had of his approach.

'Bah!' said Scrooge, 'Humbug!'

'Christmas a humbug, uncle! You don't mean that, I am sure.'

'I do. † *Out*[5] upon merry Christmas! What's Christmas time to you but a time for paying bills without money; a time for finding yourself a year older, and not an hour richer; a time for balancing your books and having every item in 'em through a round dozen of months presented dead against you? If I had my will, every idiot who goes about with "Merry Christmas" on his lips, should be boiled with his own pudding, and buried with a stake of holly through his heart.[6] He should!'

'Uncle!'

'Nephew, keep Christmas in your own way, and let me keep it in mine.'

'Keep it! But you don't keep it.'

'Let me leave it alone, then. Much good may it do you! Much good it has ever done you!'

'There are many things from which I might have derived good, by which I have not profited, I dare say: Christmas among the rest. But I am sure I have always thought of Christmas time, when it has come round—apart from the veneration due to its sacred origin, if anything belonging to it *can* be apart from that—as a good time: a kind, forgiving, charitable, pleasant time: the only time I know of, in the long calendar of the year, when men and women seem by one consent to open their shut-up hearts

[1] Marginal stage direction *Narrative* – 'changing his tone suddenly to a rich mellow note, splendidly inflected' (Hill).

[2] *clerk* doubly underlined.

[3] Dickens's enactment of Bob Cratchit's trying to warm his hands over the candle – reinforced by his inserting 'decidedly' before 'failed' – finally established his command of his audience (Hill; Field, p. 29).

[4] Marginal stage-direction *Cheerful*. The ensuing description of the nephew was deleted; he 'was visibly before us, without a word being uttered' (Kent, p. 99).

[5] *Out* doubly underlined.

[6] This sentence was emphasized 'with a good bang on his reading table' (Hill).

freely, and to think of people below them as if they really were fellow-travellers to the grave, and not another race of creatures bound on other journeys.[1] And therefore, uncle, though it has never put a scrap of gold or silver in my pocket, I believe that it *has*[2] done me good, and *will* do me good; and I say, God bless it!'

The clerk in the tank involuntarily applauded.

'Let me hear another sound from *you*,[3]' said Scrooge, 'and you'll keep your Christmas by losing your situation. You're quite a powerful speaker, sir,' he added, turning to his nephew. 'I wonder you don't go into Parliament.'

'Don't be angry, uncle. Come! Dine with us[4] to-morrow.'

Scrooge said that he would see him—yes, indeed he did. He went the whole length of the expression, and said that he would see him in that extremity first.

'But why?' cried Scrooge's nephew. 'Why?'

'Why did you get married?'

'Because I fell in love.'

'Because you fell in love!' growled Scrooge, as if that were the only one thing in the world more ridiculous than a merry Christmas. 'Good afternoon!'

'Nay, uncle, but you never came to see me before that happened. Why give it as a reason for not coming now?'

'Good afternoon.'

'I want nothing from you; I ask nothing of you; why cannot we be friends?'

'Good afternoon.'

'I am sorry, with all my heart, to find you so resolute. We have never had any quarrel, to which I have been a party. But I have made the trial in homage to Christmas, and I'll keep my Christmas humour to the last. So A Merry Christmas, uncle!'

'Good afternoon!'

'And A Happy New Year!'

'Good afternoon!'[5]

His nephew left the room without an angry word, notwithstanding. The clerk, in letting Scrooge's nephew out, had let two other people in. They were portly gentlemen, pleasant to behold, and now stood, with their hats off, in Scrooge's office. They had books and papers in their hands, and bowed to him.

---

[1] Against this sentence, Wright notes: 'Moving eyebrows'.

[2] *has* and *will* italic in *1843*.

[3] 'Pointing with right forefinger' at Bob (Wright); *you* italic in *1843*.

[4] Dickens substituted 'with me and my young wife' (Hill).

[5] The successive 'Good afternoons!' spoken crossly and 'with irresistibly humorous iteration' (Wright; Kent, p. 101).

'Scrooge and Marley's I believe,' said one of the gentlemen, referring to his list.[1] 'Have I the pleasure of addressing Mr. Scrooge, or Mr. Marley?'

'Mr. Marley has been dead these seven years. He died seven years ago, this very night.'[2]

'At this festive season of the year, Mr. Scrooge,' said the gentleman, taking up a pen, 'it is more than usually desirable that we should make some slight provision for the Poor and destitute, who suffer greatly at the present time. Many thousands are in want of common necessaries; hundreds of thousands are in want of common comforts, sir.'

'Are there no prisons?'

'Plenty of prisons. † But under the impression that they scarcely furnish Christian cheer of mind or body to the unoffending multitude, a few of us are endeavouring to raise a fund to buy the Poor some meat and drink, and means of warmth. We choose this time, because it is a time, of all others, when Want is keenly felt, and Abundance rejoices. What shall I put you down for?'

'Nothing!'

'You wish to be anonymous?'

'I wish to be left alone. Since you ask me what I wish, gentlemen, that is my answer. I don't make merry myself at Christmas and I can't afford to make idle people merry. I help to support the prisons and the work-houses—they cost enough—and those who are badly off must go there.'

'Many can't go there; and many would rather die.'

'If they would rather die, they had better do it, and decrease the surplus population.' †

At length the hour of shutting up the counting-house arrived. With an ill-will Scrooge, dismounting from his stool, tacitly admitted the fact to the expectant clerk in the Tank, who instantly snuffed his candle out, and put on his hat.

'You'll want all day to-morrow, I suppose?'

'If quite convenient, Sir.'[3]

'It's not convenient, and it's not fair. If I was to stop half-a-crown for it, you'd think yourself mightily ill used, I'll be bound?'

---

[1] Speaking with just the conciliatory voice 'in which gentlemen-beggars deliver their errands of charity'; Dickens *became* the portly gentleman (Field, p. 29).

[2] Dickens interpolated, at the beginning of this speech, 'Well, you haven't the pleasure of addressing Mr. Marley'. After '. . . these seven years,' he paused, 'opened his eyes widely, and also his mouth, and said, with tragic pauses—"He died—seven years ago—this—very—night! He died today!"' (Hill).

[3] 'When Bob Cratchit lisped [this] out in his timid, trembling tones, . . . the audience caught sight at once of the little, round-faced, deferential, simple-hearted clerk as if he had entered bodily' (*New York Times*, 10 December 1867)—one of many such encomia on this impersonation; cf. Field, p. 30; Kent, p. 101; *Critic*, 4 September 1858, p. 537. 'Sort of lisp in a high frightened timid voice' (Wright).

'Yes, Sir.'

'And yet you don't think *me*[1] ill-used, when I pay a day's wages for no work.'

'It's only once a year, Sir.'

'A poor excuse for picking a man's pocket every twenty-fifth of December! But I suppose you must have the whole day. Be here all the earlier next[2] morning!'

The clerk promised that he would; and Scrooge walked out with a growl. The office was closed in a twinkling, and the clerk, with the long ends of his white comforter dangling below his waist (for he boasted no great-coat), went down a slide, at the end of a lane of boys, twenty times, in honour of its being Christmas-eve, and then ran home as hard as he could pelt, to play at blindman's-buff.

[3] Scrooge took his melancholy dinner in his usual melancholy tavern; and having read all the newspapers, and beguiled the rest of the evening with his banker's-book, went home to bed. He lived in chambers which had once belonged to his deceased partner. They were a gloomy suite of rooms, in a lowering pile of building up a yard. The building was old enough now, and dreary enough, for nobody lived in it but Scrooge, the other rooms being all let out as offices.

Now, it is a fact, that there was nothing at all particular about the knocker on the door of this house, except that it was very large. Also, that Scrooge had seen it night and morning during his whole residence in that place; also that Scrooge had as little of what is called fancy about him as any man in the City of London. And yet Scrooge, having his key in the lock of the door, saw in the knocker, without its undergoing any intermediate process of change: not a knocker, but Marley's face.

Marley's face. With a dismal light about it, like a bad lobster in a dark cellar. It was not angry or ferocious, but it looked at Scrooge as Marley used to look: with ghostly spectacles turned up upon its ghostly forehead.

As Scrooge looked fixedly at this phenomenon, it was a knocker again. †
He said 'Pooh, pooh!' and closed the door with a bang.

The sound resounded through the house like thunder. Every room above, and every cask in the wine-merchant's cellars below, appeared to have a separate peal of echoes of its own. Scrooge was not a man to be frightened by echoes. He fastened the door, and walked across the hall, and up the stairs. Slowly too: trimming his candle as he went. †

---

[1] *me* italic in *1843*.

[2] 'next' italic in *T & F*: a mistake made because a blot from the facing page in *Berg* looked like an underlining. This is one simple proof that *T & F* was set from the prompt-copies.

[3] Marginal stage-direction *Tone to Mystery*. 'Comically' at '. . . banker's book' (Wright).

[1]Up Scrooge went, not caring a button for its being very dark: darkness is cheap, and Scrooge liked it. But before he shut his heavy door, he walked through his rooms to see that all was right. He had just enough recollection of the face to desire to do that.

Sitting-room, bed-room, lumber-room. All as they should be. Nobody under the table, nobody under the sofa; a small fire in the grate; spoon and basin ready; and the little saucepan of gruel (Scrooge had a cold in his head) upon the hob. Nobody under the bed; nobody in the closet; nobody in his dressing-gown, which was hanging up in a suspicious attitude against the wall.

Quite satisfied, he closed his door, and locked himself in; double-locked himself in, which was not his custom. Thus secured against surprise, he took off his cravat, put on his dressing-gown and slippers, and his night-cap; and sat down before the very low fire to take his gruel. †

As he threw his head back in the chair, his glance happened to rest upon a bell, a disused bell, that hung in the room, and communicated for some purpose now forgotten with a chamber in the highest story of the building.[2] It was with great astonishment, and with a strange, inexplicable dread, that as he looked, he saw this bell begin to swing. Soon it rang out loudly, and so did every bell in the house. This was succeeded by a clanking noise, deep down below; as if some person were dragging a heavy chain over the casks in the wine-merchant's cellar. Then he heard the noise much louder, on the floors below; then coming up the stairs; then coming straight towards his door. It came on through the heavy door, and a spectre passed into the room before his eyes. And upon its coming in, the dying flame leaped up, as though it cried '*I know him! Marley's ghost!*'[3]

The same face: the very same. Marley in his pig-tail, usual waistcoat, tights, and boots. His body was transparent: so that Scrooge, observing him, and looking through his waistcoat, could see the two buttons on his coat behind.[4]

Scrooge had often heard it said that Marley had no bowels, but he had never believed it until now.[5]

[1] The next two paragraphs were deleted, but *stetted* in pencil (which, in this prompt-copy, is usually a sign of a late stage of revision). *T & F* prints the paragraphs, but Wright deletes them.

[2] 'Dramatic. Hand outstretched in the air' (Wright).

[3] A much-praised moment in the Reading: a 'startling effect' as Dickens's voice 'rose to a hurried outcry' (Kent, p. 102). The 'unexpected wild vehemence and weirdness' of the dying flame's cry was 'striking in the extreme' (David Christie Murray, *Recollections* (1908), p. 50).

[4] Another much-praised moment: its 'dismal facetiousness . . . made an abundance of mirth without interrupting the spectral illusion' (*Aberdeen Journal*, 6 October 1858).

[5] 'Low voice, shaking forefinger' (Wright). It was 'said with such a merry twinkle, that the audience always roared with laughter, and sometimes received it with cheers' (Hill).

No, nor did he believe it even now. Though he looked the phantom through and through, and saw it standing before him; though he felt the chilling influence of its death-cold eyes; and noticed the very texture of the folded kerchief bound about its head and chin; he was still incredulous.

'How now!' said Scrooge, caustic and cold as ever. 'What do you want with me?'

'Much!'—Marley's voice, no doubt about it.

'Who are you?'

'Ask me who I *was*.'[1]

'Who *were* you then?'

'In life I was your partner, Jacob Marley.'

'Can you—can you sit down?'

'I can.'

'Do it then.'

Scrooge asked the question, because he didn't know whether a ghost so transparent might find himself in a condition to take a chair. But the ghost sat down on the opposite side of the fireplace, as if he were quite used to it.

'You don't believe in me.'

'I don't.'

'What evidence would you have of my reality beyond that of your senses?'

'I don't know.'

'Why do you doubt your senses?'

'Because a little thing affects them. A slight disorder of the stomach makes them cheats. You may be an undigested bit of beef, a blot of mustard, a crumb of cheese, a fragment of an underdone potato. There's more of gravy than of grave about you, whatever you are!'

Scrooge was not much in the habit of cracking jokes, nor did he feel, in his heart, by any means waggish then. The truth is, that he tried to be smart, as a means of distracting his own attention, and keeping down his horror. †

But how much greater was his horror, when the phantom taking off the bandage round its head, as if it were too warm to wear in-doors, its lower jaw dropped down upon its breast!

'Mercy! Dreadful apparition, why do you trouble me? Why do spirits walk the earth, and why do they come to me?'

'It is required of every man that the spirit within him should walk abroad among his fellow-men, and travel far and wide; and if that spirit goes not forth in life, it is condemned to do so after death.[2] † I cannot tell

---

[1] *was* and *were* italic in *1843*.

[2] 'In all passages where pathos was the main characteristic, the lines ran easily to rhythm, and the reciter's voice inflected them to almost like blank verse, as when Marley says to Scrooge, "And if that spirit . . . [*etc.*]"' (*Springfield* [Mass.] *Semi-Weekly Republican*, 21 March 1868).

you all I would. A very little more, is permitted to me. I cannot rest, I cannot stay, I cannot linger anywhere. My spirit never walked beyond our counting house—mark me!—in life my spirit never roved beyond the narrow limits of our money-changing hole; and weary journeys lie before me!'

'Seven years dead. And travelling all the time? You travel fast?'

'On the wings of the wind.'

'You might have got over a great quantity of ground in seven years.'

[1]'Oh! blind man, blind man, not to know, that ages of incessant labour by immortal creatures, for this earth must pass into eternity before the good of which it is susceptible is all developed. Not to know that any Christian spirit working kindly in its little sphere, *whatever it may be*, will find its mortal life too short for its vast means of usefulness. Not to know that no space of regret can make amends for one life's opportunities misused! Yet I was like this man! I once was like this man!'

'But you were always a good man of business, Jacob,' faltered Scrooge, who now began to apply this to himself.[2]

'Business! Mankind was my business. The common welfare was my business; charity, mercy, forbearance, benevolence, were, all, my business. The dealings of my trade were but a drop of water in the comprehensive Ocean of my business!'

It held up its chain at arm's length, as if that were the cause of its unavailing grief, and flung it heavily upon the ground again.

'At this time of the rolling year, I suffer most. Why did I walk through crowds of fellow-beings with my eyes turned down, and never raise them to that blessed Star which led the Wise Men to a poor abode? Were there no poor homes to which its light would have conducted *me*?'[3]

Scrooge was very much dismayed to hear the spectre going on at this rate, and began to quake exceedingly.

'Hear me! My time is nearly gone.'

'I will. But don't be hard upon me! Don't be flowery, Jacob! Pray!'

'I am here to-night to warn you, that you have yet a chance and hope of escaping my fate. A chance and hope of my procuring, Ebenezer.'

'You were always a good friend to me. Thank'ee!'

'You will be haunted by Three Spirits.'

'Is that the chance and hope you mentioned, Jacob? I—I think I'd rather not.'

---

[1] 'Hands upheld. Fingers outstretched' (Wright).

[2] The extent of Dickens's abbreviation hereabouts is uncertain. In *Berg*, five successive paragraphs have been deleted, at different times (from 'But you were always . . .' to '. . . quake exceedingly'). Later Dickens wrote *Stet* in the margin but (as often when there are several layers of deletion) it is unclear how much is *stetted*. *T & F* omits from 'It held up' to 'conducted *me*'; Hill records that Dickens sometimes included, and sometimes omitted these, and the following, paragraphs. The present text restores all five paragraphs, minus internal cuts.

[3] *me* italic in *1843*. This speech contains four blank verse lines.

'Without their visits, you cannot hope to shun the path I tread.[1] Expect the first to-morrow night, when the bell tolls One. Expect the second on the next night at the same hour. The third upon the next night when the last stroke of Twelve has ceased to vibrate. Look to see me no more; and look that, for your own sake, you remember what has passed between us!'

It walked backward from him; and at every step it took, the window raised itself a little, so that when the Apparition reached it, it was wide open: and [it] floated out through the self-opened window into the bleak dark night.[2] †

Scrooge closed the window, and examined the door by which the Ghost had entered. It was double-locked, as he had locked it with his own hands, and the bolts were undisturbed. Scrooge tried to say 'Humbug!' but stopped at the first syllable. And being—from the emotion he had undergone, or the fatigues of the day, or his glimpse of the Invisible World, or the dull conversation of the Ghost, or the lateness of the hour— much in need of repose; he went straight to bed, without undressing, and fell asleep on the instant.

STAVE TWO
The First of the Three Spirits

WHEN Scrooge awoke, it was so dark, that looking out of bed, he could scarcely distinguish the transparent window from the opaque walls of his chamber † until suddenly the church-clock tolled a deep dull hollow melancholy *One*.[3] † Light flashed up in the room upon the instant, and the curtains of his bed were drawn.

By a strange figure—like a child: yet not so like a child as like an old man, viewed through some supernatural medium, which gave him the appearance of having receded from the view, and being diminished to a child's proportions. Its hair, which hung about its neck and down its back, was white as if with age; and yet the face had not a wrinkle in it, and the tenderest bloom was on the skin. It held a branch of fresh green holly in its hand; and, in singular contradiction of that wintry emblem, had its dress trimmed with summer flowers. But the strangest thing about it was, that from the crown of its head there sprung a bright clear jet of light, by which all this was visible; and which was doubtless the occasion of its using, in its duller moments, a great extinguisher for a cap, which it now held under its arm. †

'Are you the Spirit, sir, whose coming was foretold to me?'

[1] 'Dramatic. Forefinger'; at 'remember . . .' (below) 'Both hands' raised (Wright).
[2] Dickens's revisions hereabouts are inconsistent; he probably omitted, in performance, some of the words after 'it was wide open'. *T & F* falters, providing no exit for Marley's Ghost.
[3] *One* (in marginal manuscript: ONE in *1843*) underlined three times.

'I am!'

'Who, and what are you?'

'I am the Ghost of Christmas Past.'

'Long past?'

'No. Your past. † The things that you will see with me, are Shadows of the things that have been; they will have no consciousness of us. Rise! And walk with me!' †

It would have been in vain for Scrooge to plead that the weather and the hour were not adapted to pedestrian purposes; that bed was warm, and the thermometer a long way below freezing; that he was clad but lightly in his slippers, dressing-gown, and nightcap; and that he had a cold upon him at that time. The grasp, though gentle as a woman's hand, was not to be resisted. He rose: but finding that the Spirit made towards the window, clasped its robe in supplication.

'I am a mortal, and liable to fall.'[1]

'Bear but a touch of my hand *there*,'[2] said the Spirit, laying it upon his heart, 'and you shall be upheld in more than this!'

As the words were spoken, they passed through the wall, and stood[3] † in the busy thoroughfares of a city. It was made plain enough by the dressing of the shops, that here too it was Christmas-Time.

The Ghost stopped at a certain warehouse door, and asked Scrooge if he knew it.

'Know it! Was I apprenticed here!'[4]

They went in. At sight of an old gentleman in a Welch wig, sitting behind such a high desk, that if he had been two inches taller he must have knocked his head against the ceiling, Scrooge cried in great excitement:

'Why, it's old Fezziwig! Bless his heart; it's Fezziwig alive again!'

Old Fezziwig laid down his pen, and looked up at the clock, which pointed to the hour of seven. He rubbed his hands; adjusted his capacious waistcoat; laughed all over himself, from his shoes to his organ of benevolence; and called out in a comfortable, oily, rich, fat, jovial voice:

'Yo ho, there! Ebenezer! Dick!'

A living and moving Picture of Scrooge's former self,[5] a young man, came briskly in, accompanied by his fellow-'prentice.

'Dick Wilkins, to be sure!' said Scrooge to the Ghost. 'My old fellow

---

[1] Elaborated to 'I beg your pardon, but being your mortal partner, you don't consider that I am liable to fall down five pairs of stairs!' (Hill).

[2] *there* italic in *1843*. This speech 'Dramatic, with hand outstretched' (Wright).

[3] Scrooge's childhood and schooldays, much amended in *Berg*, are here eventually all deleted: the first big cut.

[4] Marginal stage-direction *Scrooge melted*; also (below) *Melted* both at 'Why, it's old Fezziwig!' and at 'Dick Wilkins, to be sure!' Scrooge's 'melting' had been evident at the end of the scene with his sister, when that was performed: *Soften very much* at 'So she had. You're right . . .'

[5] Doubly underlined.

'Prentice! Bless me, yes. There he is. He was very much attached to me, was Dick. Poor Dick! Dear, dear!'

'Yo ho, my boys!' said Fezziwig.[1] 'No more work to-night. Christmas Eve, Dick. Christmas, Ebenezer! Let's have the shutters up, before a man can say, Jack Robinson! Clear away, my lads, and let's have lots of room here!'

Clear away! There was nothing they wouldn't have cleared away, or couldn't have cleared away, with old Fezziwig looking on. It was done in a minute. Every movable was packed off, as if it were dismissed from public life for evermore; the floor was swept and watered, the lamps were trimmed, fuel was heaped upon the fire; and the warehouse was as snug, and warm, and dry, and bright a ball-room, as you would desire to see upon a winter's night.

[2]In came a fiddler with a music-book, and went up to the lofty desk, and made an orchestra of it, and tuned like fifty stomach-aches. In came Mrs. Fezziwig, one vast substantial smile. In came the three Miss Fezziwigs, beaming and lovable. In came the six young followers whose hearts they broke.[3] In came all the young men and women employed in the business. In came the housemaid, with her cousin, the baker. In came the cook, with her brother's particular friend, the milkman. In they all came, one after another; some shyly, some boldly, some gracefully, some awkwardly, some pushing, some pulling; in they all came, anyhow and everyhow. Away they all went, twenty couple at once, hands half round and back again the other way; down the middle and up again; round and round in various stages of affectionate grouping; old top couple always turning up in the wrong place; new top couple starting off again, as soon as they got there; all top couples at last, and not a bottom one to help them. When this result was brought about, old Fezziwig, clapping his hands to stop the dance, cried out, 'Well done!' and the fiddler plunged his hot face into a pot of porter, especially provided for that purpose.[4]

There were more dances, and there were forfeits, and more dances, and there was cake, and there was negus, and there was a great piece of Cold Roast, and there was a great piece of Cold Boiled, and there were mince-pies, and plenty of beer. But the great effect of the evening came after the Roast and Boiled, when the fiddler struck up 'Sir Roger de

---

[1] 'Laughing' (Wright).

[2] Marginal stage-direction *Cheerful narrative*.

[3] The 'six young followers' were increased to 'ten'; similarly, the number of pairs of dancers was amplified, 'twenty' becoming 'thirty', etc. (Hill).

[4] '. . . a pot of porter, *which positively hissed* . . .' (Hill). As Fezziwig, Dickens clapped hands; at 'Sir Roger de Coverley' (below), he fiddled (Wright). The dance was made vivid through 'the incomparable action of his hands. They actually perform upon the table, as if it were the floor of Fezziwig's room, and every finger were a leg belonging to one of the Fezziwig family' (Field, p. 31).

Coverley.' Then old Fezziwig stood out to dance with Mrs. Fezziwig. Top couple too; with a good stiff piece of work cut out for them; three or four and twenty pair of partners; people who were not to be trifled with; people who *would*[1] dance, and had no notion of walking. But if they had been twice as many—four times—old Fezziwig would have been a match for them, and so would Mrs. Fezziwig. As to *her*, she was worthy to be his partner in every sense of the term. A positive light appeared to issue from Fezziwig's calves. They shone in every part of the dance. You could n't have predicted, at any given time, what would become of 'em next. And when old Fezziwig and Mrs. Fezziwig had gone all through the dance; advance and retire, turn your partner; bow and curtsey; corkscrew; thread-the-needle, and back again to your place; Fezziwig 'cut'—cut so deftly, that he appeared to wink with his legs.[2]

When the clock struck eleven, this domestic ball broke up. Mr. and Mrs. Fezziwig took their stations, one on either side the door, and shaking hands with every person individually as he or she went out, wished him or her a Merry Christmas. When everybody had retired but the two 'prentices, they did the same to them; and thus the cheerful voices died away, and the lads were left to their beds; which were under a counter in the back-shop. †

'A small matter,' said the Ghost, 'to make these silly folks so full of gratitude. He has spent but a few pounds of your mortal money: three or four, perhaps. Is that so much that he deserves this praise?'

'It is n't that,' said Scrooge, heated by the remark, and speaking unconsciously like his former, not his latter, self. 'It is n't that, Spirit. He has the power to render us happy or unhappy; to make our service light or burdensome; a pleasure or a toil. Say that his power lies in words and looks; in things so slight and insignificant that it is impossible to add and count 'em up: what then? The happiness he gives, is quite as great as if it cost a fortune.'

He felt the Spirit's glance, and stopped.

'What is the matter?'

'Nothing particular.'[3]

'Something, I think?'

'No. No. I should like to be able to say a word or two to my clerk just now! That's all.'

---

[1] *would*, and *her* (below), italic in *1843*.
[2] A much-praised moment: 'the greatest hit of the evening . . . The contagion of the audience's laughter reached Mr. Dickens himself who with difficulty brought out the inimitable drollery;' his *wink* 'was too much for Boston, and I thought the roof would go off' (*New York Tribune*, 3 December 1867). At the climactic word, 'Mr. Dickens . . . actually did wink with his eyes' (*New York Times*, 10 December 1867).
[3] 'Left finger to mouth' (Wright).

'My time grows short,' observed the Spirit. 'Quick!'

This was not addressed to Scrooge, or to any one whom he could see, but it produced an immediate effect. For again he saw himself. He was older now; a man in the prime of life.

He was not alone, but sat by the side of a fair young girl in a black dress: in whose eyes there were tears.

'It matters little,' she said, softly, to Scrooge's former self. 'To you, very little. Another idol has displaced *me*; and if it can comfort you in time to come, as I would have tried to do, I have no just cause to grieve.'

'What Idol has displaced you?'

'A golden one.[1] I have seen your nobler aspirations fall off one by one, until the master-passion, Gain, engrosses you. Have I not?'

'What then? Even if I have grown so much wiser, what then? I am not changed towards you. † Have I ever sought release from our engagement?'

'In words. No. Never.'

'In what, then?'

'In a changed nature; in an altered spirit; in another atmosphere of life; another Hope as its great end. † If you were free to-day, to-morrow, yesterday, can even I believe that you would choose a dowerless girl: or, choosing her, do I not know that your repentance and regret would surely follow? I do; and I release you. With a full heart, for the love of him you once were.'[2] †

'Spirit! remove me from this place.'

'I told you these were shadows of the things that have been,' said the Ghost. 'That they are what they are, do not blame me!'

'Remove me!' Scrooge exclaimed. 'I cannot bear it! Leave me! Take me back. Haunt me no longer!'[3] †

As he struggled with the Spirit he was conscious of being exhausted, and overcome by an irresistible drowsiness; and, further, of being in his own bedroom. He had barely time to reel to bed, before he sank into a heavy sleep.

---

[1] *T & F* here includes the sentence, later deleted: 'You fear the world too much'.

[2] The vision of Scrooge's lost love, happy in her marriage to another, is here, after sundry deletions, omitted altogether, both in *Berg* and in *T & F*. But Hill records his performing (and amplifying) part of the omitted episode: 'Spirit, show me no more *of the past*. . . . Why do you delight to torture me? *I cannot bear to see it*" (the latter words in keen agony)—and he went on—"Remove me . . ."'

[3] The paragraph following in *1843* ('In the struggle') is deleted in pencil in *Berg*; there is a marginal *Stet*, in pencil, but the paragraph is also deleted in blue ink. *T & F* does not include the paragraph. The blue-ink deletion is later, and more authoritative than, the uncancelled *Stet*.

STAVE THREE[1]

The Second of the Three Spirits

SCROOGE awoke in his own Bedroom. There was no doubt about that. But *it*, and his own adjoining sitting-room into which he shuffled in his slippers—attracted by a great Light there—had undergone a surprising transformation. The walls and ceiling were so hung with living green, that it looked a perfect grove. The leaves of holly, mistletoe, and ivy reflected back the light, as if so many little mirrors had been scattered there; and such a mighty blaze went roaring up the chimney, as that petrifaction of a hearth had never known in Scrooge's time, or Marley's, or for many and many a winter season gone. Heaped upon the floor, to form a kind of throne, were turkeys, geese, game, brawn, great joints of meat, sucking-pigs, long wreaths of sausages, mince-pies, plum-puddings, barrels of oysters, red-hot chesnuts, cherry-cheeked apples, juicy oranges, luscious pears, immense twelfth-cakes, and great bowls of punch. In easy state upon this couch, there sat a Giant, glorious to see; who bore a glowing torch, in shape not unlike Plenty's horn, and who raised it high, to shed its light on Scrooge, as he came peeping round the door.

'Come in! Come in! and know me better, man! I am the Ghost of Christmas Present. Look upon me! † You have never seen the like of me before!'

'Never.'[2]

'Have never walked forth with the *younger* members of my family; meaning (for I am very young) my elder brothers born in these later years?' pursued the Phantom.

'I don't think I have. I am afraid I have not. Have you had many brothers, Spirit?'

'More than eighteen hundred.'

'A tremendous family to provide for! Spirit, conduct me where you will. I went forth last night on compulsion, and I learnt a lesson which is working now. To-night, if you have aught to teach me, let me profit by it.'

'Touch my robe!'

Scrooge did as he was told, and held it fast.

The room, and its contents, all vanished instantly, and they stood in the city streets upon a snowy Christmas morning.[3] †

---

[1] '*Chapter 3*' in *Berg*, regularized in *T & F* to STAVE THREE. After tinkering with its opening, Dickens deleted the first three pages.

[2] 'Scrooge did *not* say "Never"; but (in a trembling voice),—"Well, I don't think I have"' (Hill).

[3] Another lengthy deletion here—the lively description of the streets and shops, and of people going to church. By contrast, the Cratchit episode which follows is hardly abbreviated at all.

Scrooge and the Ghost passed on, invisible,[1] straight to Scrooge's clerk's; and on the threshold of the door the Spirit smiled, and stopped to bless Bob Cratchit's dwelling with the sprinklings of his torch. Think of that! Bob had but fifteen 'Bob' a-week himself; he pocketed on Saturdays but fifteen copies of his Christian name; and yet the Ghost of Christmas Present blessed his four-roomed house!

Then up rose Mrs. Cratchit, Cratchit's wife, dressed out but poorly in a twice-turned gown, but brave in ribbons—which are cheap and make a goodly show for sixpence; and she laid the cloth, assisted by Belinda Cratchit, second of her daughters, also brave in ribbons; while Master Peter Cratchit plunged a fork into the saucepan of potatoes, and getting the corners of his monstrous shirt-collar (Bob's private property, conferred upon his son and heir in honour of the day) into his mouth, rejoiced to find himself so gallantly attired, and yearned to show his linen in the fashionable Parks. And now two smaller Cratchits, boy and girl, came tearing in, screaming that, outside the baker's, they had smelt the goose, and known it for their own; and basking in luxurious thoughts of sage-and-onion, these young Cratchits danced about the table, and exalted Master Peter Cratchit to the skies, while he (not proud, although his collars nearly choked him) blew the fire, until the slow potatoes bubbling up, knocked loudly at the saucepan-lid to be let out and peeled.

'What has ever got your precious father, then?' said Mrs. Cratchit. 'And your brother, Tiny Tim! And Martha warn't as late last Christmas Day by half-an-hour!'

'Here's Martha, mother!' said a girl, appearing as she spoke.

'Here's Martha, mother!' cried the two young Cratchits. 'Hurrah! There's *such*[2] a goose, Martha!'

'Why, bless your heart alive, my dear, how late you are!' said Mrs. Cratchit, kissing her a dozen times, and taking off her shawl and bonnet for her.

'We'd a deal of work to finish up last night,' replied the girl, 'and had to clear away this morning, mother!'

'Well! Never mind so long as you are come,' said Mrs. Cratchit. 'Sit ye down before the fire, my dear, and have a warm, Lord bless ye!'

'No no! There's father coming,' cried the two young Cratchits, who were everywhere at once. 'Hide, Martha, hide!'

So Martha hid herself, and in came little Bob, the father,[3] with at least three feet of comforter exclusive of the fringe, hanging down before him; and his thread-bare clothes darned up and brushed, to look seasonable;

---

[1] Doubly underlined (probably because these words, written in the margin, marked the resumption of text after a long cut).

[2] *such* italic in *1843*. 'The way those two young Cratchits hail Martha, and exclaim [this] . . . can never be forgotten' (Field, p. 32).

[3] Marginal stage-direction *Tone to Tiny Tim.*

and Tiny Tim upon his shoulder. *Alas for Tiny Tim, he bore a little crutch, and had his limbs supported by an iron frame!*[1]
'Why, where's our Martha?' cried Bob Cratchit, looking round.
'Not coming,' said Mrs. Cratchit.
'Not coming!' said Bob, with a sudden declension in his high spirits; for he had been Tim's blood horse all the way from church, and had come home rampant. 'Not coming upon Christmas Day!'
Martha didn't like to see him disappointed, if it were only in joke; so she came out prematurely from behind the closet door, and ran into his arms, while the two young Cratchits hustled Tiny Tim, and bore him off into the wash-house, that he might hear the pudding singing in the copper.
'And how did little Tim behave?' asked Mrs. Cratchit, when she had rallied Bob on his credulity and Bob had hugged his daughter to his heart's content.
'As good as gold,' said Bob, 'and better. Somehow he gets thoughtful, sitting by himself so much, and thinks the strangest things you ever heard. He told me, coming home, that he hoped the people saw him in the church, because he was a cripple, and it might be pleasant to them to remember upon Christmas Day, who made lame beggars walk and blind men see.'[2]
Bob's voice was tremulous when he told them this, and trembled more when he said that Tiny Tim was growing strong and hearty.
His active little crutch was heard upon the floor, and back came Tiny Tim before another word was spoken, escorted by his brother and sister to his stool beside the fire; and while Bob, turning up his cuffs—as if, poor fellow, they were capable of being made more shabby—compounded some hot mixture in a jug with gin and lemons, and stirred it round and round and put it on the hob to simmer; Master Peter and the two ubiquitous young Cratchits went to fetch the goose, with which they soon returned in high procession.
Mrs. Cratchit made the gravy (ready beforehand in a little saucepan) hissing hot;[3] Master Peter mashed the potatoes with incredible vigour; Miss Belinda sweetened up the apple-sauce; Martha dusted the hot plates; Bob took Tiny Tim beside him in a tiny corner at the table; the two young Cratchits set chairs for everybody, not forgetting themselves, and mounting guard upon their posts, crammed spoons into their mouths, lest they should shriek for goose before their turn came to be helped. At last the dishes were set on, and grace was said. It was succeeded by a

[1] Doubly underlined.
[2] This speech 'Feelingly, tremblingly' and 'With hkf' at 'blind men see' (Wright); its pathos was 'the most delicate and artistic rendering of the whole reading' (Field, p. 32).
[3] 'Mr Dickens . . . is one of the best of living actors,' wrote the *New York Times* critic (10 December 1867): and, instancing his 'free use of gesticulation', he described how, in this passage, he stirred the gravy, mashed the potatoes, dusted the plates, and (later) sniffed the famous pudding.

breathless pause, as Mrs. Cratchit, looking slowly all along the carving-knife, prepared to plunge it in the breast; but when she did, and when the long expected gush of stuffing issued forth, one murmur of delight arose all round the board, and even Tiny Tim, excited by the two young Cratchits, beat on the table with the handle of his knife, and feebly cried Hurrah![1]

There never was such a goose. Bob said he didn't believe there ever was such a goose cooked. Its tenderness and flavour, size and cheapness, were the themes of universal admiration. Eked out by the apple-sauce and mashed potatoes, it was a sufficient dinner for the whole family; indeed, as Mrs. Cratchit said with great delight (surveying one small atom of a bone upon the dish), they hadn't ate it all at last! Yet every one had had enough, and the youngest Cratchits in particular, were steeped in sage and onion to the eyebrows! But now, the plates being changed by Miss Belinda, Mrs. Cratchit left the room alone—too nervous to bear witnesses —to take the pudding up, and bring it in.

Suppose it should not be done enough![2] Suppose it should break in turning out! Suppose somebody should have got over the wall of the back-yard, and stolen it, while they were merry with the goose: a supposition at which the two young Cratchits became livid! All sorts of horrors were supposed.

Hallo! A great deal of steam! The pudding was out of the copper. A smell like a washing-day! That was the cloth. A smell like an eating-house, and a pastry cook's next door to each other, with a laundress's next door to that! That was the pudding! In half a minute Mrs. Cratchit entered: flushed, but smiling proudly: with the pudding, like a speckled cannon-ball, so hard and firm, blazing in half of half-a-quartern of ignited brandy, and bedight with Christmas holly stuck into the top.

Oh, a wonderful pudding![3] Bob Cratchit said, and calmly too, that he regarded it as the greatest success achieved by Mrs. Cratchit since their marriage. Mrs. Cratchit said that now the weight was off her mind, she would confess she had had her doubts about the quantity of flour. Every-body had something to say about it, but nobody said or thought it was at all a small pudding for a large family. Any Cratchit would have blushed to hint at such a thing.

At last the dinner was all done, the cloth was cleared, the hearth swept, and the fire made up. The compound in the jug being tasted and con-sidered perfect, apples and oranges were put upon the table, and a

[1] 'Very high thin voice' (Wright).

[2] 'Shaking to and fro with his body' during this paragraph (Wright).

[3] 'What cheers when Mrs. Cratchit brought in that pudding. . . . His description brought down torrents of applause, so archly was it given' (*Cambridge Independent Press*, 17 October 1859). Dickens's sniffing the pudding made Kate Field remark (p. 33) that 'What Dickens *does* is frequently infinitely better than anything he says, or the way he says it.'

shovel-full of chesnuts on the fire.[1] Then all the Cratchit family drew round the hearth, in what Bob Cratchit called a circle; and at Bob Cratchit's elbow stood the family display of glass; two tumblers, and a custard-cup without a handle.[2]

These held the hot stuff from the jug, however, as well as golden goblets would have done; and Bob served it out with beaming looks, while the chesnuts on the fire sputtered and crackled noisily. Then Bob proposed:

'A Merry Christmas to us all, my dears. God bless us!'

Which all the family re-echoed.

'God bless us every one!' said Tiny Tim, the last of all.

He sat very close to his father's side, upon his little stool. Bob held his withered little hand in his, as if he loved the child, and wished to keep him by his side, and dreaded that he might be taken from him.[3] †

Scrooge raised his head speedily, on hearing his own name.

'Mr. Scrooge!' said Bob; 'I'll give you Mr. Scrooge, the Founder of the Feast!'

'The Founder of the Feast indeed!' cried Mrs. Cratchit, reddening. 'I wish I had him here. I'd give him a piece of my mind to feast upon, and I hope he'd have a good appetite for it.'

'My dear,' said Bob, 'the children! Christmas Day.'

'It should be Christmas Day, I am sure,' said she, 'on which one drinks the health of such an odious, stingy, hard, unfeeling man as Mr. Scrooge. You know he is, Robert! Nobody knows it better than you do, poor fellow!'

'My dear,' was Bob's mild answer, 'Christmas Day.'

'I'll drink his health for your sake and the Day's,' said Mrs. Cratchit, 'not for his. Long life to him! A merry Christmas and a happy new year! He'll be very merry and very happy, I have no doubt!'[4]

The children drank the toast after her. It was the first of their proceedings which had no heartiness in it. Tiny Tim drank it last of all, but he didn't care twopence for it. Scrooge was the Ogre of the family. The mention of his name cast a dark shadow on the party, which was not dispelled for full five minutes.

After it had passed away, they were ten times merrier than before, from the mere relief of Scrooge the Baleful being done with. Bob Cratchit told them how he had a situation in his eye for Master Peter, which would

---

[1] *T & F* begins a new paragraph here.

[2] '... two *broken* tumblers, and a *cracked* custard cup ...' (Hill).

[3] 'Who can forget Bob Cratchit, holding Tiny Tim's hand, then throwing him a kiss, and brushing a tear from his eyes, as he prepares to propose the health of Scrooge? It was a little action, but it meant so much! Those only who have children and fear to lose them, or loving them *have* lost, can know how much it meant' (*New York Tribune*, 10 December 1867). Cf. Field, p. 34, on this passage.

[4] She drank the toast 'sharply' (Hill).

bring in, if obtained, full five-and-sixpence weekly. The two young Cratchits laughed tremendously at the idea of Peter's being a man of business; and Peter himself looked thoughtfully at the fire from between his collars, as if he were deliberating what particular investments he should favour when he came into the receipt of that bewildering income. Martha, who was a poor apprentice at a milliner's, then told them what kind of work she had to do, and how many hours she worked at a stretch, and how she meant to lie a-bed to-morrow morning for a good long rest; to-morrow being a holiday she passed at home. Also how she had seen a countess and a lord some days before, and how the lord 'was much about as tall as Peter;' at which Peter pulled up his collars so high that you couldn't have seen his head if you had been there. All this time the chesnuts and the jug went round and round; and bye and bye they had a song, about a lost child travelling in the snow, from Tiny Tim; who had a plaintive little voice, and sang it very well indeed.

There was nothing of high mark in this. They were not a handsome family; they were not well dressed; their shoes were far from being waterproof; their clothes were scanty; and Peter might have known, and very likely did, the inside of a pawnbroker's. But they were happy, grateful, pleased with one another, and contented with the time; and when they faded, and looked happier yet in the bright sprinklings of the Spirit's torch at parting, Scrooge had his eye upon them, and especially on Tiny Tim, until the last.[1] †

It was a great surprise to Scrooge, *as this scene vanished*,[2] to hear a hearty laugh. It was a much greater surprise to Scrooge to recognize it as his own nephew's, and to find himself in a bright, dry, gleaming room, with the Spirit standing smiling by his side, and looking at that same nephew.

It is a fair, even-handed, noble adjustment of things, that while there is infection in disease and sorrow, there is nothing in the world so irresistibly contagious as laughter and good-humour. When Scrooge's nephew laughed, Scrooge's niece, by marriage, laughed as heartily as he. And their assembled friends being not a bit behindhand, laughed out, lustily.

'He said that Christmas was a humbug, as I live!' cried Scrooge's nephew. 'He believed it too!'[3]

'More shame for him, Fred!' said Scrooge's niece, indignantly.—

[1] Scrooge's vision of the miners, lighthouse-keepers, and mariners is here deleted.

[2] A manuscript insertion, doubly underlined (cf. p. 19, note 1, above). Marginal stage-direction here, *Tone to cheerful Narrative* .

[3] Scrooge's nephew's laughter here was 'contagious' (Hill), and the ensuing account of his niece was 'irresistibly exhilarating' (Kent, p. 104). 'I hate him!' she added, after the text's 'More shame for him, Fred!' and Fred, instead of calling Scrooge 'a comical old fellow' called him 'a queer old fellow'—a great improvement (Hill noted and remarked).

Bless those women; they never do anything by halves. They are always in earnest.

She was very pretty: exceedingly pretty. With a dimpled, surprised-looking, capital face; a ripe little mouth, that seemed made to be kissed—as no doubt it was; all kinds of good little dots about her chin, that melted into one another when she laughed; and the sunniest pair of eyes you ever saw in any little creature's head. Altogether she was what you would have called provoking; but satisfactory, too. Oh, perfectly satisfactory!

'He's a comical old fellow,' said Scrooge's nephew, 'that's the truth; and not so pleasant as he might be. However, his offences carry their own punishment, and I have nothing to say against him. † Who suffers by his ill whims? Himself, always. Here, he takes it into his head to dislike us, and he won't come and dine with us. What's the consequence? He don't lose much of a dinner.'

'Indeed, I think he loses a very good dinner,' interrupted Scrooge's niece. Everybody else said the same, and they must be allowed to have been competent judges, because they had just had dinner; and, with the dessert upon the table, were clustered round the fire, by lamplight.

'Well! I am very glad to hear it,' said Scrooge's nephew, 'because I haven't any great faith in these young housekeepers. What do _you_[1] say, Topper?'

Topper clearly had his eye on one of Scrooge's niece's sisters, for he answered that a bachelor was a wretched outcast, who had no right to express an opinion on the subject. Whereat Scrooge's niece's sister—the plump one with the lace tucker: not the one with the roses—blushed. †

After tea, they had some music. For they were a musical family, and knew what they were about, when they sung a Glee or Catch, I can assure you: especially Topper, who could growl away in the bass like a good one, and never swell the large veins in his forehead, or get red in the face over it.[2] † But they didn't devote the whole evening to music. After a while they played at forfeits; _for it is good to be children sometimes, and never better than at Christmas, when its mighty Founder was a child himself._ There was first a game at blind-man's buff though. And I no more believe Topper was really blinded than I believe he had eyes in his boots.[3] _Because, the way in which_[4] he went after that plump sister in the lace tucker, was an

---

[1] _you_ italic in _1843_.

[2] Against the deleted passage which follows, in which Scrooge 'softened more and more', marginal stage-direction _Tone down to Pathos_; but _Up to cheerfulness_ at 'But they didn't devote the whole evening to music'.

[3] An episode 'never to be forgotten'. When Dickens spoke this sentence, 'his facial expression—indignant as of a man who is being put upon, and yet with a consciousness of the absurdity of the statement that makes him laugh in spite of his anger—was inimitable, and it was long before the audience would let him get on.' The plump sister was 'immortal' (_New York Tribune_, 3 December 1867).

[4] A manuscript insertion, doubly underlined (cf. p. 19, note 1).

outrage on the credulity of human nature. Knocking down the fire-irons, tumbling over the chairs, bumping up against the piano, smothering himself among the curtains, wherever she went, there went he. He always knew where the plump sister was. He wouldn't catch anybody else. If you had fallen up against him, as some of them did, and stood there; he would have made a feint of endeavouring to seize you, which would have been an affront to your understanding; and would instantly have sidled off in the direction of the plump sister. †

'Here is a new game,' said Scrooge.[1] 'One half hour, Spirit, only one!'

It was a Game called Yes and No, where Scrooge's nephew had to think of something, and the rest must find out what; he only answering to their questions yes or no as the case was. The fire of questioning to which he was exposed, elicited from him that he was thinking of an animal, a live animal, rather a disagreeable animal, a savage animal, an animal that growled and grunted sometimes, and talked sometimes, and lived in London, and walked about the streets, and wasn't made a show of, and wasn't led by anybody, and didn't live in a menagerie, and was never killed in a market, and was not a horse, or an ass, or a cow, or a bull, or a tiger, or a dog, or a pig, or a cat, or a bear. At every new question put to him, this nephew burst into a fresh roar of laughter; and was so inexpressibly tickled, that he was obliged to get up off the sofa and stamp. At last the plump sister cried out:

'I have found it out! I know what it is, Fred! I know what it is!'

'What is it?' cried Fred.

'It's your uncle Scro-o-o-o-oge!'[2]

Which it certainly was. Admiration was the universal sentiment, though some objected that the reply to 'Is it a bear?' ought to have been 'Yes.' †

Uncle Scrooge had imperceptibly become so gay and light of heart, that he would have drank to the unconscious company in an inaudible speech. But the whole scene passed off in the breath of the last word spoken by his nephew; and he and the Spirit were again upon their travels.

Much they saw, and far they went, and many homes they visited, but always with a happy end. The Spirit stood beside sick beds, and they were cheerful; on foreign lands, and they were close at home; by struggling men, and they were patient in their greater hope; by poverty, and it was rich. In almshouse, hospital, and jail, in misery's every refuge, where vain man in his little brief authority had not made fast the door, and barred

[1] 'This scene he treated quite freely,' notes Hill, who records Dickens's textual variations hereabouts. This speech 'Laughingly and cryingly' (Wright).

[2] 'In high key' (Wright); an 'abiding memory' for many witnesses—'the blood-curdling and yet almost loving way in which the name ... was pronounced—long-drawn-out and with tremendous emphasis' (Walter Pine, in *Dickensian*, xxxiv (1939), 206).

the Spirit out, he left his blessing, and taught Scrooge his precepts.[1] Suddenly, as they stood together in an open place, the bell struck *Twelve*.[2] †

Scrooge looked about him for the Ghost, and saw it no more. As the last stroke ceased to vibrate, he remembered the prediction of old Jacob Marley, and lifting up his eyes, beheld a solemn Phantom, draped and hooded, coming, like a mist along the ground, towards him.

STAVE FOUR

The Last of the Spirits

THE Phantom slowly, gravely, silently, approached.[3] When it came near him, Scrooge bent down upon his knee; for in the air through which this Spirit moved it seemed to scatter gloom and mystery.

It was shrouded in a deep black garment, which concealed its head, its face, its form, and left nothing of it visible *save one outstretched hand*.[4] He knew no more, for the Spirit neither spoke nor moved.

'I am in the presence of the Ghost of Christmas Yet To Come? † Ghost of the Future! I fear you more than any Spectre I have seen. But, as I know your purpose is to do me good, and as I hope to live to be another man from what I was, I am prepared to bear you company, and do it with a thankful heart.[5] Will you not speak to me?'

It gave him no reply. The hand was pointed straight before them.

'Lead on! Lead on! The night is waning fast, and it is precious time to me, I know. Lead on, Spirit!'

They scarcely seemed to enter the city; for the city rather seemed to spring up about them. But there they were, in the heart of it; on Change, amongst the merchants.

The Spirit stopped beside one little knot of business men. Observing that the hand was pointed to them, Scrooge advanced to listen to their talk.

'No,' said a great fat man with a monstrous chin, 'I don't know much about it, either way. I only know he's dead.'[6]

---

[1] 'Pause. Look from one side to the other' (Wright).

[2] The encounter with the two terrible children, Ignorance and Want (preluded by the marginal stage-direction *Stern Pathos*), is here deleted.

[3] Marginal stage-direction *Mystery*: and, above STAVE FOUR, *Throughout, Monotonous Hand*.

[4] Here 'he stretched out his right arm at full length, and soon bent the hand down very definitely' (Hill).

[5] 'A very long pause' here: 'Dickens's face looked so anxious that the audience watched him in breathless silence. "Will you not *speak* to me?" with great emphasis on the one word "speak"' (Hill).

[6] 'Low guttural voice' (Wright). This fat man was often mentioned as an instance of Dickens's power of giving an unforgettable individuality to minor characters; e.g., see Kent, p. 96.

'When did he die?' inquired another.

'Last night, I believe.'

'Why, what was the matter with him? I thought he'd never die.'

'God knows,' said the first, with a yawn.

'What has he done with his money?' asked a red-faced gentleman.

'I haven't heard,' said the man with the large chin. 'Company, perhaps. He hasn't left it to *me*.[1] That's all I know. Bye, bye!' †

Scrooge was at first inclined to be surprised that the Spirit should attach importance to conversation apparently so trivial; but feeling assured that it must have some hidden purpose, he set himself to consider what it was likely to be. It could scarcely be supposed to have any bearing on the death of Jacob, his old partner, for that was Past, and this Ghost's province was the Future.

He looked about in that very place for his own image; *but another man stood in his accustomed corner*,[2] and though the clock pointed to his usual time of day for being there, *he saw no likeness of himself* among the multitudes that poured in through the Porch. It gave him little surprise, however; for he had been revolving in his mind a change of life, and he thought and hoped he saw his new-born resolutions carried out in this.

They left this busy scene, and went into an obscure part of the town, to a low shop where iron, old rags, bottles, bones, and greasy offal, were bought by a gray-haired rascal, of great age; who sat smoking his pipe.

Scrooge and the Phantom came into the presence of this man, just as a woman with a heavy bundle slunk into the shop. But she had scarcely entered, when another woman, similarly laden, came in too; and she was closely followed by a man in faded black. After a short period of blank astonishment, in which the old man with the pipe had joined them, they all three burst into a laugh.[3]

'Let the charwoman alone to be the first!' cried she who had entered first. 'Let the laundress alone to be the second; and let the undertaker's man alone to be the third. Look here, old Joe, here's a chance! If we haven't all three met here without meaning it!'

'You couldn't have met in a better place. You were made free of it long ago, you know; and the other two an't strangers. What have you got to sell, what have you got to sell?'

'Half a minute's patience, Joe, and you shall see. What odds then! What odds, Mrs. Dilber?' said the woman. 'Every person has a right to take care of themselves. *He*[4] always did! Who's the worse for the loss of a few things like these? Not a dead man, I suppose.'

[1] *me* italic in *1843*.

[2] This, and the next italicized phrase, doubly underlined.

[3] Marginal stage-direction *Weird*. 'There was something positively and Shakespearianly weird in the laugh and tone of the charwoman' (Field, p. 35). 'Miserable high wheezing voice' for Old Joe (Wright).

[4] *He* italic in *1843*.

Mrs. Dilber, whose manner was remarkable for general propitiation, said, 'No, indeed, Ma'am.'

'If he wanted to keep 'em after he was dead, a wicked old screw, why wasn't he natural in his lifetime? If he had been, he'd have had somebody to look after him when he was struck with Death, instead of lying gasping out his last there, alone by himself.'

'It's the truest word that ever was spoke. It's a judgement on him.'

'I wish it was a little heavier judgement; and it should have been, you may depend upon it, if I could have laid my hands on anything else. Open that bundle, old Joe, and let me know the value of it. Speak out plain. I'm not afraid to be the first, nor afraid for them to see it.' †

Joe went down on his knees for the greater convenience of opening the bundle, and dragged out a large and heavy roll of some dark stuff.

'What do you call this? Bed-curtains!'

'Ah! Bed-curtains! Don't drop that oil upon the blankets, now.'

'*His* blankets?'

'Whose else's do you think? He isn't likely to take cold without 'em, I dare say. Ah! You may look through that shirt till your eyes ache; but you won't find a hole in it, nor a threadbare place. It's the best he had, and a fine one too. They'd have wasted it by dressing him up in it, if it hadn't been for me.'

Scrooge listened to this dialogue in horror.

'Spirit! I see, I see. The case of this unhappy man might be my own. My life tends that way, now. *Merciful Heaven, what is this!*'[1]

The scene had changed, and now he almost touched a bare, uncurtained bed. A pale light, rising in the outer air, fell straight upon this bed; and on it, unwatched, unwept, uncared for, was the body of this plundered man unknown.[2] †

'*Spirit! Let me see some tenderness connected with a death*, or this dark chamber, Spirit, will be for ever present to me.'

[3] The Ghost conducted him to poor Bob Cratchit's house; the dwelling he had visited before; and found the mother and the children seated round the fire.

Quiet. Very quiet. The noisy little Cratchits were as still as statues in one corner, and sat looking up at Peter, who had a book before him. The mother and her daughters were engaged in needlework. But surely they were very quiet!

'"And He took a child, and set him in the midst of them."'

Where had Scrooge heard those words? He had not dreamed them.

---

[1] Doubly underlined. Marginal stage-direction *Scrooge's start and change to terror*.
[2] 'Pause. Look to left' (Wright). *T & F* has '. . . plundered unknown man'. In the next line '*Spirit!*' (a marginal insertion) is doubly underlined, the rest singly.
[3] Marginal stage-direction *Pathos*. 'Looking about' (Wright).

The boy must have read them out, as he and the Spirit crossed the threshold. Why did he not go on?

The mother laid her work upon the table, and put her hand up to her face.

'The colour hurts my eyes,' she said.[1]

The colour? *Ah, poor Tiny Tim!*

'They're better now again. It makes them weak by candle-light; and I wouldn't show weak eyes to your father when he comes home, for the world. It must be near his time.'

'Past it rather,' Peter answered, shutting up his book. 'But I think he has walked a little slower than he used, these few last evenings, mother.'

'I have known him walk with—I have known him walk with Tiny Tim upon his shoulder, very fast indeed.'

'And so have I,' cried Peter. 'Often.'

'And so have I,' exclaimed another. So had all.

'But he was very light to carry, and his father loved him so, that it was no trouble: no trouble. And there is your father at the door!'

She hurried out to meet him; and little Bob in his comforter—he had need of it, poor fellow—came in. His tea was ready for him on the hob, and they all tried who should help him to it most. Then the two young Cratchits got upon his knees and laid, each child a little cheek, against his face, as if they said, 'Don't mind it, father. Don't be grieved!'

Bob was very cheerful with them, and spoke pleasantly to all the family. He looked at the work upon the table, and praised the industry and speed of Mrs. Cratchit and the girls. They would be done long before Sunday, he said.

'Sunday! You went to-day, then, Robert?'

'Yes, my dear,' returned Bob. 'I wish you could have gone. It would have done you good to see how green a place it is. But you'll see it often. I promised him that I would walk there on a Sunday.[2] My little, little child! My little child!'

He broke down all at once. He couldn't help it. *If he could have helped it, he and his child would have been farther apart perhaps than they were.* †

---

[1] 'Sigh. Handkerchief to eyes', a gesture repeated below at 'Sunday!...' (Wright). 'The pathos which he throws into [this] one short line . . . cannot be described' (*Town Talk*, 1858, quoted in *Dickensian*, xxxvii (1941), 223); a passage 'breathing an exquisite tenderness . . . that thrilled to the hearts of all who heard [it], and still, we doubt not, haunts their recollections' (Kent, p. 104).

[2] '3 or 4 seconds of painful silence. Then Bob's grief burst out, almost in a suppressed scream' (Hill); 'Cry with head thrown back' (Wright). Some critics thought Dickens over-played this moment (e.g., Field, p. 35). He made 'more of a "point" of it than of any other passage' in the Reading (New York *Nation*, 12 December 1867, p. 483). Kent, who praises Dickens's rendering, notes how much of this pathetic episode is deleted, e.g. Bob's visit to the deathbed (pp. 104–5).

'Spectre,' said Scrooge, 'something informs me that our parting moment is at hand. I know it, but I know not how. Tell me what man that was with the covered face whom we saw lying dead?'

The Ghost of Christmas Yet To Come conveyed him † to a dismal, wretched, ruinous churchyard.

The Spirit stood among the graves, and pointed down to One.

'Before I draw nearer to that stone to which you point, answer me one question. *Are these the shadows of the things that Will be, or are they shadows of the things that May be, only?*'[1]

Still the Ghost pointed downward to the grave by which it stood.

'Men's courses will foreshadow certain ends, to which, if persevered in, they must lead. But if the courses be departed from, the ends will change. Say it is thus with what you show me!'

The Spirit was immovable as ever. Scrooge crept towards it, trembling as he went; and following the finger, read upon the stone of the neglected grave his own name, EBENEZER SCROOGE.[2]

'Am *I*[3] that man who lay upon the bed? No, Spirit! Oh no, no! Spirit! hear me! I am not the man I was. I will not be the man I must have been but for this intercourse. Why show me this, if I am past all hope? Assure me that I yet may change these shadows you have shown me, by an altered life.'

For the first time, the kind hand faltered.

'I will honour Christmas in my heart, and try to keep it all the year. I will live in the Past, the Present, and the Future. The Spirits of all Three shall strive within me. I will not shut out the lessons that they teach. Oh, tell me I may sponge away the writing on this stone!'

Holding up his hands in one last prayer to have his fate reversed, he saw an alteration in the Phantom's hood and dress. It shrunk, collapsed, and dwindled down into a bedpost.[4]

Yes! and the bedpost was his own. The bed was his own, the room was his own. Best and happiest of all, the time before him was his own, to make amends in! †

He was checked in his transports by the churches ringing out the lustiest peals he had ever heard. Running to the window, he opened it, and put out

---

[1] *Will* underlined three times, *May* four times, the rest singly. Dickens also much emphasized the concluding word, 'only' (Hill).

[2] The Ghost's right hand pointed downwards to the grave. 'Dickens put great terror into the tones of Scrooge' in 'Am *I* that man . . .' The silent Ghost's finger continued to point downwards, and in the rest of his speech 'Scrooge's voice lost all its stern, hard character' (Hill). He put both hands up, then clasped them (Wright). Then, at 'I will honour Christmas . . .' his voice 'became fully charged with firm tones and a humaner outlook' (Hill).

[3] *I* italic in *1843*.

[4] The text here runs straight into the story's STAVE FIVE, without any break, Dickens reading its opening paragraph 'in his richest, fullest, happiest voice' (Hill).

his head. No fog, no mist, no night; clear, bright, stirring, golden Day!

'What's to-day?' cried Scrooge, calling downward to a boy in Sunday clothes, who perhaps had loitered in to look about him.

'EH?'[1]

'What's to-day, my fine fellow?'

'To-day! Why, CHRISTMAS DAY.'

'It's Christmas Day! I haven't missed it. Hallo, my fine fellow!'

'Hallo!'

'Do you know the Poulterer's, in the next street but one, at the corner?'

'I should hope I did.'

'An intelligent boy! A remarkable boy! Do you know whether they've sold the prize Turkey that was hanging up there? Not the little prize Turkey; the big one?'

'What, the one as big as me?'

'What a delightful boy! It's a pleasure to talk to him. Yes, my buck!'

'It's hanging there now.'

'Is it? Go and buy it.'

'Walk-ER!'[2] exclaimed the boy.

'No, no, I am in earnest. Go and buy it, and tell 'em to bring it here, that I may give them the direction where to take it. Come back with the man, and I'll give you a shilling. Come back with him in less than five minutes, and I'll give you half-a-crown!'

The boy was off like a shot.

'I'll send it to Bob Cratchit's! He sha'n't know who sends it. It's the size of Tiny Tim. Joe Miller never made such a joke as sending it to Bob's will be!'

The hand in which he wrote the address was not a steady one, but write it he did, somehow, and went down stairs to open the street door, ready for the coming of the poulterer's man.

It *was*[3] a Turkey! He never could have stood upon his legs, that bird. He would have snapped 'em short off in a minute, like sticks of sealing-wax. †

He[4] dressed himself 'all in his best,' and at last got out into the streets. The people were by this time pouring forth, as he had seen them with

---

[1] Capitals here, and in the boy's next speech, in *1843*: also in his 'Walk-ER' below. 'Boy's voice very high' (Wright). A famous moment: every word of it was 'watched for and listened to by audiences like celebrated passages from a great standard play' (*Critic*, 4 September 1858, p. 537). After one performance, Dickens wrote to Forster: 'if you could have seen [the audience during this dialogue] . . . I doubt if you would ever have forgotten it' (*N*, iii. 62). He sometimes amplified the dialogue, e.g., 'What a conversational boy!' (Hill).

[2] 'Dickens, as the boy, put his thumb to his nose, and spread out his fingers, with a jeer' (Hill).

[3] *was* italic in *1843*.

[4] 'Scrooge' in *T & F*: presumably Dickens's correction.

the Ghost of Christmas Present; and walking with his hands behind him, Scrooge regarded every one with a delighted smile. He looked so irresistibly pleasant, in a word, that three or four good-humoured fellows said, 'Good morning, sir! A merry Christmas to you!' And Scrooge said often afterwards, that of all the blithe sounds he had ever heard, those were the blithest in his ears. †

In the afternoon, he turned his steps towards his nephew's house.

He passed the door a dozen times, before he had the courage to go up and knock. But he made a dash, and did it.

'Is your master at home, my dear?' said Scrooge to the girl. Nice girl! Very.[1]

'Yes, sir.'

'Where is he, my love?'

'He's in the dining-room, sir, along with mistress.'

'He knows me,' said Scrooge, with his hand already on the dining-room lock. 'I'll go in here, my dear. Fred!'

'Why bless my soul!' cried Fred, 'who's that?'

'It's I. Your uncle Scrooge. I have come to dinner. Will you let me in, Fred?'

Let him in! It is a mercy he didn't shake his arm off. He was at home in five minutes. Nothing could be heartier. His niece looked just the same. So did Topper when *he*[2] came. So did the plump sister, when *she* came. So did every one when *they* came. Wonderful party, wonderful games, wonderful unanimity, won-der-ful happiness!

But he was early at the office next morning. Oh he was early there. If he could only be there first, and catch Bob Cratchit coming late! That was the thing he had set his heart upon.

And he did it! The clock struck nine. No Bob. A quarter past. No Bob. Bob was full eighteen minutes and a half, behind his time.

Bob's hat was off, before he opened the door; his comforter too. He was on his stool in a jiffy; driving away with his pen, as if he were trying to overtake nine o'clock.

'Hallo!' growled Scrooge, in his accustomed voice as near as he could feign it.[3] 'What do you mean by coming here at this time of day?'

'I am very sorry, sir. I *am*[4] behind my time.'

'You are? Yes. I think you are. Step this way, if you please.'

'It's only once a year, sir. It shall not be repeated. I was making rather merry yesterday, sir.'

[1] 'There was a sort of parenthetical smack of the lips in [this] self-communing of Scrooge . . ."*Nice girl! very!*" Then, as to the cordiality of his reception by his Nephew, what could possibly have expressed it better than the look, voice, manner of the Reader?' (Kent, pp. 106–7).

[2] *he . . . she . . . they* italic in *1843*.

[3] Several reports noted Scrooge's comic inability to 'feign' his old gruff voice.

[4] *am* italic in *1843*. Bob's speech 'full of hesitancy and timidity' (Hill).

'Now, I'll tell you what, my friend. I am not going to stand this sort of thing any longer.—And therefore,' Scrooge continued, leaping from his stool, and giving Bob such a dig in the waistcoat that he staggered back into the Tank again: 'and therefore I am about to raise your salary!'

Bob trembled, and got a little nearer to the ruler.

'A merry Christmas, Bob!' said Scrooge, with an earnestness that could not be mistaken, as he clapped him on the back. 'A merrier Christmas, Bob, my good fellow, than I have given you, for many a year! I'll raise your salary, and endeavour to assist your struggling family, and we will discuss your affairs this very afternoon, over a Christmas bowl of smoking bishop, Bob![1] Make up the fires, and buy a second coal-scuttle before you dot another i, Bob Cratchit!'

Scrooge was better than his word. He did it all, and infinitely more; and to Tiny Tim, who did NOT die,[2] he was a second father. He became as good a friend, as good a master, and as good a man, as the good old city knew, or any other good old city, town, or borough, in the good old world. Some people laughed to see the alteration in him, but his own heart laughed: and that was quite enough for him.

He had no further intercourse with Spirits, but lived in that respect upon the Total Abstinence Principle, ever afterwards; *and it was always said of him, that he knew how to keep Christmas well, if any man alive possessed the knowledge. May that be truly said of us, and all of us! And so, as Tiny Tim observed, God Bless Us, Every One!*[3]

[1] Stage-direction *Quick on*—needed because the *1843* text is here interrupted by an engraving.

[2] NOT in small capitals in *1843*. At this point, in one of the Charity Readings, 'a universal feeling of joy seemed to pervade the whole assembly, who rising spontaneously, greeted the renowned and popular author with a tremendous burst of cheering' (*Sheffield Daily Telegraph*, 11 December 1855). Dickens reported this 'most prodigious shout and roll of thunder' exultantly, to a friend (*N*, ii, 715).

[3] At the end of his American début (Boston, 2 December 1867), with this item, 'a dead silence seemed to prevail—a sort of public sigh as it were—only to be broken by cheers and calls, the most enthusiastic and uproarious, causing Mr. Dickens to break through his rule, and again presenting himself before his audience, to bow his acknowledgements' (Dolby, p. 174). Three weeks later, on Christmas Eve, he again read the *Carol* in Boston, with another kind of gratifying result: a local industrialist was so moved by hearing this reading that, next day, he changed his firm's practice of working on Christmas Day, and next year began the custom of giving a turkey to every employee (Gladys Storey, *Dickens and Daughter* (1939), pp. 120–1, quoted in the 1971 facsimile of the *Carol* Reading, pp. 205–6).

Additional Note on A CHRISTMAS CAROL

THE *Carol* was, apparently, given its first semi-formal reading at the British Consulate at Genoa during the summer of 1845. Dickens, who was then living in Genoa, became friendly with the Consul, Timothy Yeats Brown, who invited him to give a reading. He hesitated, but eventually agreed. As his wife explained on his behalf, he 'has made up his mind to read the Christmas Carol *through*, instead of any detached pieces from his other works . . . He feels so much, he says, the want of effect and interest in the extracts that it is in fact for that reason he has so long deferred fixing the evening for the reading, but he is sure he can make a very effective thing of the Carol'. At the last minute, however, he withdrew, having discovered how many guests had been invited: what had begun as a 'pleasant recreation' now risked becoming an exhibition of himself. The performance did take place, eventually, and Yeats Brown recalled that 'Dickens was extremely nervous and insisted that no one should sit behind him' (an authentic detail, that, for he always insisted on this). See F. Yeats-Brown, 'Dickens in Genoa', *Spectator*, 22 September 1928, p. 358, and *The Pilgrim Edition of the Letters of Charles Dickens*, Vol. 4 (forthcoming). I owe this reference to Professor Kathleen Tillotson.

THE CRICKET ON THE HEARTH

OF the Christmas Books, *The Cricket on the Hearth* had been even more popular than *A Christmas Carol*. As a Reading, it featured both in Dickens's first charity performances in 1853 and in his first paid series in 1858; but, while the *Carol* enjoyed sustained popularity, *The Cricket* proved much less successful, and it soon disappeared from the repertoire.

Dickens had promised to read at Birmingham on three evenings in December 1853. The *Carol* would occupy two of these, and he sought the local committee's opinion about which of the Christmas Books he should read on the other night. They suggested *The Cricket*, but he was doubtful, and replied:

> The Cricket on the Hearth would answer exceedingly well for the purpose in a smaller place, but the Town Hall at Birmingham requires a more dramatic and forcible subject. I have not the least doubt of this. The best book would be The Chimes or The Haunted Man. I could make the greater effect with The Chimes which I read privately on several occasions at the time it was written and know the power of with an audience. (Rachel E. Waterhouse, *The Birmingham and Midland Institute 1854–1954* (Birmingham 1954), p. 18)

The committee stuck to their choice, however, and Dickens complied with their request. His colleague W. H. Wills reported that the single performance of *The Cricket*, on 29 December 1853, had gone off 'quite as well as the "Carol"' but 'Dick [*sic*] does not like it so well; and indeed it is not nearly so well adapted for reading. But the audience were delighted—such attention, such laughing and crying I never saw anywhere. All the characters seem to live—no monotony, no hesitation, but all smooth and uncommonly lifelike without effort or staginess' (Lady Priestley, *The Story of a Lifetime* (1904), p. 174). Press reports agreed that, though it lacked the dramatic interest of the *Carol* and did not tell so strongly, it was much liked by the audience.

The Cricket was not performed again in the charity series, but in November 1855, when he was staying in Paris, he gave a private reading of it, 'by special entreaty', in the studio of his friend the painter, Ary Shaffer, to an audience of sixty (*Life*, p. 618; see also Patrick Waddington's essay, cited above in Introduction, p. lviii, note 1). When the paid readings began, however, *The Cricket* was chosen to open the series (on 29 April 1858), and it was followed by *The Chimes* (6 May) before the ever-popular *Carol* was introduced (13 May). This must have resulted from Dickens's wish to offer his public some novelties rather than from any expectation of surpassing the appeal of the *Carol*, and in fact neither *The Cricket* nor *The Chimes* succeeded as a Reading, in competition with the other items in the repertoire. *The Cricket* was only given once more in the first London series (on 20 May 1858); *The Chimes*, with four performances, and the *Carol* with five, were evidently more congenial. During the provincial tour that followed, *The Cricket* seems to have been given only once (at a 'morning', or matinée, performance in Edinburgh on 29 September), and I can trace no later performances at all.

It is therefore the more surprising that two prompt-copies exist, quite distinct from each other. One, in the Berg Collection, conforms to the usual pattern of the Christmas Book adaptations made early in his Readings career: pages of an ordinary copy of the story (here a 7th edn, 1846) have been inlaid into larger pages. The other prompt-copy, in the William M. Elkins Collection, Free Library of Philadelphia, deviates from this pattern: it is an ordinary copy (of the 1st edition, 1846[*for* 1845]) still in its original binding. Both these copies contain much writing in Dickens's autograph, and the texts of both are much cut: *Berg* by nearly a half, and *Elkins* by just over a quarter. The cuts, and other textual alterations, in the two copies are quite different: it is not a case of *Berg* taking further a process of abbreviation and adaptation begun in *Elkins*. Only nine of the 174 pages of the two versions are textually identical (and five of these are pages entirely deleted).

The *Elkins* copy of *The Cricket* differs from all but one of the other prompt-copies in that it left Dickens's possession during his lifetime. It is inscribed, in the flyleaf: 'Ernest Acton Burnell / The gift of his / dear Mamma / 12 February 1868'. The surname might possibly be Busnell; but anyway I do not know who Mrs. Burnell (or Busnell) was. The inscription does not have the air of having been written by someone who had obtained the book illegitimately; more likely, Dickens had given it to her, or to someone else from whom she had acquired it. But it is most unlikely that he would have given away the effective prompt-copy of an item which, though rarely performed, he might wish to restore to the repertoire some time. Moreover he rarely infringed his evident sense that his manuscripts, etc., constituted an archive which would pass, on his death, to John Forster. So, if (as seems likely) he gave away this copy, it must have been because it was dispensable, being (at that time) not the true prompt-copy. It has indeed much less the 'look' of a prompt-copy than *Berg*. Though the deletions are substantial, they are of a simpler kind than in most of the others: most of the cuts are in simple longish blocks. All the deletions and writing are in one ink (a light brown), whereas *Berg* has been revised in at least two inks; this reinforces the impression that *Elkins* had not been worked over, during a prolonged period of rehearsal and performance—rather, that it represents a single one-day attempt to shape up a reading-text. Similarly, it contains fewer marginal stage-directions ('Sigh', 'Loud', etc.) than *Berg*—five, compared with twenty-five. Its deletions total, as was noted above, little more than half of those in *Berg*, and this would suggest that *Berg* is the later text, for the universal tendency of the Readings texts was to diminish in length over the period during which they were in repertoire.

A likely explanation of the date and purpose of *Elkins* is that this was the copy from which he read in Paris, in 1855. This hypothesis would account for all the anomalies about it—his having to prepare a second prompt-copy (he was away from home when Schaffer 'entreated' him to perform), his having done only a rough-and-ready job on it (he was knocking up a passable text for a not very taxing private occasion), and his giving it away to some friend, maybe in Paris (he knew that the real prompt-copy was safe in the Tavistock House library). Another, but less plausible, explanation is that *Elkins* was prepared for the 1853 performance, and used again in Paris in 1855, and that *Berg* was prepared for the 1858 paid Readings. But if this was the case, the question arises why the

Elkins text of *The Cricket* is unlike the *Berg* prompt-copy of the *Carol*? Two answers are possible: either that there was an *Elkins*-like copy of the *Carol*, prepared in 1853 but subsequently destroyed or lost; or that, from the start, Dickens took more trouble over the *Carol* than over *The Cricket*. Altogether, the hypothesis that *Elkins* is a text hurriedly prepared in Paris in 1855 is simpler and more persuasive.

If so, *Elkins* is in one sense the 'later' of the two prompt-copies: but the text printed below is that of *Berg*. Almost certainly—whatever the date and provenance of *Elkins*—it was the *Berg* text that Dickens read in 1858 (and, as was noted above, he seems never to have read it thereafter). It is so much more thoroughly worked over, and more fully abbreviated, that it must represent his maturer treatment of the text. The deletions in *Berg*, it may be remarked, do not appear to have been determined by a desire to emphasize one element in the narrative, or to diminish another, as happened in the other Christmas Book Reading texts.

Dickens's young journalistic colleague Edmund Yates recalled the first professional performance of *The Cricket*—a script less obviously attractive (as he and everyone else remarked) than the *Carol*:

There was, however, no doubt of its interest and attraction to the audience present—ordinary upper and lower middle-class people, amongst whom the Dickens books find their most numerous and most enthusiastic readers. From first to last they sat in rapt suspense, broken only by outbursts of laughter and applause; and at the conclusion the vehement cheering [which had greeted his first appearance on the platform] was renewed. The success of the readings was assured. (*Recollections and Experiences* (1885 edn.), p. 303)

The qualities which had won *The Cricket* its great popularity in 1845 and later—qualities more highly valued then than in the twentieth century—gave the Reading some charm for audiences in 1853 and 1858: the pathos, the comedy, the genial sympathy for the domestic affections of simple folk. Dickens's voice and manner as Tilly Slowboy were particularly relished (see below, p. 40, note 1, and Kent, p. 136). Despite this and other successes, however, the Reading was, in the number of performances given, the least popular in the repertoire.

The Cricket on the Hearth

A Fairy Tale of Home

CHIRP THE FIRST

KETTLE began the song. *Mrs. Peerybingle*[1] may leave it on record to the end of time that she couldn't say which of the two—the Cricket, or the Kettle—began the Song; but I *Know* the Kettle did.

As if the little wax-y faced Dutch clock in the corner hadn't finished striking, and the convulsive little Haymaker at the top of it, jerking away right and left with a scythe in front of a Moorish Palace, hadn't mowed down half an acre of imaginary grass before the Cricket joined in at all![2] †

That the Kettle's *song*, was a song of invitation and welcome to somebody out of doors coming on, towards the snug home and the crisp fire Mrs. Peerybingle knew perfectly, as she sat musing, before the hearth. It's a dark night, sang the Kettle, and the rotten leaves are lying by the way; and above, all is mist and darkness, and below, all is mire and clay—and there's only one relief in all the sad and murky air—and I don't know that it is one, for it's nothing but a glare—of deep and angry crimson, where the sun and wind together—set a brand upon the clouds for being guilty of such weather—and the widest open country is a long dull streak of black—and there's hoar-frost on the finger-post, and thaw upon the track—and the ice it isn't water, and the water isn't free—and you couldn't say that anything is what it ought to be—but he's coming, coming, coming!——

And here it was that the Cricket chimed in; † its shrill sharp voice resounding through the house, and seeming to twinkle in the darkness outside, like a star. They went very well together, the Cricket and the Kettle; † but so fast and so furiously, that whether the Kettle chirped and the Cricket hummed, or the Cricket chirped and the Kettle hummed, or they both chirped and both hummed, it would have taken a clearer head than mine to decide. But of this, there is no doubt: that the Kettle and the Cricket sent, each, his fireside song streaming into a ray of the candle that shone out through the window; and a long way down the lane. And this light, bursting on a certain person who approached towards it through

[1] Doubly underlined. In *Elkins*, Dickens inserts 'Pretty little' before 'Mrs. Peerybingle'.
[2] The substantial cut here—from p. 2 to p. 7—is made by wafering the pages together. Dickens does this several times later in this prompt-copy.

the gloom, expressed the whole thing to him—literally in a twinkling—
and cried, 'Welcome home, old fellow! Welcome home, my Boy!'

Mrs. Peerybingle then went running to the door, where, what with the
wheels of a cart, the tramp of a horse, the voice of a man, the tearing in
and out of a dog, and the mysterious appearance of a Baby, there was soon
the very What's-his-name to pay.

Where this Baby came from, or how Mrs. Peerybingle got hold of it
in that flash of time, *I*[1] don't know. But a live Baby there was, in Mrs.
Peerybingle's arms; and a pretty tolerable amount of pride she seemed to
have in it, too, when she was drawn to the fire, by a sturdy figure of a man,
much taller and much older than herself; who had to stoop a long way
down, to kiss her. But she was worth the trouble. Six foot six, with the
lumbago, might have done it.

'Oh goodness, John! What a state you're in with the weather!'

John made answer, as he unrolled a shawl from about his throat; and
warmed his hands; 'Why you see Dot, it—it an't exactly summer weather.
So, no wonder.'

'I wish you wouldn't call me Dot, John. I don't like it.'

'Why what else are you?' looking down upon her with a smile, and
giving her waist as light a squeeze as his huge hand could give. 'A dot
and'—here he glanced at the Baby—'a dot and carry—I won't say it, for
fear I should spoil it; but I was very near a joke. I don't know as ever I was
nearer.'

He was often near to something or other very clever, by his own
account: this lumbering, slow, honest John; this John so heavy but so
light of spirit; so rough upon the surface, but so gentle at the core;
so dull without, so quick within; so stolid, but so good! *Oh Mother Nature,
give thy children the true Poetry of Heart that hid itself in this poor Carrier's
breast*—he was but a Carrier by the way—*and we can bear to have them
talking Prose, and leading lives of Prose; and bless Thee for their company!*

It was pleasant to see Dot, with her little figure and her Baby in her
arms (a very doll of a Baby) glancing at the fire, and inclining her delicate little head just enough on one side to let it rest in a half-natural, half-
affected, wholly nestling and agreeable manner, on the great rugged
figure of the Carrier. It was pleasant to see him, with his tender awkwardness, endeavouring to adapt his rude support to her slight need, and make
his burly middle-age a leaning-staff not inappropriate to her blooming
youth. It was pleasant to observe how *Tilly Slowboy*,[2] waiting in the back-
ground for the Baby, took special notice (though in her earliest teens) of

---

[1] *I* italic in *1846*. (*The Cricket* bore the date 1846 on its title-page, though it was in fact
published in December 1845.)

[2] Doubly underlined. The underlining later in this paragraph is of the double-
interrupted kind, often used in this prompt-copy; but, as it does not seem to indicate
any special degree of emphasis, this will not in future be noted.

this grouping; and stood with her mouth and eyes wide open, and her head thrust forward, taking it in as if it were air.[1] Nor was it less agreeable to observe how John the Carrier, reference being made by Dot to the aforesaid Baby, checked his hand when on the point of touching the infant, *as if he thought he might crack it*; and bending down, surveyed it from a safe distance, with a kind of puzzled pride: *such as an amiable mastiff might be supposed to show, if he found himself, one day, the father of a young canary.*

'An't he beautiful, John? Don't he look precious in his sleep?'

'Very precious. Very much so.—He generally *is*[2] asleep, an't he?'

'Lor John! Good gracious no! You don't deserve to be a father, you don't—you don't know anything about children, John.'

'No,' said John, pulling off his outer coat. 'It's very true, Dot. I only know that I've been fighting pretty stiffly with the Wind to-night. It's been blowing north-east, straight into the cart, the whole way home.'

'Poor old man, so it has![3] Here! Take the precious darling, Tilly, while I make myself of some use.[4] Bless it, I could smother it with kissing it; I could! Hie then, good dog! Hie Boxer, boy! Only let me make the tea first, John; and then I'll help you bring in the parcels out of the Cart, like a busy bee. "How doth the little"—and all the rest of it, you know John. Did you ever learn "how doth the little," when you went to school, John?'

'Not to quite know it. I was very near it once. But I should only have spoilt it.'

'*Oh my Goodness.* What a dear old darling of a dunce you are, John, to be sure!'

Not at all disputing this position, John went out to see that the boy with the lantern took due care of the horse; who was fatter than you would quite believe, if I gave you his measure, and so old that his birthday was lost in the mists of antiquity. †

'There! There's the teapot, ready on the hob!' said Dot.[5] 'And there's the cold knuckle of ham; and there's the butter; and there's the crusty loaf, and all! Here's a basket for the small parcels, John, if you've got any there —where are you, John? Don't let the dear child fall under the grate, Tilly, whatever you do!'

[1] 'The awkward form of the slow-witted and eccentric Tilly stood out with all the rich effect of comedy, heightened as the impersonation was by the graphic aids of gesture and mimicry. Many of us may recall with a smile [Edward] Wright's ludicrous acting of the part; but Mr. Dickens' reading, while losing none of the oddity of the character, had the rare merit of being entirely free of caricature' (Edinburgh *Courant*, 30 September 1858).

[2] *is* italic in *1846*.

[3] Marginal stage-direction *Bustle*.

[4] *Elkins* has a marginal stage-direction here, *Kiss*.

[5] Marginal stage-direction *Bustle*.

It may be noted of Miss Slowboy, in spite of her rejecting the caution with some vivacity, that she had a surprising talent for getting this Baby into difficulties: and had several times imperilled its short life, in a quiet way peculiarly her own. She was of a spare and straight shape, this young lady, insomuch that her garments appeared to be in constant danger of sliding off those sharp pegs, her shoulders, on which they were loosely hung. Her costume was remarkable for the partial development on all possible and *im*possible occasions *of some flannel vestment of a singular structure*; also for affording glimpses, in the region of the back, of a pair of stays, in colour a dead-green. Being always in a state of gaping admiration at everything, and absorbed, besidse, in the perpetual contemplation of her mistress's perfections and the Baby's, Miss Slowboy, in her little errors of judgement, may be said to have done equal honour to her head and to her heart; and though these did *less* honour to the *Baby's* head, which they were the occasional means of bringing into contact with doors, dressers, stair-rails, bedposts, and other foreign substances, still they were the honest results of Tilly Slowboy's astonishment at finding herself installed in such a comfortable home.

To have seen little Mrs. Peerybingle come back with her husband; tugging at the basket of parcels from the Cart, and making the most strenuous exertions to do nothing at all (for he carried it) may have entertained the Cricket, for anything I know; but, certainly, it now began to chirp again, vehemently.

'Heyday! It's merrier than ever, to-night, I think.'

'And it's sure to bring us good fortune, John! To have a Cricket on the Hearth is the luckiest thing in all the world!'

John looked at her as if he had very nearly got the thought into his head, that she was his Cricket in chief. But it was probably one of his narrow escapes, for he said nothing.

[1]'*The first time I heard its little cheerful note, John, was on that night when you brought me to my new home here; its little mistress. Nearly a year ago. You recollect, John?*'

Oh yes. John remembered. I should think so!

'*Its chirp was such a welcome to me! It seemed to say, you would be kind and gentle with me, and would not expect (I had*[2] *a fear of that, John, then) to find an old head on the shoulders of your foolish little wife.*'

John thoughtfully patted one of the shoulders, and then the head, as though he would have said No, No; he had had no such expectations; he had been quite content to take them as they were. And really he had reason. They were very comely.

'*It spoke the truth, John, when it seemed to say so: for you have ever been, I am sure, the best, the most considerate, the most affectionate of husbands*

[1] Marginal stage-direction *Domestic Pathos*.
[2] *had* doubly underlined.

to me. This has been a happy home, John; and I love the Cricket for its sake!'
'Why so do I then. So do *I*, Dot.'
'*I love it for the many times I have heard it, and the many thoughts its harmless music has given me. Sometimes, in the twilight, when I have felt a little solitary and down-hearted, John—before Baby was here, to keep me company and make the house gay;*[1] *when I have thought how lonely you would be if I should die; how lonely I should be, if I could know that you had lost me, dear; its Chirp, upon the hearth, has seemed to tell me of another little voice, so sweet, so very dear to me, before whose coming sound, my trouble vanished like a dream.*[2] *And when I used to fear—I did fear once, John; I was very young you know*[3]*—that ours might prove to be an ill-assorted marriage: I being such a child, and you more like my guardian than my husband: and that you might not, however hard you tried, be able to learn to love me, as you hoped and prayed you might; its Chirp has cheered me up again, and filled me with new trust and confidence.* I was thinking of these things to-night, dear, when I sat expecting you; and I love the Cricket for their sake!'
'And so do I. But Dot? *I*[4] hope and pray that I might learn to love you? How you talk! I had learnt that, long before I brought you here, to be the Cricket's little mistress, Dot!'
She laid her hand, an instant, on his arm, and looked up at him with an agitated face, as if she would have told him something.[5] Next moment, she was down upon her knees before the basket; speaking in a sprightly voice, and busy with the parcels.
'Why what's this round box? Heart alive, John, it's a wedding-cake!'
'There! *There!!* Leave a woman alone, to find out that. Now a man would never have thought of it! whereas, it's my belief that if you was to pack a wedding-cake up in a tea-chest, or a turn-up bedstead, or a pickled salmon keg, or any unlikely thing, a woman would be sure to find it out directly. Yes; I called for it at the pastry-cook's.'
'Whose is it, John? Where is it going?'
'Read the writing on the other side.'
'Why, John! My Goodness, John!'
'Ah! who'd have thought it!'
'You never mean to say, John, that it's *Gruff and Tackleton*[6] the toy-maker!'
John nodded.

---

[1] *before Baby* to *make the house gay* doubly underlined.
[2] *has seemed to tell me* to *like a dream* doubly underlined.
[3] *I was very young you know* doubly underlined; so is *I being such a child* to *than my husband*.
[4] *I* italic in *1846*, but also underlined.
[5] Double-interrupted underlining, but *as if she* is trebly underlined.
[6] Doubly underlined.

Mrs. Peerybingle nodded also, fifty times at least. Miss Slowboy, in the mean time, who had a mechanical power of reproducing scraps of conversation for the delectation of the Baby, with all the sense struck out of them, and all the Nouns changed into the Plural number, enquired aloud of that young creature, Was it Gruffs and Tackletons the toymakers then, and Would it call at Pastry-cooks for wedding-cakes, and Did its mothers know the boxes when its fathers brought them homes; and so on.

'And that is really to come about!' said Dot. 'Why, she and I were girls at school together, John. *And he's as old! As unlike her!—Why, how many years older than you, is Gruff and Tackleton John?*'

'How many more cups of tea shall I drink to-night at one sitting, than Gruff and Tackleton ever took in four, I wonder!' replied John, good-humouredly, as he drew a chair to the round table, and began at the cold Ham. Absorbed in thought, Dot stood there, heedless alike of the tea and him (although he called to her, and rapped the table with his knife to startle her), until he rose and touched her on the arm. Then she looked at him for a moment, and hurried to her place behind the teaboard, laughing at her negligence. *But not as she had laughed before. The manner, and the music, were quite changed.*[1]

The Cricket, too, had stopped. Somehow the room was not so cheerful as it had been. Nothing like it.

'So these are all the parcels; are they, John?'[2]

'That's all. Why—no—I—I declare—I've clean forgotten the old gentleman!'

'*The old gentleman?*'

'In the cart. He was asleep, among the straw, the last time I saw him. I've very nigh remembered him, twice, since I came in; but he went out of my head again. Halloa! Yahip there! rouse up! That's my hearty!'

Miss Slowboy, conscious of some mysterious reference to The Old Gentleman, and connecting in her mystified imagination certain associations of a religious nature with the phrase, was so disturbed, that hastily rising from the low chair by the fire to seek protection near her mistress, and coming into contact as she crossed the doorway with an ancient Stranger, she instinctively made a charge at him with the only offensive instrument within her reach. This instrument happening to be the Baby, great commotion ensued. †

The Stranger, who had long white hair; good features, *singularly bold and well defined for an old man*; and dark, bright, penetrating eyes; looked round with a smile, and saluted the Carrier's wife by gravely inclining his head.

---

[1] These two sentences, and the next two, doubly underlined. Against the paragraph beginning 'The Cricket, too, had stopped', *Elkins* has the marginal stage-direction *Sigh.*

[2] Marginal stage-direction *Old gentleman coming.*

His dress was very quaint and odd—a long, long way behind the time. Its color, brown, all over. In his hand he held a great brown club or walking-stick; and striking this upon the floor, it fell asunder, and became a chair. On which he sat down, quite composedly.

'There, Dot my dear! That's the way I found him, sitting by the roadside! upright as a milestone. And almost as deaf.'

'Sitting in the open air, John!'

'In the open air, just at dusk. "Carriage Paid," he said; and gave me eighteenpence. Then he got in. And there he is.'

[1]'He's going, John, I think!'

Not at all. He was only going to speak.

'If you please, I was to be left till called for. Don't mind me.'

With that, he took a pair of spectacles from one of his large pockets, and a book from another; and leisurely began to read.

The Carrier and his wife exchanged a look of perplexity. The Stranger raised his head; and glancing from the latter to the former, said:

'Your daughter, my good friend?'

'*Wife.*'[2]

'Niece?'

'*Wife.*'

'Indeed? Surely? *Very young!* Baby, yours?'

John gave him a gigantic nod; equivalent to an answer in the affirmative, delivered through a speaking-trumpet.

'Girl?'

'*Bo-o-oy!*'

'Also very young, eh?'

Mrs. Peerybingle instantly struck in.

'*Two months and three da-ays! Vaccinated just six weeks ago-o! Took very fine-ly! Considered, by the doctor, a remarkably beautiful chi-ild! Equal to the general run of children at five months o-old! Takes notice, in a way quite won-der-ful! May seem impossible to you,[3] but feels his legs already!*'

Here the breathless little mother, who had been shrieking these short sentences into the old man's ear, until her pretty face was crimsoned, held up the Baby before him as a stubborn and triumphant fact; while Tilly Slowboy, with a melodious cry of Ketcher, Ketcher, performed some cow-like gambols round that all unconscious Innocent.

---

[1] Marginal stage-direction *Slow*.

[2] Here 'the comic influence of the Reading became irresistible', with John roaring his answers to the deaf 'old gentleman', and giving the 'gigantic nod' described in the text; but 'the merriment . . . became fairly irresistible' when Dickens, as Dot, described the wonderful baby 'at the highest pitch of his voice, that is, of *her* voice (the comic effect of this being simply indescribable) . . .' (Kent, pp. 136–7).

[3] *you* doubly underlined.

'Hark! old gentleman called for, sure enough. There's somebody at the door. Open it. Tilly.'

Before she could reach it, however, it was opened from without; being a primitive sort of door, with a latch, that any one could lift if he chose. It gave admission to a little, meagre, thoughtful, dingy-faced man, who seemed to have made himself a great-coat from the sack-cloth covering of some old box.

'Good evening John! Good evening Mum. Good evening Tilly. Good evening Unbeknown! How's Baby Mum? Boxer's pretty well I hope?'

'Busy in the Toy making trade just now, Caleb?'

'Why, pretty well John,' with the distraught air of a man who was casting about for the Philosopher's stone, at least. 'Pretty much so. There's rather a run on Noah's Arks at present. I could have wished to improve upon the Family, but I don't see how it's to be done at the price. It would be a satisfaction to one's mind, to make it clearer which was Shems and Hams, and which was Wives. Flies an't on that scale neither, as compared with elephants you know! Ah! well! Have you got anything in the parcel line for me John?'

The Carrier put his hand into a pocket of the coat he had taken off; and brought out, carefully preserved in moss and paper, a tiny flower-pot.

'There it is! Not so much as a leaf damaged. Full of Buds! Dear, Caleb. Very dear at this season.'

'Never mind that. It would be cheap to me, whatever it cost. Anything else, John?'

'A small box. Here you are!'

'"For Caleb Plummer. With Cash." With Cash John? I don't think it's for me.'

'With Care. Where do you make out cash?'

'Oh! To be sure! It's all right. With care! Yes, yes; that's mine. Care's mine, John. *It might have been with cash, indeed, if my dear Boy in the Golden South Americas had lived, John.*[1] *You loved him like a son; didn't you? You needn't say you did. I know, of course.*[2] "Caleb Plummer. With care." Yes, yes, it's all right. It's a box of dolls' eyes for my daughter's work. *I wish it was her own sight in a box, John.*'

'I wish it was, or could be!'

'Thankee. You speak very hearty. To think that she should never see the Dolls we make; and them a staring at her, so bold, all day long! That's where it cuts. †—You couldn't have the goodness to let me pinch Boxer's tail, Mum, for half a moment, could you?'

'Why Caleb! what a question!'

'Oh never mind, Mum. *He mightn't like it perhaps.* There's a small

<hr />

[1] In *Elkins*, this sentence is heavily emphasized, by double underlining and treble strokes in the margin.

[2] *I* italic in *1846*.

order just come in, for barking dogs; and I should wish to go as close to Natur' as I could, for sixpence. That's all. Never mind Mum.'

It happened opportunely, that Boxer, without receiving the proposed stimulus, began to bark with great zeal. But as this implied the approach of some new visitor, Caleb, postponing his study from the life to a more convenient season, shouldered the round box, and took a hurried leave. He might have spared himself the trouble, for he met the visitor upon the threshold.

'Oh! You are here, are you? Wait a bit. I'll take you home. John Peerybingle, my service to you. More of my service to your pretty wife. Handsomer every day! Better too, if possible! And younger, that's the Devil of it.'

Tackleton the Toy merchant, pretty generally known as Gruff and Tackleton—for that was the firm, though Gruff had been bought out long ago—was a man whose vocation had been quite misunderstood by his Parents and Guardians. If they had made him a Money-Lender, or a sharp Attorney, or a Sheriff's Officer, he might have sown his discontented oats in his youth, and might have turned out amiable, at last. But, chafing in the pursuit of toy-making, he was a domestic Ogre, who had been living on children all his life, and was their implacable enemy. He despised all playthings—wouldn't have bought one for the world—delighted in making them grim and hideous. †

What he was in toys, he was (as most men are) in all other things. You may easily suppose, therefore, that within the large green cape, which reached down to the calves of his legs, there was buttoned up to the chin an uncommonly pleasant fellow; and that he was as agreeable a companion, as ever stood in a pair of bull-headed looking boots with mahogany tops.

Still, Tackleton, the Toy-merchant, was going to be married. In spite of all this, he was going to be married. And to a young wife, too; a beautiful young wife.[1]

'In three days' time. Next Thursday. The last day of the first month in the year. That's my wedding-day,' said Tackleton, rattling his money.

'Why, it's the anniversary of our wedding-day, too.'

'Ha! Odd! I say! A word! I say! A word with you. You'll come to the wedding? We're in the same boat, you know.'

'How the same boat?'

'A little disparity, you know. Come and spend an evening with us, beforehand. † The truth is you have a—what tea-drinking people call a sort of comfortable appearance together: you and your wife. We know better, you know, but—'

'No, we don't know better. What are you talking about?'

'Well! We *don't*[2] know better then. As you like. I was going to say, as

---

[1] This paragraph underlined in *Elkins*, and with heavy strokes in the margin.
[2] *don't* italic in *1846*.

you have that sort of appearance, your company will produce a favourable effect on Mrs. Tackleton that will be. You'll say you'll come?'

'We have arranged to keep our Wedding-Day (as far as that goes) at home. We have made the promise to ourselves these six months. We think, you see, that home—'

'Bah! what's home? Four walls and a ceiling! (*why don't you kill that Cricket*; I *would!*[1] I always do. I hate their noise.) There are four walls and a ceiling at my house. Come to me!'

'You kill your Crickets, eh?'

'Scrunch 'em, sir. You'll say you'll come? It's as much your interest as mine, you know, that the women should persuade each other that they're quiet and contented, and couldn't be better off. I know their way. Whatever one woman says, another woman is determined to clinch, always. There's that spirit of emulation among 'em, Sir, that if your wife says to my wife, "I'm the happiest woman in the world, and mine 's the best husband in the world, and I dote on him," my wife will say the same to your's, or more, and half believe it.'

'Do you mean to say she don't, then?'

'Don't what? †—now look there.'[2]

He pointed to where Dot was sitting, thoughtfully, before the fire; leaning her dimpled chin upon her hand, and watching the bright blaze. The Carrier looked at her, and then at him, and then at her, and then at him again.

'*She*[3] honors and obeys, no doubt, you know, and that, as I am not a man of sentiment, is quite enough for *me*. But do you think there's anything more in it?'

'I think that I should chuck any man out of window, who said there wasn't.'

'Exactly. To be sure![4] † Thankee. *What's that!*'

It was a loud cry from the Carrier's wife; a loud, sharp, sudden cry, that made the room ring, like a glass vessel. She had risen from her seat, and stood like one transfixed by terror and surprise. *The Stranger had advanced towards the fire, to warm himself, and stood within a stride of her chair*. But quite still.

'Dot! Mary! Darling! What's the matter? Mary! Are you ill! what is it? Tell me dear!'

She only answered by beating her hands together, and falling into a

---

[1] *I* italic in *1846*.

[2] Marginal stage-directions *Break* (at 'Don't what?') and *Point* (at 'look there').

[3] *She* doubly underlined; *me*, later in the sentence, italic in *1846*.

[4] *What's that!* doubly underlined. Marginal stage-direction against the preceding lines (which are deleted), *Surprise coming*. Marginal stage-direction against the next paragraph ('It was a loud cry . . .'), *Mystery*.

wild fit of laughter. Then, sinking from his grasp, she covered her face
with her apron, and wept. *The old man standing, as before; quite still.*[1]
'I'm better, John. I'm quite well now—I—'
*John! But John was on the other side of her. Why turn her face towards
the strange old gentleman, as if addressing him!*[2]
'Only a fancy, John dear—a kind of shock—a something coming
suddenly before my eyes—I don't know what it was. It's quite gone;
quite gone.'
'I'm glad it's gone,' muttered Tackleton. 'I wonder where it's gone,
and what it was.' †
'Oh quite gone! Quite gone!' waving him hurriedly away. 'Good
night!'
'Good night. Good night, John Perrybingle! (*Very* odd) Take care
how you carry that box, Caleb. Let it fall, and I'll murder you! (*Very*
odd) Dark as pitch, and weather worse than ever, eh? (*Very* odd)[3] Good
night!'
The Carrier had been so much astounded by his little wife, and so
busily engaged in soothing her, that he had scarcely been conscious of the
Stranger's presence, until now, when he again stood there, their only guest.
'I beg your pardon, friend; the more so, as I fear your wife has not
been well; but the Attendant whom my infirmity renders almost indispensable, not having arrived, I fear there must be some mistake. The
bad night which made the shelter of your comfortable cart (may I never
have a worse!) so acceptable, is still as bad as ever. Would you, in your
kindness, suffer me to rent a bed here?'
'*Yes, yes,*' *cried Dot.*[4] '*Yes! Certainly!*'
'Oh! Well! I don't object; but still I'm not quite sure that—'
'Hush! Dear John!'
'Why, he's stone deaf.'
'I know he is, but—Yes Sir, certainly. Yes! certainly! I'll make him
up a bed, directly, John.'
*As she hurried off to do it, the flutter of her spirits, and the agitation of
her manner, were so strange, that the Carrier stood looking after her, quite
confounded.*
'Did its mothers make it up a Beds then!' cried Miss Slowboy to the
Baby; 'and did its hair grow brown and curly, when its caps was lifted
off, and frighten it, a precious Pets, a sitting by the fires!' †
'And frighten it a Precious Pets, a sitting by the fire. What frightened
Dot, I wonder!'

---

[1] Doubly underlined.
[2] *John* and *him* doubly underlined; in *Elkins, him* is underlined six times.
[3] The three asides of '(*Very* odd)' are interjected in manuscript. The emphasis on
Very mounts: the word being underlined, successively, once, twice and three times.
[4] Marginal stage-direction *Quick.*

He scouted the insinuations of the Toy merchant, and yet they filled him with a vague uneasiness; for Tackleton was quick and sly; and he had that painful sense, himself, of being a man of slow perception, that a broken hint was always worrying to him. The bed was soon made ready; and the visitor, declining all refreshment but a cup of tea, retired. Then Dot—quite well again, she said: quite well again—arranged the great chair in the chimney corner for her husband; filled his pipe and gave it him; and took her usual little stool beside him on the hearth.

She always *would*[1] sit on that little stool; I think she must have had a kind of notion that it was a coaxing little stool. †

And the Cricket and the Kettle, tuning up again, acknowledged it! The bright fire, blazing up again, acknowledged it! The little Mower on the clock, in his unheeded work, acknowledged it! The Carrier, in his smoothing forehead and expanding face, acknowledged it, the readiest of all.

And as he soberly and thoughtfully puffed at his old pipe; and as the Dutch clock ticked; and as the red fire gleamed; and as the Cricket chirped; that *Genius of his Hearth and Home* (*for such the Cricket was*) came out, in fairy shape, into the room, and summoned many forms of Home about him. Dots of all ages, and all sizes, seemed to fill the chamber. † Old Carriers, too, appeared, with blind old Boxers lying at their feet; and sick old Carriers, tended by the gentlest hands; and graves of dead and gone old Carriers, green in the churchyard. And as the Cricket showed him all these things—he saw them plainly, though his eyes were fixed upon the fire—the Carrier's heart grew light and glad, and he blessed his Household Gods and cared no more for Gruff and Tackleton than you do.

[2] *But what was that young figure of a man, unseen by him, which the same Fairy Cricket set so near Her stool, and which remained there, singly and alone? Why did it linger still, so near her, with its arm upon the chimney-piece, ever repeating 'Married! and not to me!'*

Oh Dot! Oh failing Dot! There is no place for that figure, in all your husband's visions; why has its shadow fallen on his hearth!

CHIRP THE SECOND

CALEB Plummer and his Blind Daughter lived all alone by themselves, as the Story-Books say—and my blessing, with yours to back it I hope, on the Story-books, for saying anything in this workaday world!—Caleb Plummer and his Blind Daughter lived all alone by themselves, in a little

---

[1] *would* italic in *1846*

[2] Marginal stage-direction *Mystery*. In this paragraph, *Her* and '*Married! and not to me!*' are doubly underlined. In *Elkins*, the whole paragraph is doubly underlined and there are treble strokes in the margin.

cracked nut-shell of a wooden house, which was no better than a pimple on the prominent red-brick nose of Gruff and Tackleton. The premises of Gruff and Tackleton were the great feature of the street; but you might have knocked down Caleb Plummer's dwelling with a hammer, and carried off the pieces in a cart. Yet it was the germ from which the full-grown trunk of Gruff and Tackleton had sprung; and under its crazy roof, the Gruff before last, had, in a small way, *made toys for a generation of old boys and girls, who had played with them, and found them out, and broken them, and gone to sleep.*

[1] I have said that Caleb and his poor Blind Daughter lived here; but I *should* have said that Caleb lived here, and his poor Blind Daughter somewhere else; in an enchanted home of Caleb's furnishing, where scarcity and shabbiness were not, and trouble never entered. Caleb was no Sorcerer, but in the only magic art that still remains to us—the magic of devoted, deathless love—Nature had been the mistress of his study; and from her teaching, all the wonder came. The Blind Girl never knew that sorrow and faint-heartedness were in the house; that her father's scanty hairs were turning greyer and more grey before her sightless face. The Blind Girl never knew they had a master, cold, exacting, and un-interested: never knew that Tackleton was Tackleton in short; but lived in the belief of an eccentric humourist who loved to have his jest with them; and who, while he was the Guardian Angel of their lives, disdained to hear a word of thankfulness.

All this was the doing of her simple father! *But he too had a Cricket on his Hearth;* and listening sadly to its music when the motherless Blind Child was very young, that Spirit had inspired him with the thought that even *her* great deprivation might be almost changed into a blessing, and the girl made happy by these little means. *For all the Cricket Tribe are potent Spirits, even though the people who hold converse with them do not know it (which is frequently the case); and there are not in the Unseen World, Voices more gentle and more true than those in which the Spirits of the Fire-side and the Hearth, address themselves to human kind.*

Caleb and his daughter were at work together in their usual working-room, which served them for their ordinary living room as well. A strange place it was. There were houses in it, finished and unfinished, for Dolls of all stations in life. The nobility and gentry and public in general, for whose accommodation these tenements were designed, lay, here and there, in baskets, staring straight up at the ceiling; but in denoting their degrees in society, and confining them to their respective stations (which experience shows to be difficult in real life), the makers of these Dolls had far improved on Nature. Thus, the Doll-lady of Distinction had *wax* limbs of perfect symmetry; the next grade in the social scale being made of *leather*; and the next of coarse *stuff.* As to the common-people, they

[1] Marginal stage-direction *Pathos, Narrative.*

had so many matches out of tinder-boxes for *their* arms and legs, and there *they* were—established in *their* sphere at once.

There were various other samples of his handicraft besides Dolls, in Caleb Plummer's room. † As it would have been hard to count the dozens of grotesque figures there, that were always ready to commit all sorts of absurdities, on the turning of a handle; so it would have been no easy task to mention any human folly, vice, or weakness, that had not its type there. And in no exaggerated form; for very little handles will move men and women to as strange performances, as any Toy was ever made to undertake.

In the midst of all these objects, Caleb and his daughter were at work. The Blind Girl busy as a Doll's dressmaker; and Caleb painting and glazing the four-pair front of a desirable family mansion. †

'So you were out in the rain last night, father, in your beautiful, new, great-coat.'

'In my beautiful new great-coat,' answered Caleb, glancing towards a clothes-line in the room, on which the sackcloth garment previously described, was carefully hung up to dry. †

'A blue coat, father.'

'Bright blue.'

'Yes, yes! Bright blue! the colour I can just remember in the blessed sky! A bright blue coat. And in it you, dear father, with your merry eye, your smiling face, your free step, and your dark hair: looking so young and handsome!'

How different the picture in her mind, from her father as he sat observing her! She had spoken of his free step. She was right in that. For years and years, he never once had crossed that threshold at his own slow pace; never had he, when his heart was heaviest, forgotten the light tread that was to render her's so cheerful. †

'You were speaking quite softly. You are not tired father?'

'Tired, what should tire me, Bertha? *I*[1] was never tired. What does it mean?'

To give greater force to his words, he hummed a fragment of a song. It was a Bacchanalian song, something about a Sparkling Bowl;[2] and he sang it with an assumption of a Devil-may-care voice, that made his face a thousand times more meagre and more thoughtful than it had been before.

'What! you're singing, are you?' said Tackleton, putting his head in, at the door. 'Go it! *I*[3] can't sing. I can't afford to sing. I'm glad *you* can. I hope you can afford to work too. Hardly time for both, I should think?'

(—'If you could only see him, Bertha, how he's winking at me! Such a man to joke! you'd think, if you didn't know him, he was in earnest—wouldn't you now?')

[1] *I* italic in *1846*.   [2] Marginal stage-direction *Tackleton coming*.
[3] *I* italic in *1846*.

The Blind Girl smiled, and nodded.

'Always merry and light-hearted with us!'

'Oh! you're there, are you? Poor Idiot!'

He really did believe she was almost an Idiot; and he founded the belief upon her being fond of *him*.

'Well! and being there,—how are you?'

'Oh! well; quite well. And as happy as even you can wish me to be.'

The Blind Girl took his hand and kissed it; with such unspeakable affection and gratitude in the act, that Tackleton himself was moved to say, in a milder growl than usual:

'What's the matter now?'

'I stood it close beside my pillow when I went to sleep last night, and remembered it in my dreams. And when the day broke, and the glorious red sun—the *red*[1] sun, father?'

'Red in the mornings and the evenings, Bertha.'

'When it rose, *and the bright light I almost fear to strike myself against in walking*, came into the room, I turned the little tree towards it, and blessed Heaven for making things so precious, and you for sending them to cheer me!'

Caleb, with his hands hooked loosely in each other, stared vacantly before him while his daughter spoke, as if he really were uncertain (I believe he was) whether Tackleton had done anything to deserve her thanks, or not. *Yet Caleb knew that with his own hands he had brought the little rose tree home for her, so carefully; and knew that with his own lips he had forged the innocent deception which should help to keep her from suspecting how very much, he every day denied himself, that she might be the happier.*

'Bertha! I know this is the day on which little what's-her-name; the spoilt child; Peerybingle's wife; pays her regular visit to you and makes her fantastic Pic-Nic here. I should like to join the party. You see, I—I want to bring the Peerybingles a little more into company with May Fielding. I am going to be married to May.'

'Married!'

'She's such a con-founded idiot, that I was afraid she'd never comprehend me. Ah, Bertha! Married! Church, parson, clerk, beadle, glass-coach, bells, breakfast, bride-cake, favours, marrow-bones, cleavers, and all the rest of the tom-foolery. A wedding, you know; a wedding. Well! on that account I want to join the party, and to bring May and her mother. I'll send in a little something or other, before the afternoon. A cold leg of mutton, or some comfortable trifle of that sort.' †

Having delivered himself of which generous promise, old Gruff and Tackleton withdrew.

Bertha remained where he had left her, lost in meditation. It was not

[1] *red* italic in *1846*.

until Caleb had been occupied, some time, in yoking a team of horses to a waggon by nailing the harness to the vital parts of their bodies, that she drew near to his working-stool, and sitting down beside him, said:

[1]'Father, I am lonely in the dark. I want my patient, willing eyes.'

'Here they are. Always ready. They are more your's than mine, Bertha, any hour in the four and twenty. What shall your eyes do for you, dear?' †

'Father, tell me something about May. She is very fair? Her hair is dark—darker than mine. Her voice is sweet and musical, I know. I have often loved to hear it. Her shape—'

'There's not a Doll's in all the room to equal it. And her *eyes*!'[2]—

He stopped; for Bertha had drawn closer round his neck; and, from the arm that clung about him, came a warning pressure which he understood too well.

'Mr. Tackleton, our friend, father; our benefactor. † He is older than May, father.'

'Ye-es. He's a little older than May. But that don't signify.'

'Oh father, yes! To be his patient companion in infirmity and age; to be his gentle nurse in sickness, and his constant friend in suffering and sorrow; to know no weariness in working for his sake; to watch him, tend him; sit beside his bed, and talk to him, awake; and pray for him asleep; what privileges these would be! Would she do all this, dear father?'

'No doubt of it.'

'I can love her, father; I can love her from my heart!' And saying so, she laid her poor blind face on Caleb's shoulder, and so wept and wept, that he wondered very much—and was almost sorry—to have brought that tearful happiness upon her.

In the mean time, there had been a pretty sharp commotion at John Peerybingle's; for little Mrs. Peerybingle couldn't think of going anywhere without the Baby; and to get the Baby under weigh, took time. Not that there was much *of*[3] the Baby: speaking of it as a thing of weight and measure: but there was a vast deal to do about and about it, and it had to be done by easy stages. For instance: when the Baby was got to a certain point of dressing, and you might have supposed that another touch or two would finish him off, and turn him out a tip-top Baby, he was unexpectedly extinguished in a flannel cap, and hustled off to bed; where he simmered between two blankets for the best part of an hour. From this state of inaction he was then recalled, shining very much and roaring violently, to partake of—a slight repast. After which, he went to sleep again. Mrs. Peerybingle took advantage of this interval, to make

---

[1] Marginal stage-direction *Tone to Pathos.*
[2] *eyes* doubly underlined.
[3] *of* doubly underlined.

herself as smart in a small way as ever you saw anybody in all your life; and Miss Slowboy insinuated herself into a spencer of a fashion so surprising and ingenious, that it had no connection with herself or anything else in the universe, but was a shrunken, dog's-eared, independent fact, pursuing its lonely course without the least regard to anybody. By this time, the Baby, being all alive again, was invested, by the united efforts of Mrs. Peerybingle and Miss Slowboy, with a cream-coloured mantle for its body, and a sort of nankeen raised-pie for its head; and so in course of time they all three got down to the door, where the old horse had already taken more than the full value of his day's toll out of the Turnpike Trust, by tearing up the road with his impatient autographs.

As to a chair, or anything of that kind for helping Mrs. Peerybingle into the cart, you know very little of John, if you think *that*[1] was necessary. Before you could have seen him lift her from the ground, there she was in her place, fresh and rosy, saying, 'John! How can you! Think of Tilly!'

If I might be allowed to mention a young lady's legs, on any terms, I would observe of Miss Slowboy's that there was a fatality about them which rendered them singularly liable to be grazed; and that she never effected the smallest ascent or descent, without recording the circumstance upon them with a notch, as Robinson Crusoe marked the days upon his wooden calendar.

'John?' said Dot. 'You've got the basket with the Veal and Ham-Pie and things; and the bottles of Beer? I could not think of going to Bertha's —I wouldn't do it, John, on any account—without the Veal and Ham-Pie and things, and the bottles of Beer. Way!'

This was addressed to the Horse, who didn't mind it at all.

'Oh *do*[2] Way, John! Please!'

'It'll be time enough to do that, when I begin to leave things behind me. The basket's here, safe enough. † By the bye, Dot. That old gentleman,'—

Again so visibly, and instantly embarrassed.[3]

'He's an odd fish. I can't make him out. I don't believe there's any harm in him. It's curious that he should have taken it into his head to ask leave to go on lodging with us; an't it? Things come about so strangely.'

'O so very, very strangely!'

'However, he's a good-natured old gentleman, and pays *as* a gentleman, and I think his word is to be relied upon, *like* a gentleman's. I had quite a long talk with him this morning: he can hear me better already, he says, as he gets more used to my voice. He told me a deal about himself, and I told him a deal about myself, and a rare lot of questions he asked me. I gave him information about my having two beats, you know, in my business; one day to the right from our house and back again; another

---

[1] *that* italic in *1846*.   [2] *do* italic in *1846*.
[3] Doubly underlined. Marginal stage-direction *Mystery*.

day to the left from our house and back again (for he's a stranger and don't know the names of places about here); and he seemed quite pleased. "Why, then I shall be returning home to-night your way," he says, "when I thought you'd be coming in an exactly opposite direction. That's capital. I may trouble you for another lift perhaps, but I'll engage not to fall so sound asleep again." He *was*[1] sound asleep, sure-ly!—Dot! what are you thinking of?'

'Thinking of, John? I—I was listening to you.'

'Oh! That's all right! I was afraid, from the look of your face, that I had gone rambling on so long, as to set you thinking about something else. I was very near it, I'll be bound.'

Dot making no reply, they jogged on, for some little time, in silence. But it was not easy to remain silent very long in John Peerybingle's cart, for everybody on the road had something to say. † Boxer, alone, gave occasion to more recognitions, than half a dozen Christians could have done! Everybody knew him, all along the road—especially the fowls and pigs, who when they saw him approaching, immediately withdrew into remote back settlements, without waiting for the honor of a nearer acquaintance. He had business everywhere; going down all the turnings, looking into all the wells, bolting in and out of all the cottages, dashing into the midst of all the Dame-Schools, fluttering all the pigeons, magnifying the tails of all the cats, and trotting into the public houses like a regular customer. Wherever he went, somebody or other might have been heard to cry, "Halloa! Here's Boxer!' and out came that somebody forthwith, accompanied by at least two or three other somebodies, to give John Peerybingle and his pretty wife, Good Day. † And so, in no time as it seemed, they reached the house where Caleb and his daughter lived; and Mrs. Peerybingle and the Baby, and Miss Slowboy, and the basket, were all got safely within doors.

May Fielding was already come; and so was her mother—a little querulous chip of an old lady with a peevish face, who, in right of having preserved a waist like a bedpost, was supposed to be a most transcendent figure; and who, in consequence of having once been better off—or of labouring under an impression that she might have been, if something had happened which never did happen, and which seemed to have never been particularly likely to come to pass—but it's all the same—was very genteel and patronising indeed.[2] Gruff and Tackleton was also there, doing the agreeable; with the evident sensation of being as perfectly at home, as a fresh young salmon on the top of the Great Pyramid. † He had brought his leg of mutton, and, wonderful to relate, a tart besides—but we don't mind a little dissipation when our brides are in the case; we don't get married every day—and in addition to these dainties, there were

---

[1] *was* italic in *1846*.

[2] Mrs. Fielding was a 'wonderfully comic minor character' (Kent, pp. 138–9).

the Veal and Ham-Pie, and 'things,' as Mrs. Peerybingle called them; which were chiefly nuts and oranges, and cakes, and such small deer. When the repast was set forth on the board, flanked by Caleb's contribution, which was a great wooden bowl of smoking potatoes, Tackleton led his intended mother-in-law to the Post of Honour. For the better gracing of this place at the high Festival, the majestic old Soul had adorned herself with a cap, calculated to inspire the thoughtless with sentiments of awe. She also wore her gloves. But let us be genteel, or die!

Caleb sat next his daughter; Dot and her old schoolfellow were side by side; the good Carrier took care of the bottom of the table. Miss Slowboy was isolated, for the time being, from every article of furniture but the chair she sat on, in order that she might have nothing else to knock the Baby's head against.

As † to Tackleton, he couldn't get on at all; and the more cheerful his intended Bride became in Dot's society, the less he liked it, though he had brought them together. For he was a regular Dog in the Manger, was Tackleton; and when they laughed, and he couldn't laugh, he took it into his head, immediately, that they *must*[1] be laughing at him.

'Ah May!' said Dot. 'Dear dear, what changes! To talk of those merry school-days of ours makes one young again. † Dear dear![2] Only to remember how we used to chatter about the husbands we would choose. I don't know how young, and how handsome, and how gay, and how lively, mine was not to be! and as to yours! If I had told you, you were ever to be married to Mr. Tackleton, why you'd have slapped me. Wouldn't you, May?'

Though May didn't say yes, she certainly didn't say no.

'You couldn't help yourselves, for all that. You couldn't resist us, you see. Here *we* are! Here *we* are![3] Where are you gay young bridegrooms now!'

[4]'*Some of them are dead; and some of them forgotten. Some of them, if they could stand among us at this moment, would not believe we were the same creatures; would not believe that what they saw and heard was real, and we could[5] forget them so. No! they would not believe one word of it!*'

'Why, Dot! How you go on! Why, Dot! Little woman!'

She had spoken with such earnestness and fire, that she stood in need of some recalling to herself, without doubt. Her husband's check was very gentle; but it proved effectual; for she stopped, and said no more.

May said no word, good or bad, but sat quite still. The good lady her mother now interposed: observing that girls were girls, and byegones byegones, and that so long as young people were young and thoughtless, they would probably conduct themselves like young and thoughtless persons:

---

[1] *must* doubly underlined.
[2] Marginal stage-direction *Earnest*.
[3] *we . . . we* doubly underlined.
[4] Marginal stage-direction *Very Earnest*.
[5] *could* italic in *1846*.

with two or three other positions of a no less incontrovertible character. She then remarked that she thanked Heaven she had always found in her daughter May, a dutiful and obedient child; for which she took no credit to herself, though she had every reason to believe it was entirely owing to herself. With regard to Mr. Tackleton she said, That he was in a moral point of view an undeniable individual; and That he was in an eligible point of view a son-in-law to be desired, *no one in their senses could doubt*.[1] (She was very emphatic here). With regard to the family into which he was about, after some solicitation, to be admitted, she believed Mr. Tackleton knew that, although reduced in purse, it had some pretentions to gentility; and that if certain circumstances, not wholly unconnected, she would go so far as to say, with the Indigo Trade, had happened differently, it might perhaps have been in possession of Wealth. She then remarked that she would not allude to the past, and would not mention that her daughter had for some time rejected the suit of Mr. Tackleton; *and that she would not say a great many other things which she did say, at great length*. Finally, she delivered it as the general result of her experience, that those marriages in which there was least of what was romantically called love, were always the happiest; and that she anticipated the greatest possible amount of bliss—not rapturous bliss; but the solid, steady-going article—from the approaching nuptials. She concluded by informing the company that to-morrow was the day she had lived for, expressly; and that when it was over, she would desire nothing better than to be disposed of, in any genteel place of burial.

As these remarks were quite unanswerable—which is the happy property of all remarks that are sufficiently wide of the purpose—they changed the current of the conversation until John Peerybingle proceeded on his journey.

For he only rested there, and gave the old horse a bait. He had to go some four or five miles farther on; and as he returned in the evening, he would call for Dot, and take another rest on his way home.

'So good bye!' said the stout Carrier, pulling on his dreadnought coat. 'I shall be back at the old time. Good bye all! Good bye young shaver! Time will come, I suppose, when *you*'ll[2] turn out into the cold, my little friend, and leave your old father to enjoy his pipe and his rheumatics in the chimney-corner.'[3] †

With these good-natured words, he strode away; and presently was heard, in company with Boxer, and the old horse, and the cart, making lively music down the road. What time the dreamy Caleb stood, watching his Blind Daughter.

'Bertha, how changed you are, my Darling, since the morning! †

---

[1] Doubly underlined.   [2] *you* italic in *1846*.

[3] Another marginal stage-direction *Mystery* appears against the paragraph (later deleted) beginning 'But it was not so soon done . . .'

To be—to be blind, my poor dear, *is*[1] a great affliction; but—'

'I have never felt it in its fulness. I have sometimes wished that I could see you, or could see our Benefactor; only once, dear father; only for one little minute; that I might know what it is I treasure up, and hold here![2] And sometimes (but then I was a child) I have wept, in my prayers at night, to think that when your images ascended from my heart to Heaven, they might not be the true resemblance of yourselves. But I have never had these feelings long. They have passed away, and left me tranquil and contented.'

'And they will again'.

'But father! This is not the sorrow that weighs me down! I cannot hold it closed and shut within myself. Bring May!'

May heard the mention of her name, and coming quietly towards her, touched her on the arm. The Blind Girl turned immediately, and held her by both hands.

'Look into my face, Sweet heart! Read it with your beautiful eyes, and tell me if the Truth is written on it. There is not, in my Soul, a wish or thought that is not for your good! There is not, in my Soul, a grateful recollection stronger than the deep remembrance which is stored here, of the many times when, in the full pride of Sight and Beauty, you have had consideration for me, even when we two were children, *or when I was as much a child as ever blindness can be*! Every blessing on your head, my dear, and on your happy course! Not the less, my Bird, because, to-day, the knowledge that you are to be *His* wife has wrung my heart! Father, May, Mary! forgive me that it is so, for the sake of all he has done to relieve the weariness of my dark life: and when I call Heaven to witness that I could not wish him married to a wife more worthy of his Goodness!'

'Great Power!' exclaimed her father, smitten with the truth, '*have I deceived her from her cradle, only to break her heart at last!*'

[3] It was well for all of them that Dot, that beaming, useful, busy little Dot—*for such she was, whatever faults she had, and however you may learn to hate her in good time*—it was well for all of them, I say, that she was there. †

She was a noble little Dot in such things, and it must have been an obdurate nature indeed that could have withstood her influence. When she had got poor Caleb and his Bertha away, that they might comfort each other, as she knew they only could, she presently came bouncing back, to mount guard over that bridling little piece of consequence in the cap and gloves, and prevent the dear old creature from making discoveries.

'So bring me the precious Baby, Tilly,' said she, drawing a chair to the fire; 'and while I have it in my lap, here's Mrs. Fielding, Tilly, will tell

---

[1] *is* doubly underlined.

[2] A deleted phrase explains 'here': 'she laid her hands upon her breast'.

[3] Marginal stage-direction *Bustle, Cheerful.*

me all about the management of Babies, and put me right in twenty points where I'm as wrong as can be. Won't you, Mrs. Fielding!'

The fact of Tackleton having walked out; and of two or three people having been talking together, for two minutes, was quite enough to have put Mrs. Fielding on the bewailment of that mysterious convulsion in the Indigo trade, for four-and-twenty hours. But this becoming deference to her experience was so irresistible, that, sitting bolt upright before the wicked Dot, she did, in half an hour, deliver more infallible recipes and precepts, than would have utterly destroyed and done for that Young Peerybingle, though he had been an Infant Samson.

To change the theme, Dot did a little needlework—then did a little nursing; then a little more needle-work; then had a little whispering chat with May, while the old lady dozed; and so in little bits of bustle, found it a very short afternoon. Then, as it grew dark, she trimmed the fire, and swept the hearth, and set the tea-board out, and drew the curtain, and lighted a candle. Then, she played an air or two on a rude kind of harp, which Caleb had made for Bertha; and played them very well; for Nature had made her delicate little ear as choice a one for music as it would have been for jewels, if she had had any to wear. By this time it was the established hour for having tea; and Tackleton, and Bertha, and Caleb, came back again, to share the meal, and spend the evening.[1] When it was night, and tea was done, and she had nothing more to do in washing up the cups and saucers; in a word—*for I must come to it, and there is no use in putting it off*[2]—*when the time drew nigh for expecting the Carrier's return; her manner changed again; her colour came and went; and she was very restless. Not as good wives are, when listening for their husbands. No, no, no. It was another sort of restlessness from that.*

Wheels heard. A horse's feet. The barking of a dog. The gradual approach of all the sounds. The scratching paw of Boxer at the door!

[3]*'Whose step is that!' cried Bertha, starting up.*

'Whose step?' returned the Carrier, standing in the portal, with his brown face ruddy as a winter berry. 'Why, mine.'

'No! *The other step. The man's tread behind you!*'

'She is not to be deceived. *Come along Sir. You'll be welcome heer, never fear.*'

He spoke in a loud tone; *and as he spoke, the deaf old gentleman entered.*

'He's not so much a stranger, that you haven't seen him once, Caleb. You'll give him house-room till we go? Thankee. He's the best company on earth, to talk secrets in. I have reasonable good lungs myself,

---

[1] Marginal stage-direction *Mystery*.

[2] This clause doubly underlined; so are, below, *Not as good wives* (to end of paragraph), *The man's tread behind you* and *and as he spoke, the deaf old gentleman entered.*

[3] *Elkins* has the marginal stage-direction *Blind*: and, against Peerybingle's speeches below to the 'old gentleman' ('*Come along Sir . . .*' and '*Sit down Sir . . .*') it has *Loud.*

but he tries 'em, I can tell you. *Sit down Sir. All friends here, and glad to see you!'*

Bertha, who had been listening intently, called Caleb to her side, when he had set a chair, and asked him, in a low voice, *to describe their visitor.* When he had done so (truly now; with scrupulous fidelity), she moved, for the first time since the stranger had come in; and seemed to have no further interest concerning him.

The Carrier was in high spirits, good fellow that he was; and fonder of his little wife than ever.

'A curious Dot she was, this afternoon! and yet I like her somehow. See yonder, Dot!'

He pointed to the old man. She looked down. I think she trembled.[1]

'He's—ha ha ha!—he's full of admiration for you! Talked of nothing else, the whole way here. Why, he's a brave old boy. I like him for it!'

'I wish he had had a better subject, John.'

'A better subject! There's no such thing. Come! off with the great-coat, off with the thick shawl, off with the heavy wrappers! and a cosy half-hour by the fire! My humble service, Mistress Fielding. A game at cribbage, you and I? That's hearty. The cards and board, Dot. And a glass of beer here, if there's any left, small wife!'

They were soon engaged upon the game. At first, the Carrier now and then called Dot to peep over his shoulder at his hand, and advise him on some knotty point. But his adversary being a rigid disciplinarian, *and subject to an occasional weakness in respect of pegging more than she was entitled to,*[2] required such vigilance on his part, as left him neither eyes nor ears to spare. Thus, his whole attention gradually became absorbed upon the cards; and he thought of nothing else, until a hand upon his shoulder restored him to a consciousness of Tackleton.

'John, John Peerybingle, I am sorry to disturb you—but a word, directly. Come here, man!'

There was that in his pale face which made the other rise immediately, and ask him, in a hurry, what the matter was.

'Hush! John Peerybingle. I am sorry for this. I am indeed. I have been afraid of it. I have suspected it from the first.'

'What is it?'

'Hush! I'll show you, if you'll come with me.'

The Carrier accompanied him, without another word. They went across a yard, where the stars were shining; and by a little side door, into Tackleton's counting-house, where there was a window, commanding the ware-room: which was closed for the night. There was no light in the

---

[1] Marginal stage-direction *Mystery*. The sentences *She looked down. I think she trembled* doubly underlined.

[2] Phrase doubly underlined. Marginal stage-direction *Mystery* against the next sentence ('Thus, his whole attention . . .').

counting-house itself, but there were lamps in the long narrow ware-room; and consequently the window was bright.

[1] '*A moment! Can you bear to look through that window, do you think?*'

'*Why not?*'

'*A moment more. Don't commit any violence. It's of no use. It's dangerous too. You're a strong-made man; and you might do Murder before you know it.*'

The Carrier looked him in the face, and recoiled a step as if he had been struck. In one stride he was at the window, and he saw—

Oh Shadow on the Hearth! Oh truthful Cricket! Oh perfidious Wife!

He saw her, with the old man—*old no longer, but erect and gallant*—bearing in his hand the false white hair which had won his way into their desolate and miserable home. He saw her listening to him, as he bent his head to whisper in her ear; and suffering him to clasp her round the waist, as they moved slowly down the dim wooden gallery. He saw them stop, and saw her turn—to have the face he loved so, so presented to his view!—and saw her, with her own hands, adjust the Lie upon his head, laughing, as she did it, at her husband's unsuspicious nature!

He clenched his strong right hand at first, as if it would have beaten down a lion. But unclasping it immediately, *he spread it out before the eyes of Tackleton (for he was tender of her, even then),*[2] and so dropped down upon a desk, and was as weak as any infant.[3] †

CHIRP THE THIRD

[4]THE Dutch clock in the corner struck Ten, when the Carrier sat down by his fireside. So troubled and grief-worn, that he seemed to scare the Cuckoo, who, having cut his ten melodious announcements as short as possible, plunged back into the Moorish Palace again, and clapped his little door behind him, as if the unwonted spectacle were too much for his feelings.

Ah! If the little Haymaker had had the sharpest of scythes, and had cut at every stroke into the Carrier's heart, he never could have gashed and wounded it, as Dot had done.

It was a heart so full of love for her; so bound up by innumerable threads of winning remembrance, spun from the daily working of her many

[1] Marginal stage-direction *Very strong. To the end.*

[2] The bracketed phrase doubly underlined, as it is in *Elkins* too. The underlinings in the preceding paragraph are different in *Elkins* (as is often the case). Thus, the whole of the first sentence ('He saw her . . .') is underlined, with 'desolate' and 'miserable' doubly underlined. The exclamation '—to have the face, the face he loved so, so presented to his view!—' and the participle 'laughing' are also underlined in *Elkins*.

[3] *Elkins*, too, ends 'Chirp the Second' here, two pages short of the *1846* ending. Both other 'Chirps' end, in both Readings texts, as in *1846*.

[4] Marginal stage-direction *Very pathetic.*

qualities of endearment; it was a heart in which she had enshrined herself so gently; a heart so single and so earnest in its Truth: so strong in right, so weak in wrong: that it could cherish neither anger nor revenge at first, and had only room to hold the broken image of its Idol.

[1] But slowly, slowly; as the Carrier sat brooding on his hearth, now cold and dark; other and fiercer thoughts began to rise within him, as an angry wind comes rising in the night. The Stranger was beneath his outraged roof. Three steps would take him to his chamber door. One blow would beat it in. 'You might do Murder before you know it,' Tackleton had said. How could it be Murder, if he gave the Villain time to grapple with him hand to hand! He was the younger man.

He was the younger man! Yes, yes; some lover who had won the heart that he had never touched.[2] *Some lover of her early choice; of whom she had thought and dreamed: for whom she had pined and pined: when he had fancied her so happy by his side.*

She had been above stairs with the Baby, getting it to bed. As he sat brooding on the hearth, she came close beside him, without his hearing— in the turning of the rack of his great misery, he lost all other sounds— and put her little stool at his feet. He only knew it, when he felt her hand upon his own, and saw her looking up into his face.

With wonder? No, not with wonder. With an eager and enquiring look; but not with wonder. At first it was alarmed and serious; then it changed into a strange, wild smile of recognition of his thoughts; then there was nothing but her clasped hands on her brow, and her bent head, and falling hair.

Though the power of Omnipotence had been his to wield at that moment, he had too much of its Diviner property of Mercy in his breast, to have turned a feather's weight of it against her. But he could not bear to see her crouching down upon the little seat where he had often looked on her, with love and pride, so innocent and gay; and when she rose and left him, sobbing as she went, he felt it a relief to have the vacant place beside him rather than her so long cherished presence. This in itself was anguish keener than all: reminding him how desolate he was become, and how the great bond of his life was rent asunder.

The more he felt this, and the more he knew he could have better borne to see her lying dead before him with their little child upon her breast, the higher and the stronger rose his wrath against his enemy. He looked about him for a weapon. †

When, suddenly, the struggling fire illumined the whole chimney with a glow of light; and the Cricket on the Hearth began to chirp! † He clasped his hands before his face, sat down again beside the fire, and found relief in tears. The Cricket on the Hearth came out into the room, and stood in Fairy shape before him.

[1] Marginal stage-direction *Anger*.   [2] *he* italic in *1846*.

'"I love it,"' said the Fairy Voice, repeating what he well remembered to have heard her say; '"I love it for the many times I have heard it, and the many thoughts its harmless music has given me."'

'She said so! True!'

'"This has been a happy Home, John; and I love the Cricket for its sake!"'

'It has been a happy home, Heaven knows. She made it happy, always, —until now.'

The Figure, in an attitude of invocation, raised its hand and said:

'Upon your own hearth'—

'The hearth she has blighted.'

'The hearth she has—how often!—blessed and brightened: the hearth which, but for her, were only a few stones and rusty bars, but which has been, through her, the Altar of your Home; on which you have nightly sacrificed some petty passion, selfishness, or care, and offered up the homage of a tranquil mind, a trusting nature, and an overflowing heart; so that the smoke from this poor chimney has gone upward with a better fragrance than the richest incense that is burnt before the richest shrines in all the Temples of this World!—Upon your own hearth; in its quiet sanctuary; surrounded by its gentle influences; hear her! Hear me! Hear everything that speaks the language of your hearth and home!'

While the Carrier, with his head upon his hands, continued to sit brooding in his chair, the Presence stood beside him; suggesting his reflections by its power, and presenting them before him, as in a magic Glass or Picture. It was not a solitary Presence. From the hearthstone, from the chimney; from the clock, the pipe, the kettle, and the cradle; from the floor, the walls, the ceiling, and the stairs; from the cart without, and the cupboard within, and the household implements; from every thing and every place with which she had ever been familiar; Fairies came trooping forth. To busy and bestir themselves and to do all honor to Her image when it appeared. To cluster round it, and embrace it, and strew flowers for it to tread on. To try to crown its fair head with their tiny hands. To show that they were fond of it and loved it; and that there was not one ugly, wicked, or accusatory creature to claim any knowledge of it.

His thoughts were constant to her Image. It was always there. † Sometimes, a shadow fell upon the mirror or the picture—call it what you will—a great shadow of the Stranger, covering its surface. But the nimble fairies worked like Bees to clear it off again; and Dot again was there— still bright and pure, and beautiful.

The night—I mean the real night: not going by Fairy clocks—was wearing now; and in this stage of the Carrier's thoughts, the moon burst out, and shone brightly in the sky. Perhaps some quiet light rose also, in his mind; and he could think more soberly of what had happened. † The moon went down; the stars grew pale; the cold day broke; the sun rose.

All night the faithful Cricket had been Chirping on the Hearth. All night the Carrier had listened to its voice. All night, the household Fairies had been busy with him. All night, she had been amiable and blameless in the Glass, except when that one shadow fell upon it.

He expected that Tackleton would pay him an early visit; and he was right. He had not walked to and fro before his own door in the fresh bright morning, many minutes, when he saw the Toy Merchant coming in his chaise along the road. As the chaise drew nearer, he perceived that Tackleton was dressed out, for his marriage: and had decorated his horse's head with flowers and favors.

'John Peerybingle! My good fellow, how do you find yourself this morning?'

'I have had but a poor night, Master Tackleton, for I have been a deal disturbed in my mind. But it's over now! Coom in!' †

When they entered the kitchen, Tilly Slowboy was kicking and knocking at the Stranger's door; which was only removed from it by a few steps. One of her very red eyes (for Tilly had been crying all night long, because her mistress cried) was at the keyhole; and she was knocking very loud; and seemed frightened. So Tackleton went to Tilly Slowboy's relief; and he too kicked and knocked; and he too failed to get the least reply. But he thought of trying the handle of the door; and as it opened easily, he went in, and soon came running out again.

'John Peerybingle, I hope there has been nothing—nothing rash in the night. Because he's gone!'

'Make yourself easy. He went into that room last night, without harm in word or deed from me; and no one has entered it since. He is away of his own free will. I'd go out gladly at that door, and beg my bread from house to house, for life, if I could so change the past that he had never come. But he has come and gone. And I have done with him!'

'Oh!—Well, I think he has got off pretty easily,' said Tackleton, taking a chair.

The sneer was lost upon the Carrier, who shaded his face with his hand, for some little time, before proceeding.

'You showed me last night,' he said at length, 'my wife; my wife that I love; secretly conniving at that man's disguise, and giving him opportunities of meeting of her alone. I think there's no sight I wouldn't have rather seen than that. I think there's no man in the world I wouldn't have rather had to show it me.'

'I confess to having had my suspicions always. And that has made me objectionable here, I know.'

'But as you did show it me, and as you saw her; my wife; *my wife that I love*, at that sad disadvantage, it is right that you should know what my mind is, upon the subject. For it's settled. And nothing can shake it now.'

Tackleton muttered a few general words about its being necessary to vindicate something or other; but he was overawed by the manner of his companion. Plain as it was, it had a something dignified and noble in it, which nothing but the soul of generous Honor dwelling in the man, could have imparted.

'I am a plain, rough man, with very little to recommend me. I am not a clever man, as you very well know. I am not a young man. I loved my little Dot, because I had seen her grow up, from a child, in her father's house; because I knew how precious she was; because she had been my Life, for years and years. There's many men I can't compare with, who never could have loved my little Dot like me, I think! † But did I consider that I took her; at her age, and with her beauty; from her young companions, and the many scenes of which she was the ornament; to shut her up from day to day in my dull house, and keep *my*[1] tedious company? Did I consider how little suited I was to her sprightly humour, and how wearisome a plodding man like me *must* be, to one of her quick spirit? Did I consider that it was no merit in me, that I loved her, when everybody must who knew her? Never. Never! I took advantage of her hopeful nature and her cheerful disposition; and I married her. I wish I never had! For her sake; not for mine!'

The Toy Merchant gazed at him, without winking. †

'She has tried; I only now begin to know how hard she has tried; to by my dutiful and zealous wife.' † In an unhappy moment some old lover, better suited to her tastes and years than me; forsaken, perhaps, for me, against her will; returned. In an unhappy moment: taken by surprise, and wanting time to think of what she did: she made herself a party to his treachery, by concealing of it. Last night she saw him, in the interview we witnessed. It was wrong. But otherwise than this, she is innocent if there is Truth on earth! So, let her go! Go, with my blessing for the many happy hours she has given me, and my forgiveness for any pang she has caused me. Let her go, and have the peace of mind I wish her! She'll never hate me. She'll learn to like me better, when I'm not a drag upon her. Her father and mother will be here to-day—we had made a little plan for keeping of it together—and they shall take her home. I can trust her, there, or anywhere. She leaves me without blame, and she will live so I am sure. This is the end of what you showed me. Now, it's over!'

[2]*'Oh no, John, not over. Do not say it's over yet! I have heard your noble words. I could not steal away, pretending to be ignorant of what has affected me with such deep gratitude. Do not say it's over, 'till the clock has struck again!'*

She had entered shortly after Tackleton; and had remained there. She never looked at Tackleton, but fixed her eyes upon her husband. But

---

[1] *my* and *must* (below) doubly underlined.

[2] Marginal stage-direction *Dot. Very Earnest.* Paragraph doubly underlined.

she kept away from him, setting as wide a space as possible between them.

'No hand can make the clock which will strike again for me such hours as are gone. But let it be so, if you will, my dear. It will strike soon. I'd try to please you in a harder case than that.'

'Well! *I* must be off: for when the clock strikes again, it'll be necessary for *me* to be upon my way to church. Good morning, John Peerybingle. I'm sorry to be deprived of the pleasure of your company. Sorry for the loss, and the occasion of it too!' †

The Carrier stood at the door looking after him; and then, with a deep sigh, went strolling like a broken man, among some neighbouring elms; unwilling to return until the clock was on the eve of striking.

His little wife, being left alone, sobbed piteously; but often dried her eyes and checked herself, to say how good he was! and once or twice she laughed—so heartily, triumphantly, and incoherently (still crying all the time), that Tilly was quite horrified, † and trailed off into such a deplorable howl, that she must infallibly have awakened the Baby, and frightened him into something serious, if her eyes had not encountered Caleb Plummer, leading in his daughter. †

'Bertha couldn't stay at home this morning. She was afraid, I know, to hear the Bells ring. So we started in good time, and came here. I have been thinking of what I have done. I have been blaming myself 'till I hardly knew what to do or where to turn, and I've come to the conclusion that I'd better, if you'll stay with me, Mum, the while, tell her the truth. You'll stay with me the while? I don't know what effect it may have upon her. † Bertha, my dear! Hear me kindly! I have a confession to make to you, my Darling. † The world you live in, heart of mine, doesn't exist as I have represented it. The eyes you have trusted in, have been false to you. Your road in life was rough, my poor one, and I meant to smooth it for you. I have altered objects, changed the characters of people, invented many things that never have been. I have had concealments from you, put deceptions on you, God forgive me! and surrounded you with fancies.'

'But living people are not fancies?' she said hurriedly, and turning very pale. 'You can't change *them*.'[1]

'I have done so, Bertha. The marriage that takes place to-day is with a stern, sordid, grinding man. A hard master to you and me, my dear, for many years. Unlike what I have painted him to you in everything, my child. In everything.'

'Oh Father, why did you ever do this! Why did you ever fill my heart so full, and then come in like Death, and tear away the objects of my love! Oh Heaven, how blind I am! Oh Heaven, how helpless and alone!'

She had been but a short time in this passion of regret, when the

---

[1] *them* doubly underlined.

Cricket on the Hearth, unheard by all but her, began to chirp. She heard the Cricket-voice more plainly soon; and was conscious, through her blindness, that the Presence which had been beside the Carrier in the night, was hovering near her father.

'Mary, tell me what my Home is. What it truly is.'

'It is a poor place, Bertha; very poor and bare indeed. The house will scarcely keep out wind and rain another winter. *It is as roughly shielded from the weather, Bertha, as your poor father in his sackcloth coat.*'

'Those presents that I took such care of; that came almost at my wish, and were so dearly welcome to me; where did they come from? Did *you*[1] send them?'

'No.'

'Who then?'

Dot saw she knew, already; and was silent.

'Dear Mary, a moment. You are true, I know. You'd not deceive me now; would you?'

'No, Bertha, indeed!'

'No, I am sure. You have too much pity for me. Look across the room where we were just now; to where my father is—and tell me what you see.'

'I see,' said Dot, *who understood her well;* 'an old man sitting in a chair, and leaning sorrowfully on the back, with his face resting on his hand. He is an old man, worn with care and work, a spare, dejected, thoughtful, grey-haired man. I see him now, despondent and bowed down, and striving against nothing. But Bertha, I have seen him many times before; and striving hard in many ways for one great sacred object. And I honor his grey head, and bless him!'

The Blind Girl broke away from her; and throwing herself upon her knees, took the grey head to her breast.

'It is my sight restored. It is my sight! I have been blind, and now my eyes are open. *I never knew him!* To think I might have died, and never truly seen the father, who has been so loving to me! The greyer, and more worn, the dearer, father! † Everything I had—the Soul of all that was dearest and best to me—is here, in you! The Benefactor whom I loved so well—the father whom I never loved enough, and never knew— both are here—here with the dear worn face and the dear grey head. And I am *not*[2] blind, father, any longer!'

Dot's whole attention had been concentrated upon the two: but looking, now, towards the little Haymaker in the Moorish meadow, she saw that the clock was within a few moments of striking; and fell, immediately, into a highly nervous state. †

---

[1] *you* doubly underlined.

[2] *not* doubly underlined. This is a manuscript passage in *Berg*. In the equivalent passage in *1846* the word is printed in small capitals.

'These are changes, but more changes than you think for, may happen, my dear. Changes for the better; changes for great joy to some of us. You mustn't let them startle you too much, if any such should happen, and affect you.—Are those wheels upon the road? You've a quick ear, Bertha. Are those wheels?'

'Yes, coming very fast.' †

'They *are*[1] wheels indeed! coming nearer! Nearer! Very close! And now you hear them stopping at the garden gate! And now you hear a step outside the door—*the same step as last night, Bertha, is it not!*[2]—and now!'—

She uttered a wild cry of delight; and running up to Caleb put her hands upon his eyes, as a young man rushed into the room.

'Is it over?'

'Yes!'

'Happily over?'

'Yes!'

'Do you recollect the voice, dear Caleb? Did you ever hear the like of it before?'

'If my boy in the Golden South Americas was alive'—

'He is[3] alive! look at him! See where he stands before you, healthy and strong! Your own dear son! Your own dear living, loving brother, Bertha!'

All honor to the little creature for her transports! when the three were locked in one another's arms! All honor to the heartiness with which she met the sunburnt Sailor-fellow and never turned her rosy little mouth aside, but suffered him to kiss it, freely, and to press her to his bounding heart!

And honor to the Cuckoo too for bursting out of the trap-door in the Moorish Palace like a housebreaker, and hiccoughing twelve times on the assembled company, as if he had got drunk for joy!

The Carrier, entering, started back: and well he might: to find himself in such good company.

'Look, John!' cried Caleb, 'look here! My own boy from the Golden South Americas! My own son! *Him that you fitted out, and sent away yourself; him that you were always such a friend to!*'

The Carrier advanced to take him by the hand; but recoiling, *as some feature in his face awakened a remembrance of the Deaf Man in the Cart,*[4] said:

---

[1] *are* doubly underlined.

[2] Phrase doubly underlined.

[3] In *Elkins*, 'is' is trebly underlined, and fuller emphasis is given also to another climax, shortly after: Dot's speech 'Now tell him all! . . .' is both underlined and strongly scored in the margin.

[4] Phrase doubly underlined.

'Edward! Was it you?'

'*Now tell him all!*' cried Dot. '*Tell him all, Edward; and don't spare me, for nothing shall make me spare myself in his eyes, ever again.*'

'I was the man,' said Edward. † 'You must know that when I left here, a boy, I was in love: and my love was returned. She was a very young girl, who perhaps (you may tell me) didn't know her own mind. But I knew mine; and I had a passion for her.'

'*You* had *! You!*'[1]

'Indeed I had. And she returned it. I have never since believed she did; and now I am sure she did. Constant to her, and returning, full of hope, after many hardships and perils, to redeem my part of our old contract, I heard, twenty miles away, that she was false to me; that she had forgotten me; and had bestowed herself upon another and a richer man. I had no mind to reproach her; but I wished to see her, and to prove beyond dispute that this was true. That I might see the real truth, I dressed myself unlike myself—you know how; and waited on the road—you know where. You had no suspicion of me; neither had—had she,' pointing to Dot, 'until I whispered in her ear at that fireside, and she so nearly betrayed me.'

[2]'But when she knew that Edward was alive, and had come back,' sobbed Dot, now speaking for herself, as she had burned to do, all through this narrative; 'and when she knew his purpose, she advised him by all means to keep his secret close; for his old friend John Peerybingle was much too open in his nature, and too clumsy in all artifice—being a clumsy man in general—to keep it for him. And when she—*that's me, John*,[3]—told him all, and how his sweetheart had believed him to be dead; and how she had at last been over-persuaded by her mother into a marriage which the silly, dear old thing called advantageous; and when she— *that's me again, John*—told him they were not yet married (though close upon it), and that it would be nothing but a sacrifice if it went on, for there was no love on her side; and when he went nearly mad with joy to hear it; *then*[4] she—*that's me again*—said she would go between them, as she had often done before in old times, John, and would sound his sweetheart and be sure that what she—*me again, John*—said and thought was right. And it WAS right, John! And they were brought together, John! And they were married, John, an hour ago! And here's the Bride! And Gruff and Tackleton may die a bachelor! And I'm a happy little woman, May, God bless you!'

The honest Carrier had stood, confounded. Flying, now, towards her, Dot stretched out her hand to stop him, and retreated as before.

---

[1] *You . . . You* doubly underlined.

[2] Marginal stage-direction *Dot. Great. Elkins* has, a few lines earlier, *Dot. Ready.*

[3] *that's me, John* doubly underlined: so are the repetitions of this phrase, later in this speech.

[4] *then* underlined trebly: and, in the margin, there are four heavy vertical lines.

'No John, no! Hear all! *Don't love me any more John, 'till you've heard every word I have to say.*[1] It was wrong to have a secret from you, John. I'm very sorry. I didn't think it any harm, till I came and sat down by you on the little stool last night; but when I knew by what was written in your face, that you had seen me walking in the gallery with Edward; I felt how giddy and how wrong it was. But oh, dear John, how could you, could you, think so!'

John Peerybingle would have caught her in his arms. But no; she wouldn't let him.

'*Don't love me yet, please John! Not for a long time yet!* When I was sad about this intended marriage, dear, it was because I remembered May and Edward such young lovers; and knew that her heart was far away from Tackleton. You believe that, now. Don't you John?'

John was going to make another rush; but she stopped him again.

'*No: keep there, please John!* When I laugh at you, as I sometimes do, John; and call you clumsy, and a dear old goose, and names of that sort, it's because I love you John, so well; and I take such pleasure in your ways; and because I wouldn't see you altered in the least respect to have you made a King tomorrow. And when I speak of people being middle-aged, and steady, John, and pretend that we are a humdrum couple, going on in a jog-trot sort of way, it's only because I'm such a silly little thing, John, that I like, sometimes, to act a kind of Play with Baby, and all that: and make believe.'

She saw that he was coming; and stopped him again. But she was very nearly too late.

'*No, don't love me for another minute or two, if you please John!* What I want most to tell you, I have kept to the last. My dear, good, generous John; when we were talking the other night about the Cricket, I had it on my lips to say, that at first I did *not*[2] love you quite so dearly as I do now; that when I first came home here, I was half afraid I mightn't learn to love you every bit as well as I hoped and prayed I might—being so very young, John. But, dear John, every day and hour, I loved you more and more. And if I could have loved you better than I do, the noble words I heard you say this morning, would have made me. But I can't. All the affection that I had (it was a great deal John) I gave you, as you well deserve, long, long, ago, and I have no more left to give. Now, my dear Husband, take me to your heart again! That's my home, John; and never, never think of sending me to any other!'

You never will derive so much delight from seeing a glorious little woman in the arms of a third party, as you would have felt if you had seen Dot run into the Carrier's embrace.

---

[1] This sentence, and the similar exclamations to John in the remainder of this episode, have heavy double-interrupted underlining.

[2] Doubly underlined. In *Elkins*, 'quite' (three words later) is also underlined.

You may be sure the Carrier was in a state of perfect rapture; and you may be sure Dot was likewise; and you may be sure they all were, inclusive of Miss Slowboy, who cried copiously for joy, and, wishing to include her young charge in the general interchange of congratulations, *handed round the Baby to everybody in succession, as if it were something to drink.* †

[1]Of course it became a serious duty now, to make a great day of it! Accordingly, Dot went to work to produce such a feast, as should reflect undying honour on the house and every one concerned; and in a very short space of time, she was up to her dimpled elbows in flour, and whitening the Carrier's coat, every time he came near her, by stopping him to give him a kiss. That good fellow washed the greens, and peeled the turnips, and broke the plates, and upset iron pots full of cold water on the fire, and made himself useful in all sorts of ways: [while] everybody tumbled over Tilly Slowboy and the Baby, everywhere. The Baby's unfortunate head was a touchstone for every description of matter. Nothing was in use that day that didn't come, at some time or other, into close acquaintance with that Baby's head.

Then, there was a great Expedition set on foot to go and find out Mrs. Fielding; and to be dismally penitent to that excellent lady; and to bring her back, by force if needful, to be happy. And when the Expedition discovered her, she would listen to no terms at all, but said, an unspeakable number of times, that ever she should have lived to see the day! and couldn't be got to say anything else, except 'Now carry me to the grave;'—which seemed absurd, on account of her not being dead. After a time, she lapsed into a state of dreadful calmness, and observed, that when that unfortunate train of circumstances had occurred in the Indigo Trade, she had foreseen that she would be exposed, during her whole life, to every species of insult. From this sarcastic mood, she passed into an angry one, in which she gave vent to the remarkable expression that the worm would turn if trodden on; and after that, she yielded to a soft regret, and said, if they had only given her their confidence, what might she not have had it in her power to suggest! Taking advantage of this crisis in her feelings, the Expedition embraced her; and she very soon had her gloves on, and was on her way to John Peerybingle's in a state of unimpeachable gentility.

Then, there were Dot's father and mother to come, in another little chaise; and they were behind their time; and fears were entertained; and there was much looking out for them down the road; and Mrs. Fielding *always would*[2] *look in the wrong and morally impossible direction; and being apprised thereof, hoped she might take the liberty of looking where she pleased.*

[1] Marginal stage-direction *Jolly* (trebly underlined; generally these marginalia have double underlining).

[2] *would* doubly underlined.

At last they came: a chubby little couple, jogging along in a snug and comfortable little way that quite belonged to the Dot family: and Dot and her mother, side by side, were wonderful to see. They were so like each other. †

After dinner, Caleb sang the song about the Sparkling Bowl! And a most unlooked-for incident occurred, just as he finished the last verse.

There was a tap at the door; and a man came staggering in, without saying with your leave, or by your leave, with something heavy on his head. Setting this down in the middle of the table, he said:

'Mr. Tackleton's compliments, and as he hasn't got no use for the cake himself, p'raps you'll eat it.'—And with those words, walked off.

I don't think any one had tasted the cake, when there came another tap at the door; and the same man appeared again, having under his arm a vast brown paper parcel.

'Mr. Tackleton's compliments, and he's sent a few toys for the Babby. They ain't ugly.'

After the delivery of which expressions, he retired again. He had scarcely shut the door, when there came another tap, and Tackleton himself walked in.

'Mrs. Peerybingle! I'm sorry. I'm more sorry than I was this morning. I have had time to think of it. Friends, one and all, my house is very lonely tonight. I have not so much as a Cricket on my Hearth. I have scared them all away. Be gracious to me; let me join this happy party!' †

There was a dance in the evening. With which general mention, I should have left it alone, if I had not some reason to suppose that it was a dance of an uncommon figure. It was formed in an odd way; in this way.

Edward, that sailor-fellow, had been telling them various marvels concerning parrots, and mines, and Mexicans, and gold dust, when all at once he took it in his head to jump up from his seat and propose a dance; for Bertha's harp was there, and she had such a hand upon it as you seldom hear. Dot said her dancing days were over;—*I*[1] think because the Carrier was smoking his pipe, and she liked sitting by him, best. Mrs. Fielding had no choice, of course, but to say *her* dancing days were over, after that; and everybody said the same, except May; May was ready.

So, May and Edward get up, amid great applause, to dance alone.

If you'll believe me, they have not been dancing five minutes, when suddenly the Carrier flings his pipe away, takes Dot round the waist, dashes out into the room, and starts off with her, toe and heel, quite wonderfully. Tackleton no sooner sees this, than he skims across to Mrs. Fielding, takes *her*[2] round the waist, and follows suit. Old Dot no sooner sees this, than up he is, all alive, whisks off Mrs. Dot into the

[1] *I* (italic in *1846*) doubly underlined; so is *her*, below in this paragraph.
[2] *her* doubly underlined.

middle of the dance, and is the foremost there. Caleb no sooner sees this, than he clutches Tilly Slowboy and goes off at score; Miss Slowboy, firm in the belief that diving in among all the other couples, and effecting any number of concussions with them, is your only principle of Dancing.

How the Cricket joined the music with its Chirp, and how the kettle hummed!

But what is this! Even as I listen to them, and turn towards Dot, for one last glimpse of a little figure very pleasant to me, she and the rest have vanished into air. A Cricket sings upon the Hearth; a broken child's-toy lies upon the ground; and nothing else remains.

THE CHIMES

DICKENS'S two pre-publication readings of *The Chimes* to groups of his friends, in December 1844, were the germ of his later career as a public reader, as John Forster recognized (*Life*, pp. 355–6, 363–4). So it was not surprising that he thought of including this piece in his first charity readings in 1853 (see above, p. 35), and that he did include it early in his professional platform career. *The Chimes* constituted, in fact, the second programme which he gave during his first 'paid' series. By then, however, he had more than one reason for feeling unsure about it. On 1 May 1858, five days before its first performance, Dickens told a friend that people seemed to be 'a little afraid of the Chimes' (presumably advance bookings were disappointing), and he continued: 'To tell you the truth, I am—as yet—a little so myself, for I *can not* yet (and I have been at it all the morning) command sufficient composure at some of the more affecting parts, to project them with the necessary force, the requisite distance. I must harden my heart, like Lady Macbeth' (*N*, iii, 20). After the first public performance, however, he reported that it had been a 'tremendous success'—'I think there is no doubt that it topped the others by a great height last night. I have heard in all directions today that the effect was amazingly strong' (*N*, iii, 21). Later, on his first provincial tour, he noted that it was 'always a surprise. They fall into it with a start, and look at me in the strangest way before they begin to applaud' (*Coutts*, p. 363). At Edinburgh, the judgement of whose audiences he always greatly respected, 'a brilliant victory' was recorded: 'The city was taken by storm, and carried. The Chimes shook it; Little Dombey blew it up' (*N*, iii. 60–1).

Certainly *Little Dombey* proved much more popular; and, among the Christmas Book readings, the *Carol* always impressed audiences and critics as altogether more varied, genial, and attractive. After performances in Scotland in September–October 1858, *The Chimes* was rarely performed again. '*Very* dramatic, but very melancholy on the whole', he described it as being, when he offered it, unpersuasively, for a charity Reading at Chatham (*To* H. G. Adams, 30 November 1858; MS. Morgan)—but the organizers chose another item. It was not included in the American repertoire. 'I have not read The Chimes for two years', he wrote on 20 January 1869. 'I am afraid it is a little dismal, but have shortened and brightened it as much as possible' (*N*, iii, 700). This is the version in the only prompt copy now extant: *The Chimes/A Reading./In Three Parts./By Charles Dickens./(Not Published)*. (printed by William Clowes and Sons, London; text paginated 3–75). This text certainly belongs to 1868, when he was preparing *Sikes and Nancy*, the prompt-copy of which is printed and bound with it, its text being paginated 79–112. They were doubtless printed at a date close to 29 September 1868, when he mentioned both Readings in a letter to George Dolby: 'I think I can make a good thing out of The Chimes . . . When you come to me on Monday, you shall look through the Murder as I have arranged it' (*Huntington Library Quarterly*, v (1941), 138). There must have been an earlier prompt-copy of *The Chimes*, though no record of it can be traced in catalogues, bibliographies, etc. Doubtless, in 1858, Dickens made a prompt-copy as for the other Christmas Books readings, inlaying pages from an ordinary copy into a larger page. The 1858 trade edition of *The Chimes*, published by Bradbury & Evans, is simply a cheap reprint of the 1844 text.

The 1868 prompt-copy was manifestly printed from the 1858 one (with further recent revisions). One sign of this is that some phrases in the 1868 text are printed in small capitals. This was an easy mistake for the printer to make (it had occurred in the *David Copperfield* prompt-copy, in similar circumstances): Dickens had doubly underlined these phrases, in the first prompt-copy, to indicate a special vocal emphasis, but this is also the proof-reading convention to indicate small capitals. The printed text of 1868 is just under two-fifths of the length of the 1844 text. Dickens's manuscript alterations, made in at least two different inks, further reduce its length, so that the final length of the Reading is about one-third of the 1844 text's. The cuts already made before the 1868 text was printed include drastic reductions in the supernatural machinery of the Bells and their Goblins, and in the high-aspiring rhetorical passages about 'the Sea of Thought', 'the Sea of Time', and suchlike; these mostly occur at the beginnings and endings of the four 'Quarters'. (The three 'Parts' into which the Reading is divided do not correspond to these 'Quarters', except the last one—though originally the four-quarter structure had been retained, as 1858 press reports show.) Also, significantly, Will Fern's big speech of protest at Sir Joshua Bowley's and his rick-burning speech (in the third and fourth 'Quarters' respectively) had been deleted by this time, though some of the reviewers of early performances had praised the power which Dickens generated in the first of these (e.g., *Clifton Chronicle*, 4 August 1858), and had judged the 'tall, gaunt, fierce, hungry, magistrate-hunted labourer, Will Fern' to be 'one of the most powerfully-drawn and impressive portraits in the whole range of Mr. Dickens's present readings' (*The Critic*, 4 September 1858, p. 538).

The deletion of these social-protest passages is in line with what was noticed above (p. 2) about the *Carol*. As Dickens realized, *The Chimes* set a particularly difficult problem in this respect, for it was very much the expression of a particular moment in recent British history. During his 1858 tour, he prefaced this Reading by a little speech:

I have been accustomed to remark in England, when reading the parts of this fancy, that it was written about a dozen years ago, at a time when I was living in Italy, and when some circumstances recorded in the home newspapers—all within the compass of a single week—appeared to me to render the utterance of a few earnest words very necessary. If there be in our United Kingdom, as I hope and believe, less direct need of such utterance now than there was then, so much the better for us all: we have only to assume tonight that a few hints for compassionate and merciful remembrance are never out of date in the Christian calendar. (*Applause*)

This report appeared in *Saunders' News-Letter* (Dublin), 25 August 1858, whose critic surmized that Dickens's having to make this prefatory speech showed that he was somewhat uneasy about how acceptable this Reading could now be. Similar reports appear in other newspapers, including the *Clifton Chronicle*, 4 August 1858, which adds the further detail that he remarked that

'Though the cause for this remonstrance was now to some extent removed, and in part, he hoped, by the aid of his little work, yet a plea for the poor and distressed was never out of season . . .'

Critics praised his evocation of the domestic affections in this Reading, and his rendering of the pathos of Lilian's situation in the third Quarter. His performance 'rivetted' the attention of his audiences, and added much to his admirers' awareness of the qualities to be found in this story. John Hollingshead, in *The Critic* (4 September 1858), went so far as to maintain that Trotty Veck's appearances produced 'more tears and laughter combined than anything within the whole range of the acted drama'. But it is not surprising that, in competition with other items in the expanding repertoire, *The Chimes* did not become an established favourite. What is surprising is that Dickens went to so much trouble over revising it in 1868; only one performance of it was given thereafter (London, 19 January 1869). It had nevertheless seemed very impressive to some people who heard it. Nearly fifty years afterwards, the novelist 'Dick Donovan' (J. E. Preston Murdock) recalled that hearing this Reading, when a young man, had been an epoch in his life:

To me it was a revelation. I had previously read many of his works, and for a long time had had an unconquerable yearning to see and know the author whom all England was talking about. The man's beautiful, sympathetic voice, the wonderfully expressive eyes, his marvellous eloquence, his magnetic presence seemed to throw me under a spell, and I regarded him as something more than a human being, or at anyrate as a man who was quite different from other men I had so far known. The power that Dickens had over the hearts of the people at this time, was little short of marvellous. On the occasion I allude to the great hall [the Free Trade Hall, Manchester] was literally packed from floor to ceiling. Yet that audience was placed under the spell wielded by the man whose voice was like a silver bell, and who acted what he read. The pathos moved the people to tears, the humour stirred them to roars of laughter. There were no accessories of music or scenery, simply one man at a reading-desk; but what a man! What a gift to be able to charm and sway a multitude! Sometimes you could have heard a pin drop, at others the roof seemed rent with the roars of the people as they gave vent to their strained feelings. And when it came to the peroration there was a silence which was almost painful, even a woman's sob here and there only served to intensify it. ['Dick Donovan' then quotes the final words.]

. . . Gently, slowly the book was closed, and the solitary figure seemed to glide from the stage, yet the vast audience remained silent—for hours; it was only seconds, but the seconds seemed hours. Then the people let themselves go; they had the weary man back, and they thundered their approval. He stood there slowly bowing, the tears of heartfelt emotion running down his pale cheeks. I passed out into the frosty night. I was a dreamer; I was dreaming dreams. Charles Dickens had carved his name on my heart. For many days afterwards he seemed to haunt me, and to stir within me feelings and desires of which up to then I had only had a vague consciousness. (*Pages from an Adventurous Life* (1907), pp. 53–5)

The Chimes

FIRST PART

* HIGH UP in the steeple of an old church, far above the town and far below the clouds, dwelt the Chimes I tell of.

Old Chimes,* but not speechless. They had clear, loud, lusty, sounding voices; and they rang out far and wide—'beating all other bells to fits,' as *Toby Veck*[1] said; for though they chose to call him Trotty Veck, his name was Toby. And I take my stand by Toby Veck, though he *did* stand all day long in all weathers, outside the church-door. In fact he was a ticket-porter, Toby Veck, and waited there for jobs. *

They called him Trotty from his pace, which meant speed if it didn't make it. He could have walked faster than he trotted; but rob him of his trot, and Toby would have taken to his bed and died. A weak, small, spare old man, he was a very Hercules, this Toby, in his strong intentions.

One day—*one New Year's Eve*[2]—Toby was trotting up and down before the Church, when *The Chimes*, his old daily companions, struck Twelve at Noon.

'Dinner-time, eh! Ah! * There's nothing more regular in its coming round than dinner-time, and there's nothing less regular in its coming round than dinner. I wonder whether it would be worth any gentleman's while, now, to buy that obserwation for the Papers; or the Parliament!'[3]

Toby was only joking with himself.

'Why! Lord! The Papers is full of obserwations as it is; and so's the Parliament. Here's last week's paper, now; full of obserwations! Full of obserwations! I like to know the news as well as any man; but it almost goes against the grain with me to read a paper now. It frightens me, almost. *I don't know what we poor people are coming to, our characters is so bad.*[4] Lord send we may be coming to something better in the New Year nigh upon us!'

'Father, father!'

Toby didn't hear.

'It seems as if we can't go right, or do right, or be righted. I hadn't

[1] *Toby Veck* in small capitals in *Berg*; *did* (in the next sentence) italic in *Berg* and in *1844*.

[2] Like *The Chimes* later in this sentence, this is doubly underlined in the manuscript insertion in *Berg*.

[3] Trotty spoke in 'a voice modified from Bob Cratchit's' (*Critic*, 4 September 1858, p. 538).

[4] Small capitals in *Berg*.

much schooling, myself, when I was young; and I can't make out whether we have any business on the face of the earth, or not. Sometimes I think we must have a little; and sometimes I think we must be intruding. I get so puzzled sometimes that I am not even able to make up my mind *whether there is any good at all in us, or whether we are born bad.*[1] We seem to do dreadful things; we seem to give a deal of trouble; we are always being complained of and guarded against. One way or another, we fill the papers. Talk of a New Year! Supposing it should really be that we have no right to a New Year—supposing we really *are*[2] intruding——'

'Why, father, father!'

Toby heard the pleasant voice, this time; started; stopped; and found himself face to face with his own child, and looking into her eyes.

Bright eyes they were. Eyes that would bear a world of looking in. Eyes that were beautiful and true, and beaming with Hope. With Hope so young and fresh; with Hope so buoyant, vigorous, and bright, despite the twenty years of work and poverty on which they had looked; that they became a Voice to Trotty Veck, and said: 'I think we have some business here—a little!'

Trotty kissed the lips belonging to the eyes, and squeezed the blooming face between his hands.

'Why Pet. What's to-do? I didn't expect you to-day, Meg.'

'Neither did I expect to come, father. But here I am! And not alone!'

'Why you don't mean to say,' *looking curiously at a covered basket which she carried in her hand*, 'that you have brought——'

'Smell it, father dear. Only smell it! Now. What's that?'

'Why, it's hot!'

'It's burning hot! It's scalding hot! But what is it, father? Come! You must guess what it is. I can't think of taking it out, till you guess what it is.' *

'Ah! It's very nice. It an't—I suppose it an't Polonies?'[3]

'No, no, no! Nothing like Polonies!'

'No. It's—it's mellower than Polonies. It's too decided for Trotters. Liver? No. There's a mildness about it that don't answer to liver. Pettitoes? No. It an't faint enough for pettitoes. It wants the stringiness of Cocks' heads. And I know it an't sausages. I'll tell you what it is. No, it is n't, neither. Why, what am I thinking of! I shall forget my own name next. It's tripe!'

Tripe it was; and Meg protested he should say, in half a minute more, it was the best tripe ever stewed.

---

[1] Small capitals in *Berg*.

[2] Italic in *Berg* and in *1844*.

[3] Much 'by-play' here by 'the Humorist . . . when he syllabled, with watering lips, guess after guess at the half-opened basket. "It ain't—I suppose it ain't polonies? [sniffing] . . .' (Kent, p. 165).

'And so I'll lay the cloth at once, father; for I have brought the tripe in a basin, and tied the basin up in a pocket handkerchief; and if I like to spread that for a cloth, and call it a cloth, there's no law to prevent me; is there, father?'

'Not as I knows of, my dear. But they're always a bringing up some new law or other.'*

'Make haste, father, for there's a hot potato besides, and half a pint of fresh-drawn beer in a bottle. Where will you dine, father? On the Post, or on the Steps? How grand we are. Two places to choose from!'

'The Steps to-day, my Pet. Steps in dry weather. Post in wet. There's a greater conveniency in the Steps at all times, because of the sitting down; but they're rheumatic in the damp.' *

As he was stooping to sit down, the Chimes rang.

'Amen!'

'Amen to the Bells, father?'

'They broke in like a grace, my dear. They'd say a good one, I am sure, if they could. For many's the kind thing they say to me. Why bless you, my dear,' *pointing at the tower with his fork*, 'how often have I heard them bells say "*Toby Veck, Toby Veck, keep a good heart, Toby! Toby Veck, Toby Veck, keep a good heart, Toby!*"[1] Have I heard 'em say it, a million times? More! When things are very bad indeed, then it's "*Toby Veck, Toby Veck, job coming soon, Toby! Toby Veck, Toby Veck, job coming soon, Toby!*" that way. * But Lord forgive me! My love! Meg! why did n't you tell me what a beast I was? Sitting here, cramming, and stuffing, and gorging myself; and you before me there, never so much as breaking your precious fast——'

'But I have broken it, father, all to bits. I have had my dinner, father. And if you 'll go on with yours I'll tell you how and where; and how your dinner came to be brought; and—and something else besides.'

So Trotty took up his knife and fork again.

'I had my dinner, father, with—with Richard. His dinner-time was early; and as he brought his dinner with him when he came to see me, we —we had it together, father.'

'Oh!'

'And Richard says, father——'

'What does Richard say, Meg?'

'Richard says, father——'

'Richard's a long time saying it.'

'He says then, father, another year is nearly gone, and where is the use of our waiting on from year to year, when it is so unlikely we shall ever be better off than we are now? He says we are poor now, father, and we shall be poor then; but we are young now, and years will make us old

---

[1] This and the following 'speech' of the Bells printed in small capitals in *Berg*.

before we know it. And how hard, father, to grow old, and die, and think
we might have cheered and helped each other! How hard in all our lives
to love each other; and to grieve, apart, to see each other working, changing, growing old and grey. So Richard says, father; as his work was yesterday made certain for some time to come, and as I love him and have loved
him full three years—ah! longer than that, if he knew it!—will I marry
him tomorrow—New Year's Day; the best and happiest day, he says, in
the whole year. And he said so much, that I said I 'd come and talk to you,
father. And as they paid the money for that work of mine this morning,
and as you have fared very poorly for a whole week, and as I could n't
help wishing there should be something to make this day a sort of holiday
to you as well as a dear and happy day to me, father, I made a little treat
and brought it to surprise you.'

'And see how he leaves it cooling on the step!'

The voice of this same Richard, looking down upon them with a face as
glowing as the iron on which his stout sledge-hammer daily rang. A
handsome, well-made, powerful youngster; with eyes that sparkled like
the red-hot droppings from his furnace fire. *

Trotty reached up his hand to Richard, when the house door opened
without any warning, and a footman very nearly put his foot in the tripe.

'Out of the vays here, will you! You must always go and be a settin on
our steps, must you! You can't go and give a turn to none of the neighbours never, can't you! *Will*[1] you clear the road or won't you?'

Strictly speaking, the last question was irrelevant, because they had
already done it.

'What's the matter, what's the matter!' *said the gentleman for whom
the door was opened: coming out of the house.* 'What's the matter. What's
the matter?'

'You 're always a being begged, and prayed, upon your bended knees
you are, to let our doorsteps be. Why don't you let 'em be? CAN'T you
let 'em be?'[2]

'There! That'll do, that'll do! Halloa there! Porter! Come here. What's
that? Your dinner?'

'Yes, sir,' *leaving it behind him in a corner.*

'Don't leave it there. Bring it here, bring it here. So! This is your
dinner, is it?'

'Yes, sir,' *looking, with a fixed eye and watery mouth, at the piece of
tripe he had reserved for a last delicious tit-bit; which the gentleman was
now turning over and over on the end of his fork.*

[1] Italic in *Berg* and in *1844*.

[2] CAN'T printed in capitals in *1844* as well as in *Berg*. Kent (p. 166), quoting this
speech, notes that 'Nothing more was seen or heard of that footman, and yet in the
utterance of those few words of his the individuality of the man somehow was thoroughly
realized . . . he stood palpable there before us.'

Two other gentlemen had come out with him.†

He called to the first one by the name of Filer; and they both drew near together. Mr. Filer being exceedingly short-sighted, was obliged to go so close to the remnant of Toby's dinner before he could make out what it was, that Toby's heart leaped up into his mouth. But Mr. Filer did n't eat it.

'This is a description of animal food, *Alderman Cute*,'[1] *making little punches in it, with a pencil-case,* 'commonly known to the labouring population of this country, by the name of tripe. But who eats tripe? Tripe is without an exception the most wasteful article of consumption that the markets of this country can by possibility produce. The loss upon a pound of tripe has been found to be, in the boiling, seven eighths of a fifth more than the loss upon a pound of any other animal substance whatever. Tripe is more expensive, properly understood, than the hothouse pineapple. Taking into account the number of animals slaughtered yearly within the bills of mortality alone; and forming a low estimate of the quantity of tripe which the carcases of those animals, reasonably well butchered, would yield; I find that the waste on that amount of tripe, if boiled, would victual a garrison of five hundred men for five months of thirty-one days each, and a February over. The Waste, the Waste!'

Trotty stood aghast. He seemed to have starved a garrison of five hundred men with his own hand.

'Who eats tripe? Who eats tripe?'

Trotty made a miserable bow.

'You do, do you? Then I'll tell you something. You snatch your tripe, my friend, out of the mouths of widows and orphans.'

'I hope not, Sir. I'd sooner die of want!'

'Divide the amount of tripe before-mentioned, Alderman, by the estimated number of existing widows and orphans, and the result will be one pennyweight of tripe to each. Not a grain is left for that man. Consequently, he's a robber.'

Trotty was so shocked, that it gave him no concern to see the Alderman finish the tripe himself. It was a relief to get rid of it, anyhow.

'And what do you say?' asked the Alderman, jocosely, of his other friend. 'You have heard friend Filer. What do *you*[2] say?'

'What's it possible to say? What *is* to be said? Who can take any interest in a fellow like this? Look at him! What an object! Look into Strutt's Costumes, and see what a Porter used to be in any of the good old English reigns. Ah! the good old times, the grand old times, the great old times!'

The gentleman did n't specify what particular times he alluded to. †

---

[1] *Alderman Cute* in small capitals in *Berg*; the phrase that follows is simply underlined.

[2] *you* (and *is* in the next sentence) italic in *Berg* and in *1844*.

'Now, you know,' *said the Alderman, addressing his two friends,* 'I am a plain man, and a practical man; and I go to work in a plain practical way. That's my way. There is not the least mystery or difficulty in dealing with this sort of people if you only understand 'em, and can talk to 'em in their own manner. Now, you Porter! Don't you ever tell me, or anybody else my friend, that you have n't always enough to eat, and of the best; because I know better. I have tasted your tripe, you know, and you can't "chaff" me. You understand what "chaff" means, eh? That's the right word is n't it? Ha, ha, ha! Lord bless you, it's the easiest thing on earth to deal with this sort of people, if you only understand 'em. You see my friend, there's a great deal of nonsense talked about Want—"hard up," you know: that's the phrase is n't it?—and I intend to Put it Down. That's all! Lord bless you, you may Put Down anything among this sort of people, if you only know the way to set about it!'

Trotty took Meg's hand and drew it through his own.

'Your daughter, eh? Where's her mother?'

'Dead!'

'Oh! and you're making love to her, are you? you young smith?'

'Yes. And we are going to be married on New Year's Day.'

'What do you mean! Married?' said Mr. Filer.

'Why, yes, we're thinking of it, Master. We're rather in a hurry you see, in case it should be Put Down first.'

'Ah! Put *that*[1] down indeed, Alderman, and you'll do something. Married! Married!! A man may live to be as old as Methusaleh, and may labour all his life for the benefit of such people as those; and may heap up facts on figures, facts on figures, facts on figures, mountains high and dry; and he can no more hope to persuade 'em that they have no right or business to be married, than he can hope to persuade 'em that they have no earthly right or business to be born. And *that* we know they have n't. We reduced it to a mathematical certainty long ago.'

Alderman Cute laid his right forefinger on the side of his nose, as much as to say to both his friends, 'Observe me, will you? Keep your eye on the practical man!'—and called Meg to him.

'Come here, my girl! * You are going to be married, you say. Rather unbecoming and indelicate in one of your sex! But never mind that. After you are married, you'll quarrel with your husband, and come to be a distressed wife. You may think not: but you will, because I tell you so. Now I give you fair warning, that I have made up my mind to Put distressed wives Down. So don't be brought before me. You'll have children—boys. Those boys will grow up bad of course, and run wild in the streets, without shoes and stockings. Mind, my young friend! I am determined to Put boys without shoes and stockings, Down. Perhaps

---

[1] *that* here, and *that* again at the end of the paragraph, italic in *Berg* and in *1844*.

your husband will die young (most likely) and leave you with a baby. Then you'll be turned out of doors, and wander up and down the streets. Now don't wander near me, my dear, for I am resolved to Put all wandering mothers Down. And, above all, don't you attempt to drown yourself, or hang yourself, for I have made up my mind to Put all suicide Down. As for you, you dull dog, what are you thinking of being married for? What do you want to be married for, you silly fellow? If I was a fine young, strapping chap like you, I should be ashamed of being milksop enough to pin myself to a woman's apron-strings! Why, she'll be an old woman before you're a middle-aged man! And a pretty figure you'll cut then, with a draggle-tailed wife and a crowd of squalling children crying after you wherever you go! There! Go along with you and repent. †—Porter, don't you go. As you happen to be here, you shall carry a letter for me. Can you be quick? You're an old man.—How old are you?'

'I'm over sixty-eight, Sir,' said Toby.[1]

'Oh! This man's a great deal past the average age, you know,' cried Mr. Filer, *breaking in as if his patience would bear some trying, but this really was carrying matters a little too far.*

'Yes: I feel I'm intruding, Sir,' said Toby. 'I—I misdoubted it this morning!'

The Alderman cut him short by giving him the letter from his pocket. Toby would have got a shilling too; but Mr. Filer clearly showing that in that case he would rob a certain given number of persons of ninepence-halfpenny a-piece, he only got sixpence; and thought himself very well off to get that.[2] *

The letter was addressed to a great man in the great district of town. The greatest district of the town. It must have been the greatest district of the town, because it was commonly called The World by its inhabitants. *

'*Put 'em down, put 'em down, Facts and Figures, facts and figures, Good old Times, good old times. Put 'em down, put 'em down.*'[3] The unfaithful and unfeeling Chimes went to that measure, and Toby's trot went to that measure, and neither Chimes nor Trot would go to any other burden.

But even that burden brought him, in due time, to the end of his journey. To the mansion of Sir Joseph Bowley, Member of Parliament. The door was opened by a Porter. Such a Porter![4] When he had found

---

[1] *1844* has 'over sixty'—a characteristic example of the raising of numerals in the Readings.

[2] The rest of the 'First Quarter' is here omitted, and a much abbreviated version of the opening of the 'Second Quarter' follows.

[3] These sentences printed in small capitals in *Berg*.

[4] This porter (Tugby) was 'a platform creation of the highest dramatic order, built up out of a few lines in the book, which an ordinary reader would pass by' (*Critic*, 4 September 1858, p. 537). His voice was 'a fat whisper' (Kent, p. 167, quoting a phrase from the novel, here omitted).

his voice—which it took him some time to do, for it was a long way off, and hidden under a load of meat—he said:

'Who's it from?'

Toby told him.

'You're to take it in, yourself. Everything goes straight in, on the last day of the old year.'

Toby wiped his feet (which were quite dry already) and took the way pointed out to him; observing as he went that it was an awfully grand house. Knocking at the room door, he was told to enter from within; and, doing so, found himself in a library, where, at a table strewn with files and papers, were a stately lady in a bonnet; and a not very stately gentleman in black who wrote from dictation; while another, and an older, and a much statelier gentleman walked up and down, with one hand in his breast.

'What is this?' said the last-named gentleman. 'Mr. Fish, will you have the goodness to attend?'

Mr. Fish begged pardon, and taking the letter from Toby, handed it, with great respect.

'From Alderman Cute, Sir Joseph.'

'Is this all? Have you nothing else, Porter? You have no bill or demand upon me (my name is Bowley, Sir Joseph Bowley) of any kind from anybody, have you? I allow nothing to be carried into the New Year. Every description of account is settled in this house at the close of the old one. So that if death was to—to—sever the cord of existence—my affairs would be found, I hope, in a state of preparation.'

'My dear Sir Joseph! How shocking!'

'My lady Bowley, at this season of the year we should think of—of—ourselves. We should look into our—our —accounts. We should feel that every return of so eventful a period in human transactions, involves matters of deep moment between a man and his—and his banker.' *

'Ah! you are the Poor Man's Friend, you know, Sir Joseph.'

'I *am*[1] the Poor Man's Friend.'

'Bless him for a noble gentleman!'

'I don't agree with Cute here, for instance. I don't agree with the Filer party. I don't agree with any party. My friend the Poor Man, has no business with anything of that sort, and nothing of that sort has any business with him. My friend the Poor Man, in my district, is my business. Your only business, my good fellow,' looking abstractedly at Toby; 'your only business in life is with me. You need n't trouble yourself to think about anything. I will think for you; I know what is good for you; I am your perpetual parent. Such is the dispensation of an all-wise Providence! Now, the design of your creation is: not that you should swill, and guzzle, and associate your enjoyments, brutally, with food'—

[1] Italic in *Berg* and in *1844*.

Toby thought remorsefully of the tripe[1]—'but that you should feel the Dignity of Labor; go forth erect into the cheerful morning air, and—and stop there.' *

'Ah! you have a thankful family, Sir Joseph!'

'My lady, ingratitude is known to be the sin of that class. I expect no other return.'

'*Ah! Born bad!* Nothing melts us!' *

Sir Joseph opened the Alderman's letter.

'Very polite and attentive, I am sure! My lady, the Alderman is so obliging as to inquire whether it will be agreeable to me to have *Will Fern* put down.'

'*Most*[2] agreeable! The worst man among them! He has been committing a robbery, I hope?'

'Why, no; not quite. Very near. Not quite. He came up to London, it seems, to look for employment (trying to better himself—that's his story), and being found at night asleep in a shed, was taken into custody and carried next morning before the Alderman. The Alderman observes (very properly) that he is determined to put this sort of thing down; and that if it will be agreeable to me to have Will Fern put down, he will be happy to begin with him.'

'Let him be made an example of, by all means,' returned the lady. 'Last winter, when I introduced pinking and eyelet-holeing among the men and boys in the village, as a nice evening employment, and had the lines—

> Oh let us love our occupations,
> Bless the squire and his relations,
> Live upon our daily rations,
> And always know our proper stations—

set to music on the new system, for them to sing the while; this very Fern —I see him now—touched that hat of his, and said, "I humbly ask your pardon my lady, but *an't* I something different from a great girl?" Make an example of him.'

'Hem! Mr. Fish, if you'll have the goodness to attend'——

Mr. Fish seized his pen, and wrote from Sir Joseph's dictation.

'Private. My dear Sir. I am very much indebted to you for your courtesy in the matter of the man William Fern, of whom, I regret to add, I can say nothing favourable. I have uniformly considered myself in the light of his Friend and Father, but have been repaid (a common case, I grieve to say) with ingratitude, and constant opposition to my plans. He is a turbulent and rebellious spirit. His character will not bear investigation. Nothing will persuade him to be happy when he might. Under these circumstances, it appears to me, I own, that when he comes before you

---

[1] This and the next two emphases (*Ah! Born bad!* and *Will Fern*) in small capitals in *Berg*.

[2] *Most*, and the next emphasis (*an't* at the end of the next paragraph but one) italic in *Berg* and in *1844*.

again his committal for some short term as a Vagabond, would be a service to society. And I am,' and so forth.

'With my compliments and thanks, Porter. Stop! You have heard, perhaps, certain remarks into which I have been led respecting the solemn period of time at which we have arrived, and the duty imposed upon us of settling our affairs, and being prepared. Now, my friend, can you lay your hand upon your heart, and say, that you also have made preparation for a New Year?'

'I am afraid, Sir, that I am a—a—little behind-hand with the world.'

'Behind-hand with the world!'

'I am afraid, Sir, that there's a matter of ten or twelve shillings owing to Mrs. Chickenstalker.'

'To Mrs. Chickenstalker!'

'A Shop, Sir, in the general line. Also I'm fearful there's a—a little money owing on account of rent. A very little, Sir. It ought n't to be owing, I know, but we have been hard put to it, indeed!'

Sir Joseph looked at his lady, and at Mr. Fish, and at Trotty, one after another, twice all round. He then made a despondent gesture with both hands at once, as if he gave the thing up altogether.

'There! Take the letter. Take the letter! Take the letter, take the letter!'

He had nothing for it but to make his bow and leave the house. In the street, he pulled his old hat down upon his head, to hide the grief he felt at getting no hold on the New Year, anywhere. *

Unfaithful and unfeeling Chimes! They would n't cheer up Toby now. '*Facts and figures, facts and figures. Good old times, good old times. Born bad, born bad! Put 'em down, put 'em down!*'[1] He could hear the Chimes ring nothing better.

He discharged himself of his commission, and set off trotting homeward. But what with his pace, and what with his hat over his eyes, he soon trotted against somebody.

'I beg your pardon, I'm sure! I hope I have n't hurt you!'

The man against whom he had run; a sun-browned country-looking man, replied:

'No, friend. You have not hurt me.'

'Nor the child, I hope?'

'Nor yet the child. I thank you kindly.'

He glanced at a little girl he carried in his arms, asleep. *

'You can tell me, perhaps—and if you can I am sure you will, and I'd rather ask you than another—where Alderman Cute lives.'

'It's impossible your name's Fern! Will Fern!'

'That's my name.'

'Why then, for Heaven's sake don't go to him! Don't go to him! He'll

---

[1] Small capitals in *Berg*.

put you down as sure as ever you were born. Here! come up this alley, and I'll tell you what I mean. Don't go to *him*.'¹

His new acquaintance looked as if he thought him mad; but he bore him company. When they were shrouded from observation, Trotty told him what he knew, and what character he had received, and all about it. The countryman did not contradict. He nodded his head now and then; and threw back his hat, and passed his hand over a brow, *where every furrow he had ploughed seemed to have set its image in little.*²

'It's true enough in the main, master. I could sift grain from husk here and there, but let it be as 't is. What odds? I have gone against his plans; to my misfortun'. I can't help it; I should do the like to-morrow. As to character, them gentlefolks will search and search, and pry and pry, and have it as free from spot or speck in us, afore they'll help us to a dry good word! —Well! I hope they don't lose good opinion as easy as we do, or their lives is strict indeed. For myself, master, I never took with that hand what was n't my own; and never held it back from work, however hard, or poorly paid. Whoever can deny it, let him chop it off! But when work won't maintain me like a human creetur; when my living is so bad, that I am Hungry, out of doors and in; then I say to the gentlefolks "Keep away from me! Let my cottage be. My doors is dark enough without your darkening of 'em more. We've nought to do with one another. I'm best let alone!" '

Seeing that the child was awake, he checked himself to say a word or two of prattle in her ear, and stand her on the ground beside him. Then, while she hung about his dusty leg, he said to Trotty:

'I'm not a cross-grained man by natur', I believe; and easy satisfied, I'm sure. I bear no ill will against none of 'em; but I've got a bad name this way, and I'm not likely, I'm afeard, to get a better. 'T an't lawful to be out of sorts, and I AM³ out of sorts, though God knows I'd sooner bear a cheerful spirit if I could. Well! I don't know as this Alderman could hurt *me* much by sending of me to gaol; but without a friend to speak a word for me, he might do it; and you see—!' *pointing downward with his finger, at the child.*

'She has a beautiful face.'

'Why yes! I've thought so, many times. I've thought so, when my hearth was very cold, and cupboard very bare. I thought so t'other night, when we were taken like two thieves. But they—they shouldn't try the little face too often, should they, Lilian? That's hardly fair upon a man!'

'Is your wife alive?'

'I never had one. She's little Lilian—my brother's child: a orphan. Nine year old. They'd have took care on her, the Union; *eight and twenty*

¹ Italic in *Berg* and in *1844*.   ² Small capitals in *Berg*.
³ AM in small capitals, and *me* (just below) in italics, in *1844* as well as in *Berg*. The final words of the paragraph are in small capitals in *Berg* only.

mile away from where we live[1] (as they took care of my old father when he could n't work no more, though he did n't trouble 'em long); but I took her instead, and she's lived with me ever since. Her mother had a friend once, in London here. We are trying to find her, and to find work too; but it's a large place. Never mind. More room for us to walk about in, Lilly!'

Meeting the child's eyes with a smile which melted Toby more than tears, he shook him by the hand.

'I don't so much as know your name; but I've opened my heart free to you, for I'm thankful to you. I'll take your advice. And to-morrow Lilly and me will try whether there's better fortun' to be met with, somewheres near London. Good night. A Happy New Year!'

'Stay! Stay! The New Year never can be happy to me, if we part like this. The New Year never can be happy to me, if I see the child and you go wandering away, you don't know where, without a shelter for your heads. Come home with me! I'm a poor man, living in a poor place; but I can give you lodging for one night and never miss it. Come home with me! Here! I'll take her! A pretty one! I'd carry twenty times her weight, and never know I'd got it. Why, she's as light as a feather.—*Here*[2] we are, and here we go!—Round this first turning to the right, Uncle Will, and past the pump, and sharp off up the passage to the left, right opposite the public-house.—*Here* we are, and here we go.—Cross over, Uncle Will, and mind the kidney pieman at the corner!—*Here* we are, and here we go! —Down the Mews here, Uncle Will, and stop at the black door, with "T. Veck, Ticket-Porter," wrote upon a board; and—*here* we are, and here we go—and here we are indeed, my precious Meg, surprising of you!'

He set the child down before his daughter in the middle of the floor. The little visitor looked once at Meg; and doubting nothing in that face, but trusting everything she saw there, ran into her arms.

'Here we are and here we go!' *running round the room, and choking audibly.* '*Here*! *Uncle Will*! Why don't you come to the fire?—Oh here we are and here we go!—Meg, my precious darling, where's the kettle?— Here it is and here it goes, and it 'll bile in no time!'[3]

Trotty really had picked up the kettle somewhere or other, and now put it on the fire: while Meg, seating the child in a warm corner, kneeled down on the ground before her, and pulled off her shoes, and dried her wet feet.

'Why father! You're crazy to-night, I think. I don't know what the Bells would say to that.—Poor little feet. How cold they are! Why father! Good gracious me! He's crazy! He's put the dear child's bonnet on the kettle, and hung the lid behind the door!'

[1] Small capitals in *Berg*.

[2] *Here* throughout this paragraph printed in small capitals in *Berg*.

[3] 'It was in the touching scenes of home affection [such as this], . . . that both as an author and a highly cultivated elocutionist, he was most unquestionably at home' (*Saunders' News-letter*, 26 August 1858).

'I didn't go to do it, my love. Meg, my dear!'

Behind the chair of their male visitor, he was holding up the sixpence he had earned.

'I see, my dear, as I was coming in, half an ounce of tea lying somewhere on the stairs; and I'm pretty sure there was a bit of bacon too. As I don't remember where it was, exactly, I'll go myself and try to find 'em.'

With this inscrutable artifice, Toby withdrew to purchase the viands at Mrs. Chickenstalker's; and presently came back, pretending that he had not been able to find them, at first, in the dark.

'But here they are at last,' *said Trotty, setting out the tea-things,* 'all correct! I was pretty sure it was tea, and a rasher. So it is. Meg, my Pet, if you'll just make the tea, while your unworthy father toasts the bacon, we shall be ready, immediate. It's a curious circumstance,' said Trotty, proceeding in his cookery, 'curious, but well known to my friends, that I never care, myself, for rashers, nor for tea. I like to see other people enjoy 'em,' speaking very loud, to impress the fact upon his guest, 'but to me, as food, they're disagreeable.' *

No. Trotty's occupation was to see Will Fern and Lilian eat and drink. And so was Meg's. *

'Now, I'll tell you what,' *said Trotty after tea.* 'The little one, she sleeps with Meg, I know. * Will Fern, you come along with me. You're tired to death, and broken down for want of rest. You come along with me. I'll show you where you lie. It's not much of a place: only a loft: but there's plenty of sweet hay up there belonging to a neighbour; and it's as clean, as hands and Meg can make it. Cheer up! Don't give way. A new heart for a New Year, always!'

It was some short time before the foolish little old fellow, left to himself, could compose himself to mend the fire, and draw his chair to the warm hearth. But when he had done so, and had trimmed the light, he took his newspaper from his pocket, and began to read. Carelessly at first, and skimming up and down the columns; but with an earnest and a sad attention, very soon.

For this same dreaded paper re-directed Trotty's thoughts into the channel they had taken all that day. His interest in the two wanderers had set him on another course of thinking, and a happier one; but being alone again, and reading of the crimes and violences of the people, he relapsed into his former train.

In this mood, he came to an account (and it was not the first he had ever read) of a woman who had laid her desperate hands not only on her own life; but on that of her young child.[1] A crime so terrible, and so revolting to his soul, dilated with the love of Meg, that he let the journal drop.

'Unnatural and cruel! Unnatural and cruel! None but people who were bad at heart: born bad: who had no business on the earth: could do such

---

[1] Small capitals in *Berg.*

deeds. It's too true, all I've heard to-day in the Chimes, and out of them; it's too just, too full of proof. Put us Down. We're Bad!'

The Chimes took up the words so suddenly that the Bells seemed to strike him out of his chair.

And what was that, they said?

'*Toby Veck, Toby Veck, waiting for you, Toby! Toby Veck, Toby Veck, waiting for you, Toby! Toby Veck, Toby Veck, door open wide, Toby; Toby Veck, Toby Veck, door open wide, Toby!*[1] Haunt his slumbers, Haunt his slumbers! Come and see us, Come and see us!——'

'Meg,' *tapping at her door*. 'Do you hear anything?'

'I hear the Bells, father. Surely they're very loud to-night.'

He resumed his seat by the fire, and once more listened. *He fell off into a doze; then roused himself.* It was impossible to bear the Bells; their energy was dreadful. †

So he slipped out into the street * and went in to the Bell-Tower, feeling his way.[2] It was very dark. And very quiet, for the Chimes were silent now. He groped his way, and went up, until, ascending through the floor, and pausing with his head just raised above its beams, he came among the Bells. * Then did he see in every Bell a bearded figure, of the bulk and stature of the Bell—incomprehensibly, a figure and the Bell. Gigantic, grave, and darkly watchful of him, as he stood rooted to the ground. Mysterious and awful figures! Resting on nothing; poised in the night air of the tower, motionless and shadowy! *

The Great Bell, or the Goblin of the Great Bell, spoke. 'What visitor is this!'

'I thought my name was called by the Chimes. I hardly know why I am here, or how I came here. I have listened to the Chimes these many years. They have cheered me often.'

'And you have thanked them?'

'A thousand times!'

'How?'

'I am a poor man, and could only thank them in words.'

'Have you never done us wrong in words?' *

'I never did so, to my knowledge, Sir; it was quite by accident if I did. I would n't go to do it, I'm sure.' *

'Who hears in us, the Chimes, one note bespeaking disregard, or stern regard, of any hope, or joy, or pain, or sorrow, of the many-sorrowed throng; who hears us make response to any creed that gauges human passions and affections, as it gauges the amount of miserable food on

---

[1] Small capitals in *Berg*. The remainder of the Bells' 'speech' was inserted, in manu-script, in *Berg*. Also printed in small capitals in *Berg* is the sentence below, *He fell off into a doze; then roused himself.*

[2] This paragraph is a drastically condensed version of the closing pages of the 'Second Quarter' and the opening of the 'Third Quarter'.

which humanity may pine and wither; does us wrong. That wrong you have done us! * Lastly, and most of all, who turns his back upon the fallen and disfigured of his kind; abandons them as Vile from the beginning; and does not trace with pitying eyes the unfenced precipice by which they fell from Good; who does this wrong to Heaven and Man, to Time and to Eternity. And you have done that wrong.'

'I hope not, spirits of the Bells. I should be sorry to do such wrong at any time, but most of all upon a New Year's Eve.'

'A New Year's Eve! Listen![1] The New Year is past—nine years ago. You ceased from among the living, nine years ago. You missed your foothold on the outside of this tower in the dark, and fell into the deep street, nine years ago. Your child is living. *Learn from her life, a living truth.*[2] *Learn from the creature dearest to your heart, how bad the Bad are born.* See every bud and leaf plucked one by one from the fairest stem, and know how bare and wretched it may become! *Follow her! To Desperation!*'

Each of the figures stretched its right arm forth, and pointed downward. And then, where the Figures had been, the Bells were.

SECOND PART

WITH a confused and stunned sensation of not being able to make himself seen, or heard—of being a mere shade without substance—not alive and yet sentient—Trotty Veck looked into a strange unearthly atmosphere before him.

In a poor, mean room; working at the same kind of embroidery which he had often, often, seen before her; Meg, his own dear daughter, was presented to his view.

Changed. Changed. The light of the clear eye, how dimmed. The bloom, how faded from the cheek.

She looked up from her work, at a companion. Following her eyes, the old man started back. For, in the woman grown, he recognized Lilian Fern. *

Hark. They were speaking!

'Meg, how often you raise your head from your work to look at me!'

'Are my looks so altered, that they frighten you?'

'Nay dear! But when you think I'm busy, and don't see you, you look so anxious and so doubtful, that I hardly like to raise my eyes. There is little cause for smiling, in this hard and toilsome life of ours; but you were once so cheerful.'

---

[1] The next two paragraphs are a condensed and re-arranged version of the 1844 text (Oxford Illustrated edition, pp. 124–5).

[2] This sentence in small capitals in *Berg*; the next sentence is printed in italic, but with *how* in small capitals. The last four words of this speech are also printed in small capitals.

'Am I not now! Do *I*[1] make our weary life more weary to you, Lilian!'

'You have been the only thing that made it life, sometimes the only thing that made me care to live so, Meg. Such work, such work! So many hours, so many days, so many nights of hopeless, cheerless, never-ending work—not to heap up riches; but to earn bare bread! Oh Meg, Meg! How can the cruel world go round, and bear to look upon such lives!'

'Lilly! Why Lilly! You! So pretty and so young!'

'Oh Meg! *The worst of all, the worst of all! Strike me old, Meg! Wither me and shrivel me, and free me, from the dreadful thoughts that tempt me in my youth!*'[2] *

His former stunned sensation came on Trotty, and he saw nothing but mist. It cleared; he rubbed his eyes, and looked again.

His daughter was again seated at her work.[3] But in a poorer, meaner garret than before; *and with no Lilian by her side.*

The frame at which Lilian had worked, was put away upon a shelf and covered up. The chair in which Lilian had sat, was turned against the wall. *

A knock came at Margaret's door. She opened it. A man was on the threshold. A slouching, moody, drunken sloven: wasted by intemperance and vice: and with his matted hair and unshorn beard in wild disorder: *but with some traces on him, too, of having been a man of good proportion and good features in his youth. Trotty knew him. Richard.*[4]

'May I come in, Margaret?'

'Yes! Come in. Come in!' †

'Still at work, Margaret? You work late.'

'I generally do.'

'And early?'

'And early.'

'So she said. She said you never tired; or never owned that you tired. Not all the time you lived together. But I told you that, the last time I came. Margaret! What am I to do? She has been to me again!'[5]

'Again! Oh! does she think of me so often! Has she been again!'

'Twenty times again. Margaret, she haunts me. She comes behind me in the street, and thrusts it in my hand. I hear her foot upon the ashes when

[1] Italic in *Berg* and in *1844*.

[2] Small capitals in *Berg*. The whole of the Bowley Hall episode, which follows here in *1844*, is omitted in *Berg*. This episode included Will Fern's long protest speech.

[3] Small capitals in *Berg*; so is the phrase in the next sentence.

[4] All in small capitals in *Berg*.

[5] Richard's account of Lilian was (according to the *Clifton Chronicle*, 4 August 1858) 'the finest bit of the whole reading,' enacted with 'wonderful art. . . . You saw before you the wretched, starving, pitying, loving, upright Meg, and the haggard, wild and restless Richard. . . .'

I'm at my work (ha, ha! *that*[1] an't often now), and before I can turn my head, her voice is in my ear, saying, "Richard, don't look round. For heaven's love, give her this!" She brings it where I live; she sends it in letters; she taps at the window and lays it on the sill. What *can*[2] I do? Look at it!'

'Hide it, hide it! When she comes again, tell her, Richard, that I love her in my soul. That I never lie down to sleep, but I bless her, and pray for her. That in my solitary work, I never cease to have her in my thoughts. That she is with me night and day. That if I died to-morrow, I would remember her with my last breath. But that I cannot look upon it!'

'I told her so. I told her so, as plain as words could speak. I've taken this gift back and left it at her door, a dozen times since then. But when she came at last, and stood before me, face to face, what could I do?'

'You saw her!'

'I saw her. There she stood: trembling! Says she, "How does she look, Richard? Does she ever speak of me? Richard, I have fallen very low; and you may guess how much I have suffered in having this sent back, when I can bear to bring it in my hand to you. But you loved her once, even in my memory, dearly."—(I suppose I did.—I did! That's neither here nor there now.)—"Oh Richard, if you have any memory for what is gone and lost, take it to her once more. Once more! Tell her how I laid my head upon your shoulder, *where her own head might have lain*,[3] and was so humble to you, Richard. Tell her that you looked into my face, and saw the beauty which she used to praise, all gone: all gone: and in its place, a poor, wan, hollow cheek, that she would weep to see."—You won't take it, Margaret?'

She shook her head, and motioned an entreaty to him to leave her.

'Good night, Margaret.'

'Good night!'

She sat down to her task, and plied it. Night, midnight. Still she worked. The Chimes rang half-past twelve; and there came a gentle knocking at the door. It opened.

She saw the entering figure; screamed its name; cried 'Lilian!'

It was swift, and fell upon its knees before her: clinging to her dress.

'Up, dear! Up! Lilian! My own dearest!'

'Never more, Meg; never more!'

'Sweet Lilian! Darling Lilian! Child of my heart—no mother's love can be more tender—lay your head upon my breast and let me raise you!'

'Never more, Meg. Never more! When I first looked into your face, *you*[4] kneeled before *me*. On my knees before *you*, let me die. Let it be here!'

---

[1] Small capitals in *Berg*.

[2] Italic in *Berg* and in *1844*. The 'it' referred to is a purse; Dickens deleted the text referring to it, as he could convey the sense of gesture.

[3] Small capitals in *Berg*.   [4] *you ... me ... you* italic in *Berg*.

'You have come back. We will live together, work together, hope together, die together!'

'Ah! Kiss my lips, Meg; fold your arms about me; press me to your bosom; look kindly on me; but don't raise me. Let me see the last of your dear face upon my knees! His blessing on you, dearest love. He suffered her to sit beside His feet, and dry them with her hair. Oh Meg, His Mercy and Compassion!'

Her heart was broken, and she died in the encircling arms.

THIRD PART

SOME new remembrance of the figures in the Bells, some new remembrance of the ringing of the Chimes, some new knowledge—how conveyed to him he knew not—that more years had passed, and Trotty Veck, again without the power of being heard or seen, again looked on at mortal company.

Fat company, rosy-cheeked company, comfortable company. They were but two, but they were red enough for ten.[1] They sat before a bright fire, with a small low table between them. * The fire gleamed not only in the little room, and on the panes of window-glass in the door, and on the curtain half drawn across them, but in the little shop beyond. A little shop in the chandlery-way, or general line, quite crammed and choked with the abundance of its stock. * Trotty had small difficulty in recognising in the stout old lady, Mrs. Chickenstalker. * In Mrs. Chickenstalker's partner in the general line, and in the crooked and eccentric line of life, he recognized the former porter of Sir Joseph Bowley. *

'What sort of night is it, Anne?' inquired the former porter of Sir Joseph Bowley, stretching out his legs before the fire.

'Blowing and sleeting hard, and threatening snow. Dark. And very cold.'

'I'm glad to think we had muffins for tea, my dear. It's a sort of night that's meant for muffins. Likewise crumpets. Also Sally Lunns.'

'You're in spirits, Tugby.'

(The firm was Tugby, late Chickenstalker.)

'No. Not particular. I'm a little elewated on accounts of being comfortable in-doors while it's such bad weather outside. * There's a customer, my love!'

Attentive to the rattling door, Mrs. Tugby had already risen.

'Now then. What's wanted? Oh! I beg your pardon, Sir, I'm sure. I did n't think it was you.'

She made this apology to a gentleman in black, who sat down astride on a table-beer barrel, and seemed to be some authorized medical attendant on the poor.

---

[1] 'A roar invariably greeted [this] remark' (Kent, p. 174).

'This is a bad business up-stairs, Mrs. Tugby. The man can't live.'

'Not our back-attic can't!'

'Your back-attic, Mr. Tugby, is coming down-stairs fast; and will be below the basement very soon.—The back-attic, Mr. Tugby, is Going.'

'Then,' *turning to his wife,* 'he must Go, you know, before he's Gone. It's the only subject that we've ever had a word upon, she and me, and look what it comes to! He's going to die here, after all. Going to die upon the premises. Going to die in our house!'

'And where should he have died, Tugby!'

'In the workhouse. What are workhouses made for?'

'Not for that. Not for that. Neither did I marry you for that. Don't you think it, Tugby. I won't have it. I won't allow it. I'd be separated first, and never see your face again. When my widow's name stood over that door, as it did for many, many years, I knew him, Richard, a handsome, steady, manly, independent youth; I knew her, Meg Veck, as the sweetest-looking girl eyes ever saw; and when I turn them out of house and home, may angels turn me out of Heaven. As they would! And serve me right!'

'Bless her! Bless her!'

'There's something interesting about the woman, even now. How did she come to marry him?'

'Why that is not the least cruel part of her story, Sir. You see they kept company, she and Richard, many year ago, and they were to have been married on a New Year's Day. But, somehow, Richard got it into his head, through what the gentlemen told him, that he might do better, and that he'd repent it, and the gentlemen frightened *her*,[1] and made her timid of his deserting her, and a good deal more. And in short, they lingered and lingered, and their trust in one another was broken, and so at last was the match. But never did woman grieve more truly for man, than she for Richard when he first went wrong.'

'Oh! he went wrong, did he?'

'Well, Sir, I don't know that he rightly understood himself, you see. I think his mind was troubled by their having broke with one another. He took to drinking, idling, bad companions. He lost his looks, his character, his health, his strength, his friends, his work, everything! This went on for years and years. At last, he was so cast down, and cast out, that no one would employ him. Applying for the hundredth time to one gentleman who had often and often tried him (he was a good workman to the very end); that gentleman, who knew his history, said, "I believe you are incorrigible; there is only one person in the world who has a chance of reclaiming you; ask me to trust you no more, until she tries to do it."

---

[1] Doubly underlined in *Berg.*

Something like that in his anger and vexation.—Well, Sir; Richard went to her, and made a prayer to her to save him.'

'And she—Don't distress yourself, Mrs Tugby.'

'She came to me that night to ask me about living here. "What he was once to me," she said, "is buried in a grave; side by side with what I was once to him. But I have thought of this; and I will make the trial." So they were married; and when they came home here, and I saw them, I hoped that such prophecies as parted them when they were young, may not often fulfil themselves as they did in this case, or I would n't be the makers of them for a Mine of Gold.'

'I suppose he used her ill?'

'I don't think he ever did that, Sir. He went on better for a short time; but his habits were too old and strong to be got rid of. There he has been lying now, these weeks and months. Between him *and her baby,*[1] she has not been able to do her old work; and by not being able to be regular, she has lost it, even if she could have done it. How they have lived, I hardly know!'

'*I*[2] know,' muttered Mr. Tugby; *looking at the till, and round the shop, and at his wife; and rolling his head with immense intelligence.* 'Like Fighting Cocks!'

He was interrupted by a cry from the upper story of the house. The gentleman ran up-stairs; Trotty floated up like mere air.

'*Follow her! Follow her! Follow her!*'[3] *He heard the ghostly voices in the Bells repeat their words.* 'Learn it from the creature dearest to your heart!'

It was over. It was over. The ruins of Richard cumbered this earth no more. And this was she, her father's pride and joy! This haggard, wretched woman, weeping by the bed, if it deserved that name, and pressing to her breast an infant. Who can tell how spare, how sickly, and how poor an infant? Who can tell how dear?

'Thank God!' cried Trotty, *holding up his folded hands.* '*Oh, God be thanked! She loves her child!*'[4] *

He hovered round his daughter. He flitted round the child: so wan, so prematurely old, *so dreadful in its gravity, so plaintive in its feeble, mournful, miserable wail.*[5] He saw the good woman tend her in the night; return to her when her grudging husband was asleep; encourage her, weep with her, set nourishment before her. He saw the day come, and the night again; the day, the night; the house of death relieved of death; the room left to herself and to the child; he heard it moan and cry; he saw it tire her out,

[1] Small capitals in *Berg.*

[2] Italic in *Berg* and in *1844.*

[3] This speech in small capitals, and the following sentence underlined, in *Berg.*

[4] *holding up his folded hands* underlined in Berg; the speech which follows is in small capitals.

[5] N.B.: from here onwards, all passages printed in *italics* are in SMALL CAPITALS in *Berg,* unless otherwise noted.

and when she slumbered, drag her back to consciousness, and hold her with its little hands upon the rack; but she was constant to it, gentle with it, patient with it. *

A change fell on the aspect of her love. One night.

She was singing faintly to the child in its sleep, and walking to and fro to hush it, when her door was softly opened, and a man looked in.

'For the last time.'

'William Fern!'

'For the last time. Margaret, my race is nearly run. I could n't finish it, without a parting word with you.* *Your child, Margaret*! Let me have it in my arms. *Let me hold your child!*'

He trembled as he took it, from head to foot.

'Is it a girl?'

'Yes.'

He put his hand before its little face.

'See how weak I'm grown, Margaret, when I want the courage to look at it! Let her be a moment. I won't hurt her. It's long ago, but—What's her name?'

'Margaret.'

He seemed to breathe more freely; and took away his hand. But he covered the child's face again, immediately.

'Margaret, it's Lilian over again.'

'Lilian!'

'I held just such another face in my arms when Lilian's mother died and left her.'

'*When Lilian's mother died and left her!*'

When he was gone, she sank into a chair, and pressed the infant to her breast. * She paced the room with it the livelong night, hushing it and soothing it. She said at intervals, '*Like Lilian, when her mother died and left her!*' And then it was that something fierce and terrible began to mingle with her love.

She dressed the child next morning with unusual care—ah vain expenditure of care upon such squalid robes!—and once more tried to find some means of life. *In vain.* *

It was a bleak, dark, cutting night: when, pressing the child close to her for warmth, she arrived outside the house she called her home. She was so faint and giddy, that she saw no one standing in the doorway until she was about to enter. Then she recognised the master of the house.

'Oh! you have come back?'

She appealed to him from the child in her arms.

'Don't you think you have lived here long enough without paying any rent?'

She repeated the same mute appeal.

'Now I see what you want, and what you mean. You know there are two parties in this house about you. But you shan't come in. That I am determined.'

She put her hair back with her hand, and looked at the sky, and the dark lowering distance. *

'*Follow her! To desperation!*'

The Bell-figures hovered in the air, and pointed where she went, down the dark street.

'She loves it! Chimes! She loves it!'

'*Follow her!*' The shadows swept upon the track she had taken, like a cloud.

He joined in the pursuit; he kept close to her; he looked into her face. He saw the fierce and terrible expression mingling with her love, and kindling in her eyes. He heard her say, '*Like Lilian! To be changed like Lilian!*' *

Putting its tiny hand up to her neck, and holding it there, within her dress: next to her distracted heart: she set its sleeping face against her, and sped onward *to the river.*

To the rolling River, swift and dim, where Winter Night sat brooding like the last dark thoughts of many who had sought a refuge there before her. Where lights upon the banks gleamed sullen, red, and dull, like torches that were burning there, to show the way to Death.

Her father followed her. She paused a moment on the river's margin. He implored the figures in the Bells now hovering above them.

'Goblins of the Bells! Spirit of the Chimes! I *have* learnt it! I *have* learnt it from the creature dearest to my heart! Oh save her, save her! * Spirits of the Chimes, think what her misery must have been, when such seed bears such fruit! Heaven meant her to be Good. Oh have mercy on my child, who, even at this pass, means mercy to her own, and dies herself, and perils her Immortal Soul, to save it!'

He could touch her, now. He could hold her, now. His strength was like a giant's.[1]

'*Spirits of the Chimes! I know that* we must trust and hope, and neither doubt ourselves, nor doubt the Good in one another. I have learnt it from the creature dearest to my heart. I clasp her in my arms again. Oh Spirits, merciful and good, I am grateful!'

He might have said more, but the Bells; the old familiar Chimes; began to ring the joy-peals for a New Year, so lustily, so merrily, so happily, so gaily, that he leaped upon his feet, and broke the spell that bound him.

'*And whatever you do, father,*' said Meg, '*don't eat tripe again, without asking some doctor whether it's likely to agree with you; for how you have*[2] *been going on, Good gracious!*'

[1] The first two sentences of this paragraph are printed in small capitals in *Berg*, but the whole paragraph is also underlined discontinuously.

[2] *have* italic in *Berg* and in *1844*; the rest of the speech in small capitals in *Berg*.

She was working with her needle, at the little table by the fire; dressing her simple gown with ribbons for her wedding. So quietly happy, so blooming and youthful, so full of beautiful promise, that he uttered a great cry as if it were An Angel in his house.

But he caught his feet in the newspaper, which had fallen on the hearth when he had fallen asleep: and somebody came rushing in between them.

'No! Not even you. Not even you. The first kiss of Meg in the New Year is mine. I have been waiting outside the house, this hour, to hear the Bells and claim it. Meg, my precious prize, a happy year! A life of happy years, my darling wife! * To-day is our Wedding Day!' *

'Richard my boy!' *cried Trotty, in an ecstacy.*[1] 'You was turned up Trumps originally; and Trumps you must be till you die!'

The child, who had been awakened by the noise, came running in half-dressed.

'Why, here she is!' *cried Trotty, catching her up.* 'Ha, ha, ha! Here's little Lilian! Here we are and here we go! Oh here we are and here we go again! And Uncle Will too! Oh, *Uncle Will, the Vision that I've had to-night, through lodging you!'*

Before Will Fern could reply, a Band of Music burst into the room, attended by the marrowbones and cleavers, the handbells, and a flock of neighbours. † They were ready for a dance in half a second, and the Drum in the Band of Music was on the brink of leathering away with all his power; when a combination of prodigious sounds was heard outside, and a comely matron came running in, attended by a man bearing a stone pitcher of terrific size.[2]

'It's Mrs. Chickenstalker!'

'Married, and not tell me, Meg! Never! So here I am; and as it's New Year's morning, and the morning of your wedding too, my dear, I had a little flip made, and brought it with me.'

Mrs. Chickenstalker's notion of *a little flip*, did honour to her character. The pitcher reeked like a volcano; and the man who carried it was faint.

'Mrs. Tugby! I *should*[3] say, Chickenstalker—Bless your heart and soul! A happy New Year, and many of 'em! Mrs. Tugby—I *should* say, Chickenstalker—This is William Fern and Lilian.'

'Not Lilian Fern whose mother died in Dorsetshire!'

Her uncle answered 'Yes,' and meeting, they exchanged some words; of which the upshot was, that Mrs. Chickenstalker shook him by both hands, and took the child to her capacious breast.

---

[1] Underlined, not in small capitals, in *Berg*; so, just below is *cried Trotty, catching her up.* The words *in an ecstacy* are not in *1844*: an unusual example of Dickens's adding, instead of deleting, such a phrase describing a character's tones.

[2] The audience roared at this entry of Mrs. Chickenstalker, and there were renewed bursts of laughter during the paragraph below about her notion of 'a little flip' (Kent, p. 174).

[3] *should . . . should* italic in *Berg* and in *1844*.

'Will Fern! Not the friend that you was hoping to find?'

'Aye! And like to prove a'most as good a friend (if that can be) as one I found.'

'*Oh! Please to play up there. Will you have the goodness!*'

To the music of the band, the bells, the marrow-bones and cleavers, all at once; and while The Chimes were yet in lusty operation out of doors; Trotty led off Mrs. Chickenstalker down the dance, and danced it in a step unknown before or since.

Had Trotty dreamed? Or are his joys and sorrows, and the actors in them, but a dream; himself a dream; the teller of this tale a dreamer, waking but now? If it be so, O Listener, dear to him in all his visions, try to bear in mind the stern realities from which these shadows come; and in your sphere endeavour to correct, improve, and soften them. So may the Rolling Year be a Happy one to You, Happy to many more whose Happiness depends on You! So may each Year be happier than the last, and not the meanest of our brethren or sisterhood debarred their rightful share, in what our Great Creator formed them to enjoy.

THE END OF THE READING

THE HAUNTED MAN

The Haunted Man was Dickens's Christmas Book for 1848, and on 11 December that year he read it at his home to a group of friends, 'with his usual energy and spirit', as one of them recorded (*Dickensian*, xlvii (1951), 20). During the summer of 1853, when he was determining the programme of readings to be given in Birmingham the following December, he suggested that, besides reading the *Carol*, he would give one of his other Christmas Books. *The Chimes* or *The Haunted Man* would be most suitable, he thought, but eventually he submitted to the local committee's decided preference for *The Cricket on the Hearth* (see above, p. 35). The idea of reading *The Haunted Man* was revived early in 1858, when he was planning his first professional season. As late as 5 April 1858, less than a month before the Readings began, he was telling a friend that his repertoire would consist of *The Cricket*, *The Chimes*, and *The Haunted Man* (*N*, iii, 17). It was doubtless about this time that he prepared the prompt-copy (now in the Suzannet Collection), using the same method as with the other Christmas Books he was then turning into Readings: pages from an ordinary edition (1848) of the book were inlaid into large octavo pages. His deletions, too, were made in the fashion he favoured in 1858; the longer deletions were made with a paint-brush, usually in red water-colour paint (or ink?), but sometimes the brush was used with blue ink, too. All the deletions made with a pen are in blue ink.

This reading was never performed, however, and Dickens obviously decided that it would not be suitable before he had completed the process of abbreviating and revising the text. His manuscript emendations end at p. 137 (just after the beginning of Chapter III, and nearly fifty pages before the end). Until then, the editing had been drastic, about two-thirds of the text being deleted; but this revision had only been made in a rough-and-ready fashion, for at several points the continuity of the story is lost at the end of a deletion, or the syntax breaks down because the appropriate connecting phrases have not been written in.

Dickens had evidently decided to concentrate the Reading on Redlaw's character and fate. Thus, at the beginning of Chapter II the presentation of the Tetterby family is drastically reduced (little, indeed, remains of the first half of this chapter), and the revelation that the sick student (Edward Denham) is really the son of Redlaw's lost love is omitted. Charles Kent, probably the only reader of this prompt-copy until now (except its owners), very reasonably considered this 'about the least likely of all his stories . . . to have been thus selected' (p. 90); but Dickens, persistent in his intention to perform it, must have been convinced that it had possibilities, until he got down to the task in detail.

The present edition does not reprint the text from p. 137 of the prompt-copy onwards, as the rest of Chapter III can be read in any edition of the *Christmas Books*.

The Haunted Man

AND

The Ghost's Bargain
A Fancy for Christmas Time

CHAPTER I
The Gift Bestowed

† EVERYBODY said he looked like a haunted man.

Who could have seen his hollow cheek; sunken brilliant eye; black-attired figure; his grizzled hair hanging, like tangled sea-weed, about his face,—as if he had been, through his whole life, a lonely mark for the chafing and beating of the great deep of humanity,—but might have said he looked like a haunted man?

Who could have observed his manner, taciturn, thoughtful, gloomy, shadowed by habitual reserve, retiring always and jocund never, with an air of reverting to a byegone place and time, or of listening to some old echoes in his mind, but might have said it was the manner of a haunted man?

Who could have heard his voice, slow-speaking, deep, and grave, [1] but might have said it was the voice of a haunted man?

Who that had seen him in his inner chamber, part library and part laboratory, upon a winter night, alone, surrounded by his drugs and instruments and books; the shadow of his shaded lamp a monstrous beetle on the wall, motionless among a crowd of spectral shapes raised there by the flickering of the fire upon the quaint objects around him; pondering in his chair before the rusted grate and red flame, moving his thin mouth as if in speech, but silent as the dead, would not have said that the man seemed haunted and the chamber too? †

His dwelling,—within doors—at his fireside—was so lowering and old, so crazy, yet so strong, with its worm-eaten beams of wood in the ceiling, and its sturdy floor shelving downward to the great oak chimney-piece; so environed and hemmed in by the pressure of the town, yet so remote in fashion, age, and custom.

You should have seen him in his dwelling about twilight, in the dead winter time.

---

[1] In the margin here, there is what seems to be the letter *l*: purpose unknown, though it recurs in this script. Possibly means *Leave*?

When the wind was blowing, shrill and shrewd, with the going down of the blurred sun. When it was just so dark, as that the forms of things were indistinct, but not wholly lost. When sitters by the fire began to see wild faces and figures, mountains and abysses, ambuscades and armies, in the coals. When people in the streets bent down their heads, and ran before the weather. When those who were obliged to meet it, were stopped at angry corners, stung by wandering snow-flakes alighting on the lashes of their eyes. When windows of private houses closed up tight and warm. When lighted gas began to burst forth in the busy and the quiet streets, fast blackening otherwise. When stray pedestrians looked down at glowing fires in kitchens, and sharpened their sharp appetites by sniffing up the fragrance of *whole miles of dinners*.[1]

When travellers by land were bitter cold, and looked wearily on gloomy landscapes, rustling and shuddering in the blast. When mariners at sea, outlying upon icy yards, were tossed and swung above the howling ocean dreadfully. When lighthouses, on rocks and headlands, showed solitary and watchful; and benighted sea-birds breasted on against their ponderous lanterns, and fell dead.

When, in rustic places, the last glimmering of daylight died away from the ends of avenues; and the trees were sullen and black. When, in parks and woods, the high wet fern and sodden moss, and beds of fallen leaves, and trunks of trees, were lost to view, in masses of impenetrable shade. When mists arose from dyke, and fen, and river. When lights in old halls and in cottage windows, were a cheerful sight. When the mill stopped, the wheelwright and the blacksmith shut their workshops, the turnpike-gate closed, the plough and harrow were left lonely in the fields, the labourer and team went home, and the striking of the church-clock had a deeper sound than at noon, and the church-yard wicket would be swung no more that night.

When twilight everywhere released the shadows, prisoned up all day, that now closed in and gathered like mustering swarms of ghosts. When they stood lowering, in corners of rooms, and frowned out from behind half-opened doors. When they had full possession of unoccupied apartments. When they danced upon the floors, and walls, and ceilings of inhabited chambers, while the fire was low, and withdrew like ebbing waters when it sprung into a blaze.

When these shadows brought into the minds of older people, other thoughts, and showed them different images, and they stole from their retreats, in the likenesses of forms and faces from the past, from the grave, from the deep, deep gulf, where the things that might have been, and never were, are always wandering; you should have seen him then. †

When a knock came at his door, and roused him.

[1] One of the few underlinings in this script: and there are three vertical lines in the margin against this phrase.

'Who's that?' said he. 'Come in!'

Surely there had been *no* figure leaning on the back of his chair; *no* face looking over it. It is certain that *no* gliding footstep touched the floor, as he lifted up his head, with a start, and spoke. And yet there was *no* mirror in the room on whose surface his own form could have cast its shadow for a moment; and Something *had* passed darkly and gone![1]

'I'm humbly fearful, sir,' said a fresh-coloured busy man, holding the door open with his foot for the admission of himself and a wooden tray, and letting it go by very gentle and careful degrees, when he and the tray had got in, 'that it's a good bit past the time to-night. But Mrs. William has been taken off her legs so often——'

'By the wind? I have heard it rising.'

'—By the wind, sir—that it's a mercy she got home at all. Oh dear, yes! It was by the wind, Mr. Redlaw. By the wind. † Mrs. William is of course subject at any time, sir, to be taken off her balance by the elements. She is not formed superior to *that*.'[2] †

'True, William,' was the abstracted answer.

'Quite ready for the fowl and mashed potatoes, sir? Mrs. William said she'd dish in ten minutes when I left the Lodge.'

'I am quite ready,' said the other, waking as from a dream, and walking slowly to and fro. †

He brought the plate to the table, upon which he half laid and half dropped it, with a lively sense of its being thoroughly heated, just as *she* entered the room, bearing another tray and a lantern, and followed by a venerable old man with long grey hair.

Mrs. William was a simple, innocent-looking person, in whose smooth cheeks the cheerful red of her husband's official waistcoat was very pleasantly repeated. †

Without any show of hurry or noise, or any show of herself even, she was so calm and quiet, Milly set the dishes she had brought upon the table.

'What is that the old man has in his arms?' asked Mr. Redlaw, as he sat down to his solitary meal.

'Holly, sir,' replied the quiet voice of Milly.

'That's what I say, sir,' interposed Mr. William. 'Berries is so seasonable to the time of year!'

'Another Christmas come, another year gone!' murmured the Chemist, with a gloomy sigh. 'More figures in the lengthening sum of recollection that we work and work at to our torment, till Death idly jumbles all together, and rubs all out. So, Philip!'[3]

---

[1] All underlinings in this paragraph double. In the margin, at the end of the paragraph is the letter *l* (or *e*?): again, purpose unknown.

[2] *that* italic in *1848*.

[3] This paragraph has been ringed by Dickens, and in the margin there is again the letter *l*.

'My duty to you, sir,' returned the old man. 'Merry Christmas, sir, and happy New Year, and many of 'em. Have had a pretty many of 'em myself—ha, ha!—and may take the liberty of wishing 'em. I'm eighty-seven!'

'Have you had so many that were merry and happy?' asked the other.

'Ay, sir, ever so many,' returned the old man.

'Is his memory impaired with age? It is to be expected now,' said Mr. Redlaw, turning to the son, and speaking lower.

'Not a morsel of it, sir,' replied Mr. William. 'There never was such a memory as my father's. He's the most wonderful man in the world. He don't know what forgetting means.'

The Chemist, rising, walked across the room to where the old man stood looking at a little sprig of holly in his hand.

'It recals the time when many of those years were old and new, then?' he said, observing him attentively, and touching him on the shoulder. 'Does it?'

'Oh many, many!' said Philip, half awaking from his reverie. 'I 'm eighty-seven!'

'Merry and happy, was it?' asked the Chemist in a low voice. 'Merry and happy, old man?'

'May-be as high as that, no higher,' said the old man, holding out his hand a little way above the level of his knee, 'when I first remember 'em! Cold, sunshiny day it was, out-a-walking, when some one—it was my mother as sure as you stand there, though I don't know what her blessed face was like, for she took ill and died that Christmas-time—told me they were food for birds. The pretty little fellow thought—that's me, you understand—that birds' eyes were so bright, perhaps, because the berries that they lived on in the winter were so bright. I recollect that. And I 'm eighty-seven!'

'Merry and happy!' mused the other. 'Merry and happy—and remember well?'

'Ay, ay, ay!' resumed the old man, 'I remember 'em well in my school time, year after year, and all the merry-making that used to come along with them. His mother and I, have sat among 'em all, boys and girls, little children and babies, many a year, when the berries like these were not shining half so bright all round us, as their bright faces. Many of 'em are gone; she's gone; and my son George is fallen very low: but I can see them, when I look here, alive and healthy, as they used to be in those days; and I can see him, thank God, in his innocence. It is a blessed thing to me, at eighty-seven. When my circumstances got to be not so good as formerly, through not being honestly dealt by, and I first come here to be custodian,' said the old man, '—which was more than half a century ago. It was quite a pleasure to know that one of our founders—or more correctly speaking,' said the old man, with a great glory in his subject, 'one of the learned gentlemen that helped endow us in Queen Elizabeth's time, for we were founded afore her day—left in his will, among the other bequests he made us, so much to buy holly, for garnishing the walls and windows, come Christmas. There was something homely and friendly in it. Being but strange here, then, and coming at Christmas time, we took a liking for his very picter that hangs in what used to be our great Dinner Hall.—A sedate gentleman in a peaked beard, with a ruff round his neck, and a scroll below him, in old English letters, "Lord! keep my memory green!" He has helped to keep *my*[1] memory green, I thank him; for going round the building every year, as I 'm a doing now, and freshening up the bare rooms with these branches and berries, freshens up my bare old brain. One year brings back another, and that year another, and those other numbers!

'So you see, sir,' pursued old Philip, whose hale wintry cheek had warmed into a ruddier glow, and whose blue eyes had brightened, while he spoke, 'I have plenty to keep, when I keep this present season. Now, where's my quiet Mouse? Chattering's the sin of my time of life, and there's half the building to do yet, if the cold don't freeze us first, or the wind don't blow us away, or the darkness don't swallow us up.'

The quiet Mouse had brought her calm face to his side, and silently taken his arm, before he finished speaking.

'Come away, my dear,' said the old man. 'Mr. Redlaw won't settle to his dinner, otherwise, till it's cold as the winter. I hope you'll excuse me rambling on, sir, and I wish you good night, and once again, a merry—'

'Stay!' said Mr. Redlaw, resuming his place. 'Spare me another moment, Philip. William, you were going to tell me something to your excellent wife's honour. It will not be disagreeable to her to hear you praise her. What was it?'

'Why, that's where it is, you see, sir,' returned Mr. William Swidger, looking towards his wife in considerable embarrassment. 'Mrs. William 's got her eye upon me.' †

'I didn't know,' said Milly, with a quiet frankness, free from any haste or confusion, 'that William had said anything about it, or I wouldn't have come. I asked him not to. It's a sick young gentleman, sir—and very poor, I am afraid—who is too ill to go home this holiday-time, and lives, unknown to any one, in but a common kind of lodging for a gentleman, down in Jerusalem Buildings. That's all, sir.'

'Why have I never heard of him?' said the Chemist, rising hurriedly. 'Why has he not made his situation known to me? Sick!—give me my hat and cloak. Poor!—what house?—what number?'

'Oh, you mustn't go there, sir,' said Milly, leaving her father-in-law, and calmly confronting him with her collected little face and folded hands.

---

[1] *my* italic in *1848*.

'Not go there?'

'Oh dear, no! It could n't be thought of!'

'What do you mean? Why not?' †

'He said that of all the world he would not be known to you, or receive help from you—though he is a student in your class. I have made no terms of secrecy with you, but I trust to your honour completely.'

'Why did he say so?'

'Indeed I can't tell, sir,' said Milly, after thinking a little, 'because I am not at all clever, you know; and I wanted to be useful to him in making things neat and comfortable about him, and employed myself that way. But I know he is poor, and lonely, and I think he is somehow neglected too.'

The room had darkened. There was a shadow gathering behind the Chemist's chair.

'What more about him?' he asked.

'He is engaged to be married when he can afford it,' said Milly, 'and is studying, I think, to qualify himself to earn a living. I have seen, a long time, that he has studied hard and denied himself much.—He muttered in his broken sleep yesterday afternoon, after talking to me' (this was to herself) 'about some one dead, and some great wrong done that could never be forgotten; but whether to him or to another person, I don't know. Not *by*[1] him, I am sure.'

'And, in short, Mrs. William, you see,' said Mr. William, † 'not content with this, sir, finds, this very night, when she was coming home, a creature more like a young wild beast than a young child, shivering upon a door-step. What does Mrs. William do, but brings it home to dry, feed, and keep it, till our old Bounty of food and flannel is given away, on Christmas morning! If it ever felt a fire before, it 's as much as it ever did; for it 's sitting in the old Lodge chimney, staring at ours as if its ravenous eyes would never shut again. It's sitting there, at least,' said Mr. William, correcting himself, on reflection, 'unless it 's bolted!'

'Heaven keep her happy!' said the Chemist aloud, 'and you too, Philip! and you, William.'

'I thankee, sir, I thankee!' said the old man, 'for Mouse, and for my son William, and for myself. "Lord keep my memory green!" It 's a very good prayer, Mr. Redlaw, "Lord keep my memory green!" It 's very pious, sir. Amen!'

As they passed out, the room turned darker.

As he fell a-musing in his chair alone, the healthy holly withered on the wall, and dropped—dead branches.

As the gloom and shadow thickened behind him, in that place where it had been gathering so darkly, it took, by slow degrees—an awful likeness of himself!

[1] *my* italic in *1848*.

Ghastly and cold, colourless in its leaden face and hands, but with his features, and his bright eyes, and his grizzled hair, and dressed in the gloomy shadow of his dress, it came into its terrible appearance of existence, motionless, without a sound. As *he*[1] leaned his arm upon the elbow of his chair, ruminating before the fire, *it* leaned upon the chairback, close above him, with its appalling copy of his face looking where his face looked, and bearing the expression his face bore.

This, then, was the Something that had passed and gone already. This was the dread companion of the haunted man!

At length he spoke; without moving or lifting up his face.

'Here again!' he said.

'Here again,' replied the Phantom.

'I see you in the fire,' said the haunted man; 'I hear you in music, in the wind, in the dead stillness of the night. Why do you come, to haunt me thus?'

'I come as I am called,' replied the Ghost.

'No. Unbidden,' exclaimed the Chemist.

'Unbidden be it,' said the Spectre. 'It is enough. I am here.'

Hitherto the light of the fire had shone on the two faces—if the dread lineaments behind the chair might be called a face—both addressed towards it, as at first, and neither looking at the other. But, now, the haunted man turned, suddenly, and stared upon the Ghost. The Ghost, as sudden in its motion, passed to before the chair, and stared on him.

An awful survey, in a lonely and remote part of an empty old pile of building, on a winter night, with the loud wind going by upon its journey of mystery—whence, or whither, no man knowing since the world began—and the stars, in unimaginable millions, glittering through it, from eternal space, where the world's bulk is as a grain, and its hoary age is infancy.

'Look upon me!' said the Spectre. 'I am he, neglected in my youth, and miserably poor, who strove and suffered, and still strove and suffered. No mother's self-denying love, no father's counsel, aided *me*.[2] A stranger came into my father's place when I was but a child, and I was easily an alien from my mother's heart. I am he who, in this struggle upward, found a friend. I made him—won him—bound him to me! We worked together, side by side. All the love and confidence that in my earlier youth had had no outlet, and found no expression, I bestowed on him.'

'Not all,' said Redlaw.

'No, not all,' returned the Phantom. 'I had a sister. Such glimpses of the light of home as I had ever known, streamed from her. How young she was, how fair, how loving! I took her to the first poor roof that I was master of, and made it rich. She came into the darkness of my life, and

---

[1] *he* and *it* below italic in *1848*.
[2] *me* italic in *1848*.

made it bright.—She is before me! *Did* he love her?' said the Phantom, echoing his contemplative tone.[1] 'I think he did, once. I am sure he did. Better had she loved him less—less secretly, less dearly, from the shallower depths of a more divided heart! A dream, like hers, stole upon my own life. A love, as like hers,' pursued the Phantom, 'as my inferior nature might cherish, arose in my own heart. I was too poor to bind its object to my fortune then, by any thread of promise or entreaty. I loved her far too well, to seek to do it. But, more than ever I had striven in my life, I strove to climb! Only an inch gained, brought me something nearer to the height. I toiled up! In the late pauses of my labour at that time,—my sister (sweet companion!) still sharing with me the expiring embers and the cooling hearth,—when day was breaking, what pictures of the future did I see!

'—Pictures of my own domestic life, in after-time, with her who was the inspiration of my toil. Pictures of my sister, made the wife of my dear friend, on equal terms—for he had some inheritance, we none—pictures of our sobered age and mellowed happiness, and of the golden links, extending back so far, that should bind us, and our children, in a radiant garland,' said the Phantom.

'Pictures,' said the haunted man, 'that were delusions.'

'Delusions,' echoed the Phantom in its changeless voice, and glaring on him with its changeless eyes. 'For my friend (in whose breast my confidence was locked as in my own), passing between me and the centre of the system of my hopes and struggles, won her to himself, and shattered my frail universe. My sister lived on to see me famous, and then—'

'Then died,' he interposed. 'Died, gentle as ever.' †

'Thus,' said the Phantom, 'I bear within me a Sorrow and a Wrong. Thus I prey upon myself. Thus, memory is my curse; and, if I could forget my sorrow and my wrong, I would!' †

'Evil spirit of myself,' returned the haunted man, in a low, trembling tone, 'my life is darkened by that incessant whisper.'

'It is an echo,' said the Phantom.

'If it be an echo of my thoughts—as now, indeed, I know it is,' rejoined the haunted man, 'why should I, therefore, be tormented? It is not a selfish thought. I suffer it to range beyond myself. All men and women have their sorrows,—most of them their wrongs; ingratitude, and sordid jealousy, and interest, besetting all degrees of life. Who would not forget their sorrows and their wrongs?'

'Who would not, truly, and be the happier and better for it?' said the Phantom. †

'Tempter, I hear again an echo of my own mind.'

---

[1] *Did* italic in *1848*. The 'contemplative tone' was Redlaw's, in a passage deleted; so this phrase too should have been deleted or amended.

'Receive it as a proof that I am powerful,' returned the Ghost. 'Hear what I offer! Forget the sorrow, wrong, and trouble you have known!' 'Forget them!' he repeated.

'I have the power to cancel their remembrance—to leave but very faint, confused traces of them, that will die out soon,' returned the Spectre. 'Say! Is it done?'

'Stay!' cried the haunted man. 'What shall I lose, if I assent to this? What else will pass from my remembrance?'

'No knowledge; no result of study; nothing but the intertwisted chain of feelings and associations, each in its turn dependent on, and nourished by, the banished recollections. Those will go.'

'In nothing else?'[1]

The Phantom held its peace.

But having stood before him, silent, for a little while, it moved towards the fire; then stopped. †

'Say,' said the Spectre, 'is it done?'

'Yes, I close the bargain. Yes! I WILL[2] forget my sorrow, wrong, and trouble!'

'Say,' said the Spectre, 'is it done?'

'It is!'

'IT IS. And take this with you, man whom I here renounce! The gift that I have given, you shall give again, go where you will. Without recovering yourself the power that you have yielded up, you shall henceforth destroy its like in all whom you approach. Your wisdom has discovered that the memory of sorrow, wrong, and trouble is the lot of all mankind, and that mankind would be the happier, in its other memories, without it. Go! Be its benefactor! Freed from such remembrance, from this hour, carry involuntarily the blessing of such freedom with you. Its diffusion is inseparable and inalienable from you. Go! Be happy in the good you have won, and in the good you do!'

The Phantom, which had held its bloodless hand above him while it spoke, as if in some unholy invocation, or some ban; and which had gradually advanced its eyes so close to his, that he could see how they did not participate in the terrible smile upon its face, but were a fixed, unalterable, steady horror; melted from before him, and was gone.

As he stood rooted to the spot, a shrill cry reached his ears. †

'Halloa!' he cried. 'This way! Come to the light!' When, as he held the curtain with one hand, and with the other raised the lamp and tried to pierce the gloom.[3]

A bundle of tatters, held together by a hand, in size and form almost an infant's, but, in its greedy, desperate little clutch, a bad old man's. A

---

[1] Dickens should have deleted 'In', which refers to phrases in a preceding speech which has been deleted.　　[2] WILL, and IS (below), small capitals in *1848*.
[3] *sic*: Dickens has deleted the terrible boy's entrance.

face rounded and smoothed by some half-dozen years, but pinched and twisted by the experiences of a life. Bright eyes, but not youthful. Naked feet, beautiful in their childish delicacy,—ugly in the blood and dirt that cracked upon them. A baby savage, a young monster, a child who had never been a child, a creature who might live to take the outward form of man, but who, within, would live and perish a mere beast.

Used, already, to be worried and hunted like a beast, the boy crouched down as he was looked at, and looked back again, and interposed his arm to ward off the expected blow.

The time had been, and not many minutes since, when such a sight as this would have wrung the Chemist's heart. He looked upon it now, coldly; but, with a heavy effort to remember something—he did not know what—he asked the boy what he did there, and whence he came.

'Where's the woman? Her that brought me here, and set me by the large fire. She was so long gone, that I went to look for her, and lost myself. I don't want you. I want the woman.' †

The Chemist led him to the door. 'This way,' he said. 'I'll take you to her.' †

'The gift that I have given, you shall give again, go where you will!'

The Phantom's words were blowing in the wind, and the wind blew chill upon him.

'Boy! straight down this long-arched passage, and past the great dark door into the yard,—you will see the fire shining on a window there.'

'The woman's fire?' inquired the boy.

He nodded, and the naked feet had sprung away. He came back with his lamp, locked his door hastily, and sat down in his chair, covering his face like one who was frightened at himself.

For now he was, indeed, alone.

CHAPTER II

The Gift Diffused

A SMALL man sat in a small parlour, in company with any amount of small children you may please to name. † The small man was the father of the family, and the chief of the firm described in the inscription over the little shop front, by the name of A. TETTERBY AND CO., NEWSMEN.[1] †

Mrs. Tetterby laid the cloth, but rather as if she were punishing the table than preparing the family supper; hitting it unnecessarily hard with the knives and forks, slapping it with the plates, denting it with the salt-cellar, and coming heavily down upon it with the loaf. †

Mrs. Tetterby finished her preparations, and took, from her ample basket, a substantial slab of hot pease pudding wrapped in paper, and a

[1] Small capitals in *1848*. Here 26 pages are reduced to 400 words.

basin covered with a saucer, which, on being uncovered, sent forth an odour so agreeable, that the three pair of eyes in the two beds opened wide and fixed themselves upon the banquet. †

There might have been more pork on the knucklebone,—which knucklebone the carver at the cook's shop had assuredly not forgotten in carving for previous customers,—but there was no stint of seasoning, and that is an accessory dreamily suggesting pork, and pleasantly cheating the sense of taste. The pease pudding, too, the gravy and mustard, if they were not absolutely pork, had lived near it; so, upon the whole, there was the flavour of a *middle*-sized pig!!! It was irresistible to the Tetterbys in bed, who, though professing to slumber peacefully, crawled out when unseen by their parents, and silently appealed to their brothers for any gastronomic token of fraternal affection. They, not hard of heart, presenting scraps in return, it resulted that a party of light skirmishers in nightgowns were careering about the parlour all through supper, which harassed Mr. Tetterby exceedingly, and once or twice imposed upon him the necessity of a charge, before which these guerilla troops retired in all directions and in great confusion. †

MRS. T.[1] started up with a scream, and ran behind her husband. Her cry was so terrified, that the children started from their sleep and from their beds, and clung about her. Nor did her gaze belie her voice, as she pointed to a pale man in a black cloak who had come into the room.

'Look at that man! Look there! What does he want?' †

Her husband, who had not been altogether free from the present strangeness of her manner, addressed himself to the pale visitor in the black cloak, who stood still, and whose eyes were bent upon the ground.

'What may be your pleasure, sir?' he asked.

'I fear that my coming in unperceived,' returned the visitor, 'has alarmed you.'

'My little woman says that it's not the first time you have alarmed her.'

'My name is Redlaw. I come from the old college hard by. A young gentleman who is a student there, lodges in your house, does he not?'

'Mr. Denham?' said Tetterby.

'Yes.' †

'The gentleman's room,' said Tetterby, 'is up stairs, sir. There's a more convenient private entrance: go up to him that way, if you wish to see him.'

'Yes, I wish to see him,' said the Chemist. 'Can you spare a light?'

The watchfulness of his haggard look, and the inexplicable distrust that darkened it, seemed to trouble Mr. Tetterby. He paused; and at length said, 'I'll light you, sir, if you'll follow me.'

---

[1] Dickens has written in 'MRS. T'; and in the left margin there is a pointing finger, and in the right margin three vertical lines: probably not a sign of emphasis, but rather Dickens's indication to himself that the script resumes here after a six-page deletion.

'No,' replied the Chemist, 'I would rather go alone. Please give me the light, if you can spare it, and I'll find the way.'

In taking the candle from the newsman, he touched him on the breast. Withdrawing his hand hastily, almost as though he had wounded him by accident, he turned and ascended the stair. †

There was a door before him, and he knocked at it. Being invited, by a voice within, to enter, he complied.

'Is that my kind nurse?' said the voice.

It spoke cheerfully, though in a languid tone, and attracted his attention to a young man lying on a couch, drawn before the chimney-piece, with the back towards the door. †

The student raised himself on the couch, and turned his head.

'Mr. Redlaw!' he exclaimed, and started up.

Redlaw put out his arm.

'Don't come nearer to me. I will sit here. Remain you, where you are! I heard, by an accident, by what accident is no matter, that one of my class was ill and solitary. I received no other description of him, than that he lived in this street. Beginning my inquiries at the first house in it, I have found him.'

'I have been ill, sir,' returned the student, not merely with a modest hesitation, but with a kind of awe of him, 'but am greatly better. An attack of fever—of the brain, I believe—has weakened me, but I am much better. I cannot say I have been solitary, in my illness, or I should forget the ministering hand that has been near me.' †

'And why?' said the Chemist; not with the least expression of interest, but with a moody, wayward kind of curiosity. 'Why? How comes it that you have sought to keep especially from me, the knowledge of your remaining here, at this season, when all the rest have dispersed, and of your being ill? I want to know why this is?' †

'Mr. Redlaw,' said the student, 'as a just man, and a good man, think how innocent I am, except in name and descent, of participation in any wrong inflicted on you, or in any sorrow you have borne.'

'Sorrow!' said Redlaw, laughing. 'Wrong! What are those to me?'

'For Heaven's sake,' entreated the shrinking student, 'do not let the mere interchange of a few words with me change you like this, sir! Let me pass from your knowledge and notice. Let me occupy my old reserved and distant place among those whom you instruct. † From infancy, I have heard you spoken of with[1] honour and respect—with something that was almost reverence. I have heard of such devotion, of such fortitude and tenderness, of such rising up against the obstacles which press men down, that my fancy, since I learnt my little lesson from my mother, has shed a lustre on your name.' †

---

[1] The words 'From infancy, I have heard you spoken of with' (one line in *1848*) are deleted in *Suzannet*: Dickens's mistake—he deleted one line too many.

'The past is past,' said the Chemist. 'It dies like the brutes. Who talks to me of its traces in my life? He raves or lies! What have I to do with your distempered dreams? If you want money, here it is. I came to offer it; and that is all I came for. There can be nothing else that brings me here.'

He tossed his purse upon the table.

'Take it back, sir,' he said proudly, though not angrily.

The Chemist went close to him, for the first time, and took the purse, and turned him by the arm, and looked him in the face.

'There is sorrow and trouble in sickness, is there not?' he demanded with a laugh.

The wondering student answered, 'Yes.'

'In its unrest, in its anxiety, in its suspense, in all its train of physical and mental miseries?' said the Chemist, with a wild unearthly exultation. 'All best forgotten, are they not?'

The student did not answer, but Redlaw still held him by the sleeve, when Milly's voice was heard outside.

Redlaw released his hold, as he listened.

'Of all the visitors who could come here, this is the one I should desire most to avoid. Hide me!'

The student opened a frail door in the wall, communicating, where the garret-roof began to slope towards the floor, with a small inner room. Redlaw passed in hastily, and shut it after him. †

When she went away, Redlaw came out of his concealment.

'When sickness lays its hand on you again,' he said, looking fiercely back at him, '—may it be soon!—Die here! Rot here!'

'What have you done?' returned the other, catching at his cloak. 'What change have you wrought in me? What curse have you brought upon me? Give me back myself!'

'Give me back *my*self!'[1] exclaimed Redlaw like a madman. 'I am infected! I am infectious! I am charged with poison for my own mind, and the minds of all mankind. Where I felt interest, compassion, sympathy, I am turning into stone. Selfishness and ingratitude spring up in my blighting footsteps. I am only so much less base than the wretches whom I make so, that in the moment of their transformation I can hate them.'

As he spoke—the young man still holding to his cloak—he cast him off, and struck him: then, wildly hurried out into the night air where the wind was blowing, the snow falling, the cloud-drift sweeping on, the moon dimly shining; and where, blowing in the wind, falling with the snow, drifting with the clouds, shining in the moonlight, and heavily looming in the darkness, were the Phantom's words, 'The gift that I have given, you shall give again, go where you will!'

Whither he went, he neither knew nor cared, so that he avoided company. The change he felt within him made the busy streets a desert, and

[1] *my* italic in *1848*.

himself a desert, and the multitude around him, in their manifold en-
durances and ways of life, a mighty waste of sand, which the winds
tossed into unintelligible heaps and made a ruinous confusion of. Those
traces in his breast which the Phantom had told him would 'die out soon,'
were not, as yet, so far upon their way to death, but that he understood
enough of what he was, and what he made of others, to desire to be alone. †

He directed his steps back to the old college, and to that part of it
where the general porch was, and where, alone, the pavement was worn
by the tread of the students' feet.

The keeper's house stood just within the iron gates, forming a part of
the chief quadrangle. There was a little cloister outside, and from that
sheltered place he knew he could look in at the window of their ordinary
room, and see who was within. The iron gates were shut, but his hand was
familiar with the fastening, and drawing it back by thrusting in his wrist
between the bars, he passed through softly, shut it again, and crept up to
the window, crumbling the thin crust of snow with his feet.

The fire, to which he had directed the boy last night, shining brightly
through the glass, made an illuminated place upon the ground. Instinctively avoiding this, and going round it, he looked in at the window. At
first, he thought that there was no one there, and that the blaze was
reddening only the old beams in the ceiling and the dark walls; but
peering in more narrowly, he saw the object of his search coiled asleep
before it on the floor. He passed quickly to the door, opened it, and went
in.

The creature lay in such a fiery heat, that, as the Chemist stooped to
rouse him, it scorched his head. So soon as he was touched, the boy, not half
awake, clutching his rags together with the instinct of flight upon him,
half rolled and half ran into a distant corner of the room, where, heaped
upon the ground, he struck his foot out to defend himself.

'Get up!' said the Chemist. 'You have not forgotten me?'

'You let me alone!' returned the boy. 'This is the woman's house—not
yours.'

The Chemist's steady eye controlled him somewhat, or inspired him
with enough submission to be raised upon his feet, and looked at. †

'Where are they?' he inquired.

'The woman's out.'

'I know she is. Where is the old man with the white hair, and his son?'

'Out. Something's the matter, somewhere. They were fetched out in a
hurry, and told me to stop here.'

'Come with me,' said the Chemist, 'and I'll give you money.' †

'Will you let me walk by myself, and never hold me, nor yet touch me?'
said the boy.

'I will!'

'And let me go before, behind, or anyways I like?'

'I will!'

'Give me some money first then, and I'll go.'

The Chemist laid a few shillings one by one, in his extended hand.

Redlaw then wrote with his pencil on a leaf of his pocket-book, that the boy was with him; and laying it on the table, signed to him to follow. Keeping his rags together, as usual, the boy complied, and went out with his bare head and his naked feet into the winter night. †

Three times, in their progress, they were side by side. Three times they stopped, being side by side. Three times the Chemist glanced down at his face, and shuddered as it forced upon him one reflection.

The first occasion was when they were crossing an old churchyard, and Redlaw stopped among the graves, utterly at a loss how to connect them with any tender, softening, or consolatory thought.

The second was, when the breaking forth of the moon induced him to look up at the Heavens, where he saw her in her glory, surrounded by a host of stars he still knew by the names and histories which human science has appended to them; but where he saw nothing else he had been wont to see, felt nothing he had been wont to feel, in looking up there, on a bright night.

The third was when he stopped to listen to a plaintive strain of music, but could only hear a tune, made manifest to him by the dry mechanism of the instruments and his own ears, with no address to any mystery within him, without a whisper in it of the past, or of the future, powerless upon him as the sound of last year's running water, or the rushing of last year's wind.

At each of these three times, he saw with horror that, in spite of the vast intellectual distance between them, and their being unlike each other in all physical respects, the expression on the boy's face was the expression on his own.

They journeyed on for some time—until they arrived at a ruinous collection of houses, and the boy touched him and stopped.

'In there!' he said, pointing out one house with 'Lodgings for Travellers' painted on it.

Redlaw looked about him; from the houses, to the child, close to him, cowering and trembling with the cold, and limping on one little foot while he coiled the other round his leg to warm it, yet staring at all these things with that frightful likeness of expression so apparent in his face, that Redlaw started from him.

'In there!' said the boy, pointing out the house again. 'I'll wait.'

'Will they let me in?' asked Redlaw.

'Say you're a doctor,' he answered with a nod. †

He gathered his cloak about him, and glided swiftly up the stairs. Opposite to him, on the landing, was a door, which stood partly open, and which, as he ascended, a man with a candle in his hand, came forward from within to shut. But this man, on seeing him, drew back, with much emotion in his manner, and, as if by a sudden impulse, mentioned his name aloud.

In the surprise of such a recognition there, he stopped, endeavouring to recollect the wan and startled face. He had no time to consider it, for, to his yet greater amazement, old Philip came out of the room, and took him by the hand.

Redlaw, with a bewildered look, submitted to be led into the room. A man lay there, on a truckle-bed, and William Swidger stood at the bedside.

'Too late!' murmured the old man, looking wistfully into the Chemist's face; and the tears stole down his cheeks.

Redlaw paused at the bedside, and looked down on the figure that was stretched upon the mattress. It was that of a man, who should have been in the vigour of his life, but on whom it was not likely that the sun would ever shine again. The vices of his forty or fifty years' career had so branded him, that, in comparison with their effects upon his face, the heavy hand of time upon the old man's face who watched him, had been merciful and beautifying.

'Who is this?' asked the Chemist, looking round.

'My son George, Mr. Redlaw,' said the old man, wringing his hands. 'My eldest son, George, who was more his mother's pride than all the rest!'

Redlaw's eyes wandered from the old man's grey head, as he laid it down upon the bed, to the person who had recognized him, and who had kept aloof, in the remotest corner of the room. He seemed to be about his own age; and although he knew no such hopelessly decayed and broken man as he appeared to be, there was something in the turn of his figure, as he stood with his back towards him, and now went out at the door, that made him pass his hand uneasily across his brow. †

Redlaw retired a little, debating with himself whether to shun the house that moment, or remain.

But he stayed, and, shrouded in his black cloak with his face turned from them, stood away from the bedside, listening to what they said, as if he felt himself a demon in the place.

'Father!' murmured the sick man, rallying a little from his stupor.

'My boy! My son George!' said old Philip.

'You spoke, just now, of my being mother's favourite, long ago. It's a dreadful thing to think now, of long ago!'

'No, no, no;' returned the old man. 'Think of it. Don't say it's dreadful. It's not dreadful to me, my son.'

'It cuts you to the heart, father.' For the old man's tears were falling on him.

'Yes, yes,' said Philip, 'so it does; but it does me good. It's a heavy sorrow to think of *that* time, but it does me good, George. Oh, think of it too, think of it too, and your heart will be softened more and more! Where's my son William? William, my boy, your mother loved him dearly to the last, and with her latest breath said, "Tell him I forgave him, blessed him, and prayed for him." Those were her words to me. I have never forgotten them, and I'm eighty-seven!'

'Father!' said the man upon the bed, 'I am dying, I know. I am so far gone, that I can hardly speak, even of what my mind most runs on. Is there any hope for me, beyond this bed?'

'There is hope,' returned the old man, 'for all who are softened and penitent. I was thankful, only yesterday, that I could remember this unhappy son when he was an innocent child. But what a comfort is it, now, to think that even God himself has that remembrance of him!'

Redlaw spread his hands upon his face, and shrunk, like a murderer.

'Ah!' feebly moaned the man upon the bed. 'The waste since then, the waste of life since then!'

'But he was a child once,' said the old man. 'He played with children. Before he lay down on his bed at night, and fell into his guiltless rest, he said his prayers at his poor mother's knee. I have seen him do it, many a time; and seen her lay his head upon her breast, and kiss him. Sorrowful as it was to her, and me, to think of this, when he went so wrong, and when our hopes and plans for him were all broken, this gave him still a hold upon us, that nothing else could have given. Oh, Father, so much better than the fathers upon earth! Oh, Father, so much more afflicted by the errors of thy children! take this wanderer back! Not as he is, but as he was then, let him cry to thee, as he has so often seemed to cry to us!'

As the old man lifted up his trembling hands, the son, for whom he made the supplication, laid his sinking head against him for support and comfort, as if he were indeed the child of whom he spoke.

When did man ever tremble, as Redlaw trembled, in the silence that ensued! He knew it must come upon them, knew that it was coming fast.

'My time is very short, my breath is shorter,' said the sick man, supporting himself on one arm, and with the other groping in the air, 'and I remember there is something on my mind concerning the man who was here just now. Father and William—wait!—is there really anything in black, out there?'

'Yes, yes, it is real,' said his aged father.

'Is it a man?'

'It's Mr. Redlaw.'

'I thought I had dreamed of him. Ask him to come here.'

The Chemist, whiter than the dying man, appeared before him. Obedient to the motion of his hand, he sat upon the bed.

'It has been so ripped up, to-night, sir,' said the sick man, laying his hand upon his heart, with a look in which the mute, imploring agony of his condition was concentrated, 'by the sight of my poor old father, and the thought of all the trouble I have been the cause of, and all the wrong and sorrow lying at my door,—that what I *can*[1] do right, with my mind running on so much, so fast, I'll try to do. There was another man here. Did you see him?'

Redlaw could not reply by any word; for when he saw that fatal sign he knew so well now, of the wandering hand upon the forehead, his voice died at his lips. But he made some indication of assent.

'He is penniless, hungry, and destitute. He is completely beaten down, and has no resource at all. Look after him! Lose no time! I know he has it in his mind to kill himself.'

It was working. It was on his face. His face was changing, hardening, deepening in all its shades, and losing all its sorrow.

'Don't you remember? Don't you know him?' he pursued.

He shut his face out for a moment, with the hand that again wandered over his forehead, and then it lowered on Redlaw, reckless, ruffianly, and callous.

'Why,' he said, scowling round, 'what have you been doing to me here! I have lived bold, and I mean to die bold.'

And so lay down upon his bed, and put his arms up, over his head and ears, as resolute from that time to keep out all access, and to die in his indifference.

If Redlaw had been struck by lightning, it could not have struck him from the bedside with a more tremendous shock. But the old man, who had left the bed while his son was speaking to him, now returning, avoided it quickly likewise, and with abhorrence.

'Where's my boy William?' said the old man hurriedly. 'William, come away from here. We'll go home.'

'Home, father!' returned William. 'Are you going to leave your own son?'

'Where's my own son?' replied the old man.

'Where? why, there!'

'That's no son of mine,' said Philip, trembling with resentment. 'No such wretch as that, has any claim on me. My children are pleasant to look at, and they wait upon me, and get my meat and drink ready, and are useful to me. I've a right to it! I'm eighty-seven!'

'You're old enough to be no older,' muttered William, looking at him grudgingly, with his hands in his pockets. 'I don't know what good you are, myself. We could have a deal more pleasure without you.' †

'I—I'm eighty-seven,' said the old man, rambling on, childlishly and weakly, 'and I don't know as I ever was much put out by anything.

---

[1] *can* italic in *1848*.

I'm not a going to begin now, because of what he calls my son. He's not my son.'

In his drowsy chuckling, and the shaking of his head, he put his hands into his waistcoat pockets. In one of them he found a bit of holly (left there, probably last night), which he now took out, and looked at. 'Berries, eh?' said the old man. 'Ah! It's a pity they're not good to eat. There's good cheer when there's berries. Well; I ought to have my share of it, and to be waited on, and kept warm and comfortable; for I'm eighty-seven, and a poor old man. I'm eigh-ty-seven. Eigh-ty-seven!'

The drivelling, pitiable manner in which, as he repeated this, he nibbled at the leaves, and spat the morsels out; the cold, uninterested eye with which his youngest son (so changed) regarded him; the determined apathy with which his eldest son lay hardened in his sin; impressed themselves no more on Redlaw's observation,—for he broke his way from the spot to which his feet seemed to have been fixed, and ran out of the house.

His guide came crawling forth from his place of refuge, and was ready for him before he reached the arches.

'Back to the woman's?' he inquired.

'Back, quickly!' answered Redlaw. 'Stop nowhere on the way!'[1] †

The stillness of the room was broken by the boy (whom he had seen listening) starting up, and running towards the door.

'Here's the woman coming!' he exclaimed.

The Chemist stopped him on his way, at the moment when she knocked.

'Let me go to her, will you?' said the boy.

'Not now,' returned the Chemist. 'Stay here. Nobody must pass in or out of the room, now. Who's that?'

'It's I, sir,' cried Milly. 'Pray, sir, let me in!'

'No! not for the world!' he said.

'Mr. Redlaw, Mr. Redlaw, pray, sir, let me in.'

'What is the matter?' he said, holding the boy.

'The miserable man you saw, is worse, and nothing I can say will wake him from his terrible infatuation. William's father has turned childish in a moment. William himself is changed. The shock has been too sudden for him; I cannot understand him; he is not like himself. Mr. Redlaw! George has been muttering, in his doze, about the man you saw there,

---

[1] The remainder of this page (p. 129) in *Suzannet* is a mass of crossings-out, painting-out (in red paint), marginal crosses, a pointing hand, a marginal balloon (empty), and a long marginal squiggle. The conventions of deletion and restoration of text are not those which Dickens was to use later; in this respect, as in others, *The Haunted Man* was an experiment in his procedures as an adaptor. Probably he intended to *stet* part of the deleted words, so that the script would have included a paragraph reading thus: 'Their return was more like a flight than a walk. Shrinking from all who passed, shrouded in his cloak, and keeping it drawn closely about him, he made no pause until they reached the door by which they had come out. He unlocked it with his key, went in, accompanied by the boy, and hastened through the dark passages to his own chamber.'

who, he fears, will kill himself. He says, in his wandering, that you know him; that he was your friend once, long ago; that he is the ruined father of a student here—my mind misgives me, of the young gentlemen who has been ill.'

All this time he held the boy, who was half-mad to pass him, and let her in.

'Phantoms! Punishers of impious thoughts!' cried Redlaw, gazing round in anguish. 'Look upon me! From the darkness of my mind, let the glimmering of contrition that I know is there, shine up, and show my misery! In the material world, as I have long taught, nothing can be spared; no step or atom in the wondrous structure could be lost, without a blank being made in the great universe. I know, now, that it is the same with good and evil, happiness and sorrow, in the memories of men. Pity me! Relieve me! Shadow of myself! Spirit of my darker hours! Come back, and haunt me day and night, but take this gift away! Or, if it must still rest with me, deprive me of the dreadful power of giving it to others. Undo what I have done. Leave me benighted, but restore the day to those whom I have cursed. As I have spared this woman from the first, and as I never will go forth again, but will die here, with no hand to tend me, save this creature's who is proof against me,—hear me!' †

CHAPTER III

The Gift Reversed

THE shadows upon Redlaw's mind succeeded thick and fast to one another, and obscured its light as the night-clouds hovered between the moon and earth, and kept the latter veiled in darkness. Fitful, uncertain as the shadows which the night-clouds cast, were their imperfect revelations to him; and, like the night-clouds still, if the clear light broke forth for a moment, it was only that they might sweep over it, and make the darkness deeper than before. †

At such a time, the Christmas music he had heard before, began to play. He listened to it at first, as he had listened in the churchyard; but presently—it playing still, and being borne towards him on the night air, in a low, sweet, melancholy strain—he rose, and stood stretching his hands about him, as if there were some friend approaching within his reach, on whom his desolate touch might rest, yet do no harm. As he did this, his face became less fixed and wondering; a gentle trembling came upon him; and at last his eyes filled with tears, and he put his hands before them, and bowed down his head.

His memory of sorrow and wrong had not come back to him; he knew that it was not restored; he had no passing belief or hope that it was. But some dumb stir within him made him capable of being moved by what was hidden, afar off, in the music . . .[1]

---

[1] With two minor verbal alterations in this paragraph, Dickens's attempt to devise a *Haunted Man* script ended. The remainder of the prompt-copy (not here reprinted) is the *1848* text unamended.

THE STORY OF LITTLE DOMBEY

THIS was the first Reading to be created from one of the novels. For the first six weeks of his career as a professional reader, Dickens had read only from the Christmas Books. Then, on 10 June 1858, he performed *The Story of Little Dombey* and, the following week, another new programme of three shorter items, one of which (*Mrs. Gamp*) was extracted from a novel. At first *Little Dombey* was a two-hour Reading like those from the Christmas Books but, by mid-October 1858, he had shortened it (like the *Carol*, the only Christmas Book to survive by then) so that *Boots at the Holly-Tree Inn* or, more often, *The Trial from 'Pickwick'* could be accommodated in the same programme. 'It is our greatest triumph everywhere,' he reported during the first provincial tour (*N*, iii, 59), and it always remained in repertoire though it was not often performed in later years. George Dolby attributed this to his always finding it so painful to read that he never did so 'except by particular request and under the greatest of pressure' (p. 20). Another explanation may be found in Kate Field's remark that, being sad, it was the least popular of all the Readings given in America (Field, p. 64); certainly only one item was performed less often on that tour. It was only given one performance during the final Farewell series in London, in 1870.

Dickens's deciding in 1858 to make this his first big effort to extract a Reading from one of the novels is very understandable. The narrative, being confined to the life of Paul Dombey, is of manageable length—exactly the first quarter of the novel, though many irrelevant developments could of course be omitted. Paul's death, which had ended ch. 16 and the fifth instalment of the novel, provides an obviously effective termination of the Reading. This episode had in 1846 'thrown a whole nation into mourning' (*Life*, p. 477), and it was, with the death of Little Nell, the standard example of his pathetic powers, then very highly esteemed. Moreover, he had already discovered that the early numbers of *Dombey* read very well, for he had read them to some friends in Switzerland, during their composition, with notable success (*Dickensian*, xlvii (1951), 18–19; *Life*, pp. 417, 477, quoted above, p. xix).

He experienced considerable difficulty in devising this script. Two privately printed versions survive from 1858, both extensively amended, and in 1862 or later he worked over another version. The earlier of these is the copy in the Gimbel collection in Yale University Library. It has no title-page, and the title on the first page of the text is simply *Little Dombey*. This text, printed by Bradbury & Evans, is paginated 1–126, but pp. 18–31 (corresponding to Chapter II) are omitted. Dickens's manuscript emendations in this copy are very spasmodic, and almost all occur in the first half of the text; in the second half there are no textual alterations or performance-signs until the final four pages.

A small piece of the manuscript sent to the printers of this version has survived (in the Suzannet Collection at Dickens House, London). This consists of pp. 115 and 116 of the 1848 edition of *Dombey and Son*, much cut and amended, and a page in Dickens's manuscript to be inserted into these printed pages, as indicated by a caret. These pages, about Paul's embarking upon his studies at Blimber's, come from ch. 12 of the novel and provide the conclusion to what became Chapter III of the Reading. As will be seen from the text below, the long manuscript insertion was necessitated by Dickens's having transferred a passage (about Paul and Toots) from near the end of ch. 12 to precede a more plangent passage (about Paul and Florence, but later deleted) on which he wanted to end this Chapter. This appears to be the only scrap of printer's copy for the Readings extant, except for a part of *Mrs. Gamp*: see pp. 117–20 of John D. Gordan's facsimile, mentioned below, p. 182.

The 1858 prompt-copy is also in the Suzannet Collection. It too lacks a title-page, but the title on the first page of its text is *The Story/of/Little Dombey*. It was printed by Bradbury & Evans (text paginated 1–121). Its text is substantially the same as that of *Gimbel*, but some emendations made in *Gimbel* are not adopted in *Suzannet*, and at a few points the texts differ: so *Gimbel* was not a preliminary version leading directly to the *Suzannet* text, but simply one early attempt at selecting and then further abbreviating the text, and only some of its revisions were adopted in the second version printed (presumably) a few weeks later. For further particulars of *Gimbel*, see my account in *Yale University Library Gazette*, xlvi (1972), 153–5.

The 'trade edition' published in 1858 is identical with *Suzannet* except that it corrects a few misprints and is printed in 16mo instead of 8vo: *The Story/ of/ Little Dombey. / By/ Charles Dickens./ London :/ Bradbury & Evans, 11 Bouverie Street./ 1858* (text paginated 1–121, as in *Suzannet*).

In 1858 and later, Dickens revised the *Suzannet* prompt-copy extensively, and its much-amended text was printed in *T & F*. In England, the 1858 'trade edition' had been kept in print, though the version which Dickens was performing diverged increasingly from its text. A copy of the 1862 reprint of this trade edition (published, at that time, by Chapman & Hall) represents another attempt at revising the text. This copy is in the Berg Collection. At some point in 1862 or after, Dickens must have decided to try revising the *Little Dombey* text in another way, but he did not get far with the task. The revisions in *Berg* (all in pencil) consist mostly of long deletions; one sequence of pages simply has the word 'No' written in the top margin. There are few verbal alterations and no performance-signs. The deletions sometimes coincide with those in *Suzannet*, but often not. Clearly *Berg* is a tentative and indeterminate revision, which could never have been used as a prompt-copy.

In all these versions, except *Suzannet* as emended in manuscript (and *T & F*, which was printed from it), the Reading is divided into six Chapters, all but one of which correspond to a chapter in the novel. The Chapters usually begin, and always end, with the same words as do the corresponding chapters in the novel, but the printed text of the prompt-copy (and the 1858 trade edition) was less than half the length of the parts of the novel from which it was derived. Further cuts eventually reduced the length of the script by almost half. The sources of the narrative are as follows: Chapter I from ch. 1 of the novel; Chapter II from ch. 5; Chapter III from ch. 8; Chapter IV from chs. 11 and 12; Chapter V from ch. 14; Chapter VI from ch. 16. Often, however, a phrase or so is borrowed from another chapter. Chapter II (Paul's christening) is deleted in the *Suzannet* prompt-copy, and the Chapters renumbered I to V accordingly. This deletion is also made in *Gimbel*, but that version nevertheless has six Chapters, because what was later one chapter is two in *Gimbel* (both of them, by mistake, numbered V).

Dickens's revisions in *Suzannet*—which is the text printed below—consists largely of the progressive elimination of minor characters. The family doctor, Mr. Pilkins, disappears, and Dr. Parker Peps's role is much reduced (and his name eventually lost). Miss Tox, quite prominent in the printed version, is much cut and finally eliminated altogether. Other characters subjected to similar treatment include Mrs. Wickam, Mr. Chick, Briggs, and Tozer; Mrs. Pipchin is progressively reduced, and all references to Waltar Gay are deleted. During the opening season, as press reports show, the christening was still included, and Miss Tox was still a prominent, and much-enjoyed, character. A major revision must have taken place in October 1858, when it was abbreviated to accommodate an afterpiece in the programme; but sometimes after that *Little Dombey* was given by itself, in matinée performances, and Dickens may have restored some of the cuts on those occasions. One character, however, suffered few cuts, and indeed his speeches had sometimes been amplified beyond what appeared in the novel: Toots. Dickens had immediately, and rightly, guessed that Toots offered splendid opportunities for his gifts as a character-actor.

One other recurrent textual alteration was to alter 'Paul' to 'Little Dombey', in line with the title of the Reading. As this alteration indicates, pathos was of course insistent in this item. Audiences wept during the final chapter, and there was usually a hush before the ensuing applause:

The beautiful chapter in which the little invalid speaks of the language which the waves seemed ever speaking to him of the great hereafter, was, as it deserved to be, received with especial favour, and the applause which greeted it was a tribute, we believe, more to Mr. Dickens as its author than Mr. Dickens as its reader. ... The final words of the ever-to-be-remembered chapter, which brings little Dombey's short life to a close, were received with an applause which would have been enthusiastic but for the feeling which mellowed it and made it almost reverent. (*Cheltenham Examiner*, 28 March 1866)

According to Charles Kent (pp. 30, 178), Dickens was very restrained in his selection and rendering of the pathetic parts of the *Story*; but, in the critical reaction against Dickens's juvenile death-beds from the late 1850s onwards, some critics found self-indulgence more evident than restraint. R. H. Hutton, for instance, remarked that in the presentation of Paul's death and of the water imagery surrounding it,

... he quite fondles his own conception. He used to give it even more of the same effect of high-strung sentimental melodrama, in reading or reciting it, than the written story itself contains. We well remember the mode in which he used to read, 'The golden ripples on the wall ... [etc.]'. It was precisely the pathos of the Adelphi Theatre, and made the most painful impression of pathos feeding upon itself. ('The Genius of Dickens', *Spectator*, 18 June 1870, p. 751)

A similar, and related, difference of opinion appears in accounts of Dickens's impersonation of 'little Dombey'. Some people found this a striking and masterly characterization, 'particularly happy' in the voice he assumed, a suitable 'treble monotone' so managed as to express completely the boy's physical exhaustion and premature decay (Field, pp. 66–7). For others, however, Paul was a dramatic failure: '. . . far from pleasing; the voice instead of being childish was grotesque, and gave us an idea of a weak, fretful, irritable, and peevish child' (*Brighton Gazette*, 18 November 1858).

Most accounts agree on the adequacy (and often much more) of the other characterizations, Dickens's skill in devising and producing suitable voices being specially praised. The great success was Toots. The description of him in the novel set a challenge to any character-actor, and Dickens was judged to have met it triumphantly: '. . . a voice so deep, and a manner so sheepish, that if a lamb had roared it couldn't have been so surprising' (ch. 11, p. 148). Every time Toots had to say 'How do you do?'—and Dickens increased the number of occasions for it—the audience roared its delight. Kate Field's enthusiasm was typical of most critics' reactions:

You may have loved him since childhood, . . . but until you have made Toots's acquaintance through the medium of Dickens, you have no idea how he looks or how he talks. When Toots puts his thumb in his mouth, looks sheepish, and roars forth, 'How are you?' I feel as the man in play must feel when, for the first time, he recognises his long-lost brother with the strawberry-mark on his left arm. Dickens's Toots bears the unmistakeable strawberry-mark. His sheepishness is by no means that of a country bumpkin. Toots is a gentleman. It is such sheepishness as only can accompany a voice that appears to proceed from some cavern ingeniously concealed in Toot's boots. (pp. 70–1)

The prominence of Toots is a reminder of the fact that, although this Reading contained the illness and death of Paul, it was also often very funny.

There is an admirable discussion of the text in this Reading (not available to me when I was preparing this edition) in Appendix D of Alan Horsman's Clarendon Dickens edition of *Dombey and Son* (1974), which draws attention to features here treated less adequately. Another item which came late to hand is Frederick Trautmann, 'Philadelphia bowled clean over: Public Readings by Charles Dickens', *Pennsylvania Magazine of History of Biography*, xcviii (1974), 456–68, which contains much useful information about how Dickens performed there. Philadelphia newspaper accounts of *Little Dombey* include the following details: 'The oppressively dignified Dombey stood before us in all his pompousness and pride'; 'Mrs. Chick fussed and cackled . . . right there upon the platform'; and 'Mrs. Pipchin glared upon us with those ogreish eyes of hers, and smacked her lips over the hot mutton-chops'.

The Story of Little Dombey
Five Chapters[1]

CHAPTER I

Rich Mr. Dombey sat in the corner of his Wife's darkened bedchamber in the great arm-chair by the bedside, and rich Mr. Dombey's Son lay tucked up warm in a little basket, carefully placed on a low settee in front of the fire and close to it, as if his constitution were analogous to that of a muffin, *and it was essential to toast him brown while he was very new.*

Rich Mr. *Dombey* was about eight-and-forty years of age. Rich Mr. Dombey's *son*, about eight-and-forty minutes. *Mr. Dombey* was rather bald, rather red, and rather stern and pompous. *Mr. Dombey's son* was very bald, and very red, and rather crushed and spotty in his general effect, as yet.[2] *

Mr. Dombey, exulting in the long-looked-for event, the birth of a son, jingled his heavy gold watch-chain as he sat in his blue coat and bright buttons by the side of the bed, and said:

'Our house of business will once again be not only in name but in fact Dombey and Son; Dom-bey and Son! † He will be christened Paul— of course. His father's name, Mrs. Dombey, and his grandfather's! I wish his grandfather were alive this day!' And again he said, 'Dom-bey and Son.'

Those three words conveyed the one idea of Mr. Dombey's life. The earth was made for Dombey and Son to trade in, and the sun and moon were made to give them light. Common abbreviations took new meanings in his eyes, and had sole reference to them. A.D. had no concern with anno Domini, but stood for anno Dombei—and Son. *

He had been married ten years, and until this present day on which he sat jingling his gold watch-chain in the great arm-chair by the side of the bed, had had no issue.

—To speak of. There had been a girl some six years before, and she,

---

[1] Dickens first wrote, above the printed title, *Six Chapters*. Later he altered *Six* to *Five*.

[2] Dickens stressed the repeated *rather ... rather ...* and *very ... very ...* and the adjectives *crushed* and *spotty*: 'With Dickens, one or two adjectives answer the purpose of a whole paint-box' (Field, p. 64). The *Peterborough Advertiser*, 22 October 1859, however, wished that he would delete 'that description of the first appearance of the infant on the stage of life, and the comparison which has been so severely and, as we think, justly condemned for indelicacy and unsuitability'.

who. had stolen into the chamber unobserved, was now crouching in a corner whence she could see her mother's face. But what was a girl to Dombey and Son!

Mr. Dombey's cup of satisfaction was so full, however, that he said, 'Florence, you may go and look at your pretty brother, if you like. Don't touch him!'[1]

Next moment, the *sick* lady had opened her eyes and seen the little girl; and the little girl had run towards her; and, standing on tiptoe, to hide her face in her embrace, had clung about her with a desperate affection very much at variance with her years. The lady herself seemed to faint.

'Oh Lord bless me!' said Mr. Dombey, 'I don't like the look of this. A very ill-advised and feverish proceeding having this child here. I had better ask the Doctor if he'll have the goodness to step up stairs again.'[2] †

Which he did; returning with the Doctor himself, and closely followed by his sister Mrs. Chick, a lady rather past the middle age than otherwise, but dressed in a very juvenile manner, who flung her arms round his neck, and said,

'My dear Paul! This last child is quite a Dombey! He's such a perfect Dombey!'

'Well, well! I think he *is*[3] like the family. But what is this they have told me since the child was born about Fanny herself? How is Fanny?'

'My dear Paul, there's nothing whatever wrong with Fanny. Take my word, nothing whatever. There is exhaustion, certainly, but *nothing like what I underwent myself either with George or Frederick.* An effort is necessary. That's all. Ah! If dear Fanny were a Dombey!—But I dare say, although she is not a born Dombey herself, she'll make an effort; I have no doubt she'll make an effort. Knowing it to be required of her, as a duty, of course she'll make an effort.[4] † And that effort she must be encouraged, and really, if necessary, urged to make. Now my dear Paul, come close to her with me.'

The lady lay immoveable, upon her bed, clasping her little daughter to her breast. The girl clung close about her, with the same intensity as before, and never raised her head, or moved her soft cheek from her mother's face, or looked on those who stood around, or spoke, or moved, or shed a tear.

There was such a solemn stillness round the bed; and the Doctor seemed to look on the impassive form *with so much compassion and so*

---

[1] 'Dickens pauses and sums up "rich Mr. Dombey and Son" in a motion of the hands and that one short command, "*Don't touch him!*"' (Field, p. 65). He made a 'Warning gesture with his forefinger' (Wright).

[2] The Dr. Parker Peps episode, which followed here, is deleted in *Suzannet* by its pages being stuck together.

[3] *is* italic in *Suzannet* and in the novel.

[4] Miss Tox's entry, which followed here, is deleted in *Suzannet* by its pages being stuck together.

little hope, that Mrs. Chick was for the moment diverted from her purpose. But presently summoning courage, and what *she* called presence of mind, *she* sat down by the bedside, and said in the tone of one who endeavours to awaken a sleeper:

'Fanny! Fanny!'

There was no sound in answer but the loud ticking of Mr. Dombey's watch and the Doctor's watch, which seemed in the silence to be running a race.

'Fanny, me dear, here's Mr. Dombey come to see you. Won't you speak to him? They want to lay your little boy in bed—the baby, Fanny, you know; you have hardly seen him yet, I think; but they can't till you rouse yourself a little. Don't you think it's time you roused yourself a little? Eh?'[1] No word or sound in answer. Mr. Dombey's watch and the Doctor's watch seemed to be racing faster.

'Now, really Fanny my dear, I shall have to be quite cross with you if you don't rouse yourself. It's necessary for you to make an effort, and perhaps a very great and painful effort which you are not disposed to make; but this is a world of effort you know, Fanny, and we must never yield, when so much depends upon us. Come! Try! I must really scold you if you don't! Fanny! Only look at me. Only open your eyes to show me that you hear and understand me; will you? Good Heaven, gentlemen, what is to be done!'

The Physician, stooping down, whispered in the *little girl's* ear. Not having understood the purport of his whisper, the little creature turned her deep dark eyes towards him.

The whisper was repeated.

'Mama!'

The little voice, familiar and dearly loved, awakened some show of consciousness, even at that ebb. For a moment, the closed eye-lids trembled, and the nostril quivered, and the faintest shadow of a smile was seen.

'Mama! O dear Mama! O dear Mama!'

The Doctor gently brushed the scattered ringlets of the child, aside from the face and mouth of the mother.

Thus, clinging fast to that frail spar within her arms, the mother drifted out upon the dark and unknown sea that rolls round all the world.[2]

---

[1] 'How like a Dombey [Mrs. Chick] is, in her exhortation there in the chamber of death; how she places her ear close to the mother's face in expectation of a reply; how she touches her, and almost shakes her, in order that Mrs. Dombey may be roused "to make an effort"!' (Field, p. 66).

[2] 'The descriptive death of Mrs. Dombey was beautifully read, and an emotion ran through the audience as the reader closed his book at the end of Chapter I' (*Brighton Gazette*, 18 November 1858).

CHAPTER II[1]

WE must all be weaned.[2] After that sharp season in Little Dombey's life had come and gone, it began to seem as if no vigilance or care could make him a thriving boy. In his steeple-chase towards manhood, he found it very rough riding. Every tooth was a break-neck fence, and every pimple in the measles a stone-wall to him. He was down in every fit of the whooping-cough. Some bird of prey got into his throat, instead of the Thrush; and the very chickens turning ferocious—if they have anything to do with that infant malady to which they lend their name—worried him like Tiger-cats. *

He grew to be nearly five years old. A pretty little fellow; but with something wan and wistful in his small face, that gave occasion to many significant shakes of his nurse's head. She said he was *too old-fashioned*.[3]

He was childish and sportive enough at times; but he had a strange, weird, thoughtful way, at other times, of sitting brooding in his miniature arm-chair, when he looked (and talked) like one of those terrible little Beings in the Fairy tales, who, at a hundred and fifty or two hundred years of age, fantastically represent the children for whom they have been substituted. At no time did he fall into this mood so surely, as when—his little chair being carried down into his father's room—he sat there with him after dinner, by the fire. *

On one of these occasions, when they had both been perfectly quiet for a long time, and Mr. Dombey knew that the child was awake by occasionally glancing at his eye, where the bright fire was sparkling like a jewel, little Paul broke silence thus:

'Papa! what's money?'[4]

Mr. Dombey was in a difficulty; for he would have liked to give him some explanation involving the terms circulating-medium, currency, depreciation of currency, paper, bullion, rates of exchange, value of precious metals in the market, and so forth: but looking down at the little chair, *and seeing what a long way down it was*, he answered: 'Gold, and silver, and copper. Guineas, shillings, half-pence. You know what they are?'

---

[1] The whole of the original Chapter II (about Paul's christening) is deleted here in *Suzannet*, the pages being attached together by stamp-edging. The chapter is also deleted in *Gimbel*. It was, however, included in performances up to, at least, mid-October 1858. The beginning of the Chapter now renumbered II gave Dickens some difficulty. The present first paragraph was deleted, and a sentence (now illegible) substituted for it; later this was deleted and the original first paragraph re-inserted, with some cuts. Yet another attempt at opening this Chapter appears in *Gimbel*.

[2] This sentence was followed by another, later deleted: 'Indeed, some of us are always being weaned all our lives long; some of us never get over it.' These sentences do not occur in the novel.

[3] Wright puts inverted commas round '*too old-fashioned*'.

[4] 'Sad, high, tired voice' (Wright).

'O yes, I know what they are. I don't mean that, Papa; I mean, what's money after all?'

'What is money after all!'

'I mean, papa, what can it do?'

[1] 'You'll know better bye-and-bye, my man. Money, Paul, can do anything.' *

'It isn't cruel; is it?'

'No. A good thing can't be cruel.'

[2] 'As you are so rich, if money can do anything, and isn't cruel, I wonder it didn't save me my Mama. * It can't make me strong and quite well, either. * I am so tired sometimes and my bones ache so, that I don't know what to do!'

Mr. Dombey became uneasy about this odd child, and, † in consequence of his uneasiness, resolved to send him, *accompanied by his sister Florence and a Nurse,* to board with one *Mrs. Pipchin* at Brighton—an old lady who had acquired an immense reputation as 'a great manager' of children; and the secret of whose management was, to give them everything that they didn't like, and nothing that they did.

Mrs. Pipchin had also founded great fame on being a widow-lady whose husband had broken his heart in pumping water out of some Peruvian Mines. * This was a great recommendation to Mr. Dombey. For it had a rich sound. Broke his heart of the Peruvian mines, mused Mr. Dombey. Well! a very respectable way of doing it. *[3]

This celebrated Mrs. Pipchin was a marvellous ill-favoured, ill-conditioned old lady, of a stooping figure, with a mottled face, like bad marble, a hook nose, and a hard grey eye, that looked as if it might have been hammered at on an anvil. Forty years at least had elapsed since the Peruvian mines had been the death of Mr. Pipchin; but his relict still wore black bombazeen. And she was such a bitter old lady, that one was tempted to believe there had been some mistake in the application of the Peruvian Machinery, and that all her waters of gladness and milk of human kindness had been pumped out dry, instead of the Mines.[4]

---

[1] The preceding sentence is half-deleted and left incomplete. Wright records what Dickens read—'Rich papa patted him on the head and said:'—and what he did '(Patting table)'.

[2] 'Sigh': and later in this speech, 'Hand to forehead' (Wright).

[3] Here, and elsewhere, Dickens gave Mr. Dombey's voice 'a hard metallic ring' (Field, p. 67). 'Finger to lips' (Wright).

[4] Dickens's text becomes uncertain here. In *Suzannet*, the page which ends with this paragraph is attached by stamp-edging to one five pages further on, which begins (apart from a manuscript interpolation) with the words 'It being a part of Mrs. Pipchin's system not to encourage . . .' *T & F*, however, prints the intervening pages, so perhaps Dickens had by then (1867–8) rejected this cut. Another possibility is that this stamp-edging deletion was made after *T & F* was printed: but, if so, the sequence of the

The Castle of this Ogress was in a steep bye-street at Brighton; where the small front gardens had the unaccountable property of producing nothing but marigolds, whatever was sown in them; and where snails were constantly discovered holding on to the street doors, and other public places they were not expected to ornament, with the tenacity of cupping-glasses. There were two other very small boarders in the house, when Little Dombey (*first called so by Mrs. Pipchin*[1]) arrived. These were one Master Bitherstone from India, and a certain Miss Pankey. As to Master Bitherstone, he objected so much to the Pipchinian system, that before Little Dombey had been established in the house five minutes, he privately asked that young gentleman if he could give him any idea of the way back to Bengal. As to Miss Pankey, *she* was disabled from offering any remark, by being in solitary confinement, for the offence of having sniffed three times in the presence of visitors. * At one o'clock there was dinner, and then this young person (a mild little blue-eyed morsel of a child, who was shampooed every morning, and seemed in danger of being rubbed away altogether) was led in from captivity by the ogress herself, and instructed *that nobody who sniffed before visitors ever went to Heaven.*[2] When this great truth had been thoroughly impressed upon her, she was regaled with rice, while all the rest had cold Pork—except Mrs. Pipchin—whose constitution required warm nourishment, and who had hot mutton chops, which smelt uncommonly nice. * Also at tea, that good lady's constitution demanded hot toast while all the rest had bread and butter. *

After breakfast next morning Master Bitherstone read aloud to the rest a pedigree from Genesis (*judiciously selected by Mrs. Pipchin*), *getting over the names with the ease and clearness of a young gentleman tumbling up the treadmill.*[3] That done, Miss Pankey was borne away to be shampoo'd; and Master Bitherstone to have something else done to him with salt water, from which he always returned, very blue and dejected. Then there were Lessons. It being a part of Mrs. Pipchin's system not to encourage a child's mind to develop itself like a young flower, but to open it by force like an oyster, the moral of all her lessons was of a violent and stunning character: the hero—always a naughty boy—seldom, in the mildest catastrophe, being finished off by anything less than a lion, or a bear. † *

narration becomes very abrupt, and the above-mentioned manuscript interpolation (beginning in mid-sentence) must be ignored. There is a great deal of textual re-arrangement hereabouts, with many lengthy deletions, passages written or pasted in, etc.: one passage, for instance, appears three times, having been twice deleted. The text printed below *includes* the pages formerly deleted by stamp-edging, minus the passages deleted in them.

[1] Doubly underlined.
[2] Doubly underlined.
[3] Single underlining up to *by Mrs. Pipchin*, double underlining thereafter.

At the exemplary Pipchin, Little Dombey would sit staring in his little arm-chair by the fire, for any length of time.

Once she asked him when they were alone, what he was thinking about.[1]

'You,' said Paul, without the least reserve.

'And what are you thinking about me?'

'I have been thinking you an't like my sister. There's nobody like my sister.'

'Well! there's nobody like me, either, perhaps.'

'An't there though? I am very glad there's nobody like you!'

'Upon my word, Sir! And what else are you thinking about me?'

'I am thinking how old you must be.'

'You mustn't say such things as that, young gentleman. That'll never do.'

'Why not?' *

'Never you mind, Sir. Remember the story of the little boy that was gored to death by a mad bull for asking questions.'

'If the bull was mad, how did he know that the boy had asked questions? Nobody can go and whisper secrets to a mad bull. I don't believe that story.'

'You don't believe it, Sir?'

'No.'

'Not if it should happen to have been a tame bull, you little Infidel?'[2]

As Paul had not considered the subject in that light, and had founded his conclusions on the alleged lunacy of the bull, he allowed himself to be put down for the present. But he sat turning it over in his mind, with such an obvious intention of fixing Mrs. Pipchin presently, that even that hardy old lady deemed it prudent to retreat. *

Such was life at Mrs. Pipchin's: and Mrs. Pipchin said, *and they all said, that Little Dombey* (who watched it all from his little arm-chair by the fire), *was an old, old fashioned child.*

But as Little Dombey was no stronger at the expiration of weeks of this life, than he had been on his first arrival, a little carriage was got for him, in which he could lie at his ease, *with an alphabet and other elementary works of reference,* and be wheeled down to the sea-side.

[1] Mrs. Pipchin asked this 'in the most snappish voice possible'; Paul replied 'in the gentlest childlike voice'. His 'Why not?' was spoken 'slowly and wonderingly', and Mrs. Pipchin's 'Never you mind, sir' was 'shorter and sharper than ever'. His question about the bull followed 'in a high falsetto voice and with greater deliberation than ever' (Kent, p. 180). Mrs. Pipchin became angry, at 'You don't believe it, Sir?' (Wright).

[2] '... the comedy does not get fully under way until [this] interview between Little Dombey and the exemplary Pipchin. ... Little Paul's earnestness is inexpressibly droll' (Field, p. 68). This dialogue 'awakened invariably such bursts of hearty laughter!' (Kent, p. 179).

Consistent in his odd tastes, the child set aside a ruddy-faced lad who was proposed as the drawer of this carriage and selected, instead, a weazen old crab-faced man, who was the lad's grandfather.

With this notable attendant to pull him along, and Florence always walking by his side, he went down to the margin of the ocean every day; and there he would sit or lie in his carriage for hours together: never so distressed as by the company of children—his sister Florence alone excepted, always.

'Go away, if you please,' he would say, to any child who came to bear him company.[1] 'Thank you, but I don't want you.'

Some small voice, near his ear, would ask him how he was, perhaps.

'I am very well, I thank you. But you had better go and play, if you please.'

Then he would turn his head, and watch the child away, and would say to Florence, 'We don't want any others, do we? Kiss me, Floy.'

He had even a dislike, at such times, to the company of his nurse, and was well pleased when she strolled away, as she generally did, to pick up shells *and acquaintances*. His favorite spot was quite a lonely one, far away from most loungers; and with Florence sitting by his side at work, or reading to him, or talking to him, *and the wind blowing on his face, and the water coming up among the wheels of his bed*, he wanted nothing more.

'Floy,' he said one day, 'where's India, where the friends of that boy Bitherstone—the other boy who stays with us at Mrs. Pipchin's—live?'

'Oh, it's a long, long distance off.'

'Weeks off?'

'Yes, dear. Many weeks' journey, night and day.'

[2]'If you were in India, Floy, I should—what is it that Mama did? I forget.'

'Love me?'

'No, no. Don't I love you now, Floy? What is it?—Died. If you were in India, I should die, Floy.'

She hurriedly put her work aside, and laid her head down on his pillow, caressing him. And so would she, she said, if he were there. He would be better soon.

'Oh! I am a great deal better now! I don't mean that. I mean that I should die of being so sorry and so lonely, Floy!'[3]

Another time, in the same place, he fell asleep, and slept quietly for a long time. Awakening suddenly, he listened, started up, and sat listening.

---

[1] '. . . in a soft, drawling, half-querulous voice, and with the gravest look' (Kent, p. 181).

[2] 'Repeat to dash' (Wright).

[3] In the margin here, Dickens writes *pause*. 'That momentary pause will be very well remembered by everyone who attended this Reading' (Kent, p. 182).

Florence asked him what he thought he heard.

'I want to know what it says. The sea, Floy, what is it that it keeps on saying?'

She told him that it was only the noise of the rolling waves.

'Yes, yes.[1] But I know that they are always saying something. Always the same thing. What place is over there?' He rose up, looking eagerly at the horizon.

She told him that there was another country opposite, but he said he didn't mean that; he meant farther away—farther away!

Very often afterwards, in the midst of their talk, he would break off, to try to understand what it was that the waves were always saying; and would rise up in his couch to look towards that invisible region, far away.[2]

CHAPTER III[3]

AT length Mr. Dombey, one Saturday, when he came down at Brighton to see Paul, who was then six years old, resolved to make a change, and enrol him as a small student under *Doctor Blimber*. *

Whenever a young gentleman was taken in hand by Doctor Blimber, he might consider himself sure of a pretty tight squeeze. The Doctor only undertook the charge of ten young gentlemen, but he had, always ready, a supply of learning for a hundred; and it was at once the business and delight of his life to gorge the unhappy ten with it.

In fact, Doctor Blimber's establishment was a great hot-house, in which there was a forcing apparatus incessantly at work. All the boys blew before their time. Mental green-peas were produced at Christmas, and intellectual asparagus all the year round. No matter what a young gentleman was intended to bear, Doctor Blimber made him bear to pattern, somehow or other.

This was all very pleasant and ingenious, but the system of forcing was attended with its usual disadvantages. There was not the right taste about the premature productions, and they didn't keep well. Moreover, one young gentleman, with a swollen nose and an excessively large head (the oldest of the ten who had 'gone through' everything), suddenly left off blowing one day, and remained in the establishment a mere

---

[1] 'Slow, faint' (Wright).

[2] Strong vertical lines in both margins, against this paragraph. 'Dickens is not a reader as others are readers. He is something better. There is a death-knell in those concluding words, "far away"' (Field, p. 69). At these words, Dickens gave a 'Shake of head' (Wright).

[3] The chapter-number was altered by Dickens from IV to 3, back to 4, and finally to 3 again—presumably reflecting periods when the chapter about the christening was omitted, restored, and finally omitted again.

stalk. *And people did say that the Doctor had rather overdone it with young Toots,*[1] *and that when he began to have whiskers he left off having brains.* †
The Doctor was a portly gentleman in a suit of black, with strings at his knees, and stockings below them. He had a bald head, highly polished; a deep voice; *and a chin so very double, that it was a wonder how he ever managed to shave into the creases.* * †

His daughter, *Miss*[2] Blimber, although a slim and graceful maid, did no soft violence to the gravity of the Doctor's house. There was no light nonsense about Miss Blimber. She kept her hair short and crisp, and wore spectacles, and *she was dry and sandy with working in the graves of deceased languages.* None of your live languages for Miss Blimber. They must be dead—stone dead—and then Miss Blimber dug them up like a Ghoule.

Mrs. Blimber, her mama, was not learned herself, but she pretended to be, and that did quite as well. *She said at evening parties, that if she could have known Cicero,*[3] *she thought she could have died contented.*

As to Mr. Feeder, B.A., Dr. Blimber's assistant, he was a kind of human barrel-organ, with a little list of tunes at which he was continually working, over and over again, without any variation. †

To Dr. Blimber's Paul was taken by his father, on an appointed day.[4] The Doctor was sitting in his portentous study, with a globe at each knee, books all round him, Homer over the door, and Minerva on the mantel-shelf. 'And how do you do, Sir,' he said to Mr. Dombey, 'and how is my little friend?' When the Doctor left off, the great clock in the hall seemed (*to Paul at least*) to take him up, and to go on saying *over and over again,* 'how, is, my, lit, tle, friend, how, is, my, lit, tle, friend.' †

'Mr. Dombey,' said Doctor Blimber, 'you would wish my little friend to acquire—'

'Everything, if you please, Doctor.'

'Yes,' said the Doctor, who with his *half-shut eyes, seemed to survey Paul with the sort of interest that might attach to some choice little animal he was going to stuff.* 'Yes, exactly. Ha! We shall impart a great variety of information to our little friend, and bring him quickly forward, I dare say. I dare say. * Permit me. Allow me to present Mrs. Blimber and my daughter *Cornelia,* who will be associated with the domestic life of our young Pilgrim to Parnassus.[5] * † Who is that *at the Door?* Oh! Come in, Toots; come in. Mr. Dombey, Sir. Our head boy, Mr. Dombey.'

---

[1] *young Toots* doubly underlined.

[2] *Miss* (and *Mrs.* at the beginning of the next paragraph) doubly underlined.

[3] Mrs. Blimber went 'from the bottom to the top of a vocal staircase', in pronouncing this name (Field, p. 70). In the next sentence, Dickens inserted 'classical' before 'tunes' (Wright).

[4] Doubly underlined; so is *over and over again* (below).

[5] This sentence, deleted (by mistake?), is *stetted* by multiple vertical lines in both margins—a device also used elsewhere in this script but not, apparently, in other

The Doctor might have called him their head and shoulders boy, for he was at least that much taller than any of the rest. He blushed very red at finding himself among strangers, and chuckled aloud.

'An addition to our little portico, Toots; Mr. Dombey's son.'

Young Toots blushed again; and finding, from a solemn silence which prevailed, that he was expected to say something, said to Paul with surprising suddenness, 'How are you?' This, he did, in a voice so deep, and a manner so sheepish, that if a lamb had roared it couldn't have been more surprising. †

'Take him round the house, Cornelia,' said the Doctor, when Mr. Dombey was gone, 'take him round the house, Cornelia, and familiarise him with his new sphere. Go with that young lady, Dombey.'

So, Cornelia took him to the schoolroom, where there were eight young gentlemen *in various stages of mental prostration*, all very hard at work, and very grave indeed. Toots, as an old hand, had a desk to himself in one corner: and a magnificent man, of immense age, he looked, in Little Dombey's young eyes, behind it. † He now had license to pursue his own course of study; *and it was chiefly to write long letters to himself* [1]*from persons of distinction*, addressed 'P. Toots Esquire, Brighton, Sussex', and to preserve them in his desk with great care. †

Young Toots said, with heavy good nature:

'Sit down, Dombey.'

'Thank you, Sir.'

Little Dombey's endeavouring to hoist himself on to a very high window-seat, and his slipping down again, appeared to prepare Toots's mind for the reception of a discovery.

'I say, you know—you're a very small chap.'

'Yes, Sir, I'm small. Thank you, Sir.'

For, Toots had lifted him into the seat, and done it kindly too.

'Who's your tailor?' inquired Toots, after looking at him for some moments.

'It's a woman that has made my clothes as yet. My sister's dressmaker.'

'My tailor's Burgess and Co. Fash'nable. But very dear.'

Paul had wit enough to shake his head, as if he would have said it was easy to see *that*.[2]

---

prompt-copies (where Dickens uses the conventional directive, *Stet*). *T & F* duly prints these passages. What may have been another *Stet* sign in this script—or, more probably, was an indication that the passages indicated were, at one time, optional inclusions—is multiple horizontal lines in both margins. *T & F* does not restore any of these cuts, nor does the present edition: often, the surrounding text has been too heavily modified for the passage to be re-integrated. *Cornelia* and *at the Door* are doubly underlined.

[1] *to himself* underlined trebly.   [2] *that* italic in *Suzannet* and in the novel.

'I say! It's of no consequence, you know, but your father's regularly rich, ain't he?'

'Yes, Sir. He's Dombey and Son.'

'And which?'[1]

'And Son, Sir.'

Mr. Toots made one or two attempts to fix the firm in his mind; but not quite succeeding, said he would get Paul to mention the name again to-morrow morning, as it was rather important. *And indeed he purposed nothing less than writing himself*[2] *a private and confidential letter from Dombey and Son immediately.* †

A gong now sounding with great fury, there was a general move towards the dining-room; † where every young gentleman had a massive silver fork, and a napkin; and all the arrangements were stately and handsome. In particular, there was a butler in a blue coat and bright buttons, *who gave quite a winey flavour to the table-beer; he poured it out so superbly.*†

Tea was served in a style no less polite than the dinner; and after tea, the young gentlemen rising and bowing, withdrew to Bed. †

There were two sharers of Little Dombey's bedroom—one named Briggs—the other Tozer.[3] In the confidence of that retreat at night, Briggs said his head ached ready to split, and that he should wish himself dead if it wasn't for his mother—and a blackbird he had at home. Tozer didn't say very much, but he sighed a good deal, and told Paul to look out, for his turn would come to-morrow. After uttering those prophetic words, he undressed himself moodily, and got into bed. †

Paul had sunk into a sweet sleep, and dreamed that he was walking hand in hand with Florence through beautiful gardens, when he found that it was a dark, windy morning, with a drizzling rain: and that the gong was giving dreadful note of preparation, down in the hall.

So, he got up directly, and † proceeded softly on his journey downstairs. As he passed the door that stood ajar, a voice from within cried 'Is that Dombey?' On Paul replying, 'Yes Ma'am:' for he knew the voice to be Miss Blimber's: Miss Blimber said, 'Come in, Dombey.' And in he went.

'Now, Dombey,' said Miss Blimber. 'I'm going out for a constitutional.'[4]

Paul wondered what that was, and why she didn't send the footman out to get it in such unfavourable weather. But he made no observation

---

[1] Wright deletes this question, and Paul's answer, and substitutes 'Dom-a-dom (stuttering)'.

[2] *himself* doubly underlined.

[3] 'Briggs rubs his eyes, has a low snuffled voice' (Wright).

[4] '... as comical as ... can be. As Miss Blimber pronounces "con-sti-tu-tion-al" it sounds like a vocal illustration of a Virginia fence. It is here, there, and everywhere. Miss Blimber peppers Dombey with it' (Field, p. 72).

on the subject: his attention being devoted to a little pile of new books, on which Miss Blimber appeared to have been recently engaged.

'These are yours, Dombey. I am going out for a constitutional; and while I am gone, that is to say in the interval between this and breakfast, Dombey, I wish you to read over what I have marked in these books, and to tell me if you quite understand what you have got to learn.' *

They comprised a little English, and a deal of Latin—names of things, declensions of articles and substantives, exercises thereon, and rules—a trifle of orthography, a glance at ancient history, a wink or two at modern ditto, a few tables, two or three weights and measures, and a little general information. When poor Little Dombey had spelt out number two, he found he had no idea of number one; fragments of which afterwards obtruded themselves into number three, which slided into number four, which grafted itself on to number two. So that it was an open question with him whether twenty Romuluses made a Remus, or hic hæc hoc was troy weight, or a verb always agreed with an ancient Briton, or three times four was Taurus a bull.[1]

'Oh, Dombey, Dombey!' said Miss Blimber, when she came back, 'this is very shocking, you know.'

Miss Blimber expressed herself with a gloomy delight, as if she had expected this result. * She divided his books into tasks on subjects A, B, C, and D, and he did very well. †

It was hard work, resuming his studies, soon after dinner; and he felt giddy and confused and drowsy and dull. But all the other young gentlemen had similar sensations, and were obliged to resume *their* studies too. The studies went round like a mighty wheel, and the young gentlemen were always stretched upon it. *

Such spirits as Little Dombey had, he soon lost, of course. But he retained all that was strange and old and thoughtful in his character; and even became more strange and old and thoughtful. He loved to be alone, and liked nothing so well as wandering about the house by himself, or sitting on the stairs listening to the great clock in the hall. He was intimate with all the paper-hanging in the house; he saw things that no one else saw in the patterns; and found out miniature tigers and lions running up the bedroom walls.

The lonely child lived on surrounded by this arabesque-work of his musing fancy, and no one understood him. Mrs. Blimber thought him 'odd,' and sometimes the servants said that Little Dombey 'moped;' but that was all.

Unless young Toots had some idea on the subject. *

He would say to Little Dombey, *fifty times a-day*, 'I say—it's of no consequence, you know—but—how are you?'

Little Dombey would answer, 'Quite well, Sir, thank you.'

'Shake hands.'

[1] This was one of 'the passages in the story which were most applauded' in Dublin (*Saunders's News-Letter*, 26 August 1858).

Which Little Dombey, of course, would immediately do. Mr. Toots generally said again, after a long interval of staring and hard breathing, 'I say—it's not of the slightest consequence, you know, but I should wish to mention it—how are you, you know?'

To which Little Dombey would again reply, 'Quite well, Sir, thank you.'

One evening a great purpose seemed to flash on Mr. Toots. He went off from his desk to look after Little Dombey, and finding him at the window of his little bedroom, blurted out all at once, as if he were afraid he should forget it: 'I say—Dombey—what do you think about?'

'*O! I think about a great many things.*'[1]

'*Do you though?—I don't, myself.*'[2]

'*I was thinking when you came in, about last night. It was a beautiful moonlight night. When I had listened to the water for a long time, I got up, and looked out at it. There was a boat over there; the sail like an arm, all silver. It went away into the distance, and what do you think it seemed to do as it moved with the waves?*'

'Pitch?'

'*It seemed to beckon—seemed to beckon me to come.*'

This was on a Friday night; it made such a prodigious impression on Mr. Toots, that he had it on his mind as long afterwards as Saturday morning.

—And so the solitary child lived on and on, surrounded by the arab-esque-work of his musing fancy, and still no one understood him. *

He grew fond now, of a large engraving that hung upon the staircase, where, in the centre of a group, one figure that he knew—*a figure with a light about its head—benignant, mild and merciful—stood pointing up-ward.*[3] * He watched *the waves and clouds at twilight with his earnest eyes, and breasted the window of his solitary room when birds flew by, as if he would have emulated them,*[4] and soared away.

CHAPTER IV

WHEN the Midsummer vacation approached, no indecent manifestation of joy were exhibited by the leaden-eyed young gentlemen assembled at Dr. Blimber's. Any such violent expression as 'breaking up,' would have been quite inapplicable to that polite establishment. The young gentlemen oozed away, semi-annually, to their own homes, but they never broke up. †

Mr. Feeder, B.A., however, seemed to think that he would enjoy the

---

[1] This, and Paul's next two speeches, have lines against them in both margins.
[2] *Do* italic in *Suzannet*. 'I don't, myself' is not in the novel.
[3] Doubly underlined.
[4] *them* doubly underlined.

holidays very much. Mr. Toots projected a life of holidays from that time forth; for, as he regularly informed Paul every day, it was his 'last half' at Doctor Blimber's, and he was going to begin to come into his property directly. *

Mrs. Blimber was by this time quite sure that Paul was *the oddest child in the world*; and the Doctor did not controvert his wife's opinion. But he said that study would do much; and he said, 'Bring him on, Cornelia! Bring him on!'

Cornelia had always brought him on as vigorously as she could; and Paul had had a hard life of it. *But, over and above the getting through his tasks, he had long had another purpose always present to him, and to which he still held fast. It was, to be a gentle, useful, quiet little fellow, always striving to secure the love and attachment of the rest; and thus he was an object of general interest; a fragile little plaything that they all liked, and whom no one would have thought of treating roughly.* †

It was darkly rumoured that even the Butler, regarding him with favor such as that stern man had never shown to mortal boy, had mingled Porter with his table beer, to make him strong. But he couldn't change his nature, and so they all agreed that Little Dombey was 'old-fashioned'.

Over and above other extensive privileges, he had free right of entry to Mr. Feeder's room, from which apartment he had twice led Mr. Toots into the open air in a state of faintness, consequent on an unsuccessful attempt to smoke a very blunt cigar: one of a bundle which that young gentleman had covertly purchased on the shingle from a most desperate smuggler, who had acknowledged, in confidence, that two hundred pounds was the price set upon his head, dead or alive, by the Custom House. †

But, Mr. Feeder's great possession was a large green jar of snuff, which Mr. Toots had brought down as a present, at the close of the last vacation; and for which he had paid a high price, as having been the genuine property of the Prince Regent. Neither Mr. Toots nor Mr. Feeder could partake of this or any other snuff, even in the most moderate degree, without being seized with convulsions of sneezing. Nevertheless it was their great delight to moisten a box-full with cold tea, stir it up on a piece of parchment with a paper-knife, and devote themselves to its consumption then and there. *In the course of which cramming of their noses, they endured surprising torments, with the constancy of martyrs; and, drinking table-beer at intervals, felt all the glories of dissipation.* *

Going into this room one evening, when the holidays were very near, Paul found Mr. Feeder filling up the blanks in some printed letters, while others were being folded and sealed by Mr. Toots. Mr. Feeder said, 'Aha, Dombey, there you are, are you? That's yours.'

'Mine, Sir?'

'Your invitation, Little Dombey.'

Paul, looking at it, found that Doctor and Mrs. Blimber requested the pleasure of Mr. P. Dombey's company at an early party on Wednesday Evening the Seventeenth Instant; and that the hour was half-past seven o'clock; and that the object was Quadrilles. He also found that the pleasure of every young gentleman's company, was requested by Doctor *and Mrs. Blimber on the same genteel occasion.*[1]

Mr. Feeder then told him, to his great joy, that his sister was invited, and that he would be expected to inform Doctor and Mrs. Blimber, in superfine small-hand, that Mr. P. Dombey would be happy to have the honour of waiting on them, in accordance with their polite invitation.

Little Dombey thanked Mr. Feeder for these hints, and pocketing his invitation, sat down on a stool by the side of Mr. Toots, as usual. *But Little Dombey's head, which had long been ailing, and was sometimes very heavy, felt so uneasy that night, that he was obliged to support it on his hand. And yet it drooped so, that by little and little it sunk on Mr. Toots's knee, and rested there, as if it had no care to be ever lifted up again.*

That was no reason why he should be deaf; but he must have been, he thought, for, by and by, he heard Mr. Feeder calling in his ear, and gently shaking him to rouse his attention. And when he raised his head, quite scared, and looked about him, he found that Doctor Blimber had come into the room; and that the window was open, and that his forehead was wet with sprinkled water; though how all this had been done without his knowledge, was very curious indeed. *

It was very kind of Mr. Toots to carry him to the top of the house so tenderly; and Paul told him that it was. But, Mr. Toots said he would do a great deal more than that, if he could; and indeed he did more as it was: for he helped Paul to undress, and helped him to bed, in the kindest manner possible, and then sat down by the bedside and chuckled very much. How he melted away, and Mr. Feeder changed into Mrs. Pipchin, Paul never thought of asking; but when he saw Mrs. Pipchin standing at the bottom of the bed, instead of Mr. Feeder, he cried out, 'Mrs. Pipchin, don't tell Florence!'

'Don't tell Florence what, my little Dombey?'

'About my not being well.'

'No, no.'

'What do you think I mean to do when I grow up, Mrs. Pipchin?'

Mrs. Pipchin couldn't guess.

'I mean to put my money all together in one Bank—never try to get any more—go away into the country with my darling Florence—have a beautiful garden, fields, and woods, and live there with her all my life!'

'Indeed, Sir?'

'Yes. That's what I mean to do, when I—' He stopped, and pondered for a moment.

---

[1] Pronounced 'O casion' (Wright). The underlining here seems incomplete.

Mrs. Pipchin's grey eye scanned his thoughtful face.

—'*If*[1] *I* grow up,' said Paul. *

There was a certain calm Apothecary, who attended at the establishment, and somehow *he*[2] got into the room and appeared at the bedside, was very chatty with him, and they parted excellent friends. Lying down again with his eyes shut, he heard the Apothecary say that *there was a want of vital power (what was that,*[3] *Paul wondered?) and great constitutional weakness. That there was no immediate cause for—what? Paul lost that word. And that the little fellow had a fine mind, but was an old-fashioned boy.*[4]

What old fashion could that be, Paul wondered, that was so visibly expressed in him? *

He lay in bed all that day; but got up on the next, and went down stairs. Lo and behold, there was something the matter with the great clock; and a workman on a pair of steps had taken its face off, and was poking instruments into the works by the light of a candle! This was a great event for Paul, who sat down on the bottom stair, and watched the operation. As the workman said, when he observed Paul, 'How do you do, Sir?'[5] Paul got into conversation with him. Finding that his new acquaintance was not very well informed on the subject of the Curfew Bell of ancient days, Paul gave him an account of that institution; and also asked him, as a practical man, what he thought about King Alfred's idea of measuring time by the burning of candles? To which the workman replied, that he thought it would be the ruin of the clock trade if it was to come up again. At last the workman put away his tools, and went away. *Though not before he had whispered something, on the doormat, to the footman, in which there was the phrase 'old-fashioned'—for Paul heard it.*

[6] *What could that old fashion be, that seemed to make the people sorry! What could it be!* * †

And now it was that he began to think it must surely be old-fashioned, to be very thin and light, and easily tired, and soon disposed to lie down anywhere and rest; for he couldn't help feeling that these were more and more his habits every day.

At last the party-day arrived; and Doctor Blimber said at breakfast, 'Gentlemen, we will resume our studies on the twenty-fifth of next month.' Mr. Toots immediately threw off his allegiance, and put on a

---

[1] *If* trebly underlined.

[2] *he* italic in *Suzannet* and in the novel.

[3] Wright puts inverted commas round *What was that?* (and round *what?* in the next sentence).

[4] *but was an old-fashioned boy* doubly underlined.

[5] 'Loud' (Wright).

[6] This paragraph, and the next, have lines against them in both margins.

ring: and mentioning the Doctor in casual conversation shortly afterwards, spoke of him as 'Blimber'! This act of freedom inspired the older pupils with admiration; but the younger spirits seemed to marvel that no beam fell down and crushed him.

Not the least allusion was made to the ceremonies of the evening, either at breakfast or at dinner; but there was a bustle in the house all day, and Paul made acquaintance with various strange benches and candlesticks, and met a harp in a green great-coat standing on the landing outside the drawing-room door. There was something queer, too, about Mrs. Blimber's head at dinner-time, as if she had screwed her hair up too tight;[1] and though Miss Blimber showed a graceful bunch of plaited hair on each temple, she seemed to have her own little curls in paper underneath, and in a playbill too; for Paul read 'Theatre Royal' over one of her sparkling spectacles, and 'Brighton' over the other.

There was a grand array of white waistcoats and cravats in the young gentlemen's bedrooms as evening approached, and such a smell of singed hair, that Doctor Blimber sent up the footman with his compliments, and wished to know if the house was on fire. But, it was only the hairdresser curling the young gentlemen, and over-heating his tongs in the ardour of business.

When Paul was dressed he went down into the drawing-room; where he found Doctor Blimber pacing up and down full dressed, but with a dignified and unconcerned demeanour, as if he thought it barely possible that one or two people might drop in by and bye. Shortly afterwards, Mrs. Blimber appeared, looking lovely, Paul thought, and attired in such a number of skirts that it was quite an excursion to walk round her. Miss Blimber came down soon after her mama; a little squeezed in appearance, but very charming.

Mr. Toots and Mr. Feeder were the next arrivals. Each of these gentlemen brought his hat in his hand, as if he lived somewhere else; and when they were announced by the butler, Doctor Blimber said, 'Aye, aye, aye! God bless my soul!' and seemed extremely surprised to see them. Mr. Toots was one blaze of jewellery and buttons; and he felt the circumstance so strongly, that when he had shaken hands with the Doctor, and had bowed to Mrs. Blimber and Miss Blimber, he took Paul aside, and said, 'What do you think of this, Dombey!'

But notwithstanding his modest confidence in himself, Mr. Toots appeared to be involved in a good deal of uncertainty whether, on the whole, it was judicious to button the bottom button of his waistcoat; and whether, on a calm revison of all the circumstances, it was best to wear his wristbands turned up or turned down. Observing that Mr. Feeder's were turned up, Mr. Toots turned his up; but the wristbands

---

[1] 'Action—side of head' (Wright).

of the next arrival being turned down, Mr. Toots turned his down. The differences in point of waistcoat-buttoning, not only at the bottom, but at the top too, became so numerous and complicated as the arrivals thickened, that Mr. Toots was continually fingering that article of dress, *as if he were performing on some*[1] *instrument.*

All the young gentlemen, tightly cravatted, curled, and pumped, and with their best hats in their hands, having been at different times announced and introduced, Mr. Baps, the dancing-master, came, accompanied by Mrs. Baps, to whom Mrs. Blimber was extremely kind and condescending. Mr. Baps was a very grave gentleman; and before he had stood under the lamp five minutes, he began to talk to Toots (*who had been silently comparing pumps with him*) about what you were to do with your raw materials when they came into your ports in return for your drain of gold.[2] Mr. Toots, to whom the question seemed perplexing, suggested 'Cook 'em.' But Mr. Baps did not appear to think that would do.

Paul now slipped away from the cushioned corner of a sofa, which had been his post of observation, and went down stairs into the tea room to be ready for Florence. Presently she came: looking so beautiful in her simple ball dress, with her fresh flowers in her hand, that when she knelt down on the ground to take Paul round the neck and kiss him, he could hardly make up his mind to let her go again.

[3]'*But what is the matter, Floy?*' *asked Paul, almost sure that he saw a tear on her face.*

'*Nothing, darling; nothing.*'

Paul touched her cheek gently with his finger—and it was[4] *a tear!* '*Why, Floy!*'

'*We'll go home together, and I'll nurse you, love.*'

'*Nurse me! Floy. Do* you *think I have grown old-fashioned?*[5] *Because, I know they say so, and I want to know what they mean, Floy.*' *

From his nest among the sofa-pillows, where she came at the end of every dance, he could see and hear almost everything that passed at the Ball. * There was one thing in particular that he observed. Mr. Feeder, after imbibing several custard-cups of negus, began to enjoy himself, and told Mr. Toots that he was going to throw a little spirit into the thing.[6] After that, he not only began to dance as if he meant dancing and nothing else, but secretly to stimulate the music to perform

---

[1] 'some *curious* instrument' (Wright).

[2] Wright puts inverted commas round Mr. Baps's enquiry ('what you were . . . drain of gold').

[3] Lines in both margins, against this dialogue.

[4] *was* italic in *Suzannet* and the novel. Wright substitutes 'the child' for 'Paul' in this sentence.

[5] This sentence doubly underlined; *you* italic in *Suzannet* and in the novel.

[6] Wright puts inverted commas round 'going to throw a little spirit into the thing'.

wild tunes. Further, he became particular in his attentions to the ladies; and dancing with Miss Blimber, whispered to her—whispered to her!—though not so softly but that Paul heard him say this remarkable poetry,

'Had I a heart for falsehood framed,
    I ne'er could injure You!'

This, Paul heard him repeat to four young ladies, in succession. Well might Mr. Feeder say to Mr. Toots, that he was afraid he should be the worse for it tomorrow! * †

A buzz at last went round of 'Dombey's going!' 'Little Dombey's going!' and there was a general move after him and Florence down the staircase and into the hall. * Once for a last look he turned, surprised to see how shining, and how bright and numerous the faces were, and how they seemed like *a great dream, full of eyes.* †

There was much, soon afterwards—next day, and after that—which Paul could only recollect confusedly. As, why they stayed at Mrs. Pipchin's days and nights, instead of going home.

But he could remember, when he got to his old London home and was carried up the stairs, that there had been the rumbling of a coach for many hours together, while he lay upon the seat, with Florence still beside him, and old Mrs. Pipchin sitting opposite. He remembered his old bed too, when they laid him down in it. But, there was something else, and recent, that still perplexed him.

'I want to speak to Florence, if you please. To Florence by herself, for a moment!'

She bent down over him, and the others stood away.

'Floy, my pet, wasn't that Papa in the hall, when they brought me from the coach?'

'Yes, dear.'

'He didn't cry, and go into his room, Floy, did he, when he saw me coming in?'

She shook her head, and pressed her lips against his cheek.

'I'm very glad he didn't cry, Floy. I thought he did. Don't tell them that I asked.'

CHAPTER THE LAST[1]

LITTLE Dombey had never risen from his little bed. He lay there, listening to the noises in the street, quite tranquilly; not caring much how the time went, but watching it and watching everything.

When the sunbeams struck into his room through the rustling blinds,

---

[1] Dickens altered VI to V, and then wrote 'The Last'. According to Wright, he always, 'in other readings' too, preluded his final section by saying: 'Chapter the Last'.

and quivered on the opposite wall, like golden water, he knew that evening was coming on, and that the sky was red and beautiful. As the reflection died away, and a gloom went creeping up the wall, he watched it deepen, deepen, deepen, into night. Then, he thought how the long unseen streets were dotted with lamps, and how the peaceful stars were shining overhead. *His fancy had a strange tendency to wander to the River, which he knew was flowing through the great city; and now he thought how black it was, and how deep it would look, reflecting the hosts of stars—and more than all, how steadily it rolled away to meet the sea.*[1]

As it grew later in the night, and footsteps in the street became so rare that he could hear them coming, count them as they passed, and lose them in the hollow distance, he would lie and watch the many-coloured ring about the candle, and wait patiently for day. *His only trouble was, the swift and rapid river.*[2] *He felt forced, sometimes, to try to stop it—to stem it with his childish hands—or choke its way with sand—and when he saw it coming on, resistless, he cried out!*[3] But a word from Florence, who was always at his side, restored him to himself; and leaning his poor head upon her breast, he told Floy of his dream, and smiled.

When day began to dawn again, he watched for the sun; and when its cheerful light began to sparkle in the room, he pictured to himself— pictured! he saw—the high church towers rising up into the morning sky, the town reviving, waking, starting into life once more, the river glistening as it rolled (*but rolling fast as ever*), and the country bright with dew. Familiar sounds and cries came by degrees into the street below; the servants in the house were roused and busy; faces looked in at the door, and voices asked his attendants softly how he was. Paul always answered for himself, '*I am better. I am a great deal better, thank you! Tell Papa so!*'

By little and little, he got tired of the bustle of the day, the noise of carriages and carts, and people passing and re-passing: and would fall asleep, *or be troubled with a restless and uneasy sense again.* '*Why, will it never stop, Floy?*' he would sometimes ask her. '*It is bearing me away, I think!*'

But, she could always soothe and reassure him; and it was his daily delight to make her lay her head down on his pillow, and take some rest.

'You are always watching me, Floy. Let *me* watch *you*,[4] now!'

They would prop him up with cushions in a corner of his bed, and

---

[1] Lines in both margins, against this sentence.

[2] 'Quick' (Wright). Lines in both margins, against these two underlined sentences.

[3] *he cried out* underlined trebly. This 'one startling instant' apart, all the pathetic incidents were narrated *sotto voce*, writes Kent (p. 185); but, on these three words, Dickens's voice was suddenly raised in 'an abrupt outcry'. 'Dropping his voice . . . instantly afterwards, to the gentlest tones, . . . the Reader continued in those subdued and tender accents to the end'.

[4] *me* underlined; *you* italic in *Suzannet* and in the novel.

there he would recline, the while she lay beside him: bending forward often-times to kiss her, and whispering to those who were near that she was tired, and how she had sat up so many nights beside him.

Thus, the flush of the day, in its heat and light, would gradually decline; and again the golden water would be dancing on the wall. †

The people around him changed unaccountably—and what had been the Doctor, would be his father, sitting with his head leaning on his hand. *This figure with its head leaning on its hand returned so often, and remained so long, and sat so still and solemn, never speaking, never being spoken to, and rarely lifting up its face, that Paul began to wonder languidly, if it were real.*

'Floy! What *is*[1] that?'

'Where, dearest?'

'There! at the bottom of the bed.'

'There's nothing there, except Papa!'

The figure lifted up its head, and rose, and coming to the bedside, said: 'My own boy! Don't you know me?'[2]

Paul looked it in the face. Before he could reach out both his hands to take it between them and draw it towards him, the figure turned away quickly from the little bed, and went out at the door.

The next time he observed the figure sitting at the bottom of the bed, he called to it.

'Don't be so sorry for me, dear Papa! Indeed I am quite happy!'

His father coming, and bending down to him, he held him round the neck, and repeated those words to him several times, and very earnestly; and he never saw his father in his room again at any time, whether it were day or night, but he called out, 'Don't be so sorry for me! Indeed I am quite happy!' This was the beginning of his always saying in the morning that he was a great deal better, and that they were to tell his father so.

How many times the golden water danced upon the wall; how many nights the dark river rolled towards the sea in spite of him; Paul never sought to know. If their kindness or his sense of it, could have increased, they were more kind, and he more grateful every day; *but, whether there were many days or few, appeared of little moment now, to the gentle boy.*

One night he had been thinking of his mother and her picture in the drawing-room down stairs. The train of thought suggested to him to inquire if he had ever seen his mother? For, *he could not remember whether they had told him yes, or no; the river running very fast, and confusing his mind.*

'Floy, did I ever see mama?'

'No, darling, why?'

---

[1] *is* italic in *Suzannet* and in the novel.   [2] 'Despairingly' (Wright).

'Did I never see any kind face, like a mama's, looking at me when I was a baby, Floy?'

'Oh yes, dear!'

'Whose, Floy?'

'Your old nurse's. Often.'

'And where is my old nurse? Show me that old nurse, Floy, if you please!'

'She is not here, darling. She shall come tomorrow.'

'Thank you, Floy!'

Little Dombey closed his eyes with those words, and fell asleep. When he awoke, the sun was high, and the broad day was clear and warm. Then he awoke[1]—woke mind and body—and sat upright in his bed. He saw them now about him. There was no gray mist before them, as there had been sometimes in the night. He knew them every one, and called them by their names.

'And who is this? Is this my old nurse?' asked the child, regarding with a radiant smile, a figure coming in.

Yes, yes. No other stranger would have shed those tears at sight of him, and called him her dear boy, her pretty boy, her own poor blighted child.[2] No other woman would have stooped down by his bed, and taken up his wasted hand, and put it to her lips and breast, as one who had some right to fondle it. No other woman would have so forgotten everybody there but him and Floy, and been so full of tenderness and pity.

'Floy! this is a kind good face! I am glad to see it again. Don't go away, old nurse! Stay here! * Good-bye!'

'Good-bye, my child?' cried Mrs. Pipchin, hurrying to his bed's head. 'Not good-bye?'

'Ah, yes! Good-bye!—Where is Papa?'

His father's breath was on his cheek, before the words had parted from his lips. The feeble hand waved in the air, as if it cried, 'good-bye!' again.

'Now lay me down; and Floy, come close to me, and let me see you!'

Sister and brother wound their arms around each other, and the golden light came streaming in, and fell upon them, locked together.[3]

'How fast the river runs, between its green banks and the rushes, Floy! But, it's very near the sea now. I hear the waves! They always said so!'

Presently, he told her that the motion of the boat upon the stream was

[1] 'Then he awoke' is inserted in manuscript, to cover two short deletions. Dickens nodded here; he forgot that Paul was already awake, and had dropped off to sleep again only in the deleted passage.

[2] 'Feelingly'; at 'taken up his wasted hand . . .', Dickens put 'Hand to lips', 'Hand to breast' (Wright).

[3] This paragraph is underlined in *Gimbel*.

lulling him to rest. Now, the boat was out at sea. *And now, there was a shore before him. Who stood on the bank!*—[1]

He put his hands together, as he had been used to do, at his prayers. He did not remove his arms to do it; but they saw him fold them so, behind his sister's neck.

'Mama is like you, Floy. I know her by the face! But tell them that the picture on the stairs at school, is not Divine enough.[2] The light about the head is shining on me as I go!'

The golden ripple on the wall came back again, and nothing else stirred in the room. The old, old, fashion! The fashion that came in with our first garments, and will last unchanged until our race has run its course, and the wide firmament is rolled up like a scroll. The old, old fashion—Death![3]

Oh, thank GOD, all who see it, for that older fashion yet, of Immortality! And look upon us, Angels of young children, with regards not quite estranged, when the swift river bears us to the ocean!

---

[1] The whole of this paragraph is underlined in *Gimbel*.

[2] Wright underlines *Divine enough*, but comments: 'Too loud altogether'.

[3] *Death* underlined five times—but spoken 'In a low whispering voice' (Wright). In *Gimbel*, too, the whole paragraph is underlined, with special emphasis on *Death*. The ensuing, and final, paragraph (all underlined in *Gimbel*) was spoken 'in a tearful voice' (Kent, p. 187). See the headnote to this Reading for R. H. Hutton's severe criticism of Dickens's performance at this point ('Adelphi Theatre' pathos).

THE POOR TRAVELLER

On 17 June 1858 Dickens for the first time departed from his practice of performing only one item, and instead read three short pieces. The prompt-copy, now in the Berg Collection, is entitled *The Poor Traveller:/ Boots at the Holly-Tree Inn:/ and Mrs. Gamp./ By Charles Dickens./ London:/ 1858.* (printed by Bradbury & Evans; texts of the three items paginated 3–35, 37–60 and 61–114, but a manuscript p. 115 is added, containing a revised ending for *Mrs. Gamp*). Bradbury & Evans also printed in 1858 a 'trade edition'. of these three items. Its title-page is the same as the prompt-copy's except that the particulars of publication are fuller: *London:/ Bradbury & Evans, 11, Bouverie Street./ 1858.* On the front cover, the price appears below this: *One Shilling.* The pagination of the items is as in the prompt-copy but, as is noted below, the texts differ slightly.

The Poor Traveller is the first tale in *The Seven Poor Travellers*, the *Household Words* Christmas number for 1854. In the December of that year, Dickens had read it to his friend Miss Coutts and her guests, one of whom (the Reverend William Harness) reported that it was 'in better taste than the others' (*Mary Russell Mitford: Correspondence with Charles Boner and John Ruskin*, ed. Elizabeth Lee (1914), p. 305). One hopes that Harness meant that it surpassed the other tales in that Christmas number, written by Dickens's collaborators: for it is not in better taste, nor superior in any other way, to much else that he himself had ever written. His choosing this feeble and uncharacteristic story for one of his earliest professional Readings is, indeed, extraordinary. Perhaps he recalled that performance at Miss Coutts's in 1854 as a triumph. Certainly he must have felt that, as *Boots* and *Mrs. Gamp* were predominantly comic, the third item should offer a contrast in mode and tone: *The Poor Traveller* did that, and enabled him to exercise elocutionary gifts which the rest of his current repertoire did not demand.

Apart from altering the opening paragraph to eliminate its reference to the introductory portion of *The Seven Poor Travellers*, he did not emend the *Household Words* text before sending it to be privately printed. This item was already quite short, so the need for abbreviation was less apparent; but, on comparable occasions later, he generally cut more at this preliminary stage before having the prompt-copy printed. About a quarter of the prompt-copy text is deleted, but how soon this was done is uncertain. Deletions and other revisions were made on successive occasions, as the inks (mainly blue, but also brown and black) show: and pencil, too, was used, sometimes before and sometimes after a series of inked revisions. Moreover, as in the other two items in this programme, the text of the 1858 'trade edition' is slightly different both from the *Household Words* text and from the prompt-copy (either as printed or as emended). These differences are, however, trivial and the trade edition of *The Poor Traveller* is virtually identical with the privately printed text. It seems unlikely, however, that even in June 1858 Dickens was reading the text exactly as it appeared in either printing. As audiences now and later were to discover, what he actually said differed considerably from the text of the 'reading editions' they bought at the door.

The story, though never one of Dickens's more admired works, appealed to the taste of its period more than it is now likely to do: 'one of those slight but exquisite sketches . . . thrown off by the hand of a great master; . . . touches so felicitous and inimitable in their way . . .; the lovely idyll' (Kent, pp. 195, 206); '. . . one of the most beautiful little stories that ever was written, either by Mr. Dickens or anybody else. We do not envy the man who can read it, and not feel a tear start unbidden to his eye' (*Bradford Observer*, 21 October 1858). Accounts of Dickens's performance vary considerably. For some critics, including admirers of the story, the Reading was disappointing, and showed that Dickens's forte, as a performer, did not lie in the pathetic. Others, however, found his pathos 'deep and thrilling' (*Limerick Reporter*, 3 September 1858) and his narration of the stirring scenes in this item very exciting: 'Mr. Dickens . . . was frequently interrupted by applause' (*Belfast News-Letter*, 30 August 1858). Generally, audiences seem to have found this performance less remarkable than others in the repertoire at that time; it tended to be monotonous, and did not offer such opportunities for Dickens's gifts as a character-actor as its companion-pieces. His attempts to represent the 'thrilling tones' of Mary Marshall's voice were not thought felicitous. An interesting extended critique in the *Saturday Review* (19 June 1858, p. 636) described the story as

. . . one of the most purely melo-dramatic things he ever wrote. It is sentimental, but not so purely sentimental as *Dombey* or *David Copperfield*. The sentimentalism is confined within the bounds and moulded into the form of the melo-dramatic— that is, there are a series of little turns or tricks adopted by which an idea is continually brought round and round, and forced upon the attention of the reader or hearer. In *The Poor Traveller* these tricks are of a rather puerile kind, and Mr. Dickens, to whose fancy they are evidently peculiarly dear, threw out the whole strength of his powers of reading to make them tell. Stated in simple language, these melo-dramatic tricks sound rather simple. They principally consist in perpetually bringing in the name 'Richard Doubledick,' and in speaking of the 'deep dark eyes' of an officer. Entering the service as a dissipated private, Doubledick cuts his way up to the rank of captain. This gives occasion to the writer to read a series of paragraphs with Sergeant Richard Doubledick, Sergeant-Major Richard Doubledick, Ensign Richard Doubledick, and so on. Mr. Dickens made this a great point in his reading. He dwelt on the separate syllables, and rolled out the r's as if this little art of repeating the man's name with variations was sure to be gratifying to every one. Richard is reclaimed by the man with the eyes, and Mr. Dickens took every pains to make us feel that the eyes were coming, and that they ought to go through us as they did through Doubledick. Nothing could be more characteristic of Mr. Dickens' style of writing than the way in which he made use of these eyes; nor could anything have more forcibly recalled to the mind of the hearer the numberless instances in which he has, as we think, thrown away the genuine success he might have achieved, by having recourse to the paltry artifices of stage effect.

The Poor Traveller remained in repertoire throughout Dickens's first season, until January 1859; it was very rarely performed after that. A performance was given in London on 12 June 1863 (*N*, iii. 354), and another in Glasgow

on 25 February 1869—but the latter was due to George Dolby's having made
a mistake in announcing it in advertisements, to Dickens's annoyance (*N*, iii.
706). As it was not performed in America, it did not appear in the Ticknor &
Fields or subsequent collections. It has not been reprinted since the 1858 trade
edition.

The Poor Traveller

In the year one thousand seven hundred and ninety-nine,[1] a relative of mine went limping down, on foot, to the town of Chatham. He was a poor traveller, with not a farthing in his pocket, and he slept that night at an old foundation for Poor Travellers, where some Poor Travellers sleep every night.

He went down to Chatham, to enlist in a cavalry regiment, if a cavalry regiment would have him; if not, to take King George's shilling from any corporal or sergeant who would put a bunch of ribbons in his hat. *His object was, to get shot; but, he thought he might as well ride to death as be at the trouble of walking.*[2]

His Christian name was Richard, but he was better known as Dick. He dropped his own surname on the road down, and took up that of Doubledick. He passed as Richard Doubledick; age twenty-two; height, five foot ten. There was no cavalry in Chatham, so he enlisted into a regiment of the line, *and was glad to get drunk and forget all about it.*

He had gone wrong and run wild. His heart was in the right place, but it was sealed up. He had been betrothed to a good and beautiful girl whom he had loved better than she—or perhaps even he—believed; but, in an evil hour, he had given her cause to say to him, 'Richard, I will never marry any other man. I will live single for your sake, but Mary Marshall's lips;' her name was Mary Marshall; 'never address another word to you on earth. Go, Richard! Heaven forgive you!' This finished him. This took him down to Chatham. This made him Private[3] Doubledick, with a determination to be shot.

There was not a more reckless soldier in Chatham barracks, in the year one thousand seven hundred and ninety-nine, than Private Doubledick. He associated with the dregs of every regiment, he was as seldom sober as he could be, and was constantly under punishment. It became clear to the whole barracks, that Private Doubledick would very soon be flogged.

---

[1] Here, and at the beginning of the fifth paragraph, Dickens altered the date to 1779; in the second instance, he altered it back again to 1799, but he forgot to do so here.

[2] All the underlining in this prompt-copy (unless otherwise noted) is in Dickens's double interrupted style, and will be represented here throughout by italic without any footnoting.

[3] The deletion of 'Richard' throughout presumably took place after the initial performance reviewed in the *Saturday Review*, in which the emphatic repetition of 'Richard Doubledick' was noted (quoted above, in the headnote).

Now, *the Captain* of Doubledick's company was a young gentleman not above five years his senior, whose eyes had an expression in them which affected Private Doubledick in a very remarkable way.[1] They were bright, handsome, dark eyes—what are called laughing eyes generally, and, when serious, rather steady than severe—but, they were the only eyes now left in his narrowed world that Private Doubledick could not stand. He could not so much as salute *Captain Taunton* in the street, like any other officer. In his worst moments he would rather turn back and go any distance out of his way, than encounter those two handsome, dark, bright eyes.

One day, when Private Doubledick came out of the Black hole—where he had been passing the last eight-and-forty hours—and in which retreat he spent a good deal of his time—he was ordered to betake himself to Captain Taunton's quarters. In the squalid state of a man just out of the Black hole, he had less fancy than ever for being seen by the Captain; but, he was not so mad yet as to disobey orders, and consequently went up to the officers' quarters: twisting and breaking in his hands as he went along, a bit of straw that had formed the decorative furniture of the Black hole.

'Come in!' Private Doubledick pulled off his cap, took a stride forward, and stood in the light of the dark bright eyes.

'Doubledick, do you know where you are going to?'

'To the Devil, Sir?'

'Yes. And very fast.'

He turned the straw of the Black hole in his mouth, and made a miserable salute of acquiescence.[2]

'Doubledick, since I entered his Majesty's service, a boy of seventeen, I have been pained to see many men of promise going that road; but, I have never been *so* pained to see a man determined to make the shameful journey, as I have been, ever since *you* joined the regiment, to see *you*.'[3]

'I am only a common soldier, sir. It signifies very little what such a poor brute comes to.'

[1] '. . . when the Reader came . . . to these words . . . the effect was singularly striking. Out of the Reader's own eyes would look the eyes of that Captain, as the Author himself describes them' (Kent, p. 197). Many reminiscences of Dickens, when met socially or seen on a platform, recall the extraordinary intensity of his eyes; *The Poor Traveller* was the only Reading which gave him such a ready-made opportunity to exploit this feature of his physical presence.

[2] '. . . one did not hear the words simply, one saw it done precisely as it is described'. This interview with the Captain was 'one of the most exquisitely portrayed incidents in the whole of this Reading' (Kent, pp. 198–9).

[3] Here Dickens deleted, in *Berg*, this paragraph: 'Private Richard Doubledick began to find a film stealing over the floor at which he looked; also to find the legs of the Captain's breakfast-table turning crooked, as if he saw them through water.' As Kent remarked, Dickens obtained 'pretty nearly the effect' of these words, by the way he spoke—after a momentary pause—the speech that follows.

'You are a man of education; and if you say that, meaning what you say, you have sunk lower than I had believed. How low that must be, I leave you to consider: knowing what I know of your disgrace, and seeing what I see.'

'I hope to get shot soon, sir, and then the regiment, and the world together, will be rid of me.'

Looking up he met the eyes that had so strong an influence over him. He put his hand before his own eyes, and the breast of his disgrace-jacket swelled as if it would fly asunder.

'I would rather see this in you, Doubledick, than I would see five thousand guineas counted out upon this table for a gift to my good mother. Have you a mother?'

'I am thankful to say she is dead, sir.'

'If your praises were sounded from mouth to mouth through the whole regiment, through the whole army, through the whole country, you would wish she had lived, to say with pride and joy, "He is my son!"'

'Spare me, sir. She would never have heard any good of me. She would never have had any pride and joy in owning herself my mother. Love and compassion she might have had, and would have always had, I know; but not——Spare me, sir! I am a broken wretch, quite at your mercy!'[1]

'My friend——'

'God bless you, sir!'

'You are at the crisis of your fate, my friend. Hold your course un-changed a little longer, and you know what must happen. *I*[2] know even better than you can imagine, that after that has happened, you are lost. No man who could shed such tears, could bear such marks.'

'I fully believe it, sir.'

'But a man in any station can do his duty, and, in doing it, can earn his own respect, even if his case should be so very unfortunate and so very rare, that he can earn no other man's. A common soldier—poor brute though you called him just now—has this advantage in the stormy times we live in, that he always does his duty before a host of sympathising witnesses. Do you doubt that he may so do it as to be extolled through a whole regiment, through a whole army, through a whole country? Turn while you may yet retrieve the past, and try.'

'I will! I ask for only one witness, sir.'

---

[1] Again action replaced speech here. Dickens deleted in *Berg* the next sentence: 'And he turned his face to the wall and stretched out his imploring hand.' Kent remarks: 'How eloquently that "imploring hand" spoke in the agonised, dumb supplication of its movement, coupled as it was with the shaken frame and the averted countenance, those who witnessed this Reading will readily recall to their recollection' (p. 200).

[2] *I* italic in *Household Words* (*HW*) and in *Berg*.

'I understand you. I will be a watchful and a faithful one.'

I have heard from Private Doubledick's own lips, that he dropped down upon his knee, kissed that officer's hand, arose, *and went out of the light of the dark bright eyes, an altered man.*[1]

In that year, one thousand seven hundred and ninety-nine, the French were in Egypt, in Italy, in Germany, where not? Napoleon Buonaparte had likewise begun to stir against us in India. In the very next year, when we formed an alliance with Austria against him, Captain Taunton's regiment was on service in India. And there was not a finer non-commissioned officer in it—no, nor in the whole line—than *Corporal* Doubledick.

In eighteen hundred and one, the Indian army were on the coast of Egypt. Next year was the year of the proclamation of the short peace, and they were recalled. It had then become well-known to thousands of men, that wherever Captain Taunton led, there, close to him, ever at his side, firm as a rock, true as the sun, and brave as Mars, would be certain to be found, while life beat in their hearts, that famous soldier, *Sergeant* Doubledick.

Eighteen hundred and five saw wonders done by a *Sergeant-Major*, who cut his way single-handed through a solid mass of men, recovered the colours of his regiment, and rescued his wounded captain, who was down in a jungle of horses' hoofs and sabres—that year saw such wonders done, I say, by this brave Sergeant-Major, that he was specially made the bearer of the colours he had won; and *Ensign* Doubledick had risen from the ranks.

Sorely cut up in every battle, but always reinforced by the bravest of men, this regiment fought its way through the Peninsular war, up to the investment of Badajos in eighteen hundred and twelve. † One day,—not in the great storming, but in repelling a hot sally of the besieged upon our men at work in the trenches, who had given way,—the two officers, Major Taunton and Ensign Doubledick, found themselves hurrying forward, face to face, against a party of French infantry who made a stand. There was an officer at their head, encouraging his men,—a courageous, handsome, gallant officer of five and thirty—whom Doubledick saw hurriedly, but saw well. He particularly noticed this officer waving his sword, and rallying his men with an eager and excited cry, when they fired, *and Major Taunton dropped.*

It was over in ten minutes more, and Doubledick returned to the spot where he had laid the best friend man ever had, on a coat spread upon the wet clay. Major Taunton's uniform was opened at the breast, and on his shirt were three little spots of blood.

'Dear Doubledick, I am dying.'

'For the love of Heaven, no! Taunton! My preserver, my guardian

[1] Spoken 'in terms how manly and yet how tender in their vibration' (Kent, p. 202).

angel, my witness! Dearest, truest, kindest of human beings! Taunton! For God's sake!'[1]

The bright dark eyes—so very, very dark now, in the pale face— smiled upon him; *and the hand he had kissed thirteen years ago, laid itself on his breast.*

'Write to my mother. You will see Home again. Tell her how we became friends. It will comfort her, as it comforts me.'

He spoke no more, but faintly signed for a moment towards his hair as it fluttered in the wind. The Ensign understood him. He smiled again when he saw that, and gently turning his face over on the supporting arm as if for rest, *died, with his hand upon the breast in which he had revived a soul.*

No dry eye looked on Ensign Doubledick, that melancholy day. He buried his friend on the field, and became a lone man. Beyond his duty he appeared to have but two remaining cares in life; one, to preserve the little packet of hair he was to give to Taunton's mother; *the other, to encounter that French officer who had rallied the men under whose fire Taunton fell.* A new legend now began to circulate among our troops; and it was, that *when he and the French officer came face to face once more, there would be weeping in France.*

The war went on until the Battle of Toulouse was fought. In the returns sent home, appeared these words: 'Severely wounded, but not dangerously, *Lieutenant* Doubledick.'

At Midsummer time in the year eighteen hundred and fourteen, Lieutenant Doubledick, now a browned soldier, seven and thirty years of age, came home to England, invalided. He brought the hair with him, near his heart. *Many a French officer had he seen, since that day; many a dreadful night, in searching with men and lanterns for his wounded, had he relieved French officers lying disabled; but, the mental picture and the reality had never come together.*

Though he was weak and suffered pain, he lost not an hour in getting down to Frome in Somerset-shire, where Taunton's mother lived. *In the sweet, compassionate words of the most compassionate of books, 'he was the only son of his mother, and she was a widow.'* †

Never, from the hour when he enlisted at Chatham, had he breathed his right name, or the name of Mary Marshall, or a word of the story of his life, into any ear, except his reclaimer's. But, that night, remembering the words he had cherished for two years, 'Tell her how we became friends. It will comfort her, as it comforts me,' he related everything. It gradually seemed to him, as if in his maturity he had recovered a mother; it gradually seemed to her, as if in her bereavement she had found

---

[1] 'To listen to that agonised entreaty as it started from the trembling and one could almost have fancied whitened lips of the Reader, was to be with him there upon the instant on the far-off battle-field' (Kent, p. 203).

a son. When he was able to rejoin his regiment in the spring, he left her; thinking was this indeed the first time he had ever turned his face towards the old colours with a woman's blessing!

He followed the old colours—so ragged, scarred and pierced with shot, that they would scarcely hold together—to Quatre Bras, and to Ligny. He stood beside them, in an awful stillness of many men, shadowy through the mist and drizzle of a wet June forenoon, on the field of Waterloo.

The famous regiment was in action early in the battle, and received its first check in many an eventful year, when *he* was seen to fall. But, it swept on to avenge him, and left behind it no such creature in the world of consciousness, as Lieutenant Doubledick.

Through pits of mire and pools of rain; along deep ditches, once roads, that were ploughed to pieces by artillery, heavy waggons, tramp of men and horses, and the struggle of every wheeled thing that could carry wounded soldiers; jolted among the dying and the dead, so disfigured by blood and mud as to be hardly recognizable for humanity; undisturbed by the moaning of men and the shrieking of horses, which, newly taken from the peaceful pursuits of life, could not endure the sight of the stragglers lying by the wayside, never to resume their toilsome journey; dead, as to any sentient life that was in it, and yet alive; the form that had been Lieutenant Doubledick, with whose praises England rang, was conveyed to Brussels. There, it was tenderly laid down in hospital: and there it lay, week after week, through the long bright summer days, until the harvest had ripened and was gathered in. †

Slowly labouring, at last, through a long heavy dream of confused time and place, Lieutenant Doubledick came back to life. To the beautiful life of a calm autumn-evening sunset. To the peaceful life of a fresh quiet room with a large window standing open; a balcony beyond, in which were moving leaves and sweet-smelling flowers; beyond again, the clear sky, and the sun, pouring its golden radiance on his bed.

It was so tranquil and so lovely, that he thought he had passed into another world. And he said in a faint voice, 'Taunton, are you near me?'

A face bent over him. Not his; his mother's.

'I came to nurse you. We have nursed you, many weeks. You were moved here, long ago. Do you remember nothing?'

'Nothing. Where is the regiment? What has happened?'

'A great victory, dear. The war is over, and the regiment was the bravest in the field.'

'Thank God! Was it dark just now?'

'No.'

'It was only dark to me? Something passed away, like a black shadow. As it went, and the sun touched my face, I thought I saw a light white cloud pass out at the door. Was there nothing that went out?'

She shook her head, and, in a little while, he fell asleep, and from that time, he recovered. Slowly, for he had been desperately wounded in the head, and had been shot in the body.

One day, he awoke out of a sleep, refreshed, and asked Mrs. Taunton to read to him. But, the curtain of the bed softening the light was held undrawn; and a woman's voice spoke, which was not hers.

'Can you bear to see a stranger? Will you like to see a stranger?'[1]

'Stranger!' *The voice awoke old memories, before the days of Private Doubledick.*

'A stranger now, but not a stranger once. Richard, dear Richard, lost through so many years, my name——'

He cried out her name, 'Mary!' and his head lay on her bosom.

'I am not breaking a rash vow, Richard. These are not Mary Marshall's lips that speak. I have another name.'

She was married.

'I have another name, Richard. Did you ever hear it?'

'Never!'

'Think again, Richard. Are you sure you never heard my altered name?'

'Never!'

'Don't move your head to look at me, dear Richard. Let it lie here, while I tell my story. I loved a generous, noble man with my whole heart; loved him for years and years, faithfully, devotedly; with no hope of return; knowing nothing of his highest qualities—not even knowing that he was alive. He was a brave soldier. He was honoured and beloved by thousands, when the mother of his dear friend found me, and showed me that in all his triumphs he had never forgotten me. He was wounded in a great battle. He was brought, dying, here into Brussels. I came to watch and tend him, as I would have joyfully gone, with such a purpose, to the dreariest ends of the earth. When he knew no one else he knew me. When he lay at the point of death, he married me, that he might call me Wife before he died. And the name, my dear love, that I took on that forgotten night——'

'I know it now! The shadowy remembrance strengthens. It was my name. You are my wife!'

Well! They were happy. It was a long recovery but they were happy through it all. The snow had melted on the ground, and the birds were singing in the early spring, when those three were first able to ride out together, and when people flocked about the open carriage to cheer and congratulate *Captain* Doubledick.

But, even then, it became necessary for the Captain, instead of returning to England, to complete his recovery in the climate of Southern France.

---

[1] 'Mr. Dickens's voice . . . is not equal to the vocal expression of these fine traits of feminine feeling . . . which his own conceptions evidently demand' (*Wolverhampton Chronicle*, 10 November 1858).

They found a spot upon the Rhone, within a ride of the old town of Avignon, which was all they could desire; and they lived there, together, six months; and then the Captain and his wife returned to England. But Mrs. Taunton growing old and feeling benefited by the change, resolved to remain for a year in those parts. So, she remained: and she was to be rejoined and escorted home, at the year's end, by Captain Doubledick.

She went to the neighbourhood of Aix; and there, *in a chateau near the farmer's house she rented*,[1] she grew into intimacy with a family belonging to that part of France. The intimacy began in her often meeting among the vineyards a pretty child: a girl, who was never tired of listening to the solitary English lady's stories of her poor son and the cruel wars. The family were as gentle as the child, and at length she came to know them so well, that she accepted their invitation to pass the last month of her residence abroad, under their roof. All this intelligence she wrote home, piecemeal as it came about; and, at last, enclosed a polite note from the head of the chateau, soliciting, on the occasion of his approaching mission to that neighbourhood, the honour of the company of cet homme si justement célèbre, Monsieur le Capitaine Richard Doubledick.

Captain Doubledick; now a hardy, handsome man in the full vigour of life, broader across the chest and shoulders than he had ever been before; dispatched a courteous reply, and followed it in person. Travelling through all that extent of country after three years of Peace, he blessed the better days on which the world had fallen. The corn was golden— not drenched in unnatural red; was bound in sheaves for food—not trodden underfoot by men in mortal fight. The smoke rose up from peaceful homes, not blazing ruins. The carts were laden with the fair fruits of the earth, not with wounds and death. To him who had so often seen the terrible reverse, these things were beautiful indeed, and they brought him in *a softened spirit* to the old chateau upon a deep blue evening.

It was a large chateau of the genuine old ghostly kind, with round towers, and extinguishers and a high leaden roof, and more windows than Aladdin's Palace. The lattice blinds were all thrown open, and the entrance doors stood open too—as doors often do in that country when the heat of the day is past; the Captain saw no bell or knocker, and walked in.

He walked into a lofty stone hall, refreshingly cool and gloomy after the glare of a Southern day's travel. Extending along the four sides of this hall, was a gallery, leading to suites of rooms; and it was lighted from the top. Still, no bell was to be seen.

[1] Single continuous underlining.

'Faith,' said the Captain, halting, ashamed of the clanking of his boots, 'this is a ghostly beginning!'

He started back, and felt his face turn white. In the gallery, looking down at him, stood the French officer: the officer whose picture he had carried in his mind so long and so far.

The officer moved, and disappeared, and Captain Doubledick heard his steps coming quickly down into the hall. He entered through an archway. *There was a bright, sudden look upon his face. Such a look as it had worn in that fatal moment.*

Monsieur le Capitaine Richard Doubledick? Enchanted to receive him! A thousand apologies! The servants were all out in the air. There was a little fête among them in the garden. In effect, it was the fête day of my daughter, the little cherished and protected of Madame Taunton.

He was so gracious that Monsieur le Capitaine Richard Doubledick could not withhold his hand. 'It is the hand of a brave Englishman,' said the French officer, retaining it while he spoke. 'I could respect a brave Englishman, even as my foe; how much more as my friend! I, also, am a soldier.'

'He has not remembered me, as I have remembered him; he did not take such note of my face, that day, as I took of his. How shall I tell him!'

The French officer conducted his guest into a garden, and there presented him to his beautiful wife. His daughter came running to embrace him; and there was a boy-baby. A multitude of children-visitors were dancing to sprightly music; and all the servants and peasants about the chateau were dancing too. *It was a scene of innocent happiness that might have been invented for the climax of the scenes of Peace which had soothed the captain's journey.*

He looked on, greatly troubled in his mind, until a resounding bell rang, and the French officer begged to show him his rooms.

'You were at Waterloo?'

'I was. And I was at Badajos.'

Left alone with the sound of his own stern voice in his ears, he sat down to consider, *What shall I do, and how shall I tell him?* At that time, unhappily, many deplorable duels had been fought between English and French officers, arising out of the recent war; and these duels, and how to avoid this officer's hospitality, were the uppermost thought in Captain Doubledick's mind.

He was thinking, and letting the time run out in which he should have dressed for dinner, when Mrs. Taunton spoke to him at his chamber door. '*His mother above all. How shall I tell her?*'[1]

'You will form a friendship with your host, I hope,' said Mrs. Taunton.

---

[1] *her*, italic in *HW*, is also further underlined in *Berg*.

'He is so true-hearted and so generous, Richard, that you can hardly fail to esteem one another. If He had been spared,' she kissed the locket in which she wore his hair, 'he would have appreciated him with his own generosity, and would have been happy that the evil days were past, which made a man his enemy.'

She left the room; the Captain walked, first to one window whence he could see the dancing in the garden; then, to another window whence he could see the smiling prospect and the peaceful vineyards.

'Spirit of my departed friend,' said he, 'is it through thee, these better thoughts are rising in my mind! Is it thou who hast shown me, all the way I have been drawn to meet this man, the blessings of the altered time! Is it thou who hast sent thy stricken mother to me, to stay my angry hand! Is it from thee the whisper comes, that this man only did his duty as thou didst—and as I did, through thy guidance, which saved me, here on earth—and that he did no more!'

He made the second strong resolution of his life: That neither to the French officer, *nor* to the mother of his departed friend, *nor* to any soul while either of the two was living, would he breathe what only *he* knew. And when he touched that French officer's glass with his own, that day at dinner, he secretly forgave him—forgave him, in the name of the *Divine Forgiver*.

BOOTS AT THE HOLLY-TREE INN

THE second item in Dickens's first programme of short pieces, introduced in June 1858, was taken from the *Household Words* Christmas number for 1855, *The Holly-Tree Inn*, where 'The Boots' had provided the third story. The Reading text was printed in the prompt-copy and the 1858 trade edition described above (see p. 153). Only a few slight deletions and alterations had been made in the *Household Words* text before the prompt-copy was printed, and many of these were the omission of speech-attributions such as 'says Cobbs'. As with *The Poor Traveller*, the text of the 1858 trade edition differs slightly from that of the prompt-copy, both as printed and as emended in manuscript: but again the differences are too trivial to be worth recording or discussing.

The prompt-book text is emended in blue and brown ink, and occasionally in pencil (usually confirmed in ink). Some short deletions, and a few short additions, are made; an introductory paragraph is written in, summarizing the Holly-Tree Inn situation. Most of the alterations, however, were occasioned by the elocutionary problems arising from the story's being a mixture of what is told by 'I' (the traveller sequestered in the Holly-Tree Inn, who speaks ordinary educated English) and what is told by the Boots (Cobbs, who speaks Cockney). Dickens's first solution was to leave the text unaltered, but to indicate to himself which passages were to be spoken (by 'I') in his ordinary narrative voice; so, in blue ink, he underlined these passages and put them inside square brackets. Some other passages, to be specially emphasized, were *doubly* underlined, in blue ink. Later, he decided to deliver more of the narrative in Cobbs's voice, so he eliminated much of the narratorial 'I', by altering the words slightly and transferring them to Cobbs. The narrator's references to 'Cobbs', 'he' or 'him' are altered to 'I' or 'me' (with Cobbs now the speaker) and an occasional 'Sir' was added to these passages. Most of these alterations were made in brown (occasionally black) ink. They took place, of course, mainly in passages previously underlined and square-bracketed; the underlining and square brackets were no longer appropriate, but it was impracticable for Dickens to try to delete them.

The text printed below is therefore a compromise. The passages still intended to be spoken by the narratorial 'I' are printed (following Dickens's convention) in italics and inside square brackets. Passages which, in the final version, have been transferred from the narrator to Cobbs are *not* italicized, etc., though Dickens had perforce left them underlined and square-bracketed in the prompt-copy. For consistency, square brackets and italics are supplied in the opening paragraph, which Dickens had added in manuscript but without underlining or square-bracketing them. In a few passages transferred from the narrator to Cobbs, he had failed to alter a stray 'he' to 'I'; such oversights have been silently corrected.

Boots was included in *T & F*, where it was printed from *Berg*. A few errors in *Berg* were corrected in *T & F*, and these corrections have been silently adopted in the text below. In a few places, *T & F* introduces new readings; where these seem likely to have been Dickens's handiwork, they are footnoted. There are also some changes in punctuation and paragraphing in *T & F*; these have not been adopted, as these are as likely to be due to Ticknor & Fields's house-style as to Dickens himself; they are, anyway, of no great significance.

This story of two little children in love, running away to Gretna Green, may strike the modern reader as coy and embarrassing (see exchange in *Dickensian*, lxvi (1970), 239, and lxvii (1971), 42), and it displeased some of Dickens's contemporaries too (an 'atrocious yarn'—*New York Tribune*, 13 December 1867). His performance certainly brought a tear to the eye, but the predominant effect was comic: and some of the more heart-tugging phrases had been deleted, so he was relatively sparing in his demands upon his audience's tears. Also the sentimentality was offset by the wit and humour of Cobbs. Two months after adding it to his repertoire, Dickens reported that people laughed at it more than at any other item—'and I notice that they sit with their heads on one side, and an expression of playful pity on their faces—as if they saw the tiny boy and girl, which is tender and pleasant, I think?' (*Coutts*, pp. 362–3). Even the *Saturday Review*, which was always fiercely critical of Dickens's sentimentality, found *Boots* 'much the best' of the three items in his new programme (19 June 1858, p. 636). Its popularity was sustained: only two items in the repertoire (*The Trial* and the *Carol*) were performed more often. Early in its run, it was thought his 'most charming' item:

> The way in which Mr. Dickens read this piece is inimitable, and kept his audience convulsed with merriment. . . . The chuckling tone and merry twinkle of the eye with which he gave expression to the salient points of the story were wonderfully effective, and impossible to be described. It was evident that Mr. Dickens entered thoroughly into the spirit of the thing, and enjoyed the fun as heartily as his hearers. (*Dublin Evening Mail*, 27 August 1858)

A decade later it was described as 'perhaps the best of the readings, and certainly one of the best of his sketches' (*Cheltenham Examiner*, 13 January 1869). It had been very popular in America, where many critics considered it and *The Trial* his two best items. It was 'unalloyed pleasure', wrote Kate Field (pp. 87–9): it contained no weak patches, and Cobbs had something of the quality of Sam Weller, though softer and more poetical. George Eliot, mentioning the story, reached for another comparison: 'there is the same startling inspiration in his description of "Boots", as in the speeches of Shakespeare's mobs or numbskulls' (*Essays*, ed. Thomas Pinney (1963), p. 271).

How Dickens portrayed Cobbs is well described by John Hollingshead:

> Boots at the Holly Tree Inn, as an example of low comedy drawn from nature, is worth a hundred fancy eccentric portraits like Sam Weller, whose character is largely marked by the vices of a bygone literature, which happily is now utterly buried and forgotten. Mr. Dickens's embodiment of Boots is remarkable for ease, finish, and a thorough relish for the character. The swaying to and fro of the body, the half-closing of the eye, and the action of the head, when any point in the narrative is supposed to require particular emphasis to make it clear, and the voice sounding as if affected by

the chewing of a straw—all assist to make a perfect example of pure comedy acting. It was a very happy notion to place such a pretty story in the mouth of such a man; and the audience, while they watch with interest the progress of the fanciful episode in the life of the little runaway children, are amused by the broad humour and strong individuality of the simulated narrator. The boy-child, when he gets an opportunity of speaking in his own character, is very clearly conveyed to the audience by Mr. Dickens. (*The Critic*, 4 September 1858, p. 538)

Cobbs, though working in Yorkshire, had started his working life 'down away by Shooter's Hill there, six or seven miles from Lunnon', and Dickens brought into his conversation

... all the characteristics of emphatic humble Cockney conversation, as far as they can be rendered consonant with the graceful interest of the tale. It is quite a treat to hear Mr. Dickens pronounce the Londoner's 'w', which, as those who have nice ears are aware, is only half a 'v', and is grossly caricatured when a full 'v' is substituted for it. The pauses for general emphasis are also the result of very shrewd observation, and the sardonics of Boots are the very cream of universal humour. (*Morning Star*, 6 January 1869)

The 'great hit' of the Reading, treasured by all who heard it, was when Boots 'told of the sympathy of the women with the little pair' (*Scotsman*, 21 December 1868)—their excitement when the children are first installed in their sitting-room, and the female staff of the Inn 'was seven deep at the key-hole', and their anguish later when the children are to be parted and one of the chambermaids calls out, 'It's a shame to part 'em!' It is characteristic of Dickens's adaptations that, in both these places, the rest of the paragraph is deleted, doubtless because it had proved an anti-climax after the 'great hit' (or clap-trap). The sentences about the chambermaid which thus had to be sacrificed are pleasing: 'But this chambermaid was always a soft-hearted girl. Not that there was any harm in that girl. Far from it.'

Boots at the Holly-Tree Inn

[1][BEFORE *the days of railways, and in the time of the old great North Road, I was once snowed up at the Holly Tree Inn. Beguiling the days of my imprisonment there, by talking, at one time or other, with the whole establishment, I one day talked with the Boots when he lingered in my room.*]

Where had he been in his time? [*Boots repeated, when I asked him the question.*] Lord, he had been everywhere! [*And what had he been?*] Bless you, everything you could mention a'most.

Seen a good deal? Why, of course he had. [*I should say so, he could assure me, if I only knew about a twentieth part of what had come in his*[2] *way.*] Why, it would be easier for him, he expected, to tell what he hadn't seen, then what he had. Ah! A deal, it would.

What was the curiousest thing he had seen? Well! He didn't know.[3] He couldn't momently name what was the curiousest thing he had seen— unless it was a Unicorn—and he see *him*[4] once at a Fair. But supposing a young gentleman not eight years old, was to run away with a fine young woman of seven, might I think *that*[5] a queer start? Certainly! Then, that was a start as he himself had had his blessed eyes on—and he had cleaned the shoes they run away in—and they was so little that he couldn't get his hand into 'em.

Master Harry Walmers's father, you see, he lived at the Elmses, down away by Shooter's Hill there, six or seven miles from Lunnon. He was a gentleman of spirit, and good looking, and held his head up when he walked, and had what you might call Fire about him. He wrote poetry, and he rode, and he ran, and he cricketed, and he danced, and he acted, and he done it all equally beautiful. He was uncommon proud of Master Harry, as was his only child; but he didn't spoil him, neither. He was a gentleman that had a will of his own and a eye of his own, and that would be minded. Consequently, though he made quite a companion of the fine bright boy, and was delighted to see him so fond of reading his

---

[1] The first paragraph is added, in manuscript, in the prompt-copy (*Berg*).

[2] *his* italic in *Berg* and in *Household Words* (*HW*).

[3] 'Well! I don't know' (Wright): Dickens doubtless often altered *he* to *I*, when reading, even if not in *Berg*. He was speaking 'in character' here, pronouncing 'curiousest' as 'curious-es-est'. 'Boots . . . approaches the word "curious-es-est" with a look of admiration, clings to every syllable with affection, and only lets go his hold because conversation would otherwise come to a dead lock' (Field, p. 89).

[4] *him* italic in *Berg* and in *HW*. Improved to 'he see him once *in spirits* at a Fair' (Field, p. 89).

[5] *that* italic in *Berg* and in *HW*.

fairy books, and was never tired of hearing him say My name is Norval,[1] or hearing him sing his songs about Young May Moons is a beaming love, and When he as adores thee has left but the name, and that: still he kept the command over the child, and the child *was*[2] a child, and it's wery much to be wished more of[3] 'em was!

[*How did Boots happen to know all this?*] Why, Sir, through being under-gardener. Of course I couldn't be under-gardener, and be always about, in the summer-time, near the windows on the lawn, a mowing and sweeping, and weeding and pruning, and this and that, without getting acquainted with the ways of the family.—Even supposing Master Harry hadn't come to me one morning early, and said, 'Cobbs, how should you spell Norah, if you was asked?' and[4] when I give him my views, Sir, respectin' the spelling o' that name, he took out his little knife, and he begun a cutting it in print, all over the fence.

And the courage of the boy![5] Bless your soul, he'd have throwd off his little hat, and tucked up his little sleeves, and gone in at a Lion, he would. One day he stops, along with her, where I was hoeing weeds in the gravel, and says, speaking up, 'Cobbs,' he says, 'I like *you*.'[6] 'Do you, sir, I'm proud to hear it.' 'Yes I do, Cobbs. Why do I like you, do you think, Cobbs?' 'Don't know, Master Harry, I am sure.' 'Because Norah likes you, Cobbs.' 'Indeed, sir? That's very gratifying.' 'Gratifying, Cobbs? It's better than millions of the brightest diamonds, to be liked by Norah.' 'Certainly, sir.'[7] 'You're going away, ain't you, Cobbs?' 'Yes, sir.' 'Would you like another situation, Cobbs?' 'Well, sir, I shouldn't object, if it was a good 'un.' 'Then, Cobbs,' says that mite, 'you shall be our Head Gardener when we are married.' And he tucks her, in her little sky blue mantle, under his arm, and walks away.

[8][*Boots could assure me that it was*] better than a picter, and equal to a play, to see them babies with their long bright curling hair, their sparkling eyes, and their beautiful light tread, rambling about the garden, deep in love.[9] [*Boots was of opinion*] that the birds believed they was birds, and kept up with 'em, singing to please 'em. Sometimes, they would creep under the Tulip-tree, and would sit there with their arms

---

[1] This passage was spoken 'monotonously' (Wright).

[2] *was* italic in *Berg* and in *HW*.

[3] '... more *on* 'em ...' (Wright).

[4] 'when I' to 'little knife, and' added in manuscript. Dickens said '... give him my *individual* views ...' (Field, p. 89).

[5] 'Action' (Wright). Dickens's gestures here may be imagined.

[6] *you* italic in *Berg* and in *HW*.

[7] 'Certainly, sir' in a 'Low, quiet voice' (Wright). 'Perhaps, there was after all nothing better in the delivery of the whole of this Reading, than the utterance of [these] two words' (Kent, p. 223).

[8] 'Holding book. Say "Sir" throughout' (Wright).

[9] 'Low monotonous rhythm' (Wright).

round one another's necks, and their soft cheeks touching, a reading about the Prince, and the Dragon, and the good and bad enchanters, and the king's fair daughter. Sometimes I would hear them planning about having a house in a forest, keeping bees and a cow, and living entirely on milk and honey. Once I came upon them by the pond, and heard Master Harry say, 'Adorable Norah, kiss me, and say you love me to distraction, or I'll jump in head foremost.' On the whole, Sir, the contemplation o' them two babbies had a tendency to make me feel as if I was in love myself—only I didn't exactly know who with.

'Cobbs,' says Master Harry, one evening, *when I was watering the flowers*; 'I am going on a visit, this present Midsummer, to my grandmamma's at York.'

'Are you indeed, sir? I hope you'll have a pleasant time. I am going into Yorkshire myself, when I leave here.'

'Are you going to your grandmamma's, Cobbs?'

'No, sir. I haven't got such a thing.'

'Not as a grandmamma, Cobbs?'[1]

'No, sir.'

The boy looks on at the watering of the flowers, for a little while, and then he says, 'I shall be very glad indeed to go, Cobbs—*Norah's going*.'[2]

'You'll be all right then, sir, with your beautiful sweetheart by your side.'

'Cobbs,' returns the boy, a flushing. 'I never let anybody joke about that, when I can prevent them.'

'It wasn't a joke, sir,—wasn't so meant.'

'I am glad of that, Cobbs, because I like you, you know, and you're going to live with us. Cobbs!'

'Sir.'

'What do you think my grandmamma gives me, when I go down there?'

'I couldn't so much as make a guess, sir.'

'A Bank of England five-pound note, Cobbs.'

'Whew![3] that's a spanking sum of money, Master Harry.'

'A person could do a good deal with such a sum of money as that. Couldn't a person, Cobbs?'

'I believe you, sir!'

'Cobbs,' says that boy, 'I'll tell you a secret. At Norah's house, they have been joking her about me, and *pretending to laugh at our being engaged*.[4] Pretending to make game of it, Cobbs!'

---

[1] 'Harry's voice not high' (Wright).

[2] Doubly underlined.

[3] Instead of saying this word, Dickens whistled (Wright).

[4] 'With a wondering look' (Kent, p. 225).

'Such, sir, is the depravity of human natur.'

The boy, looking exactly like his father, stood for a few minutes, and then departed with 'Good-night, Cobbs. I'm going in.'

[*If I was to ask Boots how it happened*] that I was a going to leave that place at just that present time, well, I couldn't rightly answer you, Sir. I do suppose I might have stayed there till now, if I had been anyways inclined. But, you see, I was younger then, and I wanted change. That's what I wanted—change. Mr. Walmers, he says to me when I give him notice of my intentions to leave, 'Cobbs,' he says, 'have you anything to complain of? I make the inquiry, because if I find that any of my people really has anythink to complain of, I wish to make it right if I can.' 'No, sir, thanking you, sir, I find myself as well sitiwated here as I could hope to be anywheres. The truth is, sir, that I'm a going to seek my fortun.' 'O, indeed, Cobbs?' he says; 'I hope you may find it.' [*And Boots could assure me—which he did, touching his hair with his bootjack*—that he hadn't found it yet.]

[1] 'Well, sir! I left the Elmses when my time was up, and Master Harry he went down to the old lady's at York, which old lady were so wrapt up in that child as she would have give that child the teeth out of her head (*if she had had any*[2]). What does that Infant do—for Infant you may call him and be within the mark—but cut away from that old lady's with his Norah, on a expedition to go to Gretna Green and be married![3]

Sir, I was at this identical Holly-Tree Inn (having left it several times since to better myself, but always come back through one thing or another), when, one summer afternoon, the coach drives up, and out of the coach gets them two children. The Guard says to our Governor, 'I don't quite make out these little passengers, but the young gentleman's words was, that they was to be brought here.' The young gentleman gets out; hands his lady out; gives the Guard something for himself; says to our Governor, 'We're to stop here to-night, please. Sitting-room and two bed-rooms will be required. Mutton chops and cherry-pudding for two!' and tucks her, in her little sky-blue mantle, under his arm, and walks into the house much bolder than Brass.

Sir, I leave you to judge what the amazement of that establishment was, when those two tiny creatures all alone by themselves was marched into the Angel;—much more so when I, who had seen them without their seeing me, give the Governor my views of the expedition they was upon. 'Cobbs,' says the Governor, 'if this is so, I must set off myself to York and quiet their friends' minds. In which case you must keep

[1] Marginal stage-direction *Piano*.

[2] Doubly underlined. '. . . her 'ead (*if* she . . .' (Wright). 'The h's were perfection' (*Scotsman*, 21 December 1868).

[3] '. . . to Gretna Green *in Scotland*, and get married' (Wright).

your eye upon 'em, and humour 'em, till I come back. But, before I take these measures, Cobbs, I should wish you to find from themselves whether your opinions is correct.' 'Sir to you,'[1] says I, 'that shall be done directly.'

[*So, Boots goes upstairs to the Angel, and there he finds*] Master Harry on a e-normous sofa—immense at any time, but looking like the Great Bed of Ware, compared with him—a drying the eyes of Miss Norah with his pocket hankecher. Their little legs was entirely off the ground, of course, and it really is not possible to express how small them children looked.

'It's Cobbs! It's Cobbs!' cries Master Harry, and he comes running to me and catching hold of my hand. Miss Norah, she comes running to me on t'other side and catching hold of my t'other hand, and they both jump for joy.

'I see you a getting out, sir,' says I. 'I thought it was you. I thought I couldn't be mistaken in your heighth and figure. What's the object of your journey, sir?—Matrimonial?'

'We are going to be married, Cobbs, at Gretna Green,' returns the boy. 'We have run away on purpose. Norah has been in rather low spirits, Cobbs; but she'll be happy, now we have found you to be our friend.'

'Thank you, sir, and thank *you*,[2] miss, for your good opinion. *Did* you bring any luggage with you, sir?'

[*If I will believe Boots when he gives me his word and honour upon it,*] the lady had got a parasol, a smelling bottle, a round and a half of cold buttered toast, eight peppermint drops, and a Doll's hairbrush. The gentleman had got about half-a-dozen yards of string, a knife, three or four sheets of writing-paper folded up surprisingly small, a orange, and a Chaney mug with his name on it.[3]

'What may be the exact natur of your plans, sir?' says I.

'To go on,' replies the boy—which the courage of that boy was something wonderful!—'in the morning, and be married to-morrow.'

'Just so, sir. Would it meet your views, sir, if I was to accompany you?'

They both jumped for joy again, and cried out, 'O yes, yes, Cobbs! Yes!'

'Well, sir. If you will excuse my having the freedom to give an opinion,

---

[1] 'Sir to you' was one of 'the little chance phrases, the merest atoms of exclamation here and there, [which] will still be borne in mind as having had an intense flavour of fun about them, as syllabled in the Reading'. Another was Harry's 'Get out with you, Cobbs!' (Kent, p. 227).

[2] *you* and *Did* both italic in *Berg* and in *HW*.

[3] This 'gravely enumerated' account of the children's luggage was one of the most 'irresistibly laughable' passages in the Reading (Kent, p. 226).

what I should recommend would be this. I'm acquainted with a pony, sir, which, put[1] in a pheayton that I could borrow, would take you and Mrs. Harry Walmers Junior (driving myself, if you approved), to the end of your journey in a very short space of time. I am not altogether sure, sir, that this pony will be at liberty till to-morrow, but even if you had to wait over to-morrow for him, it might be worth your while. As to the small account here, sir, in case you was to find yourself running at all short, that don't signify; because I'm a part proprietor of this inn, and it could stand over.'

[Boots assures me that when they clapped their hands, and jumped for joy again, and called him, 'Good Cobbs!' and 'Dear Cobbs!' and bent across him to kiss one another in the delight of their confiding hearts, he felt himself] the meanest rascal for deceiving 'em, that was ever born.

'Is there anything you want, just at present, sir?' I says, mortally ashamed of myself.

'We should like some cakes after dinner,' answers Master Harry, 'and two apples—and jam. With dinner we should like to have toast and water. But, Norah has always been accustomed to half a glass of currant wine at dessert. And so have I.'

'It shall be ordered at the bar, sir,' I says.

Sir, I has the feeling as fresh upon me at this minute of speaking, as I had then, that I would far rather have had it out in half-a-dozen rounds with the Governor, than have combined with him; and that I wished with all my heart there was any impossible place where those two babies could make an impossible marriage, and live impossibly happy ever afterwards. However, as it couldn't be, I[2] went into the Governor's plans, and the Governor set off for York in half-an-hour.

The way in which the women of that house—without exception—every one of 'em—married *and*[3] single—took to that boy when they heard the story, is surprising.[4] It was as much as could be done to keep 'em from dashing into the room and kissing him. They climbed up all sorts of places, at the risk of their lives, to look at him through a pane of glass. And they was seven deep at the key-hole.[5]

In the evening, I went into the room to see how the runaway couple was getting on. The gentleman was on the window-seat, supporting the lady in his arms. She had tears upon her face, and was lying, very tired and half asleep, with her head upon his shoulder.

[1] Pronounced as in 'putty' (Wright).

[2] *Berg* here reads 'he went ...' In the rest of this paragraph, Dickens had altered 'Boots' and 'he' to 'I'; he overlooked this instance. *T & F* corrects it to 'I went ...'

[3] *and* italic in *Berg* and in *HW*.

[4] Pronounced 'suppurising' (Wright). Boots fondled this word, like 'curious-es-est' (Field, p. 90).

[5] This passage, and the chambermaid's 'It's a shame to part 'em!', 'were always the most telling hits, the chief successes of the Reading' (Kent, p. 229).

'Mrs. Harry Walmers Junior, fatigued, sir?'

[1] 'Yes, she is tired, Cobbs; but, she is not used to be away from home, and she has been in low spirits again. Cobbs, do you think you could bring a biffin,[2] please?'

'I ask your pardon, sir. What was it you?—'

'I think a Norfolk biffin would rouse her, Cobbs. She is very fond of them.'

Well, Sir, I withdrew in search of the required restorative, and the gentleman handed it to the lady, and fed her with a spoon, and took a little himself. The lady being heavy with sleep, and rather cross, 'What should you think, sir,' I says, 'of a chamber candlestick?' The gentleman approved; the chambermaid went first, up the great staircase; the lady, in her sky-blue mantle, followed, gallantly escorted by the gentleman; the gentleman embraced her at her door, and retired to his own apartment, where I locked him up.[3]

[*Boots couldn't but ·feel with increased acuteness what a base deceiver he was, when they consulted him at breakfast (they had ordered sweet milk-and-water, and toast and currant jelly, overnight), about the pony. It really was as much as he could do, he don't mind confessing to me,*] to look them two young things in the face, and think what a wicked old father of lies he had grown up to be. Howsomever, Sir, I went on a lying like a Trojan, about the pony. I told 'em that it did so unfort'nately happen that the pony was half clipped, you see, and that he couldn't be took out in that state, for fear it should strike to his inside. But that he'd be finished clipping in the course of the day, and that to-morrow morning at eight o'clock the pheayton would be ready. [*Boots's view of the whole case, looking back upon it in my room, is,*] that Mrs. Harry Walmers Junior was beginning to give in. She hadn't had her hair curled when she went to bed, and she didn't seem quite up to brushing it herself, and its getting in her eyes put her out. But, nothing put out Master Harry. He sat behind his breakfast-cup, a tearing away at the jelly, as if he had been his own father.

In the course of the morning, Master Harry rung the bell—it was surprising how that there boy did carry on—and said in a sprightly way, 'Cobbs, is there any good walks in this neighbourhood?'

'Yes, sir. There's Love Lane.'

'Get out with you, Cobbs!'[4]—that was that there boy's expression—'you're joking.'

'Begging your pardon, sir, there really is Love Lane. And a pleasant

---

[1] 'Distressed sort of voice' (Wright).

[2] Here, and for 'a Norfolk biffin' below, Dickens substituted 'a baked apple' (Wright; Field, p. 91).

[3] Stressing *locked him up* (Wright).

[4] Spoken quickly (Wright).

walk it is, and proud shall I be to show it to yourself and Mrs. Harry Walmers Junior.'

'Norah, dear,' says Master Harry, 'this is curious. *We*[1] really ought to see Love Lane. Put on your bonnet, my sweetest darling, and we will go there with Cobbs.'

[*Boots leaves me to judge what a Beast he felt himself to be, when that young pair told him, as they all three jogged along together, that they had made up their minds to give him two thousand guineas a year as head gardener, on account of his being so true a friend to 'em.*] Well, sir, I turned the conversation as well as I could, and I took 'em down Love Lane to the water-meadows, and there Master Harry would have drownded himself in a half a moment more, a-getting out a water-lily for her—but nothing daunted that boy. Well, sir, they was tired out. All being so new and strange to 'em, they was tired as tired could be. And they laid down on a bank of daisies, like the children in the wood—leastways meadows[2]—and fell asleep.

[3] I don't know, sir—perhaps you do—why it made a man fit to make a fool of himself, to see them two pretty babies a lying there in the clear still sunny day, not dreaming half so hard when they was asleep, as they done when they was awake. But Lord! when you come to think of yourself, you know, and what a game you have been up to ever since you was in your own cradle, and what a poor sort of chap you are arter all—that's where it is! Don't you see, Sir?

Well, sir, they woke up at last, and then one thing was getting pretty clear to me, namely, that Mrs. Harry Walmerses Junior's temper was on the move. When Master Harry took her round the waist, she said he 'teased her so;' and when he says, 'Norah, my young May Moon, your Harry tease you?' she tells him, 'Yes; and I want to go home!'[4]

A biled fowl, and baked bread-and-butter pudding, brought Mrs. Walmers up a little; but I could have wished, I must privately own to you, sir, to have seen her more sensible of the woice of love, and less abandoning of herself to the currants in the pudding. However, Master Harry he kep up, and his noble heart was as fond as ever. Mrs. Walmers turned very sleepy about dusk, and began to cry. Therefore, Mrs. Walmers went off to bed as per yesterday; and Master Harry ditto repeated.

About eleven or twelve at night, comes back the Governor in a chaise, along with Mr. Walmers and a elderly lady. Mr. Walmers says to our missis, 'We are much indebted to you, ma'am, for your kind care of our little children, which we can never sufficiently acknowledge. Pray

---

[1] *We* doubly underlined.
[2] The interjected 'leastways meadows' was spoken quickly (Wright).
[3] The paragraph was spoken 'Feelingly and monotonous[ly]' (Wright).
[4] 'Quick and snappishly' (Wright).

ma'am, where is my boy?' Our missis says, 'Cobbs has the dear child in charge, sir. Cobbs, show Forty!' Then, Mr. Walmers, he says: 'Ah, Cobbs! I am glad to see *you*.[1] I understood you was here!' And I says, 'Yes, sir. Your most obedient, sir. I beg your pardon, sir,' I adds, while unlocking the door; 'I hope you are not angry with Master Harry. For, Master Harry is a fine boy, sir, and will do you credit and honour.' [*And Boots signifies to me, that if the fine boy's father had contradicted him in the state of mind in which he then was, he thinks he should have*] 'fetched him a crack,' and took the consequences.

But, Mr. Walmers only says, 'No, Cobbs. No, my good fellow. Thank you!' And, the door being opened, goes in, goes up to the bedside, bends gently down, and kisses the little sleeping face. Then, he stands looking at it for a minute, looking wonderfully like it (*they do say he ran away with Mrs. Walmers*); and then he gently shakes the little shoulder.

'Harry, my dear boy! Harry!'

Master Harry starts and looks at his Pa. Looks at me too. Such is the honour of that mite, that he looks at me, to see whether he has brought me into trouble.

'I am not angry, my child. I only want you to dress yourself and come home.'

'Yes, Pa.'

Master Harry dresses himself quick.

'Please may I'—the spirit of that little creatur!—'please, dear Pa— may I—kiss Norah, before I go?'

'You may, my child.'

So he takes Master Harry in his hand, and I leads the way with the candle, to that other bedroom: where the elderly lady is seated by the bed, and poor little Mrs. Harry Walmers Junior is fast asleep. There, the father lifts the boy up to the pillow, and he lays his little face down for an instant by the little warm face of poor little Mrs. Harry Walmers Junior, and gently draws it to him—a sight so touching to the chamber-maids who are a peeping through the door, that one of them calls out 'It's a shame to part 'em!'[2]

[*Finally, Boots says,*] that's all about it. Mr. Walmers drove away in the chaise, having hold of Master Harry's hand. The elderly lady and Mrs. Harry Walmers Junior that was never to be (she married a Captain, long afterwards, and died in India), went off next day. [*In conclusion, Boots puts it to me whether I hold with him in two opinions:*] firstly, that there are not many couples on their way to be married, who are half as innocent as them two children; secondly, that it would be a jolly

---

[1] *you* italic in *Berg* and in *HW*.

[2] 'High female voice' (Wright); 'shrill' (Kent, p. 230). 'May the exclamation of the soft-hearted chambermaid ... never vanish from my memory!' (A. W. Ward, *Dickens* (1882), p. 152). See headnote, above.

good thing for a great many couples on their way to be married, if they could only be stopped in time and brought back separate.[1]

[1] 'With which cynical scattering of sugar-plums in the teeth of married and single, the blithe Reading was laughingly brought to its conclusion' (Kent, p. 230).

MRS. GAMP

Mrs. Gamp, which concluded the programme of three items first performed on 17 June 1858, was much the longest, and it gave Dickens the most trouble. This was only the second Reading he had devised from a novel instead of from one of the shorter Christmas books and stories, and his principle of selection was to base it upon one character—Mrs. Gamp being, of course, one of the most admired of all his creations. The initial process of adaptation, in 1858, was indeed considerably simpler than on comparable occasions later, when he was more experienced. A privately printed text was prepared, in two chapters. Chapter I was a slightly abbreviated version of Mrs. Gamp's first appearance in *Martin Chuzzlewit* (ch. 19): she is fetched by Mr. Pecksniff to lay out the body of Anthony Chuzzlewit; there are dialogues involving Mr. Mould, Jonas Chuzzlewit, and old Chuffey, and the chapter ends with Mrs. Gamp's feeling dispoged to put her lips to several glasses of liquor and thus dropping into somnolent silence. A few Gampisms from chs. 46 and 40 were interpolated into this narrative. Chapter II was taken entirely from Mrs. Gamp's next entry in the novel (ch. 25): she calls upon Mr. Mould, and after pleasant conversation with him goes to the Bull in Holborn, where she relieves Betsey Prig, who is nursing an unnamed young man (Mr. Lewsome) through a fever. Mrs. Gamp settles down for the night, but is disturbed by her patient's strange and incriminating ejaculations during his delirium. The Reading ended, as did ch. 25 of the novel, with Mrs. Prig's returning in the morning; Mrs. Gamp departs, commending the cucumbers.

The reception of *Mrs. Gamp* in 1858 was very mixed, critics disagreeing over this item more than any other. It was 'the strong point of the evening' (*Belfast News-Letter*, 30 August 1858)—or it was 'not so good' as the other two, though most had been expected of it (*Dundee Advertiser*, 5 October 1858). The characters were portrayed so brilliantly that 'our powers would fail us to describe the manner' (*Glasgow Herald*, 11 October 1858)—or it was such a failure, through Dickens's technical inability to produce adequate voices for the several characters, that 'the attempt does not require any detailed criticism' (*Saturday Review*, 19 June 1858, p. 636). Dickens, having shown himself a consummate actor, was loudly cheered at the end (*Manchester Guardian*, 20 September 1858)—or the performance fell flat, 'the impression left upon the audience was not gratifying', and the item was 'coldly received' (*Bradford Observer*, 21 October 1858; *Limerick Reporter*, 3 September 1858). The last-quoted of these critics complained that 'there is not much point in the story and Dickens certainly recognized this weakness, eventually making drastic alterations to his script. At first he cut and sharpened the text, much as in other Readings, and interpolated a few more favourite Gampisms from other chapters. Later, deciding that this tinkering was inadequate, he jettisoned Chapter II and wrote a much shorter new ending. Just when this major surgery was applied cannot be established, but it was certainly not during the first series of Readings, for a reminiscence of a performance in April 1861 includes Dickens rubbing his nose up and down his ivory paper knife, 'to imitate Mrs. Gamp's rubbing her nose on the fender'—an episode which occurs in Chapter II (W. Ridley Kent, 'A Dickens Reading', *Dickensian*, vii (1911), 319).

After the 1858-9 tours, *Mrs. Gamp* was performed only infrequently until, in the 1868-9 Farewell series, Dickens's fondness for it seems to have revived. It was then often used as an afterpiece, and it also became again the regular closing item in another much-performed triple bill—*Boots*, *Sikes and Nancy*, and *Mrs. Gamp*. In America it had only been given four performances—the fewest of any of the items in his repertoire there. Certainly by then the text had been revised, as described above, for *T & F* incorporates these changes.

The process of revision can be followed in the 1858 prompt-copy, now in the Berg Collection (see above, p. 153), which has been reprinted photographically with a commentary: *Mrs. Gamp, by Charles Dickens: A Facsimile of the Author's Prompt Copy*, ed. John D. Gordan (New York Public Library, 1956). As Gordan points out, none of Dickens's Readings was revised so drastically— an entirely new ending created, and the length reduced progressively from 10,000 to 4,000 words. The two-chapter division was scrapped. What had been Chapter I was abbreviated, though no more extensively than occurred in many other Readings; when Chapter II was jettisoned, some of its best detachable passages were salvaged and dexterously inserted into the surviving script. The original ending of Chapter I was deleted, and a new piece was written in. This incorporated further passages from the old Chapter II, but the narrative is given more coherence by all the action's taking place in the Chuzzlewit house. Mrs. Gamp's duties there now include helping Betsey Prig to nurse old Chuffey, and appropriate passages from Chapter II (ch. 25 of the novel) are used, simply by substituting Chuffey for Lewsome as the patient. The Reading ends with their quarrelling at Chuffey's bedside, over the existence of Mrs. Harris (a brief extract from ch. 49). Kate Field, hearing the Reading in this revised form, complained that 'What disappoints in *Mrs. Gamp* is the absence of a climax. It is the only one of Dickens's Readings that is not thoroughly worked up' (p. 125). But the revised ending is certainly a considerable improvement on the feeble 1858 one, and the elimination of Mr. Lewsome is an advantage, too: his feverish speeches incriminating Jonas Chuzzlewit lost their point outside their context in the novel, and were dramatically unimpressive in the Reading. Indeed, the 1858 text was, by the standards of Dickens's later adaptations, an unintelligent (probably a hurried) effort; he had not thought or worked hard enough to devise a coherent and relatively self-contained narrative ending on an effective 'curtain line.'

The 1858 Bradbury & Evans' trade edition of this Reading (see above, p. 153) is textually almost identical with that of the 1858 private printing; the differences are trivial. *T & F* was set from the *Berg* prompt-copy. As was noted in the Introduction, proof-sheets survive (also now in the Berg Collection) containing Dickens's corrections, made in November or December 1867: these include over twenty minor verbal alterations—an exceptionally large number, compared with other *T & F* texts—and a few changes in punctuation and paragraphing. A further stage in the evolution of this text appears in a new prompt-copy which Dickens made, while in America, 1867-8. This copy, formerly in the

Suzannet Collection, is now owned by Mr. Kenyon Law Starling. It is a copy of *T & F*, slightly cut and emended. Its title-page is endorsed in Dickens's autograph: 'Charles Dickens/ His Reading Book/ To H.M. Ticknor, 20th April, 1868.' No other prompt-copy was thus given away, and inscribed, by Dickens. The deletions in *Starling* are all short; a few words are added or altered; some passages are underlined for emphasis, but neither in this nor in the 1858 prompt-copy are there any stage-directions.

The text printed below is that of the 1867–8 prompt-copy (*Starling*), as Dickens's latest revised version. Some features of the 1858 prompt-copy (*Berg*) are described in footnotes.

There was at least one other prompt-copy of *Mrs. Gamp*. Charles Kent records (p. 141) that there are two copies of the *Mrs. Gamp* text in the Gad's Hill library in 1870, 'so slightly different that they are all but identical'. One was presumably the 1858 prompt-copy (*Berg*); the other cannot have been *Starling*, as Dickens had given it away in 1868. Sotheran's 1878 Catalogue records, among 'Charles Dickens's Public-Reading Books', a copy of *Mrs. Gamp* in the Boston 1867–8 text; presumably this was the second copy to which Kent refers. During his Farewell series, Dickens, having given Ticknor his recently devised text, must either have reverted to using the *Berg* prompt-copy or (more likely) he had transcribed the *Starling* alterations into another copy of *T & F*, and used that. It would indeed have been rash of him to give away a recently revised prompt-copy of an item still in repertoire, without first providing himself with a duplicate. The present whereabouts of this copy, sold in 1878, is unknown; as was noted in the Introduction, this is the only recorded prompt-copy which has not been available to the present editor.

Charles Kent regarded this as 'the most comic of all the Readings' (p. 219), but it was never among the most admired or beloved items in the repertoire. Even after the final revisions, the narrative is less satisfactory than that of the others. Moreover, it was found indelicate; Mrs. Gamp could distress the nice-minded, in both of her professional capacities. Laying-out corpses was 'a repulsive subject. The majority of cultivated people dislike joking about death and its accessories' (*Bradford Observer*, 21 October 1858). Her work as midwife raised even worse objections:

> ... it was a breach of good taste—a serious and needless affront to ordinary refinement—to obtrude the gross remarks of these professional nurses on the ears of the young ladies who formed so large a proportion of the audience: and it struck us that many of those present seemed half ashamed of the very partial laugh which these coarse jokes elicited. ... We do not believe that [these indelicacies] would be read by any unmarried woman without disgust, ... [and they were quite inappropriate for public performance] to a large audience of both sexes. (*Derby Mercury*, 27 October 1858)

On one occasion at least, in 1866, a troop of young ladies were bundled out of the hall within minutes of the Reading's beginning—driven by their head-mistress, 'with purple face and rigid, shocked expression' (Gladys Storey, *Dickens and Daughter* (1939), pp. 112–14). Most audiences and critics did not react so severely, but the text contained enough of the *risqué* to prevent its becoming a universal family favourite. Moreover, Dickens's acting technique proved less adequate than in other items. His Chuffey and Jonas Chuzzlewit were praised, and some critics admired his Mr. Mould, though Kate Field found it too close to his Micawber and weaker in conception. His Betsey Prig was generally found unimpressive. The big disappointment was his Pecksniff, which was universally reckoned a failure—though the script was entirely unhelpful here, containing little for Pecksniff to say or do and nothing that reminded one of his legendary qualities of character and expression. It was indeed unwise to include such a notable figure, without providing materials for an adequate impersonation.

Obviously, however, the Reading stood or fell by its Mrs. Gamp. Critics complained there was not enough of her, but the script did contain a good sample of her felicities, though it must have cost Dickens some pangs to omit or delete so many good things: thus, when reducing the length of Chapter II, he had deleted 'he'd make a lovely corpse', and when inserting a much-abbreviated version of the famous quarrel with Betsey Prig, he must have regretted having to stop far short of 'lambs could not forgive. No, Betsey! . . . nor worms forget.' His impersonation of Mrs. Gamp was much praised. He deployed a splendid variety of facial expressions—and 'Such a voice!' as Kate Field exclaimed: 'Take a comb, cover it with tissue paper, and attempt to sing through it, and you have an admirable idea of the quality of Mrs. Gamp's vocal organ, provided that you make the proper allowance for an inordinate use of snuff' (p. 129). Kent, too, praised Dickens's skill here: 'A voice snuffy, husky, unctuous, the voice of a fat old woman . . .' (p. 212). 'Slow, measured and nasal', noted W. M. Wright, with 'sighs long drawn-out'. Nevertheless, there were enough sharply dismissive assessments of his impersonation of Mrs. Gamp, particularly during the opening months of this item, to suggest that he had not immediately hit a consistent form in this difficult role. Some of the adverse criticism may, however, have arisen from the same cause as afflicted the reception of his performance in another of his most legendary creations, Sam Weller (see below, p. 197). These were the only two characters in the Readings he gave in America, the mere mention of whose names evoked a burst of applause (Field, p. 127). This rapturous recognition of these much-loved characters, while doubtless gratifying, had the disadvantage that audiences were easily disappointed by the outcome, either if it was less than superb, or if it clashed with their own cherished notions of how the character must be played. The point is made in a favourable critique by John Hollingshead:

There is no fault to find with Mr. Dickens's embodiment of the immortal nurse, for no amount of study could improve it; and if it fails to produce an impression upon the audience commensurate with its artistic merits, it is because the character, coarse in itself, is so broadly and deeply impressed upon the printed page, that nearly every reader is able to build up for himself a clear idea of this great friend and confidant of doctors and undertakers. (*Critic*, 4 September 1858, p. 538)

W. M. Wright's notes record, as usual, the voices used for the various characters: 'Quick female voices' for the troops of married ladies who embarrass Mr. Pecksniff, 'Mr. Mould's voice affectedly serious and shaking head when speaking', Jonas Chuzzlewit 'quick and nervous; finger to mouth occasionally', Chuffey 'very old man, weak and cringingly: both hands clasping head', and 'Betsey's voice like a man's'. Mrs. Gamp, of course, used Cockney pronunciations throughout: 'put' as in 'putty', 'with' as 'vith', 'Harris' as ''Arris', etc.

Mrs. Gamp

MR. Pecksniff was in a hackney-cabriolet, for Jonas Chuzzlewit had said, 'Spare no expense.' It should never be charged upon his father's son that he grudged the money for his father's funeral.

Mr. Pecksniff had been to the undertaker, and was now on his way to another officer in the train of mourning,—a female functionary, a nurse, and watcher, and performer of nameless offices about the persons of the dead,—whom the undertaker had recommended. Her name was Gamp; her residence, in Kingsgate Street, High Holborn. So Mr. Pecksniff, in a hackney-cab, was rattling over Holborn's stones, in quest of Mrs. Gamp.

This lady[1] lodged at a bird-fancier's, *next door but one to the celebrated mutton-pie shop, and directly opposite to the original cat's-meat warehouse.* It was a little house, and this was the more convenient; for Mrs. Gamp being also a monthly nurse, and lodging in the first-floor front, her window was easily assailable at night by pebbles, walking-sticks, and fragments of tobacco-pipe,—all much more efficacious than the street-door knocker; *which was so ingeniously constructed as to wake the street with ease, without making the smallest impression on the premises to which it was addressed.*

It chanced on this particular occasion that Mrs. Gamp had been up *with a distressed Lady* all the previous night. It chanced that Mrs. Gamp had not been regularly engaged, but had been called in at a crisis, to assist another professional lady with her advice; and thus it happened that, all points of interest in the case being over, Mrs. Gamp had come home again to the bird-fancier's, and gone to bed. So, when Mr. Pecksniff drove up in the hackney-cab, Mrs. Gamp's curtains were drawn close, and Mrs. Gamp was fast asleep behind them. †

Mr. Pecksniff, in the innocence of his heart, applied himself to the knocker; *but at his first double-knock, every window in the street became alive with female heads;*[2] and before he could repeat it, whole troops of married ladies came flocking round the steps, all crying out with one accord, and with uncommon interest, 'Knock at the winder, sir, knock at the winder. Lord bless you, don't lose no more time than you can help,—knock at the winder!'

Borrowing the driver's whip for the purpose, Mr. Pecksniff soon made

---

[1] 'This *excellent* lady' (Wright).

[2] Dickens stressed '*alive*', and his eyes became 'so distended at the extraordinary spectacle as to remove all doubt as to the possibility of such a commotion' (Field, p. 128).

a commotion among the first-floor flower-pots, and roused Mrs. Gamp, whose voice—to the great satisfaction of the matrons—was heard to say, 'I'm coming.'

'He's as pale as a muffin,' said one lady, in allusion to Mr. Pecksniff.

'So he ought to be, if he's the feelings of a man,' observed another.[1]

A third lady said she wished he had chosen any other time for fetching Mrs. Gamp, but it always happened so with *her*.[2]

It gave Mr. Pecksniff much uneasiness to infer, from these remarks, that he was supposed to have come to Mrs. Gamp *upon an errand touching, not the close of life, but the other end*. Mrs. Gamp herself was under the same impression, for, throwing open the window, she cried behind the curtains, as she hastily dressed herself:

'Is it Mrs. Perkins?'

'No! nothing of the sort.'

'What, Mr. Whilks! Don't say it's you, Mr. Whilks, and that poor creetur Mrs. Whilks with not even a pincushion ready. Don't say it's you, Mr. Whilks!'[3]

'It isn't Mr. Whilks. I don't know the man. Nothing of the kind. A gentleman is dead; and some person being wanted in the house, you have been recommended by Mr. Mould the undertaker. You are also wanted to relieve Mrs. Prig, the day-nurse in attendance on the book-keeper of the deceased,—one Mr. Chuffey,—whose grief seems to have affected his mind.'[4]

As she was by this time in a condition to appear, Mrs. Gamp, who had a face for all occasions, looked out of the window with her mourning countenance, and said she would be down directly.

But the matrons took it very ill that Mr. Pecksniff's mission was of so unimportant a kind; and rated him in good round terms, signifying that they would be glad to know what he meant by terrifying delicate females 'with his corpses', and giving it as their opinion that he was ugly enough to know better.

So, when Mrs. Gamp appeared, the unoffending gentleman was glad

---

[1] 'Nodding head' (Wright).

[2] *her* italic in the novel. The three ladies were 'defined with photographic accuracy': the first, 'of measured medium voice and scrutinizing eye'; the second 'of nervous-sanguine temperament', speaking quickly and with a toss of the head; the third 'of a melancholy turn of mind and cast of countenance, the born victim of circumstances' (Field, p. 129).

[3] Kate Field describes this as an 'exclamation', but then corrects herself: 'There is an intellectual ponderosity about her that renders an exclamation impossible. She carries too much ballast. ... She scorns staccato passages, and her vocalisation may be said to be confined to the use of semi-breves, on which she lingers as if desirous of developing her voice by what is technically known as "swelling". She holds all notions of light and shade in contempt, and with monotonous cadence produces effects upon her hearers undreamed of by her readers' (p. 130).

[4] This sentence (not in the novel) is written into *Berg*.

to hustle her into the cabriolet, and drive off, *overwhelmed with popular execration.*

Mrs. Gamp had a large bundle with her, a pair of pattens, and a species of gig umbrella; the latter article in color like a faded leaf, except where a circular patch of a lively blue had been let in at the top. She was much flurried by the haste she had made, and labored under the most erroneous views of cabriolets, which she appeared to confound with mail-coaches or stage-wagons, insomuch that she was constantly endeavoring for the first half-mile to force her luggage through the little front window, and clamoring to the driver to 'put it in the boot.' When she was disabused of this idea, her whole being resolved itself into an absorbing anxiety about her pattens, *with which she played innumerable games of quoits on Mr. Pecksniff's legs.* It was not until they were close upon the house of mourning that she had enough composure to observe:—

'And so the gentleman's dead, sir! Ah! The more's the pity,'—*she didn't even know his name.* 'But it's what we must all come to. It's as certain as being born, except that we can't make our calculations as exact. Ah! Poor dear!'

She was a fat old woman, with a husky voice and a moist eye. Having very little neck, it cost her some trouble to look over herself, if one may say so, at those to whom she talked. She wore a rusty black gown, rather the worse for snuff, and a shawl and bonnet to correspond. * *The face of Mrs. Gamp—the nose in particular—was somewhat red and swollen, and it was difficult to enjoy her society without becoming conscious of a smell of spirits.*

'Ah!' repeated Mrs. Gamp, *for that was always a safe sentiment in cases of mourning,*—'ah, dear! When Gamp was summonsed to his long home, and I see him a lying in the hospital with a penny-piece on each eye, and his wooden leg under his left arm, I thought I should have fainted away. But I bore up.'

If certain whispers current in the Kingsgate Street circles had any truth in them, Mrs. Gamp had borne up surprisingly, *and had indeed exerted such uncommon fortitude as to dispose of Mr. Gamp's remains for the benefit of science.*

'You have become indifferent since then, I suppose? Use is second nature, Mrs. Gamp.'

'You may well say second natur, sir. One's first ways is to find sich things a trial to the feelings, and such is one's lasting custom.[1] If it wasn't for the nerve a little sip of liquor gives me (which I was never able to do more than taste it), I never could go through with what I sometimes has to do. "Mrs. Harris," I says, at the wery last case as ever

---

[1] The spellings *sich*, *such* and *sech* all occur in the Reading text.

I acted in, which it was but a young person,[1]—"Mrs. Harris," I says, "leave the bottle on the chimley-piece, and don't ask me to take none, but let me put my lips to it when I am so dispoged, and then I will do what I am engaged to do, according to the best of my ability." "Mrs. Gamp," she says, in answer, "if ever there was a sober creetur to be got at eighteen-pence a day for working people, and three and six for gentlefolks,—*night watching being a extra charge*—you are that inwallable person." "Mrs. Harris," I says to her, "don't name the charge, for if I could afford to lay all my fellow-creeturs out for nothink, I would gladly do it, sich is the love I bears 'em."'[2]

At this point, she was fain to stop for breath. And advantage may be taken of the circumstance, *to state that a fearful mystery surrounded this lady of the name of Harris*, whom no one in the circle of Mrs. Gamp's acquaintance had ever seen; neither did any human being know her place of residence. The prevalent opinion was that she was a phantom of Mrs. Gamp's brain, created for the purpose of holding complimentary dialogues with her on all manner of subjects.

'The bottle shall be duly placed on the chimney-piece, Mrs. Gamp, and you shall put your lips to it at your own convenience.'

'Thank you, sir. Which it is a thing as hardly ever occurs with me, unless when I am indispoged, and find my half a pint o' porter settling heavy on the chest. Mrs. Harris often and often says to me, "Sairey Gamp," she says, "you raly do amaze me!" "Mrs. Harris," I says to her, "why so? Give it a name, I beg!" "Telling the truth then, ma'am," says Mrs Harris, "and shaming him as shall be nameless betwixt you and me, never did I think, till I know'd you, as any woman could[3] sick-nurse and monthly likeways, on the little that you takes to drink." "Mrs. Harris," I says to her, "none on us knows what we can do till we tries; and wunst *I*[4] thought so, too. But now," I says, "my half a pint of porter fully satisfies; perwisin', Mrs. Harris, that it is[5] brought reg'lar, and draw'd mild."'

The conclusion of this affecting narrative brought them to the house.

[1] In *Berg*, the words 'which it was but a young person' are underlined. Wright notes here: 'Head moving from side to side'.

[2] 'The expression of her glowing face at this juncture defies language, however live, particularly as she remarks to Mrs. Harris, with a pendulum wag to her head in the *tempo* of a funeral march, "If I could possible afford to lay . . . [*etc.*]' (Field, p. 134). Maybe Dickens inserted a 'possible' here: or maybe Kate Field was misquoting from memory.—The next three paragraphs are an interpolation, made in *Berg* when the Reading was shortened; the first and third paragraphs were transferred from Chapter II of the *Berg* text (ch. 25 of the novel), and the middle paragraph was a newly written bridge-passage.

[3] *could* doubly underlined in *Berg*.

[4] *I* italic in *Starling*.

[5] *is* doubly underlined in *Berg*. Wright notes an additional phrase here: Dickens read '. . . perwisin', Mrs. Harris, *which I makes a condition*, that it is . . .'

In the passage they encountered Mr. Mould, the undertaker, a little elderly gentleman, bald, and in a suit of black; with a note-book in his hand, and a face in which a queer attempt at melancholy was at odds with a smirk of satisfaction.

'Well, Mrs. Gamp, and how are *you*,[1] Mrs. Gamp?'

'Pretty well, I thank you, sir.'

'You'll be very particular here, with the deceased party upstairs, Mrs. Gamp. This is not a common case, Mrs. Gamp. Let everything be very nice and comfortable, about the deceased, Mrs. Gamp, if you please.'[2]

'It shall be so, sir; you knows me of old, I hope, and so does Mrs. Mould, your ansome pardner, sir; and so does the two sweet young ladies, your darters; although the blessing of a daughter was deniged myself, which, if we had had one, Gamp would certainly have drunk its little shoes right off its feet, as with our precious boy he did, and arterwards send the child a errand, to sell his wooden leg *for any liquor it would fetch as matches in the rough*; which was truly done beyond his years, for ev'ry individgle penny that child lost at tossing for kidney-pies, and come home arterwards quite[3] bold, to break the news, *and offering to drown himself if sech would be a satisfaction to his parents*. But wery different is them two sweet young ladies o' yourn, Mister Mould, as I know'd afore a tooth in their pretty heads was cut, and have many a time seen—ah! the dear creeturs!—a playing at berryin's down in the shop, and a follerin' the order-book to its long home in the iron safe. Young ladies with such faces as your darters thinks of something else besides berryin's; don't they, sir? Thinks o' marryin's; don't they, sir?'

'I'm sure I don't know, Mrs. Gamp. * Very shrewd woman, Mr. Pecksniff, sir. Woman whose intellect is immensely superior to her station in life; sort of woman one would really almost feel disposed to bury for nothing, and do it neatly, too. Mr. Pecksniff, sir. This Funeral is one of the most impressive cases, sir, that I have seen in the whole course of my professional experience.'

'Indeed, Mr. Mould!'

'Such affectionate regret I never saw. There is no limitation; there is positively NO[4] limitation in point of expense! I have orders, sir, in short, to turn out something absolutely gorgeous.'

'My friend Mr. Jonas is an excellent man.'

---

[1] *you* italic in *Starling* and in the novel.

[2] The next two paragraphs (up to Mr. Mould's 'and do it neatly, too, Mr. Pecksniff, sir') were interpolated into *Berg*, being a rearranged version of some passages from the discarded Chapter II (ch. 25 of the novel).

[3] Here Ticknor, to whom Dickens gave this prompt-copy, inserted, with a caret, 'sweet and', and noted: 'So read by C.D.'

[4] Small capitals in *Starling* and in the novel.

'Well, I have seen a good deal of what is filial in my time, sir, and of what is unfilial, too! It is the lot of parties in my line, sir. We come into the knowledge of those secrets. But anything so filial as this—anything so honorable to human nature, anything so expensive, so calculated to reconcile all of us to the world we live in—never yet came under my observation. It only proves, sir, what was so forcibly observed by the lamented poet,[1]—*buried at Stratford,*—that there is good in everything.'

'It is very pleasant to hear you say so, Mr. Mould.'

'You are very kind, sir. And what a man the late Mr. Chuzzlewit was, sir! Ah! what a man he was. * Mr. Pecksniff, sir, good morning!'

Mr. Pecksniff returned the compliment; and Mould was going away with a brisk smile, when he remembered the occasion. Quickly becoming depressed again, he sighed; *looked into the crown of his hat, as if for comfort; put it on*[2] *without finding any; and slowly departed.*

Mrs. Gamp and Mr. Pecksniff then ascended the staircase; and Mrs. Gamp, having been shown to the chamber in which all that remained of old Anthony Chuzzlewit lay covered up, with but one loving heart, and that the heart of his old book-keeper, to mourn it, left Mr. Pecksniff free to enter the darkened room below in search of Mr. Jonas.

He found that example to bereaved sons, and pattern in the eyes of all performers of funerals, so subdued, that he could scarcely be heard to speak, and only seen to walk across the room.[3]

'Pecksniff, you shall have the regulation of it all, mind! You shall be able to tell anybody who talks about it, that everything was correctly and freely done. There isn't any one you'd like to ask to the funeral, is there?'

'No, Mr. Jonas, I think not.'

'Because if there is, you know, ask him. We don't want to make a secret of it.'

'No; I am not the less obliged to you on that account, Mr. Jonas, for your liberal hospitality; but there really is no one.'

'Very well; then you, and I, and the doctor, will be just an easy coachful. We'll have the doctor, Pecksniff, because he knows what was the matter with my father, and that it couldn't be helped.' *

With that, they went up to the room where the old book-keeper was, attended by Mrs. Betsey Prig. And to them entered Mrs. Gamp soon

---

[1] In *Berg*, it is 'lamented theatrical poet'; Dickens failed to notice that 'theatrical' had been omitted in *T & F*, but (as Wright notes) he said the omitted word.

[2] 'Put on hat' (Wright).

[3] 'The brief glimpse of Jonas Chuzzlewit gave an opportunity for the display of the highest dramatic power. The suspicious glance; the morose, churlish voice; the incessant biting of the thumb-nail, betrayed the conscious parricide' (*Belfast News-Letter*, 30 August 1858).

afterwards, who saluted Mrs. Prig as one of the sisterhood, and 'the best of creeturs.'[1]

The old book-keeper sat beside the bed, with his head bowed down; until Mrs. Gamp took him by the arm, when he meekly rose, saying:—[2]

'My old master died at threescore and ten,—ought and carry seven. Some men are so strong that they live to fourscore—four times ought's an ought, four times two's an eight—eighty. Oh! why—why—why—didn't he live to four times ought's an ought, and four times two's an eight—eighty? Why did he died before his poor old crazy servant! Take him from me, and what remains? I loved him. He was good to me. I took him down once, six boys, in the arithmetic class at school. God forgive me! Had I the heart to take him down!'

[3] 'Well I'm sure,' said Mrs. Gamp, 'you're a wearing old soul, and that's the blessed truth. You ought to know that you was born in a wale, and that you live in a wale, and that you *must take the consequences of sich a sitivation.* As a good friend of mine has frequent made remark to me, Mr. Jonage Chuzzlewit, which her name, sir,—I will not deceive you,—is Harris,—Mrs. Harris through the square and up the steps a turnin' round by the tobacker shop,—and which she said it the last Monday evening as ever dawned upon this Pilgrim's Progress of a mortal wale,[4]—"O Sairey, Sairey, little do we know wot lays afore us!" "Mrs. Harris, ma'am," I says, "not much, it's true, but more than you suppoge. Our calcilations, ma'am," I says, "respectin' wot the number of a family will be, comes most times within one, and oftener than you would suppoge, exact." "Sairey," says Mrs. Harris, in a awful way, "tell me wot is my individgle number." "No, Mrs. Harris," I says to her, "ex-cuge me, if you please. My own family," I says, "has fallen out of three-pair backs, and has had damp doorsteps settled on their lungs, and one was turned up smilin' in a bedstead unbeknown.[5] Therefore, ma'am," I says, "seek not to protigipate, but take 'em as they come and as they

[1] This paragraph was written in, in *Berg*, where the next two pages were wafered together. It draws on ch. 25.

[2] 'Chuffey . . . stands out vividly. . . . The fine "points" of this short monologue are seized by Dickens. The picture of the meek, heart-broken, maundering, faithful servant, with decrepit figure, quavering voice, and trembling hands, . . . is painted in natural colors; nor is there exaggeration in the drawing' (Field, p. 131).

[3] The following speech is made up of Gampisms from several chapters; it was printed here in *Berg*, but Dickens interpolated, in manuscript, the phrases about being 'born in a wale' and the 'Pilgrim's Progress' (*sic*: *Berg* has the compromise 'Pilgian's Progress', but *Starling* regularizes 'Piljian's Projiss' entirely). Wright alters it to 'Projiss'. The interpolations come from chs. 46, 49 and 40 (pp. 705, 751, 625).

[4] 'There is a sibylline tendency in her look as she ecstatically gazes towards heaven' at this point (Field, p. 136).

[5] 'Here Mrs. Gamp suits the action to the word and smiles the smile of confiding youth and innocence. Its appeal is irresistible' (Field, p. 135).

go. Mine," I says to her,—"mine is all gone, my dear young chick.[1] And as to husbands, there's a wooden leg gone likewise home to its account, which, in its constancy of walking into public-'ouses, and never coming out again till fetched by force, was quite as weak as flesh, if not weaker."'[2]

Mrs. Gamp, now left to the live part of her task, formally relieved Mrs. Prig for the night. That interesting lady had a gruff voice and a beard, and straightway got her bonnet and shawl on. *

'Anythink to tell afore you goes, Betsey, my dear?'

'The pickled salmon in this house is delicious. I can partickler recommend it. The drinks is all good. His physic and them things is on the drawers and mankleshelf. He took his last slime draught at seven. The easy-chair ain't soft enough. You'll want his piller.'[3]

Mrs. Gamp thanked Mrs. Prig for these friendly hints and gave her good night. † She then entered on her official duties: firstly, she put on a yellow-white nightcap of prodigious size, in shape resembling a cabbage: *having previously divested herself of a row of bald old curls, which could scarcely be called false, they were so innocent of anything approaching to deception*;[4] secondly, and lastly, she summoned the housemaid, to whom she delivered this official charge, in tones expressive of faintness:—

'I think, young woman, as I could peck a little bit o' pickled salmon, with a little sprig o' fennel, and a sprinkling o' white pepper. I takes new bread, my dear, with jest a little pat o' fredge butter and a mossel o' cheese. With respect to ale, if they draws the Brighton old tipper at any 'ouse nigh here, I takes that[5] ale at night, my love; not as I cares for it myself, but on accounts of it being considered wakeful by the doctors; and whatever you do, young woman, don't bring me more than a shillingsworth of gin-and-water, warm, when I rings the bell a second time; for that is always my allowange, and I never takes a drop beyond. In case there should[6] be sich a thing as a cowcumber in the 'ouse, I'm rather partial to 'em, though I am but a poor woman. *Rich folks may ride on camels, but it ain't so easy for them to see out of a needle's eye.* That is my comfort, and I hopes I knows it.'

---

[1] In *Berg*, the last four words are underlined.

[2] This is the penultimate paragraph of Chapter I of the *Berg* text. At this point, Dickens interpolated two closely-written manuscript pages, and then directed himself to a further page mostly made up from stuck-in extracts from ch. 49 (about Mrs. Gamp's quarrel with Mrs. Prig). These three pages constituted the revised ending of the Reading, replacing the thirty-three pages of Chapter II: but most of the two manuscript pages were versions of passages salvaged from that Chapter.

[3] Voice too mannish: a demoralized Dickens, not really a Betsey Prig (Field, p. 133).

[4] According to Charles Kent (p. 216), Dickens later omitted the address to the housemaid, which follows here.

[5] In *Berg*, Dickens underlined 'that': also the next phrase from 'not as I cares for it' to 'by the doctors'.

[6] In *Berg*, 'should' is underlined.

The supper and drink being brought and done full justice to, she administered the patient's medicine by the simple process of clutching his windpipe to make him gasp, and immediately pouring it down his throat.

'Drat the old wexagious creetur,[1] I a'most forgot your piller, I declare!' she said, drawing it away. 'There! Now you're as comfortable as you need be, I'm sure! and *I*'m[2] a going to be comfortable too.'

All her arrangements made, she lighted the rushlight, coiled herself up on her couch, and fell asleep.

Ghostly and dark the room, and full of shadows. The noises in the streets were hushed, the house was quiet, the dead of night was coffined in the silent city. * When Mrs. Gamp awoke, she found that the busy day was broad awake too. Mrs. Prig relieved punctually, having passed a good night at another patient's. But Mrs. Prig relieved in an ill temper.

The best among us have their failings,[3] and it must be conceded of Mrs. Prig, that if there were a blemish in the goodness of her disposition, it was a habit she had of not bestowing all its sharp and acid properties upon her patients (*as a thoroughly amiable woman would have done*), but of keeping a considerable remainder for the service of her friends. * She looked offensively at Mrs. Gamp, and winked her eye. Mrs. Gamp felt it necessary that Mrs. Prig should know her place, and be made sensible of her exact station in society. * So she began a remonstrance with:—

'Mrs. Harris, Betsey—'

'Bother Mrs. Harris!'[4]

Mrs. Gamp looked at Betsey with amazement, incredulity, and indignation. Mrs. Prig, winking her eye tighter, folded her arms and uttered these tremendous words:—

'I don't believe there's no sich a person!'[5]

With these expressions, she snapped her fingers once, twice, thrice, each time nearer to the face of Mrs. Gamp, and then turned away as one who felt that there was now a gulf between them which nothing could ever bridge across.

---

[1] 'Drat the old wexagious creetur,' inserted in manuscript in *Starling*, is a conflation of two phrases from ch. 46 (pp. 705, 709).

[2] *I* italic in *Starling*. In *Berg*, 'you' in 'you need' is underlined.

[3] This passage was spoken by 'the Reader with a hardly endurable gravity of explanation' (Kent, p. 218). This final episode comes from ch. 49.

[4] 'Sneeringly' (Wright).

[5] 'Shaking head' (Wright).

BARDELL AND PICKWICK

Bardell and Pickwick (more often advertised and referred to as *The Trial from Pickwick*) was Dickens's most popular reading after the *Carol*, and was the item he read most often both in Britain and in America. As was noted above (p. 1), he particularly relied upon the combination of these two favourite items for such outstanding occasions as his American débuts and his final farewell performances. It was first performed, on impulse but obviously after thorough preparation, in Birmingham on 19 October 1858; it had not been announced, but 'I took it into my head' to read it, as he explained (*N*, iii. 64). It had been devised during the previous months. The humorist 'Cuthbert Bede' (the Reverend Edward Bradley) claimed that it was upon his suggestion, in August 1858, that Dickens began to work this Reading up, though at first afraid that it contained too many characters for one reader to sustain (*Dickensian*, xii (1916), 209). It immediately became a great favourite, and for the rest of his 1858-9 tour was his most frequently performed item; during his London season that Christmas, it was included in every performance. In later seasons, it was the most frequently used afterpiece with the *Copperfield* and *Marigold* readings, as well as with the *Carol*.

The original prompt-copy has apparently not survived, and its existence has never been recorded. Charles Kent, working on the prompt-copies in 1870-2, noted that the *Trial* text displayed a 'very striking peculiarity', in that it contained no deletions or other manuscript writings or performance-signs (p. 109); what he failed to remark was that this unique copy of the *Trial* was printed with two other Readings, one of which (*Mr. Chops*) was certainly, and the other (*Bob Sawyer*) most likely, devised in the summer of 1861 (see below, p. 213). This prompt-book, containing three items, was doubtless also printed in 1861. Maybe Dickens, despite having had this clean new prompt-copy printed, continued to use the old one—though, if so, it is surprising that it has not survived (or been recorded). More likely, he threw away the old 1858 copy, but, because by 1861 he knew the text so well, never bothered to mark up the new one with performance-signs. He continued to make textual changes extempore, and then to keep some of them in his memory without writing them into the script. The prompt-copy is entitled *Bardell and Pickwick. | Mr. Chops, the Dwarf. | Mr. Bob Sawyer's Party. | Three Readings. | Each in One Chapter. | Privately Printed.* (printed by William Clowes and Sons, London; texts of the three items paginated 3-31, 33-52 and 53-82). The *Trial* was not included in the Bradbury & Evans 'Readings editions' in 1858, but appeared in the Ticknor & Fields series of 1867-8. The *T & F* text is identical with that of the prompt-copy, except in correcting a few printing errors and altering the punctuation, etc., slightly.

The script comes entirely from *Pickwick Papers*, ch. 34, except for a few added phrases and the strengthening of Tony Weller's speech about the 'alleybi' (which ends the Reading, as it had concluded the chapter and the serial instalment) by a phrase from ch. 33 about a successful 'alleybi'. The Reading reduces the length of the original chapter by about a half—too severe a truncation, as Kate Field (p. 100) and others thought:

> This is one of the most dramatic passages in the whole range of his writings, and it appears to us that Mr. D. hardly bestows upon it the care that it deserves. Not that what he reads is not delivered admirably, and does not provoke roars of laughter; but we have not enough of it. Even the scene, as given in the classic pages of *Pickwick*, is very considerably curtailed in reading; and we think that Mr. D. errs in not preceding it by the scene in the lodging-house when Mr. Pickwick is discovered by his friends holding the fainting widow in his arms . . .; and those who have not read the book—there may be such persons—could hardly come to any other conclusion from the evidence at the trial than that Mr. Pickwick had really been a gay deceiver. (*Berwick and Kelso Warder*, 29 November 1861)

(Mr. Emlyn Williams, it may be noted, does include the lodging-house scene in his version: see his *Readings from Dickens* (1954), pp. 100–11.) The *Berwick Warder* critic found some compensation, however, in Dickens's having introduced 'many sly impromptu bits of humour not to be found in the text'. There was no Reading in which he improvised more liberally (Kent, p. 100), and 'As nearly every line of *Pickwick* was as well known to the audience as to himself, . . . these occasional liberties with the text were the more enjoyed, and . . . were regarded more in the light of a new edition, direct from the author, than anything else' (Dolby, p. 175).

These emendations to the text, impromptu or otherwise, did not please everyone. The New York *Nation* critic, noting how Dickens departed from the *T & F* (and thus also from the prompt-copy) text, remarked that these omissions and interpolations were 'very many, some advantageous, some injurious' (12 December 1867, p. 482). Professor Adolphus W. Ward, reviewing the performance in the *Manchester Guardian*, 4 February 1867—he repeats much of this review in his *Dickens* (1882), pp. 152–3—found his 'otherwise perfect enjoyment' of the Reading marred by the 'horrible suspicion' that Dickens had been 'tampering with his text . . . *Pickwick* cannot be improved—even by Mr. Dickens.' The author, he said, was not the only man to know this scene by heart, though 'he is the only man who can add to its infinite humour'. The footnotes below record some of the impromptu 'tamperings' which became a regular part of the script.

The *Trial*, a favourite comic episode ever since 1837, had been very popular in theatrical adaptations and, long before Dickens started doing it, had been 'done to death' in Penny-readings and other such performances. It was, as reviewers said, in the repertoire of every public reader, amateur or professional. Dickens's performance did not prove a disappointment, however, and his conception of the characters differed significantly from the usual interpretations. To quote two critics on this: not merely was his 'the best impersonation of the characters', but also 'the author's conception of his well-known creations' was strikingly different from the comedians'—

> Serjeant Buzfuz . . . was not the fat pluffy lawyer he is sometimes represented, who utters five words and then stops like a hippopotamus to blow, but a grave and keenly suasive advocate, who, while he has acquired the usual pauses and swings of the head common to old practitioners, utters his words with an apparent conviction of their

truth, and with an evident grasp of the plaintiff's view of the whole subject. So Sam Weller, as Dickens thought of him, is not the slangy dried-up cockney, who jerks out his drolleries with a consciousness of their force, and gives a self-satisfied smirk when he sees how they sting, but rather a pleasant, smart young fellow, shrewd as he is quick of motion, ready with a flooring joke as he is amusing with his comical smile, but doing it all with a perfectly natural and almost artless air. (*Chester Chronicle*, 26 January 1867)

Those public readers or actors ... who have read or performed this scene have un-avoidably given it an air of burlesque or farce ... Mr. Dickens, with the privilege of the author, has done what no one else has ventured to do. He has omitted, added, and altered, and has in this way succeeded in giving the scene an air of probability which in the original version it does not wear. The greatest change has been in the character of Mr. Winkle, who in the original is represented as a weak, timid and almost idiotic young man, but who in Mr. Dickens's new version gets into something like a passion with the opposing barrister, and shows a certain amount of courage and resolu-tion. The humour is still exaggerated but it no longer runs riot with excess of caricature. (*Bath Chronicle*, 14 February 1867)

A characterization which everyone commented upon was that of Mr. Justice Stareleigh. For him, Dickens created a marvellously comic face ('a wonderfully stolid expression'—Edinburgh *Courant*, 29 November 1861) and an equally comic voice, variously described as sepulchral and drawling and said by Percy Fitzgerald to have been based upon Samuel Rogers's (*Memories of Charles Dickens* (Bristol, 1913), p. 49). Physically, he seemed to take on the shape of the fat little judge:

Dickens steps out of his own skin which, for the time being, is occupied by Mr. Justice Stareleigh. His little round eyes, wide open and blinking; his elevated eyebrows that are in a constant state of interrogation; his mouth, drawn down by the weight of the law; the expression of the *ensemble*, which clearly denotes that everybody *is* a rascal whether found guilty or not; and the stern, iron-clad voice, apparently measuring out justice in as small quantities as possible, and never going faster than a dead march,— make up an impersonation that is extraordinary, even for Dickens. (Field, p. 103)

Most of the eight characters in this item, indeed, were described with relish and high admiration by various critics; some further quotations will be given in the footnotes. As Professor Ward exclaimed,

Talk to us of Garrick and his Protean powers! Mr. Justice Stareleigh, and Mr. Serjeant Buzfuz, and Mr. Nathaniel Winkle himself, all appeared in succession in Mr. Dickens's face and voice, and, like the image of Mrs. Bardell's departed exciseman, will remain 'stamped on' us for ever. If Mr. Samual Weller failed to attain to a similar incarnation, it is only because, like his own personal illustrations, he has already become to all of us a mythical personage incapable of realisation in this imperfect world. (*Manchester Guardian*, 4 February 1867)

This disappointment with Sam Weller—doubtless partly for the reason Ward suggests—was often expressed, most vividly perhaps by the Yankee who walked out of a performance at Boston, in a state of high dudgeon, maintaining that Dickens 'knows no more about Sam Weller 'n a cow does of pleatin' a shirt, at all events that ain't *my* idea of Sam Weller, anyhow' (Dolby, p. 176). Some critics, indeed, regarded his characterization of Sam as successful—and perhaps it improved markedly, as was claimed by the artist W. P. Frith, who took the credit for it. Dickens had given him tickets for a performance of the *Trial*; Frith went, but was disappointed, feeling that Dickens had misconceived the character of Sam Weller, in reading whose repartees and quaint sayings he 'lowered his voice to the tones of one who was rather ashamed of what he was saying, and afraid of being reproved for the freedom of his utterances'. Plucking up courage, Frith told Dickens what he thought was wrong; Dickens smiled and said nothing. A few days later, one of Frith's friends went to a performance, and afterwards told him that Sam's sayings came from Dickens 'like pistol-shots'. When Frith mentioned this, Dickens replied, 'with a twinkle in his eye which those who knew him must so well remember, "I altered it a little—made it smarter. . . . Whenever I am wrong I am obliged to any one who will tell me of it; but up to the present I have never been wrong."' (W. P. Frith, *Autobiography and Reminiscences* (1887), i. 311–12)

The impersonation of Sam Weller was, it seems clear, not untalented (and Dickens made great hits with two somewhat kindred figures, the Boots at the Holly-Tree Inn, and Doctor Marigold). But, while other characters in the *Trial* were unimaginably satisfying, splendid improvements upon everyone's comprehension of the text, many people thought they could imagine Sam's being better done. He was indeed, as Ward said, too 'mythical' not to be a disappointment in the flesh. The one indubitable success associated with Sam in this Reading was the applause, even cheering, which greeted the first mention of his name. At the first performance, in 1858, as Dickens recorded, 'they gave a thunder of applause, as if he were really coming in', when Buzfuz named him (*N*, iii. 64). This compliment to one of the best-loved of Dickens's characters became customary. Fifty years afterwards, a man wrote: 'No one who ever heard it can forget the roar of delight that came from the vast audience [in St. James's Hall] when Serjeant Buzfuz said "Call Samuel Weller!"' (W. Ridley Kent, 'A Dickens Reading', *Dickensian*, vii (1911), 319). As a critic wrote, of Dickens's New York début:

A thousand things might be said of the impressions which Monday evening made upon Mr. Dickens's audience, most of whom saw for the first time a friend whom they had long loved. To us the most impressive thing was the burst of applause which followed the mention of Sam Weller's name. It was such an unaffected tribute of admiration as few authors have ever obtained. Mr. Dickens stood before us in the flesh——listening to that voice of human sympathy and admiration which only the posterity of most other great men hear. (*Nation*, 12 December 1867, p. 483)

Altogether, *The Trial* contained, as an Edinburgh journalist thought, 'more genuine amusement than perhaps has ever been afforded by any other public entertainment in this city' (*Courant*, 29 November 1861). Many other such superlatives could be quoted: and Dickens's own unconcealed enjoyment of this Reading was infectious—'he "goes in" for his own amusement as well as that of his audience' (*Scotsman*, 8 December 1868); 'in it, Mr. Dickens seems absolutely to revel with delight' (*Manchester Guardian*, 27 January 1862). Certainly *The Trial* was among the best two or three of the Readings, and, being a short one (it lasted about thirty minutes), it was a very convenient item to be paired with one of the longer and less hilarious Readings (the *Carol*, *Little Dombey*, *Copperfield*, or *Marigold*). Having figured as the concluding item in so many programmes, it was appropriately the last item that Dickens ever read in public, on 15 March 1870.

W. M. Wright's extensive marginalia on this Reading, which were discovered too late for inclusion in the text, are summarised in an Additional Note (p. 212).

Bardell and Pickwick

ON the morning of the trial of the great action for breach of promise of marriage—Bardell against Pickwick—the defendant, Mr. Pickwick, being escorted into court, stood up in a state of agitation, and took a glance around him. There were already a pretty large sprinkling of spectators in the gallery, and a numerous muster of gentlemen in wigs, in the barristers' seats: who presented, as a body, all that pleasing and extensive variety of nose and whisker for which the bar of England is justly celebrated. Such of the gentlemen as had a brief to carry, carried it in as conspicuous a manner as possible, and occasionally scratched their noses with it, to impress it more strongly on the observation of the spectators. Other gentlemen who had no briefs, carried under their arms goodly octavos, with a red label behind, and that under-done-pie-crust-coloured cover, which is technically known as 'law calf.' Others, who had neither briefs nor books, thrust their hands into their pockets, and looked as wise as they could. The whole, to the great wonderment of Mr. Pickwick, were divided into little groups, who were chatting and discussing the news of the day in the most unfeeling manner possible,—just as if no trial at all were coming on. *

A loud cry of 'Silence!' announced the entrance of the judge: who was most particularly short, and so fat, that he seemed all face and waistcoat. He rolled in, upon two little turned legs, and having bobbed to the bar, who bobbed to him, put his little legs underneath his table, and his little three-cornered hat upon it.[1] * A sensation was then perceptible in the body of the court; and immediately afterwards Mrs. Bardell, the plaintiff, supported by Mrs. Cluppins, her bosom friend number one, was led in in a drooping state. An extra-sized umbrella was then handed in by Mr. Dodson, and a pair of pattens by Mr. Fogg (Dodson and Fogg being the plaintiff's attornies), each of whom had prepared a sympathizing and melancholy face for the occasion. Mrs. Sanders, bosom friend number two, then appeared, leading in Master Bardell, * whom she placed on the floor of the court in front of his hysterical mother,—a commanding position in which he could not fail to awaken the sympathy of both judge and jury. This was not done without considerable opposition on the part of the young gentleman himself, who had misgivings that his being placed in the full glare of the judge's eye was only a formal prelude to his being immediately ordered away for instant execution.

[1] *Suzannet* reads '... hat upon it; a sensation ...' *1883* correctly begins a new sentence here. *Suzannet* is punctuated thus because, after a long deletion (the swearing-in of the jury) the text resumes in the middle of a sentence.

'I am for the plaintiff, my Lord,' said Mr. Serjeant Buzfuz.

COURT.—'Who is with you, brother Buzfuz?' Mr. Skimpin bowed, to intimate that he was.

'I appear for the defendant, my Lord,' said Mr. Serjeant Snubbin.

COURT.—'Anybody with you, brother Snubbin?'

'Mr. Phunky, my Lord.' *

COURT.—'Go on.'

Mr. Skimpin proceeded to 'open the case;' and the case appeared to have very little inside it when he had opened it, for he kept such particulars as he knew, completely to himself.

Serjeant Buzfuz then rose with all the majesty and dignity which the grave nature of the proceedings demanded, and having whispered to Dodson, and conferred briefly with Fogg, pulled his gown over his shoulders, settled his wig, and addressed the jury.

Serjeant Buzfuz began by saying,[1] that never, in the whole course of his professional experience—never, from the very first moment of his applying himself to the study and practice of the law—had he approached a case with such a heavy sense of the responsibility imposed upon him— a responsibility he could never have supported, were he not buoyed up and sustained by a conviction so strong, that it amounted to positive certainty that the cause of truth and justice, or, in other words, the cause of his much-injured and most oppressed client, *must* prevail[2] with the high-minded and intelligent dozen of men whom he now saw in that box before him.

Counsel always begin in this way, because it puts the jury on the best terms with themselves, and makes them think what sharp fellows they must be. A visible effect was produced immediately; several jurymen beginning to take voluminous notes.

'You have heard from my learned friend, gentlemen,' continued Serjeant Buzfuz, well knowing that, from the learned friend alluded to, the gentlemen of the jury had heard nothing at all—'you have heard from my learned friend, gentlemen, that this is an action for a breach of promise of marriage, in which the damages are laid at 1500*l*. But

---

[1] 'The oration of the learned Serjeant ... was a triumph in its way—Mr. Dickens ingeniously contriving to accent every word that the rules of elocution would forbid to be accented' (*Scotsman*, 21 April 1866). Charles Kent writes of Buzfuz's 'extraordinarily precise, almost mincing pronunciation'; for instance, he pronounced *responsibility* 'respon-see-bee-lee-ty' (pp. 112–13). Kate Field remarks on his 'rising inflection', and uses a quasi-musical notation to indicate the pitch and stress of various phrases (pp. 103–7). Wright annotates Buzfuz extensively: see p. 212.

[2] The word *must*, like all words italicized in this Reading, is printed italic in *Suzannet*. Dickens would repeat the phrase 'must prevail', and 'The intonation of these final words are delightfully burlesque. Serjeant Buzfuz draws back his head and then throws it forward to add impressiveness to speech, while a muscular contortion going on at the back of his neck and rippling down his shoulders suggests memories of a heavy swell on the ocean' (Field, pp. 104–5).

you have not heard from my learned friend, inasmuch as it did not come within my learned friend's province to tell you, what are the facts and circumstances of this case. Those facts and circumstances, gentlemen, you shall hear detailed by me, and proved by the unimpeachable female whom I will place in that box before you.[1] The plaintiff is a widow; yes, gentlemen, a widow. The late Mr. Bardell, after enjoying, for many years, the esteem and confidence of his sovereign, as one of the guardians of his royal revenues, glided almost imperceptibly from the world, to seek elsewhere for that repose and peace which a custom-house can never afford.'

This was a pathetic description of the decease of Mr. Bardell, who had been knocked on the head with a quart-pot in a public-house cellar.

'Some time before Mr. Bardell's death, he had stamped his likeness on a little boy.[2] With this little boy, the only pledge of her departed exciseman, Mrs. Bardell shrunk from the world, and courted the retirement and tranquillity of Goswell Street; and here she placed in her front parlour-window a written placard, bearing this inscription—"Apartments furnished for a single gentleman. Inquire within."' Here Serjeant Buzfuz paused, while several gentlemen of the jury took a note of the document.

'There is no date to that, is there, sir?' inquired a juror.

'There is no date, gentlemen, but I am instructed to say that it was put in the plaintiff's parlour-window just this time three years. Now, I entreat the attention of the jury to the wording of this document— "Apartments furnished for a single gentleman!" "Mr. Bardell," said the widow; "Mr. Bardell was a man of honour—Mr. Bardell was a man of his word—Mr. Bardell was no deceiver—Mr. Bardell was once a single gentleman himself; *in* single gentlemen I shall perpetually see something to remind me of what Mr. Bardell was, when he first won my young and untried affections; to a single gentleman shall my lodgings be let." Actuated by this beautiful and touching impulse, (among the best impulses of our imperfect nature, gentlemen,) the desolate widow dried her tears, furnished her first floor, caught her innocent boy to her maternal bosom, and put the bill up in her parlour-window. Did it remain there long? No. Before the bill had been in the parlour-window three days—three days, gentlemen—a Being, erect upon two legs, and bearing all the outward semblance of a man, and not of a monster, knocked at Mrs. Bardell's door. He inquired within; he took the lodgings; and on the very next day he entered into possession of them. This man was Pickwick—Pickwick the defendant.'

Serjeant Buzfuz here paused for breath. The silence awoke Mr. Justice

---

[1] Here 'Buzfuz' gave a mighty thump on the desk, as the novel text indicates (Field, p. 105).

[2] Pronounced '*lit*-tle bo—*hoy*' (Field, p. 105).

Stareleigh, who immediately wrote down something with a pen without any ink in it, and looked unusually profound, to impress the jury with the belief that he always thought most deeply with his eyes shut.

'Of this man Pickwick I will say little; the subject presents but few attractions; and I, gentlemen, am not the man, nor are you, gentlemen, the men, to delight in the contemplation of revolting heartlessness, and of systematic villany.'

Here Mr. Pickwick, who had been writhing in silence, gave a violent start, as if some vague idea of assaulting Serjeant Buzfuz, in the august presence of justice and law, suggested itself to his mind.

'I say systematic villany, gentlemen,' said Serjeant Buzfuz, looking through Mr. Pickwick, and talking *at* him; 'and when I say systematic villany, let me tell the defendant Pickwick—if he be in court, as I am informed he is[1]—that it would have been more decent in him, more becoming, in better judgment, and in better taste, if he had stopped away.[2] * I shall show you, gentlemen, that for two years Pickwick continued to reside without interruption or intermission, at Mrs. Bardell's house. I shall show you that, on many occasions, he gave halfpence, and on some occasions even sixpences, to her little boy; and I shall prove to you, by a witness whose testimony it will be impossible for my learned friend to weaken or controvert, that on one occasion he patted the boy on the head, and, after inquiring whether he had won any *alley tors* or *commoneys* lately (both of which I understand to be a particular species of marbles much prized by the youth of this town), made use of this remarkable expression—"How should you like to have another father?" I shall prove to you, gentlemen, * on the testimony of three of his own friends—most unwilling witnesses, gentlemen—most unwilling witnesses —that on that morning he was discovered by them holding the plaintiff in his arms, and soothing her agitation by his caresses and endearments.[3] And now, gentlemen, but one word more. Two letters have passed between these parties—letters which are admitted to be in the handwriting of the defendant. * Let me read the first:—"Garraway's, twelve o'clock. Dear Mrs. B.—Chops and Tomata sauce. Yours, PICKWICK." Gentlemen, what does this mean? Chops! Gracious heavens! and Tomata[4] sauce! Gentlemen, is the happiness of a sensitive and confiding female to be trifled away by such shallow artifices as these? The next has no date whatever, which is in itself suspicious.—"Dear Mrs. B., I shall not be at home till to-morrow. Slow coach." And then follows

---

[1] Rising to a *crescendo* on 'he is'. 'When Serjeant Buzfuz . . . [here] aims a forefinger at the defendant's head, it becomes a query, whether grotesque action is not as difficult to excel in as absolute grace. Dickens has learned its secret' (Field, p. 106).

[2] *T & F* begins a new paragraph here, as does the novel.

[3] *T & F* again begins a new paragraph here, as does the novel.

[4] Spelled *Tomato* in *T & F*, throughout.

this very remarkable expression—"Don't trouble yourself about the warming-pan." Why, gentlemen, who *does* trouble himself about a warming-pan? Why is Mrs. Bardell so earnestly entreated not to agitate herself about this warming-pan, unless it is, as I assert it to be, a mere cover for hidden fire—a mere substitute for some endearing word or promise, agreeably to a preconcerted system of correspondence, artfully contrived by Pickwick with a view to his contemplated desertion, and which I am not in a condition to explain?[1] * Enough of this: my client's hopes and prospects are ruined. * But Pickwick, gentlemen, Pickwick, the ruthless destroyer of this domestic oasis in the desert of Goswell Street—Pickwick, who has choked up the well, and thrown ashes on the sward—Pickwick, who comes before you to-day with his heartless Tomata sauce and warming-pans—Pickwick still rears his head with un-blushing effrontery, and gazes without a sigh on the ruin he has made. Damages, gentlemen—heavy damages—are the only punishment with which you can visit him; the only recompense you can award to my client. And for those damages she now appeals to an enlightened, a high-minded, a right-feeling, a conscientious, a dispassionate, a sympa-thising, a contemplative[2] jury of her civilized countrymen.'

With this beautiful peroration, Mr. Serjeant Buzfuz sat down, and Mr. Justice Stareleigh woke up.

'Call Elizabeth Cluppins,' said Sergeant Buzfuz, rising a minute after-wards, with renewed vigour. *

'Do you recollect, Mrs. Cluppins? Do you recollect being in Mrs. Bardell's back one pair of stairs, on one particular morning in July last, when she was dusting Pickwick's apartment?'

'Yes, my Lord and Jury, I do.'

'Mr. Pickwick's sitting-room was the first floor front, I believe?'

'Yes, it were, sir.'

COURT.—'What were you doing in the back room, ma'am?'[3]

'My Lord and Jury, I will not deceive you.'

COURT.—'You had better not, ma'am.'

'I was there, unbeknown to Mrs. Bardell; I had been out with a little basket, gentlemen, to buy three pound of red kidney purtaties, which was three pound tuppence ha'penny, when I see Mrs. Bardell's street door on the jar.'

COURT.—'On the what?'[4]

'Partly open, my Lord.'

---

[1] Again, *T & F* begins a new paragraph here, as does the novel.

[2] Amplified by Dickens to 'and, it is not going too far to say, a highly poetical jury . . .' (New York *Nation*, 12 December 1867, p. 482). See also Wright, p. 212, below.

[3] Mr. Justice Stareleigh's inquiry was suspicious; Mrs. Cluppins replied lacka-daisically, and Stareleigh's 'You had better not, ma'am' was very fierce (Kent, p. 114).

[4] Spoken 'in a state of owl-like astonishment' (Field, p. 108).

COURT.—'She *said* on the jar.'

'It's all the same, my Lord.'

The little judge looked doubtful, and said he'd make a note of it.

'I walked in, gentlemen, just to say good mornin', and went, in a permiscuous manner, up stairs, and into the back room. Gentlemen, there was the sound of voices in the front room, and—'

'And you listened, I believe, Mrs. Cluppins?'

'Beggin' your pardon, sir, I would scorn the haction. The voices was very loud, sir, and forced themselves upon my ear.'

'Well, Mrs. Cluppins, you were not listening, but you heard the voices. Was one of those voices, Pickwick's?'

'Yes, it were, sir.'

And Mrs. Cluppins, after distinctly stating that Mr. Pickwick addressed himself to Mrs. Bardell, repeated, by slow degrees, and by dint of many questions, the conversation she had heard. Which, like many other conversations repeated under such circumstances, or indeed like many other conversations repeated under any circumstances, was of the smallest possible importance in itself, but looked big now.[1]

Mrs. Cluppins having broken the ice, thought it a favourable opportunity for entering into a short dissertation on her own domestic affairs; so, she straightway proceeded to inform the court that she was the mother of eight children at that present speaking, and that she entertained confident expectations of presenting Mr. Cluppins with a ninth, somewhere about that day six months. At this interesting point, the little judge interposed most irascibly, and the worthy lady was taken out of court.

'Nathaniel Winkle!' said Mr. Skimpin.

'Here!'[1] Mr. Winkle entered the witness-box, and having been duly sworn, bowed to the judge: who acknowledged the compliment by saying:

COURT.—'Don't look at me, sir; look at the jury.'

Mr. Winkle obeyed the mandate, and looked at the place where he thought the jury might be.

Mr. Winkle was then examined by Mr. Skimpin.[2]

'Now, sir, have the goodness to let his Lordship and the jury know what your name is, will you?' Mr. Skimpin inclined his head on one

---

[1] Sentence added by Dickens, maybe recalling rumours about his marital troubles.

[2] '"He-ah, he-ah", replies an embarrassed voice' (Field, p. 108). 'Don't we remember how, even before he could open his lips, he was completely disconcerted?' (Kent, p. 116). Mr. Winkle's speech was 'lively and nervously rapid', in contrast to Dickens's narrative pace, which was 'generally slow and measured' (*Western Daily Mercury*, 7 January 1862). There was also a happy contrast between 'the sepulchral tone' of Mr. Justice Stareleigh and what the *Scotsman* (21 April 1866) described as Winkle's 'sharp curt speech'. See also Wright, in Appendix.

[3] Mr. Skimpin remained 'as vividly as anything at all about this Reading in our recollection' (Kent, p. 117). During his badgering of Mr. Winkle, 'the expression of his countenance denoted positive delight in the work before him' (Field, p. 108).

side and listened with great sharpness for the answer, as if to imply that he rather thought Mr. Winkle's natural taste for perjury would induce him to give some name which did not belong to him.

'Winkle.'

COURT.—'Have you any Christian name, sir?'[1]

'Nathaniel, sir.'

COURT.—'Daniel,—any other name?'

'Nathaniel, Sir—my Lord, I mean.'

COURT.—'Nathaniel Daniel, or Daniel Nathaniel?'

'No, my Lord, only Nathaniel—not Daniel at all.'

COURT.—'What did you tell me it was Daniel for then, sir?'

'I didn't, my Lord.'

COURT.—'You did, sir. How could I have got Daniel on my notes, unless you told me so, sir?'

'Mr. Winkle has rather a short memory, my Lord; we shall find means to refresh it before we have quite done with him, I dare say. Now, Mr. Winkle, attend to me, if you please, sir; and let me recommend you be careful. I believe you are a particular friend of Pickwick, the defendant, are you not?'

'I have known Mr. Pickwick now, as well as I recollect at this moment, nearly—'

'Pray, Mr. Winkle, do not evade the question. Are you, or are you not, a particular friend of the defendant's?'

'I was just about to say, that—'

'Will you, or will you not, answer my question, sir?'[2]

COURT.—'If you don't answer the question, you'll be committed to prison, sir.'

'Yes, I am.'

'Yes, you are. And couldn't you say that at once, sir? Perhaps you know the plaintiff too—eh, Mr. Winkle?'

'I don't know her; but I've seen her.'

'Oh, you don't know her, but you've seen her? Now, have the goodness to tell the gentlemen of the jury what you mean by *that*, Mr. Winkle.'

'I mean that I am not intimate with her, but that I have seen her when I went to call on Mr. Pickwick, in Goswell Street.'[3]

'How often have you seen her, sir?'

[1] This improvement on the novel—where the Judge had asked 'What's your Christian name, sir?'—is typical of many small changes made before this text was printed. Mr Justice Stareleigh's 'slow, authoritative tone, as if founded on the Rock of Ages' (Field, p. 109), during this exchange, was much admired.

[2] Here Winkle was given an extra speech: 'Why, God bless my soul, I was just about to say that—' (Kent, p. 111).

[3] Winkle preluded this speech too with 'God bless my soul!' (Field, p. 110).

'How often?'

'Yes, Mr. Winkle, how often? I'll repeat the question for you a dozen times, if you require it, sir.'

On this question there arose the edifying brow-beating, customary on such points. First of all, Mr. Winkle said it was quite impossible for him to say how many times he had seen Mrs. Bardell. Then he was asked if he had seen her twenty times, to which he replied, 'Certainly,— more than that.' Then he was asked whether he hadn't seen her a hundred times—whether he couldn't swear that he had seen her more than fifty times—whether he didn't know that he had seen her at least seventy-five times—and so forth.

'Pray, Mr. Winkle, do you remember calling on the defendant Pickwick at these apartments in the plaintiff's house in Goswell Street, on one particular morning, in the month of July last?'

'Yes, I do.'

'Were you accompanied on that occasion by a friend of the name of Tupman, and another of the name of Snodgrass?'

'Yes, I was.'

'Are they here?'

'Yes, they are,' looking very earnestly towards the spot where his friends were stationed.

'Pray attend to me, Mr. Winkle, and never mind your friends,' with an expressive look at the jury. 'They must tell their stories without any previous consultation with you, if none has yet taken place (another look at the jury). Now, sir, tell the gentlemen of the jury what you saw on entering the defendant's room, on this particular morning. Come; out with it, sir; we must have it, sooner or later.'

'The defendant, Mr. Pickwick, was holding the plaintiff in his arms, with his hands clasping her waist, and the plaintiff appeared to have fainted away.'

'Did you hear the defendant say anything?'

'I heard him call Mrs. Bardell a good creature, and I heard him ask her to compose herself, for what a situation it was, if anybody should come, or words to that effect.'

'Now, Mr. Winkle, I have only one more question to ask you. Will you undertake to swear that Pickwick, the defendant, did not say on the occasion in question, "My dear Mrs. Bardell, you're a good creature; compose yourself to this situation, for to this situation you must come," or words to *that* effect?'

'I—I didn't understand him so, certainly. I was on the staircase, and couldn't hear distinctly; the impression on my mind is—'

'The gentlemen of the jury want none of the impressions on your mind, Mr. Winkle, which I fear would be of little service to honest straightforward men. You were on the staircase, and didn't distinctly hear; but you will not swear that Pickwick did not make use of the expressions I have quoted? Do I understand that?'

'No I will not.' *

'You may leave the box, sir.'

Tracy Tupman, and Augustus Snodgrass, were severally called into the box; both corroborated the testimony of their unhappy friend; and each was driven to the verge of desperation by excessive badgering.

Susannah Sanders was then called, and examined by Serjeant Buzfuz, and cross-examined by Serjeant Snubbin. Had always said and believed that Pickwick would marry Mrs. Bardell; knew that Mrs. Bardell's being engaged to Pickwick was the current topic of conversation in the neighbourhood, after the fainting in July. Had heard Pickwick ask the little boy how he should like to have another father. Did not know that Mrs. Bardell was at that time keeping company with the baker, but did know that the baker was then a single man and is now married. Thought Mrs. Bardell fainted away on the morning in July, because Pickwick asked her to name the day; knew that she (witness) fainted away stone dead when Mr. Sanders asked *her* to name the day, and believed that anybody as called herself a lady would do the same under similar circumstances. During the period of her keeping company with Mr. Sanders she had received love letters, like other ladies. In the course of their correspondence Mr. Sanders had often called her a 'duck,' but he had never called her 'chops,' nor yet 'tomata sauce.'[1]

Serjeant Buzfuz now rose with more importance than he had yet exhibited, if that were possible, and said 'Call Samuel Weller.'[2]

It was quite unnecessary to call Samuel Weller; for Samuel Weller stepped into the box the instant his name was pronounced; and placing his hat on the floor, and his arms on the rail, took a bird's-eye view of the bar, and a comprehensive survey of the bench with a remarkably cheerful and lively aspect.

COURT.—'What's your name, sir?'

'Sam Weller, my Lord.'

COURT.—'Do you spell it with a "V" or with a "W"?'[3]

'That depends upon the taste and fancy of the speller, my Lord. I never had occasion to spell it more than once or twice in my life, but I spells it with a "V."'

---

[1] Strangely, Dickens omits the next sentences, which provide the pay-off to this joke: 'He was particularly fond of ducks. Perhaps if he had been as fond of chops and tomata sauce, he might have called her that, as a term of affection.' Mr. Emlyn Williams, in his version, retains them, in abbreviated form. Mr. Williams's version, about the same length as Dickens's, is superior to it in retaining more joke-lines and a better continuity; his abbreviations, however, damage the prose-rhythms more than Dickens's do.

[2] See above, p. 198, for the applause which invariably greeted this line.

[3] On the niceties of Cockney *v*/*w* sounds, see above, p. 169.

Here a voice in the gallery exclaimed, 'Quite right too, Samivel; quite right. Put it down a we, my Lord, put it down a we.'

COURT.—'Who is that, who dares to address the court? Usher.'

'Yes, my Lord.'

COURT.—'Bring that person here instantly.'

'Yes, my Lord.'

But as the usher didn't find the person, he didn't bring him; and, after a great commotion, all the people who had got up to look for the culprit, sat down again. The little judge turned to the witness as soon as his indignation would allow him to speak, and said,

COURT.—'Do you know who that was, sir?'

'I rayther suspect it was my father, my Lord.'

COURT.—'Do you see him here now?'

Sam stared up into the lantern in the roof of the court, and said, 'Why no, my Lord, I can't say that I *do* see him at the present moment.'

COURT.—'If you could have pointed him out, I would have sent him to jail instantly.'

Sam bowed his acknowledgments.

'Now, Mr. Weller,' said Serjeant Buzfuz.

'Now, sir.'

'I believe you are in the service of Mr. Pickwick, the defendant in this case. Speak up, if you please, Mr. Weller.'

'I mean to speak up, sir. I am in the service o' that 'ere gen'l'man, and a wery good service it is.'

'Little to do, and plenty to get, I suppose?'

'Oh, quite enough to get, sir, as the soldier said ven they ordered him three hundred and fifty lashes.'

COURT.—'You must not tell us what the soldier said, unless the soldier is in court, and is examined in the usual way; it's not evidence.'[1]

'Wery good, my Lord.'

'Do you recollect anything particular happening on the morning when you were first engaged by the defendant; eh, Mr. Weller?'

'Yes I do, sir.'

'Have the goodness to tell the jury what it was.'

'I had a reg'lar new fit out o' clothes that mornin', gen'l'men of the jury, and that was a wery partickler and uncommon circumstance vith me in those days.'

---

[1] The novel does not contain 'unless the soldier is in court, and is examined in the usual way'. Dickens further amplified this famous moment: sometimes, apparently, making the Judge inquire whether the soldier was in court (*Berwick and Kelso Warder*, 29 November 1861), sometimes restoring from the novel the phrase '... what the soldier, *or any other man*, said ...' (*Northern Whig*, 21 March 1867), sometimes specifying that 'You cannot possibly be allowed to inform the Court' (etc.) unless the soldier 'is in court, in full Regimentals' (Wright).

The judge looked sternly at Sam, but Sam's features were so perfectly serene that the judge said nothing.

'Do you mean to tell me, Mr. Weller, that you saw nothing of this fainting on the part of the plaintiff in the arms of the defendant, which you have heard described by the witnesses?'

'Certainly not, sir, I was in the passage 'till they called me up; and then the old lady as you call the plaintiff, she warn't there, sir.'

'You were in the passage and yet saw nothing of what was going forward. Have you a pair of eyes, Mr. Weller?'

'Yes, I have a pair of eyes, and that's just it. If they wos a pair o' patent double million magnifyin' gas microscopes of hextra power, p'r'aps I might be able to see through two flights o' stairs and a deal door; but bein' only eyes, you see, my wision's limited.' *

'Now, Mr. Weller, I'll ask you a question on another point, if you please.'

'If you please, sir.'

'Do you remember going up to Mrs. Bardell's house, one night in November?'

'Oh yes, wery well.'

'Oh, you *do* remember that, Mr. Weller. I thought we should get at something at last.'

'I rayther thought that, too, sir.'

'Well; I suppose you went up to have a little talk about the trial—eh, Mr. Weller?'

'I went up to pay the rent; but we *did* get a talkin' about the trial.'

'Oh, you did get a talking about the trial. Now what passed about the trial; will you have the goodness to tell us, Mr. Weller?'

'Vith all the pleasure in life, sir. Arter a few unimportant observations from the two wirtuous females as has been examined here to-day, the ladies gets into a wery great state o' admiration at the honourable conduct of Mr. Dodson and Mr. Fogg—them two gen'l'men as is settin' near you now.'

'The attornies for the plaintiff. Well, they spoke in high praise of the honourable conduct of Messrs. Dodson and Fogg, the attornies for the plaintiff, did they?'

'Yes; they said what a wery gen'rous thing it was o' them to have taken up the case on spec, and not to charge nothin' at all for costs, unless they got 'em out of Mr. Pickwick.'

'It's perfectly useless, my Lord, attempting to get at any evidence through the impenetrable stupidity of this witness. I will not trouble the court by asking him any more questions. Stand down, sir. * That's my case, my Lord.'

Serjeant Snubbin then addressed the jury on behalf of the defendant; *

and did the best he could for Mr. Pickwick; and the best, as everybody knows, could do no more.

Mr. Justice Stareleigh summed up, in the old-established form. He read as much of his notes to the jury as he could decipher on so short a notice; he didn't read as much of them as he couldn't make out; and he made running comments on the evidence as he went along. If Mrs. Bardell were right, it was perfectly clear Mr. Pickwick was wrong; and if they thought the evidence of Mrs. Cluppins worthy of credence, they would believe it; and, if they didn't, why they wouldn't.[1] The jury then retired to their private room to talk the matter over, and the judge retired to *his* private room to refresh himself with a mutton chop and a glass of sherry.

An anxious quarter of an hour elapsed; the jury came back; and the judge was fetched in. Mr. Pickwick put on his spectacles, and gazed at the foreman.

'Gentlemen, are you all agreed upon your verdict?'

'We are.'

'Do you find for the plaintiff, gentlemen, or for the defendant?'

'For the plaintiff.'

'With what damages, gentlemen?'

'Seven hundred and fifty pounds.'

Mr. Pickwick having drawn on his gloves with great nicety, and stared at the foreman all the while, * allowed himself to be assisted into a hackney-coach, which had been fetched for the purpose by the ever-watchful Sam Weller.

Sam had put up the steps, and was preparing to jump on the box, when he felt himself gently touched on the shoulder; and his father stood before him.

'Samivel! The gov'nor ought to have been got off with a alleybi. Ve got Tom Vildspark off o' that 'ere manslaughter (that come of hard driving) vith a alleybi, ven all the big vigs to a man, said as nothing couldn't save him.[2] I know'd what 'ud come o' this here way o' doin' bisniss. O Sammy, Sammy, vy worn't there a alleybi!'

THE END OF BARDELL AND PICKWICK

---

[1] *T & F* begins a new paragraph here.

[2] These sentences are adapted from ch. 33, but the Reading adds the bracketed admission about Tom Wildspark's culpability.

Additional Note on Bardell and Pickwick

When this edition was in page-proof, two further copies of Readings text with marginalia by W. M. Wright were discovered at Dickens House: *T & F* booklets containing the *Carol* and *Trial*, and *Copperfield* and *Bob Sawyer*. Most of these marginal notes appear in—were copied into?—the two-volume *T & F* drawn upon in the present edition, but some are new. Where possible, the more useful of these have been added to the headnotes or footnotes. But his notes on *The Trial*—very sparse in his two-volume collection—are too numerous to be introduced into the page-proofs, so a selection of them is given below.

Bardell and Pickwick: Stareleigh 'Sleepily' at 'Who is with you . . . ?', and Snubbin answered 'Very quick' (p. 201). Buzfuz turned indirect into direct speech (p. 201), e.g., 'the responsibeeleety imposed *upon* me'. At 'The plaintiff is a widow' (p. 202), 'Brushes tear from right eye with handkerchief and crushes tear from left eye with left hand.' Pronounced her name 'Bardill', and, when reading the letter, said 'Mistress B.' The placard (p. 202): '*In*quire with*in*.' Deleted 'inquired a juror' (p. 202), and substituted action: 'Leaning forward.' Omitted the two paragraphs from 'Serjeant Buzfuz here paused' to 'systematic villainy' (pp. 202–3) and sometimes the next nine lines, to 'if he had stopped away'. After reading the first letter, 'slapped book' at 'Chops!', 'sauce!', 'happiness', 'sensitive' and 'confiding'. Second letter: 'Don't/ trouble/ yourself/ *about* the warming-*pan*' (p. 204). Further amplification of his peroration (p. 204, note 2): '. . . a contemplative, and I am persuaded I'm not going too far in saying, an eminently practical, and a highly philosophical and poetical, jury. . . .' Dickens was 'Too slow and tame as Buzfuz'. He sometimes omitted the paragraph 'Mrs. Cluppins having broken the ice . . .' (p. 205). 'Winkle stutters and leans over table during part of his answers,' 'Very rapid and stammering;' at 'I am not intimate' (p. 206) spoke 'Crossly, rising on toes and coming down by way of emphasis;' 'gulping and pausing' at Pickwick's 'holding the plaintiff in his arms' (p. 207). Stareleigh 'writing in book' at 'Daniel', etc. (p. 206), and Winkle would be 'sent to moulder in gaol' instead of 'committed to prison' (p. 206). Skimpin, dramatizing 'the occasion in question' (p. 207), put 'Arm out as if enclosing waist'. The 'Tracy Tupman' paragraph (p. 208) was omitted. 'Leaning forward on right arm on table every time he answers as Weller.' After Sam's 'Wery good, my Lord' (p. 209), an extra speech for Skimpin: 'Come, come, come, Mr. Weller. We are rather travelling out of the record.' Sam pointed out Dodson and Fogg when he mentioned them (p. 210). Skimpin, at 'asking him any more questions' (p. 210): 'Motion straight ahead.'

DAVID COPPERFIELD

In the summer of 1861, having finished writing *Great Expectations*, Dickens began to think about his new series of Readings, due to start in late October. He had given very few performances since the conclusion of his first provincial tour in February 1859: only a fortnight's tour in October 1859, three readings in London for the Christmas of 1859, and a season of six performances given weekly in London in March–April 1861. He had of course been preoccupied with the establishment of *All the Year Round* (30 April 1859) and with writing, for publication in its pages, *A Tale of Two Cities* and *Great Expectations*. The short seasons of Readings in 1859 and 1861 had been devoted to his established repertoire; the last new item he had introduced was *The Trial from Pickwick*, in October 1858.

He now, therefore, needed to rehearse his old repertoire again, and he decided also to amplify it by devising some new items. About the end of August, he wrote to Forster:

> Every day for two or three hours, I practise my new readings, and (except in my office work) do nothing else. With great pains I have made a continuous narrative out of *Copperfield*, that I think will reward the exertion it is likely to cost me. Unless I am much mistaken, it will be very valuable in London. I have also done *Nicholas Nickleby* at the Yorkshire school, and hope I have got something droll out of Squeers, John Browdie, & Co. Also, the Bastille prisoner from the *Tale of Two Cities*. Also, the Dwarf from one of our Christmas numbers. (*Life*, pp. 687–8)

Probably about this time he also devised two other Readings, *Great Expectations* and *Mr. Bob Sawyer's Party*. Of these items, *Copperfield* and *Nickleby* opened his provincial tour (Norwich, 28 and 29 October 1861), and *Bob Sawyer* came into repertoire just after Christmas. The other items remained unperformed, for the time being or forever.

Dickens had thought of devising a Reading from *Copperfield* several years earlier. When discussing plans to give another charity performance in Birmingham in 1855 (which came to nothing), he wrote to his friend Arthur Ryland there:

> Having already read two Christmas books at Birmingham, I should like to get out of that restriction, and have a swim in the broader waters of one of my long books. I have been poring over Copperfield (which is my favourite), with the idea of getting a reading out of it, to be called by some such name as 'Young Housekeeping and Little Emily.' But there is still the huge difficulty that I constructed the whole with immense pains, and have so woven it up and blended it together, that I cannot yet so separate the parts as to tell the story of David's married life with Dora, and the story of Mr. Peggotty's search for his niece, within the time. This is my object. If I could possibly bring it to bear, it would make a very attractive reading, with a strong interest in it, and a certain completeness.
>
> This is exactly the state of the case. I don't mind confiding to you, that I never can approach the book with perfect composure (it had such perfect possession of me when

I wrote it), and that I no sooner begin to try to get it into this form, than I begin to read it all, and to feel that I cannot disturb it. (*N*, ii. 619)

In 1858 he again 'began to sketch out' a Reading from *Copperfield*, along the same lines; he failed to complete it then, though a year later he was still hoping to do so (*To* the Rev. W. H. Brookfield, 20 June 1859: MS. New York Public Library).

The script devised in 1861 was on the plan sketched out in 1855 and 1858. It was the most ambitious exercise in selection and revision he had yet undertaken. His earlier Readings taken from the novels had concentrated on a single character (*Mrs. Gamp*) or episode (*The Trial from Pickwick*), or a limited stretch of the story (*Little Dombey*). Only the *Great Expectations* Reading—probably devised about this time, but never even prepared for performance—tried to do more, by including the whole main plot from the first chapter until very near the end. That Dickens made what he soon decided was a false start is evident from the prompt-copy: *David Copperfield.*/ *A Reading.*/ *In Five Chapters.*/ *Privately Printed* (printed by William Clowes and Sons; text paginated i–xx, 3–104). The 'Introduction' (pp. i–xx) was evidently written after the five-chapter version had been printed. Indeed, pp. i–iii correspond to parts of pp. 3–5 of 'Chapter the First', and were printed from them; one sign of this is that a passage on pp. ii–iii is printed in small capitals—a mistake easy for the printer to make, for Dickens had doubly-underlined this passage (on p. 3) to indicate a vocal emphasis. Evidently, Dickens had decided that the Reading had opened too abruptly with the original 'Chapter the First', which, after a brief reminder of David's childhood memories of the Peggotty household (pp. 1–3), had been concerned with Emily's disappearance and Mr. Peggotty's determination to seek her out. So he added the Introduction, which (after the short childhood-memories passage) dealt with David's introducing Steerforth to the Peggotty family, and with the premonitory signs that trouble would ensue. Then, in the prompt-copy, Dickens renumbered the chapters, I to VI.

Before having the prompt-copy printed, Dickens had effected a great deal of condensation and rearrangement, conflating into one episode passages from various chapters, raiding various chapters for happy phrases or speeches (by the Micawbers, for instance), and drastically reducing the length of the narrative retained. The printed text of the prompt-copy contains almost 26,500 words; the corresponding parts of the novel total about 35,500 words, though the total would be much larger if one counted the full wordage of the chapters from which various snippets were taken. Then, in manuscript, Dickens deleted over 10,000 words; only nine of the 120 pages of the text are left unemended. It is difficult to determine which emendations were made sooner, and which later, in the prompt-copy. Light and dark brown ink, light and dark blue ink, and pencil, are all used. Certainly a major revision must have been made in late 1861. When *Copperfield* was first performed, it was a two-hour Reading, as the *Carol* and other Christmas Books, and *Little Dombey*, had originally been. In January 1862, however, he began giving a shortened version, at first in his 'morning' readings (at 2.30 p.m. or 3 p.m., sometimes advertised to take 'about an hour and a half', sometimes 'within two hours'), and then in the evenings (still two hours) together with a shorter item. This was usually *Bob Sawyer* ('to finish merrily' [*N*, iii. 289]), introduced into the repertoire about this time: but *The Trial, Boots, Mrs. Gamp*, or another of the after-pieces was sometimes paired with it.

A summary of the sources of the narrative may be useful—and it can be given largely in Dickens's words, for Professor E. W. F. Tomlin has recently discovered a holograph summary of this Reading (date and purpose uncertain). But, as Dickens's summary does not refer to some incidents, I insert a description of these, and the chapter-numbers, in square brackets:

Chapter I. [Childhood memories of the Peggotty family, from ch. 3.] Copperfield (as a young man of 19 or 20) takes his friend, Steerforth, to the old boat where Mr. Peggotty lives, and introduces Steerforth to Little Emily [ch. 21]. It is foreshadowed in this chapter, that Steerforth admires her in a profligate way, and begins to form designs upon her [ch. 22; and David's final meeting with Steerforth, from ch. 29.]

Chapter II. Copperfield goes alone to the old boat, to pass with the family, the last evening of Little Emily's single life; because she has engaged herself to be married to Ham (Mr. Peggotty's nephew) that day fortnight. Ham suddenly brings the news that she has eloped with Steerforth—a last letter from her is read—and Mr. Peggotty sets forth to seek her 'through the world' [ch. 31].

Chapter III. Copperfield describes his love for Dora [chs. 28, 26], and the dinner that he gave to Mr. and Mrs. Micawber and Traddles [ch. 28, with interpolations from chs. 27, 16 and 36].

Chapter IV. [David's mind is haunted by Mr. Peggotty's quest (ch. 32).] Mr. Peggotty returns from his search, unsuccessful, and relates where he has been in France and Italy [ch. 40].

Chapter V. Copperfield describes how he made proposals to Dora [ch. 33; courtship, chs. 37, 41]—how he married Dora [ch. 43]—and what their little menage was [chs. 44, 48].

Chapter VI describes the storm at Yarmouth, in the words of the book, and the Death of Steerforth [ch. 55: preceded by Mr. Peggotty's announcement that he has discovered Emily (ch. 50) and intends to take her overseas (ch. 51), and David's journey to Yarmouth (chs. 51, 55)].[1]

Many episodes and inessential characters are omitted: Clara Barkis from ch. 31, Littimer and Steerforth from ch. 28, Martha from chs. 40 and 51, Betsey Trotwood from ch. 51. The selection and rearrangement are adroit, but the Reading narrative is awkward in two ways. First, the emotional transitions are

---

[1] I am obliged to Professor Tomlin for drawing my attention to this MS. summary, in advance of his publishing it. I am unaware of any other such summary of a Reading by the novelist. It is difficult to date this document, which could belong to 1855, 1858, 1859, or 1861. One phrase, from the account of Chapter VI, is curious: 'in the words of the book'—for this Chapter is no closer to the novel text than any of the others. This inclines Tomlin towards the earliest date, when Dickens was least experienced in devising Readings. This is very possible, though it is odd that—if so—Dickens started with the six-chapter idea, then devised the five-chapter reading, and then reverted to his original six-chapter narrative. So I incline, marginally, to 1861 as the date. For Tomlin's account of this MS., and of the Dickens letters associated with it, see his 'Newly Discovered Dickens Letters', *TLS*, 22 February 1974, pp. 183–6.

sometimes over-rapid, through compression—Steerforth's sudden self-criticism at the end of Chapter I, or Mr. Peggotty's narrative and plans at the beginning of Chapter VI (especially after Dickens had made an eight-page cut in the prompt-copy). Second, the 'Young Housekeeping' chapters, though delightful, are irrelevant to the Emily–Steerforth–Peggotty story, which provides the main plot of the Reading. Dickens secures variety here at the expense of unity: this is the 'streaky-bacon' technique of story-telling, discussed at the beginning of ch. 17 of *Oliver Twist*, and indicated in the Number-plan for the tenth instalment of *David Copperfield*—'First chapter funny   Then on *to Emily*.'

Like the novel from which it was taken, this Reading was Dickens's favourite (Dolby, p. 19; *N*, iii. 354, 465, 579). 'It is far more interesting to me than any of the other Readings,' he told Mrs. Monckton Milnes, 'and I am half-ashamed to confess, even to you, what a tenderness I have for it' (T. Wemyss Reid, *Life of Richard Monckton Milnes* (1890), ii. 80). He rejoiced in its great effect upon a responsive audience. At Plymouth, for instance, in January 1862, he

... positively enthralled the people. It was a most overpowering effect, and poor Andrew [Lieutenant Andrew Gordon, R.N.] came behind the screen, after the storm, and cried in the best and manliest manner. Also there were two or three lines of his shipmates and other sailors, and they were extraordinarily affected. But its culminating effect was on Macready at Cheltenham. When I got home after Copperfield, I found him quite unable to speak, and able to do nothing but square his dear old jaw all on one side, and roll his eyes (half closed), like Jackson's picture of him. And when I said something light about it, he returned: 'No—er—Dickens! I swear to Heaven that, as a piece of passion and playfulness—er—indescribably mixed up together, it does—er—no, really, Dickens!—amaze me as profoundly as it moves me. But as a piece of art—and you know—er—that I—no, Dickens! By——! have seen the best art in a great time—it is incomprehensible to me. How is it got at—er—how is it done—er—how one man can—well? It lays me on my—er—back, and it is of no use talking about it!' With which he put his hand upon my breast and pulled out his pocket-handkerchief, and I felt as if I were doing somebody to his Werner. (*N*, iii. 276-7; cf. above, p. lvii)

It was a very exhausting Reading for him to give: 'I have now got to the point of taking so much out of myself with Copperfield, that I might as well do Richard Wardour' [his great dramatic role in Wilkie Collins's *The Frozen Deep*] (*N*, iii. 277); he was 'half dead' the day after giving it (*N*, iii. 288). Also, its success depended much more than that of any of the other Readings upon the auditorium, the audience, and his own strength and spirits. Kate Field opens her interesting chapter on it by saying how disappointed she was, the first time she heard it, and how unrecognizably different it was on subsequent evenings. Another observer in Boston, his hostess Annie Fields, noted in her diary one day: 'Dickens was very ill yesterday ... Copperfield was never more tragic than last night, but it was no longer "vif". I should hardly have known it for the same reading and reader' (*James T. Fields: Biographical Notes and Personal Sketches* (1881), p. 158). He sometimes avoided giving it in unsuitable auditoria: or he moved elsewhere, as in his short 1863 series in London, when he abandoned the St. James's Hall for the Hanover Square Room ('quite a wonderful room for sound') for the sake of 'the finer effects', principally in this item (*N*, iii. 346-7). At first, in America, he feared that it might be 'a thought too delicate for them' (*N*, iii. 579), particularly as most of the halls were larger than those he was used to in Britain: but it soon became a success there, though not one of the most popular items. Wright notes that, in Boston, it took 85 minutes to perform.

Forty-odd years after Dickens's death, the *Copperfield* Reading was remembered by two people who had seen it, and both stressed the same moment. 'Never shall I forget', wrote Lord Redesdale, 'the effect produced by his reading of the death of Steerforth; it was tragedy itself, and when he closed the book and his voice ceased, the audience for a moment seemed paralysed, and one could almost hear a sigh of relief' (*Memories* (1915), ii. 518). Thackeray's daughter Annie (Lady Ritchie) also recalled the storm scene as more thrilling than anything she had ever seen in a theatre. She was present at Dickens's last performance of *Copperfield* (1 March 1870), and was impressed by the power of this 'slight figure (so he appeared to me)' to hold a huge audience 'in some mysterious way. . . . It was not acting, it was not music, nor harmony of sound and colour, and yet I still have an impression of all these things as I think of that occasion' (*From the Porch* (1913), pp. 43–4; *Dickensian*, xxxiii (1937), 68). This finale was, for most people who heard it, the great moment in the Reading, indeed the most sublime moment in all the Readings: and, for many critics, this storm scene had seemed, anyway, the finest thing Dickens ever wrote. Charles Kent was expressing a common opinion when he wrote:

In all fiction there is no grander description than that of one of the sublimest spectacles in nature. The merest fragments of it conjured up the entire scene—aided as those fragments were by the look, the tones, the whole manner of the Reader. . . . There, in truth, the success achieved was more than an elocutionary triumph—it was the realisation to his hearers, by one who had the soul of a poet, and the gifts of an orator, and the genius of a great and imaginative author, of a convulsion of nature when nature bears an aspect the grandest and the most astounding. (Kent, p. 35)

The only criticism that was made of his rendering was that, to 'the most hypercritical, . . . there seemed a lack of something which, for want of a better term, may be denominated "physical energy"' (*Manchester Guardian*, 16 December 1861). Kate Field made the same point, though thrilled by the tragic power Dickens here displayed: the passage was, nevertheless, 'capable of even greater effect. The scene admits of wonderful scope for a mighty voice and mighty action' (Field, p. 49).

The Reading as a whole was, however, as Kate Field continued, 'an extraordinary performance . . . and no one actor living can embody the twelve characters of this reading with the individuality given them by Dickens, unaided, too, as he is, by theatrical illusion.' Mr. Peggotty in his anguish reminded one critic of King Lear, while Steerforth's dark destructiveness was 'as magically suggestive as anything imagined of Faust' (*Manchester Examiner*, 19 October 1868). Micawber, with his all-pervading cough (a mannerism not made much of in the novel), Traddles vivid though his 'part' was so minimal, and all of the many female characters in this item, were praised:

Every little trait and turn of character was indicated by some delicate inflection of voice, or equally appropriate facial expression. . . . Mr. Dickens's power of infusing femininity into his voice and gestures, in the dialogue and description of his female characters, is marvellous—his command over the ludicrous, in this as in the whole reading, never, however, for a moment exceeding the strictest limits of good taste. (*Scotsman*, 28 November 1861)

After a performance in 1867, Robert Lytton (the poet 'Owen Meredith', and son of Bulwer Lytton) wrote enthusiastically to Dickens that these were

... two hours so perfect in their uninterrupted intensity of delight, that the memory of them has become an integral part of myself. ... You play with the heart, like the Japanese juggler with his paper butterfly, as tho' it were a creature of your own construction, turn it this way and that at a breath, and make it rise or sink just as you will. Certainly, 'Voice' was never more felicitously 'married to immortal words' than yours during those two wonderful hours on Tuesday night, when I had the delight of listening to its magical utterance in a luxury of tears and laughter. For the multitudinous creations of your surpassing genius stimulated every emotion, and I confess that I was heartily *blubbering* at the time that Mr. Peggotty was talking to us. (MS. Dickens House)

Another, and more illustrious, blubberer might be cited to show how parts of this Reading could appeal to contemporary taste which may now seem unconvincing: Thackeray emphatically remarked that Emily's letter to her uncle (below, p. 227) was 'a masterpiece' (Anne Thackeray, *Chapters from Some Memories* (1894), p. 78). Dickens read it 'As if Emily was speaking,' 'Slow and pausing' (Wright).

The Reading was included in the Ticknor & Fields edition of 1867–8. It was printed from the prompt-copy (*Berg*), from which it differs, however, both in a few minor respects (different paragraphing and punctuation, a few accidentals, etc.) and, more interestingly, by including a dozen passages deleted in the prompt-copy. Clearly Dickens continued revising—mainly abbreviating—his text during or after his American tour. He also restored some passages cut earlier; *T & F* observes all but one of these 'Stet' instructions (Dickens had even deleted Micawber's letter, which ends Chapter III, but later relented and restored it). Most of the final cuts were made in the light-relief scenes with the Micawbers and with Dora, but some from the storm scene. When in a hurry, Dickens also made extempore cuts; at Glasgow, for instance, in 1868, 'I cut Copperfield with a bold dexterity that amazed myself and utterly confounded George [Allison, the gasman] at the wing; knocking off that and Bob [Sawyer's Party] by ten minutes to ten' (*N*, iii. 688).

The Reading has also been reprinted in its earliest form: *David Copperfield: a Reading, in Five Chapters, by Charles Dickens*, ed. John Harrison Stonehouse (1922). This is a facsimile of the original five-chapter version (text paginated 3–104), without the added 'Introduction' and without any of Dickens's other textual revisions and deletions. Stonehouse's own Introduction is devoted to 'the romantic history of Charles Dickens and Maria Beadnell', and he does not say where he found a copy of this edition (I must confess to not knowing the whereabouts of any copy). Anyone curious to see the text from which Dickens started should consult Stonehouse's reprint of the Reading, though it is not easy to obtain, since only 250 copies were offered for sale.

David Copperfield

CHAPTER I[1]

I had known Mr. Peggotty's house very well in my childhood, and I am sure I could not have been more charmed with it, if it had been Aladdin's palace, roc's egg and all. It was an old black barge or boat, high and dry on Yarmouth Sands, with an iron funnel sticking out of it for a chimney. There was a delightful door cut in the side, and it was roofed in, and there were little windows in it. It was beautifully clean and as tidy as possible. There were some lockers and boxes, and there was a table, and there was a Dutch clock, and there was a chest of drawers, and there was a tea-tray with a painting on it, and the tray was kept from tumbling down, by a Bible; and the tray, if it *had*[2] tumbled down, would have smashed a quantity of cups and saucers and a teapot that were grouped around the book. On the walls were coloured pictures of Abraham in red going to sacrifice Isaac in blue; and of Daniel in yellow being cast into a den of green lions.[3] Mr. Peggotty, as honest a seafaring man as ever breathed, dealt in lobsters, crabs and crawfish. *

As in my childhood, so in these days when I was a young man, Mr. Peggotty's household consisted of *his orphan nephew Ham Peggotty, a young shipwright; his adopted niece Little Emily, once my small sweetheart, now a beautiful young woman; and Mrs. Gummidge.*[4] All three had been maintained at Mr. Peggotty's sole charge for years and years; and Mrs. Gummidge was the widow of his partner in a boat, who had died poor. * She was very grateful, but she certainly would have been more agreeable[5] if she had not constantly complained, as she sat in the most comfortable corner by the fireside, that she was a 'lone lorn creetur and everythink went contrary with her.'

Towards this old boat, I walked one memorable night, with *my former*

---

[1] *Berg* has the heading INTRODUCTION TO DAVID COPPERFIELD. Dickens did not delete this but wrote above it 'In all, Six chapters'. At the top of the page is a (rejected?) alternative opening phrase: 'I had known the odd dwelling house inhabited by Mr. Peggotty'. He began the reading 'Quickly' (Wright).

[2] *had* printed italic in *Berg* here and in the corresponding passage in the original Chapter I; it was not italic in the novel.

[3] Two passages in the remainder of this paragraph were deleted in *Berg* but had been printed in *T & F*: the first of a number of such late deletions.

[4] Small capitals in *Berg* here, because doubly underlined in the corresponding passage in the original Chapter I.

[5] *T & F* here includes some words deleted in *Berg*: '... more agreeable company in a small habitation ...'

schoolfellow and present dear friend, Steerforth;[1] Steerforth, half a dozen years older than I; brilliant, handsome, easy, winning; whom I admired with my whole heart; for whom I entertained the most romantic feelings of fidelity and friendship. He had come down with me from London, and had entered with the greatest ardour into my scheme of visiting the old simple place and the old simple people.

There was no moon; and as he and I walked on the dark wintry sands towards the old boat, the wind sighed mournfully.

'This is a wild place, Steerforth, is it not?'

'Dismal enough in the dark, and the sea has a cry in it, as if it were hungry for us. Is that the boat, where I see a light yonder?'

'That's the boat.'

We said no more as we approached the light, but made softly for the door. I laid my hand upon the latch; and whispering Steerforth to keep close to me, went in, † and I was in the midst of the astonished family, whom I had not seen from my childhood, face to face with Mr. Peggotty, and holding out my hand to him, when Ham shouted:

'Mas'r Davy! It's Mas'r Davy!'

In a moment we were all shaking hands with one another, and asking one another how we did, and telling one another how glad we were to meet, and all talking at once. Mr. Peggotty was so overjoyed to see me, and to see my friend, that he did not know what to say or do, but kept over and over again shaking hands with me, and then with Steerforth, and then with me, and then ruffling his shaggy hair all over his head, and then laughing with such glee and triumph, that it was a treat to see him.

'Why, that you two gentl'men—gentl'men growed—should come to this here roof to-night, of all nights in my life, is such a merry-go-rounder as never happened afore, I do rightly believe![2] Em'ly, my darling, come here! Come here, my little witch! *Theer's Mas'r Davy's friend, my dear! Theer's the gentl'man as you've heerd on, Em'ly.* He comes to see you, along with Mas'r Davy, on the brightest night of your uncle's life as ever was or will be, horroar for it!' Then he let her go;[3] and as she ran into her little chamber, looked round upon us, quite hot and out of breath with his uncommon satisfaction.

'If you two gentl'men—gentl'men growed now, and such gentl'men— don't ex-cuse me for being in a state of mind, when you understand

---

[1] Doubly underlined. The description of Steerforth does not appear in the novel.

[2] On 'such a merry-go-rounder' see Introduction, p. xxxiv. For Mr. Peggotty's voice, Dickens did not use 'the regular Yarmouth dialect, as I could not make it sufficiently intelligible in so large a place' as the halls where he performed (*N*, iii. 764).

[3] In the Reading text, as now printed, Mr. Peggotty had never had hold of her (he had, however, in a deleted passage 'put one of his large hands on each side of his niece's face'). But Dickens, as Peggotty, had in gesture chucked her under his arm 'just as if she were there *to* be chucked' (Field, p. 38).

matters, I'll arks your pardon. Em'ly, my dear!—She knows I'm agoing to tell, and has made off.[1] This here little Em'ly, sir,' to Steerforth, '—her as you see a blushing here just now—this here little Em'ly of ours, has been, in our house, sir, what I suppose (I'm a ignorant man, but that's my belief) no one but a little bright-eyed creetur *can*[2] be in a house. She ain't my child; I never had one; but I couldn't love her more, if she was fifty times my child. You understand! I couldn't do it!'

'I quite understand.'

'I know you do, sir, and thank'ee. † Well, Sir, there was a certain person as had know'd our Em'ly, from the time when her father was drownded; as had seen her constant when a babby, when a young gal, when a woman. Not much of a person to look at, he warn't—something o' my own build—rough—a good deal o' the sou'wester in him—wery salt—but, on the whole, a honest sort of a chap too, with his art in the right place.'

I had never seen Ham grin to anything like the extent to which he sat grinning at us now.

'What does this here blessed tarpaulin go and do, but he loses that there art of his to our little Em'ly. He follers her about, he makes hisself a sort o' servant to her, he loses in a great measure his relish for his wittles, and in the long run he makes it clear to me wot's amiss. † Well! I counsels him to speak to Em'ly. He's big enough, but he's bashfuller than a little un, and he says to me he doen't like. So *I* speak.[3] "What! *Him!*" says Em'ly. "*Him* that I've know'd so intimate so many year, and like so much! Oh, Uncle! I never can have *him*. He's such a good fellow!" I gives her a kiss, and I says no more to her than "My dear, you're right to speak out, you're to choose for yourself, you're as free as a little bird." Then I aways to him, and I says, "I wish it could have been so, but it can't. But you can both be as you was, and wot I say to you is, Be as you was with her, like a man." He says to me, a shaking of my hand, "I will!" he says. And he was—honourable, trew, and manful—going on for two year.

'All of a sudden, one evening—as it might be to-night—comes little Em'ly from her work, and him with her! There ain't so much in *that*, you'll say. No, sure, because he takes care on her, like a brother, arter dark, and indeed afore dark, and at all times. But this heer tarpaulin chap, he takes hold of her hand, and he cries out to me, joyful, "Lookee here! This is to be my little wife!" And she says, half bold and half shy, and half a laughing and half a crying, "Yes, uncle! If you please."— If I please! Lord, as if I should do anythink else!—"If you please,"

---

[1] Marginal stage-direction *Low*.

[2] *can* italic in *Berg* and in the novel.

[3] *I*, and all the other words italic in the rest of this speech, italic in *Berg* and in the novel.

she says, "I am steadier now, and I have thought better of it, and I'll be as good a little wife as I can to him, for he's a dear good fellow!" Then Missis Gummidge, she claps her hands like a play, and you come in. There! The murder's out! You come in! It took place this here present hour; and here's the man as'll marry her, the minute she's out of her time at the needlework.'

Ham staggered, as well he might, under the blow Mr. Peggotty dealt him, as a mark of confidence and friendship; but feeling called upon to say something to us, he stammered:[1]

'She warn't no higher than you was, Mas'r Davy—when you first come heer—when I thought what she'd grow up to be. I see her grow up—gentl'men—like a flower. I'd lay down my life for her—Mas'r Davy—Oh! most content and cheerful! There ain't a gentl'man in all the land—nor yet a sailing upon all the sea—that can love his lady more than I love her, though there's many a common man—as could say better—what he meant.'

I thought it affecting to see such a sturdy fellow trembling in the strength of what he felt for the pretty little creature who had won his heart. I thought the simple confidence reposed in us by Mr. Peggotty and by himself, was touching. I was affected by the story altogether. I was filled with pleasure; but at first, with an indescribably sensitive pleasure, that a very little would have changed to pain.

Therefore, if it had depended upon *me* to touch the prevailing chord among them with any skill, I should have made a poor hand of it. But it depended upon Steerforth; and he did it with such address, that in a few minutes we were all as easy as possible.

'Mr. Peggotty,' he said, 'you are a thoroughly good fellow, and deserve to be as happy as you are to-night. My hand upon it! Ham, I give you joy, my boy. My hand upon that, too![2] Davy, stir the fire, and make it a brisk one! And Mr. Peggotty, unless you can induce your gentle niece to come back, I shall go. Any gap at your fireside on such a night—such a gap least of all—I wouldn't make, for the wealth of the Indies!'

So, Mr. Peggotty went to fetch little Em'ly. At first little Em'ly didn't

---

[1] 'Feelingly' (Wright).

[2] A famous moment in the Reading: Dickens modified Steerforth's tone of voice, and hand-grip, as he 'turned' from Peggotty to Ham. It gave Dickens great satisfaction when, during a reading of *Copperfield* in Paris, a Frenchman in the front row 'suddenly exclaimed to himself, under his breath, "Ah-h!"'—having instantly caught the situation!' (Kent, p. 124). According to another account, 'When I was impersonating Steerforth . . . and gave that peculiar grip of the hand to Emily's lover, the French audience burst into cheers and rounds of applause' (J. T. Fields, *Yesterdays with Authors* (1872), p. 241). Maybe Dickens later sought too hard for further 'Ah-h's or cheers; certainly Kate Field thought he over-dramatized this moment—'for had Steerforth exhibited the hatred of Ham that darkens Dickens's face, it could not have passed unnoticed' (p. 39).

like to come, and then Ham went. Presently they brought her to the fireside, very much confused, and very shy,—but she soon became more assured when she found how Steerforth spoke to her; how skilfully he avoided anything that would embarrass her; how he talked to Mr. Peggotty of boats, and ships, and tides, and fish; how delighted he was with that boat and all belonging to it; how lightly and easily he carried on, until he brought us, by degrees, into a charmed circle. †

But he set up no monopoly of the conversation.[1] He was silent and attentive when little Emily talked across the fire to me of our old childish wanderings upon the beach, to pick up shells and pebbles; he was very silent and attentive, when I asked her if she recollected how I used to love her, and how we used to walk about that dim old flat, hours and hours, and how the days sported by us as if Time himself had not grown up then, but were a child like ourselves, and always at play.[2] She sat all the evening, in her old little corner by the fire—Ham beside her. *I could not satisfy myself whether it was in her little tormenting way, or in a maidenly reserve before us, that she kept quite close to the wall, and away from Ham; but I observed that she did so, all the evening.*

As I remember, it was almost midnight when we took our leave. We had had some biscuit and dried fish for supper, and Steerforth had produced from his pocket a flask of Hollands. We parted merrily; and as they all stood crowded round the door to light us on our road, I saw the sweet blue eyes of little Em'ly peeping after us, from behind Ham, and heard her soft voice calling to us to be careful how we went.

'A most engaging little Beauty!' *said Steerforth, taking my arm.*[3] 'Well! It's a quaint place, and they are quaint company; and it's quite a new sensation to mix with them.'

'How fortunate we are, too, Steerforth, to have arrived to witness their happiness in that intended marriage! I never saw people so happy. How delightful to see it!'

'Yes—that's rather a chuckle-headed fellow for the girl. Isn't he?'

I felt a shock in this cold reply. But turning quickly upon him, and seeing a laugh in his eyes, I answered:

'Ah, Steerforth! It's well for you to joke about the poor! But when I see how perfectly you understand them, and how you can enter into happiness like this plain fisherman's, I know there is not a joy, or sorrow, or any emotion, of such people, that can be indifferent to you. And I admire and love you for it, Steerforth, twenty times the more!' *

To my surprise, he suddenly said, with nothing, that I could see, to lead to it:[4]

'Daisy, I wish to God I had had a judicious father these last twenty

---

[1] 'Leaning on table' (Wright).   [2] From ch. 3 (p. 37).   [3] 'Rough' (Wright).
[4] Indeed not: the text jumps here from ch. 21 to ch. 22.

years! You know my mother has always doted on me and spoilt me. I wish with all my soul I had been better guided! I wish with all my soul, I could guide myself better!'

There was a passionate dejection in his manner that quite amazed me. He was more unlike himself than I could have supposed possible.

'It would be better to be this poor Peggotty, or his lout of a nephew,[1] than be myself, twenty times richer and twenty times wiser, and be the torment to myself that I have been in that Devil's bark of a boat within the last half-hour.'

I was so confounded by the change in him that at first I could only regard him in silence as he walked at my side. At length I asked him to tell me what had happened to cross him so unusually.

'Tut, it's nothing—nothing, Davy! I must have had a nightmare, I think. What old women call the horrors, have been creeping over me from head to foot. I have been afraid of myself.'

'You are afraid of nothing else, I think.'

'Perhaps not, and yet may have enough to be afraid of, too. Well! so it goes by![2] * Daisy—for though that's not the name your godfathers and godmothers gave you, you're such a fresh fellow that it's the name I best like to call you by—and I wish, I wish, I wish, you could give it to me!'

'Why, so I can, if I choose.'

'Daisy, if anything should ever happen to separate us, you must think of me at my best, old boy. Come! let us make that bargain. Think of me at my best, if circumstances should ever part us!'

'You have no best to me, Steerforth, and no worst. You are always equally loved and cherished in my heart.' *

I was up, to go away alone, next morning with the dawn, and, having dressed as quietly as I could, looked into his room. He was fast asleep; lying, easily, with his head upon his arm, as I had often seen him lie at school.

The time came in its season, and that was very soon, when I almost wondered that nothing troubled his repose, as I looked at him then.[3] But he slept—let me think of him so again—as I had often seen him sleep at school; and thus, in this silent hour I left him.

—Never more, O God forgive you, Steerforth! to touch that passive hand in love and friendship. Never, never, more!

---

[1] 'Looking up occasionally with a sneer' (Wright).   [2] Jump to ch. 29.

[3] This paragraph 'Solemnly, slowly, measuredly, and with feeling' (Wright). Dickens's rendering of 'Never more, . . . Steerforth! . . .' was widely admired. Kate Field doubted whether any actor could equal his rendering of 'the solemn yet tender sorrow' of this exclamation (p. 39). 'Sigh' on final words (Wright).

CHAPTER II[1]

SOME months elapsed, before I again found myself down in that part of the country, and approaching the old boat by night.[2]

It was a dark evening, and rain was beginning to fall, when I came within sight of Mr. Peggotty's house, and of the light within it shining through the window. A little floundering across the sand, which was heavy, brought me to the door, and I went in. I was bidden to a little supper; Emily was to be married to Ham that day fortnight, and this was the last time I was to see her in her maiden life.

It looked very comfortable, indeed. Mr. Peggotty had smoked his evening pipe, and there were preparations for supper by-and-by. The fire was bright, the ashes were thrown up, *the locker was ready for little Emily in her old place.* Mrs. Gummidge appeared to be fretting a little, in her own corner: and consequently looked quite natural.

'You're first of the lot, Mas'r Davy! Sit ye down, sir. It ain't o' no use saying welcome to you, but you're welcome, kind and hearty.' *

Here Mrs. Gummidge groaned.

'Cheer up, cheer up, Mrs. Gummidge!' said Mr. Peggotty. *

'No, no, Dan'l. It ain't o' no use telling *me* to cheer up, when everythink goes contrairy with me. Nothink's nat'ral to me but to be lone and lorn.'

After looking at Mrs. Gummidge for some moments, with great sympathy, Mr. Peggotty glanced at the Dutch clock, rose, snuffed the candle, and put it in the window.

'Theer! Theer we are, Missis Gummidge!'[3] *Mrs. Gummidge slightly groaned again.* 'Theer we are, Mrs. Gummidge, lighted up, accordin' to custom! You're a wonderin' what that's fur, sir! Well, it's fur our little Em'ly. You see, the path ain't over light or cheerful arter dark; and when I'm here at the hour as she's a comin' home from her needle-work down-town, I puts the light in the winder. That, you see, meets two objects. She says to herself, says Em'ly, "Theer's home!" she says. And likeways, says Em'ly, "My uncle's theer!" Fur if I ain't theer, I never have no light showed. You may say this is like a Babby, sir. Well, I doen't know but what I *am* a babby in regard o' Em'ly. Not to look

---

[1] In *Berg*, CHAPTER THE FIRST is amended to SECOND. Similar changes are made throughout, and will not further be noted. The opening pages of this Chapter are deleted, having been transferred to the new beginning; a new opening paragraph is written in.

[2] The paragraph continued: 'I remember the occasion well. Events of later date have floated from me to the shore where all forgotten things will re-appear; but *this* stands like a high rock in the Ocean.' These sentences (drawn from ch. 9, Oxford Illustrated edn., p. 131) were later deleted.

[3] 'Jolly' (Wright). Later in the paragraph, near 'That, you see, meets two objects', Wright has: 'Facial expression. Elevating eyebrows'.

at, but to—to consider on, you know. *I* doen't care, bless you![1] Now I
tell you. When I go a looking and looking about that theer pritty house
of our Em'ly's, all got ready for her to be married, if I doen't feel as if
the littlest things was her, a'most. I takes 'em up, and I puts 'em down,
and I touches of 'em as delicate as if they was our Em'ly. So 't is with
her little bonnets and that. I couldn't see one on 'em rough used a
purpose—not fur the whole wureld.

'It's my opinion, you see, as this is along of my havin' played with
Em'ly so much when she was a child, and havin' made believe as we
was Turks, and French, and sharks, and every variety of forinners—
bless you, yes; and lions and whales, and I don't know what all!—when
she warn't no higher than my knee. I've got into the way on it, you
know. Why, this here candle, now! *I*[2] know wery well that arter she's
married and gone, I shall put that candle theer, just the same as now,
and sit afore the fire, pretending I'm expecting of her, like as I'm a
doing now. Why, at the present minute, when I see the candle sparkle
up, I says to myself, "She's a looking at it! Em'ly's a coming!" Right
too, fur here she is!'

No; it was only Ham. The night should have turned more wet since
I came in, for he had a large sou'wester hat on, slouched over his face.

'Where's Em'ly?'

Ham made a movement, as if she were outside. Mr. Peggotty took the
light from the window, trimmed it, put it on the table, and was stirring
the fire, when Ham, who had not moved, said:

'Mas'r Davy, will you come out a minute, and see what Em'ly and
me has got to show you?'[3]

As I passed him, I saw, to my astonishment and fright, that he was
deadly pale. He closed the door upon us. Only upon us two.

'Ham! What's the matter?'

'My love, Mas'r Davy—the pride and hope of my art—her that I'd
have died for, and would die for now—she's gone!'

'Gone!'

'Em'ly's run away![4] You're a scholar, and know what's right and best.
What am I to say, in-doors? How am I ever to break it to him, Mas'r
Davy?'

I saw the door move, and tried to hold the latch, to gain a moment's
time.[5] It was too late. Mr. Peggotty thrust forth his face; and never could
I forget the change that came upon it when he saw us, if I were to live
five hundred years.

---

[1] *I* italic in *Berg* and in the novel.

[2] *I* italic in *Berg* and in the novel.

[3] 'Breathlessly and slow' (Wright).

[4] 'D D D' (Wright)—i.e. very Dramatic. Dickens had, however, deleted from this
episode Ham's weeping; Kent (p. 127) regretted this.

[5] 'Fast' (Wright).

I remember a great wail and cry, and the women hanging about him, and we all standing in the room; I with an open letter in my hand, which Ham had given me; Mr. Peggotty, with his vest torn open, his hair wild, his face and lips white, and blood trickling down his bosom (it had sprung from his mouth, I think).

'Read it, sir; slow, please. I doen't know as I can understand.'

In the midst of the silence of death, I read thus, from the blotted letter Ham had given me. In Em'ly's hand—addressed to himself:

'"When you, who love me so much better than I ever have deserved, even when my mind was innocent, see this, I shall be far away. When I leave my dear home—my dear home—oh, my dear home!—in the morning,"'—the letter bore date on the previous night: '"—it will be never to come back, unless he brings me back a lady. This will be found at night, many hours after, instead of me. For mercy's sake, tell uncle that I never loved him half so dear as now. Oh, don't remember you and I were ever to be married—but try to think *as if I died when I was little,*[1] *and was buried somewhere.* Pray Heaven *that I am going away from,* have compassion on my uncle! Be his comfort. Love some good girl, that will be what I was once to uncle, and that will be true to you, and worthy of you, *and know no shame but me.* God bless all! If he don't bring me back a lady, and I don't pray for my own self, I'll pray for all. My parting love to uncle. My last tears, and my last thanks, for uncle!"'

That was all.

He stood, long after I had ceased to read, still looking at me. Slowly, at last, he moved his eyes from my face, and cast them round the room.

'Who's the man? I want to know his name.'

Ham glanced at me, and suddenly I felt a shock.

'Mas'r Davy! Go out a bit, and let me tell him what I must. You doen't ought to hear it, sir.'

I sank down in a chair, and tried to utter some reply; but my tongue was fettered, and my sight was weak. For I felt that the man was my friend— the friend I had unhappily introduced there—Steerforth, my old schoolfellow and my friend.

'I want to know his name!' †

'Mas'r Davy's frend. He's the man. Mas'r Davy, it ain't no fault of yourn—and I am far from laying of it to you—but it is your friend Steerforth, and he's a damned villain!'

Mr. Peggotty moved no more, until he seemed to wake all at once, and pulled down his rough coat from its peg in a corner.

'Bear a hand with this! I'm struck of a heap, and can't do it. Bear a hand, and help me. Well! Now give me that theer hat!'

Ham asked him whither he was going?

---

[1] *T & F* reads 'very little'. On this **letter**, see headnote.

'I'm a going to seek my niece. I'm a going to seek my Em'ly. I'm a going, first, to stave in that theer boat as he gave me, and sink it where I would have drownded *him*,[1] as I'm a livin' soul, if I had had one thought of what was in him! As he sat afore me, in that boat, face to face, strike me down dead, but I'd have drownded him, and thought it right!— I'm a going fur to seek my niece.'[2]

'Where?'

'Anywhere! I'm a going to seek my niece through the wureld. I'm a going to find my poor niece in her shame, and bring her back wi' my comfort and forgiveness. No one stop me! I tell you I'm a going to seek my niece! I'm a going to seek her fur and wide!'

Mrs. Gummidge came between them, in a fit of crying. 'No, no, Dan'l, not as you are now. Seek her in a little while, my lone lorn Dan'l, and that'll be but right; but not as you are now. Sit ye down, and give me your forgiveness for having ever been a worrit to you, Dan'l—what have *my*[3] contrairies ever been to this!—and let us speak a word about them times when she was first a orphan, and when Ham was too, and when I was a poor widder woman, and you took me in.[4] It'll soften your poor heart, Dan'l, and you'll bear your sorrow better; for you know the promise, Dan'l, "As you have done it unto one of the least of these, you have done it unto me;" and that can never fail under this roof, that's been our shelter for so many, many year!'

He was quite passive now; and when I heard him crying, the impulse that had been upon me to go down upon my knees, and curse Steerforth, yielded to a better feeling. My overcharged heart found the same relief as his, and I cried too.

CHAPTER III

At this period of my life I lived in my top set of chambers in Buckingham Street, Strand, London, and was over head and ears in love with Dora. I lived principally on Dora and coffee. My appetite languished and I was glad of it, for I felt as though it would have been an act of perfidy towards Dora to have a natural relish for my dinner. * I bought four sumptuous waistcoats—not for myself; *I*[5] had no pride in them—for Dora. I took to wearing straw-coloured kid gloves in the streets. I laid the foundations of all the corns I have ever had. *If the boots I wore at that period could only be produced and compared with the natural size of*

---

[1] *him* italic in *Berg* and in the novel.

[2] It was the rendering of Peggotty here, as his mind wandered in rage, grief and bewilderment, that reminded one critic of King Lear (*Manchester Examiner*, 19 October 1868; cf. Field, p. 41).

[3] *my* italic in *Berg* and in the novel.

[4] 'Both hands up. Monotone' (Wright).

[5] *I* italic in *Berg* and in the novel.

my feet, they would show in a most affecting manner what the state of my heart was.[1] *

Mrs. Crupp, the housekeeper of my chambers, must have been a woman of penetration; for, when this attachment was but a few weeks old, she found it out. She came up to me one evening when I was very low, to ask (she being afflicted with spasms) if I could oblige her with a little tincture of cardamums, mixed with rhubarb and flavoured with seven drops of the essence of cloves—or, if I had not such a thing by me—with a little brandy. As I had never even heard of the first remedy, and always had the second in the closet, I gave Mrs. Crupp a glass of the second; which (that I might have no suspicion of its being devoted to any improper use) she began to take immediately.

'Cheer up, sir,' said Mrs. Crupp. 'Excuse me. I know what it is, sir. There's a lady in the case.'

'Mrs. Crupp?'

'Oh, bless you! Keep a good heart, sir! Never say die, sir! If she don't smile upon you, there's a many as will. You're a young gentleman to *be*[2] smiled on, Mr. Copperfull, and you must learn your walue, sir.'

Mrs. Crupp always called me Mr. Copperfull: firstly, no doubt, because it was not my name; and secondly, I am inclined to think, in some indistinct association with a washing-day.

'What makes you suppose there is any young lady in the case, Mrs. Crupp?'

'Mr. Copperfull, I'm a mother myself. * Your boots and your waist is equally too small, and you don't eat enough, sir, nor yet drink. Sir, I have laundressed other young gentlemen besides you. † It was but the gentleman which died here before yourself, that fell in love—with a barmaid—and had his waistcoats took in directly, though much swelled by drinking.'

'Mrs. Crupp, I must beg you not to connect the young lady in my case with a barmaid, or anything of that sort, if you please.'

'Mr. Copperfull, I'm a mother myself, and not likely. I ask your pardon, sir, if I intrude. I should never wish to intrude where I were not welcome. But you are a young gentleman, Mr. Copperfull, and my adwice to you is, to cheer up, sir, to keep a good heart, and to know

---

[1] With a 'falling inflection' to the end of the sentence (Wright). The effect was helped by the phrase 'in a most affecting manner' having been moved from the end of the sentence, where it occurs in the novel, to its present place.—The present editor, having often performed this item, might draw attention to this, as an instance of Dickens's professional skill, because the alteration makes all the difference. David's *heart*, thus brought to the end of the paragraph, and played off against his emotionally ignominious *feet*, can hardly fail to make an audience laugh. No laugh here, indeed, presages a tough evening ahead.

[2] *be* italic in *Berg* and in the novel. Against this dialogue with Mrs. Crupp, Wright has: 'No action.'Look about from place to place.'

your own walue. If you was to take to something, sir; if you was to take to skittles, now, which is healthy, you might find it divert your mind, and do you good.'

I turned it off and changed the subject by informing Mrs. Crupp that I wished to entertain at dinner next day, my esteemed friends Traddles, and Mr. and Mrs. Micawber. And I took the liberty of suggesting a pair of soles, a small leg of mutton, and a pigeon pie. Mrs. Crupp broke out into rebellion on my first bashful hint in reference to *her* cooking the fish and joint. But, in the end, a compromise was effected; and Mrs. Crupp consented to achieve this feat, on condition that I dined from home for a fortnight afterwards. * †

Having laid in the materials for a bowl of punch, to be compounded by Mr. Micawber; having provided a bottle of lavender-water, two wax candles, a paper of mixed pins, and a pin-cushion, to assist Mrs. Micawber in her toilette, at my dressing-table; having also caused the fire in my bed-room to be lighted for Mrs. Micawber's convenience; and having laid the cloth with my own hands; I awaited the result with composure.

At the appointed time, my three visitors arrived together. Mr. Micawber with more shirt-collar than usual, and a new ribbon to his eye-glass; Mrs. Micawber with her cap in a parcel; Traddles carrying the parcel, and supporting Mrs. Micawber on his arm. They were all delighted with my residence. When I conducted Mrs. Micawber to my dressing-table, and she saw the scale on which it was prepared for her, she was in such raptures, that she called Mr. Micawber to come in and look.

'My dear Copperfield,' said Mr. Micawber, 'this is luxurious.[1] This is a way of life which reminds me of the period when I was myself in a state of celibacy. * I am at present established on what may be designated as a small and unassuming scale; but, you are aware that I have, in the course of my career, surmounted difficulties, and conquered obstacles. You are no stranger to the fact, that there have been periods of my life, when it has been requisite that I should pause, until certain expected events should turn up—when it has been necessary that I should fall back, before making what I trust I shall not be accused of presumption in terming—a spring. The present is one of those momentous stages in the life of man. You find me, fallen back, *for*[2] a spring; and I have every reason to believe that a vigorous leap will shortly be the result.'

I informed Mr. Micawber that I relied upon him for a bowl of punch, and led him to the lemons. I never saw a man so thoroughly enjoy himself, as he stirred, and mixed, and tasted, and looked as if he were

---

[1] Micawber 'Shaking head', 'Slight cough. Swinging eyeglass' (Wright). Kate Field notes also that Dickens, as Micawber, tipped 'backward and forward, first on his heels and then on his toes' and that he savoured his words, e.g. 'lux-u-rious' (p. 43).
[2] *for* italic in *Berg* and in the novel.

making, not mere punch, but a fortune for his family down to the latest posterity. As to Mrs. Micawber, I don't know whether it was the effect of the cap, or the lavender-water, or the pins, or the fire, or the wax-candles, but she came out of my room, comparatively speaking, lovely.[1]

I suppose—I never ventured to inquire, but I suppose—that Mrs. Crupp, after frying the soles, was taken ill. Because we broke down at that point. The leg of mutton came up, very red inside, and very pale outside: besides having a foreign substance of a gritty nature sprinkled over it, as if it had had a fall into ashes. But we were not in a condition to judge of this fact from the appearance of the gravy, forasmuch as it had been all dropped on the stairs. The pigeon-pie was not bad, but it was a delusive pie[2]: the crust being like a disappointing phrenological head: *full of lumps and bumps, with nothing particular underneath*. In short, the banquet was such a failure that I should have been quite unhappy—about the failure, I mean, for I was always unhappy about Dora—if I had not been relieved by the great good-humour of my company.

'My dear friend Copperfield,' said Mr. Micawber, 'accidents will occur in the best-regulated families; and especially in families not regulated by that pervading influence which sanctifies while it enhances the—a—I would say, in short, by the influence of Woman in the lofty character of Wife. If you will allow me to take the liberty of remarking that there are few comestibles better, in their way, than a Devil, and that I believe, with a little division of labour, we could accomplish a good one if the young person in attendance could produce a gridiron, I would put it to you, that this little misfortune may be easily repaired.'

There *was* a gridiron in the pantry, on which my morning rasher of bacon was cooked. We had it out, in a twinkling; Traddles cut the mutton into slices; Mr. Micawber covered them with pepper, mustard, salt, and cayenne;[3] I put them on the gridiron, turned them with a fork, and took them off, under Mr. Micawber's direction; and Mrs. Micawber heated some mushroom ketchup in a little saucepan. † Under these circumstances, my appetite came back miraculously. I am ashamed to confess it, but I really believe I forgot Dora for a little while. *

'Punch, my dear Copperfield,' said Mr. Micawber, tasting it as soon as dinner was done,[4] 'like time and tide, waits for no man. Ah! it is at the present moment in high flavour. My love, will you give me your opinion?'

---

[1] Dickens's audiences roared with laughter when, as David, he prolonged the final word, 'l-l-lovely!' (Kent, p. 129).

[2] Dickens paused before the adjective 'delusive' (Wright), and made much of it (Field, p. 46).

[3] 'Motions over table' (Wright); *was* (above) doubly underlined.

[4] Marginal stage-direction *Tasting*. Littimer's entrance here is omitted.

Mrs. Micawber pronounced it excellent. †

'As we are quite confidential here, Mr. Copperfield,' said Mrs. Micawber sipping her punch,[1] '(Mr. Traddles being a part of our domesticity), I should much like to have your opinion on Mr. Micawber's prospects. I have consulted branches of my family on the course most expedient for Mr. Micawber to take, and it was, that he should immediately turn his attention to coals.'

'To what, ma'am?'

'To coals. To the coal trade. Mr. Micawber was induced to think, on inquiry, that there might be an opening for a man of his talent in the Medway Coal Trade. Then, as Mr. Micawber very properly said, the first step to be taken clearly was, to go and *see*[2] the Medway. Which we went and saw. I say "we," Mr. Copperfield; for I never will desert Mr. Micawber.[3] I am a wife and mother, and I never will desert Mr. Micawber.'

Traddles and I murmured our admiration.

'That,' said Mrs. Micawber, 'that, at least, is *my*[4] view, my dear Mr. Copperfield and Mr. Traddles, of the obligation which I took upon myself when I repeated the irrevocable words "I Emma, take thee, Wilkins." I read the service over with a flat-candle, on the previous night, and the conclusion I derived from it was that I never could or would desert Mr. Micawber.'

'My dear,' said Mr. Micawber, *a little impatiently*, 'I am not conscious that you are expected to do anything of the sort.'

'We went,' repeated Mrs. Micawber, 'and saw the Medway. My opinion of the coal trade on that river, was, that it might require talent, but that it certainly requires capital. Talent, Mr. Micawber has; capital, Mr. Micawber has not. We saw, I think, the greater part of the Medway; and that was my individual conclusion.[5] My family were then of opinion that Mr. Micawber should turn his attention to corn—on commission. But corn, as I have repeatedly said to Mr. Micawber, may be gentlemanly, but it is not remunerative. Commission to the extent of two and ninepence in a fortnight cannot, however limited our ideas, be considered remunerative.'

We were all agreed upon that.

'Then,' said Mrs. Micawber, *who prided herself on taking a clear view of things, and keeping Mr. Micawber straight by her woman's wisdom, when he might otherwise go a little crooked*, * 'then I naturally look round

---

[1] Marginal stage-direction *Sipping*. Wright notes further sips, during the ensuing speeches. The ensuing Coal Trade passage is from ch. 17.

[2] *see* italic in *Berg* and in the novel.

[3] 'Affectedly' (Wright). This 'never desert . . .' passage is from ch. 36.

[4] *my* italic in *Berg*, but not in the novel.

[5] 'Very affectedly' (Wright). Back to ch. 28, for corn and banking.

the world, and say, "What is there in which a person of Mr. Micawber's talent is likely to succeed?" † I may have a conviction that Mr. Micawber's manners peculiarly qualify him for the Banking business. I may argue within myself, that if I^1 had a deposit at a banking-house, the manners of Mr. Micawber, as representing that banking-house, would inspire confidence, and extend the connexion. But if the various banking-houses refuse to avail themselves of Mr. Micawber's abilities, or receive the offer of them with contumely, what is the use of dwelling upon *that*[2] idea? None. As to originating a banking-business, I may know that there are members of my family who, if they chose to place their money in Mr. Micawber's hands, might found an establishment of that description. But if they do *not* choose to place their money in Mr. Micawber's hands—which they don't—what is the use of that?[3] Again I contend that we are no farther advanced than we were before.'

I shook my head, and said, 'Not a bit.' Traddles also shook his head, and said, 'Not a bit.'

'What do I deduce from this?' *Mrs Micawber went on to say, still with the same air of putting a case lucidly.* 'What is the conclusion, my dear Mr. Copperfield, to which I am irresistibly brought? Am I wrong in saying, it is clear that we must live?'

I answered, 'Not at all!'[4] and Traddles answered, 'Not at all!' and I found myself afterwards sagely adding, alone, that a person must either live or die.

'Just so,' returned Mrs. Micawber. 'It is precisely that. † And here is Mr. Micawber without any suitable position or employment. Where does that responsibility rest? Clearly on society. Then I would make a fact so disgraceful known, and boldly challenge society to set it right. It appears to me, my dear Mr. Copperfield, that what Mr. Micawber has to do is to throw down the gauntlet to society, and say, in effect, "Show me who will take that up. Let the party immediately step forward." It appears to me, that what Mr. Micawber has to do, is to advertise in all the papers; to describe himself plainly as so and so, with such and such qualifications, and to put it thus: "*Now*[5] employ me, on remunerative terms, and address, post paid, to *W. M.*, Post Office, Camden Town." † For this purpose, I think Mr. Micawber ought to raise a certain sum of money—on a bill. If no member of my family is possessed of sufficient natural feeling to negotiate that bill, then, my opinion is, that Mr. Micawber should go into the City, should take that bill into the Money Market, and should dispose of it for what he can get.'

[1] *I* italic in *Berg*, but not in the novel.

[2] *that*, like *not* (below), italic in *Berg* and in the novel.

[3] 'Elevate chin' (Wright).

[4] 'Quickly' (Wright). Traddles, writes Kate Field (p. 43), sprang to life with his 'Not at all!' as a distinct character 'with a propensity to eat his own fingers'.

[5] *Now*, like *W.M.* (below), italic in *Berg* and in the novel.

I felt, but I am sure I don't know why, that this was highly self-denying and devoted in Mrs. Micawber, and I uttered a murmur to that effect. Traddles, who took his tone from me, did likewise, * and really I felt that she was a noble woman—the sort of woman who might have been a Roman matron, and done all manner of troublesome heroic public actions.[1]

In the fervour of this impression, I congratulated Mr. Micawber on the treasure he possessed. So did Traddles. Mr. Micawber extended his hand to each of us in succession, and then covered his face with his pocket-handkerchief—which I think had more snuff upon it than he was aware of. He then returned to the punch in the highest state of exhilaration. †

Mrs. Micawber made tea for us in a most agreeable manner; and after tea we discussed a variety of topics before the fire; and she was good enough to sing us (in a small, thin, flat voice, which I remembered to have considered, when I first knew her, the very table-beer of acoustics) the favourite ballads of 'The Dashing White Sergeant,' and 'Little Tafflin.' For both of these songs Mrs. Micawber had been famous when she lived at home with her papa and mamma. Mr. Micawber told us, that when he heard her sing the first one, on the first occasion of his seeing her beneath the parental roof, she had attracted his attention in an extraordinary degree; but that when it came to Little Tafflin, he had resolved to win that woman, or perish in the attempt.

It was between ten and eleven o'clock when Mrs. Micawber rose to replace her cap in the parcel, and to put on her bonnet. Mr. Micawber took the opportunity to slip a letter into my hand, with a whispered request that I would read it at my leisure. I[2] also took the opportunity of my holding a candle over the bannisters to light them down, when Mr. Micawber was going first, leading Mrs. Micawber, to detain Traddles for a moment on the top of the stairs.

'Traddles, Mr. Micawber don't mean any harm; but, if I were you, I wouldn't lend him anything.'

'My dear Copperfield, I haven't got anything to lend.'

'You have got a name, you know.'

'Oh! you call *that*[3] something to lend?'

'Certainly.'

'Oh! Yes, to be sure! I am very much obliged to you, Copperfield, but—I am afraid I have lent him that already.'

'For the bill that is to go into the Money Market?'

---

[1] A long deletion follows in *Berg*, with the next two pages being joined by stamp-edging: the text resumed at 'It was between ten and eleven o'clock'. Later, Dickens *stetted* some passages, and had to break the stamp-edging.

[2] *I* doubly underlined.

[3] *that* italic in *Berg* and in the novel.

'No. Not for that one. This is the first I have heard of that one. I have been thinking that he will most likely propose that one, on the way home. Mine's another.'

'I hope there will be nothing wrong about it.'

'I hope not. I should think not, though, because he told me, only the other day, that it was provided for. That was Mr. Micawber's expression, "Provided for."'

Mr. Micawber looking up at this juncture, I had only time to repeat my caution. Traddles thanked me, and descended. But I was much afraid, when I observed the good-natured manner in which he went down with Mrs. Micawber's cap in his hand, that he would be carried into the Money Market, neck and heels.[1]

I returned to my fireside, and[2] * read Mr. Micawber's letter, which was dated an hour and a half before dinner. I am not sure whether I have mentioned that, when Mr. Micawber was at any particularly desperate crisis, he used a sort of legal phraseology: which he seemed to think equivalent to winding up his affairs.

This was the letter.

'Sir—for I dare not say my dear Copperfield,

'It is expedient that I should inform you that the undersigned is Crushed. Some flickering efforts to spare you the premature knowledge of his calamitous position, you may observe in him this day; but hope has sunk beneath the horizon, and the undersigned is Crushed.

'The present communication is penned within the personal range (I cannot call it the society) of an individual, in a state closely bordering on intoxication, employed by a broker. That individual is in legal possession of the premises, under a distress for rent. His inventory includes, not only the chattels and effects of every description belonging to the undersigned, as yearly tenant of this habitation, but also those appertaining to Mr. Thomas Traddles, lodger, a member of the Honourable Society of the Inner Temple.

'If any drop of gloom were wanting in the overflowing cup, which is now "commended" (in the language of an immortal Writer) to the lips of the undersigned, it would be found in the fact, that a friendly acceptance granted to the undersigned, by the before-mentioned Mr. Thomas Traddles, for the sum of £23 4s. 9½d., is over due, and is NOT provided for. Also, in the fact, that the living responsibilities clinging to the undersigned will, in the course of nature, be increased by the sum of one more helpless victim; whose miserable appearance may be looked for—in round numbers—at the expiration of a period not exceeding six lunar months from the present date.

[1] Chapter III ended at this point, Dickens having deleted the rest. Later he *stetted* it.
[2] A long omission here—Steerforth's visit to David.

'After premising thus much, it would be a work of supererogation to add, that dust and ashes are for ever scattered

'On

'The

'Head

'Of

'WILKINS MICAWBER.'

CHAPTER IV

SELDOM did I wake at night, seldom did I look up at the moon or stars or watch the falling rain, or hear the wind, but I thought of the solitary figure of the good fisherman toiling on—poor Pilgrim!—and recalled his words, 'I'm a going to seek my niece. I'm a going to seek her fur and wide.'

Months passed, and he had been absent—no one knew where—the whole time.

It had been a bitter day in London, and a cutting north-east wind had blown. The wind had gone down with the light, and snow had come on. My shortest way home,—and I naturally took the shortest way on such a night—was through Saint Martin's Lane. * On the steps of the church, there was the figure of a man. And I stood face to face with Mr. Peggotty!

'Mas'r Davy! It do my art good to see you, sir. Well met, well met!'

'Well met, my dear old friend!'

'I had thowts o' coming to make inquiration for you, sir, to-night, but it was too late. I should have come early in the morning, sir, afore going away agen.'

'Again?'

'Yes, sir, I'm away to-morrow.'

In those days there was a side entrance to the stable-yard of the Golden Cross Inn. Two or three public-rooms opened out of the yard: and looking into one of them, and finding it empty, and a good fire burning, I took him in there. †

'I'll tell you, Mas'r Davy, wheer-all I've been, and what-all we've heerd.[1] I've been fur, and we've heerd little; but I'll tell you!'

As he sat thinking, there was a fine massive gravity in his face, which I did not venture to disturb.

'You see, sir, when she was a child, she used to talk to me a deal about the sea, and about them coasts where the sea got to be dark blue, and to lay a shining and a shining in the sun. When she was—lost, I

---

[1] 'Feelingly' (Wright)—repeated against Peggotty's next speech.

know'd in my mind, as he would take her to them countries.[1] I know'd in my mind, as he'd have told her wonders of 'em, and how she was to be a lady theer, and how he first got her to listen to him along o' sech like. I went across-channel to France, and landed theer, as if I'd fell down from the skies. I found out a English gentleman, as was in authority, and told him I was going to seek my niece. He got me them papers as I wanted fur to carry me through—I doen't rightly know how they're called—and he would have give me money, but that I was thankful to have no need on. I thank him kind, for all he done, I'm sure! I told him, best as I was able, what my gratitoode was, and went away through France, fur to seek my niece.'

'Alone, and on foot?'

'Mostly a-foot; sometimes in carts along with people going to market; sometimes in empty coaches. Many mile a day a-foot, and often with some poor soldier or another, travelling fur to see his friends. I couldn't talk to him, nor he to me; but we was company for one another, too, along the dusty roads. When I come to any town, I found the inn, and waited about the yard till some one came by (some one mostly did) as know'd English. Then I told how that I was on my way to seek my niece, and they told me what manner of gentlefolks was in the house, and I waited to see any as seemed like her, going in or out. When it warn't Em'ly, I went on agen. By little and little, when I come to a new village or that, among the poor people, I found they know'd about me. They would set me down at their cottage doors, and give me what-not fur to eat and drink, and show me where to sleep.[2] And many a woman, Mas'r Davy, as has had a daughter of about Em'ly's age, I've found a-waiting for me, at Our Saviour's Cross outside the village, fur to do me sim'lar kindnesses. Some has had daughters as was dead. And God only knows how good them mothers was to me!' *

I laid my trembling hand upon the hand he put before his face. 'Thankee, sir, doen't take no notice.'

'At last I come to the sea. It warn't hard, you may suppose, for a seafaring man like me to work his way over to Italy. When I got theer, I wandered on as I had done afore. I got news of her being seen among them Swiss mountains yonder. I made for them mountains, day and night. Ever so fur as I went, ever so fur them mountains seemed to shift *away from me*. But I come up with 'em, and I crossed 'em. I never doubted her. No! Not a bit! On'y let her see my face—on'y let her heer my voice—on'y let my stanning still afore her bring to her thoughts the home she had fled away from, and the child she had been—and if

---

[1] 'Slow, low, monotonous' (Wright). Against the next paragraph but one ('Mostly a-foot . . .') Wright again puts 'Monotonously': but, as others of his marginalia show, the term was not intended pejoratively.

[2] 'Hand over eyes' (Wright).

she had growed to be a royal lady, she'd have fell down at my feet! I know'd it well! I bought *a country dress* to put upon her. To put that dress upon her, and to cast off what she wore—to take her on my arm again, and wander towards home—to stop sometimes upon the road, and heal her bruised feet and her worse-bruised heart—was all I thowt of now. But, Mas'r Davy, it warn't to be—not yet! I was too late, and they was gone. Wheer, I couldn't learn. Some said heer, some said theer. I travelled heer, and I travelled theer, but I found no Em'ly, and I travelled home.'

'How long ago?'

'A matter o' fower days. I sighted the old boat arter dark, and I never could have thowt, I'm sure, that the old boat would have been so strange!'

From some pocket in his breast, he took out with a very careful hand, a small paper bundle containing two or three letters or little packets, which he laid upon the table.[1]

'The faithful creetur Mrs. Gummidge gave me these. This first one come afore I had been gone a week. A fifty pound Bank note, in a sheet of paper, directed to me, and put underneath the door in the night. She tried to hide her writing, but she couldn't hide it from Me! This one come to Missis Gummidge, two or three months ago. * Five pounds.'

It was untouched like the previous sum, and he refolded both. *

'Is that another letter in your hand?'

'It's money too, sir. Ten pound, you see. And wrote inside, "From a true friend." But the two first was put underneath the door, and this come by the post, day afore yesterday. I'm going to seek her at the postmark.'

He showed it to me. It was a town on the Upper Rhine. He had found out, at Yarmouth, some foreign dealers who knew that country, and they had drawn him a rude map on paper, which he could very well understand.

I asked him how Ham was?

'He works as bold as a man can. He's never been heerd fur to complain. But my belief is ('twixt ourselves) as it has cut him deep. * Well! Having seen you to-night, Mas'r Davy (and that doos me good!), I shall away betimes to-morrow morning. You have seen what I've got heer;' putting his hand on where the little packet lay; 'all that troubles me is, to think that any harm might come to me, afore this money was give back. If I was to die, and it was lost, or stole, or elseways made away with, and it was never know'd by him but what I'd accepted of it, I believe the t'other wureld wouldn't hold me! I believe I must come back!'

He rose, and I rose too. We grasped each other by the hand again, and as we went out into the rigorous night, everything seemed to be

---

[1] 'Note from Pocket book'; below, at 'he refolded both', 'Kiss letter' (Wright).

hushed in reverence for him, when he resumed his solitary journey through the snow.

CHAPTER V

ALL this time I had gone on loving Dora harder than ever. * If I may so express it, I was steeped in Dora. I was not merely over head and ears in love with her; I was saturated through and through. I took night walks to Norwood where she lived, and perambulated round and round the house and garden for hours together; looking through crevices in the palings, using violent exertions to get my chin above the rusty nails on the top, blowing kisses at the lights in the windows, and romantically calling on the night to shield my Dora.—*I don't exactly know from what—I suppose from fire—perhaps from mice, to which she had a great objection.* *

Dora had a discreet friend, comparatively stricken in years—*almost of the ripe age of twenty, I should say*—whose name was Miss Mills. Dora called her Julia, and she was the bosom friend of Dora. Happy Miss Mills! *

One day Miss Mills said, 'Dora is coming to stay with me. She is coming the day after to-morrow. If you would like to call, I am sure papa would be happy to see you.' *

I passed three days in a luxury of wretchedness, and at last, arrayed for the purpose at a vast expense, I went to Miss Mills's *fraught with a declaration.*[1]

Mr. Mills was not at home. I didn't expect he would be. Nobody wanted *him.*[2] Miss Mills was at home. Miss Mills would do.

I was shown into a room up-stairs, where Miss Mills and Dora were. Dora's little dog Jip was there. Miss Mills was copying music, and Dora was painting flowers.—*What were my feelings when I recognized flowers I had given her!*

Miss Mills was very glad to see me, and very sorry her papa was not at home: *though I thought we all bore that with fortitude.* Miss Mills was conversational for a few minutes, and then, laying down her pen, got up and left the room.

I began to think I would put it off till to-morrow.[3]

'I hope your poor horse was not tired, when he got home at night from that pic-nic,' said Dora, lifting up her beautiful eyes. 'It was a long way for him.'

---

[1] Doubly underlined.

[2] *him* italic in *Berg* and in the novel.

[3] This, and the two subsequent 'I began ...' paragraphs, and 'I saw now ...', all doubly underlined. They were spoken 'Aside' (Wright).

I began to think I would do it to-day.

'It was a long way for *him*, for *he*[1] had nothing to uphold him on the journey.'

'Wasn't he fed, poor thing?' asked Dora.

I began to think I would put it off till to-morrow.

'Ye-yes, he was well taken care of. I mean he had not the unutterable happiness that I had in being so near you.'

I saw now that I was in for it, and it must be done on the spot.

'I don't know why you should care for being near me,' said Dora, 'or why you should call it a happiness. But of course you don't mean what you say. Jip, you naughty boy, come here!'

I don't know how I did it, but I did it in a moment.[2] I intercepted Jip. I had Dora in my arms. I was full of eloquence. I never stopped for a word. I told her how I loved her. I told her I should die without her. I told her that I idolized and worshipped her.—*Jip barked madly all the time.*

My eloquence increased and I said, if she would like me to die for her, she had but to say the word, and I was ready. I had loved her to distraction every minute, day and night, since I first set eyes upon her. I loved her at that minute to distraction. I should always love her, every minute, to distraction. Lovers had loved before, and lovers would love again; but no lover had ever loved, might, could, would, or should, ever love, as I loved Dora.—*The more I raved, the more Jip barked. Each of us, in his own way, got more mad every moment.*

Well, well! Dora and I were sitting on the sofa by-and-by, quiet enough, and Jip was lying in her lap, winking peacefully at me. *It was off my mind. I was in a state of perfect rapture. Dora and I were engaged.* *[3]

Being poor, I felt it necessary the next time I went to my darling, to expatiate on that unfortunate drawback. I soon carried desolation into the bosom of our joys—not that I meant to do it, but that I was so full of the subject—by asking Dora, without the smallest preparation, *if she could love a beggar?*

'How can you ask me anything so foolish?[4] Love a beggar!'

'Dora, my own dearest, *I*[5] am a beggar!'

'How can you be such a silly thing,' replied Dora, slapping my hand, 'as to sit there, telling such stories? I'll make Jip bite you if you are so ridiculous.'

But I looked so serious, that Dora began to cry. She did nothing but exclaim Oh dear! Oh dear! And oh, she was so frightened! And where

---

[1] *him* . . . *he* italic in *Berg* and in the novel.
[2] 'Quickly' (Wright).
[3] These three sentences doubly underlined. The narrative now jumps to ch. 37.
[4] Marginal stage-direction *Sprightly laugh*; contrast the novel's 'pouted Dora' here.
[5] *I* italic in *Berg* and in the novel.

was Julia Mills! And oh, take her to Julia Mills, and go away, please! until I was almost beside myself. *

I thought I had killed her. I sprinkled water on her face. I went down on my knees. I plucked at my hair. I implored her forgiveness. I besought her to look up. *I ravaged Miss Mills's work-box for a smelling-bottle, and in my agony of mind applied an ivory needle-case instead, and dropped all the needles over Dora.*

At last, I got Dora to look at me, with a horrified expression, which I gradually soothed until it was only loving, and her soft, pretty cheek was lying against mine. *

'Is your heart mine still, dear Dora?'

'Oh, yes! Oh, yes, it's all yours. Oh, don't be dreadful!'

I[1] dreadful! To Dora!

'Don't talk about being poor, and working hard! Oh, don't, don't!'

'My dearest love, the crust well earned—'

'Oh, yes; but I don't want to hear any more about crusts. And after we are married, Jip must have a mutton-chop every day at twelve, or he'll die!'

I was charmed with her childish, winning way, and I fondly explained to her that Jip should have his mutton-chop with his accustomed regularity. * †

When we had been engaged some half a year or so, Dora delighted me by asking me to give her that cookery-book I had once spoken of, and to show her how to keep housekeeping accounts, as I had once promised I would. I brought the volume with me on my next visit (*I got it prettily bound, first, to make it look less dry and more inviting*); and showed her an old housekeeping-book of my aunt's, and gave her a set of tablets, and a pretty little pencil-case, and a box of leads, to practise house-keeping with.

But the cookery-book made Dora's head ache, and the figures made her cry. *They wouldn't add up, she said.* So she rubbed them out, and drew little nosegays, and likenesses of me and Jip, all over the tablets. †

Time went on, and at last, here in this hand of mine I held the wedding licence. There were the two names in the sweet old visionary connexion, David Copperfield and Dora Spenlow; and there in the corner was that parental Institution the Stamp-office, looking down upon our union; and there, in the printed form of words, was the Archbishop of Canterbury invoking a blessing on us, *and doing it as cheap as could possibly be expected!* *

I doubt whether two young birds could have known less about keeping house, than I and my pretty Dora did. We had a servant, of course. *She*[2] kept house for us. We had an awful time of it with Mary Anne.

---

[1] *I* italic in *Berg* and in the novel.   [2] *she* doubly underlined.

Her name was Paragon. Her nature was represented to us, when we engaged her, as being feebly expressed in her name. She had a written character, as large as a Proclamation; and, according to this document, could do everything of a domestic nature that I ever heard of, and a great many things that I never did hear of. She was a woman in the prime of life: of a severe countenance; and subject (particularly in the arms) to a sort of perpetual measles. She had a cousin in the Life Guards, with such long legs that he looked like the afternoon shadow of somebody else. She was warranted sober and honest. And I am therefore willing to believe that she was in a fit when we found her under the boiler; and that the deficient teaspoons were attributable to the dustman. She was the cause of our first little quarrel.

'My dearest life.' I said one day to Dora, 'do you think Mary Anne has any idea of time?'

'Why, Doady?'

'My love, because it's five, and we were to have dined at four.'

My little wife came and sat upon my knee, to coax me to be quiet, and drew a line with her pencil down the middle of my nose: *but I couldn't dine off that, though it was very agreeable.*

'Don't you think, my dear, it would be better for you to remonstrate with Mary Anne?'

'Oh no, please! I couldn't, Doady!'

'Why not, my love?'

'Oh, because I am such a little goose, and she knows I am!'

I thought this sentiment so incompatible with the establishment of any system of check on Mary Anne, that I frowned a little. †

'My precious wife, we must be serious sometimes. Come! Sit down on this chair, close beside me! Give me the pencil! There! Now let us talk sensibly. You know, dear;' what a little hand it was to hold, and what a tiny wedding-ring it was to see! 'You know, my love, it is not exactly comfortable to have to go out without one's dinner. Now, is it?'

'N—n—no!' replied Dora, faintly.

'My love, how you tremble!'

'Because I KNOW[1] you're going to scold me.'

'My sweet, I am only going to reason.'

'Oh, but reasoning is worse than scolding! I didn't marry to be reasoned with. If you meant to reason with such a poor little thing as I am, you ought to have told me so, you cruel boy!' †

'Now, my own Dora, you are childish, and are talking nonsense. You must remember, I am sure, that I was obliged to go out yesterday when dinner was half over; and that, the day before, I was made quite unwell

---

[1] Small capitals in *Berg* and in the novel. Against the passage which follows, Wright has 'Innocently'.

by being obliged to eat underdone veal in a hurry; to-day, I don't dine at all—and I am afraid to say how long we waited for breakfast—and *then*[1] the water didn't boil. I don't mean to reproach you, my dear, but this is not comfortable.'

'I wonder, I do, at your making such ungrateful speeches. When you know that the other day, when you said you would like a little bit of fish, I went out myself, miles and miles, and ordered it, to surprise you.'

'And it was very kind of you, my own darling, and I felt it so much that I wouldn't on any account have mentioned that you bought a salmon—which was too much for two. Or that it cost one pound six— which was more than we can afford.'

'You enjoyed it very much,' sobbed Dora. 'And you said I was a mouse.'

'And I'll say so again, my love, a thousand times!' *

I said it a thousand times, and more, and went on saying it until Mary Anne's cousin deserted into our coal-hole, and was brought out, to our great amazement, by a piquet of his companions in arms, who took him away handcuffed, in a procession that covered our front-garden with disgrace. †

Everybody we had anything to do with, seemed to cheat us. Our appearance in a shop was a signal for the damaged goods to be brought out immediately. If we bought a lobster, it was full of water. All our meat turned out tough, and there was hardly any crust to our loaves. * As to the *washerwoman*[2] pawning the clothes, and coming in a state of penitent intoxication to apologize, I suppose that might have happened several times to anybody. Also the chimney on fire, the parish engine, and perjury on the part of the *Beadle*. But I apprehend we were personally unfortunate in our *page*: whose principal function was to quarrel with the cook and who lived in a hail of saucepan-lids.[3] We wanted to get rid of him, but he was very much attached to us, and wouldn't go, * until one day he stole Dora's watch, and spent the produce (he was always a weak-minded boy) in riding up and down between London and Uxbridge outside the coach. He was taken to the Police Office, on the completion of his fifteenth journey; when four-and-sixpence, and a second-hand fife which he couldn't play, were found upon his person. *

He was tried and ordered to be transported. Even then he couldn't be quiet, but was always writing us letters; and he wanted so much to see Dora before he went away, that Dora went to visit him, and fainted when she found herself inside the iron bars. I had no peace of my life until he was expatriated, and made (as I afterwards heard) a shepherd of, 'up the country' somewhere; I have no geographical idea where.

---

[1] *then* italic in *Berg* and in the novel.

[2] *Washerwoman*, and *Beadle* and *page* (below), all doubly underlined.

[3] In *Berg*, Dickens deleted 'and who' and may have intended to delete the rest of the sentence (as is done in *T & F*). The 'page' episode is from ch. 48.

'I am very sorry for all this, Doady,' said Dora. * 'Will you call me a name I want you to call me?'

'What is it, my dear?'

'It's a stupid name—Child-wife. When you are going to be angry with me, say to yourself "it's only my Child-wife."[1] When I am very disappointing, say, "I knew, a long time ago, that she would make but a Child-wife." When you miss what you would like me to be, and what I should like to be, and what I think I never can be, say, "Still my foolish Child-wife loves me." For indeed I do.' *

I invoke the innocent figure that I dearly loved, to come out of the mists and shadows of the Past, and to turn its gentle head towards me once again, and to bear witness that it was made happy by what I answered.

CHAPTER VI

I HEARD a footstep on the stairs one day. I knew it to be Mr. Peggotty's. It came nearer, nearer, rushed into the room.

'Mas'r Davy, I've found her! I thank my Heavenly Father for having guided of me in His own ways to my darling!'[2] †

'You have made up your mind as to the future, good friend?'

'Yes, Mas'r Davy, theer's mighty countries, fur from heer. Our future life lays over the sea.' *

As he gave me both his hands, hurrying to return to the one charge of his noble existence, I thought of Ham and who would break the intelligence to him? Mr. Peggotty thought of everything. He had already written to the poor fellow, and had the letter in the pocket of his rough coat, ready for the post. I asked him for it, and said I would go down to Yarmouth, and talk to Ham myself before I gave it him, and prepare him for its contents. He thanked me very earnestly, and we parted, with the understanding that I would go down by the Mail that same night. In the evening I started.

'Don't you think that,' I asked the coachman,[3] in the first stage out

---

[1] 'Feelingly' (Wright). This final dialogue comes from ch. 44.

[2] Dickens made successive attempts to shorten Peggotty's long narrative (from ch. 51), which followed here. There are many deletions in *Berg*; then pp. 81–4 were stuck together with stamp-edging; finally Dickens jettisoned the whole narrative and, on p. 80, indicated a jump to p. 88, and again used stamp-edging to eliminate the unwanted pages.

[3] 'Looking up at ceiling' (Wright). The storm-scene which follows was greatly admired (see headnote). Accounts about its rendering differ—though performances doubtless differed, too. Thus, one critic wrote: it 'was a brilliant bit of elocution; intensely powerful, yet perfectly quiet; subdued, though telling, in every phrase' (*Scotsman*, 28 November 1861). Another did not find it quiet or subdued: 'it was, if anything, a little too dramatic for the platform, and . . . scarcely so easy and natural as many of the other passages' (*Carlisle Journal*, 13 December 1861). Wright puts 'Exaggerated' at several points in the final pages.—The *Berg* text is extremely heavily cut here. The narrative jumps from ch. 51 to ch. 55.

of London, 'a very remarkable sky? I don't remember to have ever
seen one like it.'

'Nor I. That's wind, sir. There'll be mischief done at sea before long.'

It was a murky confusion of flying clouds tossed up into most remarkable heaps, through which the wild moon seemed to plunge headlong,
as if, in a dread disturbance of the laws of nature, *she had lost her way.*
There had been a wind all day; and it was rising then, with an extraordinary great sound. In another hour it had much increased, and the
sky was more overcast, and it blew hard.

But, as the night advanced, it came on to blow, harder and harder.[1] †
I had been in Yarmouth when the seamen said it blew great guns, but
I had never known the like of this, or anything approaching to it. * †

The tremendous sea itself, when I came to my journey's end, confounded me. As the high watery walls came rolling in, and tumbled
into surf, † I seemed to see a rending and upheaving of all nature.

Not finding Ham among the people whom this memorable wind had
brought together on the beach, I made my way to his house. I learned
that he had gone, on a job of shipwright's work, some miles away, but
that he would be back to-morrow morning, in good time.

So, I went back to the inn; and when I had washed and dressed, and
tried to sleep, but in vain, it was late in the afternoon. I had not sat
five minutes by the coffee-room fire, when the waiter coming to stir
it, told me that two colliers had gone down, with all hands, a few miles
off; and that some other ships had been seen labouring hard in the
Roads, and trying, in great distress, to keep off shore. Mercy on them,
and on all poor sailors, said he, if we had another night like the last! *

I could not eat, I could not sit still, I could not continue stedfast to
anything. My dinner went away almost untasted, and I tried to refresh
myself with a glass or two of wine. In vain.[2] I walked to and fro, tried
to read an old gazetteer, listened to the awful noises: looked at faces,
scenes, and figures in the fire. At length the ticking of the *undisturbed*
clock on the wall, tormented me to that degree that I resolved to go to
bed.

For hours, I lay in bed listening to the wind and water; imagining,
now, that I heard shrieks out at sea; now, that I distinctly heard the
firing of signal guns; now, the fall of houses in the town. At length,
my restlessness attained to such a pitch, that I hurried on my clothes,
and went down-stairs. In the large kitchen, all the inn servants and some
other watchers were clustered together. One man asked me when I went

---

[1] Dickens deleted too much here, and it is uncertain whether he meant to *stet* 'it
came on to blow, harder and harder' or a similar phrase, later, 'the wind blew harder
and harder'.

[2] 'Dramatic. Impatiently' (Wright).

in among them whether I thought the souls of the collier-crews who had gone down, were out in the storm?

There was a dark gloom in my lonely chamber, when I at length returned to it; but I was tired now, and, getting into bed again, fell into the depths of sleep until broad day; when I was aroused, at eight or nine o'clock, by some one knocking and calling at my door.

'What is the matter?'

'A wreck! Close by!'[1]

'What wreck?'

'A schooner, from Spain or Portugal, laden with fruit and wine. Make haste, sir, if you want to see her! It's thought, down on the beach, she'll go to pieces every moment.'

[2]I wrapped myself in my clothes as quickly as I could, and ran into the street, where numbers of people were before me, all running in one direction—to the beach.

When I got there,—in the difficulty of hearing anything but wind and waves, and in the crowd, and the unspeakable confusion, and my first breathless efforts to stand against the weather, I was so confused that I looked out to sea for the wreck, and saw nothing but the foaming heads of the great waves. A boatman laid a hand upon my arm, and pointed. Then, I saw it, close in upon us!

One mast was broken short off, six or eight feet from the deck, and lay over the side, entangled in a maze of sail and rigging; and all that ruin, as the ship rolled and beat—which she did with a violence quite inconceivable—beat the side as if it would stave it in. Some efforts were being made, to cut this portion of the wreck away; for, as the ship, which was broadside on, turned towards us in her rolling, I plainly descried her people at work with axes—especially one active figure with long curling hair.[3] But, a great cry, audible even above the wind and water, rose from the shore; *the sea, sweeping over the wreck, made a clean breach, and carried men, spars, casks, planks, bulwarks, heaps of such toys, into the boiling surge.*

The second mast was yet standing, with the rags of a sail, and a wild confusion of broken cordage flapping to and fro. The ship had struck once, the same boatman said, *and then lifted in and struck again.* I understood him to add that she was parting amidships. As he spoke, there was another great cry of pity from the beach. *Four men arose with the wreck out of the deep, clinging to the rigging of the remaining mast; uppermost, the active figure with the curling hair.*[4]

[1] 'High voice' (Wright).

[2] Marginal stage-direction *Quick.*

[3] The final phrase—*especially one active figure with long curling hair*—doubly underlined. Later references to Steerforth are similarly distinguished. Wright has, against the rest of this paragraph, 'Quick'.

[4] *Four men arose* and *uppermost, the active figure with the curling hair* doubly underlined.

There was a bell on board; and as the ship rolled and dashed, this bell rang; and its sound, the knell of those unhappy men, was borne towards us on the wind. Again we lost her, and again she rose. Two of the four men were gone.[1] †

I noticed that some new sensation moved the people on the beach, and I saw them part, and Ham come breaking through them to the front.

Instantly, I ran to him, for I divined that he meant to wade off with a rope. I held him back with both arms; and implored the men not to listen to him, not to let him stir from that sand!

Another cry arose; and we saw the cruel sail, with blow on blow, beat off the lower of the two men, and fly up in triumph round the active figure left alone upon the mast.[2]

Against such a sight, and against such determination as that of the calmly desperate man who was already accustomed to lead half the people present, I might as hopefully have entreated the wind.

I was swept away to some distance, where the people around me made me stay; urging, as I confusedly perceived, that he was bent on going, with help or without, and that I should endanger the precautions for his safety by troubling those with whom they rested. I saw hurry on the beach, and men running with ropes, and penetrating into a circle of figures that hid him from me. Then, I saw him standing alone, in a seaman's frock and trowsers: a rope in his hand: another round his body: and several of the best men holding to the latter.

The wreck was breaking up. I saw that she was parting in the middle, and that the life of the solitary man upon the mast hung by a thread.[3] *He had a singular red cap on, not like a sailor's cap, but of a finer colour; and as the few planks between him and destruction rolled and bulged, and as his death-knell rung, he was seen by all of us to wave this cap.* I saw him do it now, *and thought I was going distracted, when his action brought an old remembrance to my mind of a once dear friend—the once dear friend—Steerforth.*[4]

Ham watched the sea, until there was a great retiring wave; when he dashed in after it, and in a moment was buffeting with the water, rising with the hills, falling with the valleys, lost beneath the foam: † *borne in towards the shore, borne on towards the ship. At length he neared the wreck. He was so near, that with one more of his vigorous strokes he would be clinging to it,—when, a high green vast hill-side of water, moving on*

---

[1] *Two men were gone* doubly underlined; *of the four* is a marginal insertion.

[2] *beat off the lower of the two men* and *round the active figure left alone upon the mast* doubly underlined.

[3] *and that the life . . . by a thread* doubly underlined.

[4] *and thought I was* to the end of the paragraph doubly underlined; *the* italic in *Berg* and in the novel. Wright notes 'Quick' against '*and thought I was . . .*', and a 'Pause' before '*Steerforth*'.

shoreward, from beyond the ship, he seemed to leap up into it with a mighty bound—and the ship was gone![1]
They drew him to my very feet—insensible—dead.[2] He was carried to the nearest house; and every means of restoration were tried; but he had been beaten to death by the great wave, and his generous heart was stilled for ever.

As I sat beside the bed,[3] when hope was abandoned and all was done, a fisherman, who had known me when Emily and I were children, and ever since, whispered my name at the door.

'Sir, will you come over yonder?'

The old remembrance that had been recalled to me, was in his look, and I asked him:

'Has a body come ashore?'

'Yes.'[4]

'Do I know it?'

He answered nothing. But, he led me to the shore. And on that part of it where she and I had looked for shells, two children—on that part of it where some lighter fragments of the old boat, blown down last night, had been scattered by the wind—among the ruins of the home he had wronged—I saw him[5] lying with his head upon his arm, as I had often seen him lie at school.

THE END OF THE READING

[1] 'Long pause' after *a mighty bound* (Wright); *and the ship was gone!* doubly underlined.

[2] Marginal stage-direction *Low*. Wright's note is 'Solemn and slow'.

[3] Marginal stage-direction *Lower*.

[4] Here 'Mr. Dickens displayed his dramatic power in a very remarkable manner. The tone in which David, knowing what the answer will be, and yet dreading to hear it, asks, "Has a body come ashore?"—strikes to the heart of every person within reach of his voice. And the answer! In the book it is simply "yes"; but Mr. Dickens, in the person of the old fisherman, does not speak,—he only bows his head; and in that simple action conveys the whole story which the lips cannot speak. Acting more impressive than this we have never witnessed. The whole audience felt its power, and the hush that fell upon the room was for the moment almost painful' (*New York Times*, 11 December 1867).

[5] Wright deletes 'him' and substitutes 'Steerforth'. 'Do you cry when you read aloud?' a twelve-year-old American girl asked Dickens, when she waylaid him on a train. 'We all do in our family. And we never read about Tiny Tim, or about Steerforth when his body is washed up on the beach, on Saturday nights, or our eyes are too swollen to go to Sunday School.'—'Yes, I cry when I read about Steerforth,' Dickens answered quietly (Kate Douglas Wiggin, *A Child's Journey with Dickens* (Boston and New York, 1912), p. 27).

'I have got the Copperfield reading ready for delivery,' Dickens told Wilkie Collins on 28 August 1861, 'and am now going to blaze away at Nickleby, which I don't like half as well' (*N*, iii. 231). *Copperfield* opened his provincial tour, in Norwich on 28 October 1861, and *Nickleby* followed, the next night, after which he reported more cheerfully: 'I think Nickleby tops all the readings. Somehow it seems to have got in it, by accident, exactly the qualities best suited to the purpose, and it went last night not only with roars, but with a general hilarity and pleasure that I have never seen surpassed' (*N*, iii. 246). It continued 'to go in the wildest manner' later in the tour, and the audience's merriment during the letter-reading scene could even make Dickens himself collapse in laughter (*N*, iii. 252–3). Two years later, however, he admitted that 'it was a long time before I could take a pleasure in reading it. But I got better, as I found the audience always taking to it' (*N*, iii. 353). It always remained in repertoire, though at one period in an abbreviated 'short-time' version.

Unlike *Copperfield*, it was never a two-hour reading. It took about an hour and a quarter and, during the 1861–2 season, was usually paired with *The Trial*, but occasionally with *Bob Sawyer*. In later seasons when this version was being given, the afterpiece was usually either *Bob Sawyer* or *Boots*; during the London Farewells in 1870 it was paired with *Mr. Chops*. During one season, however, April–June 1866, it was paired with *Dr. Marigold*, which was a long (seventy-minute) Reading, so during this period a 'short-time' version was used. (This version may have been prepared four years earlier, for on 17 May 1862 Dickens gave a triple-bill consisting of *Nickleby*, *Boots*, and *Bob Sawyer*, and could not have used the full-length *Nickleby* then.) The 'short-time' version was longer, however, than the other afterpieces. Its main difference from the original version is that the third of the four chapters is omitted, and there are a few other minor adjustments.

There are two prompt-copies, and a further (but dubious) unique copy of a privately-printed version. These are now respectively in the Berg, Suzannet, and Gimbel collections. The 1861 prompt-copy (*Berg*) is entitled *Nicholas Nickleby/at the Yorkshire School./A Reading./In Four Chapters./Privately Printed.* (printed by William Clowes and Sons, London; text paginated 3–71). The narrative starts with short extracts from chs. 3, 4, and 5 of the novel, but most of Chapter I is from ch. 7 (Nicholas joins Mr. Squeers at the Saracen's Head, in London, and travels with him to Dotheboys Hall). Chapter II (the school) and Chapter III (Fanny Squeers's tea-party) correspond to chs. 8 and 9, with a little from ch. 42 inserted; Chapter IV (Nicholas thrashes Squeers, leaves Dotheboys Hall, and is joined on the road by Smike) derives from chs. 12 and 13, with a paragraph from ch. 64 ('Dotheboys Hall breaks up for ever'). After the preliminary pages, selected drastically from chs. 3–5, the printed text is about three-fifths the length of the corresponding parts of the novel; manuscript deletions reduce it further, to about a half.

The 'short-time' version (*Suzannet*) is simply another copy of the 1861 privately printed text, with Chapter III removed by its pages being tied together with red tape. Some of the *Berg* deletions and verbal alterations were transcribed into *Suzannet*, but then Dickens made further cuts and alterations in the latter, the text of which thus gradually diverged from the 1861 version. In particular Dickens was, as often, troubled by the beginnings and endings of his chapters, and in both prompt-copies he tried several variants, writing in new material or pasting-in passages from a cut-up copy of the novel.

The *Gimbel* copy is unlike all of Dickens's privately printed texts, typographically and in other ways (no printer or publisher is named). It contains no writing or underlining by Dickens, and indeed there is no evidence that he had anything to do with it. It is entitled *Nicholas Nickleby/at/Dotheboys Hall* (text paginated 1–22), and its narrative covers that of Chapter I, and most of Chapter II, of the 1861 version. It ends with the letter-writing scene—a less satisfactory conclusion than that of the 1861 text. The only indication known to me that Dickens may have performed the *Gimbel* text at some time is an Edinburgh critic's remark, in 1868 that on 'previous occasions' Dickens had included the scene of Mrs. Squeers giving the boys brimstone and treacle (see p. 259, note 3). This scene appears in the *Gimbel* text, but not in the others. Not too much reliance may be placed on undocumented reminiscences of past performances, however; people were apt to 'remember' Dickens's reading episodes, or whole items, which were never in the repertoire. For further discussion of the *Gimbel* text, see my essay 'Dickens Reading-copies in the Beinecke Library', *Yale University Library Gazette*, xl (1972), 153–8: but I have since grown more sceptical about Dickens's association with it.

The *T & F* four-chapter version was set up from *Berg*, but Dickens subsequently made quite a number of alterations to this text, mainly deletions, but also some verbal alterations and a few additions. The three-chapter version was set up from *Suzannet*, which was not altered thereafter; indeed, the *Suzannet* 'short-time' version was only in use during the 1866 season (and possibly at that single performance in 1862). The 'short-time' version had not been popular in 1866; most people 'had an evident preference' for the longer version, remarks Charles Kent (p. 141), and there is indeed a marked contrast between press reports in 1866 and in other years. The reception of the longer version, in 1861 and later, was very favourable, but many critics in 1866 found it, while still enjoyable, rather an anti-climax after *Marigold*, with which it was then paired. So Dickens, in the 1867 and later seasons, returned to the longer version, but incorporated into his performance some successful passages which appear only in the *Suzannet* 'short-time' text. He did not transcribe these into *Berg*, however, nor did he write down some amplifications of the jokes which had become a standard part of his performance. Some examples will be cited in the footnotes.

The text printed below is that of *Berg*—the four-chapter version as emended up to and beyond 1867–8. It does not seem useful to print also the *Suzannet* 'short-time' text, but some of its more interesting verbal variants from *Berg* will be indicated in the footnotes. Anyone curious to read the *Suzannet* text can consult the facsimile published in 1973 by the Ilkley (Yorkshire) Literature

Festival;[1] also it was accurately printed in *T & F* and in the 1883 and 1907 collected *Readings*. The authenticity of the *Gimbel* copy is too dubious for its text to the printed or cited.

The Reading was usually advertised under the title of *Nicholas Nickleby at Mr. Squeers's School*, the naming of Squeers being a reminder of the dominant character in the piece. Squeers was very droll, particularly in the letter-reading scene, but audiences' righteous indignation against him mounted, and the moment which they were perceptibly waiting for (as Charles Kent said) was Nicholas's intervention to protect Smike. His 'battle with the tyrant' was 'narrated with a stirring manliness and vigour that told greatly' (*Manchester Guardian*, 27 January 1862). Audiences 'actually exulted in the punishment' that Squeers received, and cheered Nicholas as the thrashing proceeded (Edinburgh *Courant*, 15 December 1868). The best comic moment was Fanny Squeers's tea-party; everyone delighted in Fanny's lisp and John Browdie's blunt heartiness, expressed in a Yorkshire accent that was at least found convincing in Lancashire. The Reading contained many good character-parts, and Dickens was said to have assumed them well:

... the facility with which Mr. Dickens suited his voice to the various characters comprised in his selection was most striking. The harsh dissonant voice of Squeers, the well-modulated tones of Nickleby, the grating treble of Mrs. Squeers, the mincing language and hysterical passion of Miss Squeers, the broad hearty speech of the Yorkshire miller, and above all, the dispirited, heart-broken utterance of poor Smike, were each admirably rendered, and gave increased effect to the wonderful descriptive power of the author. The scene in which the poor drudge Smike first realises the fact that there is one in the world who still cares for him, ... was 'painted' with a vividness and pathos which told with thrilling effect upon the audience, and well deserved the burst of applause with which it was received. (*Cheltenham Examiner*, 8 January 1862)

Opinions differed, however, on the rendering of Smike. Most people found it very affecting; applause was general at the 'tender touches', and tears flowed at the conclusion. For some critics, indeed, Smike was the great success of the piece, 'a very masterpiece of art', Dickens portraying his terror 'in such a way— and we speak without exaggeration—as actually to appal his hearers' (Edinburgh *Courant*, 29 November 1861). A similar verdict appeared years later: 'John Browdie captivated the audience most, but we must give the palm to the far more difficult character of poor Smike, which, in any other hands, of very doubtful success, in Mr. Dickens's is a gem of pure pathos' (*Birmingham Gazette*, 3 April 1869). Kate Field's assessment, however, was less favourable, and one is inclined to accept her judgement, not only because she avoids phrases like 'a gem of pure pathos' but also because of her general level-headedness. 'Impartial criticism', she wrote, must declare that

... of the eight characters portrayed, Fanny Squeers, 'Tilda Price, and John Browdie are unapproachable; that Mr. and Mrs. Squeers could be equally well done by actors

---

[1] This facsimile, though clearly printed and useful, is bibliographically curious, for it bears no particulars of date or publisher except, on the inside cover, an acknowledgement of the (unnamed) Festival Committee's gratitude for permission to print it. An unnumbered manuscript page (the beginning of Chapter III) is printed facing p. 34: it should appear facing p. 52. A loose typescript 'Editorial Note' gives brief particulars of this prompt-copy and how to read it.

born for the purpose; that Nicholas Nickleby *might* be done better on the stage, but never *is*; and that Smike is the only character wherein Dickens fails . . . Smike is not poorly done, but it can be better done. Dickens's Smike is earnest, pathetic, and his sighing is as truly touching as it is artistically fine. But Smike is not pathetic enough, and his monotonous voice frequently degenerates into a whine . . . the monotonous intonation is unnatural, and therefore unworthy of Dickens, whose best manner is thorough naturalness. (Field, pp. 61–2)

W. M. Wright annotated his copy of *Nickleby* very fully, often noting the gestures which Dickens's numerous stage-directions enjoined: his notes here, indeed, attest his accuracy as an observer. His account of the characters' voices is useful: 'Natural voice for Nickleby', 'Mrs. Cluppins's voice' for Mrs. Squeers, 'Quick slight voices' for the boys at their class in 'English spelling and philosophy', 'High dismal voice' and 'Breathlessly' for Smike, 'High laugh' for Browdie. Squeers pronounces 'put' as in 'putty', and is apt to aspirate words like 'angel': he is evidently a Londoner.

Nicholas Nickleby

4 Chapters[1]

CHAPTER I

NICHOLAS NICKLEBY, in the nineteenth year of his age, arrived at eight o'clock of a November morning at the sign of the Saracen's Head, Snow Hill, London, *to join Mr. Squeers, the cheap—the terribly cheap—Yorkshire schoolmaster.*[2] Inexperienced, sanguine, and thrown upon the World with no adviser, and his bread to win, he had engaged himself to Mr. Squeers as his *scholastic assistant*, on the faith of the following advertisement in the London papers:

'EDUCATION.—At Mr. Wackford Squeers's Academy, Dotheboys Hall, at the delightful village of Dotheboys, near Greta Bridge in Yorkshire, Youth are boarded, clothed, booked, furnished with pocket-money, provided with all necessaries, instructed in all languages living and dead, mathematics, orthography, geometry, astronomy, trigonometry, the use of the globes, algebra, single stick (if required), writing, arithmetic, fortification, and every other branch of classical literature. Terms, twenty guineas per annum. *No extras, no vacations, and diet unparalleled.*[3] Mr. Squeers is in town, and attends daily, from one till four, at the Saracen's Head, Snow Hill. N.B. An able assistant wanted. *Annual Salary £5. A Master of Arts would be preferred.*' *

Mr. Squeers was standing by one of the coffee-room fireplaces, and his appearance was not prepossessing. He had but one eye, and the popular prejudice runs in favour of two. The blank side of his face was much puckered up, which gave him a sinister appearance, especially when he smiled; at which times his expression bordered on the villanous. He wore a white neckerchief with long ends, and a scholastic suit of black; but his coat-sleeves being a great deal too long, and his trousers a great

---

[1] *IN FOUR* deleted, *3* inserted and then deleted, and *4* inserted. At one stage, Dickens made this (full-length) version of *Nickleby* a three-chapter Reading, by running Chapters I and II into one. Later, he reverted to the four-chapter division. Wright notes Dickens's brief introduction: 'I am to have the pleasure of reading to you first tonight ...' The opening paragraph is a summary, not in the novel.

[2] Doubly underlined, as is *scholastic assistant* below. The words 'cheap—the terribly cheap—' and the phrase from 'Inexperienced' to 'bread to win' do not appear in *T & F*, so are a late manuscript addition.

[3] *and diet unparalleled* doubly underlined. Dickens 'laid particular stress' upon this sentence (Kent, p. 192). The underlining in the *Suzannet* 'short-time' copy is generally similar to that in *Berg*, as here; only significant differences will be noted. Against this paragraph, Wright notes: 'Holding handkerchief both hands'.

deal too short, *he appeared ill at ease in his clothes, and as if he were in a perpetual state of astonishment at finding himself so respectable.* *

The learned gentleman had before himself, a breakfast of coffee, hot toast, and cold round of beef; but he was at that moment intent on preparing another breakfast for five little boys.

[1]'This is twopenn'orth of milk is it, waiter?' said Mr. Squeers, looking down into a large mug.

'That's twopenn'orth, sir.'

'What a rare article milk is, to be sure, in London! Just fill that mug up with lukewarm water, William, will you?'

'To the wery top, sir? Why, the milk will be drownded.'

'*Serve it right for being so dear.* You ordered that thick bread and butter for three, did you?'

'Coming directly, sir.'

[2]'You needn't hurry yourself; there's plenty of time. *Conquer your passions, boys, and don't be eager after vittles.*' As he uttered this moral precept, Mr. Squeers took a large bite out of the cold beef, and recognized Nicholas.

[3]'Sit down, Mr. Nickleby. Here we are, a breakfasting you see!' *Nicholas did not see that anybody was breakfasting, except Mr. Squeers.*[4]

'Oh! that's the milk and water, is it, William?[5] Here's richness! Think of the many beggars and orphans in the streets that would be glad of this, little boys. When I say number one, the boy on the left hand, nearest the window, may take a drink; and when I say number two, the boy next him will *go in*,[6] and so till we come to number five. Are you ready?'

'Yes, sir.'

[7]'Keep ready till I tell you to begin. Subdue your appetites, and you've conquered human natur. This is the way we inculcate strength of mind, Mr. Nickleby.'

Nicholas murmured something in reply; and the little boys remained in torments of expectation.

---

[1] Marginal stage-direction *The Mug* (in both margins). 'The mug is *not* on that desk, but it seems to be, as Mr. Squeers looks into it and gives his order' (Field, p. 55).

[2] Marginal stage-directions *Chuckle* (in the left margin) and *Chuckling* (in the right margin).

[3] Marginal stage-direction *Breakfasting*. Just below, opposite the paragraph (deleted in *Berg*) beginning 'At this fresh mention . . .', there is the stage direction *Stir*. This piece of business was retained: 'Stirring all time' (Wright; Kent, p. 143).

[4] *not* doubly underlined in *Berg*; whole sentence doubly underlined in *Suzannet*. Wright, however, deletes the sentence.

[5] Marginal stage-direction *Smack*.

[6] *go in* doubly underlined. The boys' reply, 'Yes, sir', came in a 'High voice' (Wright).

[7] Marginal stage-directions *Chuckle* (in the left margin) and *Chuckling* (in the right margin).

[1]'Thank God for a good breakfast. Number one may take a drink.'

Number one seized the mug ravenously, and had just drunk enough to make him wish for more, when Mr. Squeers gave the signal for number two, who gave up at the like interesting moment to number three; and the process was repeated until the milk and water terminated with number five.

'And now,' said the schoolmaster, dividing the bread and butter for three into five portions, 'you had better look sharp with your breakfast, for the coach-horn will blow in a minute or two, and then every boy leaves off.'

The boys began to eat voraciously, while the schoolmaster (who was in high good humour after his meal) picked his teeth with a fork, and looked on. In a very short time, the horn was heard.

[2] 'I thought it wouldn't be long' said Squeers, jumping up and producing a little basket; 'put what you haven't had time to eat, in here, boys! You'll want it on the road!' *

They certainly *did*[3] want it on the road, and very much, too; for the journey was long, the weather was intensely cold, a great deal of snow fell from time to time, and the wind was intolerably keen. Mr. Squeers got down at almost every stage—*to stretch his legs, he said*[4]—and as he always came back with a very red nose, and composed himself to sleep directly, *the stretching seemed to answer.* * It was a long journey, but the longest lane has a turning at last, and late in the night the coach put them down at a lonely roadside Inn where they found in waiting two labouring men, a rusty pony-chaise, and a cart.

'Put the boys and the boxes into the cart, and this young man and me will go on in the chaise. Get in, Nickleby.'

Nicholas obeyed. Mr Squeers with some difficulty inducing the pony to obey too, they started off, leaving the cart-load of infant misery to follow at leisure.

[5]'Are you cold, Nickleby?'

'Rather, sir, I must say.'

'Well, I don't find fault with that. It's a long journey this weather.'

'Is it much further to Dotheboys Hall, sir?'

'About three mile. But you needn't call it a Hall down here.'

Nicholas coughed, as if he would like to know why.

[1] Marginal stage-direction *Wiping mouth*. Wright, who notes this piece of business, writes at the bottom of this page of *T & F*, 'Slow, monotonous', and at the top of the next 'Reading in a low key'.

[2] Marginal stage-direction *Glee*. At the end of this paragraph there is a long deletion of the novel's text.

[3] *did* italic in *Berg*.

[4] Doubly underlined.

[5] Marginal stage-direction *Driving*. Against the dialogue following, Wright notes: 'Natural voice for Nickleby'.

'The fact is, it ain't a Hall.'

'Indeed!'

'No. We call it a Hall up in London, because it sounds better, but they don't know it by that name in these parts. A man may call his house an island if he likes; there's no act of Parliament against that, I believe?'

Squeers eyed him at the conclusion of this little dialogue, and finding that he had grown thoughtful, contented himself with lashing the pony until they reached their journey's end,[1] * when he ushered him into a small parlour scantily furnished, where they had not been a couple of minutes, when a female bounced into the room, and, seizing Mr. Squeers by the throat, gave him two loud kisses: *one close after the other, like a postman's knock.* This lady was of a large raw-boned figure, about a head taller than Mr. Squeers, and was dressed in a dimity night-jacket; with her hair in papers and a dirty nightcap. (She was accustomed to boast that she was no grammarian, thank God; and also that she had tamed a high spirit or two in her day. Truly, in conjunction with her worthy husband, she had broken many and many a one.)[2]

'How is my Squeery?'

'Quite well, my love. How's the cows?'

'The cows is all right, every one of 'em.'

'And the pigs?'

'The pigs is as well as they was when you went away.'

'Come! That's a blessing! The boys are all as they were, I suppose?'

'Oh, yes, the boys is well enough. Only that young Pitcher's had a fever.'

'No! Damn that chap, he's always at something of that sort.'

Pending these endearments, Nicholas had stood, awkwardly enough, in the middle of the room: not very well knowing whether he was expected to retire into the passage. He was now relieved from his perplexity by Mr. Squeers.

'This is the new young man, my dear.'[3]

Here, a young servant-girl brought in some cold beef, and this being set upon the table, *a boy addressed by the name of Smike appeared with a jug of ale.*[4]

---

[1] *T & F* contains a short passage here (deleted in *Berg*) describing the arrival at Dotheboys Hall. Smike had a brief first entrance here, and there is in *Berg* a marginal stage-direction *Smike*. Nicholas's lengthy first impressions of Smike here had been omitted, however, before *Berg* was printed.

[2] The bracketed sentences, drawn from ch. 9, are added in the margin of *Berg*.

[3] Dickens's stage-business here may be surmised from Mrs. Squeers's 'Oh!' which was printed, but deleted, in *Berg*. Dickens had there omitted the following words, 'replied Mrs. Squeers, nodding her head at Nicholas, and eyeing him coldly from top to toe': he performed, instead of reading, such sentences.

[4] Marginal stage-direction *Smike*. The phrase referring to him is doubly underlined. Against the following paragraph, Wright notes: 'As if pulling letters out of pocket'.

Mr. Squeers was emptying his greatcoat pockets of letters and other small documents he had brought down. The boy glanced, with an anxious and timid expression, at the papers, as if with a sickly hope that one among them might relate to him. The look was a very painful one, and went to Nicholas's heart at once; for it told a long and very sad history.

It induced him to consider the boy more attentively, and he was surprised to observe the extraordinary mixture of garments which formed his dress. Although he could not have been less than eighteen or nineteen, and was tall for that age, he wore a skeleton suit, such as was then[1] usually put upon a very little boy. In order that the lower part of his legs might be in keeping with this singular dress, he had a very large pair of boots, originally made for tops, which might have been once worn by some stout farmer, but were now too patched and tattered for a beggar. God knows how long he had been there, but he still wore a tattered child's frill, only half concealed by a coarse, man's neckerchief. He was lame; and as he feigned to be busy in arranging the table, he glanced at the letters with a look so keen, and yet so dispirited and hopeless, that Nicholas could hardly bear to watch him.

'What are you bothering about there, Smike?' cried Mrs. Squeers; 'let the things alone, can't you?'

'Eh! Oh! it's you, is it?'

'Yes, sir. Is there—'

'Well! What are you stammering at?'

'Have you—did anybody—has nothing been heard—about me?'[2]

'Devil a bit, not a word, and never will be. Now this is a pretty sort of thing, isn't it, that you should have been left here, all these years, and no money paid after the first six—nor no notice taken, nor no clue to be got who you belong to? It's a pretty sort of thing that I should have to feed a great fellow like you, and never hope to get a penny for it, isn't it?'

The boy put his hand to his head as if he were making an effort to recollect something, and then, looking vacantly at his questioner, gradually broke into a smile, and limped away.

'I'll tell you what, Squeers, I think that young chap's turning silly.'

[3]'I hope not, for he's a handy fellow out of doors, and worth his meat and drink, any way. Hows'ever, I should think he'd have wit enough for us, if he was[4] silly. But come! Let's have supper, for I'm hungry and tired, and want to get to bed.'[5]

---

[1] 'was then' substituted in *Berg* for 'is'—an example of the up-dating sometimes needed in the Readings.

[2] 'Breathlessly' (Wright). Against the next paragraph (Squeers's speech), marginal stage direction *Bullying*.

[3] Marginal stage-direction *Yawning*. 'Squeers's right eye closed' (Wright).

[4] *was* italic in *Berg*.

[5] The printed text of Chapter I of *Berg* (and *Suzannet*) ends here. The remainder is written in, or pasted in from a cut-up copy of the novel.

This reminder brought in an exclusive steak for Mr. Squeers, * and Nicholas had a tough bit of cold beef. Mr. Squeers then took a Bumper of hot brandy and water of a stiff nature, and Mrs. Squeers made the new young man the Ghost of a small glassful of that compound.

Then: Mr. Squeers yawned again, and opined that it was time to go to bed;[1] upon which signal, Mrs. Squeers and the girl dragged in a straw mattress and a couple of blankets, and arranged them into a couch for Nicholas.

'We'll put you into your regular bed-room to-morrow, Nickleby. Let me see! Who sleeps in Brooks's bed, my dear?'

'In Brooks's? There's Jennings, little Bolder, Graymarsh, and what's his name.'

'So there is. Yes! Brooks is full. There's a place somewhere, I know, but I can't at this moment call to mind where. However, we'll have that all settled to-morrow. Good night, Nickleby. Seven o'clock in the morning, mind.'

'I shall be ready, sir. Good night.'[2]

'I don't know, by the bye, whose towel to put you on; but if you'll make shift with something to-morrow morning, Mrs. Squeers will arrange that, in the course of the day. My dear, don't forget.'

Mr. Squeers then nudged Mrs. Squeers[3] to bring away the brandy bottle, lest Nicholas should help himself in the night; and the lady having seized it with great precipitation, they retired together. *

CHAPTER 11[4]

A ride of two hundred and odd miles in winter weather, is a good softener of a hard bed. Perhaps it is even a sweetener of dreams, for those which came to Nicholas, and whispered their airy nothings, were of a happy kind. He was making his fortune very fast indeed—in his sleep—when the faint glimmer of a candle shone before his eyes, and Mr. Squeers's voice admonished him that it was time to get up.

[5]'Past seven, Nickleby!'

'Has morning come already?'

'Ah! that has it, and ready iced too. Now, Nickleby, come; tumble up!'

---

[1] 'Rubbing forehead'; at the end of this paragraph, 'Action with both hands' (Wright).

[2] An unwritten exchange followed here: Squeers enquired, 'Do you wash?' to which Nicholas replied, 'Occasionally' (Field, p. 56). Another elaboration of the ablutions at Dotheboys Hall appears in *Suzannet*: 'make shift with something', in Squeers's next speech, becomes 'make shift with your pocket handkerchief.'

[3] 'With elbow' (Wright).

[4] 'No pause between chapters' (Wright).

[5] Marginal stage-direction *Waking cold*. The first paragraph is cut in *Suzannet*.

Nicholas 'tumbled up,' and proceeded to dress himself by the light of Mr. Squeers's candle.

'Here's a pretty go,' said that gentleman; 'the pump's froze.'

'Indeed!'

'Yes. You can't wash yourself this morning.'

'Not wash myself!'

'Not a bit of it.[1] So you must be content with giving yourself a dry polish till we break the ice in the well, and get a bucketful out for the boys. Don't stand staring at me, but look sharp!'

Nicholas huddled on his clothes; * and Squeers, arming himself with his cane, led the way across a yard, to a door in the rear of the house.

'There! This is our shop, Nickleby!'[2]

A bare and dirty room, with a couple of windows, of which a tenth part might be of glass, the remainder being stopped up with old copybooks and paper. A couple of old desks, cut and notched, and inked, and damaged, in every possible way; two or three forms; a detached desk for Squeers; another for his assistant. Walls so discoloured, that it was impossible to tell whether they had ever been touched with paint or whitewash.[3] *†

The boys took their places and their books, *of which latter commodity the average might be about one to a dozen*[4] *learners.* A few minutes having elapsed, *during which Mr. Squeers looked very profound, as if he had a perfect apprehension of what was inside all the books, and could say every word of their contents by heart if he chose,* that gentleman called up the first class.

There ranged themselves in front of the schoolmaster's desk, a dozen haggard scarecrows, out at knees and elbows, one of whom placed a filthy book beneath his learned eye.

'This is the first class in English spelling and philosophy, Nickleby. We'll get up a Latin one, and hand that over to you. Now, then, where's the first boy?'

[1] 'Rubbing hands' (Wright).

[2] 'Open hand to right with a flourish' (Wright).

[3] *T & F* prints here the paragraph, beginning 'But the pupils!' which is deleted— obviously later—in *Berg*. (Wright, too, deletes it.) It is left standing in *Suzannet*. This deletion is interesting, for it contains the grimmest account of the boys' plight, and had been very effective when read: e.g., the *Western Daily Mercury*, 7 January 1862, noted that 'the deeply pathetic passages' in this Reading 'fell with their full force . . . effectually upon the ear, through the slow and simple cadences of the reader. Thus nothing could be finer than those passages descriptive of the wretched misery of the poor boys at Dotheboys Hall as they were first seen by Nickleby . . .' The brimstone and treacle, and the porridge, episodes which followed this description were not printed in *Berg* (or *Suzannet*); one reviewer recalled Dickens's including them in a performance a few years back—but was probably misremembering (Edinburgh *Courant*, 15 December 1868). As was noted above, in the headnote, the episode does appear in *Gimbel*.

[4] *a dozen* substituted for *eight* in manuscript: the usual rounding up and amplifying of figures in the Readings texts. Similarly, in the next paragraph, 'half a dozen' becomes 'a dozen'.

'Please, sir, he's cleaning the back parlour window,' said the temporary head of the philosophical class.

'So he is, to be sure. We go upon the practical mode of teaching, Nickleby; the regular education system. C-l-e-a-n, clean, verb active, to make bright, to scour. W-i-n, win, d-e-r, der, winder, a casement.[1] *When the boy knows this* out of book, *he goes and does it.*[2] It's just the same principle as the use of the globes. Where's the second boy?'

'Please, sir, he's weeding the garden.'

'To be sure. So he is. B-o-t, bot, t-i-n, tin, bottin, n-e-y, bottinney, noun substantive, a knowledge of plants. When he has learned that bottiney means a knowledge of plants, *he goes and knows 'em.* That's our system, Nickleby. Third boy, what's a horse.'

'A beast, sir.'

'So it is. Ain't it, Nickleby?'

'I believe there is no doubt of that, sir.'[3]

'Of course there ain't. A horse is a quadruped, and quadruped's Latin for beast. As you're perfect in that, boy, go and look after *my*[4] horse, and rub him down well, or I'll rub you down. The rest of the class go and draw water up, till somebody tells you to leave off, for it's washing-day to-morrow, and they want the coppers filled.'

So saying, he dismissed the first class *to their experiments in practical philosophy*, and eyed Nicholas with a look, half cunning and half doubtful, *as if he were not altogether certain what he might think of him by this time.*

[5]'That's the way we do it, Nickleby, and a very good way it is. Now, just take them fourteen little boys and hear them some reading, because, you know, you must begin to be useful, and idling about here, won't do.' *

It was Mr. Squeers's custom to call the boys together, and make a sort of report, after every half-yearly visit to the metropolis. So, in the afternoon, the boys were recalled from house-window, garden, stable, and cow-yard, and the school were assembled in full conclave.

[6]'Let any boy speak a word without leave,' said Mr. Squeers, 'and I'll take the skin off that boy's back.'

Death-like silence immediately prevailed.

---

[1] Dickens increased the absurdity of Mr. Squeers's pedagogy, though these improvements do not appear in *Berg* or *Suzannet*. Kate Field (p. 57) records the happy inventions—'. . . winder, *preposition*, a casement . . . bottiney, *adjective*, a knowledge of plants . . .' and, best of all, 'and quadruped's Latin, *or Greek, or Hebrew, or some other language that's dead and deserves to be*, for beast . . .'

[2] *he goes and does it* doubly underlined, as is *he goes and knows 'em* below.

[3] 'With a sigh' (Wright).

[4] *my* italic in the novel and in *Berg*. Wright notes against this speech, 'Threatening with forefinger': also that Dickens altered 'coppers' to 'boilers'.

[5] Wright deletes this paragraph.

[6] Marginal stage-direction *Slapping desk*. Kent (p. 145) describes it as a 'ferocious slash on the desk with his cane'.

'Boys, I've been to London, and have returned to my family and you, as strong and as well as ever.'

The boys gave three feeble cheers at this refreshing intelligence. Such cheers!

'I have seen the parents of some boys,' continued Squeers, turning over his papers, 'and they're so glad to hear how their sons are getting on, that there's no prospect at all of their sons' going away.—Which of course is a very pleasant thing to reflect upon, for all parties.'

Two or three hands went to two or three eyes, but the greater part of the young gentlemen—having no particular parents to speak of—were uninterested in the thing one way or other.

'I have had disappointments to contend against. Bolder's father was two pound ten short. Where is Bolder? Come here, Bolder.'

An unhealthy-looking boy, with warts all over his hands, stepped from his place to the master's desk, and raised his eyes to the face[1]; his own, quite white from the rapid beating of his heart.

'Bolder,' *speaking slowly, for he was considering, as the saying goes, where to have him.* 'Bolder, if your father thinks that because—why, what's this, sir?'

He caught up the boy's hand by the cuff of his jacket.

'What do you call this, sir?'

'I can't help the warts indeed, sir. They will come; it's the dirty work I think, sir—at least I don't know what it is, sir, but it's not my fault.'

'Bolder, you're an incorrigible young scoundrel, and as the last thrashing did you no good, we must see what another will do towards beating it out of you.'

Mr. Squeers fell upon the boy and caned him soundly.

'There; rub away as hard as you like, you won't rub that off in a hurry. Now let us see. A letter for Cobbey. Stand up, Cobbey.'

Another boy stood up, and eyed the letter very hard while Squeers made a mental abstract of it.[2]

'Oh! Cobbey's grandmother is dead, and his uncle John has took to drinking. Which is all the news his sister sends, *except eighteenpence, which will just pay for that broken square of glass. Mrs. Squeers, my dear, will you take the money?* Graymarsh, he's the next. Stand up, Graymarsh.'

Another boy stood up.

'Graymarsh's maternal aunt is very glad to hear he's so well and happy, and sends her respectful compliments to Mrs. Squeers, *and thinks she must be a angel.*[3] She likewise thinks Mr. Squeers is too good for this

---

[1] *sic:* 'Squeers's' deleted, 'the' inserted: but Dickens probably intended 'the master's'. Bolder replied, below ('I can't help the Warts...'), with 'Both Hands supplicatingly' (Wright).

[2] Here and during Graymarsh's aunt's letter, Squeers 'Reads from Book'; at 'Mrs. Squeers, ... will you take the money?' he 'Hands money' (Wright). The words from *except eighteenpence* are doubly underlined.

[3] *an angel* altered in *Berg* to *a angel*: but pronounced *a hangel* (Wright).

world; but hopes he may long be spared to carry on the business.[1] Would have sent the two pair of stockings as desired, but is short of money, so forwards a tract instead. Hopes, above all things, that Graymarsh will study to please Mr. and Mrs. Squeers, and look upon them *as his only friends;*[2] and that he will love Master Squeers; *and not object to sleeping five in a bed, which no Christian should.* Ah! a delightful letter. Very affecting indeed.'

It was[3] *affecting in one sense, for Graymarsh's maternal aunt was strongly supposed, by her more intimate friends, to be his maternal parent.*

'Mobbs's mother-in-law took to her bed on hearing that he wouldn't eat fat, and has been very ill ever since.[4] She wishes to know, by an early post, where he expects to go to, if he quarrels with his vittles; and with what feelings he *could*[5] turn up his nose at the cow's liver broth, after his good master had asked a blessing on it. This was told her in the London newspapers—not by Mr. Squeers, for he is too kind and too good to set anybody against anybody. Mobbs's mother-in-law is sorry to find Mobbs is discontented, which is sinful and horrid, and hopes Mr. Squeers will flog him into a happier state of mind; with this view, she has also stopped his halfpenny a week pocket-money, and given a double-bladed knife with a corkscrew in it, which she had bought on purpose for him, to the Missionaries.[6] A sulky state of feeling won't do. Cheerfulness and contentment must be kept up. Mobbs, come to me!'

The unhappy Mobbs moved slowly towards the desk, rubbing his eyes in anticipation of good cause for doing so; and soon afterwards retired by the side door, with as good cause as a boy need have.

Mr. Squeers then proceeded to open a miscellaneous collection of letters; some enclosing money, *which Mrs. Squeers 'took care of;'* and others referring to small articles of apparel, as caps and so forth, all of which the same lady stated to be too large, or too small, for anybody but young Squeers, *who would appear to have had most accommodating limbs, since everything that came into the school fitted him.*

In course of time, Squeers retired to his fireside, leaving Nicholas to take care of the boys in the school-room, which was very cold, and where a meal of bread and cheese was served out shortly after dark.

---

[1] Squeers repeated 'She likewise thinks Mr. Squeers is too good for this world' (Wright), and hereabouts, reflecting on this eulogy, he sagely observed that 'a good man struggling with his destiny is—a spectacle for things in general' (Field, p. 58); these words do not appear in Dickens's copies. Then, downcast by Graymarsh's aunt's having sent no money, his tone altered to a 'sulky sort of voice' (Wright).

[2] Doubly underlined, as is the next italicized phrase.

[3] *was* doubly underlined, the rest singly.

[4] For these words, Dickens substituted (according to Kate Field, p. 58)—'and has had a succession of cold and boiling water alternately running down her back ever since'.

[5] *could* italic in *Berg*.

[6] 'This is a very disagreeable letter' interpolated (Wright).

There was a small stove at that corner of the room which was nearest to the master's desk, and by it Nicholas sat down, depressed and self-degraded. * As he was absorbed in meditation he encountered the up-turned face of *Smike*, on his knees before the stove, picking a few cinders from the hearth and planting them on the fire. When he saw that he was observed, he shrunk back, expecting a blow.[1]

'You need not fear me. Are you cold?'[2]

'N-n-o.'

'You are shivering.'

'I am not cold. I am used to it.'

'Poor broken-spirited creature!'

If he had struck the wretched object, he would have slunk away without a word. But, now, he burst into tears.

'Oh, dear, oh dear! My heart will break. It will, it will.'

'Hush! Be a man; you are nearly one by years, God help you.'

'By years! Oh, dear, dear, how many of them! How many of them since I was a little child, younger than any that are here now! Where are they all!'

'Whom do you speak of?'

'My friends, myself—my—oh! what sufferings mine have been!'

'There is always hope.'

'No, no; none for me. Do you remember the boy that died here?'

'I was not here, you know, but what of him?'

'I was with him at night, and when it was all silent he cried no more for friends he wished to come and sit with him, but began to see faces round his bed that came from home; he said they smiled, and talked to him; and he died at last lifting his head to kiss them. What faces will smile on *me*[3] when *I* die here! Who will talk to *me* in those long long nights? They cannot come from home; they would frighten me, if they did, for I don't know what home is. Pain and fear, pain and fear for me, alive or dead. No hope, no hope!'[4]

The bell rang to bed; and the boy crept away. With a heavy heart Nicholas soon afterwards retired—no, not retired; there was no retirement there—followed—to the dirty and crowded dormitory.

[1] 'Hand to forehead' (Wright). Against the dialogue with Nicholas which follows, Wright has: 'Hands clasped as if in supplication', 'Sighs several times', 'Breathlessly'. It is unclear at which points Smike acted thus.

[2] This scene between Nicholas and Smike was 'painted with a vividness and pathos which told with thrilling effect upon the audience, and well deserved the burst of applause with which it was received' (*Cheltenham Examiner*, 8 January 1862).

[3] *me . . . I . . . me* all doubly underlined. 'Head from side to side' here (Wright).

[4] 'Oh!' with both hands up (Wright).

CHAPTER III[1]

MISS Fanny Squeers was in her three-and-twentieth year. If there be any grace of loveliness quite inseparable from that period of life, Miss Squeers must be presumed to have been possessed of it.[2] She was not tall like her mother, but short like her father—*from whom she inherited a remarkable expression of the right eye, something akin to having none at all.*

Miss Squeers had been spending a few days with a neighbouring friend, and had only just returned to the parental roof. * Questioning the servant, regarding the outward appearance and demeanour of Mr. Nickleby, the girl returned such enthusiastic replies, coupled with so many praises of his beautiful dark eyes, and his sweet smile, and his straight legs—*upon which last-named articles she laid particular stress; the general run of legs at Dotheboys Hall being crooked*—that Miss Squeers was not long in arriving at the conclusion that the new usher must be a very remarkable person, or, as she herself significantly phrased it, 'something quite out of the common.' And so Miss Squeers made up her mind that she would take a personal observation of Nicholas the very next day.

In pursuance of this design, the young lady watched the opportunity of her mother being engaged, and her father absent, and went *accidentally* into the school-room to get a pen mended: where, seeing nobody but Nicholas presiding over the boys, she blushed very deeply, and exhibited great confusion.

'I beg your pardon, I thought my Pa was—or might be—dear me, how very awkward!'

'Mr. Squeers is out.'

'Do you know will he be long, sir?'

'He said about an hour.'

'Thank you![3] I am very sorry I intruded, I am sure.' Miss Squeers said this, glancing from the pen in her hand, to Nicholas at his desk, and back again.

'If that is all you want,' said Nicholas, pointing to the pen, 'perhaps I can supply his place.'

Miss Squeers glanced at the door, as if dubious of the propriety of advancing nearer to a male stranger; then glanced round the school-room, as though in some measure reassured by the presence of forty boys; then sidled up to Nicholas, and delivered the pen into his hand.

'Shall it be a hard or a soft nib?'

[1] *III* altered to *2*, then back to *3*; cf. above, the footnote on the subtitle *4 Chapters.* Wright has a tantalizing note above this chapter-heading: 'Narration with forefinger and little finger'.

[2] Sentence deleted by Wright.

[3] '. . . that simper, lisp, and mien certainly belong to Mr. Squeers's offspring. Her "thank you" is perfect, and her . . . "As soft as possible, if you please" deserves to be perpetuated by a John Leech' (Field, p. 60).

'He *has*[1] a beautiful smile,' thought Miss Squeers. 'As soft as possible, if you please.'[2] Miss Squeers sighed. *It might be, to give Nicholas to understand that her heart was soft, and that the pen was wanted to match.*

Upon these instructions Nicholas made the pen; and when he gave it to Miss Squeers, Miss Squeers dropped it; and when he stooped to pick it up, Miss Squeers stooped too, and they knocked their heads together; whereat five-and-twenty little boys laughed: *being positively for the first and only time that half-year*. *

[3]Said Miss Squeers, as she walked away, 'I never saw such a pair of legs in the whole course of my life!'

In fact, Miss Squeers was in love with Nicholas Nickleby.

To account for the rapidity with which this young lady had conceived a passion for Nicholas, it may be necessary to state, that the friend from whom she had so recently returned, was a miller's daughter of only eighteen, who had engaged herself unto the son of a small corn-factor, resident in the nearest market town. Miss Squeers and the miller's daughter, being fast friends, had agreed together some two years before[4] (*according to a custom prevalent among young ladies*) that whoever was first engaged to be married, should straightway confide the mighty secret to the bosom of the other; in fulfilment of which pledge the miller's daughter, when her engagement was formed, came out express—*at eleven o'clock at night, as the corn-factor's son made an offer of his hand and heart at twenty-five minutes after ten by the Dutch clock in the kitchen*—and rushed into Miss Squeers's bed-room with the gratifying *intelligence*. Now Miss Squeers being five years older, had, since, been more than commonly anxious to return the compliment; but, either in consequence of finding it hard to please herself, or harder still to please anybody else, she had never had an opportunity so to do. The little interview with Nicholas had no sooner passed, than Miss Squeers, putting on her bonnet, made her way, with great precipitation, to her friend's house, and revealed how that she was— *not exactly engaged, but going to be*—to a gentleman's son (*none of your corn-factors*)—to a gentleman's son[5] of high descent, who had come down as teacher to Dotheboys Hall, under most mysterious and remarkable circumstances. Indeed, as Miss Squeers more than hinted, induced by the fame of her many charms, to seek her out, and woo and win her. *

'How I should like to see him!' exclaimed the friend.

'So you shall, 'Tilda; I should consider myself one of the most dis-

---

[1] *has* italic in *Berg* and in the novel.
[2] Marginal stage-direction *Sighing.*
[3] Marginal stage-direction *Legs.*
[4] *T & F* has 'ago' not 'before'.
[5] *not exactly engaged* and *none of your corn-factors* doubly underlined. Wright puts inverted commas round 'not exactly engaged, but going to be' and deletes 'to a gentleman's son (none of your corn-factors)'.

honorable creatures alive, if I denied you. Mother's going away tomorrow for two days to fetch some boys; and when she does, I'll ask you and your Intended, *John Browdie*,[1] up to tea, and have him to meet you.'[2]*

When such an opportunity occurred, it was Mr. Squeers's custom to drive over to the market town, every evening, on pretence of urgent business, and stop till ten or eleven o'clock at a tavern he much affected. As the contemplated party was not in his way, therefore, but rather afforded a means of compromise with Miss Squeers, he readily yielded his assent, and willingly told Nicholas that he was expected to take his tea in the parlour that evening, at five o'clock.

To be sure Miss Squeers was in a flutter, and to be sure she was dressed out to the best advantage: with her hair—she wore it in a crop—curled in five distinct rows,[3] up to the very top of her head, and arranged over the doubtful eye; to say nothing of the blue sash which floated down her back, or the worked apron, or the long gloves, or the scarf of green gauze, worn over one shoulder and under the other; or any of the numerous devices which were to be as so many arrows to the heart of Mr. Nickleby. She had scarcely completed these arrangements, when the friend arrived.†

The servant brought in the tea-things, and, soon afterwards, somebody tapped at the room door.

'There he is! Oh 'Tilda! I do so palpitate!'

'Hush! Hem! Say, come in.'

'Come in.'[4] And in walked Nicholas.

'Good evening,' *said that young gentleman, all unconscious of his conquest.* 'I understood from Mr. Squeers that I was expected?'

'Oh yes; it's all right. (Don't, 'Tilda!) Father don't tea with us, but you won't mind that, I dare say. We are only waiting for one more gentleman. ('Tilda, don't!).'[5] *

'Well,' thought Nicholas, 'as I am here, and seem expected to be amiable, it's of no use looking like a goose. I may as well accommodate myself to the company.' So he saluted Miss Squeers and the friend with gallantry, and drew a chair to the teatable, and began to make himself probably as much at home as ever an Usher was in his principal's parlor.

The ladies were in full delight at this, when the expected swain arrived

---

[1] Doubly underlined.

[2] *T & F* here has a paragraph (beginning 'It so fell out'), deleted in *Berg*. Wright deletes it in his copy of *T & F*, and correctly notes other such minor textual differences between *T & F* and *Berg*.

[3] 'Dramatic Both Hands' (Wright).

[4] Pronounced 'Coh/m/e' (Wright)—presumably Fanny's attempt at gentility.

[5] The bracketed asides to 'Tilda are late additions, not printed in *T & F*. Earlier, Dickens had interpolated Fanny's formal introduction 'Mr. Nickelby, 'Tilda; 'Tilda, Mr. Nickleby'—a fitting overture, wrote Kate Field, to 'one of the cleverest of *petite* comedies'. Dickens, she thought, was not at his best in this Reading until this scene (Field, pp. 59–60).

(with his hair damp from washing) in a clean shirt, whereof the collar might have belonged to some giant ancestor, and a white waistcoat of similar dimensions.

'Well, John,' said Miss Matilda Price (*which, by-the-by, was the name of the miller's daughter*).

'Weel,' said John *with a grin that even the collar could not conceal.*

'I beg your pardon,' interposed Miss Squeers, hastening to do the honours, 'Mr. Nickleby—Mr. John Browdie.'

'Servant, sir,' said John, who was about six feet six, with a face and body rather above the due proportion.

'Yours, sir,' replied Nicholas, *making fearful ravages on the bread and butter.*[1]

Mr. Browdie was not a gentleman of great conversational powers, so he grinned twice more, and having now bestowed his customary mark of recognition on every person in company, grinned at nothing particular, and helped himself to food.

'Old wooman awa', bean't she?'

Miss Squeers nodded assent.

Mr. Browdie gave a grin of special width, as if he thought that really was something to laugh at, and went to work at the bread and butter with vigour. It was quite a sight to behold how he and Nicholas emptied the plate between them.

'Ye wean't get bread and butther ev'ry neight, I expect, mun,' said Mr. Browdie, *after he had sat staring at Nicholas a long time over the empty plate.* 'Ecod, they dean't put too much intiv 'em. Ye'll be nowt but skeen and boans if you stop here long eneaf. Ho! ho! ho!'

'You are facetious, sir.'

'Na; I dean't know, but t'oother teacher, 'cod he wur a learn 'un, he wur.'

The recollection of the last teacher's leanness seemed to afford Mr. Browdie the most exquisite delight.

'I don't know whether your perceptions are quite keen enough, Mr. Browdie, to enable you to understand that your remarks are offensive, but they are——'

Miss Price stopped her admirer's mouth as he was about to answer.[2] 'If you say another word, John, I'll never forgive you, or speak to you again.'

[3]'Weel, my lass, I dean't care aboot 'un; let 'un gang on, let 'un gang on.'

It now became Miss Squeers's turn to intercede with Nicholas and the

---

[1] 'High laugh' (Wright)—John Browdie's, of course, which was a great feature of his characterization. His height is increased by six inches, in the Reading (above).

[2] 'Quick' (Wright). Miss Price is 'Quick' in other speeches, too, he notes.

[3] Marginal stage-direction *Snapping fingers.*

effect of the double intercession, was, that he and John Browdie shook hands across the table with much gravity. Such was the imposing nature of this ceremonial, that Miss Squeers shed tears.

'What's the matter, Fanny?' said Miss Price.

'Nothing, 'Tilda.'

'There never was any danger,' said Miss Price, 'was there, Mr. Nickleby?'

'None at all. Absurd.'

'Say something kind to her, and she'll soon come round. Here! Shall John and I go into the little kitchen, and come back presently?'

'Not on any account! What on earth should you do that for?'

'Well, you *are*[1] a one to keep company.'

'What do you mean? I am not a one to keep company at all. You don't mean to say that you think—'

'O no! I think nothing at all. Look at her, dressed so beautiful, and looking so well—really *almost* handsome. I am ashamed at you.'

'My dear girl, what have I got to do with her dressing beautifully or looking well?'

'Come, don't call me a dear girl!'[2] (*She smiled a little though, for she was pretty, and a coquette in her small way, and Nicholas was good-looking, and she supposed him the property of somebody else, which were all reasons why she should be gratified to think she had made an impression on him.*)

'Come; we're going to have a game at cards.' *She tripped away and rejoined the big Yorkshireman, and they sat down to play speculation.*

'There are only four of us, 'Tilda,' *said Miss Squeers, looking slyly at Nicholas*: 'so we had better go partners, two against two.'[3]

'What do you say, Mr. Nickleby?'

'With all the pleasure in life.' *And quite unconscious of his heinous offence, he 'went partners' with Miss Price.*

[4]'Mr. Browdie, shall we make a bank against them?'

The Yorkshireman assented—apparently quite overwhelmed by the usher's impudence—and Miss Squeers darted a spiteful look at her friend.

The deal fell to Nicholas, and the hand prospered.

'We intend to win everything.'

''Tilda *has*[5] won something she didn't expect, I think, haven't you, dear?'

'Only a dozen and eight, love.'

'How dull you are to-night!'

'No, indeed. I am in excellent spirits. I was thinking *you* seemed out of sorts.'

---

[1] *are*, like *almost* just below, italic in the novel and in *Berg*.

[2] 'Slappingly' (Wright).

[3] 'Back of fingers of left hand to mouth' (Wright).

[4] Marginal stage-direction *Spiteful*.

[5] *has*, like *you* just below, italic in the novel and in *Berg*.

'Me? Oh no!'

'Your hair's coming out of curl, dear.'

'Never mind me;[1] you had better attend to your partner, Miss.'

'Thank you for reminding her. So she had.'

[2] *The Yorkshireman flattened his nose, once or twice, with his clenched fist, as if to keep his hand in, till he had an opportunity of exercising it upon the nose of some other gentleman; and Miss Squeers tossed her head with such indignation, that the gust of wind raised by the multitudinous curls in motion, nearly blew the candle out.*

'I never had such luck, really,' exclaimed Miss Price, after another hand or two. 'It's all along of you, Mr. Nickleby, I think. I should like to have you for a partner always.'

'I wish you had.'

'You'll have a bad wife, though, if you always win at cards.'

'Not if your wish is gratified. I am sure I shall have a good one in that case.'

To see how Miss Squeers tossed her head, and [3]how the corn-factor flattened his nose, the while!

'We have all the talking to ourselves, it seems,' *said Nicholas, looking good-humouredly round the table as he took up the cards for a fresh deal.*

'You do it so well, that it would be a pity to interrupt, wouldn't it, Mr. Browdie?'

'Nay, we do it in default of having anybody else to talk to.'

'We'll talk to you, you know, if you'll say anything.'

'Thank you, 'Tilda.'

'Or you can talk to each other, if you don't choose to talk to us. John, why don't *you*[4] say something?'

'Say summat?'

'Ay, and not sit there so silent and glum.'

[5]'Weel, then! what I say's this—Dang my boans and boddy, if I stan' this ony longer. Do ye gang whoam wi' me; and do yon loight an' tight young whipster, look sharp out for a brokken head, next time he cums under my hond.'

'Mercy on us, what's all this?'

'Cum whoam, tell 'e, cum whoam!'

Here, Miss Squeers burst into tears; in part from vexation, and in part from an impotent desire to lacerate somebody's countenance with her fair finger-nails. *

[1] 'Snappishly' (Wright).

[2] Marginal stage-direction *Nose*. Dickens's enactment of this piece of business was delightful (Kent, p. 147).

[3] Marginal stage-direction *Nose* repeated. Browdie slapped his nose again at 'Say summat?' (Wright).

[4] *you* doubly underlined.

[5] Marginal stage-direction *Striking Table*.

'Why, and here's Fanny in tears now! What can be the matter?'
'Oh! you don't know, Miss, of course you don't know. Pray don't trouble yourself to inquire,' said Miss Squeers, *producing that change of countenance which children call, making a face.*
'Well, I'm sure!'
'And who cares whether you are sure or not, ma'am?'
'You are monstrous polite, ma'am.'
'I shall not come to you to take lessons in the art, ma'am!'
'Oh! you needn't take the trouble to make yourself plainer than you are, ma'am, however, because that's quite unnecessary.'
Miss Squeers, in reply, turned very red, and thanked God that she hadn't got the bold faces of some people. Miss Price, in rejoinder, congratulated herself upon not being possessed of the envious feeling of other people; whereupon Miss Squeers made some general remark touching the danger of associating with low persons.[1] *In which Miss Price entirely coincided.*
''Tilda, artful and designing 'Tilda! I wouldn't have a child named 'Tilda—not to save it from its grave!'
(*Here John Browdie, a little nettled,* wound up the evening by remarking, 'Weel, weel, weel! As to the matther o' thot, Fonny, it'll be time eneaf to think aboot neaming of it when it cooms.')[2]

CHAPTER IV[3]

THE poor creature, Smike, since the night Nicholas had spoken kindly to him in the school-room, had followed him to and fro, content only to be near him.[4] He would sit beside him for hours; and a word would brighten up his care-worn face, and call into it a passing gleam, even of happiness.

Upon this poor being, all the spleen and ill-humour that could not be vented on Nicholas were bestowed. It was no sooner observed that he had

---

[1] Wright puts inverted commas round 'low persons'. Fanny's next words, he notes, spoken 'Cryingly'.

[2] This brief exchange, from ch. 42, was printed in *Berg*, but slightly altered after *T & F* was printed. *Berg* contains one more printed page, to conclude Chapter III, but it is all deleted. *T & F*, however, retains one paragraph from this page, based upon the paragraph (near the end of ch. 9 of the novel) beginning 'There were no sooner gone . . .' and ending with Fanny 'moaning in her pocket-handkerchief'. Wright deletes it.

[3] The 1858 printing began Chapter IV with 'The cold, feeble, dawn of a January day' (the opening of ch. 13 of the novel). Dickens then decided to amplify the text here, so with scissors and paste he stuck in some extracts from the end of ch. 12; these, subsequently much cut and amended, now precede 'The cold, feeble, dawn . . .', but the paragraph which followed that in the novel ('It needed a quick eye . . .'), printed in the 1858 copies, is deleted in both *Berg* and *Suzannet*. A slightly different, and shorter, version of the extracts from ch. 12 is written and pasted in to the *Suzannet* text at this point, to begin its Chapter III. Wright heads this chapter: 'Holding book over box'.

[4] Wright deletes from here until the end of the next paragraph ('. . . Smike paid for all').

become attached to Nicholas, than stripes and blows, morning, noon, and night, were his portion. Squeers was jealous of the influence his man had so soon acquired in the school, and the slighted Miss Squeers now hated Nicholas, and Mrs. Squeers hated him, and Smike paid for all.

One night the poor soul was poring hard over a book, vainly endeavouring to master some task which a child of nine years old could have conquered with ease, but which, to the brain of the crushed boy of nineteen, was a hopeless mystery.

Nicholas laid his hand upon his shoulder.

'I can't do it.'

'Do not try. * You will do better, poor fellow, when I am gone.'

'Gone! Are you going?'

'I cannot say.[1] I was speaking more to my own thoughts than to you. I shall be driven to that at last!' said Nicholas. 'The world is before me, after all.'

'Is the world as bad and dismal as this place?'

'Heaven forbid,'[2] replied Nicholas, pursuing the train of his own thoughts, 'it's hardest, coarsest toil, is happiness to this.'

[3] 'Should I ever meet you there?'

'Yes,' willing to soothe him.

'No, no! Should I—should I— Say I should be sure to find you.'

'You would, and I would help you, and not bring fresh sorrow on you as I have done here.'

The boy caught both his hands and uttered a few broken sounds which were unintelligible. Squeers entered, at the moment, and he shrunk back into his old corner.

Two days later, the cold, feeble dawn of a January morning was stealing in at the windows of the common sleeping-room, when Nicholas, raising himself on his arm, looked among the prostrate forms in search of one. * †

'Now, then,' *cried Squeers, from the bottom of the stairs,* 'are you going to sleep all day, up there—'

'We shall be down directly, sir.'

'Down directly! Ah! you had better be down directly, or I'll be down upon some of you in less time than directly. Where's that Smike?'

Nicholas looked round again. *

'He is not here, sir.'

'Don't tell me a lie. He is.'

'He is not. Don't tell me one.'

Squeers bounced into the dormitory, and, swinging his cane in the air ready for a blow, darted into the corner where Smike usually lay at night. The cane descended harmlessly. There was nobody there.

---

[1] 'Hand to brow' (Wright).
[2] 'Hand uplifted' (Wright).
[3] Wright inserts: 'If I was to go into the world, should I . . .'

'What does this mean? Where have you hid him?'

'I have seen nothing of him, since last night.'

'Come, you won't save him this way. Where is he?'

'At the bottom of the nearest pond for anything I know.'

'D—n you, what do you mean, by that?' In a fright, Squeers inquired of the boys whether any one of them knew anything of their missing schoolmate.

There was a general hum of denial, in the midst of which, one shrill voice was heard to say (as, indeed, everybody thought[1]):—

'Please, sir, I think Smike's run away, sir.'

'Ha! who said that?'

Mr. Squeers made a plunge into the crowd, and caught a very little boy, the perplexed expression of whose countenance as he was brought forward, seemed to intimate that he was uncertain whether he was going to be punished or rewarded for his suggestion. He was not long in doubt.

'You think he has run away, do you, sir?'

'Yes, please sir.'

'And what reason have you to suppose that any boy would want to run away from this establishment? Eh?'

The child raised a dismal cry, by way of answer, and Mr. Squeers beat him until he rolled out of his hands. He mercifully allowed him to roll away.

'There! Now if any other boy thinks Smike has run away, I shall be glad to have a talk with him.'

Profound silence.[2]

'Well, Nickleby, you[3] think he has run away, I suppose?'

'I think it extremely likely.'

'Maybe you know he has run away?'

'I know nothing about it.'[4]

'He didn't tell you he was going, I suppose?'

'He did not. I am very glad he did not, for it would then have been my duty to have told you.'

'Which no doubt you would have been devilish sorry to do.'

'I should, indeed.'

Mrs. Squeers had listened to this conversation, from the bottom of the stairs; but, now losing all patience, she hastily made her way to the scene of action.

'What's all this here to do? What on earth are you talking to him[5] for,

---

[1] thought doubly underlined.

[2] Wright alters 'Profound' to 'Dead'.

[3] you italic in the novel and in Berg. Wright notes that, after 'Well, Nickleby', Dickens interpolated: 'you look to me'.

[4] 'Determinedly' (Wright).

[5] him, like must . . . must just below, doubly underlined.

Squeery! * The cow-house and stable are locked up, so Smike can't be there; and he's not down stairs anywhere, for the girl has looked. He *must* have gone York way, and by a public road. * He *must* beg his way, and he could do that nowheres but on the public road. Now, if you takes the chaise and goes one road, and I borrows Swallows's chaise, and goes t'other, what with keeping our eyes open, and asking questions, one or other of us is moral sure to lay hold of him.'

The lady's plan was put in execution without delay, * Nicholas remaining behind, in a tumult of feeling.[1] Death, from want and exposure, was the best that could be expected from the prolonged wandering of so helpless a creature, through a country of which he was ignorant. There was little, perhaps, to choose between this and a return to the tender mercies of the school: but Nicholas lingered on, in restless anxiety, until the evening of next day, when Squeers returned, alone.

'No news of the scamp!' *

Another day came, and Nicholas was scarcely awake when he heard the wheels of a chaise approaching the house. It stopped, and the voice of Mrs. Squeers was heard, ordering a glass of spirits for somebody— *which was in itself a sufficient sign that something extraordinary had happened*. Nicholas hardly dared to look out of window, but he did so, and the first object that met his eyes was wretched Smike: bedabbled with mud and rain, haggard and worn, and wild.

[2]'Lift him out,' said Squeers. 'Bring him in; bring him in!'

'Take care,' cried Mrs. Squeers. 'We tied his legs under the apron and made 'em fast to the chaise, to prevent his giving us the slip again.'

With hands trembling with delight, Squeers unloosened the cord; and Smike, more dead than alive, was brought in and locked up in a cellar, until such time as Mr. Squeers should deem it expedient to operate upon him. *

The news that the fugitive had been caught and brought back, ran like wild-fire through the hungry community, and expectation was on tiptoe all the morning. On tiptoe it remained until the afternoon; when Squeers, having refreshed himself with his dinner, and an extra libation or so, made his appearance (accompanied by his amiable partner) with a fearful instrument of flagellation, strong, supple, wax-ended, and new.

'Is every boy here?'[3]

Every boy was there, but every boy was afraid *to speak*; so Squeers glared along the lines to assure himself.[4]

---

[1] Wright deletes from here until the paragraph beginning 'Another day came'.

[2] Marginal stage-direction *Savage glee*; very dramatic, Wright noted.

[3] 'Hand down at side' (Wright).

[4] 'As Squeers was represented as "glaring along the lines" . . ., the Reader, instead of uttering one word of what the ruffianly schoolmaster ought then to have added: 'Each boy keep his place. Nickleby! You go to your desk, sir!'" [speech deleted in *Berg*]

There was a curious expression in the usher's face; but he took his seat, without opening his lips in reply. Squeers left the room, and shortly afterwards returned, dragging Smike by the collar—*or rather by that fragment of his jacket which was nearest the place where his collar ought to have been.* *

'Now, what have you got to say for yourself? (*Stand a little out of the way, Mrs. Squeers, my dear; I've hardly got room enough.*)'[1]

'Spare me, sir!'

'Oh! that's all you've got to say, is it? Yes, I'll flog you within an inch of your life, and spare you that.'[2] *

One cruel blow had fallen on him, when Nicholas Nickleby cried, 'Stop!'[3]

'Who cried stop?'

'I did. This must not go on.'

'Must not go on!'

'Must not! Shall not! I will prevent it. You have disregarded all my quiet interference in this miserable lad's behalf; you have returned no answer to the letter I wrote you, in which I begged forgiveness for him, and offered to be responsible that he would remain quietly here. Don't blame me for this public interference. You have brought it upon yourself; not I.'

'Sit down, you beggar!'

'Touch him again at your peril! I will not stand by, and see it done. My blood is up, and I have the strength of ten such men as you. By Heaven I will not spare you, if you drive me on! I have personal insults to avenge, and my indignation is aggravated by the cruelties practised in this wicked den. Take care; for if you raise the devil in me, the consequences will fall heavily upon your head!'

Squeers, in a violent outbreak of wrath, spat at him, and struck him a blow across the face. Nicholas instantly sprang upon him, wrested his weapon from his hand, pinned him by the throat, and beat the ruffian till he roared for mercy. *

He flung him away with all the force he could muster, and the violence of his fall precipitated *Mrs. Squeers over an adjacent form; Squeers, striking*

—instead of uttering one syllable of this, contented himself with his own manuscript direction [in *Berg*], in one word—*Pointing*. The effect of this simple gesture was startling —particularly when, after the momentary hush with which it was always accompanied, he observed quietly,—"There was a curious expression in the usher's face; but he took his seat, without opening his lips in reply"' (Kent, p. 149).

[1] Doubly underlined; spoken with 'a horrible relish' (Kent, p. 150).

[2] 'Threateningly—clenched' (Wright).

[3] '"Stop!" was cried out in a voice that made the rafters ring—even the lofty rafters of St. James's Hall.' Squeers replied 'with the glare and snarl of a wild beast', gave another 'frightful look' on 'Must not go on!' and 'screamed out' his final speech, 'Sit down, you beggar!' (Kent, p. 150).

his head against the same form in his descent, lay at his full length on the ground, stunned and motionless.[1]

Having brought affairs to this happy termination, and having ascertained, to his satisfaction, that Squeers was only stunned, and not dead (*upon which point he had had some unpleasant doubts at first*), Nicholas packed up a few clothes in a small valise, and, finding that nobody offered to oppose his progress, marched boldly out by the front door, and struck into the road. Then such a cheer arose as the walls of Dotheboys Hall had never echoed before, and would never respond to again. When the sound had died away, the school was empty; and of the crowd of boys, *not one remained*.[2]

When Nicholas had cooled, sufficiently to give his present circumstances some reflection, they did not appear in an encouraging light; he had only four shillings and odd pence in his pocket, and was something more than two hundred and fifty miles from London.

Lifting up his eyes, he beheld a horseman coming towards him, discovered to be no other than Mr. John Browdie, carrying a thick ash stick.

'I am in no mood for more noise and riot, and yet, do what I will, I shall have an altercation with this honest blockhead, and perhaps a blow or two from yonder cudgel.'

There appeared reason to expect it, for John Browdie no sooner saw Nicholas, than he reined in his horse, and waited until such time as he should come up.

'Servant, young genelman.'

'Yours.'

'Weel; we ha' met at last.'

'Yes.—Come! We parted on no very good terms the last time we met; it was my fault; but I had no intention of offending you, and no idea that I was doing so. I was very sorry for it, afterwards. Will you shake hands?'

[1] The episode of Squeer's castigation was performed with a 'startling reality' (*Manchester Guardian*, 26 October 1868). Squeers's 'ruffianism ... so much scandalized the audience ... that, when the reader came to the fight ..., there came a loud outburst of applause as [Squeers] fell senseless to the floor, just as if they had all been witnesses of an actual combat' (Edinburgh *Courant*, 19 April 1866). This reviewer noted, however, that 'One scarcely knows whether to take Mr. Squeers for a mere ruffian or a humorist in disguise.' The Reading, if not reconciling these two roles, fully exploited the dramatic possibilities of both.

[2] Underlined trebly. These two sentences from ch. 64 are pasted into *Berg*. They do not appear in *Suzannet*, which at this point makes a large deletion (the whole of the John Browdie episode). Its text jumps from Nicholas's leaving Dotheboys Hall ('... marched boldly out by the front door, and struck into the road') to the paragraph beginning 'He did not travel far ...' From there to the end, the *Suzannet* text is virtually identical with *Berg*.

[1]'Shake honds! Ah! that I weel! But wa'at be the matther wi' thy feace, mun? It be all brokken loike.'

'It is a cut—a blow; but I returned it to the giver, and with good interest.'

'Noa, did'ee though? Well deane! I loike 'un for thot.'

'The fact is, I have been ill-treated.'

'Noa! Dean't say thot.'

'Yes, I have, by that man Squeers, and I have beaten him soundly, and am leaving this place in consequence.'

'What!' cried John Browdie, *with such an ecstatic shout, that the horse shyed at it.* 'Beatten the schoolmeasther! Ho! ho! ho! Beatten the school-measther. Who ever heard o' the loike o' that noo! Giv' us thee hond agean, yoongster. Beatten the schoolmeasther! Dang it, I loove thee for't.'[2]

When his mirth had subsided, he inquired what Nicholas meant to do? On his replying, to go straight to London, he shook his head, and inquired if he knew how much the coaches charged, to carry passengers so far?

'No, I do not; but it is of no great consequence to me, for I intend walking.'

'Gang awa' to Lunnun afoot! (Stan' still, tellee, old horse.) Hoo much cash hast thee gotten?'

'Not much, but I can make it enough. Where there's a will, there's a way, you know.'

John Browdie pulled out an old purse, and insisted that Nicholas should borrow from him whatever he required.

'Dean't be afeard, mun, tak' eneaf to carry thee whoam. Thee'lt pay me yan day, a' warrant.'

Nicholas would by no means be prevailed upon to borrow more than a sovereign, with which loan Mr. Browdie was fain to content himself after many entreaties that he would accept of more. (*He observed, with a touch of Yorkshire caution, that if Nicholas didn't spend it all, he could put the surplus by, till he had an opportunity of remitting it carriage free*).

'Tak' that bit o' timber to help thee on wi', mun; keep a good heart, and bless thee. Beatten the schoolmeasther! 'Cod it's the best thing a've heerd this twonty year!'[3]

John set spurs to his horse, and went off at a smart canter. Nicholas watched the horse and rider until they disappeared over the brow of a distant hill, and then set forward on his journey.

He did not travel far, that afternoon, for by this time it was nearly dark;

---

[1] Marginal stage-direction *Shaking hands*. Wright deletes the *e* in 'shake'.

[2] After 'I loove thee for 't' Wright interpolates: 'Givens thee hand again'.

[3] 'Shaking hands closed or clasped together up and down and out and in from his [*word(s) lost*]' (Wright).

so, he lay, that night, at a cottage, where beds were let cheap; and, rising betimes next morning, made his way before night to Boroughbridge. There he stumbled on an empty barn; and in a warm corner stretched his weary limbs, and fell asleep.

When he awoke next morning, he sat up, rubbed his eyes, and stared at some motionless object in front of him.

'Strange! It cannot be real—and yet I—I am awake! Smike!'

It was Smike indeed.[1]

'Why do you kneel to me?'

'To go with you—anywhere—everywhere—to the world's end—to the churchyard. Let me go with you, oh do let me.[2] You are my home—my kind friend—take me with you, pray!'

He had followed Nicholas, it seemed; had never lost sight of him all the way; had watched while he slept, and when he halted for refreshment; and had feared to appear, sooner, lest he should be sent back.

'Poor fellow! Your hard fate denies you any friend but one, and he is nearly as poor and helpless as yourself.'

'May I—may I go with you? I will be your faithful hard-working servant. I want no clothes; these will do very well. I only want to be near you.'

'And you shall. And the world shall deal by you as it does by me, till one or both of us shall quit it for a better.[3] Come!'

So, he strapped his burden on his shoulders, and, taking his stick in one hand, extended the other to his delighted charge. And so they passed out of the old barn, together.[4]

THE END OF THE READING

[1] Wright deletes this sentence.

[2] 'Both hands supplicatingly' (Wright).

[3] 'Beckoningly'; below, at 'extended the other', 'Thrust out his hand' (Wright).

[4] 'I am inclined to suspect', Dickens wrote to Wilkie Collins after the first performance of *Nickleby*, 'that the impression of protection and hope derived from Nickleby's going away protecting Smike is exactly the impression—this is discovered by chance—that an Audience most likes to be left with' (*N*, iii. 248).

THE BASTILLE PRISONER

OF the four Readings which Dickens mentioned he was preparing in the late summer of 1861 (see above, p. 213), *The Bastille Prisoner* alone remained unperformed, to the regret of Charles Kent who thought it would certainly have been one of his 'most powerful delineations' (p. 90). The prompt-copy (now in the Suzannet Collection) was entitled *The/Bastille Prisoner./A Reading./From 'A Tale of Two Cities'./In Three Chapters./Privately Printed.* (printed by William Clowes and Sons, London, text paginated 3–45). Dickens worked hard on this item, both in selecting drastically from the corresponding chapters of the novel and then in preparing the prompt-copy, cutting the text and adding many performance signs.

The Reading is confined to Book I of the novel (much the shortest of the Books), and from this it selects the passages dealing with Doctor Manette's being 'restored to life'. The rumblings of the French Revolution are omitted almost entirely, as are various other episodes and characters from these early chapters which are more relevant to other plot-developments. Thus, Defarge is retained (as the Doctor's old servant) but passages about Madame Defarge and the 'Jacques' conspirators are omitted, as had been Jerry Cruncher's appearance in the opening chapter. Chapter I of the Reading consists mainly of Mr. Lorry's encounter with Lucie Manette at the Royal George Hotel, Dover, though it begins with the opening paragraph of the novel and takes up phrases from chs. 1 and 2. Chapter II is a shortened version of Book I, ch. 5; it retains the opening and closing paragraphs of that chapter but much reduces the description of the plight of the poor of Saint Antoine, and the suggestions of the threat which they represent. Chapter III is taken from Book I, ch. 6, somewhat abbreviated; it ends with Manette's sinking peacefully into his daughter's arms. Lucie's speeches, both here and in the Dover scene, are cut very little. The pages which conclude ch. 6 (and Book I) of the novel are omitted; these deal with Manette and his party's setting out upon their journey from Paris to London.

The prompt-copy is much revised, in blue ink and in pencil. The deletions amount to a total of five out of the forty-three pages of text. For a fuller discussion of this item see Michael Slater, '*The Bastille Prisoner*: a Reading Dickens Never Gave', *Études Anglaises*, xxxiii (1970), 190–6.

The Bastille Prisoner
In Three Chapters

CHAPTER I

IT was the best of times, it was the worst of times, it was the age of wisdom, it was the age of foolishness, it was the epoch of belief, it was the epoch of incredulity, it was the season of Light, it was the season of Darkness, it was the spring of hope, it was the winter of despair, we had everything before us, we had nothing before us, we were all going direct to Heaven, we were all going direct the other way—in short, the period was so far like the present period, that some of its loudest authorities insisted on its being received, for good or for evil, in the superlative degree of comparison only.

It was the year of Our Lord one thousand seven hundred and seventy-five. *

Upon a certain November day in that year, the London mail got to Dover in the course of the forenoon, and the head-drawer at the Royal George Hotel opened the coach-door, as his custom was. The inside of the coach, with its damp and dirty straw, its disagreeable smell, and its obscurity, was rather like a larger sort of dog-kennel. The only passenger, shaking himself out of it, a tangle of wrapper and straw, was rather like a larger sort of dog.

'There will be a packet to Calais to-morrow, drawer?'

'Yes, sir, if the weather holds and the wind sets tolerably fair. The tide will serve pretty nicely at about two in the afternoon, sir. Bed, sir?'

'I shall not go to bed till night; but I want a bedroom, and a barber.'

'And then breakfast, sir? Yes, sir. That way, sir, if you please. Show Concord! Gentleman's valise and hot water to Concord. Pull off gentleman's boots in Concord. (You will find a fine sea-coal fire, sir.) Fetch barber to Concord. Stir about there, now, for Concord!'

The Concord bed-chamber being always assigned to a passenger by the mail, and passengers by the mail being always wrapped up from head to foot, the room had the odd interest for the establishment of the Royal George, that although but one kind of man was seen to go into it, all kinds and varieties of men came out of it. The gentleman who came out of it on this occasion, was a gentleman of sixty, formally dressed in a brown suit of clothes, pretty well worn but very well kept, with large square cuffs, and large flaps to the pockets.

The coffee-room had no other occupant, that forenoon, than the gentleman in brown. Very methodical he looked, with a hand on each knee, and a loud watch ticking under his flapped waistcoat, as though it set its gravity against the levity of the brisk fire. The gentleman had a good leg, and was a little vain of it, for his brown stockings fitted sleek and close, and were of a fine texture; his shoes and buckles, too, though plain, were trim. His linen was as white as the tops of the waves that broke upon the neighbouring beach, or the specks of sail that glinted in the sunlight far at sea. His face, habitually quieted, was still lighted up under his flaxen wig by a pair of moist bright eyes; and he had a healthy colour in his cheeks.

'I wish accommodation prepared for a young lady who may come here at any time to-day. She may ask for me—Mr. Jarvis Lorry—or she may only ask for a gentleman from Tellson's Bank. Please to let me know.'

'Yes, sir. Tellson's Bank in London, sir.'

'Yes.'

'Yes, sir. We have oftentimes the honour to entertain your gentlemen in their travelling backwards and forwards betwixt London and Paris, sir. A vast deal of travelling, sir, in Tellson and Company's house.'

'Yes. We are quite a French house, as well as an English one.'

'Yes, sir. Not much in the habit of such travelling yourself, I think, sir?'

'Not of late years. It is fifteen years since we—since I—came last from France.'

'Indeed, sir? That was before my time here, sir. Before our people's time here, sir. The George was in other hands at that time, sir.'

'I believe so.'

'But I would hold a pretty wager, sir, that a House like Tellson and Company was flourishing, a matter of fifty, not to speak of fifteen years ago?'

'You might treble that, and say a hundred and fifty, yet not be far from the truth.'

'Indeed, sir!'

Rounding his mouth and both his eyes, as he stepped back from the table, the waiter shifted his napkin from his right arm to his left, dropped into a comfortable attitude, and stood surveying the guest while he ate and drank, as from an observatory or watch-tower. According to the immemorial usage of waiters in all ages.

When Mr. Lorry had finished his breakfast, he went out for a stroll on the beach. The little narrow, crooked town of Dover at that time hid itself away from the beach, and ran its head into the chalk cliffs, like a marine ostrich. The beach was a desert of heaps of sea and stones tumbling wildly about, and the sea did what it liked, and what it liked was destruction. It thundered at the town, and thundered at the cliffs, and brought the coast down, madly. The air among the houses was of so strong a piscatory flavour that one might have supposed sick fish went up to be dipped in it, as sick people went down to be dipped in the sea. A little fishing was done in the port, and a quantity of strolling about by night, and looking seaward—particularly at those times when the tide made, and was near flood. Small tradesmen, who did no business whatever, sometimes unaccountably realized large fortunes, and *it was remarkable that nobody in the neighbourhood could endure a lamplighter*. *

Mr. Lorry had got through the day, and had had his dinner, and had poured out his last glass of good claret—*with as complete an appearance of satisfaction as is ever to be found in an elderly gentleman of a fresh complexion who has got to the end of a bottle*—when a rattling of wheels came up the narrow street, and rumbled into the inn-yard.

'This is Mam'selle!' said he.

In a very few minutes the waiter came in, to announce that MISS MANETTE[1] had arrived from London, and would be happy to see the gentleman from Tellson's. * So, the gentleman from Tellson's followed the waiter to Miss Manette's apartment—a large, dark room, furnished in a funereal manner with black horsehair, * and lighted by two tall candles. He saw standing to receive him, a young lady of not more than seventeen, in a riding-cloak, and still holding her straw travelling hat by its ribbon, in her hand. His eyes rested on a short, slight, pretty figure, a quantity of golden hair, a pair of blue eyes that met his own with an inquiring look, and a forehead with a singular capacity (remembering how young and smooth it was), of lifting itself into an expression that was not quite one of perplexity, or wonder, or alarm, or merely of a bright fixed attention, though it included all the four expressions. *

'Pray take a seat, sir.' In a very clear and pleasant young voice: a little foreign in its accent, but a very little indeed.

'I kiss your hand, miss.'

'I received a letter from the Bank, sir, yesterday, in London, informing me that some new intelligence—or discovery——'

'The word is not material, miss; either word will do.'

'—respecting the small property of my poor father whom I never saw—so long dead—rendered it necessary that I should go to Paris, there to communicate with a gentleman of the Bank, so good as to be despatched to Paris for the purpose.'

'Myself.'

'As I was prepared to hear, sir.'

She curtseyed to him (young ladies made curtseys in those days), with a pretty desire to convey to him that she felt how much older and wiser he was than she. He made her another bow.

'I replied to the Bank, sir, that as it was considered necessary, by those who know, and who are so kind as to advise me, that I should go to France,

---

[1] Capitals thus in *Suzannet*. Probably Dickens, when preparing copy for the printer, had doubly underlined these words.

and that as I am an orphan and have no friend who could go with me, I should esteem it highly if I might be permitted to place myself, during the journey, under that worthy gentleman's protection. The gentleman had left London, but I think a messenger was sent after him to beg the favour of his waiting for me here.'

'I was happy, miss, to be intrusted with the charge.'

'Sir, I thank you very gratefully. It was told me by the Bank that the gentleman would explain to me the details of the business, and that I must prepare myself to find them of a surprising nature. I have done my best to prepare myself, and I naturally have a strong and eager interest to know what they are.'

'Naturally. Yes—I—It is very difficult to begin.'

He did not begin, but met her glance. The young forehead lifted itself into that singular expression—but it was pretty and characteristic, besides being singular—and she raised her hand.

'Are you quite a stranger to me, sir?'

'Am I not?'

He watched her as she mused, and, the moment she raised her eyes again, went on:

'In your adopted country, I presume, I cannot do better than address you as a young English lady, Miss Manette?'

'If you please, sir.'

'Miss Manette, I am a man of business. I have a business charge to acquit myself of. In your reception of it, don't heed me any more than if I was a speaking machine—truly, I am not much else. I will, with your leave, relate to you, miss, the story of one of our customers.'

'Story!'

He seemed wilfully to mistake the word she had repeated, when he added, 'Yes, customers; in the banking business we usually call our connexion our customers. He was a French gentleman; a scientific gentleman; a man of great acquirements—a Doctor.'

'Not of Beauvais?'

'Why, yes, of Beauvais. Like Monsieur Manette, your father, the gentleman was of Beauvais. Like Monsieur Manette, your father, the gentleman was of repute in Paris. I had the honour of knowing him there. Our relations were business relations, but confidential. I was at that time in our French House, and had been—oh! twenty years.'

'At that time—I may ask, at what time, sir?'

'I speak, miss, of twenty years ago. He married—an English lady—and I was one of the trustees. His affairs, like the affairs of many other French gentlemen and French families, were entirely in Tellson's hands. In a similar way, I am, or I have been, trustee of one kind or other for scores of our customers. I have passed from one to another, in the course of my business life, just as I pass from one of our customers to another in the course of my business day; in short, I have no feelings; I am a mere machine. To go on——'

'But this is my father's story, sir; and I begin to think that when I was left an orphan, through my mother's surviving my father only two years, it was you who brought me to England. I am almost sure it was you.'

[1] *Mr. Lorry took the little hand that confidingly advanced to take his, and put it with some ceremony to his lips.*

'Miss Manette, it *was*[2] I. And you will see how truly I spoke of myself just now, in saying I had no feelings, and that all the relations I hold with my fellow-creatures are mere business relations, when you reflect that I have never seen you since. No; you have been the ward of Tellson's House since, and I have been busy with the other business of Tellson's House since. Feelings! I have no time for them, no chance of them. I pass my whole life, miss, in turning an immense pecuniary Mangle.'

After this odd description of his daily routine of employment, Mr. Lorry flattened his wig upon his head with both hands (which was most[3] unnecessary, for nothing could be flatter than it was before), and resumed his former attitude.

'So far, miss (as you have remarked), this is the story of your regretted father. Now comes the difference. *If your father had not died when he did*[4] ——Don't be frightened! How you start!'

She did, indeed, start. *

'As I was saying—if Monsieur Manette had not died; if he had suddenly and silently disappeared; if he had been spirited away; if it had not been difficult to guess to what dreadful place, though no art could trace him; if he had had an enemy in some compatriot who could exercise a privilege that I in my own time have known the boldest people afraid to speak of in a whisper, across the water, there; for instance, the privilege of filling up blank forms for the consignment of any one to the oblivion of a prison for any length of time; if his wife had implored the king, the queen, the court, the clergy, for any tidings of him, and all quite in vain;— *then the history of your father would have been the history of this unfortunate gentleman, the Doctor of Beauvais.'*[5]

'I entreat you to tell me more, sir.'

'I will. I am going to. You can bear it?'

'I can bear anything but the uncertainty you leave me in at this moment.'

'You speak collectedly, and you—*are*[6] collected. That's good! A matter of business. Regard it as a matter of business—business that must be

[1] Marginal stage-direction *Kissing hand.*
[2] *was* italic in *Suzannet* and in the novel.
[3] Dickens here turned the page, and forgot to continue his underlining.
[4] Doubly underlined.
[5] Doubly underlined.
[6] *are* italic in *Suzannet* and in the novel.

done. Now, if this Doctor's wife, though a lady of great courage and spirit, had suffered so intensely from this cause before her little child was born——'

'The little child was a daughter, sir?'

'A daughter. A—a—matter of business—don't be distressed. Miss, if the poor lady had suffered so intensely before her little child was born, that she came to the determination of sparing the poor child the inheritance of any part of the agony *she* had known the pains of, *by rearing her in the belief that her father was dead*[1]——No, don't kneel! In Heaven's name why should you kneel to me!'

'For the truth. O dear, good, compassionate sir, for the truth!'

'A—a matter of business. You confuse me, and how can I transact business if I am confused? Let us be clear-headed. If you could kindly mention now, for instance, what nine times nine pence are, or how many shillings in twenty guineas, it would be so encouraging. I should be so much more at my ease about your state of mind.'

Without directly answering to this appeal, she sat so still when he had very gently raised her, and the hands that clasped his wrists were so much more steady than they had been, that she communicated some reassurance to Mr. Jarvis Lorry.

'That's right, that's right. Courage! Business! You have business before you; useful business. Miss Manette, your mother took this course with you. And when she died—I believe broken-hearted—having never slackened her unavailing search for your father, she left you, at two years old, to grow to be blooming, beautiful, and happy, without the dark cloud upon you of living in uncertainty whether your father soon wore his heart out in prison, or wasted there through many lingering years.'

As he said the words, he looked down, with admiring pity, on the flowing golden hair; as if he pictured to himself that it might have been already tinged with gray.[2]

'You know that your parents had no great possessions, and that what they had was secured to your mother and to you. There has been no new discovery of money, or of any other property; but——'

He felt his wrist held closer, and he stopped. The expression in the forehead had deepened into one of pain and horror.

'But he has been—been found. He is alive. Greatly changed, it is too probable; almost a wreck, it is possible; though we will hope the best. Still, alive. Your father has been taken to the house of an old servant in Paris, who now keeps a wine-shop in that city, and we are going there; *I*, to identify him, if I can; *you*[3], to restore him to life, love, duty, rest, comfort. * He has been found under another name; his own, long for-

---

[1] *she* and the following phrase both doubly underlined.

[2] Underlined singly until *admiring pity*, and doubly thereafter.

[3] *I* and *you* doubly underlined.

gotten or long concealed. It would be worse than useless now to inquire which; it would be dangerous. * But what is the matter! She doesn't notice a word! Miss Manette! Miss Manette!'

*Perfectly still and silent, and not even fallen back in her chair, she sat insensible, with her eyes open and fixed upon him, and with that last expression looking as if it were carved into her forehead. ***

CHAPTER II

A large cask of wine had been dropped and broken, in the street. The accident had happened in getting it out of a cart; the cask had tumbled out with a run, the hoops had burst, and it lay on the stones just outside the door of the wine-shop, shattered like a walnut-shell.

All the people within reach had suspended their business, or their idleness, to run to the spot and drink the wine. The rough irregular stones of the street had dammed it into little pools; and these were surrounded, each by its own jostling group or crowd, according to its size. * There was no drainage to carry off the wine, and not only did it all get taken up, but so much mud got taken up along with it, that one might have supposed there had been a scavenger in the street—if anybody acquainted with it could have believed in such a miraculous presence. *

The wine was red wine, and had stained the ground of the narrow street in the suburb of St. Antoine, in Paris, where it was spilled. It had stained many hands, too, and many faces, and many naked feet, and many wooden shoes. The hands of the man who sawed wood, left red marks on the billets; and the forehead of the woman who nursed her baby, was stained with the stain of the old rag she wound about her head again. Those who had been greediest, had acquired a tigerish smear about the mouth; and one tall joker so besmirched—his head more out of a long squalid bag of a nightcap than in it—scrawled upon a wall with his finger dipped in muddy wine lees—BLOOD.[1]

*The time was to come, when that wine too would be spilled on the street stones, and when the stain of it would be red upon many there. * But, the time was not come yet; and every wind that blew over France shook the rags of the scarecrow People in vain, for the birds, fine of song and feather, took no warning. ***

Monsieur Defarge, the wine-shop keeper, was a martial-looking dark man, with good eyes and a good bold breadth between them.* He rolled his eyes about his shop, until they rested upon an elderly gentleman and a young lady, who were seated in a corner. Other company were there: playing cards, playing dominoes, standing by the counter lengthening out a short supply of wine. He took notice that the elderly gentleman said in a look to the young lady, 'This is our man.'

[1] Capitals thus in *Suzannet* and in the novel.

'What the devil do *you*[1] do in that galley there!' said Monsieur Defarge to himself; 'I don't know you.' *

The elderly gentleman advanced and begged the favour of a word.

'Willingly, sir.' Monsieur Defarge stepped with him to the door.

Their conference was very short, but very decided. Almost at the first word, Monsieur Defarge started and became deeply attentive. It had not lasted a minute, when he nodded and went out. The gentleman then beckoned to the young lady, and they, too, went out.

Mr. Jarvis Lorry and Miss Manette, emerging from the wine-shop thus, joined Monsieur Defarge in a doorway opening from a nauseous little black court-yard, which was the general public entrance to a great pile of house, inhabited by a great number of people. In the gloomy tile-paved entry to the gloomy tile-paved staircase, Monsieur Defarge bent down on one knee to the child of his old master, and put her hand to his lips.

'It is very high; it is a little difficult. Better to begin slowly.' Thus, Monsieur Defarge, in a stern voice, to Mr. Lorry, as they began ascending the stairs.

'Is he alone?'

'Alone! God help him who should be with him!'

'Is he always alone, then?'

'Yes.'

'Of his own desire?'

'Of his own necessity. As he was, when I first saw him—after they found me and demanded to know if I would take charge of him, and, at my peril, be discreet—as he was then, so he is now.'

'He is greatly changed?'

'Changed!'

No direct answer could have been half so forcible. Mr. Lorry's spirits grew heavier and heavier, as he and his two companions ascended higher and higher. †

At last, high up, they stopped for the third time. There was yet an upper staircase to be ascended, before the garret story was reached. The keeper of the wine-shop, always going a little in advance, and always going on the side which Mr. Lorry took—as though he dreaded to be asked any question by the young lady—turned himself about here, and, carefully feeling in the pockets of the coat he carried over his shoulder, took out a key.

'The door is locked then, my friend?'

'Ay. Yes.'

'You think it necessary to keep the unfortunate gentleman so retired?'

'I think it necessary to turn the key.'

---

[1] *you* italic in *Suzannet* and in the novel.

'Why?'

'Why! Because he has lived so long, locked up, that he would be frightened—rave—tear himself to pieces—die—come to I know not what harm—if his door was left open.'

'Is it possible!'

'Is it possible? Yes. And a beautiful world we live in, when it *is*[1] possible, and when many other such things are possible, and not only possible, but done—done, see you!—under that sky there, every day. Long live the Devil. Let us go on.'

This dialogue had been held in so low a whisper, that not a word of it had reached the young lady's ears. But, by this time, she trembled under such strong emotion, and her face expressed such deep anxiety, and, above all, such terror, that Mr. Lorry felt it incumbent on him to speak a word of reassurance.

'Courage, dear miss! Courage! The worst will be over in a moment; it is but passing the room door, and the worst *is*[2] over. Then, all the good you bring to him, all the relief, all the happiness, you bring to him, begin. Let our good friend here assist you on that side. That's well, friend Defarge. Come, now. Business, business!'

[3] They went on slowly and softly, until they reached the top. There, * with a gesture to keep them back, Defarge stooped, and looked in through a crevice in the wall beside a door. Soon raising his head again,[4] he struck twice or thrice upon the door—evidently with no other object than to make a noise there. Then he put the key into the lock, and turned it as heavily as he could.

The door slowly opened inward under his hand, and he looked into the room and said something. A faint voice answered something. Little more than a single syllable could have been spoken on either side.

[5] He then looked back over his shoulder, and beckoned them to enter. †

The garret, built to be a dry depository for firewood and the like, was dim and dark: for, the window was in truth a door in the roof, with a little crane over it for the hoisting up of stores from the street: unglazed, and closing up the middle in two pieces, like any other door of French construction. To exclude the cold, one half of this door was fast closed, and the other was opened but a very little way. Such a scanty portion of light was admitted through these means, that it was difficult, on first coming in, to see anything; and long habit alone could have formed in any one, the ability to do work requiring nicety in such obscurity. Yet work of that kind was being done in the garret; for, with his back towards the door,

---

[1] *is* italic in *Suzannet* and in the novel.
[2] Doubly underlined.
[3] Marginal stage-direction *Dialogue ends*.
[4] Marginal stage-direction *Knocking*.
[5] Marginal stage-direction *Beckoning*.

and his face towards the window, where the keeper of the wine-shop stood looking at him, a white-haired man sat on a low bench, stooping forward and very busy, making shoes.

CHAPTER III

'Good day!' said Monsieur Defarge, looking down at the white head that bent low over the shoemaking.

The white head was raised for a moment, and a very faint voice responded to the salutation.

'Good day!'

'You are still hard at work, I see?'

[1]'Yes—I am working.'

The faintness of the voice was pitiable and dreadful. It was not the faintness of physical weakness, though confinement and hard fare no doubt had their part in it; its deplorable peculiarity was, that it was the faintness of solitude and disuse. It was like the last feeble echo of a sound made long and long ago. So entirely had it lost the life and resonance of the human voice, that it affected the senses like a once beautiful colour, faded away into a poor weak stain. So sunken and suppressed it was, that it was like a voice underground. So expressive it was, of a hopeless and lost creature, that a famished traveller, wearied out by wandering in a wilderness, might have remembered home and friends in such a tone before lying down to die.

'I want to let in a little more light here. You can bear a little more?'

'What did you say?'

'You can bear a little more light?'

'I must bear it, if you let it in.'

As the half-door was opened a little further and secured at that angle, a broad ray of light fell into the garret, and showed the workman, with an unfinished shoe upon his lap. His few common tools and various scraps of leather were at his feet and on his bench. He had a white beard raggedly cut, a hollow face, and exceedingly bright eyes. His yellow rags of shirt lay open at the throat, and showed his body to be withered and worn. He, and his old canvas frock, and his loose stockings, and all his poor tatters of clothes, had, in a long seclusion from light and air, faded down to such a dull uniformity of parchment-yellow, that it would have been hard to say which was which. *

'Are you going to finish that pair of shoes to-day?' asked Defarge, motioning to Mr. Lorry to come forward.

'What did you say?'

'Do you mean to finish that pair of shoes today?'

'I can't say that I mean to. I suppose so. I don't know.'

The question reminded him of his work, and he bent over it again.

[1] Marginal stage-direction *Sigh*.

Mr. Lorry came silently forward, leaving the daughter by the door.
When he had stood, for a minute or two, by the side of Defarge, the shoe-
maker looked up. He showed no surprise at seeing another figure, but the
unsteady fingers of one of his hands strayed to his lips as he looked at it (his
lips and his nails were of the same pale lead-colour), and then the hand
dropped to his work, and he once more bent over the shoe.
'You have a visitor, you see. Come! Here is monsieur, who knows a
well-made shoe when he sees one. Show him that shoe you are working at.
(Take it, monsieur.)'
Mr. Lorry took it in his hand.
'Tell monsieur what kind of shoe it is, and the maker's name.'
'I forget what it was you asked me. What did you say?'
'I said, couldn't you describe the kind of shoe, for monsieur's informa-
tion?'
'It is a lady's shoe. It is a young lady's walking-shoe. It is in the present
mode. I never saw the mode. I have had a pattern in my hand.' *He glanced*
at the shoe, with some passing touch of pride.
'*And the maker's name?*'
The task of recalling him from the vacancy into which he always sank
when he had spoken was like endeavouring, in the hope of some disclosure, to
stay the spirit of a fast-dying man.
'Did you ask me for my name?'
'Assuredly I did.'
'One Hundred and Five, North Tower.'
'Is that all?'
'One Hundred and Five, North Tower.'
[1] *With a weary sound that was not a sigh, nor a groan, he bent to work*
again, until the silence was again broken.
'You are not a shoemaker by trade?' said Mr. Lorry.
'I am not a shoemaker by trade? No, I was not a shoemaker by trade. I—
I learnt it here. I taught myself. I asked leave to—I asked leave to teach
myself, and I got it with much difficulty after a long while, and I have
made shoes ever since.'
As he held out his hand for the shoe that had been taken from him, Mr.
Lorry said:
'Monsieur Manette, do you remember nothing of me?'
The shoe dropped to the ground, and he sat looking fixedly at the questioner.
'Monsieur Manette;' *Mr. Lorry laid his hand upon Defarge's arm*; 'do
you remember nothing of this man? Look at him. Look at me. Is there no
old banker, no old business, no old servant, no old time, rising in your
mind, Monsieur Manette?' †
Darkness had fallen on him. He looked at the two, less and less atten-

---

[1] Marginal stage-direction *Moan.*

tively, and his eyes in gloomy abstraction sought the ground. Finally, with a deep long sigh, he took the shoe up, and resumed his work.

'Have you recognized him, monsieur?'

'Yes; for a moment. At first I thought it quite hopeless, but I have unquestionably seen, for a single moment, the face that I once knew well. Hush! Let us draw further back. Hush!'

She had moved from the wall of the garret, very near to the bench on which he sat. There was something awful in his unconsciousness of the figure that could have put out its hand and touched him as he stooped over his labour.

Not a word was spoken, not a sound was made. She stood, like a spirit, beside him, and he bent over his work.[1]

It happened, at length, that he had occasion to change the instrument in his hand, for his shoemaker's knife, which lay on that side of him which was *not* the side on which she stood. He had taken it up, and was stooping to work again, when his eyes caught the skirt of her dress. He raised them, and saw her face. The two spectators started forward, but she stayed them with a motion of her hand. S*he* had no fear of his striking at her with the knife, though *they* had. [2]

'What is this!'

With the tears streaming down her face, she put her two hands to her lips, and kissed them to him; then clasped them on her breast, as if she laid his ruined head there.

'You are not the gaoler's daughter?'

'No.'

'Who are you?'

Not yet trusting the tones of her voice, she sat down on the bench beside him and laid her head upon his arm. He[3] *laid the knife down softly, as he sat staring at her.*

Her golden hair, which she wore in long curls, had been hurriedly pushed aside, and fell down over her neck. Advancing his hand by little and little, he took it up, and looked at it. He laid down his work, put his hand to his neck, and took off a blackened string with a scrap of folded rag attached. He opened this, carefully, on his knee, and it contained a very little quantity of hair—not more than one or two long golden hairs, which he had, in some old day, wound off upon his finger.

'She had laid her head upon my shoulder, that night when I was summoned out—she had a fear of my going, though I had none—and when I was brought to the North Tower they found these upon my sleeve. "You will leave me them? They can never help me to escape in the body, though they may in the spirit." Those were the words I said. I remember them very well. How was this?—*Was it you?*'[4]

---

[1] *She* and *he* doubly underlined.   [2] *She* and *they* doubly underlined.
[3] *He* doubly underlined.   [4] *Was it you?* italic in *Suzannet* and in the novel.

She sat perfectly still in his grasp, and only said, 'I entreat you, good gentlemen, do not come near us, do not speak, do not move!'

'No, no, no; you are too young, too blooming. It can't be. See what the prisoner is. These are not the hands she knew, this is not the face she knew, this is not a voice she ever heard. No, no. She was—and He was—before the slow years of the North Tower—ages ago. What is your name, my gentle angel?'

She fell upon her knees before him, with her appealing hands upon his breast.

'O, sir, at another time you shall know my name, and who my mother was, and who my father, and how I never knew their hard, hard history. But I cannot tell you at this time, and I cannot tell you here. All that I may tell you, here and now, is, that I pray to you to touch me and to bless me. Kiss me, kiss me! O my dear, my dear!'

His cold white head mingled with her radiant hair, which warmed and lighted it as though it were the light of Freedom shining on him.

'If you hear in my voice—I don't know that it is so, but I hope it is—if you hear in my voice any resemblance to a voice that once was sweet music in your ears, weep for it, weep for it! If you touch, in touching my hair, anything that recalls a beloved head that lay in your breast when you were young and free, weep for it, weep for it! If, when I hint to you of a Home there is before us, where I will be true to you with all my duty and with all my faithful service, I bring back the remembrance of a Home long desolate, while your poor heart pined away, weep for it, weep for it!'

She held him closer round the neck, and rocked him on her breast like a child.

'If, when I tell you, dearest dear, that your agony is over, and that I have come here to take you from it, and that we go to England to be at peace and at rest, I cause you to think of your useful life laid waste, and of our native France, so wicked to you, weep for it, weep for it! And if, when I shall tell you of my name, and of my father who is living, and of my mother who is dead, you learn that I have to kneel to my honoured father, and implore his pardon for having never for his sake striven all day and lain awake and wept all night, because the love of my poor mother hid his torture from me, weep for it, weep for it! Weep for her, then, and for me! Good gentlemen, thank God! I feel his sacred tears upon my face, and his sobs strike against my heart. O, see! Thank God for us, thank God!'

[1]He had sunk in her arms, with his face dropped on her breast: a sight so touching, yet so terrible in the tremendous wrong and suffering which had gone before it, that the two beholders covered their faces.

[2]When the quiet of the garret had been long undisturbed, and his heaving breast and shaken form had yielded to the calm that must follow all

---

[1] Marginal stage-direction *Dialogue ends.*   [2] Marginal stage-direction *Low.*

storms—*emblem to humanity, of the rest and silence into which the storm called Life must hush at last*—they came forward to raise the father and daughter from the ground. *He*[1] had gradually drooped to the floor, and lay there in a lethargy, worn out. *She* had nestled down with him, that his head might lie upon her arm; and her hair drooping over him curtained him from the light.

THE END OF THE READING

[1] *He* and the *She* of the next sentence both doubly underlined.

MR. CHOPS, THE DWARF

Mr. Chops the Dwarf was prepared during the summer of 1861 (see above, p. 213), from the story 'Going into Society' which Dickens had contributed to the *Household Words* Christmas Number for 1858, *A House to Let*. The prompt-copy was printed in the volume containing also *Bardell and Pickwick* and *Mr. Bob Sawyer's Party* (see above, p. 195). Dickens made only a few abbreviations and rearrangements of the *Household Words* text before having the prompt-copy printed. He subsequently worked over the text, not very intensively, adding or deleting a sentence here and there, and underlining passages for emphasis. Only one ink is used, except in the emendation of one passage, so probably most of this work was done at one period. Two minor curiosities about the adaptation may be mentioned. In the prompt-copy, *ain't* is consistently spelt *aint* (*Household Words* always has *an't*). Other such contractions have the normal apostrophes. Perhaps Dickens was trying to suggest some trick of pronunciation by deleting these apostrophes, but it is difficult to imagine what. In the narrative, he was in two minds about Mr. Chops's unhappy love-life and jealous feelings towards his successful rival, the Red Indian. Among the few omissions and deletions are some amusing details about this (*Christmas Stories*, pp. 214, 215): but the Readings passage about the canvas depicting the Fat Lady is a manuscript addition, and Mr. Chops's eventual forgiveness of the loving couple is a manuscript expansion of the original text (below, pp. 297, 303).

Of the new items prepared that summer, only *Copperfield* and *Nickleby* were immediately introduced into the repertoire of the ensuing 1861–2 tour. *Bob Sawyer* was kept in reserve until after Christmas, *The Bastille Prisoner* and *Great Expectations* were never performed, and *Mr. Chops* apparently remained un-performed for some years. Its first performance seems to have been given during the Farewell tour, in Liverpool on 28 October 1868. It was repeated twice in London in the ensuing months—and that ended its brief career except that, surprisingly, Dickens chose to read it twice again during the dozen London Farewell performances in 1870. So after waiting seven years to be given at all, it remained among the three least-often performed items in the repertoire.

It is quite an amusing character-monologue, as Mr. Emlyn Williams has lately shown (see his shorter version, in his *Readings from Dickens* (1954), pp. 26–34). Dickens was always fascinated by circuses, show-people, freaks, patterers of various kinds, and this story is a genial if mildly satirical evocation of the lower reaches of show-business and of 'society'. His correspondence is silent about *Mr. Chops*, after the mention of its being devised in 1861, so one can only sur-mise why he read it so little. Perhaps he felt that, as a character-monologue, it did not match such favourites as *Boots* and *Marigold*, while as a comic anecdote it was both slighter and less amusing than the *Trial*, *Bob Sawyer*, and other afterpieces. It has more vitality, however, than *The Boy at Mugby*, another item to which he never became attached, though it was given more performances.

His rendering of *Mr. Chops* was memorable, at least for one intelligent witness. Some years after Dickens's death, Frank T. Marzials was recalling the Readings —'there are tones of the reader's voice that still linger in my ears!'—and he cited four examples. Three of these were crucial and widely-praised moments from the most esteemed items in the repertoire, the *Carol* and *Sikes and Nancy*. Unpredictably, the fourth was from *Mr. Chops*:

> As of old I listen to poor little Chops, the dwarf, declaring very piteously, that his 'fashionable friends' don't use him well, and put him on the mantel-piece when he refuses to 'have in more champagne-wine', and lock him in the sideboard when he 'won't give up his property'. (*Life of Charles Dickens* (1887), p. 125)

Charles Kent's account is less enchanted, and gives more credit to the reader than to the author: as 'rattled through by Dickens, the laughter awakened seems now in retrospect to have been altogether out of proportion' (p. 189).

This is one of the items of minor Dickens which Mr. Emlyn Williams has revived, with success: see his *Readings from Dickens* (1954), pp. 26–34, and hear his rendering in the album *Emlyn Williams as Charles Dickens* (Decca LXT 5295–6). On Dickens's selection of items, and on his textual policies and his performance, Mr. Williams has commented interestingly in his prefatory Note to that collection and, more fully, in his essay 'Dickens and the Theatre' contributed to *Charles Dickens 1812–1870*, ed. E. W. F. Tomlin (1970), pp. 177–95.

Mr. Chops's friend Normandy is described, in Mr. Williams's version, as an 'assistant decoy-duck' at a gaming booth—a justifiable gloss on Dickens's term 'Bonnet' (below, p. 300) for members of a modern audience unversed in the slang of Victorian roguery. Readers anxious for a more precise notion of a *bonnet* (in this sense) may welcome the *OED* definition: 'a pretended player at a gaming-table . . . secretly in league with the proprietor . . . to lure others to play'. As his avocation suggests, and the narrative proves, Normandy is not a man to be relied upon.

Mr. Chops, The Dwarf

ONCE upon a time there was a certain house to let, and it was necessary to make many inquiries concerning the house.[1] In particular it was important to know why the old tenants had all left it. *At one period it had been occupied by a showman, by name Mr. Magsman*[2]—Mr. Magsman being found out was asked if he would object to state why *he* left the house? He said, 'Not at all. Why should he? He left it along of a Dwarf.'

Might it be compatible with Mr. Magsman's inclination and convenience, to enter, as a favour, into a few particulars?

Mr. Magsman entered into the following particulars.

It was a long time ago, to begin with;—afore lotteries and a deal more, was done away with, I was a looking about for a good pitch, and I see that house, and I says to myself, 'I'll have you, if you're to be had. If money'll get you, I'll have you.'

The neighbours cut up rough, and made complaints; but I don't know what they *would*[3] have had. It was a lovely exhibition. The ole outside of the house was covered with painting. First of all, there was the canvass, representin *the picter of the giant*[4] who was himself the heighth of the house, and was run up with a line and pulley to a pole on the roof, so that his Ed was coeval with the parapet. Then, there was the canvass, representing *the picter of the Albina lady*, shewing her white air to the Army and Navy in correct uniform. Then, there was the canvass representin *the picter of the Wild Indian* a scalpin a member of some foreign nation. Then there was the canvas representing the fat lady from Norfolk in a plaid frock and sash several yards round. Then, there was the canvass, representing the *picter of a child of a British Planter*, seized by two Boa Constrictors—*not that we*[5] *never had no child, nor no Constrictors neither*. Similarly, there was the canvass, representing *the picter of the Wild Ass of the Prairies—not that we*[5] *never had no wild asses, nor wouldn't have had 'em at a gift.* Last, there was the canvass, *representin the picter of the Dwarf*, and like him too (considerin), with George the Fourth in such a state of astonishment

---

[1] The opening sentences are a summary of the initial situation in the *Household Words* (*HW*) story.

[2] Doubly underlined.

[3] *would* italic in *Suzannet* and in *HW*.

[4] This and other phrases in this paragraph about other *picters* are all doubly underlined. The *not that we never had . . .* phrases are underlined singly.

[5] *we* italic in *Suzannet* and in *HW*

at him as His Majesty couldn't with his utmost politeness and stoutness express. †

The Dwarf was wrote up as Major Tpschoffki, of the Imperial Bulgraderian Brigade. Nobody couldn't pronounce the name, and it never was intended as anybody should. The public always turned it, as a regular rule, into Chopski. In the line he was called Chops; partly on that account, and partly because his real name, if he ever had any real name (which was very dubious), was Stakes.

He was a un-common small man, he really was. *Certainly, not so small as he was made out to be, but where is*[1] *your Dwarf as is?* He was a most uncommon small man with a most uncommon large Ed; and what he had inside that Ed, nobody never knowed but himself.

The kindest little man as never growed! Spirited, but not proud. When he travelled with the Spotted Baby—though he knowed hisself to be a nat'ral Dwarf, and knowed the Baby's spots to be put upon him artificial, he nursed that Baby like a mother. You never heerd him give a ill-name to a Giant. He *did*[2] allow himself to break out into strong language respectin the Fat Lady from Norfolk; *but that was an affair of the 'art; and when a man's 'art has been trifled with by a lady, and the preference giv to a Indian, he aint master of his actions.*

He was always in love, of course; every human nat'ral phenomenon is. And he was always in love with a large woman; I[3] *never knowed the Dwarf as could be got to love a small one. Which helps to keep 'em the Curiosities they are.*

One sing'ler idea he had in that Ed of his, which must have meant something, or it wouldn't have been there. It was always his opinion that he was entitled to property. He never would put his name to anything. He had been taught to write, by the young man without arms, who got his living by writing with his toes, but Chops would have starved to death, afore he'd have gained a bit of bread by putting his hand to a paper. This is the more curious to bear in mind, because HE[4] had no property, nor hope of property, except his house and a sarser. When I say his house, I mean the box, painted and got up outside like a reg'lar six-roomer, that he used to creep into, with a diamond ring (*or quite as good to look at*) on his forefinger, and ring a little bell out of what the Public believed to be the Drawing-room winder. And when I say a sarser, I mean a Chaney sarser in which he made a collection for hisself at the end of every Entertainment. His cue for that, he took from me: 'Ladies and gentlemen, the little man will now walk three times round the Cairawan, and retire behind the curtain.' When he said anything important, in private life, he

---

[1] *is* italic in *Suzannet* and in *HW*.
[2] *did* italic in *Suzannet* and in *HW*.
[3] *I* italic in *Suzannet* and in *HW*.
[4] Small capitals in *Suzannet* and in *HW*.

mostly wound it up with this form of words, and they was generally the
last thing he said to me at night afore he went to bed.

He had what I consider a fine mind—a poetic mind. His ideas respectin
his property, never come upon him so strong as when he sat upon a
barrel-organ and had the handle turned. Arter the wibration had run
through him a little time, he would screech out, 'Toby, I feel my property
coming—grind away! Toby, I feel the Mint a jingling in me, Toby,
and I'm a swelling out into the Bank of England!' Such is the influence
of music on a poetic mind. *Not that he was partial to any other music but a
barrel-organ; on the contrairy, hated it.*

He had a kind of everlasting grudge agin the Public: *which is a thing
you may notice in many phenomenons that get their living out of it.* What
riled him most, in the natur of his occupation was, that it kep him out of
Society. He was continiwally sayin to me, 'Toby, my ambition is, to go
into Society. The curse of my position towards the Public is, that it keeps
me hout of Society. This don't signify to a low beast of a Indian; he aint
formed for Society. This don't signify to a Spotted Baby; *he*[1] aint formed
for Society.—I am.'

Nobody never could make out what Chops done with his money. He
had a good salary, down on the drum every Saturday as the day come
round, besides having the run of his teeth—*and he was a Woodpecker to
eat—but all Dwarfs are.* And the sarser was a little income, bringing him
in so many halfpence that he'd carry 'em, for a week together, tied up in a
pocket handkercher. And yet he never had money.

Most unexpected, the mystery come out one day at Egham Races.
Chops was a ringin his little bell out of his drawing-room winder, with
his legs out at the back-door—for he couldn't be shoved into his house
without kneeling down, and the premises wouldn't accommodate his legs
—when a man in the crowd holds up a carrier-pigeon, and cries out, 'If
there's any person here as has got a ticket, the Lottery's just drawed, and
the number as has come up for the great prize is three, seven, forty-two!
Three, seven, forty-two!' I was giving the man to the Furies myself, for
calling off the Public's attention, when I see Chops's little bell fly out of
winder at a old lady, and he gets up and kicks his box over, exposin the
whole secret, and he catches hold of the calves of my legs and he says to
me, 'Carry me into the wan, Toby, and throw a pail of water over me or
I'm a dead man, for I've come into my property!'

Twelve thousand odd hundred pound, was Mr. Chops's winnins. He
had bought a half-ticket for the twenty-five thousand prize, and it had
come up.

Arter he had been mad for a week, Mr. Chops come round, and be-
haved liberal and beautiful to all. He then sent for a young man he knowed,

---

[1] *he* italic in *Suzannet* and in *HW*.

as had a wery genteel appearance and was a Bonnet at a gaming-booth (most respectable brought up, father having been imminent in the livery stable line but unfort'nate in a commercial crisis through painting a old grey, ginger-bay, and sellin him with a Pedigree), and Mr. Chops said to this Bonnet, who said his name was Normandy, which it warn't:

'Normandy, I'm a goin into Society. Will you go with me?'

Says Normandy: 'Do I understand you, Mr. Chops, to hintimate that the 'ole of the expenses of that move will be borne by yourself?'

'Correct,' says Mr. Chops. 'And you shall have a Princely allowance too.'

The Bonnet lifted Mr. Chops upon a chair, to shake hands with him, and replied in poetry, with his eyes seemingly full of tears:

> 'My boat is on the shore,
> And my bark is on the sea,
> And I do not ask for more,
> But I'll Go;—along with thee.'

They went into Society, in a chay and four greys with silk jackets. They took lodgings in Pall Mall, London, and they blazed away.

In consequence of a note that was brought to Bartlemy Fair in the autumn of next year by a servant, most wonderful got up in milk-white cords and tops, I cleaned myself and went to Pall Mall, one evenin appinted. The gentlemen was at their wine arter dinner, and Mr. Chops's eyes was more fixed in that Ed of his than I though good for him. There was three of 'em (not his eyes—in company, I mean), and I knowed the third well. *When last met, he had on a white Roman shirt, and a bishop's-mitre covered with leopard-skin, and played the clarionet all wrong, in a band at a Wild Beast Show.*

This gent took on not to know me, and Mr. Chops said: 'Gentlemen, this is a old friend of former days:' and Normandy looked at me through a eye-glass, and said, 'Magsman, glad to see you!'—which I'll take my oath he warn't. Mr. Chops, to get him convenient to the table, had his chair on a throne, much of the form of George the Fourth's in the canvass. They was all dressed like May-Day—goregous!—and as to Wine they swam in all sorts.

I made the round of the bottles, first separate (to say I had done it), and then mixed 'em all together (to say I had done it), and then tried two of 'em as half-and-half, and then t'other two. Altogether, I passed a pleasin evenin, but with a tendency to feel muddled, until I considered it good manners to get up and say, 'Mr. Chops, the best of friends must part. I thank you for the wariety of foreign drains you have stood so 'ansome, I looks towards you in red wine, and I takes my leave.' Mr. Chops replied, 'If you'll just hitch me out of this over your right arm, Magsman, and carry me down stairs, I'll see you out.' I said I couldn't think of such a thing, but he would have it, so I lifted him off his throne. He smelt strong of Maideary, and I couldn't help thinking as I carried him down that it was like carrying a large bottle full of wine, with a rayther ugly stopper, a good deal out of proportion.

When I set him on the door-mat in the hall, he kep me close to him by holding on to my coat collar, and he whispers:

'I aint appy, Magsman.'

'What's on your mind, Mr. Chops?'

'They don't use me well. They aint grateful to me. They puts me on the mantelpiece when I won't have in more Champagne-wine, and they locks me in the sideboard when I won't give up my property.'

'Get rid of 'em, Mr. Chops.'

'I can't. We're in Society together, and what would Society say?'

'Come out of Society.'

'I can't. You don't know what you're talking about. You're a good feller, but you don't understand. Good night, go along. Magsman, the little man will now walk three times round the Cairawan, and retire behind the curtain.' The last I see of him on that occasion was his trying, on the extremest werge of insensibility, to climb up the stairs, one by one, with his hands and knees.

It warn't long after that, as I read in the newspaper of Mr. Chops's being presented at court. It was printed, 'It will be recollected'—*and I've noticed in my life, that it is sure to be printed that it will*[1] *be recollected, whenever it won't*—'that Mr. Chops is the indiwidual of small stature, whose brilliant success in the last State Lottery attracted so much attention.' Well, I says to myself, Such is life! He has been and done it in earnest at last! He has astonished George the Fourth!

(*On account of which, I had that canvass new-painted; him with a bag of money in his hand, a presentin it to George the Fourth; and a lady in Ostrich Feathers fallin in love with him in a bag-wig, sword, and buckles correct.*)

I took the House as is the subject of present inquiries, and I run Magsman's Amusements in it thirteen months—sometimes one thing, sometimes another, *sometimes nothin particular, but always all the canvasses outside.* One night, when we had played the last company out, which it was a shy company through its raining heavens hard, I was takin a pipe in the one pair back along with the young man with the toes, *which I had taken on for a month (though he never drawed—except on paper),* and I heard a kickin at the street door. '*Halloa!*' I says to the young man, 'what's up!' He rubs his eyebrows with his toes, and he says, 'I can't imagine, Mr. Magsman'—*which that young man never could imagine nothin, and was monotonous company.*

The noise not leavin off, I laid down my pipe, and I took up a candle,

---

[1] *will* italic in *Suzannet* and in *HW*.

and I went down and opened the door. I looked out into the street; but nothin could I see, and nothin was I aware of, until I turned round quick, because some creetur run between my legs into the passage. There was Mr. Chops!

'Magsman,' he says, 'take me, on the hold terms, and you've got me; if it's done, say done!'

I was all of a maze, but I said, 'Done, sir.'

'Done to your done, and double done!' says he. 'Have you got a bit of supper in the house?'

Bearin in mind them sparklin warieties of foreign drains as we'd guzzled away at in Pall Mall, I was ashamed to offer him cold sassages and gin-and-water; but he took 'em both and took 'em free.

It was arter he had made a clean sweep of the sassages (beef, and to the best of my calculations two pound and a quarter), that the wisdom as was in that little man, began to come out of him like prespiration.

'Magsman,' he says, 'look upon me! You see afore you, One as has both gone into Society and come out.'

'Oh! You *are*[1] out of it, Mr. Chops? How did you get out, sir?'

'SOLD OUT!' says he. You never saw the like of the wisdom as his Ed expressed, when he made use of them two words.

'My friend Magsman, I'll impart to you a discovery I've made. It's wallable; it's cost twelve thousand five hundred pound; it may do you good in life.—The secret of this matter is, that it aint so much that a person goes into Society, as that Society goes into a person. Magsman, Society has gone into me, to the tune of every penny of my property.'

I felt that I went pale, and though nat'rally a bold speaker, I couldn't hardly say, 'Where's Normandy?'

'Bolted. With the plate,' said Mr. Chops.

'And t'other one?' meaning him as formerly wore the bishop's mitre.

'Bolted. With the jewels,' said Mr. Chops.

I sat down and looked at him, and he stood up and looked at me.

'Magsman,' he says, and he seemed to myself to get wiser as he got hoarser; 'Society, taken in the lump, is all dwarfs. At the court of St. James's they was all a doin my hold business—all a goin three times round the Cairawan, in the hold Courtsuits and properties. Elsewheres, they was most of 'em ringing their little bells out of make-believes. Everywheres, the sarser was a goin round. Magsman, the sarser is the uniwersal Institution!'

I perceived, you understand, that he was soured by his misfortuns, and I felt for Mr. Chops.

'As to Fat Ladies,' says he, *giving his Ed a tremendious one agin the wall*, 'there's lots of *them*[2] in Society. Lay in Cashmeer shawls, buy bracelets,

---

[1] *are* italic, and SOLD OUT (in the next speech) in small capitals, in *Suzannet* and in *HW*.   [2] *them* italic in *Suzannet* and in *HW*.

strew 'em and a lot of 'andsome fans and things about your rooms, let it
be known that you give away like water to all as come to admire, and the
Fat Ladies that don't exhibit for so much down upon the drum, will
come from all the pints of the compass to flock about you. And when
you've no more left to give they'll laugh at you to your face, and leave you
to have your bones picked dry by Wulturs, like the dead Wild Ass of the
prairies that you deserve to be !' *Here he giv himself a most tremendious
one, and dropped.*

I thought he was gone. His Ed was so heavy, and he knocked it so hard,
and he fell so stoney, *and the sassagerial disturbance in him must have
been so immense,* that I thought he was gone. But he soon come round
with care, and he sat up on the floor, and he reached out his poor little
hand, and his tears dropped down on the moustachios *which it was a credit
to him to have done his best to grow, but it is not in mortals to command
success.* 'Magsman,' he says, 'give me out through the trumpet, in the
hold way, to-morrow.'

Arter that, he slid into the line again as easy as if he had been iled all
over. But the organ was kep from him, and no allusions was ever made,
when a company was in, to his property.

He took well, and pulled 'em in most excellent for nine weeks. At the
expiration of that period, when his Ed was a sight, he expressed one evenin,
the last Company havin been turned out, and the door shut, a wish to have
a little music.

'Mr. Chops,' I said (*I*[1] *never dropped the 'Mr.' with him; the world
might do it, but not me*); 'Mr. Chops, are you sure as you are in a state of
mind and body to sit upon the organ?'

His answer was this: 'Toby, I am. And when next met with on the
tramp, I forgive a certain developed party from Norfolk, and also a
certain foreign member of the scalping persuasion.'

It was with fear and trembling that I began to turn the handle; but he
sat like a lamb. It will be my belief to my dying day, that I see his Ed
expand as he sat; you may therefore judge how great his thoughts was. He
sat out all the changes, and then he come off.

'Toby,' he says, with a quiet smile, 'the little man will now walk
three times round the Cairawan, and retire behind the curtain.'

When we called Mr. Chops in the morning, we found him gone into a
much better Society that either mine or Pall Mall's. I giv Mr. Chops as
comfortable a funeral as lay in my power, I followed myself as Chief, and I
had the George the Fourth canvass carried first, in the form of a banner.
But, the House was so dismal arterwards, that I giv it up, and I took to the
Wan again.

THE END OF MR. CHOPS, THE DWARF

[1] *I* underlined doubly, the rest singly.

GREAT EXPECTATIONS

DICKENS finished writing the novel *Great Expectations* in June 1861. In a letter to Forster later that summer (see above, p. 213) he mentioned four new items he was devising for his new series of Readings due to start that October. Neither there, nor, it would seem, anywhere else does he mention a *Great Expectations* Reading, but this is the most likely period for its having been devised. It was never performed. At least two copies of the privately printed text are extant, in the Berg and Gimbel collections: *Great Expectations. | A Reading. | In Three Stages. | Privately Printed* (printed by William Clowes and Sons, London; text paginated 3–160). Neither copy contains any manuscript alterations or notes. It is possible that another copy of this Reading (and of *Mrs. Lirriper* and *The Signalman*, the other two unperformed Readings, the privately-printed texts of which contain no manuscript alterations) will come to light which do contain Dickens's alterations, and would thus be the true, though unperformed, prompt-copy. This, however, is unlikely. Probably in all these cases Dickens decided, when he contemplated his privately printed text, that—for one reason or another—he would not perform it, so would not embark on the considerable labour of rehearsing and emending it.

He had, however, gone to great pains to prepare the privately printed text of the *Great Expectations* Reading. He departed from his usual practice when creating a Reading out of one of his novels, which had been either to take a single episode or short span of the narrative, or to centre the Reading on one prominent character (as in *Mrs. Gamp*). Instead, the *Great Expectations* Reading attempts to narrate the whole of one of the central plots, from ch. 1 to ch. 56, besides including some of the incidental delights of the novel (such as Wemmick, the Aged P., and Miss Skiffins) which are not strictly relevant to that plot. The result is quite impressive, though too long for even a two-hour performance such as *David Copperfield* was when it first came into Dickens's repertoire in 1861. He could, however, have reduced the text to a more manageable length, had he persisted; at nearly 160 pages, it was not so very much longer than the *Copperfield* text, which was over 120 pages before he began cutting it. Charles Kent's regret (p. 90) that Dickens did not attempt the task seems justified; this script contains some excellent narrative and character possibilities.

Dickens's most obvious economy, in creating even so lengthy a Reading out of the complete novel, was to omit Pip's love-life entirely. Neither Biddy nor Estella is ever mentioned. Inevitably, many other characters and episodes are omitted—Orlick, Trabb's boy, Drummle, the Barleys, and others. The narrative runs from Pip's first meeting with Magwitch in the churchyard to Magwitch's death in prison. The three 'stages' into which the Reading is divided do not correspond to the three 'stages' of the novel. The 'First Stage. Pip's Childhood' is an abbreviated version of chs. 1–7 (omitting the short ch. 6); beginning as the novel does, it ends with Pip's setting off for Satis House for the first time. The 'Second Stage. Pip's Minority' begins with his visits to Miss Havisham, from chs. 8, 11, 12, and 13; here and elsewhere in the Reading, passages from several episodes in the novel are conflated into one continuous episode. A brief extract from Chapter 14 then acts as a bridge to Pip's hearing from Mr. Jaggers about his 'great expectations' and his departure from the Forge (chs. 18–19). The rest of this 'Stage' deals with Pip's life in Barnard's Inn with Herbert Pocket (chs. 21, 22, 27, and 34), his coming of age (ch. 36), and his visit to Wemmick's 'castle' at Walworth (chs. 25 and 37). The 'Third Stage. Pip's Majority' starts with Magwitch's re-entering the story (chs. 39–43) and then jumps to his unsuccessful attempt to escape from England (chs. 54–6).

The Reading ends, as ch. 56 does, with Pip's prayer for Magwitch: 'O Lord, be merciful to him, a sinner!' This misquotation from the New Testament has been regarded, by some recent commentators, as deliberate (on Dickens's part); Pip thus appears, ironically, as more Pharisee-like than truly charitable or humble. Dickens's choosing to end his Reading on this prayer surely confirms, however, one's suspicion that this interpretation is over-ingenious. Clearly it was not Dickens's intention that this massive Reading should end on an ironical or ambivalent note.

Great Expectations

FIRST STAGE

Pip's Childhood

My father's family name being Pirrip, and my christian name Philip, my infant tongue could make of both names nothing longer than Pip. So I called myself Pip, and I came to be called Pip.

I give my family name on the authority of the family tombstones and of my sister—Mrs. Joe Gargery, who married the blacksmith. * The tombstones recorded that Philip Pirrip, late of this parish, was dead and buried, and also Georgiana, wife of the above. But my childish construction even of their simple meaning was not very correct, for I read 'Wife of the Above' as a complimentary reference to my father's exaltation to a better world: and if any of my deceased relatives had been referred to as 'Below,' I have no doubt I should have formed the worst opinions of that member of the family.

Ours was the marsh country, down by the river, within twenty miles of the sea. My first most vivid impression of the identity of things, seems to me to have been gained on a memorable raw winter's afternoon towards evening. At such a time I found out for certain, that the bleak place overgrown with nettles, into which I had wandered alone, was the churchyard; and that the dark flat wilderness beyond the churchyard, intersected with dykes and mounds and gates, with cattle feeding on it, was the marshes; and that the low leaden line beyond, was the river; and that the distant lair from which the wind was rushing, was the sea; and that the small bundle of shivers growing afraid of it all and beginning to cry, was myself.

'Hold your noise!' cried a terrible voice, as a man started up from among the graves at the side of the church porch. 'Keep still, you little devil, or I'll cut your throat!'

A fearful man, all in coarse grey, with a great iron on his leg. A man with no hat, and with broken shoes, and with an old rag tied round his head. A man who had been soaked in water, and smothered in mud, and lamed by stones, and cut by flints, and stung by nettles, and torn by briars; a man who limped and shivered, and glared and growled; and whose teeth chattered in his head as he seized me by the chin.

'O! Don't cut my throat, sir,' I pleaded in terror. 'Pray don't do it, sir.'

'Show us where you live. Pint out the place!'

I pointed to where our village lay, on the flat in-shore, among the alder-trees and pollards; a mile or more from the church. *

'Now then, lookee here!' said the man, seating me on a high tombstone. 'Where's your mother?'

'There, sir!'

He started, made a short run, and stopped and looked over his shoulder. 'There, sir! Also Georgiana. That's my mother.'

'Oh! And is that your father alonger your mother?'

'Yes, sir; him too; late of this parish.'

'Ha! Who d'ye live with—supposin' you're kindly let to live, which I han't made up my mind about?'

'My sister, sir—Mrs. Joe Gargery—wife of Joe Gargery, the black-smith, sir.'

'Blacksmith, eh?' said he. And looked down at his leg. 'Now lookee here, the question being, whether you're to be let to live. You know what a file is.'

'Yes, sir.'

'And you know what wittles is.'

'Yes, sir.'

After each question he tilted me over, as I sat perched on the high tombstone; so as to give me a greater sense of helplessness and danger. 'You get me a file.' He tilted me again. 'And you get me wittles.' He tilted me again. 'You bring 'em both to me.' He tilted me again. 'Or I'll have your heart and liver out.' He tilted me again. 'You bring me, to-morrow morning early, that file and them wittles. You bring the lot to me at that old Battery over yonder. You do it, and you never dare to say a word nor dare to make a sign concerning your having seen such a person as me, or any person sumever, and you shall be let to live. You fail, or you go from my words in any partickler, no matter how small, and your heart and your liver shall be tore out, roasted and ate. * Now, what do you say?'

I said that, under those circumstances, I would certainly get him the file,[1] and I would get him what broken bits of food I could, and I would come to him at the Battery early in the morning.

'Say Lord strike you dead if you don't!'

I said so, and he took me down. I set my face towards home, and made the best use of my legs. But presently I looked over my shoulder, and saw him going on towards the river. The marshes were just a long black hori-zontal line then; and the river was just another horizontal line, not nearly so broad nor yet so black; and the sky was just a row of long angry red lines and dense black lines intermixed. On the edge of the river I could faintly make out the only two black things in all the prospect that seemed

---

[1] 'under those circumstances' and 'certainly' are not in the novel. There are many other such small alterations to the novel text; they will not normally be noted.

to be standing upright; one of these was the beacon by which the ships steered—like an unhooped cask upon a pole—an ugly thing when you were near it—the other, a gibbet with some chains hanging to it which had once held a pirate. The man was limping on towards this latter, as if he were the pirate come to life and come down, and going back to hook himself up again. It gave me a terrible turn when I thought so; and as I saw the cattle lifting their heads to gaze after him, I wondered whether they thought so too. But now I was frightened again, and ran home without stopping.

My sister, Mrs. Joe Gargery, was more than twenty years older than I, and had established a great reputation with herself and the neighbours because she had brought me up 'by hand.' Having at that time to find out for myself what the expression meant, and knowing her to have a hard and heavy hand, and to be much in the habit of laying it upon her husband as well as upon me, I supposed that Joe Gargery and I were both brought up by hand.

She was not a good-looking woman, my sister; and I had a general impression that she must have made Joe Gargery marry her by hand. Joe was a fair man, with curls of flaxen hair on each side of his smooth face, and with eyes of such a very undecided blue that they seemed to have somehow got mixed with their own whites. He was a mild, good-natured, sweet-tempered, easy-going, foolish, dear fellow—a sort of Hercules in strength, and also in weakness. *

Joe's forge adjoined our house, which was a wooden house, as many of the dwellings in our country were—most of them, at that time. When I ran home from the churchyard, the forge was shut up, and Joe was sitting alone in the kitchen. Joe and I being fellow-sufferers, and having confidences as such, Joe imparted a confidence to me the moment I raised the latch of the door.

'Mrs. Joe has been out a dozen times, looking for you, Pip. And she's out now, making it a baker's dozen.'

'Is she?'

'Yes, Pip, and what's worse, she's got Tickler with her.'

At this dismal intelligence I twisted the only button on my waistcoat round and round, and looked in great depression at the fire. Tickler was a wax-ended piece of cane, worn smooth by collision with my tickled frame.

'She sot down,' said Joe, 'and she got up, and she made a grab at Tickler, and she Ram-paged out, Pip.'

'Has she been gone long, Joe?' I always treated him as a larger species of child, and as no more than my equal.

'Well,' said Joe, glancing up at the Dutch clock, 'she's been on the Ram-page, this last spell, about five minutes, Pip. She's a coming! Get behind the door, old chap, and have the jack-towel betwixt you.'

I took the advice. My sister, Mrs. Joe, throwing the door wide open, and finding an obstruction behind it, immediately divined the cause, and applied Tickler to its further investigation. She concluded by throwing me—I often served her as a connubial missile—at Joe, who, glad to get hold of me on any terms, passed me on into the chimney, and quietly fenced me up there with his great leg.

'Where have you been, you young monkey?' said Mrs. Joe, stamping her foot. 'Tell me directly what you have been doing to wear me away with fret and fright and worrit, or I'd have you out of that corner if you was fifty Pips and he was five hundred Gargerys.'

'I have only been to the churchyard,' said I from my stool, crying and rubbing myself.

'Churchyard!' repeated my sister. 'If it warn't for me you'd have been to the churchyard long ago, and stayed there. Who brought you up by hand?'

'You did.'

'And why did I do it, I should like to know!'

I whimpered, 'I don't know.'

'*I*[1] don't!' said my sister. 'I'd never do it again! I know that. It's bad enough to be a blacksmith's wife (and him a Gargery) without being your mother.' *

My sister had a trenchant way of cutting our bread-and-butter for us (it was tea-time now), that never varied. First, with her left hand she jammed the loaf hard and fast against her bib—where it sometimes got a pin into it, and sometimes a needle, which we afterwards got into our mouths. Then she took some butter (not too much) on a knife and spread it on the loaf, in an apothecary kind of way, as if she were making a plaister. Then she gave the knife a final smart wipe on the edge of the plaister, and then sawed a very thick round off the loaf: which she finally, before separating from the loaf, hewed into two halves, of which Joe got one, and I the other.

On the present occasion, though I was hungry, I dared not eat my slice. I felt that I must have something in reserve for my dreadful acquaintance. Therefore I resolved to put my hunk of bread-and-butter down the leg of my trousers.

The effort of resolution necessary to the achievement of this purpose I found to be awful. And it was made the more difficult by the unconscious Joe. It was our evening habit to compare the way we bit through our slices, by silently holding them up to each other's admiration now and then—which stimulated us to new exertions. To-night, Joe several times invited me, by the display of his fast-diminishing slice, to enter upon our usual friendly competition; but he found me, each time, with my yellow

---

[1] Like all italics in this Reading, this does *not* represent an underlining in the prompt-copy but was printed as italic both in the prompt-copy and in the novel. This will not be noted in further instances.

mug of tea on one knee, and my untouched bread-and-butter on the other. At last, I desperately considered that the thing I contemplated must be done, and that it had best be done in the least improbable manner consistent with the circumstances. So I took advantage of a moment when Joe had just looked at me, and got my bread-and-butter down my leg.

Joe was about to take another bite at his slice, and had just got his head on one side for a good purchase on it, when his eye fell on me, and he saw that my bread-and-butter was gone.

The wonder and consternation with which Joe stopped on the threshold of his bite and stared at me, were too evident to escape my sister's observation.

'What's the matter now?' said she.

'I say, you know!' muttered Joe, shaking his head at me in very serious remonstrance. 'Pip, old chap! You'll do yourself a mischief. It'll stick somewhere. You can't have chawed it, Pip?'

'What's the matter *now*?' repeated my sister.

'If you can cough any trifle on it up, Pip, I'd recommend you to do it,' said Joe, all aghast. 'Manners is manners, but still your elth's your elth.'

By this time my sister was quite desperate; so she pounced on Joe, and, taking him by the two whiskers, knocked his head for a little while against the wall behind him, while I sat in the corner looking guiltily on.

'Now, perhaps you'll mention what's the matter,' said my sister, out of breath, 'you staring great stuck pig.'

Joe looked at her in a helpless way; then took a helpless bite, and looked at me again.

'You know, Pip,' said Joe, solemnly, with his last bite in his cheek, and speaking in a confidential voice, as if we two were quite alone, 'you and me is always friends, and I'd be the last to tell upon you, any time. But such a'—he moved his chair and looked about the floor between us, and then again at me—'such a most oncommon Bolt as that!'

'Been bolting his food, has he?' cried my sister.

'You know, old chap,' said Joe, looking at me, and not at Mrs. Joe, with his bite still in his cheek, 'I Bolted, myself, when I was your age—frequent—and as a boy I've been among a many Bolters; but I never see your Bolting equal yet, Pip, and it's a mercy you ain't Bolted dead.'

My sister made a dive at me, and fished me up by the hair, saying nothing more than the awful words, 'You come along and be dosed.'

Some medical beast had revived Tar-water in those days as a fine medicine, and Mrs. Joe always kept a supply of it in the cupboard, having a belief in its virtues correspondent to its nastiness. At the best of times, so much of this elixir was administered to me as a choice restorative, that I was conscious of going about smelling like a new fence. On this particular evening the urgency of my case demanded a pint of this mixture, which was poured down my throat for my greater comfort, while Mrs. Joe held my head under her arm, as a boot would be held in a boot-jack. Joe got off with half-a-pint; but was made to swallow that, 'because he had had a turn.' Judging from myself, I should say he certainly had a turn afterwards, if had had none before.

Conscience is a dreadful thing when it accuses man or boy; but when, in the case of a boy, that secret burden co-operates with another secret burden down the leg of his trousers, it is (as I can testify) a great punishment. The guilty knowledge that I was going to rob Mrs. Joe—I never thought I was going to rob Joe, for I never thought of any of the house-keeping property as his—united to the necessity of always keeping one hand on my bread-and-butter as I sat, or when I was ordered about the kitchen on any small errand, almost drove me out of my mind. *

If I slept at all that night, it was only to imagine myself drifting down the river on a strong spring tide, to the Hulks; a ghostly pirate calling out to me through a speaking-trumpet, as I passed the gibbet-station, that I had better come ashore and be hanged there at once, and not put it off. At the first faint dawn of morning I got up and went down stairs to the pantry. I had no time for selection.[1] I stole some bread, some rind of cheese, about half a jar of mincemeat (which I tied up in my pocket-handkerchief with my last night's slice), some brandy from a stone bottle, a meat bone with very little on it, and a beautiful round compact pork pie. There was a door in the kitchen communicating with the forge; I unlocked and unbolted that door, and got a file from among Joe's tools. Then I put the fastenings as I had found them, opened the door at which I had entered when I ran home last night, shut it, and ran for the misty marshes. *

The mist was very dense when I got out upon the marshes, so that instead of my running at everything, everything seemed to run at me. This was very disagreeable to a guilty mind. The gates and dykes and banks came bursting at me through the mist, as if they cried as plainly as could be, 'A boy with Somebody else's pork pie! Stop him!' The cattle came upon me seeming to stare out of their eyes, and steam out of their nostrils, 'Holloa, young thief!' One black ox, with a white cravat on—who even had to my awakened conscience something of a clerical air—fixed me so obstinately with his eyes, and moved his blunt head round in such an accusatory manner as I moved round, that I blubbered out to him, 'I couldn't help it, sir! It wasn't for myself I took it!' Upon which he put down his head, blew a cloud of smoke out of his nose, and vanished with a kick-up of his hind-legs and a flourish of his tail. *

Making my way along with all despatch, I had just crossed a ditch which I knew to be very near the Battery, and had just scrambled up the

---

[1] The preceding two sentences, devised from a considerably longer passage in the novel, are a good example of Dickens's process of reduction of this text.

mound beyond the ditch, when I saw the man sitting before me. His back was towards me, and he had his arms folded, and was nodding forward, heavy with sleep.

I thought he would be more glad if I came upon him with his breakfast in that unexpected manner, so I went forward softly and touched him on the shoulder. He instantly jumped up, and it was not the same man, but another man!

And yet this man was dressed in coarse grey, too, and had a great iron on his leg, and was lame, and hoarse, and cold, and was everything that the other man was; except that he had not the same face, and had a flat broad-brimmed low-crowned felt hat on. All this, I saw in a moment, for I had only a moment to see it in. He swore an oath at me, made a hit at me—it was a round weak blow that missed me and almost knocked himself down, for it made him stumble—and then he ran into the mist, and I lost him.

I was soon at the Battery after that, and there was the right man. He was awfully cold, to be sure. I half expected to see him drop down before my face, and die of cold. His eyes looked so awfully hungry, too, that when I handed him the file, and he laid it down on the grass, it occurred to me he would have tried to eat it if he had not seen my bundle.

He took some of the liquor, shivering all the while so violently, that it was quite as much as he could do to keep the neck of the bottle between his teeth without biting it off. * He gobbled mincemeat, meat-bone, bread, cheese, and pork pie, all at once; staring about at the mist all round us, and often stopping—even stopping his jaws—to listen. Some real or fancied sound, some clink upon the river or breathing of beast upon the marsh, gave him a start, and he said, suddenly:

'You're not a deceiving imp? You brought no one with you?'

'No, sir! No!'

'Nor giv' no one the office to follow you?'

'No!'

'Well, I believe you. You'd be but a fierce young hound indeed, if at your time of life you could help to hunt a wretched warmint, hunted as near death and dunghill as this poor wretched warmint is!'

Something clicked in his throat, as if he had works in him like a clock, and was going to strike.

Pitying his desolation, and watching him as he settled down upon the pie, I made bold to say, 'I am glad you enjoy it. * But I am afraid you won't leave any for him.'

'Leave any for him? Who's him?' *

'Yonder,' said I, pointing; 'over there, where I found him nodding asleep, and thought it was you.'

He took me by the collar and stared at me so, that I began to think his first idea about cutting my throat had revived.

'Dressed like you, you know, only with a hat—and—and'—I was very anxious to put this delicately—'and with—the same reason for wanting to borrow a file. Didn't you hear the cannon last night?'

'Then, there *was* firing!'

'I wonder you shouldn't have been sure of that, for we heard it up at home.'

'Why, see now! When a man's alone on these flats, with a light head and a light stomach, perishing of cold and want, he hears nothin' all night but guns firing and voices calling. Hears? He sees the soldiers, with their red coats lighted up by the torches carried afore, closing in round him. Hears his number called, hears himself challenged, hears the rattle of the muskets. Why, if I see one pursuing party last night—coming up in order, damn 'em, with their tramp, tramp—I see a hundred. But this man; did you notice anything in him?'

'He had a badly bruised face.'

'Not here?' Striking his left cheek mercilessly with the flat of his hand.

'Yes, there!'

'Where is he?' He crammed what little food was left into the breast of his grey jacket. 'Show me the way he went. I'll pull him down, like a bloodhound. Curse this iron on my sore leg! Give us hold of the file, boy.'

I indicated in what direction the mist had shrouded the other man, and he looked up at it for an instant. But he was down on the rank wet grass, filing at his iron like a madman, and not minding me or minding his own leg, which had an old chafe upon it and was bloody, but which he handled as roughly as if it had no more feeling in it than the file. I told him I must go, but he took no notice, so I thought the best thing I could do was to slip off.

When I got back, I fully expected to find a Constable in the kitchen, waiting to take me up. But not only was there no Constable there, but no discovery had yet been made of the robbery. *

It was Christmas Day, and we were to have a superb dinner, consisting of a leg of pickled pork and greens, and a pair of roast stuffed fowls. A handsome mince-pie had been made yesterday morning (which accounted for the mince-meat not being missed), and the pudding was already on the boil. These extensive arrangements occasioned us to be cut off unceremoniously in respect of breakfast; 'for I an't,' said Mrs. Joe, 'I an't a going to have no formal cramming and busting and washing up now, with what I've got before me, I promise you!'

So Joe and I had our slices served out as if we were two thousand troops on a forced march, instead of a man and boy at home; and we took gulps of milk and water, with apologetic countenances, from a jug on the dresser. *

Mr. Wopsle, the clerk at church, was to dine with us; and Mr. Hubble the village wheelwright and Mrs. Hubble; and Uncle Pumblechook (Joe's

uncle, but Mrs. Joe appropriated him), who was a well-to-do corn-chandler in the nearest town, and drove his own chaise-cart. The dinner hour
was half-past one. The time came without bringing with it any relief to
my feelings, and the company came. Mr. Wopsle, united to a Roman nose
and a large shining bald forehead, had a deep voice which he was uncommonly proud of; indeed it was understood among his acquaintance
that if you could only give him his head, he would read the clergyman
into fits; he punished the Amens tremendously; and when he gave out the
psalm—always giving the whole verse—he looked all round the congrega-
tion first, as much as to say, 'You have heard my friend overhead; will you
oblige me with your opinion of this style!'

'Mrs. Joe,' said Uncle Pumblechook, a large hard-breathing middle-
aged slow man, with a mouth like a fish, dull staring eyes, and sandy
hair standing upright on his head, so that he looked as if he had just been
all but choked, and had that moment come to; 'I have brought you,
as the compliments of the season—I have brought you, Mum, a bottle of
sherry wine—and I have brought you, Mum, a bottle of port wine.'

Every Christmas Day he presented himself, as a profound novelty,
with exactly the same words, and carrying the two bottles like dumb-bells.
Every Christmas Day Mrs. Joe replied, as she now replied, 'Oh Un—cle
Pum—ble—chook! This is kind!' Every Christmas Day he retorted, as he
now retorted, 'It's no more than your merits. And now are you all bob-
bish, and how's Sixpennorth of halfpence?' meaning me. (As to me, I was
always considered in the way, and was treated as if I had insisted on being
born, in opposition to the dictates of reason, religion, and morality, and
against the dissuading arguments of my best friends.) My sister was
uncommonly lively on the present occasion, and indeed was generally
more gracious in the society of Mrs. Hubble than in any other company.
I remember Mrs. Hubble as a little curly sharp-edged person in sky-blue,
who held a conventionally juvenile position, because she had married Mr.
Hubble—I don't know at what remote period—when she was much
younger than he. I remember Mr. Hubble as a tough high-shouldered
stooping old man, of a sawdusty fragrance, with his legs extraordinary
wide apart; so that in my short days I always saw some miles of open
country between them when I met him coming up the lane.

Among this good company I should have felt myself, even if I hadn't
robbed the pantry, in a false position. Not because I was squeezed in at
an acute angle of the tablecloth, with the table in my chest, and the
Pumblechookian elbow in my eye, nor because I was not allowed to speak
(I didn't want to speak), nor because I was regaled with the scaly tips of
the drumsticks of the fowls, and with those obscure corners of pork of
which the pig, when living, had had the least reason to be vain. I should
not have minded that, if they would only have left me alone. But they
wouldn't leave me alone. They seemed to think the opportunity lost, if

they failed to point the conversation at me, every now and then, and stick the point into me. I might have been an unfortunate little bull in a Spanish arena, I got so smartingly touched up by these moral goads.

It began the moment we sat down to dinner. Mr. Wopsle said grace with theatrical declamation—as it now appears to me, something like a religious cross of the Ghost in Hamlet with Richard the Third—and ended with the very proper aspiration that we might be truly grateful. Upon which my sister fixed me with her eye, and said, in a low reproachful voice, 'Do you hear that? Be grateful.'

Mrs. Hubble shook her head, and contemplating me with a mournful presentiment that I should come to no good, asked, 'Why is it that the young are never grateful?' This moral mystery seemed too much for the company until Mr. Hubble tersely solved it by saying, 'Naterally wicious.' Everybody then murmured 'True!' and looked at me in a particularly unpleasant and personal manner.

Joe's station and influence were something feebler (if possible) when there was company than when there was none. But he always aided and comforted me when he could, in some way of his own, and he always did so at dinner-time by giving me gravy, if there were any. There being plenty of gravy to-day, Joe spooned into my plate, at this point, about half a pint.

A little later on in the dinner, Mr. Wopsle reviewed the sermon with some severity, and remarked that he considered the subject of the day's homily ill chosen; which was the less excusable, he added, when there were so many subjects 'going about.'

'True again,' said Uncle Pumblechook. 'You've hit it, sir! Plenty of subjects going about, for them that know how to put salt upon their tails. That's what's wanted. A man needn't go far to find a subject if he's ready with his salt-box.' Mr. Pumblechook added, after a short interval of re-flection, 'Look at Pork alone. There's a subject! If you want a subject, look at Pork!'

'True, sir. Many a moral for the young,' returned Mr. Wopsle; and I knew he was going to lug me in, before he said it; 'might be deduced from that text.'

('You listen to this,' said my sister to me, in a severe parenthesis.)

Joe gave me some more gravy.

'Swine,' pursued Mr. Wopsle, in his deepest voice, and pointing his fork at my blushes, as if he were mentioning my christian name; 'Swine were the companions of the prodigal. The gluttony of Swine is put before us as an example to the young.' (I thought this pretty well in him who had been praising up the pork for being so plump and juicy.) 'What is detestable in a pig is more detestable in a boy.'

'Besides,' said Mr. Pumblechook, turning sharp on me, 'think what you've got to be grateful for. If you'd been born a Squeaker——'

'He *was*, if ever a child was,' said my sister.

Joe gave me some more gravy.

'Well, but I mean a four-footed Squeaker,' said Mr. Pumblechook. 'If you had been born such, would you have been here now? Not you——'

'Unless in that form,' said Mr. Wopsle, nodding towards the dish.

'But I don't mean in that form, sir,' returned Mr. Pumblechook, who had an objection to being interrupted; 'I mean, enjoying himself with his elders and betters, and improving himself with their conversation, and rolling in the lap of luxury. Would he have been doing that? No, he wouldn't. And what would have been your destination?' turning on me again. 'You would have been disposed of for so many shillings according to the market price of the article, and Dunstable the butcher would have come up to you as you lay in your straw, and he would have whipped you under his left arm, and with his right he would have tucked up his frock to get a penknife from out of his waistcoat-pocket, and he would have shed your blood and had your life.'

Joe offered me more gravy, which I was afraid to take.

'He was a world of trouble to you, ma'am,' said Mrs. Hubble.

'Trouble?' echoed my sister; 'trouble?' And then entered on a fearful catalogue of all the illnesses I had been guilty of, and all the acts of sleeplessness I had committed, and all the high places I had tumbled from, and all the low places I had tumbled into, and all the injuries I had done myself, and all the times she had wished me in my grave, and I had contumaciously refused to go there.

I think the Romans must have aggravated one another very much with their noses. Perhaps they became the restless people they were, in consequence. Anyhow, Mr. Wopsle's Roman nose so aggravated me, during the recital of my misdemeanours, that I should have liked to pull it until he howled. But * the apparition of a file of soldiers ringing down the butt-ends of their loaded muskets on our door-step changed the current of my thoughts, and caused us all to rise from the table in confusion. *

'Excuse me, ladies and gentlemen,' said the sergeant, 'I am on a chase in the name of the King, and I want the blacksmith.'

'And pray what might you want with *him*?' retorted my sister.

'Missis,' returned the gallant sergeant; 'speaking for myself, I should reply, the honour and pleasure of his fine wife's acquaintance: speaking for the King, I answer, a little job done.'

This was received as rather neat in the sergeant; insomuch that Mr. Pumblechook cried audibly, 'Good again!'

'You see, blacksmith,' said the sergeant, who had by this time picked out Joe with his eye, 'we have had an accident with these handcuffs, and I find the lock of one of 'em goes wrong, and the coupling don't act pretty. As they are wanted for immediate service, will you throw your eye over them?'

Joe threw his eye over them, and pronounced that the job would necessitate the lighting of his forge fire, and would take nearer two hours than one. *

'Just gone half-past two,' said the sergeant. 'How far might you call yourselves from the marshes hereabouts? Not above a mile, I reckon? That'll do. We begin to close in upon 'em about dusk. A little before dusk my orders are. That'll do. Convicts. Two of 'em. They're pretty well known to be out on the marshes still, and they won't try to get clear of 'em before dusk. Anybody here seen anything of any such game?'

Everybody, myself excepted, said no, with confidence. Nobody thought of me.

'Well! they'll find themselves trapped in a circle, I expect, sooner than they count on. Now, blacksmith! If you're ready, His Majesty the King is.'

Joe had got his coat and waistcoat and cravat off, and his leather apron on, and passed into the forge. One of the soldiers opened its wooden windows, another lighted the fire, another turned to at the bellows, the rest stood round the blaze, which was soon roaring. Then Joe began to hammer and clink, hammer and clink, and we all looked on.

The interest of the impending pursuit even made my sister liberal. She drew a pitcher of beer from the cask for the soldiers, when Mr. Pumblechook invited the sergeant to take a glass of wine. *

'With you. Hob and nob,' returned the sergeant. 'The top of mine to the foot of yours—the foot of yours to the top of mine—Ring once, ring twice—the best tune on the Musical Glasses! Your health. May you live a thousand years, and never be a worse judge of the right sort than you are at the present moment of your life!'

The sergeant tossed off his glass again, and seemed quite ready for another glass. I noticed that Mr. Pumblechook in his hospitality appeared to forget that he had made a present of the wine, but took the bottle from Mrs. Joe, and had all the credit of handing it about in a gush of joviality. Even I got some. And he was so very free of the wine that he even called for the other bottle, and handed that about with the same liberality. *

At last Joe's job was done, and the ringing and roaring stopped. As Joe got on his coat, he mustered courage to propose that some of us should go down with the soldiers and see what came of the hunt. The others declined, on the plea of a pipe and ladies' society; but Joe said he would take me, if Mrs. Joe approved. We never should have got leave to go, I am sure, but for Mrs. Joe's curiosity to know all about it. As it was, she merely stipulated, 'If you bring the boy back with his head blown to bits by a musket, don't look to me to put it together again.'

The sergeant took a polite leave of the ladies, and parted from Mr. Pumblechook as from a comrade; though I doubt if he were quite as fully sensible of that gentleman's merits under arid conditions as when some-

thing moist was going. His men resumed their muskets and fell in. Joe
and I received strict charge to keep in the rear, and to speak no
word after we reached the marshes. When we were all out in the
raw air, I treasonably whispered to Joe, 'I hope, Joe, we shan't find
them.' And Joe whispered to me, 'I'd give a shilling if they had cut and
run, Pip.'

We were joined by no stragglers from the village, for the weather was
cold and threatening, the way dreary, the footing bad, darkness coming
on, and the people had good fires in-doors and were keeping the day. We
struck out on the open marshes through the gate at the side of the churchyard. A bitter sleet came rattling against us here on the east wind, and
Joe took me on his back.

Now that we were out upon the dismal wilderness—where they little
thought I had been within eight or nine hours and had seen both men
hiding—I considered for the first time, with great dread, if we should
come upon them, would my particular convict suppose that it was I who
had brought the soldiers there? It was of no use asking myself the question
now. There I was, on Joe's back, and there was Joe beneath me, charging
at the ditches like a hunter. *

All of a sudden we all stopped. For there had reached us on the wings
of the wind and rain a long shout. It was repeated. It was at a distance
towards the east, but it was long and loud. Nay, there seemed to be two or
more shouts raised together. The sergeant, a decisive man, ordered that
the sound should not be answered, but that the course should be changed,
and that his men should make towards it 'at the double.' So we slanted
to the right (where the East was), and Joe pounded away so wonderfully,
that I had to hold on tight to keep my seat.

It was a run indeed now, and what Joe called, in the only two words he
spoke all the time, 'a Winder.' Down banks and up banks, and over gates,
and splashing into dykes, and breaking among coarse rushes: no man
cared where he went. As we came nearer to the shouting, it became more
and more apparent that it was made by more than one voice. * The sergeant ran in first, when he had run the noise quite down, and two of his
men ran in close upon him. Their pieces were cocked and levelled when
we all ran in.

'Here are both men!' panted the sergeant, 'struggling at the bottom of a
ditch. Surrender, you two! and confound you for two wild beasts! Come
asunder!'

Water was splashing, and mud was flying, and oaths were being sworn,
and blows were being struck, when some more men went down into the
ditch to help the sergeant, and dragged out separately my convict and
the other one. Both were bleeding and panting and execrating and struggling; but of course I knew them both directly.

'Mind!' said my convict, wiping blood from his face with his ragged sleeves, and shaking torn hair from his fingers; '*I* took him! *I* give him up to you! Mind that!'

The other convict was livid to look at, and, in addition to the old bruised left side of his face, seemed to be bruised and torn all over. He could not so much as get his breath to speak, until they were both separately hand-cuffed, but leaned upon a soldier to keep himself from falling. His first words were:

'Take notice, guard—he tried to murder me.'

'Tried to murder him?' said my convict, disdainfully. 'Try, and not do it? I took him, and giv' him up; that's what I done. I not only pre-vented him getting off the marshes, but I dragged him here—dragged him this far on his way back. Lookee here! Single-handed I got clear of the prison-ship; I made a dash and I done it. I could ha' got clear of these death-cold flats likewise—look at my leg: you won't find much iron on it— if I hadn't made discovery that *he* was here. Let *him* go free? Let *him* profit by the means as I found out? Let *him* make a tool of me afresh and again? Once more? No, no, no.'

The other fugitive repeated, 'He tried to murder me.'

'He lies!' said my convict with fierce energy. 'He's a liar born, and he'll die a liar.' *

My convict now looked round him for the first time, and saw me. I had alighted from Joe's back on the brink of the ditch, and had not moved since. I looked at him eagerly when he looked at me, and slightly moved my hands and shook my head. I had been waiting for him to see me, that I might try to assure him of my innocence in the matter of his being taken. It was not at all expressed to me that he even comprehended my in-tention, for he gave me a look that I did not understand, and it all passed in a moment. * Suddenly he turned to the sergeant and remarked:

'I wish to say something respecting this escape. It may prevent some persons laying under suspicion alonger me. A man can't starve; at least *I* can't. I took some wittles up at the willage over yonder—where the church stands a'most out on the marshes. And I'll tell you where from. From the blacksmith's.'

'Halloa!' said the sergeant, staring at Joe.

'Halloa, Pip!' said Joe, staring at me.

'It was some broken wittles—that's what it was—and a dram of liquor, and a pie.'

'Have you happened to miss such an article as a pie, blacksmith?' asked the sergeant.

'So,' said my convict, turning his eyes on Joe in a moody manner, and without the least glance at me; 'so you're the blacksmith, are you? Then I'm sorry to say I've eat your pie.'

'God knows you're welcome to it—so far as it was ever mine,' returned Joe, with a saving remembrance of Mrs. Joe. 'We don't know what you have done, but we wouldn't have you starved to death for it, poor miserable fellow-creatur.—Would us, Pip?'

The something that I had noticed before clicked in the man's throat again, and he turned his back. We went on to the river-side, and saw him put into a boat, which was rowed by a crew of convicts like himself. By the light of torches we saw the black Hulk lying out a little way from the mud of the shore, like a wicked Noah's ark. Cribbed and barred and moored by massive rusty chains, the prison-ship seemed in my young eyes to be ironed like the prisoners. We saw the boat go alongside, and we saw him taken up the side and disappear. Then the ends of the torches were flung hissing into the water, and went out, as if it were all over with him. *

I think it must have been a full year after this hunt of ours upon the marshes—well, any way it was a long time after, and it was winter-time and a hard frost—when Joe and I again found ourselves sitting alone together in the kitchen chimney-corner. *

'How do you spell Gargery, Joe?' I asked him.

'I don't spell it at all,' said Joe.

'But supposing you did?'

'It *can't* be supposed,' said Joe. 'Tho' I'm oncommon fond of reading, too. Give me a good book, or a good newspaper, and sit me down afore a good fire, and I ask no better. Lord!' he continued, after rubbing his knees a little, 'when you *do* come to a J and a O, and says you, "Here, at last, is a J-O, Joe," how interesting reading is!'

I derived from this that Joe's education, like Steam, was yet in its infancy. Pursuing the subject, I inquired:

'Didn't you ever go to school, Joe, when you were as little as me?'

'No, Pip.'

'Why didn't you ever go to school, Joe, when you were as little as me?'

'Well, Pip, I'll tell you. My father, Pip, he were given to drink, and when he were overtook with drink he hammered away at my mother most onmerciful. It were a'most the only hammering he did, indeed, 'xcepting at myself. And he hammered at me with a wigour only to be equalled by the wigour with which he didn't hammer at his anwil. You're a listening and understanding, Pip?'

'Yes, Joe.'

"Consequence, my mother and me we ran away from my father several times; and then my mother she'd go out to work, and she'd say, "Joe," she'd say, "now, please God, you shall have some schooling, child," and she'd put me to school. But my father were that good in his hart that he couldn't abear to be without us. So he'd come with a most tremenjous crowd, and make such a row at the doors of the houses where we was, that they used to be obligated to have no more to do with us and to give us up to him. And then he took us home and hammered us. Which, you see, Pip, were a drawback on my learning.'

'Certainly, poor Joe!'

'Though, mind you, Pip, rendering unto all their doo, and maintaining equal justice betwixt man and man, my father were that good in his hart, don't you see?'

I didn't see; but I didn't say so.

'Well!' Joe pursued, 'somebody must keep the pot a biling, Pip, or the pot won't bile, don't you know?'

I saw that, and said so.

''Consequence, my father didn't make objections to my going to work; so I went to work at my present calling, which were his too, if he would have followed it, and I worked tolerable hard, I assure *you*, Pip. In time I were able to keep him, and I kep him till he went off in a purple leptic fit. And it were my intentions to have put upon his tombstone that, Whatsume'er the failings on his part, Remember reader he were that good in his hart.'

Joe recited this couplet with such manifest pride and careful perspicuity, that I asked him if he had made it himself?

'I made it,' said Joe, 'my own self. I made it in a moment. It was like striking out a horseshoe complete in a single blow. I never was so much surprised in all my life—couldn't credit my own ed—to tell you the truth, hardly believed it *were* my own ed. As I was saying, Pip, it were my intentions to have had it cut over him; but poetry costs money, cut it how you will, small or large, and it were not done. Not to mention bearers, all the money that could be spared were wanted for my mother. She were in poor elth, and quite broke. She weren't long of following, poor soul, and her share of peace come round at last.'

Joe's blue eyes turned a little watery; he rubbed, first one of them, and then the other, in a most uncongenial and uncomfortable manner, with the round knob on the top of the poker.

'It were but lonesome then, living here alone, and I got acquainted with your sister. Now, Pip;' Joe looked firmly at me, as if he knew I was not going to agree with him; 'your sister is a fine figure of a woman.'

I could not help looking at the fire in an obvious state of doubt.

'Whatever family opinions, or whatever the world's opinions on that subject may be, Pip, your sister is a—fine—figure—of—a—woman!'

'I am glad you think so, Joe.'

'So am I, *I* am glad I think so, Pip. A little redness, or a little matter of Bone here or there, what does it signify to Me?'

I sagaciously observed, if it didn't signify to him, to whom did it signify?

'Certainly! That's it. You're right, old chap! When I got acquainted with your sister, it were the talk how she was bringing you up by hand.

Very kind of her too, all the folks said, and I said along with all the folks. As to you,' Joe pursued, with a countenance expressive of seeing something very nasty indeed; 'if you could have been aware how small and flabby and mean you was, dear me, you'd have formed the most contemptible opinions of yourself!'

Not exactly relishing this, I said, 'Never mind me, Joe.'

'But I did mind you, Pip! When I offered to your sister to keep company, and to be asked in church at such times as she was willing and ready to come to the forge, I said to her, "And bring the poor dear little child. God bless the poor dear little child," I said to your sister, "there's room for *him* at the forge!"'

I broke out crying and begged pardon, and hugged Joe round the neck; who hugged me, and said, 'Ever the best of friends; an't us, Pip. Don't cry, old chap!'

When this little interruption was over, Joe resumed:

'Well, you see, Pip, and here we are! That's about where it lights; here we are! * I don't deny that your sister comes the Mo-gul over us now and again. I don't deny that she do throw us backfalls, and that she do drop down upon us heavy. At such times as when your sister is on the Rampage, Pip, candour compels fur to admit that she is a Buster.'

Joe pronounced this word as if it began with at least twelve capital Bs. *

'However, here's the Dutch-clock a working himself up to being equal to strike Eight of 'em, and she's not come home yet! I hope Uncle Pumblechook's mare mayn't have set a fore-foot on a piece o' ice, and gone down.'

Mrs. Joe made occasional trips with Uncle Pumblechook on market-days, to assist him in buying such household stuffs and goods as required a woman's judgment; Uncle Pumblechook being a bachelor and reposing no confidences in his domestic servant. This was market-day, and Mrs. Joe was out on one of these expeditions.

Joe made the fire and swept the hearth, and then we went to the door to listen for the chaise-cart.

'Here comes the mare,' said Joe, 'ringing like a peal of bells!'

The sound of her iron shoes upon the hard road was quite musical, as she came along. We got a chair out, ready for Mrs. Joe alighting, and stirred up the fire. When we had completed our preparations, they drove up, wrapped to the eyes. Mrs. Joe was soon landed, and Uncle Pumblechook was soon down too.

'Now,' said Mrs. Joe, unwrapping herself with haste and excitement, and throwing her bonnet back on her shoulders, where it hung by the strings; 'if this boy an't grateful this night, he never will be!'

I looked as grateful as any boy possibly could who was wholly uninformed why he ought to assume that expression.

'It is only to be hoped,' said my sister, 'that he won't be Pompeyed'—her reading of pampered—'but I have my fears.'

'She an't in that line, Mum,' said Mr. Pumblechook. 'She knows better.'

She? I looked at Joe, making the motion with my lips and eyebrows, 'She?' Joe looked at me, making the motion with *his* lips and eyebrows, 'She?' My sister catching him in the act, he drew the back of his hand across his nose with his usual conciliatory air on such occasions.

'Well?' said my sister, in her snappish way. 'What are you staring at? Is the house a-fire?'

'—Which some individual,' Joe politely hinted, 'mentioned—she.'

'And she is a she, I suppose? Unless you call Miss Havisham a he. And I doubt if even you'll go as far as that.'

'Miss Havisham up town?'

'Is there any Miss Havisham down town? She wants this boy to go and play there. And of course he's going. And he had better play there,' said my sister, shaking her head at me as an encouragement to be extremely light and sportive, 'or I'll work him.'

I had heard of Miss Havisham up town—everybody for miles round had heard of Miss Havisham up town—as an immensely rich and grim lady who lived in a large and dismal house barricaded against robbers, and who led a life of seclusion.

'Well to be sure!' said Joe, astounded. 'I wonder how she come to know Pip!'

'Noodle! Who said she knew him?'

'—Which some individual,' Joe again politely hinted, 'mentioned that she wanted him to go and play there.'

'And couldn't she ask Uncle Pumblechook if he knew of a boy to go and play there? Isn't it just barely possible that Uncle Pumblechook may be a tenant of hers, and that he may sometimes—we won't say quarterly or half-yearly, for that would be requiring too much of you—but sometimes—go there to pay his rent? And couldn't she then ask Uncle Pumblechook if he knew of a boy to go and play there? And couldn't Uncle Pumblechook, being always considerate and thoughtful for us—though you may not think it, Joseph,' in a tone of the deepest reproach, as if he were the most callous of nephews, 'then mention this boy, standing prancing here?' Which I solemnly declare I was not doing.

'Good again!' cried Uncle Pumblechook. 'Well put! Prettily pointed! Good indeed! Now, Joseph, you know the case.'

'No, Joseph,' said my sister, still in a reproachful manner, while Joe apologetically drew the back of his hand across and across his nose, 'you do not yet—though you may not think it—know the case. You may consider that you do, but you do *not*, Joseph. For you do not know that Uncle Pumblechook, being sensible that for anything we can tell, this boy's fortune may be made by his going to Miss Havisham's, has offered to take him into town to-night in his own chaise-cart, and to keep him to-night, and to take him with his own hands to Miss Havisham's to-morrow morning. And Lor-a-mussy me! here I stand talking to mere mooncalves, with Uncle Pumblechook waiting, and the mare catching cold at the door, and the boy grimed with crock and dirt from the hair of his head to the sole of his foot!'

With that she pounced upon me like an eagle on a lamb, and my face was squeezed into wooden bowls in sinks, and my head was put under taps of water-butts, and I was soaped, and kneaded, and towelled, and thumped, and harrowed, and rasped, until I really was quite beside my-self. When my ablutions were completed I was put into clean linen of the stiffest character, like a young penitent into sackcloth, and was trussed up in my tightest and fearfullest suit. I was then delivered over to Mr. Pumblechook, who formally received me as if he were the sheriff.

'Good-bye, Joe!'

'God bless you, Pip, old chap!'

I had never parted from him before, and what with my feelings and what with soapsuds, I could at first see no stars from the chaise-cart. But they twinkled out one by one, without throwing any light on the questions why on earth I was going to play at Miss Havisham's, and what on earth I was expected to play at.

SECOND STAGE
Pip's Minority

* MISS HAVISHAM's house was of old brick, and dismal, and had a great many iron bars to it. Some of the windows had been walled up; of those that remained, all the lower were rustily barred. There was a court-yard in front, and that was barred. At the side of the house there was a large brewery. No brewing was going on in it, and none seemed to have gone on for a long time.[1] *

The cold wind seemed to blow colder there than outside the gate; and it made a shrill noise in howling in and out at the open sides of the brewery, like the noise of wind in the rigging of a ship at sea. *

Entering, as I was directed, by a dark passage and staircase, I knocked at a door, and was told from within to enter. I entered, and found my-self in a pretty large room, well lighted with wax candles. No glimpse of daylight was to be seen in it. It was a dressing-room, as I supposed from

[1] In the novel, Estella here makes her first appearance. Her omission from the Reading accounts for many substantial cuts henceforward.

the furniture, though much of it was of forms and uses then quite unknown to me. But prominent in it was a draped table with a gilded looking-glass, and that I made out at first sight to be a fine lady's dressing-table.

Whether I should have made out this object so soon, if there had been no fine lady sitting at it, I cannot say. In an arm chair, with an elbow resting on the table and her head leaning on that hand, sat the strangest lady I have ever seen, or shall ever see.

She was dressed in rich materials—satins, and lace, and silks—all of white. Her shoes were white, and she had a long white veil dependent from her hair, and she had bridal flowers in her hair, but her hair was white. Some bright jewels sparkled on her neck and on her hands, and some other jewels lay sparkling on the table. Dresses, less splendid than the dress she wore, and half-packed trunks, were scattered about. She had not quite finished dressing, for she had but one shoe on—the other was on the table near her hand—her veil was but half arranged, her watch and chain were not put on, and some lace for her bosom lay with those trinkets, and with her handkerchief, and gloves, and flowers, and a prayer-book, all confusedly heaped about the looking-glass.

It was not in the first moments that I saw all these things, though I saw more of them in the first moments than might be supposed. But I saw that everything within my view which ought to be white, had been white long ago, and had lost its lustre, and was faded and yellow. I saw that the bride within the bridal dress had withered like the dress, and like the flowers, and had no brightness left but the brightness of her sunken eyes. I saw that the dress had been put upon the rounded figure of a young woman, and that the figure upon which it now hung loose had shrunk to skin and bone. Once I had been taken to see some ghastly wax-work at the Fair, representing I know not what impossible personage lying in state. Once I had been taken to one of our old marsh churches to see a skeleton in the ashes of a rich dress, that had been dug out of a vault under the church pavement. Now, wax-work and skeleton seemed to have dark eyes that moved and looked at me.

It was when I stood before this spectral lady, avoiding her eyes, that I took note of the surrounding objects in detail, and saw that her watch had stopped at twenty minutes to nine, and that a clock in the room had stopped at twenty minutes to nine.

'Look at me,' said Miss Havisham. 'You are not afraid of a woman who has never seen the sun since you were born?'

I regret to state that I was not afraid of telling the enormous lie comprehended in the answer 'No.'

'Do you know what I touch here?' she said, laying her hands, one upon the other, on her left side.

'Yes, ma'am.'

'What do I touch?'

'Your heart.'

'Broken!'

She uttered the word with an eager look and with strong emphasis, and with a weird smile that had a kind of boast in it. Afterwards she kept her hands there for a little while, and slowly took them away as if they were heavy.

'I am tired,' said Miss Havisham. 'I want diversion, and I have done with men and women. Play. I sometimes have sick fancies, and I have a sick fancy that I want to see some play. There, there!' with an impatient movement of the fingers of her right hand; 'Play, play, play!'

I stood looking at her, in what I suppose she took for a dogged manner, inasmuch as she said, when we had taken a good look at each other:

'Are you sullen and obstinate?'

'No, ma'am; I am very sorry for you, and very sorry I can't play just now. If you complain of me I shall get into trouble with my sister, so I would do it if I could; but it's so new here, and so strange, and so fine—and so melancholy——'

She turned her eyes from me, and looked at the dress she wore, and at the dressing-table, and finally at herself in the looking-glass.

'So new to him,' she muttered, 'so old to me; so strange to him, so familiar to me; so melancholy to both of us![1] * Since this house strikes you old and grave, boy, and you are unwilling to play, are you willing to work?'

I could answer this inquiry with a better heart than I had been able to find for the other question, and I said I was quite willing.

'Then go into that opposite room, and wait there till I come.'

From that room, too, the daylight was completely excluded, and it had an airless smell that was oppressive. A fire had been lately kindled in the damp old-fashioned grate, and it was more disposed to go out than to burn up, and the reluctant smoke which hung in the room seemed colder than the clearer air—like our own marsh mist. Certain wintry branches of candles on the high chimney-piece faintly lighted the chamber; or, it would be more expressive to say, faintly troubled its darkness. It was spacious, and I dare say had once been handsome, but every discernible thing in it was covered with dust and mould, and dropping to pieces. The most prominent object was a long table with a tablecloth spread on it, as if a feast had been in preparation when the house and the clocks all stopped together. An epergne or centre-piece of some kind was in the middle of this cloth; it was so heavily overhung with cobwebs that its form was quite undistinguishable; and, as I looked along the yellow expanse out of which I remember its seeming to grow, like a black fungus, I saw speckled-legged spiders with blotchy bodies running home to it, and running out from it, as if some circumstance of the greatest public im-

[1] The game of beggar-my-neighbour with Estella, which follows here in the novel (ch. 8), is of course omitted, and the episode continues with a passage from ch. 11.

portance had just transpired in the spider community. I heard the mice too, rattling behind the panels, as if the same occurrence were important to their interests. But the black-beetles took no notice of the agitation, and groped about the hearth in a ponderous elderly way, as if they were short-sighted and hard of hearing, and not on terms with one another.

These crawling things had fascinated my attention, and I was watching them from a distance, when Miss Havisham laid a hand upon my shoulder. In her other hand she had a crutch-headed stick on which she leaned, and she looked like the witch of the place.

'This,' said she, pointing to the long table with her stick, 'is where I will be laid when I am dead. They shall come and look at me here. Matthew Pocket shall come and look at me here.'[1]

With some vague misgiving that she might get upon the table then and there and die at once, the complete realization of the ghastly waxwork at the Fair, I shrank under her touch.

'What do you think that is?' she asked me, again pointing her stick; 'that, where those cobwebs are?'

'I can't guess what it is, ma'am.'

'It's a great cake. A bride-cake. Mine!'

She looked all round the room in a glaring manner, and then said, leaning on me while her hand twitched my shoulder—'Come, come, come! Walk me, walk me!'

I made out from this that the work I had to do was to walk Miss Havisham round and round the room. Accordingly I started at once, and she leaned upon my shoulder and we went away at an impatient fitful speed. * At last she stopped before the fire, and said, after muttering and looking at it some seconds:

'This is my birthday, Pip. On this day of the year, long before you were born, this heap of decay,' stabbing with her crutched stick at the pile of cobwebs on the table, but not touching it, 'was brought here. It and I have worn away together. The mice have gnawed at it, and sharper teeth than teeth of mice have gnawed at me. When the ruin is complete, and when they lay me dead, in my bride's dress on the bride's table—which shall be done, and which will be the finished curse upon him—so much the better if it is done on this day!'

She stood looking at the table as if she stood looking at her own figure lying there.[2] *

On the broad landing, between Miss Havisham's own room and that other room in which the long table was laid out, there was a garden-chair —a light chair on wheels, that you pushed from behind. I entered, that

---

[1] This sentence, adapted from one later in this chapter (p. 81), is inserted here, the other references to the Pockets in ch. 11 having been omitted.

[2] The episode continues with a passage from ch. 12 (in the novel, Pip's third visit to Satis House).

same day, on a regular occupation of pushing Miss Havisham in this chair (when she was tired of walking with her hand upon my shoulder) round her own room, and across the landing, and round the other room. Over and over and over again we would make these journeys, and sometimes they would last as long as three hours at a stretch. I insensibly fall into a general mention of these journeys as numerous, because it was at once settled that I should return every alternate day at noon for these purposes, and because I now sum up a period of many months. *

We went on in this way for a long time, and it seemed likely that we should continue to go on in this way for a long time; when one day Miss Havisham stopped short as she and I were walking (she leaning on my shoulder), and said with some displeasure:

'You are growing tall, Pip!'

I thought it best to hint, through the medium of a meditative look, that this might be occasioned by circumstances over which I had no control.

She said no more at the time; but she presently stopped and looked at me again; and presently again; and after that looked frowning and moody. On the next day of my attendance, when our usual exercise was over, and I had landed her at her dressing-table, she stayed me with a movement of her impatient fingers:

'Tell me the name again of that blacksmith of yours.'

'Joe Gargery, ma'am.'

'Meaning the master you were to be apprenticed to?'

'Yes, Miss Havisham.'

'You had better be apprenticed at once. Would Gargery come here with you, and bring your indentures, do you think?'

I signified that I had no doubt he would take it as an honour.

'Then let him come.' *

It was a trial to my feelings, on the next day but one, to see Joe arraying himself in his Sunday clothes to accompany me to Miss Havisham's. However, as he thought his court-suit necessary to the occasion, it was not for me to tell him that he looked far better in his working dress; the rather, because I knew he made himself so dreadfully uncomfortable entirely on my account, and that it was for me he pulled up his shirt-collar so very high behind, that it made the hair on the crown of his head stand up like a tuft of feathers. *

'Oh!' said Miss Havisham to Joe. 'You are the husband of the sister of this boy?'

I could hardly have imagined dear old Joe looking so unlike himself or so like some extraordinary bird; standing, as he did, speechless, with his tuft of feathers ruffled, and his mouth open, as if he wanted a worm.

'You are the husband,' repeated Miss Havisham, 'of the sister of this boy?'

It was very aggravating; but throughout the interview Joe persisted in addressing Me instead of Miss Havisham.

'Which I meantersay, Pip,' Joe now observed, in a manner that was at once expressive of forcible argumentation, strict confidence, and great politeness, 'as I hup and married your sister, and I were at the time what you might call (if you was anyways inclined) a single man.'

'Well!' said Miss Havisham. 'And you have reared the boy, with the intention of taking him for your apprentice; is that so, Mr. Gargery?'

'You know, Pip,' replied Joe, 'as you and me were ever friends, and it were look'd for'ard to betwixt us. Not but what, Pip, if you had ever made objections to the business—such as its being open to black and sut, or such-like—not but what they would have been attended to, don't you see?'

'Has the boy,' said Miss Havisham, 'ever made any objection? Does he like the trade?'

'Which it is well beknown to yourself, Pip,' returned Joe, strengthening his former mixture of argumentation, confidence, and politeness, 'that it were the wish of your own hart.' (I saw the idea suddenly break upon him that he would adapt his epitaph to the occasion, before he went on to say) 'And there weren't no objection on your part, and Pip it were the great wish of your hart!'

'Have you brought his indentures with you?' asked Miss Havisham.

'Well, Pip, you know,' replied Joe, as if that were a little unreasonable, 'you yourself see me put 'em in my 'at, and therefore you know as they are here.' With which he took them out, and gave them, not to Miss Havisham, but to me. I am afraid I was ashamed of the dear good fellow—I *know* I was ashamed of him. *

Miss Havisham took up a little bag from the table beside her.

'Pip has earned a premium here, and here it is. There are five-and-twenty guineas in this bag. Give it to your master, Pip.'

As if he were absolutely out of his mind with the wonder awakened in him by her strange figure and the strange room, Joe, even at this pass, persisted in addressing me.

'This is wery liberal on your part, Pip,' said Joe, 'and it is as such received and grateful welcome, though never looked for, far nor near nor nowheres. And now, old chap,' said Joe, conveying to me a sensation, first of burning and then of freezing, for I felt as if that familiar expression were applied to Miss Havisham; 'and now, old chap, may we do our duty! May you and me do our duty, both on us by one and another, and by them which your liberal present—have—conweyed—fur to be—for the satisfaction of mind—of—them as never—' here Joe showed that he felt he had fallen into frightful difficulties, until he triumphantly rescued himself with the words, 'and from myself far be it!' These words had such a round and convincing sound for him that he said them twice. *

So I was apprenticed to Joe. But when I got into my little bedroom I was truly wretched, and had a strong conviction on me that I should never like Joe's trade. I had liked it once, but once was not now. *

I had once believed in the forge as the glowing road to manhood and independence. Within a single year all this was changed. Now it was all coarse and common, and now I was utterly discontented and unhappy.[1]

How much of my ungracious condition of mind may have been my own fault, how much Miss Havisham's, how much my sister's, is of no moment to me or to any one. The change was made in me; the thing was done. Well or ill done, excusably or inexcusably, it was done. * What I wanted, who can say? How can *I* say, when I never knew?[2] *

It was in the fourth year of my apprenticeship to Joe, and it was on a Saturday night, that a strange gentleman entered the forge, just as we had left off work, and looked at Joe, and looked at me, and frowned at me, and frowned at Joe.

'I want,' said he, 'Joseph—or Joe—Gargery.'

'Here is the man,' said Joe.

'You have an apprentice commonly known as Pip? Is he here?'

'I am here!' I cried.

The stranger did not recognize me, but I recognized him as a gentleman whom I had seen long ago at Miss Havisham's, and whom I supposed to be her solicitor. I recognized his large head, his dark complexion, his deep-set eyes, his bushy black eyebrows, his large watch-chain, his strong black dots of beard and whisker, his disagreeably sharp suspicious manner, and even a peculiar smell of scented soap on his great hand. *

'My name is Jaggers, and I am a lawyer in London. I am pretty well known. I have unusual business to transact with you, and I commence by explaining that it is not of my originating. If my advice had been asked, I should not have been here. It was not asked and you see me here. What I have to do as the confidential agent of another, I do. No less, no more. Now, Joseph Gargery, I am the bearer of an offer to relieve you of this young fellow, your apprentice. You would not object to cancel his indentures, at his request and for his good? You would not want anything for so doing?'

'Lord forbid that I should want anything for not standing in Pip's way,' said Joe, staring.

'Lord forbidding is pious, but not to the purpose. The question is, Would you want anything? Do you want anything?'

'The answer is,' returned Joe, sternly, 'No.'

---

[1] The final phrase is substituted for 'and I would not have had Miss Havisham and Estella see it on any account'. Estella's being omitted from the Reading leaves Pip's shame about being 'coarse and common' insufficiently accounted for.

[2] A big jump here, from ch. 14 to ch. 18.

I thought Mr. Jaggers glanced at Joe, as if he considered him a fool for his disinterestedness. *

'Now, I return to this young fellow, and the communication I have got to make is, that he has great expectations. I am instructed to communicate to him,' said Mr. Jaggers, throwing his finger at me, sideways, 'that he will come into a handsome property. Further, that it is the desire of the present possesser of that property, that he be immediately removed from his present sphere of life and from this place, and be brought up as a gentleman.'

My secret[1] dream was out; my wild fancy was surpassed by sober fact. Miss Havisham was going to make my fortune on a grand scale.

'Now, Mr. Pip, I address the rest of what I have to say to you. You are to understand, first, that it is the request of the person from whom I take my instructions, that you always bear the name of Pip. You are to understand, secondly, Mr. Pip, that the name of the person who is your liberal benefactor remains a profound secret until the person chooses to reveal it. I am empowered to mention that it is the intention of the person to reveal it, at first hand, by word of mouth to yourself. When or where that intention may be carried out, I cannot say; no one can say. It may be years hence. Now, you are distinctly to understand that you are most positively prohibited from making any inquiry on this head, or any allusion or reference, however distant, to any individual whomsoever as *the* individual, in all the communications you may have with me. If you have a suspicion in your own breast, keep that suspicion in your own breast. * We come next to mere details of arrangement. You must know that you are not endowed with expectations only. There is already lodged in my hands a sum of money amply sufficient for your suitable education and maintenance. You will please consider me your guardian. Oh!' for I was going to thank him, 'I tell you at once, I'm paid for my services, or I shouldn't render them. It is considered that you must be better educated, in accordance with your altered position.'

I said I had always longed for it.

'Never mind what you have always longed for, Mr. Pip; keep to the record. If you long for it now, that's enough. Am I answered that you are ready to be placed at once under some proper tutor? Is that it?'

I stammered, yes, that was it.

'Good. Now, your inclinations are to be consulted. I don't think that wise, mind, but it's my trust. Have you ever heard of any tutor whom you would prefer to another?'

I had never heard of any.

'There is a certain tutor, of whom I have some knowledge, who I think might suit the purpose. I don't recommend him, observe, because I never

---

[1] 'Secret' added: a big Dickens word, hovering between 'unconscious' and 'unavowed'.

recommend anybody. The gentleman I speak of is one Mr. Matthew Pocket.'

Ah! I caught at the name directly. A relation of Miss Havisham's. She had spoken of that relation.

'You know the name?' said Mr. Jaggers, looking shrewdly at me, and then shutting up his eyes while he waited for my answer.

My answer was that I had heard of the name.

'Oh! you have heard of the name. But the question is, what do you say of the name?'

I said that I was much obliged to him for his recommendation——

'No, my young friend! recollect yourself!'

Not recollecting myself, I began again that I was much obliged to him for his recommendation——

'No, my young friend,' he interrupted, shaking his head and frowning and smiling both at once; 'no, no, no; it's very well done, but it won't do; you are too young to fix me with it. Recommendation is not the word, Mr. Pip. Try another.'

Correcting myself, I said that I was much obliged to him for his mention of Mr. Matthew Pocket——

'*That's* more like it!' cried Mr. Jaggers.

—And (I added) I would gladly try that gentleman.

'Good. You had better try him in his own house. The way shall be prepared for you, and you can see his son first, who is in London. When will you come to London? You should have some new clothes to come in, and they should not be working clothes. Say this day week. You'll want some money. Shall I leave you twenty guineas?'

He produced a long purse with the greatest coolness, and counted them out on the table and pushed them over to me.

'Well, Joseph Gargery! You look dumbfoundered!'

'I *am*!' said Joe, in a very decided manner.

'It was understood that you wanted nothing for yourself, remember.'

'It were understood,' said Joe. 'And it are understood. And it ever will be similar according.'

'But what,' said Mr. Jaggers, swinging his purse, 'what if it was in my instructions to make you a present as compensation? * Now, Joseph Gargery, I warn you this is your last chance. No half measures with me. If you mean to take a present that I have it in charge to make you, speak out, and you shall have it. If on the contrary you mean to say——'

Here, to his great amazement, he was stopped by Joe's suddenly working round him with every demonstration of a fell pugilistic purpose.

'Which I meantersay,' cried Joe, 'that if you come into my place bull-baiting and badgering me, come out! Which I meantersay as such if you're a man, come on! Which I meantersay that what I say, I meantersay and stand or fall by!'

I drew Joe away, and he immediately became placable; merely stating to me in an obliging manner, and as a polite expostulatory notice to any one whom it might happen to concern, that he were not a going to be bull-baited and badgered in his own place. Mr. Jaggers had risen when Joe demonstrated, and had backed near the door. Without evincing any inclination to come in again, he there delivered his valedictory remarks. They were these.

'Well, Mr. Pip, I think the sooner you leave here—as you are to be a gentleman—the better. Let it stand for this day week, and you shall receive my printed address in the mean time. Understand that I express no opinion, one way or other, on the trust I undertake. I am paid for undertaking it, and I do so. Now understand that finally. Understand that!'

He was throwing his finger at both of us, and I think would have gone on, but for his seeming to think Joe dangerous, and going off. *

I patronized Joe to an extent that I am ashamed to think of now, and I ordered a splendid suit of clothes, and I put them on when they were made, and I found them horridly uncomfortable, and I went to take leave of my benefactress.[1]

'I start for London, Miss Havisham, to-morrow:' I was exceedingly careful what I said; 'and I thought you would kindly not mind my taking leave of you.'

'This is a gay figure, Pip,' said she, making her crutch stick play round me, as if she, the fairy godmother who had changed me, were bestowing the finishing gift.

'I have come into such good fortune since I saw you last, Miss Havisham. And I am so grateful for it, Miss Havisham!'

'Ay, ay! I have seen Mr. Jaggers. _I_ have heard about it, Pip. So you go to-morrow?'

'Yes, Miss Havisham.'

'And you are adopted by a rich person?'

'Yes, Miss Havisham.'

'Not named?'

'No, Miss Havisham.'

'And Mr. Jaggers is made your guardian?'

'Yes, Miss Havisham.'

'Well! You have a promising career before you. Be good—deserve it—and abide by Mr. Jaggers's instructions. Good-bye, Pip!—you will always keep the name of Pip, you know.'

'Yes, Miss Havisham.'

'Good-bye, Pip!'

She stretched out her hand, and I went down on my knee and put it to my lips. *

---

[1] This paragraph is a bridge-passage covering sundry ch. 18-19 episodes.

And now those six days which were to have run out so slowly had run out fast and were gone, and to-morrow looked me in the face more steadily than I could look at it. On the last evening of all I dressed myself out in my new clothes, for Joe's delight, and had the condescension to sit in[1] my splendour until bedtime. We were very low, and none the higher for pretending to be in spirits. I was to leave our village at five in the morning, carrying my little hand-portmanteau, and I had told Joe that I wished to walk away alone. I am afraid—sore afraid—that this purpose originated in my sense of the contrast there would be between me and Joe if we went to the coach together. *

It was a hurried breakfast with no taste in it. I got up from the meal, saying with a sort of briskness, as if it had only just occurred to me, 'Well! I suppose I must be off!' And then I kissed my sister, and threw my arms round Joe's neck. Then I took up my little portmanteau and walked out. I walked away at a good pace, thinking it was easier to go than I supposed it would be. I whistled and made nothing of going. But the village was very peaceful and quiet, and the light mists were solemnly rising, as if to show me the world, and I had been so innocent and little there, and all beyond was so unknown and great, that in a moment, with a strong heave and sob, I broke into tears after all. *

[2]I found Mr. Matthew Pocket an excellent tutor, and (as he said of himself) not at all an alarming personage; and I arranged to live with his son Herbert, in Barnard's Inn, Holborn. I liked Herbert Pocket much better than Barnard's Inn, which appeared to me to be a very forlorn creation on the part of Barnard, and in fact the dingiest collection of shabby buildings ever squeezed into a rank corner as a club for Tom cats. Herbert was about my own age, very amiable and cheerful, very frank and easy, not rich, but carried off his rather old clothes much better than I carried off my very new suit.

At our very first bachelor-dinner together, he was so communicative that I felt that reserve on my part would be a bad return unsuited to our years. I therefore told him my small story, and laid stress on my being forbidden to inquire who my benefactor was. I further mentioned that as I had been brought up a blacksmith in a country place, and knew very little of the ways of politeness, I would take it as a great kindness in him if he would give me a hint whenever he saw me at a loss or going wrong.

'With pleasure,' said he, 'though I venture to prophesy that you'll want very few hints. Will you do me the favour to begin at once to call me

---

[1] The novel reads simply 'and sat in'. Biddy having been omitted from the Reading, 'Joe's delight' was substituted for 'their delight'.

[2] The following paragraph, replacing many pages about Pip's arrival in London, draws on passages from chs. 21–3 (pp. 162, 163, 167, 168, 178), and contains some summarizing phrases not in the novel.

by my christian name, Herbert? * And we are so harmonious, and you have been a blacksmith—would you mind Handel for a familiar name? There's a charming piece of music by Handel, called the Harmonious Blacksmith.'

'I should like it very much.'

'Then, my dear Handel,' said he, turning round as the door opened, 'here is the dinner; and I must beg of you to take the top of the table, because the dinner is of your providing.'

This I would not hear of, so he took the top, and I faced him. It was a nice little dinner—seemed to me then a very Lord Mayor's Feast—and it acquired additional relish from being eaten under those independent circumstances, with no old people by, and with London all around us. This again was heightened by a certain gipsy character that set the banquet off; for, while the table was, as one might say, the lap of luxury—being entirely furnished forth from the coffee-house—the circumjacent region of sitting-room was of a comparatively pastureless and shifty character; imposing on the waiter the wandering habits of putting the covers on the floor (where he fell over them), the melted butter in the arm-chair, the bread on the book-shelves, the cheese in the coal-scuttle, and the boiled fowl into my bed in the next room—where I found much of its parsley and butter in a state of congelation when I retired for the night.

'I'll tell you,' said Herbert, 'all I know about Miss Havisham. Let me introduce the topic, Handel, by mentioning that in London it is not the custom to put the knife in the mouth—for fear of accidents—and that while the fork is reserved for that use, it is not put further in than is necessary. It is scarcely worth mentioning, only it's as well to do as other people do. Also, the spoon is not generally used over-hand, but under. This has two advantages. You get at your mouth better (which after all is the object), and you save a good deal of the attitude of opening oysters, on the part of the right elbow.'

He offered these friendly suggestions in such a lively way, that we both laughed and I scarcely blushed.

'Now,' he pursued, 'concerning Miss Havisham. Miss Havisham, you must know, was a spoilt child. Her mother died when she was a baby, and her father denied her nothing. Her father was a country gentleman down in your part of the world, and was a brewer. I don't know why it should be a crack thing to be a brewer; but it is indisputable, that while you cannot possibly be genteel and bake, you may be as genteel as never was and brew. You see it every day.'

'Yet a gentleman may not keep a public-house, may he?'

'Not on any account; but a public-house may keep a gentleman. Well! Mr. Havisham was very rich and very proud. So was his daughter.'

'Miss Havisham was an only child?'

'Stop a moment, I am coming to that. No, she was not an only child;

she had a half-brother. Her father privately married again—his cook, I rather think.'

'I thought he was proud.'

'My good Handel, so he was. He married his second wife privately because he was proud, and in course of time *she* died. Whe she was dead, I apprehend he first told his daughter what he had done, and then the son became a part of the family, residing in the house you are acquainted with. As the son grew a young man, he turned out riotous, extravagant, undutiful—altogether bad. At last his father disinherited him; but he softened when he was dying, and left him well off, though not nearly so well off as Miss Havisham. Take another glass of wine, and excuse my mentioning that society as a body does not expect one to be so strictly conscientious in emptying one's glass, as to turn it bottom upwards with the rim on one's nose.'

I had been doing this, in an excess of attention to his recital. I thanked him, and apologized. He said, 'Not at all,' and resumed.

'Miss Havisham was now an heiress, and you may suppose was looked after as a great match. Her half-brother had now ample means again, but what with debts and what with new madness, again wasted them most fearfully. There were stronger differences between him and her than there had been between him and his father, and it is suspected that he cherished a deep and mortal grudge against her, as having influenced the father's anger. Now, I come to the cruel part of the story—merely breaking off, my dear Handel, to remark that a dinner-napkin will not go into a tumbler.'

Why I was trying to pack mine into my tumbler I am wholly unable to say.

'There appeared upon the scene—say at the races, or the public balls, or anywhere else you like—a certain man who made love to Miss Havisham. I never saw him, for this happened five-and-twenty years ago (before you and I were, Handel), but I have heard my father mention that he was a showy man, and the kind of man for the purpose. But that he was not to be, without ignorance or prejudice, mistaken for a gentleman, my father most strongly asseverates; because it is a principle of his that no man who was not a true gentleman at heart, ever was, since the world began, a true gentleman in manner. He says no varnish can hide the grain of the wood; and that the more varnish you put on, the more the grain will express itself. Well! This man pursued Miss Havisham closely, and professed to be devoted to her. She passionately loved him. There is no doubt that she perfectly idolized him. He practised on her affection in that systematic way, that he got great sums of money from her, and he induced her to buy her brother out of a share in the brewery (which had been weakly left him by his father) at an immense price, on the plea that when he was her husband he must hold and manage it all. Your guardian was not at that time in Miss Havisham's councils, and she was too haughty and too much in love to be advised by any one. * The marriage day was fixed, the wedding dresses were bought, the wedding tour was planned out, the wedding guests were invited. The day came, but not the bridegroom. He wrote her a letter——'

'Which she received when she was dressing for her marriage? At twenty minutes to nine?'

'At the hour and minute, at which she afterwards stopped all the clocks. What was in it, further than that it most heartlessly broke the marriage off, I can't tell you, because I don't know. When she recovered from a bad illness that she had, she laid the whole place waste, as you have seen it, and she has never since looked upon the light of day. I have forgotten one thing. It has been supposed that the man to whom she gave her misplaced confidence acted throughout in concert with her half-brother; that it was a conspiracy between them, and that they shared the profits.'

'Are they alive now?'

'I don't know. And now Handel, there is a perfectly open understanding between us. And all that I know about Miss Havisham you know.'

'And all that I know, you know.'

'I fully believe it. So there can be no competition or perplexity between you and me. And as to the condition on which you hold your advancement in life—namely, that you are not to inquire or discuss to whom you owe it—you may be very sure that it will never be encroached upon, or even approached by me, or by any one belonging to me.'

In truth, he said this with so much delicacy, that I felt the subject done with. Yet he spoke with so much meaning, too, that I felt he as perfectly understood Miss Havisham to be my benefactress as I understood the fact myself. We were very gay and sociable, and I asked him, in the course of conversation, what he was? He replied, 'A capitalist—an Insurer of Ships.'

I had grand ideas of the wealth and importance of Insurers of Ships, and * I asked him where the ships he insured mostly traded to at present?

'I haven't begun insuring yet,' he replied. 'I am looking about me.'

Somehow that pursuit seemed more in keeping with Barnard's Inn. I said (in a tone of conviction), 'Ah-h!'

'Yes. I am in a counting-house, and looking about me.'

'Is a counting-house profitable?'

'To——do you mean to the young fellow who's in it?'

'Yes: to you.'

'Why, n-no; not to me. Not directly profitable. That is, it doesn't pay me anything, and I have to——keep myself.'

This certainly had not a profitable appearance.

'But the thing is,' said Herbert, 'that you look about you. *That's* the grand thing. You are in a counting-house, you know, and you look about you. Then the time comes when you see your opening, and you go in, and you swoop upon it, and you make your capital, and then there you are!'[1]

I soon began to be always decorating the chambers in some quite unnecessary and inappropriate way or other; and very expensive those wrestles with Barnard proved to be. The rooms were soon vastly different from what I had found them, and I enjoyed the honour of occupying a few prominent pages in the books of a neighbouring upholsterer. I went on so fast, indeed, that I even started a boy in boots—top boots—in bondage and slavery to whom I might have been said to pass my days. For, after I had made this monster (out of the refuse of my washerwoman's family), and had clothed him with a blue coat, canary waistcoat, white cravat, creamy breeches, and the boots already mentioned, I had to find him a little to do and a great deal to eat; and with both of those horrible requirements he haunted my existence. *

My lavish habits by degrees led Herbert's easy nature into expenses that he could not afford, corrupted the simplicity of his life, and disturbed his peace with anxieties and regrets. * As an infallible way of making little ease great ease, I began to contract a quantity of debt. I could hardly begin but Herbert must begin too, so he soon followed suit. * In my confidence in my own resources, I would willingly have taken Herbert's expenses on myself; but Herbert was proud, and I could make no such proposal to him. So he got into difficulties in every direction, and continued to look about him. When we gradually fell into keeping late hours and late company, I noticed that he looked about him with a desponding eye at breakfast-time; that he began to look about him more hopefully about mid-day; that he drooped when he came into dinner; that he seemed to descry Capital in the distance rather clearly, after dinner; that he all but realised Capital towards midnight; and that at about two o'clock in the morning he became so deeply despondent again as to talk of buying a rifle and going to America, with a general purpose of compelling buffaloes to make his fortune. *

We spent as much money as we could, and got as little for it as people could make up their minds to give us. We were always more or less miserable, and most of our acquaintance were in the same condition. There was a gay fiction among us that we were constantly enjoying ourselves, and a skeleton truth that we never did. To the best of my belief, our case was in the last aspect a rather common one.

Every morning, with an air ever new, Herbert went into the City to look about him. I often paid him a visit in the dark back room in which he consorted with an ink-jar, a hat-peg, a coal-box, a string-box, an

---

[1] The Reading text here jumps from ch. 22 to one paragraph drawn from ch. 27, after which the text again jumps, to ch. 34.

almanack, a desk and stool, and a ruler; and I do not remember that I ever saw him do anything else but look about him. *

If we had been less attached to one another, I think we must have hated one another regularly every morning. I detested the chambers beyond expression at that period of repentance, and could not endure the sight of the Avenger's livery (I called the boy in top-boots the Avenger), which had a more expensive and a less remunerative appearance then than at any other time in the four-and-twenty hours. As we got more and more into debt, breakfast became a hollower and hollower form. At certain times—meaning at uncertain times, for they depended on our humour—I would say to Herbert, as if it were a remarkable discovery:

'My dear Herbert, we are getting on badly.'

'My dear Handel, if you will believe me, those very words were on my lips, by a strange coincidence.'

'Then, Herbert,' I would respond, 'let us look into our affairs.'

We always derived profound satisfaction from making an appointment for this purpose. We always thought this was business, this was the way to confront the thing, this was the way to take the foe by the throat.

We ordered something rather special for dinner, with a bottle of something similarly out of the common way, in order that our minds might be fortified for the occasion, and we might come well up to the mark. Dinner over, we produced a bundle of pens, a copious supply of ink, and a goodly show of writing and blotting paper. For, there was something very comfortable in having plenty of stationery.

I would then take a sheet of paper, and write across the top of it, in a neat hand, the heading, 'Memorandum of Pip's debts,' with Barnard's Inn and the date very carefully added. Herbert would also take a sheet of paper, and write across it with similar formalities, 'Memorandum of Herbert's debts.'

Each of us would then refer to a confused heap of papers at his side, which had been thrown into drawers, worn into holes in pockets, half-burnt in lighting candles, stuck for weeks into the looking-glass, and otherwise damaged. The sound of our pens going, refreshed us exceedingly, insomuch that I sometimes found it difficult to distinguish between this edifying business proceeding and actually paying the money. In point of meritorious character the two things seemed about equal.

When we had written a little while, I would ask Herbert how he got on. Herbert probably would have been scratching his head in the most rueful manner at the sight of his accumulating figures.

'They are mounting up, Handel,' Herbert would say; 'upon my life, they are mounting up.'

'Be firm, Herbert,' I would retort, plying my own pen with great assiduity. 'Look the thing in the face. Look into your affairs. Stare them out of countenance.'

'So I would, Handel, only they are staring *me* out of countenance.'

However, my determined manner would have its effect, and Herbert would fall to work again. After a time he would give up once more, on the plea that he had not got Cobbs's bill, or Lobbs's, or Nobbs's, as the case might be.

'Then, Herbert, estimate; estimate it in round numbers, and put it down.'

'What a fellow of resource you are!' my friend would reply, with admiration. 'Really your business powers are remarkable.'

I thought so too. I established with myself on these occasions the reputation of a first-rate man of business—prompt, decisive, energetic, clear, cool-headed. When I had got all my responsibilities down upon my list, I compared each with the bill, and ticked it off. My self-approval, when I ticked an entry, was quite a luxurious sensation. When I had no more ticks to make, I folded all my bills up, and tied the whole into a symmetrical bundle. Then I did the same for Herbert (who modestly said he had not my administrative genius), and felt that I had brought his affairs into a focus for him.

My business habits had one other bright feature, which I called 'leaving a margin.' For example: supposing Herbert's debts to be one hundred and sixty-four pounds four and twopence, I would say, 'Leave a margin, and put them down at two hundred.' Or, supposing my own to be four times as much, I would leave a margin, and put them down at seven hundred. I had the highest opinion of the wisdom of this same Margin, but I am bound to acknowledge, that on looking back, I deem it to have been an expensive device. For we always ran into new debt immediately, to the full extent of the margin, and sometimes in the sense of freedom and solvency it imparted, got pretty far on into another margin.

But there was a calm, a rest, a virtuous hush, consequent on these examinations of our affairs, that gave me, for the time, an admirable opinion of myself. Soothed by my exertions, I would sit among the stationery, and feel like a bank of some sort, rather than a private individual. This is a general description of our usual manners and customs when we were growing up at Barnard's Inn. *

At length and at last, I came of age.[1]

Herbert had come of age eight months before me. As he had nothing else to come into, the event did not make a profound sensation in Barnard's Inn. But we had looked forward to my one-and-twentieth birthday with a crowd of speculations and anticipations, for we had both considered that my guardian could hardly help saying something definite on that occasion.

I received an official note from Wemmick—Mr. Jagger's confidential

---

[1] A sentence from earlier in ch. 34; then on to ch. 36.

clerk, with a mouth like a post-office—informing me that Mr. Jaggers would be glad if I would call upon him at five in the afternoon of the auspicious day.

In the outer office Wemmick offered me his congratulations, and incidentally rubbed the side of his nose with a folded piece of tissue-paper that I liked the look of. But he said nothing, and motioned me with a nod into my guardian's room. It was November, and my guardian was standing before his fire leaning his back against the chimney-piece, with his hands under his coat-tails.

'Well, Pip; I must call you Mr. Pip to-day. Congratulations, Mr. Pip.'

We shook hands—he was always a remarkably short shaker—and I thanked him.

'Now, my young friend,' my guardian began, as if I were a witness in the box, 'I am going to have a word or two with you.'

'If you please, sir?'

'What do you suppose,' said Mr. Jaggers, bending forward to look at the ground, and then throwing his head back to look at the ceiling, 'what do you suppose you are living at the rate of?'

'At the rate of, sir?'

'At,' repeated Mr. Jaggers, still looking at the ceiling, 'the—rate of!' And then looked all round the room, and paused with his pocket-handkerchief in his hand, half way to his nose.

I had looked into my affairs so often that I had thoroughly destroyed any slight notion I might ever have had of their bearings. Reluctantly I confessed myself quite unable to answer the question. This reply seemed agreeable to Mr. Jaggers, who said, 'I thought so!' and blew his nose with an air of satisfaction.

'Now, I have asked *you* a question, my friend,' said Mr. Jaggers. 'Have you anything to ask *me*?'

'Of course it would be a great relief to me to ask you several questions, sir; but I remember your prohibition.'

'Ask one,' said Mr. Jaggers.

'Is my benefactor to be made known to me to-day?'

'No. Ask another.'

There appeared to be no possible escape from the inquiry, 'Have—I—anything to receive, sir?' On that, Mr. Jaggers said, triumphantly, 'I thought we should come to it!' and called to Wemmick to give him that piece of paper. Wemmick appeared, handed it in, and disappeared.

'Now, Mr. Pip,' said Mr. Jaggers, 'attend, if you please. You have been drawing pretty freely here; your name occurs pretty often in Wemmick's cash-book; but you are in debt, of course.'

'I am afraid I must say yes, sir.'

'You know you must say yes; don't you?'

'Yes, sir.'

'I don't ask you what you owe, because you don't know; and if you did know, you wouldn't tell me; you would say less. Yes, yes, my friend,' cried Mr. Jaggers, waving his forefinger to stop me, as I made a show of protesting; 'it's likely enough that you think you wouldn't, but you would. You'll excuse me, but I know better than you. Now, take this piece of paper in your hand. You have got it? Very good. Now, unfold it and tell me what it is.'

'This is a bank-note,' said I, 'for five hundred pounds.'

'That is a bank-note,' repeated Mr. Jaggers, 'for five hundred pounds. And a very handsome sum of money, too, I think. You consider it so?'

'How could I do otherwise?'

'Ah! But answer the question.'

'Undoubtedly.'

'You consider it, undoubtedly, a handsome sum of money. Now, that handsome sum of money, Mr. Pip, is your own. It is a present to you on this day, in earnest of your expectations. And at the rate of that handsome sum of money per annum, and at no higher rate, you are to live until the donor of the whole appears. That is to say, you will now take your money affairs entirely into your own hands, and you will draw from Wemmick one hundred and twenty-five pounds per quarter, until you are in communication with the fountain-head, and no longer with the mere agent.' *

'Is it likely that my patron—the fountain-head you have spoken of, Mr. Jaggers, will soon—' there I delicately stopped.

'Will soon what?'

'Will soon come to London?'

'Now here,' replied Mr. Jaggers, fixing me for the first time with his dark deep-set eyes, 'we must revert to the evening when we first encountered one another in your village. What did I tell you then, Mr. Pip?'

'You told me, Mr. Jaggers, that it might be years hence when that person appeared.'

'Just so,' said Mr. Jaggers; 'that's my answer.' *

'If that is all you have to say, sir,' I remarked, 'there can be nothing left for me to add.' *

But because Herbert was my young friend and companion, and I had a great affection for him, I wished my own good fortune to reflect some rays upon him, and I wanted advice from Wemmick's experience and knowledge of me, how I could best help Herbert to some present income—say of a hundred a year to keep him in heart and hope—and gradually buy him into some small partnership. So I thought I would go into the outer office and talk to Wemmick. *

'Mr. Wemmick,' said I, 'I want to ask your opinion. I am very desirous to serve a friend.'

Wemmick tightened his post office and shook his head, as if his opinion were dead against any fatal weakness of that sort.

'This friend is trying to get on in commercial life, but has no money, and finds it difficult and disheartening to make a beginning. Now I want to help him to a beginning with *some* money down, and perhaps some anticipation of my expectations.'

'Mr. Pip,' said Wemmick, 'I should like just to run over with you on my fingers, if you please, the names of the various bridges up as high as Chelsea Reach. Let's see; there's London, one; Southwark, two; Blackfriars, three; Waterloo, four; Westminster, five; Vauxhall, six.' He had checked off each bridge in its turn with the handle of his safe-key on the palm of his hand. 'There's as many as six, you see, to choose from.'

'I don't understand you.'

'Choose your bridge, Mr. Pip, and take a walk upon your bridge, and pitch your money into the Thames over the centre arch of your bridge, and you know the end of it. Serve a friend with it, and you may know the end of it too—but it's a less pleasant and profitable end.'

I could have posted a newspaper in his mouth, he made it so wide after saying this.

'Then is it your opinion,' I inquired, with some little indignation, 'that a man should never——'

'—Invest portable property in a friend? Certainly he should not. Unless he wants to get rid of the friend—and then it becomes a question how much portable property it may be worth to get rid of him.'

'And that is your deliberate opinion, Mr. Wemmick?'

'That is my deliberate opinion——in this office.'

'Ah!' said I, pressing him, for I thought I saw him near a loophole here; 'but would that be your opinion at your own house at Walworth?'

'Mr. Pip,' he replied, with gravity, 'Walworth is one place, and this office is another. My Walworth sentiments must be taken at Walworth, and none but my official sentiments can be taken in this office.'

'Then,' said I, 'I will go home with you this very evening if you will take me.' To which he willingly agreed, saying, I should be 'welcome in a private and personal capacity.'[1]

Wemmick's house was a little wooden cottage in the midst of plots of garden, and the top of it was cut out and painted like a battery mounted with guns.

'My own doing,' said Wemmick. 'Looks pretty; don't it?'

I highly commended it. I think it was the smallest house I ever saw; with the queerest Gothic windows (by far the greater part of them sham), and a Gothic door, almost too small to get in at.

'That's a real flagstaff, you see,' said Wemmick, 'and on Sundays I run up a real flag. Then look here. After I have crossed this bridge, I hoist it up—so—and cut off the communication.'

[1] Here the Reading text, having in the preceding paragraph slightly amended the ch. 36 wording, goes back to ch. 25.

The bridge was a plank, and it crossed a chasm about four feet wide and two deep. But it was very pleasant to see the pride with which he hoisted it up and made it fast; smiling as he did so with a relish, and not merely mechanically.

'At nine o'clock every night, Greenwich time,' said Wemmick, 'the gun fires. There he is, you observe! And when you hear him go, I think you'll say he's a Stinger.'

The piece of ordnance referred to was mounted in a separate fortress, constructed of lattice-work. It was protected from the weather by an ingenious little tarpaulin contrivance in the nature of an umbrella.

'Then, at the back,' said Wemmick, 'out of sight, so as not to impede the idea of fortifications—for it's a principle with me, if you have an idea, carry it out and keep it up—I don't know whether that's your opinion——'

I said, decidedly.

'At the back, there's a pig, and there are fowls and rabbits; then, I knock together my own little frame, you see, and grow cucumbers; and you'll judge at supper what sort of a salad I can raise. So, sir,' said Wemmick, smiling again, but seriously too, as he shook his head, 'if you can suppose the little place besieged, it would hold out a devil of a time in point of provisions.'

Then he conducted me to a bower about a dozen yards off, but which was approached by such ingenious twists of path that it took quite a long time to get at, and which stood on the margin of an ornamental lake. This piece of water (with an island in the middle which might have been the salad for supper) was of a circular form, and he had constructed a fountain in it, which, when you set a little mill going and took a cork out of a pipe, played to that powerful extent that it made the back of your hand quite wet.

'This piece of property is a freehold, by George! I am my own engineer, and my own carpenter, and my own plumber, and my own gardener, and my own Jack of all Trades,' said Wemmick, in acknowledging my compliments. 'Well; it's a good thing, you know. It brushes the Newgate cobwebs away, and pleases the Aged. You wouldn't mind being at once introduced to the Aged, would you? It wouldn't put you out?'

I expressed the readiness I felt, and we went into the Castle. There we found, sitting by a fire, a very old man in a flannel coat; clean, cheerful, comfortable, and well cared for, but intensely deaf.

'Well aged parent,' said Wemmick, shaking hands with him in a cordial and jocose way, 'how are you?'

'All right, John; all right!' replied the old man.

'Here's Mr. Pip, aged parent,' said Wemmick, 'and I wish you could hear his name. Nod away at him, Mr. Pip; that's what he likes. Nod away at him, if you please, like winking!'

'This is a fine place of my son's, sir,' cried the old man, while I nodded as hard as I possibly could. 'This is a pretty pleasure-ground, sir. This spot and these beautiful works upon it ought to be kept together by the Nation, sir, after my son's time, for the people's enjoyment.'

'You're as proud of it as Punch; ain't you, Aged?' said Wemmick, contemplating the old man with his hard face really softened; '*there's* a nod for you;' giving him a tremendous one; '*there's* another for you;' giving him a still more tremendous one; 'you like that, don't you? If you're not tired, Mr. Pip—though I know it's tiring to strangers—will you tip him one more? You can't think how it pleases him.'

I tipped him several more, and he was in great spirits. * 'Halloa! Getting near gun-fire,' said Wemmick, 'it's the Aged's treat.'

In fact, the Aged was heating the poker, with expectant eyes, as a preliminary to the performance of this great nightly ceremony. Wemmick stood with his watch in his hand, until the moment was come for him to take the red-hot poker from the Aged, and repair to the battery. He took it, and went out, and presently the Stinger went off with a Bang that shook the crazy little box of a cottage as if it must fall to pieces, and made every glass and teacup in it ring. Upon this, the Aged—who I believe would have been blown out of his armchair but for holding on by the elbows—cried out exultingly, 'He's fired! I heerd him!' and I nodded at the old gentleman until it is no figure of speech to declare that I absolutely could not see him.[1]

When Wemmick came back, he was accompanied by a lady who had just arrived, and whom he presented as Miss Skiffins. Miss Skiffins was of a wooden appearance, and might have been some two or three years younger than Wemmick, and I judged her to stand possessed of portable property. The cut of her dress from the waist upward, both before and behind, made her figure very like a boy's kite; and I might have pronounced her gown a little too decidedly orange, and her gloves a little too intensely green. But she seemed to be a good sort of fellow, and showed a high regard for the Aged. * While this lady prepared tea, the responsible duty of making the toast was delegated to the Aged, and that excellent old gentleman was so intent upon it that he seemed to me in some danger of melting his eyes. It was no nominal meal that we were going to make, but a vigorous reality. The Aged prepared such a haystack of buttered toast, that I could scarcely see him over it as it simmered on an iron stand hooked on to the top-bar; while Miss Skiffins brewed such a jorum of tea, that the pig in the back premises became strongly excited, and repeatedly expressed his desire to participate in the entertainment.

I inferred from the methodical nature of Miss Skiffins's arrangements that she made tea there on most nights; and I rather suspected that a classic brooch she wore, representing the profile of an undesirable female

---

[1] The action here jumps from ch. 25 to ch. 37.

with a very straight nose and a very new moon, was a piece of portable property that had been given her by Wemmick.

We ate the whole of the toast, and drank tea in proportion, and it was delightful to see how warm and greasy we all got after it. The Aged especially might have passed for some clean old chief of a savage tribe, just oiled. After a short pause of repose, Miss Skiffins washed up the tea-things, in a lady-like amateur manner that compromised none of us. Then she put on her gloves again, and we drew round the fire to hear the Aged read the paper.

'I won't offer an apology,' said Wemmick, 'for he isn't capable of many pleasures—are you, Aged P. ?' *

As the Aged wanted the candles close to him, and as he was always on the verge of putting either his head or the newspaper into them, he required as much watching as a powder-mill. But Wemmick was equally untiring and gentle in his vigilance, and the Aged read on, quite unconscious of his many rescues. He was altogether inaudible, but whenever he looked at us we all expressed the greatest interest and amazement, and nodded until he resumed again.

As Wemmick and Miss Skiffins sat side by side, and as I sat in a shadowy corner, I observed a slow and gradual elongation of Mr. Wemmick's mouth, powerfully suggestive of his slowly and gradually stealing his arm round Miss Skiffins's waist. In course of time I saw his hand appear on the other side of Miss Skiffins; but at that moment Miss Skiffins neatly stopped him with the green glove, unwound his arm again as if it were an article of dress, and with the greatest deliberation laid it on the table before her. Miss Skiffins's composure while she did this was one of the most remarkable sights I have ever seen. By-and-by, I noticed Wemmick's arm beginning to disappear again, and gradually fading out of view. Shortly afterwards his mouth began to widen again. After an interval of suspense on my part that was quite enthralling and almost painful, I saw his hand appear on the other side of Miss Skiffins. Instantly Miss Skiffins stopped it with the neatness of a placid boxer, took off that girdle or cestus as before, and laid it on the table. Taking the table to represent the path of virtue, I am justified in stating that during the whole time of the Aged's reading, Wemmick's arm was straying from the path of virtue and being recalled to it by Miss Skiffins.

At last the Aged read himself into a light slumber, and I took my leave.[1] Wemmick, at parting, told me (as his unofficial Walworth sentiments) that my idea in behalf of Herbert was devilish kind of me, and that he thought it could be carried out through 'Her' (Miss Skiffins's) brother, who was an accountant and agent. Wemmick was as good as his word,

---

[1] The remainder of this 'Stage' is a highly condensed, rearranged and summarized version of passages from ch. 37.

and I made a secret treaty, by virtue of which I did buy Herbert into a partnership at last, and was proud and happy to think that my expectations had at last done good to somebody.

THIRD STAGE
Pip's Majority

[1] I was three-and-twenty years of age. Not another word had I heard to enlighten me on the subject of my expectations, and my twenty-third birthday was a week gone. We had left Barnard's Inn more than a year, and lived in the Temple. Our chambers were in the last house in Garden-court, down by the river. *

Business had taken Herbert on a journey to Marseilles. I was alone, and had a dull sense of being alone.

It was wretched weather; stormy and wet, stormy and wet; mud, mud, mud, deep in all the streets. Day after day, a vast heavy veil had been driving over London from the East, and it drove still, as if in the East there were an Eternity of cloud and wind. So furious had been the gusts, that high buildings in town had had the lead stripped off their roofs; and in the country, trees had been torn up, and sails of windmills carried away; and gloomy accounts had come in from the coast, of shipwreck and death. Violent blasts of rain had accompanied these rages of wind, and the day just closed as I sat down to read had been the worst of all.

Alterations have been made in that part of the Temple since that time, and it has not now so lonely a character as it had then, nor is it so exposed to the river. The wind rushing up the river shook the house that night like discharges of cannon or breakings of a sea. When the rain came with it and dashed against the windows, I thought, raising my eyes to them as they rocked, that I might have fancied myself in a storm-beaten lighthouse. Occasionally the smoke came rolling down the chimney, as though it could not bear to go out into such a night; and when I set the doors open and looked down the staircase, the staircase lamps were blown out; and when I shaded my face with my hands and looked through the black windows (opening them ever so little was out of the question in the teeth of such wind and rain) I saw that the lamps in the court were blown out, and that the lamps on the bridges and the shore were shuddering, and that the coal fires in barges on the river were being carried away before the wind, like red-hot splashes in the rain.

I read with my watch upon the table, purposing to close my book at eleven o'clock. As I shut it, Saint Paul's, and all the many church-clocks in the City—some leading, some accompanying, some following—

---

[1] The Reading here jumps to the beginning of ch. 39.

struck that hour. The sound was curiously flawed by the wind; and I was listening, and thinking how the wind assailed and tore it, when I heard a footstep on the stair.

Remembering then that the staircase-lights were blown out, I took up my reading-lamp and went out to the stair-head. Whoever was below had stopped on seeing my lamp, for all was quiet.

'There is some one down there, is there not?'

'Yes.'

'What floor do you want?'

'The top. Mr. Pip.'

'That is my name. There is nothing the matter?'

'Nothing the matter.' And the man came on.

I stood with my lamp held over the stair-rail, and he came slowly within its light. It was a shaded lamp, to shine upon a book, and its circle of light was very contracted; so he was in it for a mere instant and then out of it. In the instant I had seen a face that was strange to me looking up with an incomprehensible air of being touched and pleased by the sight of me.

Moving the lamp as the man moved, I made out that he was substantially dressed, but roughly; like a voyager by sea. That he had a furrowed bald head, and long iron grey hair at the sides. That his age was about sixty. That he was a muscular man, strong on his legs, and that he was browned and hardened by exposure to weather. As he ascended the last stair or two, and the light of my lamp included us both, I saw, with a stupid kind of amazement, that he was holding out both his hands to me.

'Pray what is your business?'

'My business? Ah! Yes. I will explain my business, by your leave.'

'Do you wish to come in?'

'Yes, I wish to come in, Master.' *

He sat down on a chair that stood before the fire, and covered his forehead with his large brown veinous hands. I looked at him attentively then, and recoiled a little from him; but I did not know him.

'There is no one nigh; is there?'

'Why do you, a stranger coming into my rooms at this time of the night, ask that question?'

'You're a game one; I'm glad you've grow'd up a game one! But don't catch hold of me. You'd be sorry arterwards to have done it.'

I relinquished the intention he had detected, for I knew him! Even yet I could not recal a single feature, but I knew him! If the wind and the rain had driven away the intervening years, had scattered all the intervening objects, had swept us to the churchyard where we first stood face to face on such different levels, I could not have known my convict more distinctly than I knew him now, as he sat in the chair before the fire. *

He held out both his hands. Not knowing what to do—for, in my astonishment I had lost my self-possession—I reluctantly gave him my hands. He grasped them heartily, raised them to his lips, kissed them, and still held them.

'You acted noble, my boy. Noble, Pip! And I have never forgot it!'

At a change in his manner, as if he were even going to embrace me, I laid a hand upon his breast and put him away.

'Stay! Keep off! If you are grateful to me for what I did when I was a little child, I hope you have shown your gratitude by mending your way of life. If you have come here to thank me it was not necessary. Still, however, you have found me out, there must be something good in the feeling that has brought you here, and I will not repulse you; but surely you must understand that—I——'

My attention was so attracted by the singularity of his fixed look at me, that the words died away on my tongue.

'You was a saying that surely I must understand. What, surely must I understand?'

'That I cannot wish to renew that chance intercourse with you of long ago, under these different circumstances. I am glad to believe you have repented and recovered yourself. I am glad to tell you so. I am glad that, thinking I deserve to be thanked, you have come to thank me. But our ways are different ways none the less. You are wet, and you look weary. Will you drink something before you go?'

He had replaced his neckerchief loosely, and had stood, keenly observant of me, biting a long end of it. 'I think,' he answered, still with the end at his mouth and still observant of me, 'that I *will* drink (I thank you) afore I go.'

There was a tray ready on a side-table. I brought it to the table near the fire, and asked him what he would have? He touched one of the bottles without looking at it or speaking, and I mixed him some hot rum-and-water. When I put the glass to him, I saw with amazement that his eyes were full of tears. I was softened by the softened aspect of the man, and felt a touch of reproach. 'I hope,' said I, hurriedly putting something into a glass for myself, and drawing a chair to the table, 'that you will not think I spoke harshly to you just now. I had no intention of doing it, and I am sorry for it if I did. I wish you well and happy. How are you living?'

'I've been a sheep-farmer, stock-breeder, other trades besides, away in the new world; many a thousand mile of stormy water off from this.'

'I hope you have done well?'

'I've done wonderful well. There's others went out alonger me as has done well too, but no man has done nigh as well as me. I'm famous for it.'

'I'm glad to hear it.'

'I hope to hear you say so, my dear boy. * May I make so bold,' he said then, with a smile that was like a frown, and with a frown that was like a smile, 'as ask you how *you* have done well, since you and me was out on them lone shivering marshes?'

'How?'

'Ah!'

I forced myself to tell him (though I could not do it distinctly) that I had been chosen to succeed to some property.

'Might a mere warmint ask what property?'

'I don't know.'

'Might a mere warmint ask whose property?'

'I don't know.'

'Could I make a guess, I wonder, at your income since you come of age! As to the first figure now. Five? There ought to have been some guardian, or such like, whiles you was a minor. Some lawyer, maybe. As to the first letter of that lawyer's name now. Would it be J?' *

I could not have spoken one word, though it had been to save my life. I stood, with a hand on the chair-back, and a hand on my breast, where I seemed to be suffocating.

'Yes, Pip, dear boy, I've made a gentleman on you! It's me wot has done it! I swore that time, sure as ever I earned a guinea, that guinea should go to you. I swore arterwards, sure as ever I spec'lated and got rich, you should get rich. I lived rough, that you should live smooth; I worked hard, that you should be above work. What odds, dear boy? Do I tell it fur you to feel a obligation? Not a bit. I tell it, fur you to know as that there hunted dunghill dog wot you kep life in, got his head so high that he could make a gentleman—and, Pip, you're him!'

The abhorrence in which I held the man, the dread I had of him, the repugnance with which I shrank from him, could not have been exceeded if he had been some terrible beast.

'Look'ee here, Pip. I'm your second father. You're my son—more to me nor any son. I've put away money, only for you to spend. When I was a hired-out shepherd in a solitary hut, not seeing no faces but faces of sheep till I half forgot wot men's and women's faces wos like, I see yourn. I drops my knife many a time in that hut when I was a eating my dinner or my supper, and I says, "Here's the boy again, a looking at me whiles I eats and drinks!" I see you there a many times, as plain as ever I see you on them misty marshes. "Lord strike me dead!" I says each time —and I goes out in the air to say it under the open heavens—"but wot, if I gets liberty and money, I'll make that boy a gentleman!" And I done it. * Didn't you never think it might be me?'

'O no, no, no! Never, never!'

'Well, you see it *was* me, and single-handed. Never a soul in it but my own self and Mr. Jaggers! * It warn't easy, Pip, for me to leave them parts, nor yet it warn't safe. * By G—, it's Death!'

'What's death?'

'I was sent for life. It's death to come back. There's been overmuch coming back of late years, and I should of a certainty be hanged if took.'

Nothing was needed but this; the wretched man, after loading wretched me with his gold and silver chains for years, had risked his life to come to me, and I held it there in my keeping!

My first care was to close the shutters, so that no light might be seen from without, and then to close and make fast the doors. * In every rage of wind and rush of rain I heard pursuers. With these fears upon me, I began either to imagine or recal that I had had mysterious warnings of this man's approach. That for weeks gone by I had passed faces in the streets which I had thought like his. That these likenesses had grown more numerous, as he, coming over the sea, had drawn nearer. That his wicked spirit had somehow sent these messengers to mine, and that now on this stormy night he was as good as his word, and with me.[1] *

'You assumed some name, I suppose, on board ship?'

'Yes, dear boy. I took the name of Provis.'

'Do you mean to keep that name?'

'Why, yes, dear boy, it's as good as another—unless you'd like another.'

'What is your real name?'

'Magwitch, chrisen'd Abel.'

'What were you brought up to be?'

'A warmint, dear boy.'

He answered quite seriously, and used the word as if it denoted some profession. *

He ate of my supper in a ravenous way that was very disagreeable. Some of his teeth had failed him since I saw him eat on the marshes, and as he turned his food in his mouth, and turned his head sideways to bring his strongest fangs to bear upon it, he looked terribly like a hungry old dog.

'I'm a heavy grubber, dear boy,' he said, as a polite kind of apology when he had made an end of his meal; 'but I always was. If it had been in my constitution to be a lighter grubber, I might ha' got into lighter trouble. Similarly, I must have my smoke. When I was first hired out as shepherd t'other side the world, it's my belief I should ha' turned into a molloncolly-mad sheep myself, if I hadn't a had my smoke. * But this is low talk. Look'ee here, Pip. Look over it. I ain't a going to be low. Look'ee here, Pip. I was low; that's what I was; low. Look over it, dear boy.' *

Herbert's key was heard in the lock, and Herbert came bursting in, with the airy freshness of six hundred miles of France upon him. *

---

[1] The final paragraphs of ch. 39 (which in the novel end 'The Second Stage of Pip's Expectations'), and the opening pages of ch. 40 (the action of which occurs the following day), are here omitted.

'Herbert, my dear friend,' said I, shutting the double doors, while he stood staring and wondering, 'something very strange has happened. This is—a visitor of mine.'

'It's all right, dear boy!' said Provis, coming forward, with a little clasped black book, and then addressing himself to Herbert. 'Take it in your right hand, Pip's friend. Lord strike you dead on the spot, if ever you split in any way sumever! Kiss it, Pip's friend! Now you're on your oath, you know.' [1]

To state that my terrible patron carried this little black book about the world solely to swear people on in cases of emergency, would be to state what I never quite established—but this I can say, that I never knew him put it to any other use. The book itself had the appearance of having been stolen from some court of justice, and perhaps his knowledge of its antecedents, combined with his own experience in that wise, gave him a reliance on its powers as a sort of legal spell or charm. *

'Look'ee here, Pip's comrade, I know very well that once since I come back—for half a minute—I've been low. But don't you fret yourself on that score. Dear boy, and Pip's comrade, you two may count upon me always having a gen-teel muzzle on.' *

I had never felt before, so blessedly, what it is to have a friend.[2] I told Herbert of the old encounter on the marshes, and of my long and bitter mistake. Then I turned to my grim visitor, and said, 'We want to know something about that other man with whom you struggled.'

'Well!' he said, after consideration. 'You're on your oath, you know, Pip's comrade?'

'Assuredly.'

'And look'ee here? Wotever I done, is worked out and paid for.'

'So be it.' *

'Dear boy and Pip's comrade. To give it you short and handy, I'll put my life at once into a mouthful of English. In jail and out of jail, in jail and out of jail, in jail and out of jail. There, you've got it. I've been done everything to, pretty well—except hanged. I've no more notion where I was born than you have—if so much. I first became aware of myself down in Essex, a thieving turnips for my living. I know'd my name to be Magwitch, chrisen'd Abel. How did I know it? Much as I know'd the birds' names in the hedges to be chaffinch, sparrer, thrush. I might have thought it was all lies together, only as the birds' names come out true, I supposed mine did. So fur as I could find, there warn't a soul that see young Abel Magwitch, with as little on him as in him, but wot caught fright at him, and either drove him off or took him up. I was took up, took up, took up, to that extent that I reg'larly grow'd up, took up. * A bit of a poacher, a bit of a labourer, a bit of a waggoner, a bit of a haymaker, a bit of a hawker,

---

[1] Here the Reading reverts, for a paragraph, to a passage earlier in ch. 40, before jumping to ch. 41.   [2] The rest of this paragraph is a summary.

a bit of most things that don't pay and lead to trouble, I got to be a man. At Epsom races, a matter of over twenty years ago, I got acquainted wi' a man whose skull I'd crack wi' this poker, like the claw of a lobster, if I'd got it on this hob. His right name was Compeyson; and *that's* the man, dear boy, what you see me a pounding in the ditch. Compeyson (a smooth one to talk, and a dab at the ways of gentlefolks) * took me on to be his man and pardner. And what was Compeyson's business in which we was to go pardners? Compeyson's business was the swindling. He'd no more heart than a iron file, he was as cold as death, and he had the head of the Devil. There was another in with Compeyson, as was called Arthur—not as being so chrisen'd, but as a surname. He was in a Decline, and was a shadow to look at. Him and Compeyson had been in a bad thing with a rich lady some years afore, and they'd made a pot of money by it; but Compeyson betted and gamed, and he'd have run through the king's taxes. So Arthur was a dying, and a dying poor and with the horrors on him. Arthur lived at the top of Compeyson's house (over nigh Brentford it was), and Compeyson kept a careful account agen him for board and lodging, in case he should ever get better to work it out. But Arthur soon settled the account. The second or third time as ever I see him, he come a tearing down into Compeyson's parlour late at night, in only a flannel gown, with his hair all in a sweat, and he says to Compeyson's wife, "Sally, she really is up-stairs alonger me, now, and I can't get rid of her. She's all in white," he says, "wi' white flowers in her hair, and she's awful mad, and she's got a shroud hanging over her arm, and she says she'll put it on me at five in the morning." Says Compeyson: "Why, you fool, don't you know she's got a living body? And how should she be up there, without coming through the door, or in at the window, and up the stairs?" "I don't know how she's there," says Arthur, shivering dreadful with the horrors, "but she's standing in the corner at the foot of the bed, awful mad. And over where her heart's broke—*you* broke it!—there's drops of blood." Compeyson spoke hardy, but he was always a coward. Compeyson's wife and me took Arthur up to bed agen. * He rested pretty quiet till it might want a few minutes of five in the morning, and then he starts up with a scream, and screams out, "Here she is! She's got the shroud. She's unfolding it. She's coming out of the corner. She's coming to the bed. Hold me, both on you—one of each side—don't let her touch me with it. Hah! she missed me that time. Don't let her throw it over my shoulders. Don't let her lift me up to get it round me. She's lifting me up. Keep me down!" Then he lifted himself up hard, and was dead. Compeyson took it easy as a good riddance for both sides. Him and me was soon busy, and first he swore me (being ever artful) on my own book—this here little black book, dear boy, what I swore your comrade on. Not to go into the things that Compeyson planned, and I done—which 'ud take a week—I'll simply say to you, dear boy, and Pip's com-

rade, that that man got me into such nets as made me his black slave. *
At last me and Compeyson was both committed for felony—on a charge of
putting stolen notes in circulation—and there was other charges behind.
Compeyson says to me, "Separate defences, no communication," and that
was all. And I was so miserable poor, that I sold all the clothes I had
except what hung on my back, afore I could get Jaggers. * When the
defence come on at our trial, I see the Compeyson plan plainer; for, says
the counsellor for Compeyson, "My lord and gentlemen, here you has
afore you, side by side, two persons as your eyes can separate wide; one,
the younger, well brought up, who will be spoke to as such; one, the elder,
ill brought up, who will be spoke to as such; one, the younger, seldom if
ever seen in these here transactions, and only suspected: t'other, the elder,
always seen in 'em, and always wi' his guilt brought home. Can you doubt,
if there is but one in it, which is the one; and, if there is two in it, which is
much the worst one?" And such like. * And when the verdict come,
warn't it Compeyson as was recommended to mercy on account of good
character and bad company, and giving up all the information he could
agen me; and warn't it me as got never a word but Guilty? And when
we're sentenced, ain't it him as gets seven year, and me fourteen; and
ain't it him as the Judge is sorry for, because he might a done so well;
and ain't it me as the Judge perceives to be a old offender of wiolent
passions, likely to come to worse?

'Well, I had said to Compeyson that I'd smash that face of his, and I
swore Lord smash mine! to do it. We was in the same prison ship, but I
couldn't get at him for long, though I tried. At last I come behind him
and hit him on the cheek to turn him round and get a smashing one at
him, when I was seen and seized. The black-hole of that ship warn't a
strong one, to a judge of black-holes that could swim and dive. I escaped
to the shore, and I was a hiding among the graves there, envying them as
was in 'em and all over, when I first see my boy. By my boy I was giv to
understand as Compeyson was out on them marshes too. I hunted him
down. I smashed his face. "And now," says I, "as the worst thing I can
do, caring nothing for myself, I'll drag you back." I was put in irons,
brought to trial again, and sent for life. But I didn't stop for life, dear boy
and Pip's comrade, being here.'[1] *

Herbert had been writing with his pencil in the cover of a book. He
softly pushed the book over to me, and I read in it: 'Young Havisham's
name was Arthur. Compeyson is the man who professed to be Miss
Havisham's lover.'

I shut the book and nodded slightly to Herbert, and put the book by;
but we neither of us said anything on the subject, and both looked at

---

[1] The end of a very lengthy speech: an instance of the unsatisfactory expedients to
which the condensation of a complicated narrative had driven Dickens, and which remained to be reconsidered and revised.

Provis as he stood smoking by the fire. * What was pressing to be done, was, to save him from being taken.[1] If Compeyson were alive, and should discover his return, I could hardly doubt the consequence. That Compeyson stood in mortal fear of him, neither of the two could know much better than I; and that any such man as that man had been described to be, would hesitate to release himself for good from a dreaded enemy by the safe means of becoming an informer, was scarcely to be imagined.[2] With great trouble, secrecy, and precaution, we got Provis an obscure lodging on the shore down the river. Our plan was, to put him and myself (for I could not desert him now) on board a foreign steamer, and to board the steamer below Gravesend, when she would be well upon her course, and all dangerous people would have left her. To avoid suspicion, we resolved to take time, to set up a boat of our own, to be constantly seen in her on the river below bridge, and to row her ourselves (adding a trusty friend to the party) on the occasion of the escape.

These preparations occupied several weeks. At last the day came, after long seeming as though it would never come. It was one of those March days when the sun shines hot and the wind blows cold; when it is summer in the light, and winter in the shade.

We loitered down to the Temple stairs, and stood loitering there, as if we were not quite decided to go upon the water. Of course I had taken care that the boat should be ready and everything in order. After a little show of indecision, which there were none to see but the two or three amphibious creatures belonging to our Temple stairs, we went on board and cast off; Herbert in the bow: I steering. It was then about high-water —half-past eight in the morning.

The tide, beginning to run down at nine, and being with us until three, we intended still to creep on after it had turned, and row against it until dark. We should then be well in those long reaches below Gravesend, between Kent and Essex, where the river is broad and solitary, where the water-side inhabitants are few, and where lone public-houses are scattered here and there, of which we could choose one for a resting-place. There we meant to lie by, all night. The steamer for Hamburg and the steamer for Rotterdam would start from London at about nine next morning. We should know at what time to expect them, according to where we were, and would hail the first that came down; so that if by any accident we were not taken aboard, we should have another chance. We knew the distinguishing marks of each vessel.

The relief of being at last engaged in the execution of the purpose was great. The crisp air, the sunlight, the movement on the river, and the

---

[1] A summary; then on to ch. 43.

[2] The remainder of this paragraph, and the opening of the next, are a summary of relevant developments between chs. 43 and 54, at which point the action resumes.

moving river itself—the road that ran with us, seeming to sympathise with us, animate us, and encourage us on—freshened me with new hope.

At that time the steam traffic on the Thames was far below its present extent, * and we went ahead among many skiffs and wherries, briskly. * We touched the stairs that adjoined his secret lodging lightly for a single moment, and he was on board and we were off again.

'Dear boy!' he said, putting his arm on my shoulder as he took his seat. 'Faithful dear boy, well done. Thankye, thankye!' *

We certainly had not been, and at that time as certainly we were not, attended or followed by any boat. If we had been waited on by any boat, I should have run in to shore, and have obliged her to go on, or to make her purpose evident. But we held our own without any appearance of molestation. *

'If you knowed, dear boy, what it is to sit here alonger you and have my smoke, arter having been day by day betwixt four walls, you'd envy me. But you don't know what it is.'

'I think I know the delights of freedom.'

'Ah!' but you don't know it equal to me. You must have been under lock and key, dear boy, to know it equal to me—but I ain't a going to be low.' *

'If all goes well, you will be perfectly free and safe again within a few hours.'

'Well, I hope so.'

'And think so?'

He dipped his hand in the water over the boat's gunwale, and said, smiling with a softened air upon him which was not new to me:

'Ay, I s'pose I think so, dear boy. We'd be puzzled to be more quiet and easy-going than we are at present. But—it's a flowing so soft and pleasant through the water, p'raps, as makes me think it—I was a thinking just then, that we can no more see to the bottom of the next few hours, than we can see to the bottom of this river what I catches hold of. Nor yet we can't no more hold their tide than I can hold this. And it's run through my fingers and gone, you see!' holding up his dripping hand.

He put his pipe back in his mouth with an undisturbed expression of face, and sat as composed and contented as if he were already out of England.

The air felt cold upon the river, but it was a bright day, and the sunshine was very cheering. The tide ran strong, I took care to lose none of it, and our steady stroke carried us on thoroughly well. By imperceptible degrees, as the tide ran out, we lost more and more of the nearer woods and hills, and dropped lower and lower between the muddy banks, but the tide was yet with us when we were off Gravesend. As our charge was wrapped in his cloak, I purposely passed within a boat or two's length of the floating Custom House, and so out to catch the stream, alongside of two emigrant ships, and under the bows of a large transport with troops on the forecastle looking down at us. And soon the tide began to slacken, and the craft lying at anchor to swing, and presently they had all swung round, and the ships that were taking advantage of the new tide to get up to the Pool began to crowd upon us in a fleet, and we kept under the shore, as much out of the strength of the tide as we could, standing carefully off from low shallows and mud-banks. *

We rowed, and rowed, and rowed, until the sun went down. By that time the river had lifted us again a little, so that we could see above the bank. There, was the red sun, on the low level of the shore, in a purple haze, fast deepening into black; and there, was the solitary flat marsh; and far away there were the rising grounds, between which and us there seemed to be no life, save here and there in the foreground a melancholy gull.

As the night was fast falling, and as the moon, being past the full, would not rise early, we held a little council—a short one—for clearly our course was to lie by at the first lonely tavern we could find. Thus we held on, speaking little, for four or five dull miles. It was very cold, and, a collier coming by us, with her galley-fire smoking and flaring, looked like a comfortable home. The night was as dark by this time as it would be until morning; and what light we had, seemed to come more from the river than the sky, as the oars in their dipping struck at a few reflected stars.

At this dismal time, we were all possessed by the idea that we were followed. As the tide made, it flapped heavily at irregular intervals against the shore; and whenever such a sound came, one or other of us was sure to start and look in that direction. Here and there, the set of the current had worn down the bank into a little creek, and we were all suspicious of such places, and eyed them nervously. Sometimes, 'What was that ripple!' one of us would say in a low voice. Or another, 'Is that a boat yonder?' And afterwards we would fall into a dead silence, and I would sit impatiently thinking with what an unusual amount of noise the oars worked in the thowels.

At length we descried a light and a roof, and presently afterwards ran alongside a little causeway made of stones that had been picked up hard by. Leaving the rest in the boat, I stepped ashore, and found the light to be in a window of a public-house. It was a dirty place enough, and I dare say not unknown to smuggling adventurers; but there was a good fire in the kitchen, and there were eggs and bacon to eat, and various liquors to drink. Also, there were two double-bedded rooms. I went down to the boat again, and we all came ashore, and brought out the oars, and rudder, and boat-hook, and all else, and hauled her up for the night. We made a very good meal by the kitchen fire, and then apportioned the bedrooms. Herbert and our trusted friend were to occupy one—I and our charge the other.

While we were comforting ourselves by the fire after our meal, the 'Jack' of this river-side public-house—who was sitting in a corner, and who had a bloated pair of shoes on, which he had exhibited, while we were eating our eggs and bacon, as interesting relics which he had taken a few days ago from the feet of a drowned seaman washed ashore—asked me if we had seen a four-oared galley going up with the tide? When I told him No, he said she must have gone down then, and yet she 'took up too,' when she left there.

'They must ha' thought better on't for some reason or another,' said the Jack, 'and gone down.'

'A four-oared galley, did you say?'

'A four, and two sitters. * A Four and two sitters, hanging and hovering, up with one tide and down with another, and both with and against another.'

This dialogue made us all uneasy, and made me very uneasy. A four-oared galley hovering about in so unusual a way as to attract this notice, was an ugly circumstance that I could not get rid of. When I had induced Provis to go up to bed, I went outside with my two companions and held another council. Whether we should remain at the house until near the steamer's time, which would be about one next afternoon; or whether we should put off early in the morning, was the question we discussed. On the whole we deemed it the better course to lie where we were, until within an hour or so of the steamer's time, and then to get out in her track, and drift with the tide. Having settled to do this, we returned into the house and went to bed. *

Next day we got aboard our boat easily, and rowed out into the track of the steamer. By that time it wanted but ten minutes of one o'clock, and we began to look out for her smoke.

But it was half-past one before we saw her smoke, and soon afterwards we saw behind it the smoke of another steamer. They were coming on at full speed. We had all shaken hands, and neither Herbert's eyes nor mine were quite dry, when I saw a four-oared galley shoot out from under the bank but a little way ahead of us, and row out into the same track.

A stretch of shore had been as yet between us and the steamer's smoke, by reason of the bend and wind of the river; but now she was visible, coming head on. I called to Herbert to keep before the tide that she might see us lying by for her, and I adjured Provis to sit quite still, wrapped in his cloak. He sat like a statue. Meantime the galley, which was very skilfully handled, had crossed us, let us come up with her, and fallen alongside. Leaving just room enough for the play of the oars, she kept alongside, drifting when we drifted, and pulling a stroke or two when we pulled. Of the two sitters, one held the rudder lines and looked at us attentively—as did all the rowers; the other sitter was wrapped up much as Provis was, and seemed to shrink, and whisper some instruction to the steerer as he looked at us. Not a word was spoken in either boat.

Herbert could make out, after a few minutes, which steamer was first, and gave me the word 'Hamburg.' She was nearing us very fast, and the beating of her paddles grew louder and louder. I felt as if her shadow were absolutely upon us, when the galley hailed us. I answered.

'You have a returned Transport there,' said the man who held the lines. 'That's the man, wrapped in the cloak. His name is Abel Magwitch, otherwise Provis. I apprehend that man, and call upon him to surrender, and you to assist.'

At the same moment, without giving any audible direction to his crew, he ran the galley aboard of us. They had pulled one sudden stroke ahead, had got their oars in, had run athwart us, and were holding on to our gunwale, before we knew what they were doing. This caused great confusion on board the steamer, and I heard them calling to us, and heard the order to stop the paddles, and heard them stop, but felt her driving down upon us irresistibly. In the same moment I saw the steersman of the galley lay his hand on his prisoner's shoulder, and saw that both boats were swinging round with the force of the tide, and saw that all hands on board the steamer were running forward quite frantically. Still in the same moment, I saw my convict start up, lean across his captor, and pull the cloak from the neck of the shrinking sitter in the galley. Still in the same moment I saw that the face disclosed, was the face of the other convict of long ago. Still in the same moment, I saw the face tilt backward—with a white terror on it that I shall never forget—and heard a great cry on board the steamer and a loud splash in the water, and felt the boat sink from under me.

It was but for an instant that I seemed to struggle with a thousand mill-weirs and a thousand flashes of light; that instant past, I was taken on board the galley. Herbert was there, and our friend was there; but our boat was gone, and the two convicts were gone.

What with the cries aboard the steamer, and the furious blowing-off of her steam, and her driving on, and our driving on, I could not at first distinguish sky from water or shore from shore; but the crew of the galley righted her with great speed, and, pulling certain swift strong strokes ahead, lay upon their oars, every man looking silently and eagerly at the water astern. Presently a dark object was seen in it, bearing towards us on the tide. No man spoke, but the steersman held up his hand, and all softly backed water, and kept the boat straight and true before it. As it came nearer, I saw it to be Magwitch, swimming, but not swimming freely. He was taken on board, and instantly manacled at the wrists and ankles.

The galley was kept steady, and the silent eager look-out at the water was resumed. But the Rotterdam steamer now came up, and apparently not understanding what had happened, came on at speed. By the time she had been hailed and stopped, both steamers were drifting away from us, and we were rising and falling in a troubled wake of water. The look-out was kept, long after all was still again and the two steamers were gone; but everybody knew that it was hopeless now.

At length we gave it up, and pulled under the shore towards the tavern we had lately left, where we were received with no little surprise. Here I was able to get some comforts for Magwitch—Provis no longer—who had received some very severe injury in the chest and a deep cut in the head.

He told me that he believed himself to have gone under the keel of the steamer, and to have been struck on the head in rising. The injury to his chest (which rendered his breathing extremely painful) he thought he had received against the side of the galley. He added that he did not pretend to say what he might or might not have done to Compeyson, but, that in the moment of his laying his hand on his cloak to identify him, that villain and spy had staggered up and staggered back, and they had both gone overboard together; when the sudden wrenching of him (Magwitch) out of our boat, and the endeavour of his captor to keep him in it, had capsized us. He told me in a whisper that they had gone down, fiercely locked in each other's arms, and that there had been a struggle under water, and that he had disengaged himself, struck out, and swum away. *

As we returned towards the setting sun that we had yesterday left behind us, and as the stream of our hopes seemed all running back, I told him how grieved I was to think that he had come home for my sake.

'Dear boy, I'm quite content to take my chance. I've seen my boy, and he can be a gentleman without me. Look'ee here, dear boy, it's best as a gentleman should not be knowed to belong to me. Only come to see me in jail as if you come by chance alonger Wemmick. Sit where I can see you at the Trial when I shall be swore to, for the last o' many times, and I don't ask no more.'

'I will never stir from your side, when I am suffered to be near you. Please God, I will be as true to you as you have been to me!'

I felt his hand tremble as it held mine, and he turned his face away as he lay in the bottom of the boat, and I heard that old sound in his throat softened now, like all the rest of him.

He was taken to the Police Court next day, and would have been immediately committed for trial, but that it was necessary to send down for an old officer of the prison-ship from which he had once escaped, to speak to his identity. Nobody doubted it; but Compeyson, the spy who had meant to depose to it, was tumbling on the tides, dead, and it happened that there was not at that time any prison officer in London who could give the required evidence. * After three days' delay the witness came and completed the easy case. He was committed to take his trial at the next Sessions, which would come on in a month. *

He lay in prison very ill, during the interval between his committal for trial and the coming round of the Sessions. He had broken two ribs, they had wounded one of his lungs, and he breathed with great pain and difficulty, which increased daily. It was a consequence of his hurt that he spoke so low as to be scarcely audible: therefore he spoke very little. But he was ever ready to listen to me, and it became the first duty of my life to say to him, and to read to him, what I knew he ought to hear.

Being far too ill to remain in the common prison, he was removed, after the first day or so, into the infirmary. This gave me opportunities of being with him that I could not otherwise have had. And but for his illness he would have been put in irons, for he was regarded as a determined prison-breaker, and I know not what else.

Although I saw him every day, it was for only a short time; hence the regularly recurring spaces of our separation were long enough to record on his face any slight changes that occurred in his physical state. I do not recollect that I once saw any change in his face for the better; he wasted, and became slowly weaker and worse, day by day, from the day when the prison door closed upon him.

The kind of submission or resignation that he showed was that of a man who was tired out. I sometimes derived an impression, from his manner or from a whispered word or two which escaped him, that he pondered over the question whether he might have been a better man under better circumstances. But he never justified himself by a hint tending that way, or tried to bend the past out of its eternal shape. * He never knew that his possessions would be all forfeited to the crown, and that his hopes of enriching me had utterly perished.

His trial was very short and very clear. The Jury found him Guilty, * and the Judge told him that the appointed punishment for his return to the land that had cast him out, being Death, and his case being an aggravated case, he must prepare himself to Die. The sun was striking in at the great windows of the court, through glittering drops of rain upon the glass, and it made a broad shaft of light between him and the Judge, linking both together, and perhaps reminding some among the audience how both were passing on, with absolute equality, to the greater Judgment that knoweth all things and cannot err. Rising for a moment, a distinct speck of face in this way of light, the prisoner said, 'My Lord, I have received my sentence of Death from the Almighty, but I bow to yours,' and sat down again. *

The daily visits I could make him were shortened now, and he was more strictly kept. But nobody was hard with him or with me. There was duty to be done, and it was done; but not harshly. The officer on duty always gave me the assurance that he was worse, and some other sick

prisoners in the room, and some other prisoners who attended on them as
sick nurses (malefactors, but not incapable of kindness, GOD be thanked!),
always joined in the same report.

As the days went on, I noticed more and more that he would lie placidly
looking at the white ceiling, with an absence of light in his face, until
some word of mine brightened it for an instant, and then it would subside
again. Sometimes he was almost, or quite, unable to speak; then he would
answer me with slight pressures on my hand. And I grew to understand
his meaning very well.

The number of the days had risen to ten, when I saw a greater change
in him than I had seen yet. His eyes were turned towards the door, and
lighted up as I entered.

'Dear boy, I thought you was late. But I knowed you couldn't be that.'

'It is just the time. I waited for it at the gate.'

'You always does wait at the gate; don't you, dear boy?'

'Yes. Not to lose a moment of the time.'

'Thank'ee dear boy. God bless you! You've never deserted me, dear
boy. And what's best of all, you've been more comfortable alonger me,
since I was under a dark cloud, than when the sun shone. That's best of
all.'

He lay on his back, breathing with great difficulty. Do what he would,
and love me though he did, the light left his face ever and again, and a
film came over the placid look at the white ceiling.

'Are you in much pain to-day, Magwitch?'

'I don't complain of none, dear boy.'

'You never do complain.'

He had spoken his last words. He smiled, and I understood his touch
to mean that he wished to lift my hand, and lay it on his breast. I laid it
there, and he smiled again, and put both his hands upon it. *

With a last faint effort, which would have been powerless but for my
yielding to it, and assisting it, he raised my hand to his lips. The placid
look at the white ceiling came back, and passed away, and his head
dropped quietly on his breast.

Mindful, then, of what we had lately read together, I thought of the
two men who went up into the Temple to pray; and I knew there were
no better words that I could say beside his bed, than 'O Lord, be merciful
to him, a sinner!'

THE END

MR. BOB SAWYER'S PARTY

Bob, as Dickens usually called this item, must have been devised during the late summer of 1861 when (as was noted above, p. 213) the repertoire was being much expanded for the new series of Readings. It was privately printed as pages 53–82 of the volume which contains *Mr. Chops, the Dwarf* (which certainly was devised at that time) and the new *Bardell and Pickwick* prompt-copy (see above, p. 195). No other prompt-copy of *Bob* survives, and doubtless none ever existed. *T & F* was set up from this 1861 copy, which had been liberally revised by Dickens.

The Reading was first performed on 30 December 1861, as an after-piece to *Nicholas Nickleby*. It was usually linked with *Nickleby* or *David Copperfield*, though sometimes it was given as an afterpiece to *Dr. Marigold*, *A Christmas Carol*, or *Little Dombey*. During the Farewell season, when *Sikes and Nancy* entered the repertoire, a favourite programme was *Boots*, *Sikes*, and *Bob*, with the humour of *Bob* restoring the audience's spirits after the horrifics of the Murder.

The narrative is taken entirely from ch. 32 of *Pickwick Papers*, and both its beginning and the ending coincide with those of that chapter. Bob Sawyer's party had never been one of the more legendary episodes in the novel; Mr. Pickwick has little to say or do in it, Sam Weller is not present, and the two medical students (Bob Sawyer and Benjamin Allen) are relatively minor characters. In the Reading, indeed, the leading figure was Mr. Jack Hopkins, whose only appearance in the novel occurs in this chapter. Dickens's choice of the *Trial* episode from *Pickwick*, three years earlier, had been almost inevitable: as was noted above, this had long been a universal favourite in recitals and theatrical adaptations. Why Dickens chose Bob Sawyer's party, from a novel which contained so many other better-loved episodes, can only be surmized, for he never discusses this Reading in his extant published letters. It was of course a conveniently short episode, and complete in itself; also, it provided opportunities for character-acting unlike those in the rest of the repertoire (notably the group of raffish and eventually tipsy young gentlemen). Certainly he was right in his guess that the episode had great comic potential, and that he could do it justice. It was evident, wrote Kate Field, that 'Dickens was as much born to read *Mr. Bob Sawyer's Party* as he was to create it'. This episode from *Pickwick* became unforgettable, once his performance of it had been seen: 'What has struck you heretofore as a diamond no better than its fellows is magically transformed into a Kohinoor. And when I say "magically transformed", I mean it in all soberness of criticism' (Field, p. 92). The Reading became one of the most popular in the repertoire, always 'provoking unflagging merriment' (*Yorkshire Post*, 17 April 1869). 'Here every line was a hit,' pronounced the critic in the *Scotsman* (21 April 1866), who could not decide whether *Bob* or *The Trial* was the finer piece of humour, or which was the more effectively rendered: 'The only thing certain is that both are masterpieces.'

To make every line a hit, Dickens had worked hard as arranger and reviser, as well as performer. The privately printed text had differed only slightly from that of the novel. A few explanatory phrases had been inserted: thus, in the opening sentence, 'the Borough' was expanded to 'the Borough of Southwark in the county of Middlesex' (a geographical error later corrected in manuscript to 'Surrey'). Some brief deletions had been made; these included the happy suggestion that Betsey the servant-girl 'might have passed for the neglected daughter of a super-annuated dustman in very reduced circumstances'. Then Dickens worked over the script carefully, sharpening and concentrating its effects. At least two different inks were used, but the revisions doubtless took place over quite a long period.

Some of the verbal alterations were simple heightenings of the comic effect (see above, p. xxxv, for examples). Some were simplifications or up-datings. 'Mantua-makers' becomes 'milliners', 'bottles' replace 'punch', 'vingt-et-un' and 'the last "natural"' become 'a round game' and 'the last deal'. Mr. Pickwick's companions (Tupman, Winkle, and Snodgrass) are unnamed, and the final arrivals at the party, who in the novel had all been individually described, are summarized as 'the rest of the company—five in number—among whom there was, as presently appeared, a sentimental young gentleman with a very nice sense of honour'. This is Mr. Noddy, later to figure in the tipsy quarrel—but his antagonist in the quarrel is changed. In the novel this had been Mr. Gunter, the 'gentleman in a shirt emblazoned with pink anchors'. Mr. Gunter is eliminated from the Reading, and his role goes to augment Mr. Jack Hopkins's. The unnamed 'prim personage in clean linen and cloth boots' who tells the 'long story about a great public character' is not described in the Reading, and Charles Kent notes (p. 159) that eventually he and his story disappeared from the Reading text (where, in fact, his telling the inconclusive anecdote is marked as an optional cut: see p. 375, note 1). At one point, at least, there was an expansion of the script which does not appear in the prompt-copy: this was in Bob Sawyer's reproachful speech to Jack Hopkins about the over-boisterous 'chorusing' which leads to the abrupt termination of the party (see below, p. 378, note 1).

The most striking development in the text centres on Jack Hopkins. His abrupt idiom, present in the novel, is intensified. A good instance is his anecdote of the boy who swallowed his sister's beads, where Dickens deleted most of the definite and indefinite articles, and inserted the word 'necklace' five more times, to exploit the amusement caused by his pronouncing it 'neck-lass' or 'neck-luss'. According to Kate Field, 'the mere pronunciation of the word "necklace" inspired as much laughter as is usually accorded to a low-comedy man's best "point"' (p. 97). She tried to indicate how the Jack Hopkins voice—upon which so much of the Reading's success depended—was manipulated; for example—

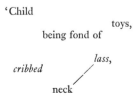

'Child

                   toys,

being fond of

                lass,

cribbed   /

           /

     neck

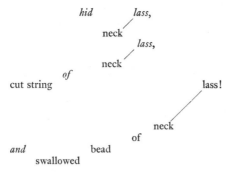

Those who have heard Dickens will understand this illustration, and may perhaps thank me for it. Those who have *not* heard him will *not* understand it, and will *not* thank me. When, after hearing a noise 'like a small hail-storm,' the father exclaims,—

and the child replies, 'I ain't a-doin' nothing,' whereupon the father rejoins,—

—fun appears to have reached its perihelion, but when, after shaking the boy, the father cries out,—

—nothing is left for human nature but to laugh at every pore. If the public eye were not upon you, you would abandon yourself to an ecstasy of delight. (pp. 97–9)

Jack Hopkins's face, stance, and manner were well remembered, as well as his voice. He stood, stiff-necked, with the inflated air of an incipient public man; his voice escaped as best it could 'between closed teeth, and from a mouth apparently full of mush'; his hands were thrust into his pantaloon-trousers, 'an attitude that, when accompanied by an oscillation of the body, as in Jack Hopkins's case, always indicates superior wisdom' (Kent, p. 158; Field, p. 96). He was one of Dickens's most comic platform creations, much enjoyed by Dickens himself, too. In the company of his Boston friends, James and Annie Fields, he 'laughed till the tears ran down his cheeks over Bob Sawyer's party and the remembrance of the laughter he had seen depicted on the faces of people the night before. Jack Hopkins was such a favorite with J[ames] that D. made up the face again and went over the necklace story until we roared aloud' (*Memories of a Hostess*, ed. M. A. DeWolfe Howe (1923), p. 146).

Bob was full of good 'faces' as well as comic lines and situations. Another was Benjamin Allen's while he was trying to console Bob over his financial difficulties, 'Mr. Dickens giving zest to Mr. Ben's remarks by the amusing action of his thumb on each side of his mouth alternately' (*Scotsman*, 21 April 1866)—this being one example, out of many in the Readings, of a characteristic gesture unspecified in the text. But the most striking of Dickens's histrionic creations in *Bob* was the servant-girl Betsey. As a critic in the *Bath Chronicle* (4 February 1869) wrote:

He excels in caricature or farce, and no better specimen of his consummate skill in this line as a 'reader' could be given than his portrait of the servant in Bob Sawyer's lodgings, or of Mrs. Raddle herself. It is impossible to forget the blank expression of his face as he assumed the character of the servant.

With only three brief entrances, and speaking a total of only sixty words, Betsey became one of the most vivid figures in all the Readings, 'an incomparably comic character':

The moment Betsey opens her mouth she is an accomplished fact. A dirtier, more slip-shod, more stolid, more irretrievably stupid girl never lived. . . . A voice never expressed more thorough individuality, for Betsey has a cold in the head . . . [which] gives a muffled sepulchral tone to her words. . . . The amiable landlady, Mrs. Raddle, is quite as well portrayed; but something is expected of Mrs. Raddle, whereas Betsey takes you entirely by surprise. If a donkey lisped in numbers you could not be more astonished. (Field, pp. 93–5)

In this Reading, wrote a Portsmouth journalist, 'Mr. Dickens's histrionic powers had full scope'. His rapid changes of face, manner, and tone of voice, from one character to another, were all 'admirably accomplished and intensely amusing', and the audience left the entertainment, which this item concluded, 'scarcely knowing which to admire most, the great and eminent novelist or the clever reciter' (quoted in *Dickensian*, xxxv (1939), 207).

Mr. Bob Sawyer's Party

THERE is a repose about Lant Street in the borough of Southwark in the county of Surrey, which sheds a gentle melancholy upon the soul. A house in Lant Street would not come within the denomination of a first-rate residence, in the strict acceptation of the term; but if a man wished to abstract himself from the world—to remove himself from the reach of temptation—to place himself beyond the possibility of any inducement to look out of window—he should by all means go to Lant Street.

In this happy retreat are colonized a few clear-starchers, a sprinkling of journeymen bookbinders, one or two prison agents for the Insolvent Court, several small housekeepers who are employed in the Docks, a handful of milliners, and a seasoning of jobbing tailors. The majority of the inhabitants either direct their energies to the letting of furnished apartments, or devote themselves to the healthful pursuit of mangling. The chief features in the still life of the street, are green shutters, lodging-bills, brass door-plates, and bell-handles; the principal specimens of animated nature are the pot-boy, the muffin youth, and the baked-potato man. *The population is migratory, usually disappearing on the verge of quarter-day, and generally by night. Her Majesty's revenues are seldom collected in this happy valley; the receipt of rent is dubious; and the water communication is frequently cut off.*

Mr. Bob Sawyer[1] embellished one side of the fire, in his first-floor front, early on the evening for which he had invited Mr. Pickwick to a friendly party; and his chum *Mr. Ben Allen* embellished the other side. The preparations for the reception of visitors appeared to be completed. The umbrellas in the passage had been heaped into the little corner outside the back-parlour door; the bonnet and shawl of the landlady's servant had been removed from the banisters; there were not more than two pairs of pattens on the street-door mat; and a kitchen candle, with a long snuff, burnt cheerfully on the ledge of the staircase window. Mr. Bob Sawyer had himself purchased the spirits, and had returned home in attendance on the bearer to preclude the possibility of their being absconded with, or delivered at the wrong house. The bottles were ready in the bed-room; a little table had been got from the parlour to play at cards on; and the glasses of the establishment, together with those which had been borrowed for the occasion from the public-house, were all drawn up in a tray on the floor of the landing outside the door.

Notwithstanding the highly satisfactory nature of these arrangements,

---

[1] Like *Mr. Ben Allen* below, this is doubly underlined.

there was a cloud on the countenance of Mr. Bob Sawyer, as he sat by the fire, and there was a sympathising expression, too, in the features of Mr. Ben Allen, and[1] melancholy in his voice, as he said,

'Well, it *is*[2] unlucky that your landlady, Mrs. Raddle, should have taken it in her head to turn sour, just on this occasion. She might at least have waited till to-morrow.'

'That's her malevolence; that's her malevolence.[3] She says that if I can afford to give a party I ought to be able to afford to pay her confounded "little bill."'

'How long has it been running?'[4] *A bill, by the bye, is the most extraordinary locomotive engine that the genius of man ever produced. It would keep on running during the longest lifetime, without ever once stopping of its own accord.*

'Only a quarter, and a month or so.'

Ben Allen coughed and directed a searching look between the two top bars of the stove.

'It'll be a deuced unpleasant thing if she takes it into her head to let out, when those fellows are here, won't it?'

'Horrible, horrible.'

Here, a low tap was heard at the room door, and Mr. Bob Sawyer looked expressively at his friend, and bade the tapper come in; whereupon a dirty slipshod girl, in black cotton stockings, thrust in her head, and said,

'Please, Mister Sawyer, Missis Raddle wants to speak to *you*.'[5]

Before Mr. Bob Sawyer could return an answer, this young person suddenly disappeared with a jerk, *as if somebody had given her a violent pull behind*. This mysterious exit was no sooner accomplished, than there was another tap at the door.

Mr. Bob Sawyer glanced at his friend with a look of abject apprehension, and once more cried 'Come in.'

The permission was not at all necessary, for, before Mr. Bob Sawyer had uttered the words, a little fierce woman bounced into the room, all in a tremble with passion, and pale with rage.

[6]'Now Mr. Sawyer, if you'll have the kindness to settle that little bill

---

[1] 'and' is supplied by *T & F*: omitted in *Suzannet*.

[2] *is* italic in *Suzannet* and in the novel.   [3] 'Sneering' (Wright).

[4] 'Sucking thumb and in a sneaking manner.' Bob Sawyer's reply ('and a month or so')—'Pulling down waistcoat' (Wright).

[5] *you* italic in *Suzannet* and in the novel. 'Slow', notes Wright. Charles Kent, like the critics quoted in the headnote, was dazzled by the impersonation of Betsey: 'No one had ever realized the crass stupidity of that remarkable young person . . . until her first introduction in these Readings, with "Please, Mister Sawyer, Missis Raddle wants to speak to *you*!"—the dull, dead-level of her voice ending on the last monosyllable with a series of inflections amounting to a chromatic passage' (p. 33).

[6] 'Very quick' (Wright).

of mine I'll thank you, because I've got my rent to pay this afternoon, and my landlord's a waiting below now.' *Here the little woman rubbed her hands, and looked steadily over Mr. Bob Sawyer's head, at the wall behind him.*

'I am very sorry to put you to any inconvenience, Mrs. Raddle, but—'

'Oh, it isn't any inconvenience. I didn't want it particular before to-day; leastways, as it has to go to my landlord directly, it was as well for you to keep it, as me. You promised me this afternoon, Mr. Sawyer, and every gentleman as has ever lived here, has kept his word, sir, as of course anybody as calls himself a gentleman, do.' *Mrs. Raddle tossed her head, bit her lips, rubbed her hands harder, and looked at the wall more steadily than ever.*

'I am very sorry, Mrs. Raddle, but the fact is, that I have been disappointed in the City to-day.'—*Extraordinary place that city. Astonishing number of men always getting disappointed there.*

'Well, Mr. Sawyer, and what is that to me, sir?'

'I—I—have no doubt, Mrs. Raddle,' *said Bob, blinking this last question,* 'that before the middle of next week we shall be able to set ourselves quite square, and go on, on a better system, afterwards.'

This was all Mrs. Raddle wanted. She had bustled up to the apartment of the unlucky Bob, so bent upon going into a passion, that, in all probability, payment would have rather disappointed her. She was in excellent order for a little relaxation of the kind: having just exchanged a few introductory compliments with Mr. Raddle in the front kitchen.

'Do you suppose, Mr. Sawyer,' *elevating her voice for the information of the neighbours,* 'do you suppose that I'm a-going day after day to let a fellar occupy my lodgings as never thinks of paying his rent, nor even the very money laid out for the fresh butter and lump sugar that's bought for his breakfast, nor the very milk that's took in, at the street door? Do you suppose as a hard-working and industrious woman which has lived in this street for twenty year (ten year over the way and nine year and three quarter in this very house) has nothing else to do, but to work herself to death after a parcel of lazy idle fellars, that are always smoking and drinking, and lounging, when they ought to be glad to turn their hands to anything that would help 'em to pay their bills?'

'My good soul,' *interposed Mr. Benjamin Allen.*

'Have the goodness to keep your observashuns to yourself, sir, I beg,' *suddenly arresting the rapid torrent of her speech, and addressing the third party with impressive slowness and solemnity.* 'I am not aweer, sir, that you have any right to address your conversation to *me.*[1] I don't think I let these apartments to *you*, sir.'

'No, you certainly did not.'

'Very good, sir. Then p'r'aps, sir, as a medical student, you'll confine

---

[1] *me* doubly underlined, as is *you* in the next sentence.

yourself to breaking the arms and legs of the poor people in the hospitals, and will keep yourself *to*[1] yourself, sir, or there may be some persons here as will make you, sir.'

'But you are such an unreasonable woman.'

'I beg your parding, young man. But will you have the goodness to call me that again, sir?'[2]

'I didn't make use of the word in any invidious sense, ma'am.'

'I beg your parding, young man. But who do you call a woman? Did you make that remark to me, sir?'

'Why, bless my heart!'

'Did you apply that name to me, I ask of you, sir?'—*with intense ferocity, and throwing the door wide open.*

'Why of course I did.'

'Yes of course you did,' *backing gradually to the door, and raising her voice for the special behoof of Mr. Raddle in the kitchen.* 'Yes, of course you did! And everybody knows that you may safely insult me in my own ouse while my husband sits sleeping down stairs, and taking no more notice than if I was a dog in the streets. He ought to be ashamed of himself (*sob*) to allow his wife to be treated in this way by a parcel of young cutters and carvers of live people's bodies, that disgraces the lodgings (*another sob*), and leaving her exposed to all manner of abuse; a base faint-hearted, timorous wretch, that's afraid to come up stairs, and face the ruffinly creatures—that's afraid—that's afraid to come!' *Mrs. Raddle paused to listen whether the repetition of the taunt had roused her better half; and, finding that it had not been successful, proceeded to descend the stairs with sobs innumerable: when there came a loud double knock at the street door. Hereupon she burst into a fit of weeping, which was prolonged until the knock had been repeated six times, when, in an uncontrollable burst of mental agony, she threw down all the umbrellas, and disappeared into the back parlour.*

'Does Mr. Sawyer live here?' said Mr. Pickwick,[3] when the door was opened.

'Yes, first floor. It's the door straight afore you, when you gets to the top of the stairs.' *Having given this instruction, the handmaid, who had been brought up among the aboriginal inhabitants of Southwark, disappeared, with the candle in her hand, down the kitchen stairs.*

Mr. Pickwick and his two friends stumbled up stairs, where they were

---

[1] *to* italic in *Suxannet* and in the novel.

[2] Here 'Mrs. Raddle's anger rose through an increasing *crescendo*.' Ben Allen replied 'meekly and somewhat uneasy on his own account,' and her response came 'louder and more imperatively' (Kent, pp. 155–6).

[3] Wright has 'Idiotic voice' in the margin here: but probably the description was meant to refer to Betsey, who has the next speech, delivered as a 'lugubrious and monotonously intoned response, all on one note' (Kent, p. 156).

received by the wretched Bob, *who had been afraid to go down, lest he should be waylaid by Mrs. Raddle.*

'How are you? Glad to see you,—take care of the glasses.' *This caution was addressed to Mr. Pickwick, who had put his foot in the tray.*

'Dear me, I beg your pardon.'

'Don't mention it, don't mention it. I'm rather confined for room here, but you must put up with all that, when you come to see a young bachelor. Walk in. You've seen Mr. Ben Allen before, I think?' *Mr. Pickwick shook hands with Mr. Benjamin Allen, and his friends followed his example.* They had scarcely taken their seats when there was another double knock.

'I hope that's Jack Hopkins! Hush. Yes, it is. Come up, Jack; come up.'

A heavy footstep was heard upon the stairs, and Jack Hopkins presented himself.[1]

'You're late, Jack?'

'Been detained at Bartholomew's.'

'Anything new?'

'No, nothing particular.[2] Rather a good accident brought into the casualty ward.'

'What was that, sir?'

'Only a man fallen out of a four pair of stairs' window; but it's a very fair case—very fair case indeed.'

'Do you mean that the patient is in a fair way to recover?'

'No. No, I should rather say he wouldn't. There must be a splendid operation though, to-morrow—magnificent sight if Slasher does it.'

'You consider Mr. Slasher a good operator?'

'Best alive. Took a boy's leg out of the socket last week—boy ate five apples and a gingerbread cake—exactly two minutes after it was all over, boy said he wouldn't lie there to be made game of; and he'd tell his mother if they didn't begin.'

'Dear me!'

'Pooh! that's nothing. Is it, Bob?'

'Nothing at all.'

'By the bye, Bob,' said Hopkins, *with a scarcely perceptible glance at Mr. Pickwick's attentive face,* 'we had a curious accident last night. A child was brought in, who had swallowed a necklace.'[3]

'Swallowed what, sir?'

'A necklace. Not all at once, you know, that would be too much—*you*

---

[1] On Jack Hopkins's physical presence and voice, see headnote.

[2] 'Hands in pocket' (Wright).

[3] On the delivery of this anecdote, see headnote. Kent reproduces (facing his p. 152) the page from *Suzannet* showing Dickens's deletion of 'a' and 'the' and his insertion of the joke-word 'necklace'. In Jack Hopkins's next speech, *you* is italic in *Suzannet* and in the novel. Some punctuation in this speech is supplied from *T & F.*

couldn't swallow that if the child did—eh, Mr. Pickwick, ha! ha! No, the way was this;—child's parents, poor people, lived in a court. Child's eldest sister bought a necklace,—common necklace—large black wooden beads. Child, being fond of toys, cribbed necklace, hid necklace, played with necklace, cut string of necklace, and swallowed a bead. Child thought it capital fun, went back next day, and swallowed another bead.'

'Bless my heart, what a dreadful thing! I beg your pardon, sir. Go on.'

'Next day, child swallowed two beads; day after that, treated himself to three beads—so on, till in a week's time he had got through the necklace—five-and-twenty beads. Sister—industrious girl, seldom treated herself to bit of finery—cried eyes out, at loss of necklace; looked high and low for necklace; but, I needn't say, didn't find necklace. Few days afterwards, family at dinner—baked shoulder of mutton, and potatoes—child wasn't hungry, playing about the room, when family suddenly heard devil of a noise, like small hail storm. "Don't do that, my boy," said father. "I ain't a doin' nothing," said child. "Well, don't do it again," said father. Short silence, and then noise worse than ever. "If you don't mind what I say, my boy," said father, "you'll find yourself in bed, in something less than a pig's whisper." Gave child a shake to make him obedient, and such a rattling ensued as nobody ever heard before. "Why, damme, it's *in*[1] the child!" said father, "he's got the croup in the wrong place!" "No, I haven't, father," said child, beginning to cry, "it's the necklace; I swallowed it, father."—Father caught child up, and ran with him to hospital: beads in boy's stomach rattling all the way with the jolting; and people looking up in the air, and down in the cellars, to see where unusual sound came from. He's in the hospital now, and makes such a devil of noise when he walks about, that they're obliged to muffle him in a watchman's coat, for fear he should wake the patients!' †

Here another knock at the door announced the rest of the company—five in number—among whom there was, as presently appeared, a sentimental young gentleman with a very nice sense of honor. The little table was wheeled out; the bottles were brought in, and the succeeding three hours were devoted to a round game at sixpence a dozen. †

When the last deal had been declared, and the profit and loss account of fish and sixpences adjusted, to the satisfaction of all parties, Mr. Bob Sawyer rang for supper, and the visitors squeezed themselves into corners while it was getting ready.

It was not so easily got ready as some people may imagine. First of all, it was necessary to awaken the girl who had fallen asleep with her face on the kitchen table; this took time, and even when she did answer the bell, another quarter of an hour was consumed in fruitless endeavours to impart to her a distant glimmering of reason. The man to whom the

---

[1] *in* italic in *Suzannet* and in the novel.

order for the oysters had been sent, had not been told to open them; it is a very difficult thing to open an oyster with a limp knife or a two-pronged fork; and very little was done in this way. Very little of the beef was done either; and the ham (which was also from the German-sausage shop round the corner) was in a similar predicament. However, there was plenty of porter in a tin can; and the cheese went a great way, for it was very strong.

After supper, more bottles were put upon the table, together with a paper of cigars.[1] Then there was an awful pause; and this awful pause was occasioned by an embarrassing occurrence.

The fact is, the girl was washing the glasses. The establishment boasted four; which is not mentioned to its disparagement, for there never was a lodging-house yet, that was not short of glasses. The establishment's glasses were little thin feeble tumblers, and those which had been borrowed from the public-house were great dropsical, bloated articles, each supported on a huge gouty leg. This would have been in itself sufficient to have possessed the company with the real state of affairs; even if the young person of all work had not prevented the possibility of any misconception arising in the mind of any gentleman upon the subject, by forcibly dragging every man's glass away, long before he had finished his beer, and audibly stating, despite the winks of Mr. Bob Sawyer, that it was to be conveyed down stairs, and washed forthwith.

It is an ill wind that blows nobody any good. The prim man in the cloth boots,[2] who had been unsuccessfully attempting to make a joke during the whole time the round game lasted, saw his opportunity and seized it. The instant the glasses disappeared, he commenced a long story 'about a great public character, whose name I have forgotten, making a particularly happy reply to another eminent and illustrious individual whom I have never been able to identify.' He enlarged with great minuteness upon divers collateral circumstances, distantly connected with the anecdote in hand, but said, 'For the life of me, I cannot recollect at this precise moment what the anecdote is,[3] although I have been in the habit of telling the story with great applause for the last ten years. Dear me, it is a very extraordinary circumstance.'

'I am sorry you have forgotten it,' *said Mr. Bob Sawyer, glancing eagerly*

---

[1] A long optional cut is here indicated in *Suzannet*, by marginal lines; it ends at the close of the paragraph (four paragraphs below) ending '. . . the very best story he had ever heard'.

[2] Unmentioned before now, because the brief description of him and his companions (in the novel paragraph beginning 'Another knock at the door') had been deleted; Dickens had substituted the brief phrase about 'the rest of the company—five in number . . .' A rare example of Dickens's having failed to make his cuts consistent.

[3] *Suzannet* has 'at that precise moment what the anecdote was . . .'; *T & F* rightly corrects this to 'this . . . is . . .', in line with Dickens's substitution here of direct speech for indirect.

at the door, as he thought he heard the noise of glasses jingling—'very sorry.'

'So am I, because I know it would have afforded so much amusement. Never mind; I dare say I shall manage to recollect it, in the course of half an hour or so.'

The prim man arrived at this point, just as the glasses came back, when Mr. Bob Sawyer, who had been absorbed in attention, said *he should very much like to hear the end of it*, for, *so far as it went*, it was, without exception, the very best story he had ever heard.

The sight of the tumblers restored Bob to a degree of equanimity he had not possessed since his interview with his landlady. His face brightened up, and he began to feel quite convivial.

'Now, Betsey,' *dispersing the tumultuous little mob of glasses the girl had collected in the centre of the table*; 'now, Betsey, the warm water: be brisk, there's a good girl.'

'You can't have no warm water.'

'No warm water!'

'No, Missis Raddle said you warn't to have none.'

'Bring up the warm water instantly—instantly!'

'No, I can't. Missis Raddle raked out the kitchen fire afore she went to bed, and locked up the kittle.'

'Never mind: never mind. Pray don't disturb yourself about such a trifle,' *said Mr. Pickwick, observing the conflict of Bob Sawyer's passions, as depicted in his countenance*, 'cold water will do very well.'[1]

'My landlady is subject to some slight attacks of mental derangement. I fear I must give her warning.'

'No, don't.'

'I fear I must. Yes, I'll pay her what I owe her, and give her warning to-morrow morning.' *Poor fellow! how devoutly he wished he could!*

Mr. Bob Sawyer's attempts to rally under this last blow communicated a dispiriting influence to the company, the greater part of whom, with the view of raising their spirits, attached themselves with extra cordiality to the cold brandy and water. The first effects of these libations were displayed in an outbreak of hostilities between the youth with the nice sense of honor and Mr. Hopkins. At last the youth with the nice sense of honor felt it necessary to come to an understanding on the matter; when the following clear understanding took place.

'Sawyer.'

'Well, Noddy.'

'I should be very sorry, Sawyer, to create any unpleasantness at any friend's table, and much less at yours, Sawyer,—very; but I must take this opportunity of informing Mr. Hopkins that he is no gentleman.'

---

[1] Another optional cut is indicated here, in *Suzannet*, by marginal lines—from 'My landlady is subject . . .' to '*how devoutly he wished he could!*'

'And *I*[1] should be very sorry, Sawyer, to create any disturbance in the street in which you reside, but I'm afraid I shall be under the necessity of alarming the neighbours by pitching the person who has just spoken, out o' window.'

'I should like to see you do it, sir.'

'You shall *feel*[2] me do it in half a minute, sir.'

'I request that you'll favour me with your card, sir.'

'I'll do nothing of the kind, sir.'

'Why not, sir?'

'Because you'll stick it up over your chimney-piece, and delude your visitors into the false belief that a gentleman has been to see you, sir.'

'Sir, a friend of mine shall wait on you in the morning.'

'Sir, I am very much obliged to you for the caution, and I'll leave particular directions with the servant to lock up the spoons.'

At this point the remainder of the guests interposed, and remonstrated with both parties on the impropriety of their conduct. A vast quantity of talking ensued, in the course of which Mr. Noddy gradually allowed his feelings to overpower him, and professed that he had ever entertained a devoted personal attachment towards Mr. Hopkins. To this, Mr. Hopkins replied that on the whole he preferred Mr. Noddy to his own mother; on hearing this admission, Mr. Noddy magnanimously rose from his seat, and proffered his hand to Mr. Hopkins. Mr. Hopkins grasped it; and everybody said the whole dispute had been conducted in a manner[3] which was highly honourable to both parties concerned.

'And now, just to set us going again, Bob, I don't mind singing a song.' *Hopkins, incited by applause, plunged at once into 'The King, God bless him,' which he sang as loud as he could, to a novel air, compounded of the 'Bay of Biscay' and 'A Frog he would a wooing go.' The chorus was the essence of the song; and, as every gentleman sang it to the tune he knew best, the effect was very striking.*

It was at the end of the chorus to the first verse, that Mr. Pickwick held up his hand in a listening attitude, and said, as soon as silence was restored,

'Hush! I beg your pardon. I thought I heard somebody calling from up stairs.'

A profound silence ensued; and Mr. Bob Sawyer was observed to turn pale.

'I think I hear it now. Have the goodness to open the door.'

The door was no sooner opened than all doubt on the subject was removed by a voice screaming from the two-pair landing, 'Mr. Sawyer! Mr. Sawyer!'

---

[1] *I* italic in *Suzannet* and in the novel.

[2] *feel* italic in *Suzannet* and in the novel.

[3] 'Here he would sometimes gag' (Kent, p. 160).

'(It's my landlady. I thought you were making too much noise.[1]—) Yes, Mrs. Raddle.'

'What do you mean by this, Mr. Sawyer? Aint it enough to be swindled out of one's rent, and money lent out of pocket besides, and insulted by your friends that dares to call themselves men, without having the house turned out of window, and noise enough made to bring the fire-engines here at two o'clock in the morning?—Turn them wretches away.'

'You ought to be ashamed of yourselves,' *said the voice of Mr. Raddle, which appeared to proceed from beneath some distant bed-clothes.*[2]

'Ashamed of themselves! Why don't you go down and knock 'em every one down stairs? You would if you was a man.'

'I should if I was a dozen men, my dear, but they've the advantage of me in numbers, my dear.'

'Ugh, you coward! *Do*[3] you mean to turn them wretches out, Mr. Sawyer?'

'They're going, Mrs. Raddle, they're going. (I am afraid you'd better go. I *thought*[4] you were making too much noise.)—They're only looking for their hats, Mrs. Raddle; they are going directly.'

Mrs. Raddle, thrusting her night-cap over the banisters just as Mr. Pickwick[5] emerged from the sitting-room. 'Going! What did they ever come for?'

'My dear ma'am'—remonstrated Mr. Pickwick, looking up.

'Get along with you, you old wretch!' said Mrs. Raddle, *hastily withdrawing the night-cap.* 'Old enough to be his grandfather, you villin! You're worse than any of 'em.'

Mr. Pickwick found it in vain to protest his innocence, so hurried down stairs into the street, closely followed by the rest.* The visitors having all departed, in compliance with this rather pressing request of Mrs. Raddle, the luckless Mr. Bob Sawyer was left alone, to meditate on the probable events of the morrow, and the pleasures of the evening.

THE END OF MR. BOB SAWYER'S PARTY

[1] 'Bob . . . turned reproachfully on the over-boisterous Jack Hopkins, with, "I *thought* you were making too much noise, Jack. You're such a fellow for chorusing! You're always at it. You came into the world chorusing; and I believe you'll go out of it chorusing"' (Kent, p. 161). Kate Field gives a slightly different version of this unwritten interpolation: Bob tells Jack that it is all his fault, 'because he will sing chorus—that he was born chorus-y, lives chorus-y, and will die chorus-y' (p. 95).

[2] The words *which appeared . . . distant bed-clothes* are underlined doubly in *Suzannet*. 'From an artistic point of view, the cleverest portions [of the Reading] were those in which the servant girl appeared . . . and the solitary ejaculation of Mr. Raddle from the recesses of the bed clothes' (*Yorkshire Post*, 17 April 1869).

[3] *Do* italic in *Suzannet* and in the novel.

[4] *thought* italic in *Suzannet* and in the novel.

[5] The underlining in *Suzannet* ends prematurely, at the end of a line.

DOCTOR MARIGOLD

THE market Cheap-jack, Doctor Marigold, had enormously delighted readers of the *All the Year Round* Christmas number for 1865, *Doctor Marigold's Prescriptions*, where his monologues occupied the first and last chapters. Most reviewers felt, as E. S. Dallas put it in *The Times* (6 December 1865), that Marigold was 'a masterly sketch, and one that deserves a place in our memories beside the best picture ever drawn by Dickens'. Dickens was due to resume his career as a public reader—which had been virtually in abeyance since 1862—in April 1866, when he began the first of his series under the management of Messrs. Chappell: so, as a new attraction, he devised *Doctor Marigold*. 'I have got him up with immense pains,' he told Forster on 11 March 1866 (*Life*, p. 701), and a week later, having now rehearsed the new piece over 200 times, he gave a highly successful trial reading to a few friends, including Browning, Wilkie Collins, Charles Kent, Forster, and the actor Charles Fechter.

Marigold (paired with *Bob Sawyer*) opened the new series, at St. James's Hall, London, on 10 April 1866, and it immediately became, as it remained, one of the most popular items in the repertoire. As George Dolby recalled (p. 9), it 'more than realized the anticipations of even the most sanguine of Mr Dickens's friends, whilst the public, and those who in various ways were more immediately interested in the Readings, were convinced that up to that time they had had but a very faint conception of Mr Dickens's power either as an adapter or an elocutionist'. His skill as an adapter was not in fact severely tested by this item. No rearrangement of episodes was necessary, only some abridgement: and he did not omit much. Indeed, he was rightly criticized for including too much: 'Why should Mr Dickens not have omitted the somewhat clumsy machinery, which was indeed admirable as an introduction to the padding of a Christmas number, but which is both dull and preposterous in a simple tale? Sophy's library might have been safely eliminated, and forgotten with the ephemeral books of which it is supposed to have consisted'—namely, the short stories contributed to the Christmas number by Dickens and his colleagues (*Manchester Guardian*, 4 February 1867).

The prompt-copy, now in the Berg Collection, is entitled *Doctor Marigold./ A Reading./ In Two Parts./ Privately Printed* (printed by William Clowes, London; text paginated 3–53). It contains fewer deletions and performance-signs than usual; perhaps another copy had been used for those 200 rehearsals. An unusual feature is that underlining is used almost entirely to distinguish the subdued or pathetic passages from the comic ones. There are no marginal stage-directions, but happily W. M. Wright, who made copious notes on this Reading, supplies plenty.

Another privately printed copy has been mentioned in various bibliographies, as having belonged to and been used by Dickens. It is now in the Huntington Library, San Marino, California. Entitled *The Readings/of/Charles Dickens/ As Arranged and Read by Himself./ Doctor Marigold*, it contains a few cuts and manuscript words—but the handwriting is not Dickens's, and several other features of this item (typographical, stylistic, etc.) make it clear that Dickens had nothing to do with it. So the text printed below is that of *Berg*.

Doctor Marigold united the appeal of several of Dickens's other readings and writings. The Cheap-jack's wry monologue is sometimes reminiscent of the Boots's in the earlier Reading; Little Sophy's ending is the only child-death since *Little Dombey*; Doctor Marigold's ingenious but unorthodox teaching methods recall Major Jackman's in *Mrs. Lirriper's Lodgings* (see below, pp. 418-20). Dickens's interest in the treatment of the deaf-and-dumb and other such unfortunates had been apparent since *American Notes*, and in his charitable activities too. Above all, Dickens had blended here his 'broadest humour' and his pathos, 'set before us in the tenderest light' (*The Times*, 6 December 1865)—or, to adopt the critical vocabulary of the *Staffordshire Sentinel* (4 May 1867), the opening moments of the Reading quickly had the audience 'primed for cacchinatory exercise', but soon 'Marigold's pathetic description of his child's death rendered humid the majority of the eyes in the room'. For many people, Little Sophy's dying moments, while her father had to maintain his comic cheap-jack patter, constituted one of the most memorable passages in all the Readings. Not that it escaped criticism: the *Scotsman*, for instance, found it 'a too real and tragic touch laid upon so otherwise light and easy-going story; too palpably a trap for tears, which are apt to be withheld when too openly bid for' (19 April 1866). Few, however, seem to have withheld their tears; indeed, one critic, who regarded this episode as 'unrivalled for its pathetic effect', noted that throughout the Farewell series 'this scene has been, as well it may, remarkable for the effect it has produced upon the audience, and every audience before whom Mr Dickens has produced it has found it too great for self-control' (*Ipswich Journal*, 20 March 1869). But the Reading was also 'one of the most humorous things he ever wrote' (*Bath Chronicle*, 14 February 1867), and Dickens's impersonation of the cheap-jack was one of his most admired performances: 'perhaps there is no character in which the great novelist appears to greater advantage' (*The Times*, 7 October 1868). As many observers noted, he *became* the cheap-jack—and not only in the comic mimicry, but also in the rich sense he conveyed of the man's heart. His voices for Mim and Pickleson were also much enjoyed.

As in some of his other minor pieces, however, he has here been much more successful in imagining a character than in devising a story worthy of him. The *Manchester Guardian* critic (probably Professor Adolphus Ward) put this point well: 'The cheap-jack himself is delightful, and was as irresistible as ever. . . . But the story is sickly, and the episode of the deaf and dumb lover courting his deaf and dumb mistress is simply painful' (4 February 1867). Clearly, much depended on Dickens's performance and his audience. As a close friend, Annie Fields, thought, this was 'Subtlest of all the readings, it requires more of the listener than any other.' This remark was provoked by one of his first American performances of this item, when 'The audience was not responsive, but we [Annie Fields and her husband] were penetrated by it' (*James T. Fields: Biographical and Personal Sketches* (1881), p. 156). Generally, however, *Marigold* was very popular in America as well as Britain, despite these technical difficulties and the accent's and the market-place patter's being somewhat alien. Dickens described his first American performance of it (New York, 2 January 1868) as 'really a tremendous hit. The people doubted it at first, having evidently not the least idea what could be done with it, and broke out at last into a perfect chorus of delight. At the end they made a great shout, and gave a rush towards the platform as if they were going to carry me off' (*Life*, p. 777).

W. M. Wright records that the Reading took 'about an hour' to perform, and that it was prefaced by these words: 'I am to have the pleasure of reading to you tonight Dr. Marigold, whom I will leave to tell you his story in his own way.' The pronunciations which he records confirm that Marigold was a Dickensian Cockney: 'opposite' as 'oppo-sight', 'put' as in 'putty', 'joints' as 'jints', 'owner' as 'howner', 'rather' as 'rayther', 'waistcoat' as 'vaistcoat'.

Doctor Marigold

I am a Cheap Jack,[1] and my own father's name was Willum Marigold. It was in his lifetime supposed by some that his name was William, but my own father always consistently said, No, it was Willum. On which point I content myself with looking at the argument this way:— If a man is not allowed to know his own name in a free country, how much is he allowed to know in a land of slavery?

I was born on the Queen's highway, but it was the King's at that time. A doctor was fetched to my own mother by my own father, when it took place on a common; and in consequence of his being a very kind gentleman, and accepting no fee but a tea-tray, I was named Doctor, out of gratitude and compliment to him. There you have me. Doctor Marigold.*

The doctor having accepted a tea-tray, you'll guess that my father was a Cheap Jack before me. You are right. He was. * And my father was a lovely one in his time at the Cheap Jack work. Now, I'll tell you what. I mean to go down into my grave declaring, that of all the callings ill-used in Great Britain, the Cheap Jack calling is the worst used. Why ain't we a profession? Why ain't we endowed with privileges? Why are we forced to take out a hawker's licence, when no such thing is expected of the political hawkers? Where's the difference betwixt us? Except that we are Cheap Jacks and they are Dear Jacks, I don't see any difference but what's in our favour.

For look here! Say it's election-time. I am on the footboard of my cart, in the market-place on a Saturday night. I put up a general miscellaneous lot. I say: 'Now here my free and independent woters, I'm a going to give you such a chance as you never had in all your born days, nor yet the days preceding. Now I'll show you what I am a going to do with you. Here's a pair of razors that'll shave you closer than the Board of Guardians; here's a flat-iron worth its weight in gold; here's a frying-pan artificially flavoured with essence of beefsteaks to that degree that you've only got for the rest of your lives to fry bread and dripping in it and there you are replete with animal food; here's a genuine chronometer watch, in such a solid silver case that you may knock at the door with it when you come home late from a social meeting, and rouse your wife and family and save up your knocker for the postman; and here's

---

[1] 'Shakes head determinedly' (Wright). He also noted that Dickens opened the monologue: 'I am known all over England.'

half a dozen dinner plates that you may play the cymbals with to charm
the baby when it's fractious. Stop! I'll throw you in another article,
and I'll give you that, and it's a rolling-pin, and if the baby can only
get it well into its mouth when its teeth is coming, and rub the gums
once with it, they'll come through double, in a fit of laughter equal to
being tickled. Stop again! I'll throw you in another article, because I
don't like the looks of you, for you haven't the appearance of buyers
unless I lose by you, and because I'd rather lose than not take money
to-night, and that article's a looking-glass in which you may see how
ugly you look when you don't bid. What do you say now? Come! Do
you say a pound? Not you, for you haven't got it. Do you say ten shillings?
Not you, for you owe more to the tallyman. Well then, I'll tell you what
I'll do with you. I'll heap 'em all on the footboard of the cart—there
they are! razors, flat-iron, frying-pan, chronometer watch, dinner-plates,
rolling-pin, and looking-glass—take 'em all away for four shillings, and
I'll give you sixpence for your trouble!' This is me, the Cheap Jack.

But on the Monday morning, in the same market-place, comes the
Dear Jack on the hustings—*his* cart—and what does *he* say?[1] 'Now my
free and independent woters, I am a going to give you such a chance'
(he begins just like me) 'as you never had in all your born days, and
that's the chance of sending Myself to Parliament. Now I'll tell you
what I am a going to do for you. Here's the interests of this magnificent
town promoted above all the rest of the civilized and uncivilized earth.
Here's your railways carried, and your neighbours' railways jockeyed.
Here's all your sons in the Post-office. Here's Britannia smiling on you.
Here's the eyes of Europe on you. Here's uniwersal prosperity for you,
repletion of animal food, golden cornfields, gladsome homesteads, and
rounds of applause from your own hearts, all in one lot, and that's
myself. Will you take me as I stand?[2] You won't? Well, then, I'll tell
you what I'll do with you. Come now! I'll throw you in anything you
ask for. There! Church-rates, abolition of church-rates, more malt-tax,
no malt-tax, uniwersal education to the highest mark or uniwersal ignorance to the lowest, total abolition of flogging in the army or a dozen
for every private once a month all round, Wrongs of Men or Rights of
Women—only say which it shall be, take 'em or leave 'em, and I'm of
your opinion altogether, and the lot's your own on your own terms.
There! You won't take it yet?[3] Well then, I'll tell you what I'll do with

---

[1] *his* and *he* italic in *All the Year Round* (*AYR*) and in *Berg*. Wright notes that Dickens
used 'Both Hands' at the beginning of the Dear Jack's speech, spreading them out
at 'Here's the interests of this magnificent town . . .'—*T & F* (but not *AYR* nor *Berg*)
begins a new paragraph at 'But on the Monday morning': a creditably authorized
clarification.

[2] 'Pause' (Wright).

[3] 'Pause and sigh and lean forward with' [other words cut away] (Wright).

you. Come![1] You *are* such free and independent woters, and I *am* so proud of you—you *are* such a noble and enlightened constituency, and I *am* so ambitious of the honour and dignity of being your member, which is by far the highest level to which the wings of the human mind can soar—that I'll tell you what I'll do with you. I'll throw you in all the public-houses in your magnificent town, for nothing. Will that content you? It won't? You won't take the lot yet? Well then, before I put the horse in and drive away, and make the offer to the next most magnificent town that can be discovered, I'll tell you what I'll do. Take the lot, and I'll drop two thousand pound in the streets of your magnificent town for them to pick up that can. Not enough? Now look here. This is the very furthest that I'm a going to. I'll make it two thousand five hundred. And still you won't? Here, missis! Put the horse—no, stop half a moment, I shouldn't like to turn my back upon you neither for a trifle, I'll make it two thousand seven hundred and fifty pound. There! Take the lot on your own terms, and I'll count out two thousand seven hundred and fifty pound on the footboard of the cart, to be dropped in the streets of your magnificent town for them to pick up that can. What do you say? Come now! You won't do better, and you may do worse. You take it? Hooray! Sold again, and got the seat!' *

I courted my wife from the footboard of the cart. I did indeed. She was a Suffolk young woman, and it was in Ipswich market-place right opposite the corn-chandler's shop. I had noticed her up at a window last Saturday that was, appreciating highly; I had took to her; and I had said to myself, 'If not already disposed of, I'll have that lot.' Next Saturday that come, I pitched the cart on the same pitch, and I was in very high feather indeed, keeping 'em laughing the whole of the time and getting off the goods briskly. At last I took out of my waistcoat pocket a small lot wrapped in soft paper, and I put it this way (looking up at the window where she was). 'Now here my blooming English maidens is a article, the last article of the present evening's sale, which I offer to only you the lovely Suffolk Dumplings biling over with beauty, and I won't take a bid of a thousand pound for, from any man alive. Now what is it? Why, I'll tell you what it is. It's made of fine gold, and it's not broke though there's a hole in the middle of it, and it's stronger than any fetter that ever was forged, though it's smaller than any finger in my set of ten. Why ten? Because when my parents made over my property to me, I tell you true, there was twelve sheets, twelve towels, twelve table-cloths, twelve knives, twelve forks, twelve table-spoons, and twelve tea-spoons, but my set of fingers was two short of a dozen and could never since be matched. Now what else is it? Come I'll tell you. It's a hoop of solid gold, wrapped in a silver curl-paper that I myself

[1] Italics in the following sentence printed in *AYR* and *Berg*.

took off the shining locks of the ever beautiful old lady in Threadneedle-street, London city. I wouldn't tell you so if I hadn't the paper to show, or you mightn't believe it even of me. Now what else is it? It's a man-trap and a handcuff, the parish stocks and a leg-lock, all in gold and all in one. Now what else is it? It's a wedding ring. Now I'll tell you what I'm a going to do with it. I'm not a going to offer this lot for money, but I mean to give it to the next of you beauties that laughs, and I'll pay her a visit to-morrow morning at exactly half after nine o'clock as the chimes go, and I'll take her out for a walk to put up the banns.' *She*[1] laughed, and got the ring handed up to her. When I called in the morning, she says 'Oh dear! It's never you, and you never mean it?' 'It's ever me,' says I, 'and I'm ever yours, and I ever mean it.' So we got married, after being put up three times—which, by-the-by, is quite in the Cheap Jack way again, and shows once more how the Cheap Jack customs pervade society.

She wasn't a bad wife, but she had a temper. If she could have parted with that one article at a sacrifice, I wouldn't have swopped her away in exchange for any other woman in England. Not that I ever did swop her away, for we lived together till she died, and that was thirteen year. Now my lords and ladies and gentlefolks all, I'll let you into a secret, though you won't believe it. Thirteen year of temper in a Palace would try the worst of you, but thirteen year of temper in a Cart would try the best of you. You are kept so very close to it in a cart, you see. There's thousands of couples among you, getting on like sweet ile upon a whet-stone, in houses five and six pairs of stairs high, that would go to the Divorce Court in a cart. Whether the jolting makes it worse, I don't undertake to decide, but in a cart it does come home to you and stick to you. Wiolence in a cart is *so* wiolent, and aggrawation in a cart is *so* aggrawating.[2]

We might have had such a pleasant life! A roomy cart, with the large goods hung outside and the bed slung underneath it when on the road, an iron pot and a kettle, a fireplace for the cold weather, a chimney for the smoke, a hanging shelf and a cupboard, a dog, and a horse. What more do you want? You draw off upon a bit of turf in a green lane or by the roadside, you hobble your old horse and turn him grazing, you light your fire upon the ashes of the last visitors, you cook your stew, and you wouldn't call the Emperor of France your father. But have a temper in the cart, flinging language and the hardest goods in stock at you, and where are you then? Put a name to your feelings.

---

[1] *She* italic in *AYR* and *Berg*.

[2] *so . . . so* italic in *AYR* and *Berg*. This description of temper in a cart 'fairly con-vulsed the audience with laughter' (*Chester Chronicle*, 26 January 1867). Wright has, at the top of the page containing the next paragraph: 'Rather nasal in tone—quiet way throughout—low tone'.

[1] My dog knew as well when she was on the turn as I did. Before she broke out, he would give a howl, and bolt.[2] How he knew it, was a mystery to me, but the sure and certain knowledge of it would wake him up out of his soundest sleep, and he would give a howl, and bolt. At such times I wished I was him.

The worst of it was we had a daughter born to us, and I love children with all my heart.[3] When she was in her furies she beat the child. This got to be so shocking, as the child got to be four or five year old, that I have many a time gone on with my whip over my shoulder, at the old horse's head, sobbing and crying worse than ever little Sophy did. For how could I prevent it? Such a thing is not to be tried with such a temper —in a cart—without coming to a fight. It's in the natural size and formation of a cart to bring it to a fight. And then the poor child got worse terrified than before, as well as worse hurt generally, and her mother made complaints to the next people we lighted on, and the word went round, 'Here's a wretch of a Cheap Jack been a beating his wife.'[4]

Little Sophy was such a brave child! She grew to be quite devoted to her poor father, though he could do so little to help her. She had a wonderful quantity of shining dark hair, all curling natural about her. It is quite astonishing to me now, that I didn't go tearing mad when I used to see her run from her mother before the cart, and her mother catch her by her hair, and pull her down by it, and beat her.

Yet in other respects her mother took great care of her. Her clothes were always clean and neat, and her mother was never tired of working at 'em. Such is the inconsistency of things. Our being down in the marsh country in unhealthy weather, I consider the cause of Sophy's taking bad low fever; but however she took it, once she got it she turned away from her mother for evermore, and nothing would persuade her to be touched by her mother's hand. She would shiver and say 'No, no, no,'[5] when it was offered at, and would hide her face on my shoulder, and hold me tighter round the neck.

The Cheap Jack business had been worse than ever I had known it, what with one thing and what with another (and not least what with railroads, which will cut it all to pieces, I expect, at last), and I was run

[1] 'Right hand uplifted' (Wright). At the bottom of the page containing the preceding and following paragraphs, Wright notes: 'Hands together working fingers'.

[2] 'And what an important character Doctor Marigold's dog becomes from just one or two references to his extraordinary sagacity! . . . The tone of the "howl" and action of the "bolt" are unutterably expressive' (Field, p. 77).

[3] 'When the good Doctor clasps his hands and presses them to his breast [here], as if he were embracing that pretty daughter . . ., you feel as if he really *did* love children. Moreover, you feel morally certain that Dickens loves children too' (Field, p. 78).

[4] 'Points' (Wright). The next paragraph was spoken 'Feelingly', and Dickens began it by interjecting 'My little Sophy! Ah!' (Wright).

[5] 'Sophy's voice' (Wright).

dry of money. For which reason, one night at that period of little Sophy's being so bad, either we must have come to a deadlock for victuals and drink, or I must have pitched the cart as I did.

I couldn't get the dear child to lie down or leave go of me, and indeed I hadn't the heart to try; so I stepped out on the footboard with her holding round my neck.[1] They all set up a laugh when they see us, and one chuckle-headed Joskin (that I hated for it) made the bidding, 'tuppence for her!'

'Now, you country boobies,' says I, *feeling as if my heart was a heavy weight at the end of a broken sash-line,*[2] † 'now let's know what you want to-night, and you shall have it. But first of all, shall I tell you why I have got this little girl round my neck? You don't want to know? Then you shall. She belongs to the Fairies. She is a fortune-teller. She can tell me all about you in a whisper, and can put me up to whether you're going to buy a lot or leave it. Now do you want a saw? No, she says you don't, because you're too clumsy to use one. Your well-known awkwardness would make it manslaughter. Now I am a going to ask her what you do want. (*Then I whispered, 'Your head burns so, that I am afraid it hurts you bad, my pet?' and she answered, without opening her heavy eyes, 'Just a little, father.'*) Oh! This little fortune-teller says it's a memorandum-book you want.[3] Then why didn't you mention it? Here it is. Look at it. Two hundred superfine hot-pressed wire-wove pages, ready ruled for your expenses, an everlastingly-pointed pencil to put 'em down with, a double-bladed penknife to scratch 'em out with, a book of printed tables to calculate your income with, and a camp-stool to sit down upon while you give your mind to it! Stop! And an umbrella to keep the moon off when you give your mind to it on a pitch dark night. Now I won't ask you how much for the lot, but how little? How little are you thinking of? Don't be ashamed to mention it, because my fortune-teller knows already. (*Then making believe to whisper, I kissed her, and she kissed me.*) Why, she says you are thinking of as little as three and threepence! I couldn't have believed it, even of you, unless she told me. Three and threepence! And a set of printed tables in the lot that'll calculate your income up to forty thousand a year! With an income of forty thousand a year, you grudge three and sixpence. Well then, I'll tell you my opinion. I so despise the threepence, that I'd sooner take three shillings. There. For three shillings, three shillings, three shillings! Gone. Hand 'em over to the lucky man.'

---

[1] 'Left Hand turned over on left breast as if holding Sophy. Smoothing back of same occasionally with Right Hand' (Wright).

[2] Like most of the underlining in this Reading, this is double; but as double underlining is not here being used to distinguish a different degree of emphasis (etc.) from single, this will not be noted henceforward.

[3] 'Right Hand slapping forehead and then throwing book on table' (Wright).

As there had been no bid at all, everybody looked about and grinned at everybody, while I touched little Sophy's face and asked her if she felt faint or giddy. 'Not very, father. It will soon be over.' *Then turning from the pretty patient eyes, which were opened now, and seeing nothing but grins across my lighted grease-pot, I went on again in my Cheap Jack style.* 'Where's the butcher?' (*My sorrowful eye had just caught sight of a fat young butcher on the outside of the crowd.*) 'She says the good luck is the butcher's. Where is he?' Everybody handed on the blushing butcher to the front, and there was a roar, and the butcher felt himself obliged to put his hand in his pocket and take the lot. The party so picked out, in general does feel obliged to take the lot. Then we had another lot the counterpart of that one, and sold it sixpence cheaper, which is always wery much enjoyed. So I went on in my Cheap Jack style till we had the ladies' lot—the tea-pot, tea-caddy, glass sugar basin, half a dozen spoons, and caudle-cup—*and all the time I was making similar excuses to give a look or two and say a word or two to my poor child. It was while the second ladies' lot was holding 'em enchained that I felt her lift herself a little on my shoulder, to look across the dark street.* 'What troubles you, darling?' 'Nothing troubles me, father. I am not at all troubled. But don't I see a pretty churchyard over there?' 'Yes, my dear.' 'Kiss me twice, dear father, and lay me down to rest upon that churchyard grass so soft and green.'[1] I staggers back into the cart with her head dropped on my shoulder, and I says to her mother, 'Quick. Shut the door! Don't let those laughing people see!' 'What's the matter?' she cries. 'O, woman, woman,' I tells her, 'you'll never catch my little Sophy by her hair again, for she's dead and flown away from you!'[2]

Maybe those were harder words than I meant 'em, but from that time forth my wife took to brooding, and would sit in the cart or walk beside it, hours at a stretch, with her arms crossed and her eyes looking

[1] 'Drop head forward'; Marigold's next speech given in a 'Hoarse voice' (Wright).

[2] As was remarked in the headnote, this episode of Sophy's death was the great moment of this Reading—indeed, one of the most celebrated moments in the repertoire. Superlatives were used liberally to describe Dickens's conception and performance of the scene: 'an irresistibly tragic power' (*Belfast Newsletter*, 21 May 1867); 'nothing could surpass in true refinement Mr. Dickens's style of rendering' it (*Manchester Guardian*, 4 February 1867); 'Incomparably the finest portion of all this wonderfully original sketch of Doctor Marigold, both in the Writing and in the Reading, . . . it was one that, by voice and look and manner, he himself most exquisitely delineated' (Kent, pp. 250–1). To conceive of such a scene showed 'certainly a surprising kind of dramatic genius', and Dickens's performance was 'worthy of the great French school of acting' (*Graphic*, 12 February 1870, p. 250). Apart from the minority view which found it sentimental clap-trap, only one technical criticism seems to have been made. Kate Field thought that Dickens made Marigold's bitter speech to his wife too loud; wanting to conceal his grief from the crowd, he would surely have 'muffled the cry of his heart. Did Doctor Marigold shout as Dickens does, he would alarm the entire neighbourhood' (p. 79).

on the ground.[1] When her furies took her (which was rather seldomer than before) they took her in a new way, and she banged herself about to the extent that I was forced to hold her. She got none the better for a little drink now and then. So sad our lives went on, till one summer evening, when as we were coming into Exeter out of the further West of England, we saw a woman beating a child in a cruel manner, who screamed, 'Don't beat me! O mother, mother, mother!'[2] *Then my wife stopped her ears and ran away like a wild thing, and next day she was found in the river.*

Me and my dog was all the company left in the cart now, and the dog learned to give a short bark when they wouldn't bid, and to give another and a nod of his head when I asked him: 'Who said half-a-crown? Are you the gentleman, sir, that offered half-a-crown?' He attained to an immense heighth of popularity, and I shall always believe taught himself entirely out of his own head to growl at any person in the crowd that bid as low as sixpence. But he got to be well on in years, and one night when I was conwulsing York with the spectacles, he took a conwulsion on his own account upon the very footboard by me, and it finished him.

Being naturally of a tender turn, I had dreadful lonely feelings on me arter this. I conquered 'em at selling times, having a reputation to keep (*not to mention keeping myself*), but they got me down in private and rolled upon me.

It was under those circumstances that I come acquainted with a giant. I might have been too high to fall into conversation with him, had it not been for my lonely feelings. For the general rule is, going round the country, to draw the line at dressing up. When a man can't trust his getting a living to his undisguised abilities, you consider him below your sort.[3] And this giant when on view figured as a Roman.

He was a languid young man, which I attribute to the distance betwixt his extremities. He had a little head and less in it, he had weak eyes and weak knees, and altogether you couldn't look at him without feeling that there was greatly too much of him both for his joints and his mind. But he was an amiable though timid young man (his mother let him out and spent the money), and we come acquainted when he was walking to ease the horse betwixt two fairs. He was called Rinaldo di Velasco, his name being Pickleson.

This giant otherwise Pickleson mentioned to me under the seal of confidence, that beyond his being a burden to himself, his life was made

[1] Marigold's compunction here, after his reproaches to his wife, 'was most affecting; and the story of the poor woman's brooding over her sorrow, and her death, . . . was given with a power that must have reached the heart of every one present' (*Birmingham Gazette*, 11 May 1866).

[2] 'Both Hands shaking to keep off the mother' (Wright).

[3] 'Sneeringly' (Wright). In the next sentence, and throughout whenever 'Roman' is mentioned, Dickens made it 'a hancient Roman' (Wright; Field, p. 79).

a burden to him, by the cruelty of his master towards a step-daughter who was deaf and dumb. Her mother was dead, and she had no living soul to take her part, and was used most hard. She travelled with his master's caravan, only because there was nowhere to leave her, and this giant otherwise Pickleson did go so far as to believe that his master often tried to lose her. He was such a very[1] languid young man, that I don't know how long it didn't take him to get this story out, but it passed through his defective circulation to his top extremity in course of time.

When I heard this account from the giant otherwise Pickleson, and likewise that the poor girl had beautiful long dark hair, and was often pulled down by it and beaten, I couldn't see the giant through what stood in my eyes. Having wiped 'em,[2] I give him sixpence (for he was kept as short as he was long), and he laid it out in two three-pennorths of gin-and-water, which so brisked him up, that he sang the Favourite Comic of Shivery Shakey, ain't it cold? A popular effect which his master had tried every other means to get out of him as a Roman, wholly in vain.

His master's name was Mim; a wery hoarse man, and I knew him to speak to. I went to that Fair as a mere civilian, leaving the cart outside the town, and I looked about the back of the Vans while the performing was going on, and at last sitting dozing against a muddy cart-wheel, I come upon the poor girl who was deaf and dumb.[3] At the first look I might almost have judged that she had escaped from the Wild Beast Show, but at the second I thought better of her, *and thought that if she was more cared for and more kindly used she would be like my child. She was just the same age that my own daughter would have been, if her pretty head had not fell down upon my shoulder[4] that unfortunate night.*

To cut it short, I spoke confidential to Mim while he was beating the gong outside betwixt two lots of Pickleson's publics, and I put it to him, 'She lies heavy on your own hands; what'll you take for her?' Mim was a most ferocious swearer. Suppressing that part of his reply, which was much the longest part, his reply was, 'A pair of braces.' 'Now I'll tell you,' says I, 'what I'm a going to do with you. I'm a going to fetch you half a dozen pair of the primest braces in the cart, and then to take her away with me.' Says Mim (again ferocious), 'I'll believe it when I've got the goods, and no sooner.' I made all the haste I could, lest he should think twice of it, and the bargain was completed: which Pickleson he was thereby so relieved in his mind that he come out at

---

[1] 'I don't know how Dickens does it, . . . but the complete vacuity of his face as he produces the word "wery", and the languor which accompanies his delivery of this sentence, absolutely makes you limp in joints and mind as Rinaldo di Velasco himself' (Field, p. 80). Kent noted that Dickens used a high falsetto voice for this giant (p. 250); it was, said Wright, 'like voice of man with fat chin in *Carol*'.

[2] 'Wipe eyes with fingers' (Wright).   [3] 'Right Hand uplifted' (Wright).

[4] 'Looking up' (Wright).

his little back door, longways like a serpent, and give us Shivery Shakey in a whisper among the wheels at parting.

It was happy days for both of us when Sophy and me began to travel in the cart. *I at once give her the name of Sophy, to put her ever towards me in the attitude of my own daughter.* We soon made out to begin to understand one another, through the goodness of the Heavens, when she knowed that I meant true and kind by her. In a very little time she was wonderful fond of me. You have no idea what it is to have any body wonderful fond of you, unless you have been got down and rolled upon by the lonely feelings that I have mentioned as having once got the better of me.

You'd have laughed—or the rewerse—it's according to your disposition —if you could have seen me trying to teach Sophy. At first I was helped— you'd never guess by what—milestones. I got some large alphabets in a box, all the letters separate on bits of bone, and say we was going to WINDSOR,[1] I give her those letters in that order, and then at every milestone I showed her those same letters in that same order again, and pointed towards the abode of royalty. Another time I give her CART,[2] and then chalked the same upon the cart. Another time I give her DOCTOR MARIGOLD, and hung a corresponding inscription out-side my waistcoat. People that met us might stare a bit and laugh, but what did *I* care if she caught the idea? She caught it after long patience and trouble, and then we did begin to get on swimmingly, I believe you! At first she was a little given to consider me the cart, and the cart the abode of royalty, but that soon wore off.

We had our signs, too, and they was hundreds in number.[3] Sometimes, she would sit looking at me and considering hard how to communicate with me about something fresh—how to ask me what she wanted ex-plained—*and then she was (or I thought she was; what does it signify?) so like my child with those years added to her, that I half believed it was herself, trying to tell me where she had been to up in the skies, and what she had seen since that unhappy night when she flied away.* She had a pretty face, and now that there was no one to drag at her bright dark hair, and it was all in order, there was a something touching in her looks that made the cart most peaceful and most quiet, though not at all melancolly.

The way she learnt to understand any look of mine was truly surprising.

---

[1] Capitals here, and below for CART and DOCTOR MARIGOLD, printed thus in *AYR* and *Berg*. Below, *I* italic in *AYR* and *Berg*.

[2] 'Spells letters along table'—C/A/R/T, etc. (Wright).

[3] 'Feelingly' (Wright)—to the end of this paragraph. Significantly, Dickens deleted the uneasy little joke which (in *AYR*, and printed in *Berg*) ended the paragraph— '[N.B. In the Cheap Jack patter we generally sound it, lemonjolly, and it gets a laugh.]'

When I sold of a night, she would sit in the cart unseen by them outside,[1] and would give a eager look into my eyes when I looked in, and would hand me straight the precise article or articles I wanted. And then she would clap her hands and laugh for joy. And as for me, seeing her so bright, and remembering what she was when I first lighted on her, starved and beaten and ragged, leaning asleep against the muddy cart-wheel, it give me such heart that I gained a greater heighth of reputation than ever, and I put Pickleson down (by the name of Mim's Travelling Giant otherwise Pickleson) for a fypunnote in my will.

This happiness went on in the cart till she was sixteen year old.[2] By which time I began to feel not satisfied that I had done my whole duty by her, and to consider that she ought to have better teaching than I could give her. It drew a many tears on both sides when I commenced explaining my views to her, but what's right is right, and you can't neither by tears nor laughter do away with its character.

So I took her hand in mine, and I went with her one day to the Deaf and Dumb Establishment in London, and when the gentleman come to speak to us, I says to him: 'Now I'll tell you what I'll do with you sir. I am nothing but a Cheap Jack, but of late years I have laid by for a rainy day notwithstanding. This is my only daughter (adopted), and you can't produce a deafer nor yet a dumber. Teach her the most that can be taught her, in the shortest separation that can be named—state the figure for it—and I am game to put the money down. I won't bate you a single farthing sir, but I'll put down the money here and now, and I'll thankfully throw you in a pound to take it. There!' The gentleman smiled, and then, 'Well, well,' says he, 'I must first know what she has learnt already. How do you communicate with her?' Then I showed him, and she wrote in printed writing many names of things and so forth, and we held some sprightly conversation, Sophy and me, about a little story in a book which the gentleman showed her and which she was able to read. 'This is very extraordinary,' says the gentleman; 'is it possible that you have been her only teacher?' 'I have been her only teacher, sir,' I says, 'besides[3] herself.' 'Then,' says the gentleman, and more acceptable words was never spoke to me, 'you're a clever fellow, and a good fellow.' This he makes known to Sophy, who kisses his hands, claps her own, and laughs and cries upon it.

We saw the gentleman four times in all, and when he took down my name, and asked how in the world it ever chanced to be Doctor, it come out that he was own nephew by the sister's side, if you'll believe me,

---

[1] '[Word illegible] forefinger to lips left and across breast'; two sentences later, 'Clap hands' (Wright).

[2] 'Feelingly'—to the end of the paragraph; next paragraph 'Quick' (Wright).

[3] '... besides her bright—beautiful—clever self (Kiss Right Hand to Sophy 3 times between [words])' (Wright).

to the very Doctor that I was called after. This made our footing still easier, and he says to me:

'Now Marigold, tell me what more do you want your adopted daughter to know?'

'I want her sir to be cut off from the world as little as can be, considering her deprivations, and therefore to be able to read whatever is wrote, with perfect ease and pleasure.'

'My good fellow,' urges the gentleman, opening his eyes wide, 'why I[1] can't do that myself!'

I took his joke and give him a laugh (knowing by experience how flat you fall without it), and I mended my words accordingly.

'What do you mean to do with her afterwards?' asks the gentleman, with a sort of a doubtful eye. 'To take her about the country?'

'In the cart sir, but only in the cart.[2] She will live a private life, you understand, in the cart. I should never think of bringing her infirmities before the public. I wouldn't make a show of her for any money.'

The gentleman nodded and seemed to approve.

'Well,' says he, 'can you part with her for two years?'

'To do her that good—yes, sir.'

'There's another question,' says the gentleman, looking towards her: 'Can she part with you for two years?'

I don't know that it was a harder matter of itself (for the other was hard enough to me), but it was harder to get over.[3] However, she was pacified to it at last, and the separation betwixt us was settled. How it cut up both of us when it took place, and when I left her at the door in the dark of an evening, I don't tell. But I know this:—remembering that night, I shall never pass that same establishment without a heart-ache and a swelling in the throat; and I couldn't put you up the best of lots in sight of it with my usual spirit—no, not for five hundred pound reward from the Secretary of State for the Home Department, and throw in the honour of putting my legs under his mahogany arterwards.

Still, the loneliness that followed in the cart was not the old loneliness, because there was a term put to it however long to look forward to, and because I could think, when I was anyways down, that she belonged to me and I belonged to her. Always planning for her coming back, I bought in a few months' time another cart, and what do you think I planned to do with it? I'll tell you. I planned to fit it up with shelves, and books for her reading, and to have a seat in it where I could sit and see her read, and think that I had been her first teacher. Not hurrying over the job, I had the fittings knocked together in contriving ways

---

[1] I italic in *AYR* and *Berg*.

[2] 'Rather crossly' (Wright).

[3] Wright heads the page which begins here: 'Action with Both Hands throughout'. Against the rest of this paragraph, he writes: 'Monotonous low voice'.

under my own inspection, and here was her bed in a berth with curtains, and there was her reading-table, and here was her writing-desk, and elsewhere was her books, in rows upon rows, picters and no picters, bindings and no bindings, gilt-edged and plain, just as I could pick 'em up for her in lots up and down the country, North and South and West and East, Winds liked best and winds liked least, Here and there and gone astray, Over the hills and far away. And when I had got together pretty well as many books as the cart would neatly hold, a new scheme come into my head: which helped me over the two years' stile.

Without being of an awaricious temper, I like to be the owner of things. I shouldn't wish, for instance, to go partners with yourself in the Cheap Jack cart. It's not that I mistrust you, but that I'd rather know it was mine. Similarly, very likely you'd rather know it was yours. Well! A kind of jealousy began to creep into my mind when I reflected that all those books would have been read by other people long before they was read by her. It seemed to take away from her being the owner of 'em like. In this way the question got into my head:—Couldn't I have a book new-made express for her, which she should be the first to read?

It pleased me, that thought did, and * having formed the resolution, then come the question of a name. How did I hammer that hot iron into shape? This way. The most difficult explanation I had ever had with her, was, how I came to be called Doctor, and yet was no Doctor. We had first discovered the mistake we had dropped into, through her having asked me to prescribe for her when she had supposed me to be a Doctor in a medical point of view; so thinks I, 'Now, if I give this[1] book the name of my Prescriptions, and if she catches the idea that my only Prescriptions are for her amusement and interest—to make her laugh in a pleasant way—or to make her cry in a pleasant way—it will be a delightful proof to both of us that we have got over our difficulty.' It fell out to absolute perfection. †

But let me not anticipate. (I take that expression out of a lot of romances I bought for her. I never opened a single one of 'em—and I have opened many—but I found the romancer saying 'let me not anticipate.' Which being so, I wonder why he did anticipate, or who asked him to it.) Let me not, I say, anticipate. This same book took up all my spare time. At last it was done, and the two years' time was gone after all the other time before it, and where it's all gone to, Who knows? The new cart was finished—yellow outside, relieved with wermilion[2] and brass fittings

---

[1] '. . . this *miscellaneous* book . . .' (Wright).

[2] 'Now the words, "relieved with wermilion", *as* words, are not funny; and yet when Dickens is "relieved with wermilion" his face looks such unutterable things that even the most stoical fancies, as did Sophy herself once, that the Doctor is the *c-a-r-t*' (Field, p. 81).

—the old horse was put in it, a new 'un and a boy being laid on for the Cheap Jack cart—and I cleaned myself up to go and fetch her.

'Marigold,' says the gentleman, giving his hand hearty, 'I am very glad to see you.'

'Yet I have my doubts, sir,' says I,[1] 'if you can be half as glad to see me as I am to see you.'

'The time has appeared so long; has it, Marigold?'

'I won't say that, sir, considering its real length; but——'[2]

'What a start, my good fellow!'

Ah! I should think it was! Grown such a woman, so pretty, so intelligent, so expressive! I knew then that she must be really like my child, or I could never have known her, standing quiet by the door.

'[3]You are affected,' says the gentleman in a kindly manner.

'[4]I feel, sir,' says I, 'that I am but a rough chap in a sleeved waistcoat.'

'*I*[5] feel,' says the gentleman, 'that it was you who raised her from misery and degradation, and brought her into communication with her kind. But why do we converse alone together, when we can converse so well with her? Address her in your own way.'

'I am such a rough chap in a sleeved waistcoat, sir,' says I, 'and she is such a graceful woman, and she stands so quiet at the door!'

'Try if she moves at the old sign,' says the gentleman.

They had got it up together o' purpose to please me. For when I give her the old sign,[6] she rushed to my feet, and dropped upon her knees, holding up her hands to me with pouring tears of love and joy; and when I took her hands and lifted her, she clasped me round the neck and lay there; and I don't know what a fool I didn't make of myself, until we all three settled down into talking without sound, as if there was a something soft and pleasant spread over the whole world for us.[7]

CHAPTER II

EVERY item of my plan was crowned with success. Our reunited life was more than all that we had looked forward to. Content and joy went with us as the wheels of the two carts went round, and the same stopped

---

[1] 'Shaking hands' (Wright).

[2] 'Gives a start' (Wright).

[3] '*My poor fellow*, you are affected' (Wright).

[4] '*I don't know, sir*. I feel, sir . . .'; Marigold meanwhile 'Rubbing eyes and forehead and speaking pantingly and tremblingly' (Wright).

[5] *I* italic in *AYR* and *Berg*.

[6] 'Slaps table'; paragraph 'Feelingly and exultingly' (Wright).

[7] This ends ch. 1 of *Doctor Marigold's Prescriptions*, apart from a paragraph introducing the stories (mostly by other hands than Dickens's) which constituted the 'book' for Sophy. The Reading text resumes half-way through the first paragraph of ch. 8.

with us when the two carts stopped. I was as pleased and as proud as a Pug-Dog with his muzzle black-leaded for an evening party and his tail extra curled by machinery.

But I had left something out of my calculations. Now, what had I left out? To help you to a guess, I'll say, a figure. Come. Make a guess, and guess right. Nought? No. Nine? No. Eight? No. Seven? No. Six? No. Five? No. Four? No. Three? No. Two? No. One? No.[1] Now I'll tell you what I'll do with you. I'll say it's another sort of a figure altogether. There. Why then, says you, it's a mortal figure. No, nor yet a mortal figure. By such means you get yourself penned into a corner, and you can't help guessing a *im*mortal[2] figure. That's about it. Why didn't you say so sooner?

Yes. It was a immortal figure that I had altogether left out of my calculations. Neither man's nor woman's, but a child's. Girl's, or boy's? Boy's. 'I says the sparrow, with my bow and arrow.'[3] Now you have got it.

We were down at Lancaster, and I had done two nights' more than fair average business in the open square there. Mim's travelling giant otherwise Pickleson happened at the selfsame time to be a trying it on in the town. The genteel lay was adopted with him. No hint of a van. Green baize alcove leading up to Pickleson in a Auction Room. Printed poster, 'Free list suspended, with the exception of that proud boast of an enlightened country, a free press. Schools admitted by private arrangement. Nothing to raise a blush in the cheek of youth or shock the most fastidious.' Mim swearing most horrible and terrific[4] in a pink calico pay-place, at the slackness of the public. Serious hand-bill in the shops, importing that it was all but impossible to come to a right understanding of the history of David without seeing Pickleson.

I went to the Auction Room in question, and I found it entirely empty of everything but echoes and mouldiness, with the single exception of Pickleson on a piece of red drugget. This suited my purpose, as I wanted a private and confidential word with him: which was: 'Pickleson. Owing much happiness to you, I did put you in my will for a fypunnote; but, to save trouble here's four-punten down, which may equally suit your views, and let us so conclude the transaction.' Pickleson, who up to that remark had had the dejected appearance of a long Roman rushlight that couldn't anyhow get lighted, brightened up at his top extremity and made his acknowledgments in a way which (for him) was parliamentary eloquence. †

But what was to the present point in the remarks of the travelling

---

[1] 'Shaking head' (Wright).

[2] *im* italic in *AYR* and *Berg*.

[3] 'As if shooting an arrow' (Wright).

[4] Wright underlines doubly *horrible* and *terrific*.

giant otherwise Pickleson, was this: 'Doctor Marigold'—I give his words without a hope of conweying their feebleness—'who is the strange young man that hangs about your carts?'[1]—'The strange young *man*?'[2] I gives him back, thinking he meant her, and his languid circulation had dropped a syllable. 'Doctor,' he returns, with a pathos calculated to draw a tear from even a manly eye, 'I am weak, but not so weak yet as that I don't know my words. I repeat them, Doctor. The strange young man.' It then appeared that Pickleson being forced to stretch his legs (not that they wanted it) only at times when he couldn't be seen for nothing, to wit in the dead of the night and towards daybreak, had twice seen hanging about my carts, in that same town of Lancaster where I had been only two nights, this same unknown young man.

It put me rather out of sorts. Howsoever, I made light of it to Pickleson, and I took leave of Pickleson. Towards morning I kept a look-out for the strange young man, and what was more—I saw the strange young man. He was well-dressed and well-looking. He loitered very nigh my carts, watching them like, as if he was taking care of them, and soon after daybreak turned and went away. I sent a hail after him,[3] but he never started nor looked round, nor took the smallest notice.

We left Lancaster within an hour or two, on our way towards Carlisle. Next morning at daybreak I looked out again for the strange young man. I did not see him. But next morning I looked out again and there he was once more. I sent another hail after him, but as before he gave not the slightest sign of being anyways disturbed. This put a thought into my head. Acting on it, I watched him in different manners and at different times not necessary to enter into, till I found that this strange young man was deaf and dumb.

The discovery turned me over, because I knew that a part of that establishment where she had been, was allotted to young men (some of them well off), and I thought to myself 'If she favours him, where am I, and where is all that I have worked and planned for?' Hoping—I must confess to the selfishness—that she might *not*[4] favour him, I set myself to find out. At last I was by accident present at a meeting between them in the open air, looking on, leaning behind a fir-tree without their knowing of it. It was a moving meeting for all the three parties concerned. I knew every syllable that passed between them as well as they did.

[1] Kate Field quotes Pickleson's words, 'without a hope of conveying their feebleness. . . .Dickens outdoes himself. The contrast between the giant's purple face, swelling with effort, and the trickle of sound squeezed out at the risk of breaking every blood-vessel in Pickleson's head, is absolute perfection. A mountain never brought forth a smaller mouse, nor one that was so much worth the trouble' (p. 82). 'Giant's voice very high and very feeble' (Wright).

[2] *man* italic in *AYR* and *Berg*. 'Start and speak crossly, surprised' (Wright).

[3] 'I sent a "Aye" loud and high after him' (Wright).

[4] *not* italic in *AYR* and *Berg*.

I listened with my eyes, which had come to be as quick and true with deaf and dumb conversation as my ears with the talk of people that can speak.[1] He was going out to China as clerk in a merchant's house, which his father had been before him. He was in circumstances to keep a wife, and he wanted her to marry him and go along with him. She persisted—no. He asked if she didn't love him? Yes, she loved him dearly, dearly, but she could never disappoint her beloved good noble generous and I don't-know-what-all father (meaning me, the Cheap Jack in the sleeved waistcoat), and she would stay with him, Heaven bless him, though it was to break her heart! Then she cried most bitterly, and that made up my mind.

While my mind had been in an unsettled state about her favouring this young man, I had felt that unreasonable towards Pickleson, that it was well for him he had got his legacy down. For I often thought 'If it hadn't been for this same weak-minded giant, I might never have come to trouble my head and wex my soul about the young man.' But, once that I knew she loved him—once that I had seen her weep for him— it was a different thing. I made it right in my mind with Pickleson on the spot, and I shook myself together to do what was right by all.

She had left the young man by that time (for it took a few minutes to get me thoroughly well shook together), and the young man was leaning against another of the fir-trees—of which there was a cluster— with his face upon his arm. I touched him on the back. Looking up and seeing me, he says, in our deaf and dumb talk: 'Do not be angry.'

'I am not angry, good boy. I am your friend. Come with me.'

I left him at the foot of the steps of the Library Cart, and I went up alone. She was drying her eyes.

'You have been crying, my dear.'

'Yes, father.'

'Why?'

'A head-ache.'

'Not a heart-ache?'

'I said a head-ache, father.'

'Doctor Marigold must prescribe for that head-ache.'

She took up the book of my Prescriptions,[2] and held it up with a forced smile; but seeing me keep still and look earnest, she softly laid it down again, and her eyes were very attentive.

'The Prescription is not there, Sophy.'

'Where is it?'

'Here, my dear.'

I brought her young husband in, and I put her hand in his, and

[1] 'Low, monotonously' (Wright).
[2] 'Taking book up' (Wright).

my only further words to both of them were these: 'Doctor Marigold's last prescription. To be taken for life.'[1] After which I bolted.

When the wedding come off, I mounted a coat (blue, and bright buttons), for the first and last time in all my days, and I give Sophy away with my own hand. There were only us three and the gentleman who had had charge of her for those two years. I give the wedding dinner of four in the Library Cart. Pigeon pie, a leg of pickled pork, a pair of fowls, and suitable garden-stuff. The best of drinks. I give them a speech, and the gentlemen give us a speech, and all our jokes told, and the whole thing went off like a sky-rocket. In the course of the entertainment I explained to Sophy that I should keep the Library Cart as my living-cart when not upon the road, and that I should keep all her books for her just as they stood, till she come back to claim them. So she went to China with her young husband, and it was a parting sorrowful and heavy, and I got the boy I had another service, and so as of old, when my child and wife were gone, I went plodding along alone, with my whip over my shoulder, at the old horse's head.

Sophy wrote me many letters, and I wrote her many letters. About the end of the first year she sent me one in an unsteady hand:[2] 'Dearest father, not a week ago I had a darling little daughter, but I am so well that they let me write these words to you. Dearest and best father, I hope my child may not be deaf and dumb, but I do not yet know.' When I wrote back, I hinted the question; but as Sophy never answered that question, I felt it to be a sad one, and I never repeated it. For a long time our letters were regular, but then they got irregular through Sophy's husband being moved to another station and through my being always on the move. But we were in one another's thoughts, I was equally sure, letters or no letters.

Five years, odd months, had gone since Sophy went away. I was at a greater heighth of popularity than ever. I had had a first-rate autumn of it, and on the twenty-third of December, one thousand eight hundred and sixty-four, I found myself at Uxbridge, Middlesex,[3] clean sold out. So I jogged up to London with the old horse, light and easy, to have my Christmas-Eve and Christmas-Day alone by the fire in the Library Cart, and then to buy a regular new stock of goods all round, to sell 'em again and get the money.

I am a neat hand at cookery, and I'll tell you what I knocked up for my Christmas-Eve dinner in the Library Cart. I knocked up a beefsteak pudding for one, with two kidneys, a dozen oysters, and a couple of mushrooms, thrown in. It's a pudding to put a man in good humour

---

[1] 'Slaps hand into left and shaking up and down and in [and] out'; at the end of paragraph, 'Wipe tear from eye' (Wright).

[2] 'Reading letter as if in left hand' (Wright).

[3] '20 miles from London' (Wright inserts).

with everything, except the two bottom buttons of his waistcoat. Having relished that pudding and cleared away, I turned the lamp low, and sat down by the light of the fire, watching it as it shone upon the backs of Sophy's books.

Sophy's books so brought up Sophy's self, that I saw her touching face quite plainly, before I dropped off dozing by the fire. This may be a reason why Sophy, with her deaf and dumb child in her arms, seemed to stand silent by me all through my nap. Even when I woke with a start, she seemed to vanish, as if she had stood by me in that very place only a single instant before.

I had started at a real sound, and the sound was on the steps of the cart. It was the light hurried tread of a child coming clambering up. That tread of a child had once been so familiar to me, that for half a moment I believed I was a going to see a little ghost.[1]

But the touch of a real child was laid upon the outer handle of the door, and the handle turned and the door opened a little way, and a real child peeped in. A bright little comely girl with large dark eyes.

Looking full at me, the tiny creature took off her mite of a straw hat, and a quantity of dark curls fell all about her face. Then she opened her lips, and said in a pretty voice:

'Grandfather!'[2]

'Ah my God!' I cries out. 'She can speak!'

In a moment Sophy was round my neck as well as the child, and her husband was a wringing my hand with his face hid, and we all had to shake ourselves together before we could get over it.[3] And when we did begin to get over it, and I saw the pretty child a talking, pleased and quick and eager and busy, to her mother, in the signs that I had first taught her mother, the happy and yet pitying tears fell rolling down my face.[4]

THE END

[1] 'Left hand to forehead [speak?] in a whisper'; at the beginning of the next paragraph, 'Dickens comes to Left end of table' (Wright).

[2] 'Child's voice' (Wright). 'And when the prattler had broken the still solitariness of the caravan with the call "Grandfather", the exclamation of the elated old man brought forth numerous pocket handkerchiefs which were still in use when genuine applause followed the talented reader into the ante-room' (*Staffordshire Sentinel*, 4 May 1867).

[3] 'Left Hand to forehead, head leaning to left. Right Hand thrust out and shaking young man's hand' (Wright).

[4] '... those tears steal into our eyes as well; and when Dickens steals away, there seems to be more love and unselfishness in the world than before we took Doctor Marigold's prescription' (Field, p. 83).

MRS. LIRRIPER'S LODGINGS

WHEN Mrs. Lirriper first appeared, in the *All the Year Round* Christmas number for 1863 (*Mrs. Lirriper's Lodgings*), the *Saturday Review* hailed her as an achievement which 'Mr. Dickens has scarcely, if ever, surpassed. Mrs. Lirriper is entitled to rank with Mrs. Nickleby and Mrs. Gamp' (12 December 1863, p. 759). She was soon a legendary figure, and Dickens revived her (a thing he rarely did, even with his most popular characters) the following year, when his journal's Christmas number was *Mrs. Lirriper's Legacy*. Some recent commentators have praised his achievement in this characterization, seeing it as one of the occasions when he produces effects more often associated with James Joyce.

The *Mrs. Lirriper* Reading is not mentioned in Dickens's letters, but it was probably devised at about the same time as *Doctor Marigold* (late 1865 or early 1866). Charles Kent records that he suggested to Dickens that a Mrs. Lirriper piece would be 'a characteristic companion or contrast to Dr. Marigold' (p. 90); very likely Dickens thought he might thus have two substantial new items for his 1866 season. He certainly worked hard—or rather, began working hard—to create this text. The opening pages, up to and including the arrival of Major Jackman, are a much condensed version of the beginning of *Mrs. Lirriper's Lodgings*, omitting about three-fifths of the original text. Then he raided *Mrs. Lirriper's Legacy* for the story of Mr. Buffle (reduced by about two-fifths). After that, he was much less stringent in his revisions. He returned to *Mrs. Lirriper's Lodgings*, and the ensuing story of the Edsons and the bringing-up of their son Jemmy is hardly cut at all. Soon, indeed, Dickens must have decided that this Reading would not enter his repertoire, for this is one of the very few of his own copies which contain no writing by him (no deletions, additions, performance-signs, etc.). Another sign of his not having worked as diligently as usual is the inconsistency over whom Mrs. Lirriper is addressing. In the 1863-4 *All the Year Round* texts, this had been 'My dear' (a friend—or the reader). When preparing the prompt-copy for the printer, Dickens deleted many of these addresses, but altered some to 'My dears' (more appropriate for a public audience); in a number of places, however, 'My dear' is left uncorrected. Mrs. Lirriper's idiom is occasionally strengthened, and more punctuation is sometimes added: but such alterations are few and trivial. It is of course possible that this is not the prompt-copy, but simply another virgin copy of the privately printed edition: but no other copy of *Mrs. Lirriper* is known to exist. The copy, in the Berg Collection, is entitled *Mrs. Lirriper's Lodgings. | A Reading. | Privately Printed.* (printed by William Clowes, London; text paginated 3-54).

The Reading was never performed. Charles Kent much regretted this, but Dickens's adverse judgement was right. The conception and idiom of Mrs. Lirriper are splendid, and not beyond Dickens's histrionic powers to present, but—as happened on some other occasions—his imagination had fallen short of inventing something adequate for this character to do or observe. More unhappily than *Doctor Marigold*, this script falls off after an excellent start: and *Doctor Marigold* at least maintained one narrative line, whereas *Mrs. Lirriper's Lodgings* consists of a sequence of ill-related episodes. The story of Mrs. Edson's tribulations, which occupies nearly a half of the Reading, is feeble. The concluding episode, about young Jemmy, has some happy moments but it ends weakly and fails to rescue the script from being an uncomfortable mixture of the brilliant and the banal.

Mrs. Lirriper's Lodgings

WHOEVER would begin to be worried with letting Lodgings that wasn't a lone woman with a living to get is a thing inconceivable to me my dears excuse the familiarity but it comes natural when wishing to open my mind to those that I can trust and I should be truly thankful if they were all mankind but such is not so, for have but a Furnished bill in the window and your watch on the mantelpiece and farewell to it if you turn your back for but a second however gentlemanly the manners. Nor is being of your own sex any safeguard as I have reason in the form of sugar-tongs to know, for that lady (and a fine woman she was) got me to run for a glass of water on the plea of going to be confined, which certainly turned out true but it was in the Station-House.

Number Eighty-one Norfolk Street Strand London—situated midway between the City and St. James's and within five minutes' walk of the principal places of public amusement—is my address.

You never have found Number Eighty-one Norfolk Street Strand advertised in Bradshaw's Railway Guide and with the blessing of Heaven you never will or shall. Some there are who do not think it lowering themselves to make their names that cheap and even going the lengths of a portrait of the house not like it with a blot in every window and a most umbrageous and outrageous oak outside which never yet was seen in Norfolk Street, and a coach and four at the door which it would have been far more to Bradshaw's credit to have drawn a cab,[1] but what will suit Wozenham's lower down on the other side of the way will not suit me, Miss Wozenham having her opinions and me having mine. *

It is forty years ago since me and my poor Lirriper got married at St. Clement's Danes where I now have a sitting in a very pleasant pew with genteel company and my own hassock and being partial to evening service not too crowded. My poor Lirriper was a handsome figure of a man with a beaming eye and a voice as mellow as a musical instrument made of honey and steel, but he had ever been a free liver being in the commercial travelling line and travelling what he called a limekiln road— 'a dry road, Emma my dear,' my poor Lirriper says to me 'where I have to lay the dust with one drink or another all day long and half the night, and it wears me Emma'—and this led to his running through a good deal and might have run through the turnpike too when that dreadful horse that never would stand still for a single instant set off, but for its being

---

[1] The phrases about the *umbrageous oak* and the *cab* are taken from *Mrs. Lirriper's Legacy*.

night and the gate shut and consequently took his wheel my poor Lirriper and the gig smashed to atoms and never spoke afterwards. He was a handsome figure of a man and a man with a jovial heart and a sweet temper, but if they had come up then they never could have given you the mellowness of his voice, and indeed I consider photographs wanting in mellowness as a general rule and making you look like a new-ploughed field. *

But it was about the Lodgings that I was intending to hold forth and certainly I ought to know something of the business having been in it so long, for it was early in the second year of my married life that I lost my poor Lirriper and I set up at Islington directly afterwards and afterwards came here, being two houses and eight and thirty years and some losses and a deal of experience. *

Servant girls are one of your first and your lasting troubles, being like your teeth which begin with convulsions and never cease tormenting you from the time you cut them till they cut you, and then you don't want to part with them which seems hard but we must all succumb or buy artificial, and even where you get a will nine times out of ten you'll get a dirty face with it and naturally lodgers do not like good society to be shown in with a smear of black across the nose or a smudgy eyebrow. Where they pick the black up is a mystery I cannot solve, as in the case of the willingest girl that ever came into a house half starved poor thing, a girl so willing that I called her Willing Sophy down upon her knees scrubbing early and late and ever cheerful but always smiling with a black face. And I says to Sophy 'Now Sophy my good girl have a regular day for your stoves and keep the width of the Airy between yourself and the blacking and do not brush your hair with the bottoms of the saucepans and do not meddle with the snuffs of the candles and it stands to reason that it can no longer be' yet there it was and always on her nose, which turning up and being broad at the end seemed to boast of it and caused warning from a steady gentleman and excellent lodger with breakfast by the week but a little irritable and use of a sitting-room when required, his words being 'Mrs. Lirriper I have arrived at the point of admitting that the Black is a man and a brother, but only in a natural form and when it can't be got off.' Well consequently I put poor Sophy on to other work and forbid her answering the door or answering a bell on any account but she was so unfortunately willing that nothing would stop her flying up the kitchen stairs whenever a bell was heard to tingle. I put it to her 'Oh Sophy Sophy for goodness goodness sake where does it come from?' To which that poor unlucky willing mortal bursting out crying to see me so vexed replied 'I took a deal of black into me ma'am when I was a small child being much neglected and I think it must be, that it works out,' so it continuing to work out of that poor thing and not having another fault to find with her I says 'Sophy what do you seriously think of my helping you away to New South Wales where it might not be noticed?' Nor did I ever repent the money which was well spent, for she married the ship's cook on the voyage (himself a Mulotter) and did well and lived happy, and so far as ever I heard it was *not*[1] noticed in a new state of society to her dying day. *

I do assure you it's a harassing thing to know what kind of girls to give the preference to, for if they are lively they get bell'd off their legs and if they are sluggish you suffer from it yourself in complaints and if they are sparkling-eyed they get made love to and if they are smart in their persons they try on your Lodger's bonnets and if they are musical I defy you to keep them away from bands and organs, and allowing for any difference you like in their heads their heads will be always out of window equally the same. And then what the gentlemen like in girls the ladies don't, which is fruitful hot water for all parties, and then there's temper though such a temper as Caroline Maxey's I hope not often. A good-looking black-eyed girl was Caroline and a comely-made girl to your cost when she did break out and laid about her, as took place first and last through a new married couple come to see London in the first floor and the lady very high and it *was* supposed not liking the good looks of Caroline having none of her own to spare, but anyhow she did try Caroline though that was no excuse. So one afternoon Caroline comes down into the kitchen flushed and flashing, and she says to me 'Mrs. Lirriper that woman in the first has aggravated me past bearing,' I says, 'Caroline keep your temper,' Caroline says with a curdling laugh 'Keep my temper? You're right Mrs. Lirriper, so I will. Capital D her!' burst out Caroline (you might have struck me into the centre of the earth with a feather when she said it) 'I'll give her a touch of the temper that *I* keep!' Caroline downs with her hair my dear, screeches and rushes up-stairs, I following as fast as my trembling legs could bear me, but before I got into the room the dinner cloth and pink and white service all dragged off upon the floor with a crash and the new married couple on their backs in the fire-grate, him with the shovel and tongs and a dish of cucumber across him and a mercy it was summer-time. 'Caroline' I says, 'be calm,' but she catches off my cap and tears it in her teeth as she passes me, then pounces on the new married lady makes her a bundle of ribbons takes her by the two ears and knocks the back of her head upon the carpet, Murder screaming all the time Policemen running down the street and Wozenham's windows (judge of my feelings when I came to know it) thrown up and Miss Wozenham calling out from the balcony with crocodile's tears 'It's Mrs. Lirriper been overcharging somebody to madness—she'll be murdered—I always thought so—Pleeseman save her!' My dear four of them and Caroline behind the chiffoniere attacking with the poker and when dis-

---

[1] Italic in *All the Year Round*. The *Berg* privately printed copy contains no underlinings, etc., by Dickens; all words italicized in it had been italicized in the *All the Year Round* text. This will not be noted henceforth.

armed prize fighting with her double fists, and down and up and up and down and dreadful! But I couldn't bear to see the poor young creature roughly handled and her hair torn when they got the better of her, and I says 'Gentlemen Policemen pray remember that her sex is the sex of your mothers and sisters and your sweethearts, and God bless them and you!' And there she was sitting down on the ground handcuffed, taking breath against the skirting-board and them cool with their coats in strips, and all she says was 'Mrs. Lirriper I am sorry as ever I touched *you*, for you're a kind motherly old thing,' and it made me think that I had often wished I had been a mother indeed and how would my heart have felt if I had been the mother of that girl! Well you know it turned out at the Police-office that she had done it before, and she had her clothes away and was sent to prison, and when she was to come out I trotted off to the gate in the evening with just a morsel of jelly in that little basket of mine to give her a mite of strength to face the world again, and there I met with a very decent mother waiting for her son through bad company and a stubborn one he was with his half boots not laced. So out came Caroline and I says 'Caroline come along with me and sit down under the wall where it's retired and eat a little trifle that I have brought with me to do you good' and she throws her arms round my neck and says sobbing 'O why were you never a mother when there are such mothers as there are!' she says, * and I never more saw or heard of that girl, except that I shall always believe that a very genteel cap which was brought anonymous to me one Saturday night in an oilskin basket by a most impertinent young sparrow of a monkey whistling with dirty shoes on the clean steps and playing the harp on the Airy railings with a hoop-stick came from Caroline.

What you lay yourself open to my dears in the way of being the object of uncharitable suspicions when you go into the Lodging business I have not the words to tell you, but it *is* a hardship hurting to the feeling that Lodgers open their mind so wide to the idea that you are trying to get the better of them and shut their minds so close to the idea that they are trying to get the better of you, but as Major Jackman says to me 'I know the ways of this circular world Mrs. Lirriper, and that's one of 'em all round it' and many is the little ruffle in my mind that the Major has smoothed, for he is a clever man who has seen much, and occupied the parlors thirteen years * though in what service I cannot truly say, whether Militia or Foreign, for I never heard him even name himself as Major but always simple 'Jemmy Jackman.' And once soon after he came when I felt it my duty to let him know that Miss Wozenham had put it about that he was no Major and I took the liberty of adding 'which you are sir' his words were 'Madam at any rate I am not a Minor, and sufficient for the day is the evil thereof' which cannot be denied to be the sacred truth, nor yet his military ways of having his boots with only the dirt brushed off taken to him in the front parlour every morning on a clean plate and varnishing them himself with a little sponge and a saucer so sure as ever his breakfast is ended. And so neat his ways that it never soils his linen which is scrupulous though more in quality than quantity, neither that nor his moustachios which to the best of my belief are done at the same time and which are as black and shining as his boots, his head of hair being a lovely white.

[1] Mr. Buffle the Assessed Taxes, was at one time so much the Major's animosity and indignation that it worried me a good deal, though allowments must ever be made for a gentleman of the Major's warmth not relishing being spoke to with a pen in the mouth, and a low-crowned broad-brimmed hat on likewise.*

Mr. Buffle's family were not liked in this neighbourhood, for when you are a householder it does not come by nature to like the Assessed, and it was considered besides that a one-horse pheayton ought not to have elevated Mrs. Buffle to that heighth especially when purloined from the Taxes which I myself did consider uncharitable. But they were *not* liked and there was that domestic unhappiness in the family in consequence of their both being very hard with Miss Buffle and one another on account of Miss Buffle's favouring Mr. Buffle's articled young gentleman, that it *was* whispered that Miss Buffle would go either into a consumption or a convent. So things stood towards Mr. Buffle when one night I was woke by a frightful noise and a smell of burning, and going to my bedroom window saw the whole street in a glow. Fortunately we had two sets empty just then and before I could hurry on some clothes I heard the Major hammering at the attics' doors and calling out 'Dress yourselves!— Fire! Don't be frightened!—Fire! Collect your presence of mind!—Fire! All right!—Fire!' most tremenjously. As I opened my bedroom door the Major came tumbling in over himself and me and caught me in his arms. 'Major' I says breathless 'where is it?' 'I don't know dearest madam' says the Major—'Fire! Jemmy Jackman will defend you to the last drop of his blood—Fire!' and altogether very collected and bold except that he couldn't say a single sentence without shaking me to the very centre with roaring Fire. We ran down to the drawing-room and put our heads out of window, and the Major calls to an unfeeling young monkey scampering by be joyful and ready to split 'Where is it?—Fire!' The monkey answers without stopping 'Oh here's a lark! Old Buffle's been setting his house alight to prevent its being found out that he boned the Taxes. Hurrah! Fire!' And then the sparks came flying up and the smoke came pouring down and the crackling of flames and spatting of water and banging of engines and hacking of axes and breaking of glass and knocking at doors, and the shouting and crying and hurrying and the heat and altogether gave me a dreadful palpitation. 'Don't be frightened dearest madam,'

[1] The episode about Mr. Buffle, which follows, is taken from *Mrs. Lirriper's Legacy.*

says the Major, '—Fire! There's nothing to be alarmed at—Fire! Don't open the street door till I come back—Fire! I'll go and see if I can be of any service—Fire! You're quite composed and comfortable ain't you?—Fire, Fire, Fire!' It was in vain for me to hold the man—his spirit was up and he went scampering off after the young monkey with all the breath he had and none to spare, and me and the girls huddled together at the parlour windows looking at the dreadful flames above the houses over the way, Mr. Buffle's being round the corner. Presently what should we see but some people running down the street straight to our door, and then the Major directing operations in the busiest way, and then some more people and then—carried in a chair similar to Guy Fawkes—Mr. Buffle in a blanket!

My dears the Major has Mr. Buffle brought up our steps and whisked into the parlour and carted out on the sofy, and then he and all the rest of them without so much as a word burst away again full speed, leaving the impression of a vision except for Mr. Buffle awful in his blanket with his eyes a rolling. In a twinkling they all burst back again with Mrs. Buffle in another blanket, which whisked in and carted out on the sofy they all burst off again and all burst back again with Miss Buffle in another blanket, which again whisked in and carted out they all burst off again and all burst back again with Mr. Buffle's articled young gentleman in another blanket—him a holding round the necks of two men carrying him by the legs, similar to the picter of the disgraceful creetur who has lost the fight, and his hair having the appearance of newly played upon. When all four of a row, we made them some hot tea and toast and some hot brandy-and-water with a little comfortable nutmeg in it, and at first they were scared and low in their spirits but being fully insured got sociable. And the first use Mr. Buffle made of his tongue was to call the Major his Preserver and his best of friends and to say 'My for ever dearest sir let me make you known to Mrs. Buffle.' Which also addressed him as her Preserver and her best of friends and was fully as cordial as the blanket would admit of. Also Miss Buffle. The articled young gentleman's head was a little light and he sat a moaning 'Robina is reduced to cinders, Robina is reduced to cinders!' Which went more to the heart on account of his having got wrapped in his blanket as if he was looking out of a violin-celler case, until Mr. Buffle says 'Robina speak to him!' Miss Buffle says 'Dear George!' and but for the Major's pouring down brandy-and-water on the instant which caused a catching in his throat owing to the nutmeg and a violent fit of coughing it might have proved too much for his strength. When the articled young gentleman got the better of it Mr. Buffle leaned up against Mrs. Buffle being two bundles, a little while in confidence, and then says with tears in his eyes which the Major noticing wiped, 'We have not been an united family, let us after this danger become so, take her George.' The young gentleman could not put his arm out far to do it, but his spoken expressions were very beautiful though of a wandering class. And I do not know that I ever had a much pleasanter meal than the breakfast we took together after we had all dozed, when Miss Buffle made tea very sweetly in quite the Roman style as depicted formerly at Covent Garden Theatre and when the whole family was most agreeable.

[1]It was the third year nearly up of the Major's being in the parlours that early one morning in the month of February when Parliament was coming on and you may therefore suppose a number of imposters were about, a gentleman and lady from the country came in to view the Second, and I well remember that I had been looking out of window and had watched them and the heavy sleet driving down the street together looking for bills. I did not quite take to the face of the gentleman though he was good-looking too but the lady was a very pretty young thing and delicate, and it seemed too rough for her to be out at all, though she had only come from the Adelphi Hotel which would not have been much above a quarter of a mile if the weather had been less severe. Now it did so happen my dear that I had been forced to put five shillings weekly additional on the second in consequence of a loss from running away full-dressed as if going out to a dinner party, which was very artful and had made me rather suspicious taking it along with Parliament, so when the gentleman proposed three months certain and the money in advance and leave then reserved to renew on the same terms for six months more, I says I was not quite certain but that I might have engaged myself to another party but would step down stairs and look into it if they would take a seat. They took a seat and I went down to the handle of the Major's door that I had already began to consult finding it a great blessing, and I knew that he was varnishing his boots which was generally considered private, however he kindly calls out 'If it's you, Madam, come in,' and I went in and told him.

'Well, Madam,' says the Major rubbing his nose—as I did fear at the moment with the black sponge but it was only his knuckle, he being always neat and dexterous with his fingers—'well, Madam, I suppose you would be glad of the money?'

I was delicate of saying 'Yes' too out, for a little extra colour rose into the Major's cheeks and there was irregularity which I will not particularly specify in a quarter which I will not name.

'I am of opinion, Madam,' says the Major, 'that when money is ready for you—when it is ready for you Mrs. Lirriper—you ought to take it. What is there against it, Madam, in this case up-stairs?'

'I really cannot say there is anything against it sir, still I thought I would consult you.'

[1] The narrative here returns to the *Mrs. Lirriper's Lodgings* text, at the point where it was interrupted by the insertion of the Mr. Buffle episode.

'You said a newly married couple, I think, Madam?' says the Major.

I says 'Ye-es. Evidently. And indeed the young lady mentioned to me in a casual way that she had not been married many months.'

The Major rubbed his nose again and stirred the varnish round and round in its little saucer with his piece of sponge and took to whistling in a whisper for a few moments. Then he says 'You would call it a Good Let, Madam?'

'Oh certainly a Good Let sir.'

'Say they renew for the additional six months. Would it put you about very much Madam if—if the worst were to come to the worst?' said the Major.

'Well I hardly know,' I says to the Major. 'It depends upon circumstances. Would *you* object Sir for instance?'

'I?' says the Major. 'Object? Jemmy Jackman? Mrs. Lirriper close with the proposal.'

So I went up-stairs and accepted, and they came in next day which was Saturday and the Major was so good as to draw up a Memorandum of an agreement in a beautiful round hand and expressions that sounded to me equally legal and military, and Mr. Edson signed it on the Monday morning and the Major called upon Mr. Edson on the Tuesday and Mr. Edson called upon the Major on the Wednesday and the Second and the parlours were as friendly as could be wished.

The three months paid for had run out and we had got without any fresh overtures as to payment into May, when there came an obligation upon Mr. Edson to go a business expedition right across the Isle of Man, which fell quite unexpected on that pretty little thing and is not a place that according to my views is particularly in the way to anywhere at any time but that may be a matter of opinion. So short a notice was it that he was to go next day, and dreadfully she cried poor pretty and I am sure I cried too when I saw her on the cold pavement in the sharp east wind—it being a very backward spring that year—taking a last leave of him with her pretty bright hair blowing this way and that and her arms clinging round his neck and him saying 'There there there! Now let me go Peggy.' And by that time it was plain that what the Major had been so accommodating as to say he would not object to happening in the house, would happen in it, and I told her as much when he was gone while I comforted her with my arm up the staircase, for I says 'You will soon have others to keep up for my pretty and you must think of that.'

His letter never came when it ought to have come and what she went through morning after morning when the postman brought none for her the very postman himself compassionated when she ran down to the door, and yet we cannot wonder at its being calculated to blunt the feelings to have all the trouble of other people's letters and none of the pleasure and doing it oftener in the mud and mizzle than not and at a rate of wages more resembling Little Britain than Great. But at last one morning when she was too poorly to come running down stairs he says to me with a pleased look in his face that made me next to love the man in his uniform coat though he was dripping wet 'I have taken you first in the street this morning Mrs. Lirriper, for here's the one for Mrs. Edson.' I went up to her bedroom with it fast as ever I could go, and she sat up in bed when she saw it and kissed it and tore it open and then a blank stare came upon her. 'It's very short!' she says lifting her large eyes to my face. 'O Mrs. Lirriper it's very short!' I says 'My dear Mrs. Edson no doubt that's because your husband hadn't time to write more just at the time.' 'No doubt, no doubt,' says she, and puts her two hands on her face and turns round in her bed.

I shut her softly in and I crept down stairs and I tapped at the Major's door, and when the Major having his thin slices of bacon in his own Dutch oven saw me he came out of his chair and put me down on the sofa. 'Hush!' says he, 'I see something's the matter. Don't speak—take time.' I says 'Oh Major I am afraid there's cruel work up-stairs.' 'Yes, yes,' says he, 'I had begun to be afraid of it—take time.' And then in opposition to his own words he rages out frightfully, and says 'I shall never forgive myself Madam, that I, Jemmy Jackman, didn't see it all that morning—didn't go straight up-stairs when my boot-sponge was in my hand—didn't force it down his throat—and choke him dead with it on the spot!'

The Major and me agreed when we came to ourselves that just at present we could do no more than take on to suspect nothing and use our best endeavours to keep that poor young creature quiet, and what I ever should have done without the Major when it got about among the organ-men that quiet was our object is unknown, for he made lion and tiger war upon them to that degree that without seeing it I could not have believed it was in any gentleman to have such a power of bursting out with fire-irons, walking-sticks, water-jugs, coals, potatoes off his table, the very hat off his head, and at the same time so furious in foreign languages that they would stand with their handles half turned fixed like the Sleeping Ugly—for I cannot say Beauty.

Ever to see the postman come near the house now gave me such a fear that it was a reprieve when he went by, but in about another ten days or a fortnight he says again 'Here's one for Mrs. Edson.—Is she pretty well?' 'She is pretty well postman, but not well enough to rise so early as she used,' which was so far gospel truth.

I carried the letter in to the Major at his breakfast and I says tottering 'Major I have not the courage to take it up to her.'

'It's an ill-looking villain of a letter,' says the Major.

'I have not the courage Major' I says again in a tremble 'to take it up to her.'

After seeming lost in consideration for some moments the Major says, raising his head as if something new and useful had occurred to his mind 'Mrs. Lirriper, I shall never forgive myself that I, Jemmy Jackman, didn't go straight up-stairs that morning when my boot-sponge was in my hand—and force it down his throat—and choke him dead with it.'

'Major,' I says a little hasty 'you didn't do it which is a blessing, for it would have done no good and I think your sponge was better employed on your own honourable boots.'

So we got to be rational, and planned that I should tap at her bedroom door and lay the letter on the mat outside and wait on the upper landing for what might happen, and never was gunpowder cannon-balls or shells or rockets more dreaded than that dreadful letter was by me as I took it to the second floor.

A terrible loud scream sounded through the house the minute after she had opened it, and I found her on the floor lying as if her life was gone. I never looked at the face of the letter which was lying open by her, for there was no occasion.

Everything I needed to bring her round the Major brought up with his own hands, besides running out to the chemist's for what was not in the house. When after a long time I saw her coming to, I slipped on the landing till I heard her cry, and then I went in and says cheerily 'Mrs. Edson you're not well my dear and it's not to be wondered at,' as if I had not been in before. Whether she believed or disbelieved I cannot say and it would signify nothing if I could, but I stayed by her for hours and then she God ever blesses me! and says she will try to rest for her head is bad.

'Major,' I whispers, looking in at the parlours, 'I beg and pray of you don't go out.'

The Major whispers 'Madam, trust me I will do no such thing. How is she?'

I says 'Major the good Lord above us only knows what burns and rages in her poor mind. I left her sitting at her window. I am going to sit at mine.'

It came on afternoon and it came on evening. Norfolk is a delightful street to lodge in—provided you don't go lower down—but of a summer evening when the dust and waste paper lie in it and stray children play in it and a kind of a gritty calm and bake settles on it and a peal of church bells is practising in the neighbourhood it is a trifle dull, and never have I seen it since at such a time and never shall I see it evermore at such a time without seeing the dull June evening when that forlorn young creature sat at her open corner window on the second and me at my open corner window (the other corner) on the third. Something merciful, something wiser and better far than my own self, had moved me while it was yet light to sit in my bonnet and shawl, and as the shadows fell and the tide rose I could sometimes—when I put out my head and looked at her window below—see that she leaned out a little looking down the street. It was just settling dark when I saw *her* in the street.

So fearful of losing sight of her that it almost stops my breath while I tell it, I went down stairs faster than I ever moved in all my life and only tapped with my hand at the Major's door in passing it and slipping out. She was gone already. I made the same speed down the street and when I came to the first corner I saw that she had turned it and was there plain before me going towards the west. O with what a thankful heart I saw her going along!

She was quite unacquainted with London and had very seldom been out for more than an airing in our own street where she knew two or three little children belonging to neighbours and had sometimes stood among them at the end of the street looking at the water. She must be going at hazard I knew, still she kept the by-streets quite correctly as long as they would serve her, and then turned up into the Strand. But at every corner I could see her head turned one way, and that way was always the river way.

It may have been only the darkness and quiet of the Adelphi that caused her to strike into it but she struck into it much as readily as if she had set out to go there, which perhaps was the case. She went straight down to the Terrace and along it and looked over the iron rail, and I often woke afterwards in my own bed with the horror of seeing her doing it. The desertion of the wharf below and the flowing of the high water there seemed to settle her purpose. She looked about as if to make out the way down, and she struck out the right way or the wrong way—I don't know which, for I don't know the place before or since—and I followed her the way she went.

It was noticeable that all this time she never once looked back. But there was now a great change in the manner of her going, and instead of going at a steady quick walk with her arms folded before her,—among the dark dismal arches she went in a wild way with her arms opened wide, as if they were wings and she was flying to her death.

We were on the wharf and she stopped. I stopped. I saw her hands at her bonnet-strings, and I rushed between her and the brink and took her round the waist with both my arms. She might have drowned me, I felt then, but she could never have got quit of me.

Down to that moment my mind had been all in a maze and not half an idea had I had in it what I should say to her, but the instant I touched her it came to me like magic and I had my natural voice and my senses and even almost my breath.

'Mrs. Edson!' I says 'My dear! Take care! How ever did you lose your way and stumble on a dangerous place like this? Why you must have come here by the most perplexing streets in all London. No wonder you are lost, I am sure. And this place too! Why I thought nobody ever got here, except me to order my coals and the Major in the parlours to smoke his cigar!'—for I saw that blessed man close by, pretending to it.

'Hah—Hah—Hum!' coughs the Major.

'And good gracious me' I says, 'why here he is!'

'Halloa! who goes there?' says the Major in a military manner.

'Well!' I says, 'if this don't beat everything! Don't you know us Major Jackman?'

'Halloa!' says the Major. 'Who calls on Jemmy Jackman?' (and more out of breath he was, and did it less like life, than I should have expected).

'Why here's Mrs. Edson Major' I says, 'strolling out to cool her poor head which has been very bad, has missed her way and got lost, and Goodness knows where she might have got to but for me coming here to drop an order into my coal merchant's letter-box and you coming here to smoke your cigar!—And you really are not well enough my dear' I says to her 'to be half so far from home without me.—And your arm will be very acceptable I am sure Major' I says to him 'and I know she may lean upon it as heavy as she likes.' And now we had both got her—thanks be Above!—one on each side.

She was all in a cold shiver and she so continued till I laid her on her own bed, and up to the early morning she held me by the hand and moaned and moaned 'O wicked, wicked, wicked!' But when at last I made believe to droop my head and be overpowered with a dead sleep, I heard that poor young creature give such touching and such humble thanks for being preserved from taking her own life in her madness that I knew she was safe.

Being well enough to do and able to afford it, me and the Major laid our little plans next day while she was asleep worn out, and so I says to her as soon as I could do it nicely:

'Mrs. Edson my dear, when Mr. Edson paid me the rent for these further six months——'

She gave a start and I felt her large eyes look at me, but I went on with it and with my needle-work.

'——I can't say that I am quite sure I dated the receipt right. Could you let me look at it?'

She laid her frozen cold hand upon mine and she looked through me when I was forced to look up from my needlework, but I had taken the precaution of having on my spectacles.

'I have no receipt,' says she.

'Ah! Then he has got it' I says in a careless way. 'It's of no great consequence. A receipt's a receipt.'

From that time she always had hold of my hand when I could spare it which was generally only when I read to her, for of course she and me had our bits of needlework to plod at and neither of us was very handy at those little things, though I am still rather proud of my share in them too considering. And though she took to all I read to her, I used to fancy that next to what was taught upon the Mount she took most of all to His gentle compassion for us poor women and to His young life and to how His mother was proud of him and treasured His sayings in her heart. She had a grateful look in her eyes that never never never will be out of mine until they are closed in my last sleep, and when I chanced to look at her without thinking of it I would always meet that look, and she would often offer me her trembling lip to kiss, much more like a little affectionate half-broken-hearted child than ever I can imagine any grown person.

One time the trembling of this poor lip was so strong and her tears ran down so fast that I thought she was going to tell me all her woe, so I takes her two hands in mine and I says:

'No my dear not now, you had best not try to do it now. Wait for better times when you have got over this and are strong, and then you shall tell me whatever you will. Shall it be agreed?'

With our hands still joined she nodded her head many times, and she lifted my hands and put them to her lips and to her bosom.

'Only one word now my dear' I says. 'Is there any one?'

She looked inquiringly 'Any one?'

'That I can go to?'

She shook her head.

'No one that I can bring?'

She shook her head.

'No one is wanted by *me* my dear. Now that may be considered past and gone.'

Not much more than a week afterwards—for this was far on in the time of our being so together—I was bending over at her bedside with my ear down to her lips, by turns listening for her breath and looking for a sign of life in her face. At last it came in a solemn way—not in a flash but like a kind of pale faint light brought very slow to the face.

She said something to me that had no sound in it, but I saw she asked me:

'Is this death?'

And I says, 'Poor dear poor dear, I think it is.'

Knowing somehow that she wanted me to move her weak right hand, I took it and laid it on her breast and then folded her other hand upon it, and she prayed a good good prayer and I joined in it poor me though there were no words spoke. Then I brought the baby in its wrappers from where it lay, and I says:

'My dear this is sent to a childless old woman. This is for me to take care of.'

The trembling lip was put up towards my face for the last time and I dearly kissed it.

'Yes my dear' I says. 'Please God! Me and the Major.'

I don't know how to tell it right, but I saw her soul brighten and leap up, and get free, and fly away in the grateful look.

So this is the why and wherefore of its coming to pass that we called him Jemmy, being after the Major his own godfather with Lirriper for a surname being after myself, and never was a dear child such a brightening thing in a Lodgings or such a playmate to his grandmother as Jemmy to this house and me, and always good and minding what he was told (upon the whole) and soothing for the temper and making everything pleasanter except when he grew old enough to drop his cap down Wozenham's Airy and they wouldn't hand it up to him, and being worked into a state I put on my best bonnet and gloves and parasol with the child in my hand and I says 'Miss Wozenham I little thought ever to have entered *your* house but unless my grandson's cap is instantly restored, the laws of this country regulating the property of the Subject shall at length decide betwixt yourself and me cost what it may.' With a sneer upon her face which did strike me I must say as being expressive of two keys but it may have been a mistake and if there is any doubt let Miss Wozenham have the full benefit of it as is but right, she rang the bell and she says 'Jane, is there a street-child's old cap down our Airy?' I says 'Miss Wozenham before your housemaid answers that question you must allow me to inform you to your face that my grandson is *not* a street-child and is *not* in the habit of wearing old caps. In fact' I says 'Miss Wozenham I am far from sure that my grandson's cap may not be newer than your own' which was perfectly savage in me, her lace being the commonest machine-make washed and torn besides, but I had been put into a state to begin with fomented by impertinence. Miss Wozenham says red in the face 'Jane you heard my question, is there any child's cap down our Airy?' 'Yes Ma'am' says Jane 'I think I did see some such rubbish a lying there.' 'Then' says Miss Wozenham 'let these visitors out, and then throw up that worthless article out of my premises.' But here the child who had been staring at Miss Wozenham with all his eyes and more, frowns down his little eyebrows purses up his little mouth puts his chubby legs far apart turns his little dimple fists round and round slowly over one another like a little coffee mill, and says to her 'Oo impdent to mi Gran, me tut oor hi!' 'Oh!' says Miss Wozenham looking down scornfully at the Mite 'this is not a street-child is it not! Really!' I bursts out laughing and I says 'Miss Wozenham if this an't a pretty sight to you I don't envy your feelings and I wish you good day. Jemmy come along with Gran.' And I was still in the best of humours though his cap came flying up into the street as if it had been just turned on out of the water-plug, and I went home laughing all the way, all owing to that dear boy.

The miles and miles that me and the Major have travelled with Jemmy in the dusk between the lights are not to be calculated, Jemmy driving on the coach box which is the Major's brass-bound writing-desk on the table, me inside in the easy-chair and the Major Guard up behind with a brown-paper horn doing it really wonderful. I do assure you my dear that sometimes when I have taken a few winks in my place inside the coach and have come half awake by the flashing light of the fire and have heard that precious pet driving and the Major blowing up behind to have the change of horses ready when we got to the Inn, I have half believed we were on the old North Road that my poor Lirriper knew so well. Then to see that child and the Major both wrapped up getting down to warm their feet and going stamping about and having glasses of ale out of the paper match-boxes on the chimney-piece was to see the Major enjoying it fully as much as the child I am very sure, and it was equal to any play when Coachee opens the coach-door to look in at me inside and says 'Wery 'past that 'tage,—'Prightened old lady?'

But what my inexpressible feelings were when we lost that child can only be compared to the Major's which were not a shade better, through his straying out at five years old and eleven o'clock in the forenoon and never heard of by word or sign or deed till half-past nine at night, when the Major had gone to the Editor of the Times newspaper to put in an advertisement, which came out next day four and twenty hours after he was found, and which I mean always carefully to keep in my lavender drawer as the first printed account of him. The more the day got on, the more I got distracted and the Major too, and both of us made worse by the composed ways of the police though very civil and obliging and what I must call their obstinancy in not entertaining the idea that he was stolen. 'We mostly find Mum' says the sergeant who came round to comfort me, which he didn't at all and he had been one of the private constables in Caroline's time to which he referred in his opening words when he said 'Don't give way to uneasiness in your mind Mum, it'll all come as right as my nose did when I got the same barked by that young woman in your second floor'—says this sergeant 'we mostly find Mum as people ain't over anxious to have what I may call second-hand children. *You'll* get him back Mum.' 'O but my dear good sir' I says clasping my hands and wringing them and clasping them again 'he is such an uncommon child!' 'Yes Mum' says the sergeant, 'we mostly find that too Mum. The question is what his clothes were worth.'

'His clothes' I says 'were not worth much sir for he had only got his playing-dress on, but the dear child!——' 'All right Mum' says the sergeant. '*You'll* get him back, Mum. And even if he'd had his best clothes on, it wouldn't come to worse than his being found wrapped up in a cabbage-leaf, a shivering in a lane.' His words pierced my heart like daggers and daggers, and me and the Major ran in and out like wild things all day long till the Major returning from his interview with the Editor of the Times at night rushes into my little room hysterical and squeezes my hand and wipes his eyes and says 'Joy joy—officer in plain clothes came up on the steps as I was letting myself in—compose your feelings—Jemmy's found.' Consequently I fainted away and when I came to, embraced the legs of the officer in plain clothes who seemed to be taking a kind of a quiet inventory in his mind of the property in my little room with brown whiskers, and I says 'Blessings on you sir where is the Darling!' and he says 'In Kennington Station House.' I was dropping at his feet Stone at the image of that Innocence in cells with murderers when he adds 'He followed the Monkey.' I says deeming it slang language 'Oh sir explain for a loving grandmother what Monkey!' He says 'him in the spangled cap with the strap under the chin, as won't keep on—him as sweeps the crossings on a round table and don't want to draw his sabre more than he can help.' Then I understood it all and most thankfully thanked him, and me and the Major and him drove over to Kennington and there we found our boy lying quite comfortable before a blazing fire having sweetly played himself to sleep upon a small accordion nothing like so big as a flat iron, which they had been so kind as to lend him for the purpose and which it appeared had been stopped upon a very young person.

The system upon which the Major commenced and as I may say perfected Jemmy's learning when he was so small that if the dear was on the other side of the table you had to look under it instead of over it to see him with his mother's own bright hair in beautiful curls, is a thing that ought to be known to the Throne and Lords and Commons.

'I'm going Madam' he says 'to make our child a Calculating Boy.'

'Major' I says, 'you terrify me and may do the pet a permanent injury you would never forgive yourself. * Major I will be candid with you and tell you openly that if ever I find the dear child fall off in his appetite I shall know it is his calculations and shall put a stop to them at two minutes' notice. Or if I find them mounting to his head' I says, 'or striking any ways cold to his stomach or leading to anything approaching flabbiness in his legs, the result will be the same, but Major you are a clever man and have seen much and you love the child and are his own godfather, and if you feel a confidence in trying try.'

'Spoken Madam' says the Major 'like Emma Lirriper. All I have to ask Madam, is, that you will leave my godson and myself to make a week or two's preparations for surprising you, and that you will give me leave to have up and down any small articles not actually in use that I may require from the kitchen.'

'From the kitchen Major?' I says half feeling as if he had a mind to cook the child.

'From the kitchen' says the Major, and smiles and swells, and at the same time looks taller.

So I passed my word and the Major and the dear boy were shut up

together for half an hour at a time through a certain while, and never
could I hear anything going on betwixt them but talking and laughing
and Jemmy clapping his hands and screaming out numbers, so I says to
myself 'it has not harmed him yet' nor could I on examining the dear find
any signs of it anywhere about him which was likewise a great relief. At
last one day Jemmy brings me a card in joke in the Major's neat writing
'The Mess.ʳˢ Jemmy Jackman' for we had given him the Major's other
name too 'request the honour of Mrs. Lirriper's company at the Jackman
institution in the front parlour this evening at five, military time, to
witness a few slight feats of elementary arithmetic.' And if you'll believe
me there in the front parlour at five punctual to the moment was the
Major behind the Pembroke table with both leaves up and a lot of things
from the kitchen tidily set out on old newspapers spread atop of it, and
there was the Mite stood up on a chair with his rosy cheeks flushing and
his eyes sparkling clusters of diamonds.

'Now Gran' says he 'oo tit down and don't oo touch ler poople'—
for he saw with every one of those diamonds of his that I was going to
give him a squeeze.

'Very well sir' I says 'I am obedient in this good company I am sure.'
And I sits down in the easy-chair that was put for me, shaking my sides.

But picture my admiration when the Major going on almost as quick as
if he was conjuring sets out all the articles he names, and says, 'Three
saucepans, an Italian iron, a hand-bell, a toasting-fork, a nutmeg-grater,
four pot-lids, a spice-box, two egg-cups, and a chopping-board—how
many?' and when that Mite instantly cries 'Tifteen, tut down tive and
carry ler 'toppin-board' and then claps his hands draws up his legs and
dances on his chair.

The pride of the Major! ('*Here's* a mind Ma'am!' he says to me behind
his hand.)

Then he says aloud, 'We now come to the next elementary rule:
which is called——'

'Umtraction!' cries Jemmy.

'Right' says the Major. 'We have here a toasting-fork, a potato in its
natural state, two pot-lids, one egg-cup, a wooden spoon, and two
skewers, from which it is necessary for commercial purposes to subtract
a sprat-gridiron, a small pickle-jar, two lemons, one pepper-castor, a
black-beetle trap, and a knob of the dresser-drawer—what remains?'

'Toating-fork!' cries Jemmy.

'In numbers how many?' says the Major.

'One!' cries Jemmy.

('*Here's* a boy, Ma'am!' says the Major to me, behind his hand.)

Then the Major goes on:

'We now approach the next elementary rule: which is entitled——'

'Tickleication' cries Jemmy.

'Correct' says the Major.

But to relate to you in detail the way in which they multiplied fourteen sticks of firewood by two bits of ginger and a larding-needle, or divided pretty well everything else there was on the table by the heater of the Italian iron and a chamber candlestick, and got a lemon over, would make my head spin round and round and round as it did at the time. So I says 'if you'll excuse my addressing the chair Professor Jackman I think the period of the lecture has now arrived when it becomes necessary that I should take a good hug of this young scholar.' Upon which Jemmy calls out from his station on the chair 'Gran oo open oor arms and me'll make a 'pring into 'em.' So I opened my arms to him as I had opened my sorrowful heart when his poor young mother lay a dying, and he had his jump and we had a good long hug together and the Major prouder than any peacock says to me behind his hand, 'You need not let him know it Madam' (which I certainly need not for the Major was quite audible) 'but he is[1] a boy!'

In this way Jemmy grew and grew and went to day-school and continued under the Major too, and in summer we were as happy as the days were long and in winter we were as happy as the days were short, and there seemed to rest a Blessing on the Lodgings for they as good as Let themselves and would have done it if there had been twice the accommodation.

THE END

[1] Lower-case in *Berg*; small capitals in *AYR*. Almost certainly a misprint in the privately printed Reading text; the sense demands the emphasis on *is*, but this word, in small capitals, can easily be mistaken for lower-case.

BARBOX BROTHERS

DICKENS'S first tour under the management of Messrs. Chappell (April–June 1866) had opened with the new Reading, *Doctor Marigold*, which had proved extremely popular. A second and longer tour, under the same management, was to open to January 1867, and Dickens decided to try to give it a similar impetus by devising some new items from his latest Christmas Stories, those contributed to *Mugby Junction* (the *All the Year Round* Christmas number for 1866). This time he devised three new items, printed together in the prompt-copy, now in the Berg Collection: *Barbox Brothers. | The Boy at Mugby. | The Signalman. | Three Readings. | Privately Printed.* (printed by William Clowes and Sons, London; the texts of the three items paginated 3–88, 89–110, and 111–38). It went to the printers in mid-November (*N*, iii. 491). There are no manuscript alterations in *The Signalman*, which was never performed. The text of *The Boy at Mugby* is considerably cut, but in a simple and hasty manner (longish block-deletions rather than numerous shorter cuts). Of the three Readings, *Barbox Brothers* is much the longest, and Dickens evidently devoted more care to preparing it.

Before printing the Reading, he had reduced the *All the Year Round* text of *Barbox Brothers* by about 7 per cent, omitting many 'he replied' phrases, some descriptive passages, and some parts which were irrelevant outside the Christmas-number context. Then, in the prompt-copy, he tightened the story up, making many brief cuts and some longer ones. Substantial revisions were made in at least two stages, first in blue ink and then in brown ink; some of the passages underlined and otherwise prepared for performance were subsequently deleted. The prompt-copy text was thus reduced in length by nearly a third.

At Christmas-time, Dickens gave a trial performance of this item and its companion-piece *The Boy at Mugby* to his family, house-guests, and neighbours at Gad's Hill. The general opinion was that this new programme would rival in popularity the fabulous *Doctor Marigold*—but, writes George Dolby (p. 53), this prognostication was regarded 'with considerable doubt and misgivings by the author and certain of the more practical judges then present, who, as matters afterwards turned out, were justified in their scepticism'. The new season opened with these two items, on 15 January 1867, at St. James's Hall, London. The programme was cordially received by the audience and the press, but it was apparent, as George Dolby recalled, that they would never take rank with other items of similar appeal already in the repertoire. Dickens, realizing this, would have dropped the programme at once, but it had already been announced for some towns early in his provincial tour. Half a dozen or so performances of *Barbox Brothers* were given and then it was finally dropped; *The Boy at Mugby* was rather more popular, but did not survive much longer. The wonder is that they endured so long; they but usurped the life so much more palpably manifest in the other Readings. As Albany says in reply to Kent, 'Bear them from hence.' Mr. Emlyn Williams showed better discrimination in devising a reading-script from the third, but unperformed, *Mugby Junction*, item, *The Signalman* (see below, p. 453), and Dickens earns more credit for so quickly dropping than for initiating the other two *Mugby* items. The quality of his *Christmas Stories*, written in his maturity, and their relation to the novels of these years, deserve more consideration than they have yet received.

'Nobody but the writer of this little freak of fancy could possibly have rendered the Reading of it in public worthy even of toleration', Charles Kent forbearingly remarked (p. 231), and he noted some of the obvious difficulties and limitations inherent in this piece. More obviously reminiscent of the original Christmas Books of the 1840s than Dickens's other recent Christmas stories in the 1860s had been, *Barbox Brothers* offers little that had not already been done better in the *Carol*, *The Haunted Man*, *Little Dorrit*, and other earlier writings. The Reading had some effective moments (Dickens's rendering of the atmosphere of the railway junction at night, for instance, was very vivid), but the verdict of the *Yorkshire Post* critic (1 February 1867) was clearly justified. There were, he wrote, a few 'capital touches' in *Mugby Junction* but, as a whole, it was painfully inferior to his previous works, and 'quite unworthy of the author of *Pickwick* and *Dombey*'. There was, he acknowledged, sufficient scope in *Barbox Brothers*

. . . for the display of Mr. Dickens's wonderful mimetic powers to render *his* reading of it, in our opinion, very much more agreeable and interesting than a private perusal. The preponderance of narrative over dialogue in *Barbox Brothers*, however, renders that story less suited to display the best features of Mr. Dickens' readings than such a sketch as *The Boy at Mugby*. This, as a monologue, has more life and individuality than the other tale . . . The whole thing, however, is such an extravagant burlesque that even the point of the satire embodied in it lost much of the piquancy which it would have possessed had the humour been more subtle and refined. We cannot but think that the choice of these stories was infelicitous, especially when we remember that Mr. Dickens has still among his best writings a store of humour and pathos upon which he has never drawn. Why, for instance, does he not read the exquisitely droll scenes from *Nicholas Nickleby*, in which the Crummles family are introduced? Why not give us Dick Swiveller, or Captain Cuttle, or the 'Fat boy' in Pickwick, or Mrs. Lirriper?

Barbox Brothers

3 Chapters[1]

CHAPTER I

'GUARD! What place is this?'

'Mugby Junction, sir.'

'A windy place!'

'Yes, it mostly is, sir.'

'And looks comfortless indeed!'

'Yes, it generally does, sir.'

'Is it a rainy night still?'

'Pours, sir.'

'Open the door. I'll get out.'

'You'll have, sir, only three minutes here.'

'More, I think.—For I am not going on.'

'Thought you had a through ticket, sir?'

'So I have, but I shall sacrifice the rest of it. I want my luggage.'

'Please to come to the van and point it out, sir. Be good enough to look very sharp, sir. Not a moment to spare.'

The guard hurried to the luggage van, and the traveller hurried after him. The guard got into it, and the traveller looked into it.

'Those two large black portmanteaus in the corner where your light shines. Those are mine.'

'Name upon 'em, sir?'

'Barbox Brothers.'

'Stand clear, sir, if you please. One. Two. Right!'

Lamp waved. Signal lights ahead already changing. Shriek from engine. Train gone.

'Mugby Junction! At past three o'clock of a tempestuous morning! So!'

He spoke to himself. There was no one else to speak to. Perhaps, though there had been any one else to speak to, he would have preferred to speak to himself. Speaking to himself, he spoke to a man within five years of fifty either way, a man with many indications on him of having been much alone, a man who had turned grey too soon, like a neglected fire. †

A place replete with shadowy shapes, this Mugby Junction in the black hours of the four-and-twenty. Mysterious goods trains, covered with

---

[1] Subheading inserted by Dickens, in manuscript.

palls and gliding on like vast weird funerals, conveying themselves guiltily away from the presence of the few lighted lamps, as if their freight had come to a secret and unlawful end. Half miles of coal pursuing in a Detective manner, following when they lead, stopping when they stop, backing when they back. Red hot embers showering out upon the ground, down this dark avenue, and down the other, as if torturing fires were being raked clear; concurrently, shrieks and groans and grinds invading the ear, as if the tortured were at the height of their suffering. Iron-barred cages full of cattle jangling by midway, the drooping beasts with horns entangled, eyes frozen with terror, and mouths too; at least they have long icicles (or what seem so) hanging from their lips. Unknown languages in the air, conspiring in red, green, and white characters. An earthquake accompanied with thunder and lightning, going up express to London. Now, all quiet, all rusty, wind and rain in possession, lamps extinguished, Mugby Junction dead and indistinct, with its robe drawn over its head, like Caesar.[1]

Now, too, as the belated traveller plodded up and down, a shadowy train went by him in the gloom which was no other than the train of his life. From whatsoever intangible deep cutting or dark tunnel it emerged, here it came, unsummoned and unannounced, stealing upon him and passing away into obscurity. Here, mournfully went by, a child who had never had a childhood or known a parent, inseparable from a youth with a bitter sense of his namelessness, coupled to a man the enforced business of whose best years had been distasteful and oppressive, linked to an ungrateful friend, dragging after him a woman once beloved. Attendant, with many a clank and wrench, were lumbering cares, dark meditations, huge dim disappointments, monotonous years, a long jarring line of the discords of a solitary and unhappy existence.

'—Yours, sir?'

The traveller recalled his eyes from the waste into which they had been staring, and fell back a step or so under the abruptness, and perhaps the chance appropriateness, of the question.

'O! My thoughts were not here for the moment. Yes. Yes. Those two portmanteaus are mine. Are you a Porter?'

'On Porter's wages, sir. But I am Lamps.'

'Who did you say you are?'

'Lamps, sir,' showing an oily cloth in his hand, as further explanation.

'Surely, surely. † I suppose I can put up in the town? There is a town here?'

'O yes, there's a town, sir. Anyways there's town enough to put up in.

---

[1] '. . . the Author . . ., in his capacity as Reader, somehow, by the mere manner of his delivery of a descriptive sentence or two, contrived to realize to his hearers in a wonder-fully vivid way the strange incidents of the traffic in a scene like this, at those blackest intervals between midnight and daybreak' (Kent, p. 232).

But this is a very dead time of the night with us, sir. The deadest time. I might a'most call it our deadest and buriedest time.'

'No porters about?'

'Well, sir, you see, they in general goes off with the gas. That's how it is. But in about twelve minutes or so, she may be up.'

'Who may be up?'

'The three forty-two, sir. She goes off in a sidin' till the Up X passes, and then she,' here an air of hopeful vagueness pervaded Lamps, 'doos all as lays in her power.'

'I doubt if I comprehend the arrangement.'

'I doubt if anybody do, sir. She's a Parliamentary, sir. And, you see, a Parliamentary, or a Skirmishun——'

'Do you mean an Excursion?'

'That's it, sir.—A Parliamentary or a Skirmishun, she mostly *doos* go off into a sidin'.[1] But when she *can* get a chance, she's whistled out of it, and she's whistled up into doin' all as lays in her power.'

He then explained that porters on duty being required to be in attendance *on the Parliamentary matron in question*,[2] would doubtless turn up with the gas. In the mean time, if the gentleman would not very much object to the smell of lamp-oil, and would accept the warmth of his little room.—The gentleman being by this time very cold, instantly closed with the proposal.

A greasy little cabin it was, suggestive to the sense of smell, of a cabin in a Whaler. But there was a bright fire burning in its rusty grate, and on the floor there stood a wooden stand of newly trimmed and lighted lamps, ready for carriage service. They made a bright show, and their light, and the warmth, accounted for the popularity of the room, as borne witness to by many impressions of velveteen trousers on a form by the fire, and many rounded smears and smudges of stooping velveteen shoulders on the adjacent wall. Various untidy shelves accommodated a quantity of lamps and oil-cans, and *also a fragrant collection of what looked like the pocket-handkerchiefs of the whole lamp family.*

As Barbox Brothers (so to call the traveller on the warranty of his luggage) warmed his hands at the fire, he glanced aside at a little desk which his elbow touched. Upon it were some scraps of paper, and a superannuated steel pen *in very reduced and gritty circumstances*.

He turned to his host, and said, with some roughness:

'Why, you are never a poet, man!'

Lamps had certainly not the conventional appearance of one, as he stood rubbing his squab nose with a handkerchief so exceedingly oily, that he might have been in the act of mistaking himself for one of his charges.

---

[1] *doos*, and *can* in the next sentence, italic in *AYR* (*All the Year Round*) and in *Berg*.

[2] All Dickens's underlinings in this Reading are of his double interrupted type, and will be represented throughout as italic without any footnote reference.

He was a spare man of about the Barbox Brothers time of life, with his features whimsically drawn upward as if they were attracted by the roots of his hair. He had a shining transparent complexion, probably occasioned by constant oleaginous application: and his attractive hair, being cut short, and being grizzled, and standing straight up on end as if it in its turn were attracted by some invisible magnet above it, the top of his head was not very unlike a lamp-wick.

'But to be sure it's no business of mine whether you are a Poet or not. That was an impertinent observation on my part. Be what you like.'

'Some people, sir, are sometimes what they don't like.'

'Nobody knows that better than I do. I have been what I don't like, all my life.'

'When I first took, sir, to composing little Comic-Songs-like—and what was more hard—to singing 'em afterwards, it went against the grain at that time, it did indeed.'

'Why did you do it, then? If you didn't want to do it, why did you do it? Where did you sing them? Public-house?'

To which Mr. Lamps returned the curious reply: 'Bedside.'

At this moment, Mugby Junction started suddenly, trembled violently, and opened its gas eyes. 'She's got up!' Lamps announced, excited. 'What lays in her power is sometimes more, and sometimes less; but it's laid in her power to get up to-night, by George!'

The legend 'Barbox Brothers' in large white letters on two black surfaces, was very soon afterwards trundling on a truck through a silent street; and, when the owner of the legend had shivered on the pavement half an hour, what time the porter's knocks at the Inn Door *knocked up the whole town first, and the Inn last*, he groped his way into the close air of a shut-up house, and groped into so cold a bed that it seemed to have been expressly refrigerated for him when last made.

CHAPTER II

[1]'YOU remember me, Young Jackson?'

'What do I remember if not you? You are my first remembrance. It was you who told me that was my name. It was you who told me that on every twentieth of December my life had a penitential anniversary in it called a birthday. I suppose the last communication was truer than the first!'

'What am I like, Young Jackson?'

'You are like a blight all through the year, to me. You changeless woman with a wax mask on. You are like the devil to me; most of all when you teach me religious things, for you make me abhor them.'

---

[1] Marginal stage-direction *On the Left.*

[1]'You remember me, Mr. Young Jackson?' In another voice from another quarter.

'Most gratefully, sir. You were the ray of hope and prospering ambition in my life. When I attended your course, I believed that I should come to be a great healer, and I felt almost happy—even though I was still the one boarder in the house with that horrible mask, and ate and drank in silence and constraint with the mask before me, every day. As I had done every, every, every, day, through my school-time and from my earliest recollection.'

[2]'You remember Me, Mr. Young Jackson?' In a grating voice from quite another quarter.

'Too well. You made your ghostly appearance in my life one day, and announced that its course was to be suddenly and wholly changed. You showed me which was my wearisome seat in the Galley of Barbox Brothers. (When *they* were, if they ever were, is unknown to me; there was nothing of them but the name when I bent to the oar.) You told me what I was to do, and what to be paid; you told me afterwards, at intervals of years, when I was to sign for the Firm, when I became a partner, when I became the Firm. I know no more of it, or of myself.'

'What am I like, Mr. Young Jackson?'

'You are like my father, I sometimes think. You are hard enough and cold enough so to have brought up an unacknowledged son. I see your scanty figure, your close brown suit, and your tight brown wig; but you, too, wear a wax mask to your death. You never by a chance remove it—it never by a chance falls off—and I know no more of you.'

Throughout this dialogue, the traveller *spoke to himself at his window in the morning, as he had spoken to himself at the Junction over-night. And as he had then looked in the darkness, a man who had turned grey too soon, like a neglected fire: so he now looked in the sunlight, an ashier grey, like a fire which the brightness of the sun put out.*

The firm of Barbox Brothers had been some offshoot or irregular branch of the Public Notary and bill-broking tree. It had gained for itself a griping reputation before the days of Young Jackson, and the reputation had stuck to it and to him. As he had imperceptibly come into possession of the den in the corner of a court off Lombard Street, London City, on whose windows the inscription Barbox Brothers had for many long years daily interposed itself between him and the sky, so he had insensibly found himself a personage held in chronic distrust, whose word was never to be taken without his attested bond. This character had come upon him through no act of his own. It was as if the original Barbox had stretched himself down upon the office-floor, and had thither caused to be

---

[1] Marginal stage-direction *On the Right*.

[2] Marginal stage-direction *In Front*. In the next paragraph, *they* italic in *Berg* and in *AYR*.

conveyed Young Jackson in his sleep, and had there effected a metempsychosis and exchange of persons with him. The discovery that he bore this character—aided in its turn by the deceit of the only woman he had ever loved, and the deceit of the only friend he had ever made: who eloped from him to be married together—the discovery, so followed up, completed what his earliest rearing had begun. He shrank, abashed, within the form of Barbox, and lifted up his head and heart no more.

But he had at last effected one great release in his condition. He broke the oar he had plied so long, and he scuttled and sank the galley. He prevented the gradual retirement of an old conventional business from him, by taking the initiative and retiring from it. With enough to live on (though after all with not too much), he obliterated the firm of Barbox Brothers from the pages of the Post-office Directory and the face of the earth, leaving nothing of it but its name on two portmanteaus.

'For one must have some name in going about, and that name at least was real once. Whereas, Young Jackson!—Not to mention its being a sadly satirical misnomer for Old Jackson.'

He took up his hat and walked out from the Inn, just in time to see, passing along on the opposite side of the way, a velveteen man, carrying his day's dinner in a small bundle *that might have been larger without suspicion of gluttony*, and pelting away towards the Junction at a great pace.

'There's Lamps! And by-the-by—'

Ridiculous, surely, that a man so serious, so self-contained, and not yet three days emancipated from a routine of drudgery, should stand rubbing his chin in the street, in a brown study about Comic Songs.

'Bedside? Sings them at the bedside? Why at the bedside, unless he goes to bed drunk? Does, I shouldn't wonder. But it's no business of mine. Let me see. Mugby Junction, Mugby Junction. Where shall I go next? As it came into my head last night when I woke from an uneasy sleep in the carriage and found myself here, I can go anywhere from here. Where shall I go? I'll go and look at the Junction by daylight and then I'll take a walk. ' †

It fell out somehow (perhaps he meant it should) that he went straight to the platform at which he had alighted, and to Lamps's room. But Lamps was not in his room. * The direction he pursued next, was into the country, keeping very near to the side of one great Line of railway, and within easy view of several others.

Ascending a gentle hill of some extent, he came to a few cottages. There, *looking about him as a very reserved man might* who had never looked about him in his life before, he saw some six or eight young children come trooping and whooping from one of the cottages, and disperse. But not until they had all turned at the little garden gate, and kissed their hands to a *face* at the upper window: a low window, although the upper, for the cottage had but a story of one room above the ground.

Now, that the children should do this was nothing; but that they should do this *to a face* lying on the sill of the open window, turned towards them in a horizontal position, *and apparently only a face*, was something notice-able.[1] He looked up at the window again. Could only see a very fragile though a very bright *face*, lying on one cheek on the window-sill. The delicate smiling *face* of a girl or woman. Framed in long bright brown hair, round which was tied a light blue band or fillet, passing under the chin.

[2] And now there were a pair of delicate hands too. They had the action of performing on some musical instrument, and yet it produced no sound that reached his ears.

'Mugby Junction must be the maddest place in England,' he said, pursuing his way back. 'The first thing I find here is a Railway Porter who composes comic songs to sing at his bedside. The second thing I find here is a face, and a pair of hands playing a musical instrument that *don't*[3] play!' *

He relished his walk so well, however, that he repeated it next day,[4] and next day, and several days. But the weather turned cold and wet again, and the window was never open. Neither did he find Lamps in his little room on any of these days.

At length, there came another streak of fine bright hardy autumn weather. He was a little earlier at the cottage, and could hear the children up-stairs singing to a regular measure and clapping out the time with their hands.

[5] 'Still, there is no sound of any musical instrument,' he said, listening at the corner, 'and yet I saw the performing hands again, as I came by. What are the children singing? Why, good Lord, they can never be singing the multiplication-table!'

They were though, and with infinite enjoyment. The mysterious face had a voice attached to it which occasionally led or set the children right. Its musical cheerfulness was delightful. The measure at length stopped, and was succeeded by a murmuring of young voices, and then by a short song. Then, there was a stir of little feet, and the children came trooping and whooping out again. And again, they all turned at the garden gate, and kissed their hands to the face on the window-sill. † Seeing it still there, as he re-passed, he acknowledged its presence with a gesture, which was not a nod, not a bow, not a removal of his hat from his head, but was a diffident compromise between or struggle with all three. The eyes in the face seemed amused, or cheered, or both, and the lips modestly said: 'Good day to you, sir.' †

---

[1] Marginal stage-direction *Look up*. [2] Marginal stage-direction *Again look up*.
[3] *don't* italic in *Berg* and in *AYR*.
[4] From here to 'autumn weather' is from the end of ch. 2 and the beginning of ch. 3.
[5] Marginal stage-direction *Listen*.

[1]'Good day. I am glad you have a fine sky again, to look at.'

'Thank you, sir. It is kind of you.'

'You are an invalid, I fear?'

'No, sir. I have very good health.'

'But are you not always lying down?'

'O yes, I am always lying down, because I cannot sit up. But I am not an invalid.'

The laughing eyes seemed highly to enjoy his great mistake.

'Would you mind taking the trouble to come in, sir? There is a beautiful view from this window. And you would see that I am not at all ill—being so good as to care.'

It was said to help him, as he stood irresolute, but evidently desiring to enter, with his diffident hand on the latch of the garden gate. It did help him, and he went in.

The room upstairs was a very clean white room with a low roof. She lay, alone, on a couch that brought her face to a level with the window. The couch was white too; and her simple dress being light blue, like the band around her hair, *she had an ethereal look, and a fanciful appearance of lying among clouds.* He touched her hand, and took a chair at the side of her couch.

'I see now, how you occupy your hands. Only seeing you from the path outside, I thought you were playing upon something.'

She was engaged in very nimbly and dexterously making lace. A lace-pillow lay upon her breast; and the quick movements and changes of her hands upon it as she worked, had given them the action he had misinterpreted.

'That is curious,' she answered, with a bright smile. 'For I often fancy, myself, that I play tunes while I am at work.'

'Have you any musical knowledge?'

She shook her head.

'I think I could pick out tunes, if I had any instrument which could be made as handy to me as my lace-pillow. But I dare say I deceive myself. At all events, I shall never know.'

He glanced at the two small forms in the room, and hazarded the speculation that she was fond of children, and that she was learned in new systems of teaching them? 'Very fond of them, but I know nothing of teaching, beyond the interest I have in it, and the pleasure it gives me when they learn. Perhaps your overhearing my little scholars sing some of their lessons has led you so far astray as to think me a grand teacher? Ah! I thought so! No, I have only read and been told about that system. It seemed so pretty and pleasant, and to treat them so like the merry Rob-

---

[1] Marginal stage-direction *Look up.* Chapter 3 of the story begins here (with its first paragraph deleted), but the Reading, having been rearranged as a three-chapter narrative, conflates chs. 2 and 3. See below, p. 436, note 1.

ins they are, that I took up with it in my little way. You don't need to be
told what a very little way mine is, sir.'

All this time her hands were busy at her lace-pillow. As they still
continued so, and as there was a kind of substitute for conversation in
the click and play of its pegs, he took the opportunity of observing her.
He guessed her to be thirty. The charm of her transparent face and large
bright brown eyes, was, not that they were passively resigned, but that
they were actively and thoroughly cheerful. Even her busy hands, which
of their thinness might have besought compassion, plied their task with
a gay courage that made mere compassion an unjustifiable assumption
of superiority, and an impertinence.

As her eyes were in the act of rising towards his, he directed his towards the prospect, saying: 'Beautiful indeed!'

'Most beautiful, sir. I have sometimes had a fancy that I would like to
sit up, for once, only to try how it looks to an erect head. But what a
foolish fancy that would be to encourage! It cannot look more lovely
to any one than it does to me. And those threads of railway, with their
puffs of smoke and steam changing places so fast, make it so lively for me.
I think of the number of people who *can*[1] go where they wish, on their
business, or their pleasure; I remember that the puffs make signs to me
that they are actually going while I look; and that enlivens the prospect
with abundance of company, if I want company. There is the great Junction, too. I don't see it under the foot of the hill, but I can very often hear
it, and I always know it is there. It seems to join me, in a way, to I don't
know how many places and things that *I*[2] shall never see.'

With an abashed kind of idea that *it might have already joined himself
to something he had never seen,* he said constrainedly: 'Just so.'

'And so you see, sir, I am not the invalid you thought me, and I am
very well off indeed.'

'You have a happy disposition.' *Perhaps with a slight excusatory touch
for his own disposition.*

'Ah! But you should know my father. His is the happy disposition!—
don't mind, sir! This is my father coming.'

The door opened.

'Why, Lamps! How do you do, Lamps?'

'The gentleman for Nowhere! How do you DO,[3] sir?'

And they shook hands, to the greatest admiration and surprise of
Lamps's daughter.

'I have looked you up, half a dozen times since that night, but have
never found you.'

'So I've heerd on, sir; so I've heerd on. It's your being noticed so
often down at the Junction, without taking any train, that has begun to

---

[1] *can* italic in *Berg* and in *AYR*.   [2] *I* italic in *Berg* and in *AYR*.
[3] Small capitals in *AYR*.

get you the name among us of the gentleman for Nowhere. No offence in my having called you by it when took by surprise, I hope, sir?'

'None at all. It's as good a name for me as any other you could call me by. But may I ask you a question in the corner here? Is this the bedside where you sing your songs?'

Lamps nodded.

The gentleman for Nowhere clapped him on the shoulder, and they faced about again.

'Upon my word, *Phœbe, my dear,*' said Lamps then to his daughter, looking from her to her visitor, 'it is such an amaze to me, to find you brought acquainted with this gentleman, that I must (if this gentleman will excuse me) take a rounder.'

Mr. Lamps demonstrated in action what this meant, by pulling out his oily handkerchief rolled up in the form of a ball, and giving himself an elaborate smear, from behind the right ear, up the cheek, across the forehead, and down the other cheek to behind his left ear.[1] After this operation he shone exceedingly.

'It's according to my custom when particular warmed up by any agitation, sir. And really I am throwed into that state of amaze by finding you brought acquainted with Phœbe, that I—that I think I will, if you'll excuse me, take another rounder.' Which he did, seeming to be greatly restored by it.

They were now both standing by the side of her couch, and she was working at her lace-pillow.

'Your daughter tells me that she never sits up.'

'No, sir, nor never has done. You see, her mother (who died when she was a year and two months old) was subject to very bad fits, and as she had never mentioned to me that she *was*[2] subject to fits, they couldn't be guarded against. Consequently, she dropped the baby when took, and this happened.'

'It was very wrong of her to marry you, making a secret of her infirmity.'

'Well, sir, you see, Phœbe and me, we have talked that over too. And Lord bless us! Such a number on us has our infirmities, what with fits, and what with misfits, of one sort and another, that if we confessed to 'em all before we got married, most of us might never get married.' *

'I wish you would tell me a little more about yourselves. I hardly know how to ask it of you, for I am conscious that I have a bad stiff manner, a dull discouraging way with me, but I wish you would. † You are hard-worked, I take for granted?'

Lamps was beginning, 'Not particular so'—when his daughter took him up.

---

[1] Dickens's enactment of Lamps's way of 'taking a rounder' was very effective (Kent, p. 233).   [2] *was* italic in *AYR* and *Berg*.

'O yes, sir, he is very hard-worked. Fourteen, fifteen, eighteen hours a day. Sometimes twenty-four hours at a time.'

'And you, what with your school, Phœbe, and what with your lace-making—'

'But my school is a pleasure to me. I began it when I was but a child, because it brought me and other children into company, don't you see? *That*[1] was not work. I carry it on still, because it keeps children about me. *That* is not work. I do it as love, not as work. Then my lace-pillow: it goes with my thoughts when I think, and it goes with my tunes when I hum any, and *that's* not work. Why, you yourself thought it was music, you know, sir. And so it is, to me.'

'Everything is!' cried Lamps, radiantly. 'Everything is music to her, sir.'

'My father is, at any rate. There is more music in my father than there is in a brass band.'

'I say! My dear! It's very fillyillially done, you know; but you are flattering your father.'

'No I am not, sir, I assure you. No I am not. If you could hear my father sing, you would know I am not. But you never will hear him sing, because he never sings to any one but me. However tired he is, he always sings to me when he comes home. *When I lay here long ago, quite a poor little broken doll*, he used to sing to me. More than that, he used to make songs, bringing in whatever little jokes we had between us. More than that, he often does so to this day. O! I'll tell of you, father, as the gentleman has asked about you. He is a poet, sir.'

'I shouldn't wish the gentleman, my dear, to carry away that opinion of your father, because it might look as if I was given to asking the stars in a molloncolly manner what they was up to. Which I wouldn't at once waste the time, and take the liberty, my dear.'

'My father, sir, is always on the bright side, and the good side. You told me just now I had a happy disposition. How can I help it?'

'Well; but my dear, how can *I*[2] help it? Put it to yourself, sir. Look at her. Always as you see her now. Always working—and after all, sir, for but a very few shillings a week—always contented, always lively, always interested in others, of all sorts.'†

'My father, sir, tells me of everything he sees down at his work. You would be surprised what a quantity he gets together for me, every day. He looks into the carriages, and tells me how the ladies are drest—so that I know all the fashions! He tells me what pairs of lovers he sees, and what new-married couples on their wedding trip—so that I know all about that! He collects chance newspapers and books—so that I have plenty to read!

---

[1] *That . . . That . . .* and *that's* all italic in *Berg* and in *AYR*.
[2] *I* italic in *Berg* and in *AYR*.

He tells me about the sick people who are travelling to try to get better—so that I know all about them! In short, as I began by saying, he tells me everything he sees and makes out, down at his work, and you can't think what a quantity he does see and make out.'

'As to collecting newspapers and books, my dear, it's clear I can have no merit in that, because they're not my perquisites. You see, sir, it's this way: A Guard, he'll say to me, "Halloo, here you are, Lamps. I've saved this paper for your daughter. How is she agoing on?" A Head-Porter, he'll say to me, "Here! Catch hold, Lamps. Here's a couple of wollumes for your daughter. Is she pretty much where she were?" And that's what makes it double welcome, you see. If she had a thousand pound in a box, they wouldn't trouble themselves about her; but being what she is—that is, you understand, not having a thousand pound in a box—they take thought for her. And as concerning the young pairs, married and un-married, it's only natural I should bring home what little I can about *them*,[1] seeing that there's not a Couple of either sort in the neighbourhood that don't come of their own accord to confide in Phœbe.'

She raised her eyes triumphantly as she said:

'Indeed, sir, that is true. If I could have got up and gone to church, I don't know how often I should have been a bridesmaid. But if I could have done that, some girls in love might have been jealous of me, *and as it is, no girl is jealous of me.* And my pillow would not have been half as ready to put the piece of cake under, as I always find it.'

The arrival of a little girl, the biggest of the scholars, now led to an understanding on the part of Barbox Brothers that she was the domestic of the cottage, and had come to take active measures in it, *attended by a pail that might have extinguished her, and a broom three times her height.* He therefore rose to take his leave, and took it; saying that if Phœbe had no objection, he would come again.

He had muttered that he would come 'in the course of his walks.' The course of his walks must have been highly favourable to his return, for he returned after an interval of a single day, * *with a kind thought in his head which her past courage had inspired.*

'We were speaking of the Junction last time. I have passed hours there since the day before yesterday, wondering where to go next. You would never guess what I am travelling from. Shall I tell you? I am travelling from my birthday. Yes; from my birthday. *I am, to myself, an unintelligible book with the earlier chapters all torn out, and thrown away. My childhood had no grace of childhood, my youth had no charm of youth*, and what can be expected from such a lost beginning? † I am travelling from my birthday because it has always been a dreary day to me. This is unintelligible to your happy disposition: I am glad it is. However';—*here he came to his kind thought*—'being perplexed among so many roads, what do you think

---

[1] *them* italic in *Berg* and in *AYR*.

I mean to do? How many of the branching roads can you see from your window?'

Looking out, full of interest, she answered, 'Seven.'

'Seven. Well! I propose to myself, at once to reduce the gross number to those very seven, and gradually to fine them down to one—the most promising one for me—and to take that.'

'But how will you know, sir, which *is*[1] the most promising?'

'Ah! To be sure. In this way. Where your father can pick up so much every day for a good purpose, I may once and again pick up a little for an indifferent purpose. The gentleman for Nowhere must become still better known at the Junction. He shall continue to explore it, until he attaches something that he has seen, heard, or found out, at the head of each of the seven roads, to the road itself. And so his choice of a road shall be determined by his choice among his discoveries. But I must not forget (having got so far) to ask a favour. I want your help in this expedient of mine. Yes! I want to bring you what I pick up at the heads of the seven roads that you lie here looking out at, and to compare notes with you about it. May I?'

She gave him her sympathetic right hand, in perfect rapture with his proposal.

'That's well! Again I must not forget (having got so far) to ask a favour. Will you shut your eyes?'

Laughing playfully at the strange nature of the request, she did so.

'Keep them shut,' *he said, going softly to the door, and coming back.* 'May I take your lace-pillow from you for a minute?'

Still laughing and wondering, she removed her hands from it, and he put it aside.

'Tell me. Did you see the puffs of smoke and steam made by the morning fast-train yesterday on road number seven from here?'

'Behind the elm-trees and the spire?'

'That's the road.'

'Yes. I watched them melt away.'

'Anything unusual in what they expressed?'

'No!'

'Not complimentary to me, for I was in that train. I went—don't open your eyes—to fetch you this, from the great ingenious town. It is not half so large as your lace-pillow, and lies easily and lightly in its place. These little keys are like the keys of a miniature piano, and you supply the air required with your left hand. May you pick out delightful music from it, my dear! For the present—you can open your eyes now—good-bye!'

He closed the door upon himself, and only saw that she ecstatically took the present to her bosom and caressed it. *The glimpse gladdened his heart, and yet saddened it; for so might she, if her youth had flourished in its*

[1] *is* italic in *Berg* and in *AYR*.

natural course, have taken to her breast that day the slumbering music of her own child's voice.

CHAPTER III[1]

WITH good will and earnest purpose, the gentleman for Nowhere began, on the very next day, his researches at the heads of the seven roads. *
His heart being in his work of good-nature, he revelled in it. There was the joy, too (it was a true joy to him), of sometimes sitting by, listening to Phœbe as she picked out more and more discourse from her musical instrument, and as her natural taste refined upon her first discoveries. *It resulted that his dreaded birthday was close upon him before he had troubled himself any more about it.* *

'But, sir,' remarked Phœbe, looking over the results of his researches as she—*with unspeakable delight and beguilement of Time*—had reduced them to fair writing, 'we have only six roads here. Is the seventh road dumb?'

'The seventh road? O! That is the road I took, you know, when I went to get your little present. That is *its*[2] story, Phœbe.'

'Would you mind taking that road again, sir? I should like you to take it, in remembrance *of your having done me so much good: of your having made me so much happier*! If you leave me by the road you travelled when you went to do me this great kindness,' *sounding a faint chord as she spoke,* 'I shall feel, lying here watching at my window, as if it *must* conduct you to a prosperous end, and bring you back some day.'

'It shall be done, my dear.'

So at last the gentleman for Nowhere took a ticket for Somewhere, and his destination was the great ingenious town. He had loitered so long about the Junction that it was the eighteenth of December when he left it. 'High time,' he reflected, as he seated himself in the train, 'that I started in earnest! *Only one clear day remains between me and the day I am running away from.* I'll push onward for the hill-country to-morrow. I'll go to Wales.'

It was with some pains that he placed before himself the advantages to be gained from going to Wales. And yet he scarcely made them out as distinctly as he could have wished. Whether the poor girl, in spite of her new resource, would have any feeling of loneliness upon her now that she had not had before; whether in telling him he had done her so much good,

---

[1] *IV* deleted, *III* inserted (cf. p. 430, note 1). In *AYR*, this episode is unnumbered, but is entitled 'Barbox Brothers and Co.' This is the first of the seven episodes introduced by the 'seven roads' device. The second and third are 'The Boy at Mugby' and 'The Signalman'; then follow four more, by other authors than Dickens. Some of the initial paraphernalia, relating to these episodes, is omitted in *Berg*.

[2] *its* italic in *Berg* and in *AYR*.

she had not unconsciously corrected *his old moody bemoaning of his station in life, by setting him thinking that a man might be a great healer, if he would, and yet not be a great doctor*; these and other similar meditations got between him and his Welsh picture. *

Having come to his journey's end for the day, and seen his portmanteaus safely housed in the hotel he chose, and having appointed his dinner-hour, Barbox Brothers went out for a walk in the busy streets. *And now it began to be suspected by him that Mugby Junction was a Junction of many branches, invisible as well as visible, and had joined him to an endless number of byways. For, whereas he would, but a little while ago, have walked these streets, blindly brooding, he now had eyes and thoughts for a new external world.*[1] †

He had walked about the town so far and so long that the lamp-lighters were now at their work in the streets, and the shops were sparkling brilliantly. Thus reminded to turn towards his quarters, he was in the act of doing so, when a very little hand crept into his, and a very little voice said:

'O! If you please, I am lost!'

He looked down, and saw a very little fair-haired girl.

'Yes,' she said, confirming her words with a serious nod. 'I am indeed, I am lost.'

'Where do you live, my child?'

'I don't know where I live. I am lost.'

'What is your name?'

'Polly.'

'What is your other name?'

The reply was prompt, but unintelligible.

Imitating the sound, as he caught it, he hazarded the guess, 'Trivits?'

'O no! Nothing like that.'

'Say it again, little one.'

An unpromising business. For this time it had quite a different sound. 'Paddens?'

'O no! Nothing like that.'

'Once more. Let us try it again, dear.'

A most hopeless business. This time it swelled into four syllables. 'It can't be Tappitarver?'

'No! It ain't! But I am lost,' said the child, nestling her little hand more closely in his, 'and you'll take care of me, won't you?'

[1] Over a page is deleted here in the prompt-copy—an interesting deletion, since the passage is one of social commentary, about 'How the toiling people lived . . .' All of it up to 'wiser than they were' (Oxford Illustrated edition, p. 501) had been underlined, and emphatic treble vertical lines were put in the margin against the phrase about how their (industrial) way of life 'did not deteriorate them as it was the fashion of the supercilious May-flies of humanity to pretend, but engendered among them a self-respect and yet a modest desire to be much wiser than they were.'

'Lost! I am sure *I*[1] am. What is to be done?'

'Where do *you* live?'

'Over there.'

'Hadn't we better go there?'

'Really, I don't know but what we had.'

So they set off, hand in hand. *He, through comparison of himself against his little companion, with a clumsy feeling on him as if he had just developed into a foolish giant.*

'We are going to have dinner when we get there, I suppose?'

'Well, I—yes, I suppose we are.'

'Do you like your dinner?'

'Why, on the whole, yes, I think I do.'

'I do mine. What,' she asked, *turning her soft hand coaxingly in his,* 'are you going to do to amuse me, after dinner?'

'Upon my soul, Polly, I have not the slightest idea!'

'Then I tell you what. Have you got any cards at your house?'

'Plenty!'

'Very well. Then I'll build houses, and you shall look at me. You mustn't blow, you know.'

'O no! No, no, no. No blowing. Blowing's not fair.'

He flattered himself that he had said this pretty well for an idiotic monster; but the child, instantly perceiving the awkwardness of his attempt to adapt himself to her level, destroyed his hopeful opinion of himself by saying, compassionately: 'What a funny man you are!'

Feeling, after this melancholy failure, as if he every minute grew bigger and heavier in person, and weaker in mind, Barbox gave himself up for a bad job. No giant ever submitted more meekly to be led in triumph by all-conquering Jack, than he to be bound in slavery to Polly. †

Thus they arrived at the hotel. And there he had to say at the bar, and said awkwardly enough: 'I have found a little girl!'

The whole establishment turned out to look at the little girl. Nobody knew her; nobody could *make out* her name, as she set it forth—*except one chambermaid, who said it was Constantinople—which it wasn't.*

'I will dine with my young friend in a private room, and perhaps you will be so good as let the police know that the pretty baby is here. I suppose she is sure to be inquired for, soon, if she had not been already. Come along, Polly.'

Perfectly at ease and peace, Polly came along, but, finding the stairs rather stiff work, was carried up by Barbox Brothers. The dinner was a most transcendent success, and the Barbox sheepishness, under Polly's directions how to mince her meat for her, and how to diffuse gravy over the plate with a liberal and equal hand, was a fine sight. † Polly, elevated on a platform of sofa-cushions in a chair at his right hand, encouraged

---

[1] *I* italic in *Berg* and in *AYR*, as is *you* in Polly's reply.

him with a pat or two on the face from the greasy bowl of her spoon, and even with a gracious kiss. In getting on her feet upon her chair, however, to give him this last reward, she toppled forward among the dishes, and caused him to exclaim as he effected her rescue: 'Gracious Angels! Whew! I thought we were in the fire, Polly!'

'What a coward you are, ain't you?'

'Yes, I am rather nervous. Whew! Don't, Polly! Don't flourish your spoon, or you'll go over sideways. Don't tilt up your legs when you laugh, Polly, or you'll go over backwards. Whew! Polly, Polly, Polly, *we are environed with dangers!*'

Indeed, he could find no security from the pitfalls that were yawning for Polly, but in proposing to her, after dinner, to sit upon a low stool. 'I will, if you will,' said Polly. So as peace of mind should go before all, he begged the waiter to wheel aside the table, bring a pack of cards, a couple of footstools, and a screen, and close in Polly and himself before the fire. *Then, finest sight of all,* was Barbox Brothers on his footstool, with a pint decanter on the rug, contemplating Polly as she built successfully, and *growing blue in the face with holding his breath, lest he should blow the house down.*

'How you stare, don't you?' said Polly.

'I am afraid I was looking rather hard at you, Polly.'

'Why do you stare?'

'I cannot recal why.—I don't know, Polly.'

'You must be a simpleton to do things and not know why, mustn't you?'

'It is impossible,' he thought, 'that I can ever have seen this pretty baby before. Can I have dreamed of her? In some sorrowful dream?'

He could make nothing of it. So he went into the building trade as a journeyman under Polly and they built three stories high, four stories high: even five.

'I say. Who do you think is coming?' asked Polly, rubbing her eyes after tea.

'The waiter?'

'No, the dustman. I am getting sleepy.'

A new embarrassment.

'I don't think I am going to be fetched to-night; what do you think?'

He thought not, either. After another quarter of an hour, *the dustman not merely impending but actually arriving,* recourse was had to the Constantinopolitan chambermaid: who cheerily undertook that the child should sleep in a comfortable and wholesome room, which she herself would share. †

Polly gave him a hug or two to keep him going, and then giving that confiding mite of a hand of hers to be swallowed up in the hand of the Constantinopolitan chambermaid, trotted off chattering, without a vestige of anxiety.

He looked after her, had the screen removed and the table and chairs replaced, and still looked after her. He paced the room for half an hour. 'A most engaging little creature, but it's not that. A most winning little voice, but it's not that. How can it be that I seem to know this child? What was it she imperfectly recalled to me when I felt her touch in the street?'

[1]'*Mr. Jackson!*'

He turned towards the sound of the subdued voice, and saw his answer standing at the door.

'O Mr. Jackson! do not be severe with me. Speak a word of encouragement to me, I beseech you.'

'You are Polly's mother.'

'Yes.'

Yes. Polly herself might come to this, one day. As you see what the rose was, in its faded leaves; as you see what the summer growth of the woods was, in their wintry branches; so Polly might be traced, one day, in a care-worn woman like this, with her hair turned grey. Before him were the ashes of a dead fire that had once burned bright. This was the woman he had loved. This was the woman he had lost. Such had been the constancy of his imagination to her, so had Time spared her under its withholding, that now, seeing how roughly the inexorable hand had struck her, his soul was filled with pity and amazement.

He led her to a chair.

'Did you see me in the street, and show me to your child?'

'Yes.'

'Is the little creature, then, a party to deceit?'

'I hope there is no deceit. I said to her, "We have lost our way, and I must try to find mine by myself. Go to that gentleman and tell him you are lost. You shall be fetched by-and-by." Perhaps you have not thought how very young she is?'

'Why did you do this?'

'O Mr. Jackson, do you ask me? In the hope that you might see something in my innocent child to soften your heart towards me. *Not only towards me, but towards my husband.*'

He walked to the opposite end of the room. He came back again with a slower step.

'I thought you had emigrated to America?'

'We did. But life went ill with us there, and we came back.'

'Do you live in this town?'

'Yes. I am a daily teacher of music here. My husband is a bookkeeper.'

'Are you—forgive my asking—poor?'

'We earn enough for our wants. That is not our distress. My husband is

---

[1] Marginal stage-direction *Beatrice*. The speech also has three vertical lines against it in the margin.

very, very ill of a lingering disorder. He will never recover. It is not that my husband's mind is at all impaired by his bodily suffering, for I assure you that is not the case. But in his weakness, and in his knowledge that he is incurably ill, he cannot overcome the ascendancy of one idea. It preys upon him, embitters every moment of his painful life, and will shorten it. We have had five children before this darling, and they all lie in their little graves. He believes that they have withered away *under a curse*, and that it will blight this child like the rest.'

'Under what curse?'

'Both I and he have it on our conscience that we tried you very heavily, and I do not know but that, if I were as ill as he, I might suffer in my mind as he does. This is the constant burden of what he says to me:—"I believe, Beatrice, I was the only friend that Mr. Jackson ever cared to make, though I was so much his junior. The more influence he acquired in the business, the higher he advanced me. And I was alone in his private confidence. I came between him and you, and I took you from him. We were both secret, and the blow fell when he was wholly unprepared. The anguish it caused a man so compressed, must have been terrible; the wrath it awakened, inappeasable. *So, a curse came to be invoked on our poor pretty little flowers, and they fall.*"'

'And you, Beatrice, how say you?'

'Until within these few weeks, I was afraid of you, and I believed that you would never, never forgive.'

'Until within these few weeks? Have you changed your opinion of me within these few weeks?'

'Yes.'

'For what reason?'

'I was getting some pieces of music in a shop in this town, when, to my terror, you came in. As I veiled my face and stood in the dark end of the shop, I heard you explain that you wanted a musical instrument for a bed-ridden girl. Your voice and manner were so softened, you showed such interest in its selection, you took it away yourself with so much tenderness of care and pleasure, that I knew you were a man with a most gentle heart. I inquired in the shop where you lived, but could get no information. As I heard you say that you were going back by the next train (but you did not say where), I resolved to visit the station at about that time of day, as often as I could, between my lessons, on the chance of seeing you again. I have been there very often, but saw you no more until to-day. You were meditating as you walked the street, but the calm expression of your face emboldened me to send my child to you. And when I saw you bend your head to speak tenderly to her, I prayed to GOD to forgive me for having ever brought a sorrow on it. I now pray to you to forgive me, and to forgive my husband. I was very young, he was young too, and in the ignorant hardihood of such a time of life we don't know what we do to those who have undergone more discipline. You generous man! You good man! So to raise me up and make nothing of my crime against you!'—*for he would not see her on her knees and soothed her*[1]—'thank you, bless you, thank you!'

'Leave Polly with me for to-morrow, Beatrice, and write me your address on this leaf of my pocket-book. In the evening I will bring her home to you—and to her father.'

'Halloo!' cried Polly, putting her sunny face in at the door next morning when breakfast was ready: 'I thought I was fetched last night?'

'So you were, Polly, but I asked leave to keep you here for the day, and to take you home in the evening.'

'Upon my word! You are very cool, ain't you?'

However, Polly seemed to think it a good idea, and added, 'I suppose I must give you a kiss though you *are*[2] cool.' The kiss given and taken, they sat down to breakfast in a highly conversational tone.

'Of course you are going to amuse me?'

'Oh, of course.'

Polly found it indispensable to put down her piece of toast, cross one of her little fat knees over the other, and bring her little fat right hand down into her left hand with a business-like slap. After this gathering of herself together, Polly, by that time *a mere heap of dimples*, asked in a wheedling manner: 'What are we going to do, you dear old thing!'

'Why, I was thinking—but are you fond of horses, Polly?'

'Ponies, I am, especially when their tails are long. But horses—n—no—too big, you know.'

'Well, I did see yesterday, Polly, on the walls, pictures of two long-tailed ponies, speckled all over——'

'No, no, NO!'[3] cried Polly, *in an ecstatic desire to linger on the charming details*. 'Not speckled all over!'

'Speckled all over. Which ponies jump through hoops—and eat pie in pinafores—and fire off guns.'

(*Polly hardly seemed to see the force of the ponies resorting to fire-arms.*)

'And I was thinking, that if you and I were to go to the Circus where these ponies are, it would do our constitutions good. There are many other wonders besides the ponies, and we shall see them all. Ladies and gentlemen in spangled dresses, and elephants and lions and tigers. I was also thinking, Polly, that if we were to look in at the toy-shop, to choose a doll——'

---

[1] Dickens deleted the words which followed—'as a kind father might have soothed an erring'—but did not delete (in the next line) the word 'daughter', which completed the phrase. Obviously he meant to do so.

[2] *are* italic in *Berg* and in *AYR*.

[3] Small capitals in *Berg* and in *AYR*, as also in the repetition of this phrase below.

'Not dressed! No, no, NO, not dressed!'

'Full dressed. Together with a house, and all things necessary for house-keeping——'

Polly gave a little scream, and seemed in danger of falling into a swoon of bliss.

The resplendent programme was carried into execution with the utmost rigour of the law. It being essential to make the purchase of the doll its first feature—or that lady would have lost the ponies—the toy-shop expedition took precedence. The lovely specimen chosen, was of Circassian descent, possessing as much boldness of beauty as was reconcilable with extreme feebleness of mouth, and combining a sky-blue silk pelisse with rose-coloured satin trousers, and a black velvet hat:—which this fair stranger to our northern shores would seem to have founded on the portraits of the late Duchess of Kent. The name of this distinguished foreigner was (on Polly's authority) Miss Melluka, and the costly nature of her outfit as a housekeeper may be inferred from the two facts that *her silver teaspoons were as large as her kitchen poker, and that the proportions of her watch exceeded those of her frying-pan*. Miss Melluka was graciously pleased to express her entire approbation of the Circus, and so was Polly. † To wind up the delicious day, there came the agreeable fever of getting Miss Melluka and all her rich possessions into a fly with Polly, to be taken home. But by that time Polly had become unable to look upon such accumulated joys with waking eyes, and had withdrawn her consciousness into the wonderful Paradise of a child's sleep.

What rustling piece of paper he took from his pocket, and carefully folded into the bosom of Polly's frock, shall not be mentioned. He said nothing about it, and nothing shall be said about it. They drove to a suburb of the great ingenious town, and stopped at the fore-court of a small house. 'Do not wake the child,' he said softly, to the driver, 'I will carry her in as she is.'

Greeting the light at the opened door which was held by Polly's mother, Polly's bearer passed on with mother and child into a room, where, stretched on a sofa, lay a wasted man, who covered his eyes with his emaciated hands.

'Tresham, I have brought you back your Polly, fast asleep. Give me your hand, and tell me you are better.'

'Thank you, thank you! I may say that I am well and happy.'

'That's brave. Tresham, I have a fancy (I am getting quite an old fellow now, you know, and old fellows may take fancies into their heads sometimes), to give up Polly, having found her, to no one but you. Will you take her from me?'

As the father held out his arms for the child, each of the two men looked steadily at the other.

'She is very dear to you, Tresham?'

'Unutterably dear.'

'God bless her! It is not much, Polly, for a blind and sinful man to invoke a blessing on something so far better than himself as a little child is; but it would be much—much upon his cruel head, and much upon his guilty soul—if he could be so wicked as to invoke a curse. He had better have a millstone round his neck, and be cast into the deepest sea. Live and thrive, my pretty baby! Live and prosper, and become in time the mother of other little children, like the Angels who behold The Father's face!'

He kissed her again, gave her up gently to both her parents, and went out.

But he never went to Wales. He went straightway for another stroll about the town, and he looked in upon the people at their work, and at their play, here, there, everywhere, and where not. *For he was Barbox Brothers and Co. now, and had* taken thousands of partners into the solitary firm.[1]

He had at length got back to his hotel room, and was standing before his fire refreshing himself with a glass of hot drink which he had stood upon the chimney-piece, when he heard the town clocks striking *Twelve*. His eyes met those of his reflection in the chimney-glass.

'Why it's your birthday already,' he said, smiling. 'You are looking very well. I wish you many happy returns of the day.'

He had never before bestowed that wish upon himself. 'By Jupiter!' he discovered, 'it alters the whole case of running away from one's birthday! It's a thing to explain to Phœbe. Besides, here is quite a long story to tell her, that has sprung out of the road with no story. I'll go back, instead of going on.'

He went back to Mugby Junction, and established himself at Mugby Junction. It was the convenient place to live in, for brightening Phœbe's life. It was the convenient place to live in, for having her taught music by Beatrice. It was the convenient place to live in, for occasionally borrowing Polly. So, he became settled there, and, his house standing in an elevated situation, it is noteworthy of him in conclusion, as Polly herself might (not irreverently) have put it:

> There was an old Barbox who lived on a hill,
> And if he ain't gone he lives there still.

---

[1] In the margin, there are three vertical lines against this sentence. The underlining should doubtless be understood as extending further.

THE BOY AT MUGBY

DICKENS had a particularly exasperating experience of railway refreshment rooms, at Rugby Junction, when on tour in April 1866. This little sketch, written later that year, was the result: and from other such experiences later (his fellow-victim George Dolby recalled) 'he derived a melancholy satisfaction in thinking how true was his satire [in this story] upon the manner in which "refreshmenting" at railway stations was then conducted' (pp. 31, 438). Ezekiel, the boy at Mugby, 'achieved immortality before he was a month old', reported the *Manchester Guardian* critic on 4 February 1867—but he spoke too soon. The Boy much tickled the fancy of readers of *Mugby Junction*, but he failed to repeat the success of his predecessors in other recent *All the Year Round* Christmas numbers, Mrs. Lirriper and Doctor Marigold. This Reading, like its companion *Barbox Brothers*, was prepared and presented very quickly. When the prompt-copy was set up, only a few slight cuts were made; then Dickens reduced the length of the prompt-copy text by about a quarter, mainly by simple deletions of a paragraph here and there. All these alterations are in one ink (blue). There are no stage-directions or underlinings.

Dickens read *The Boy at Mugby* to the ladies of his household on 20 October 1866, 'with such extraordinary peals and tears of laughter, that I think I foresee a great success [he reported]. I don't think I ever saw people laugh so much under the prosiest of circumstances' (*N*, iii. 488). What he then read was doubtless the full text to be published in *All the Year Round*, and the 'great success' he foretold probably referred to the forthcoming Christmas number, not to the public reading.

His trial performance of *The Boy* and the other new *Mugby Junction* Reading, at Christmas 1866, has been mentioned in the headnote to *Barbox Brothers*. The reception of *The Boy* at its first performance, 15 January 1867, was cordial ('. . . in the happiest spirit of fun', pronounced *The Times* two days later), but this Reading never caught on. As Charles Kent records, it was introduced among the Readings

. . . once or twice in a way only, . . . and then merely as a slight stop-gap or interlude. Thoroughly enjoying the delivery of it himself, and always provoking shouts of laughter whenever this colloquial morsel was given, the Novelist seemed to be perfectly conscious himself that it was altogether too slight and trivial of its kind, to be worthy of anything like artistic consideration . . . (pp. 239–40)

This seems the kindest possibly verdict upon it. A joke worth making in a paragraph or so (and Dickens had made it effectively, in earlier letters and essays) is here stretched out tediously and developed implausibly. His other scripts being so much better, and his audiences not being tired of them, Dickens can have felt little inducement to waste time performing this one. I have no record of his performing it after February 1867.

The Boy at Mugby

I am The Boy at Mugby. That's about what I[1] am.

You don't know what I mean? What a pity! But I think you do. I think you must. Look here. I am the Boy at what is called The Refreshment Room at Mugby Junction, and what's proudest boast is, that it never yet refreshed a mortal being.

Up in a corner of the Down Refreshment Room at Mugby Junction, in the height of twenty-seven cross draughts (I've often counted 'em while they brush the First Class hair twenty-seven ways), behind the bottles, among the glasses, bounded on the nor'-west by the beer, stood pretty far to the right of a metallic object that's at times the tea-urn and at times the soup-tureen, according to the nature of the last twang imparted to its contents which are the same groundwork, fended off from the traveller by a barrier of stale sponge-cakes erected atop of the counter, and lastly exposed sideways to the glare of Our Missis's eye—you ask a Boy so sitiwated, next time you stop in a hurry at Mugby, for anything to drink; you take particular notice that he'll try to seem not to hear you, that he'll appear in a absent manner to survey the Line through a transparent medium composed of your head and body, and that he won't serve you as long as you can possibly bear it. That's Me. †

What a delightful lark it is! I look upon us Refreshmenters as ockipying the only proudly independent footing on the Line. There's Papers for instance—my honourable friend if he will allow me to call him so—him as belongs to Smith's book-stall. Why he no more dares to be up to our Refreshmenting games, than he dares to jump atop of a locomotive with her steam at full pressure, and cut away upon her alone, driving himself, at limited-mail speed. Papers, he'd get his head punched at every compartment, first second and third, the whole length of a train, if he was to ventur to imitate my demeanour. It's the same with the porters, the same with the guards, the same with the ticket clerks, the same the whole way up to the secretary, traffic manager, or very chairman. There ain't a one among 'em on the nobly independent footing we are. Did you ever catch one of *them*, when you wanted anything of him, making a system of surveying the Line through a transparent medium composed of your head and body? I should hope not.

You should see our Bandolining Room at Mugby Junction. It's led to,

---

[1] *I* italic in *Berg* and in *All the Year Round*. *Berg* contains a few textual alterations in Dickens's autograph, but no underlining: and all words set in italic or capitals had been printed thus in *AYR*. This will not be mentioned henceforth.

by the door behind the counter which you'll notice usually stands ajar, and it's the room where Our Missis and our young ladies Bandolines their hair. You should see 'em at it, betwixt trains, Bandolining away, as if they was anointing themselves for the combat. When you're telegraphed, you should see their noses all a going up with scorn, as if it was a part of the working of the same Cooke and Wheatstone electrical machinery. You should hear Our Missis give the word 'Here comes the Beast to be Fed!' and then you should see 'em indignantly skipping across the Line, from the Up to the Down, or Wicer Warsaw, and begin to pitch the stale pastry into the plates, and chuck the sawdust sangwiches under the glass covers, and get out the—ha ha ha!—the Sherry—O my eye, my eye!—for your Refreshment.

It's only in the Isle of the Brave and Land of the Free (by which of course I mean to say Britannia) that Refreshmenting is so effective, so 'olesome, so constitutional, a check upon the public. There was a foreigner, which having politely, with his hat off, beseeched our young ladies and Our Missis for 'a leetel gloss hoff prarndee,' and having had the Line surveyed through him by all and no other acknowledgment, was a proceeding at last to help himself, as seems to be the custom in his own country, when Our Missis with her hair almost a coming un-Bandolined with rage, and her eyes omitting sparks, flew at him, cotched the decanter out of his hand, and said: 'Put it down! I won't allow that!' The foreigner turned pale, stepped back with his arms stretched out in front of him, his hands clasped, and his shoulders riz, and exclaimed: 'Ah! Is it possible this. That these disdaineous females and this ferocious old woman are placed here by the administration not only to empoison the voyagers, but to affront them! Great Heaven! How arrives it? The English people. Or is he then a slave? Or idiot?' Another time, a merry wideawake American gent had tried the sawdust and spit it out, and had tried the Sherry and spit that out, and had tried in vain to sustain exhausted natur upon Butter-Scotch, and had been rather extra Bandolined and Line-surveyed through, when, as the bell was ringing and he paid Our Missis, he says, very loud and good-tempered: 'I tell Yew what 'tis, ma'arm. I la'af. Theer! I la'af. I Dew. I oughter ha' seen most things, for I hail from the Onlimited side of the Atlantic Ocean, and I haive travelled right slick over the Limited, head on, through Jeerusalemm and the East, and like-ways France and Italy, Europe Old World, and I am now upon the track to the Chief Europian Village; but such an Institution as Yew, and Yewer young ladies, and Yewer fixin's solid and liquid, afore the glorious Tarnal I never did see yet! And if I hain't found the eighth wonder of monarchical Creation, in finding Yew, and Yewer young ladies, and Yewer fixin's solid and liquid, all as aforesaid established in a country where the people air not absolute Loo-naticks, I am Extra Double Darned with a Nip and Frizzle to the innermostest grit! Wheerfur—Theer!—I la'af! I Dew, ma'arm. I la'af!' And so he went, stamping and shaking his sides, along the platform all the way to his own compartment.[1]

I think it was her standing up agin the Foreigner, as giv' Our Missis the idea of going over to France, and droring a comparison betwixt Refreshmenting as followed among the frog-eaters, and Refreshmenting as triumphant in the Isle of the Brave and Land of the Free (by which of course I mean to say agin, Britannia). Our young ladies, Miss Whiff, Miss Piff, and Mrs. Sniff, was unanimous opposed to her going; for, as they says to Our Missis one and all, it is well beknown to the hends of the herth as no other nation except Britain has a idea of anythink, but above all of business. Why then should you tire yourself to prove what is aready proved? Our Missis however (being a teazer at all pints) stood out grim obstinate, and got a return pass by South-Eastern Tidal, to go right through, if such should be her dispositions, to Marseilles.

Sniff is husband to Mrs. Sniff, and is a regular insignificant cove. He looks after the sawdust department in a back room, and is sometimes when we are very hard put to it let in behind the counter with a corkscrew; but never when it can be helped, his demeanour towards the public being disgusting servile. How Mrs. Sniff ever come so far to lower herself as to marry him, I don't know; but I suppose *he* does, and I should think he wished he didn't, for he leads a awful life. †

But Mrs. Sniff. How different! She's the one! She's the one as you'll notice to be always looking another way from you, when you look at her. She's the one with the small waist buckled in tight in front, and with the lace cuffs at her wrists, which she puts on the edge of the counter before her, and stands a smoothing while the public foams.

When Our Missis went away upon her journey, Mrs. Sniff was left in charge. She did hold the public in check most beautiful! In all my time, I never see half so many cups of tea given without milk to people as wanted it with, nor half so many cups of tea with milk given to people as wanted it without. When foaming ensued, Mrs. Sniff would say: 'Then you'd better settle it among yourselves, and change with one another.' It was a most highly delicious lark. I enjoyed the Refreshmenting business more than ever, and was so glad I had took to it when young.

Our Missis returned. It got circulated among the young ladies, and it penetrated to me, that she had Orrors to reveal. At length it was put forth that on our slackest evening in the week, and at our slackest time of that evening betwixt trains, Our Missis would give her views of foreign Refreshmenting, in the Bandolining Room.

[1] 'There is nothing in [this monologue], and nothing in Mr. Dickens's reading of it, better than the brief sentences in which the Frenchman and the American comment upon the abuses of the refreshment room. These told upon the audience with great effect, and the exclamation of "the boy" about the sherry was equally amusing' (*Yorkshire Post*, 1 February 1867).

It was arranged tasteful for the purpose. The Bandolining table and glass was hid in a corner, a arm-chair was elevated on a packing-case for Our Missis's ockypation, a table and a tumbler of water (no sherry in it, thankee) was placed beside it. Two of the pupils, the season being autumn, and hollyhocks and daliahs being in, ornamented the wall with three devices in those flowers. On one might be read, 'MAY ALBION NEVER LEARN;' on another, 'KEEP THE PUBLIC DOWN;' on another, 'OUR REFRESHMENTING CHARTER.' The whole had a beautiful appearance, with which the beauty of the sentiments corresponded.

'Where,' said Our Missis, glancing gloomily around, 'is Sniff?'

'I thought it better,' answered Mrs. Sniff, 'that he should not be let to come in. He is such an Ass.'

'No doubt,' assented Our Missis. 'But for that reason is it not desirable to improve his mind?'

'O! Nothing will ever improve *him*,' said Mrs. Sniff.

'However,' pursued Our Missis, 'call him in, Ezekiel.'

I called him in. The appearance of the low-minded cove was hailed with disapprobation from all sides, on account of his having brought his corkscrew with him. He pleaded 'the force of habit.'

'The force!' said Mrs. Sniff. 'Don't let us have you talking about force, for Gracious sake. There! Do stand still where you are, with your back against the wall.'

He is a smiling piece of vacancy, and he smiled in the mean way in which he will even smile at the public if he gets a chance (language can say no meaner of him), and he stood upright near the door with the back of his head agin the wall, as if he was a waiting for somebody to come and measure his heighth for the Army.

'I should not enter, ladies,' says Our Missis, 'on the revolting disclosures I am about to make, if it was not in the hope that they will cause you to be yet more implacable in the exercise of the power you wield in a constitutional country, and yet more devoted to the constitutional motto which I see before me;' it was behind her, but the words sounded better so; '"May Albion never learn!"'

Here the pupils as had made the motto, admired it, and cried, 'Hear! Hear! Hear!' Sniff, showing an inclination to join in chorus, got himself frowned down by every brow. †

'Shall I be believed when I tell you that no sooner had I landed on that treacherous shore, than I was ushered into a Refreshment Room where there were, I do not exaggerate, actually eatable things to eat and drinkable things to drink?'

A murmur, swelling almost into a scream, ariz. Miss Piff, trembling with indignation, called out: 'Name!'

'I *will* name,' said Our Missis. 'There was roast fowls, hot and cold; there was smoking roast veal surrounded with browned potatoes; there was hot soup with (again I ask shall I be credited?) nothing bitter in it, and no flour to choke off the consumer: there was a variety of cold dishes set off with jelly: there was salad: there was—mark me!—*fresh* pastry, and that of a light construction: there was a luscious show of fruit. There was bottles and decanters of sound small wine, of every size and adapted to every pocket; the same odious statement will apply to brandy; and these were set out upon the counter so that all could help themselves. This was my first unconstitutional experience. Well would it have been, if it had been my last and worst. But no. As I proceeded further into that enslaved and ignorant land, its aspect became more hideous. I need not explain to this assembly the ingredients and formation of the British Refreshment sangwich?'

Universal laughter—except from Sniff, who, as sangwich-cutter, shook his head in a state of the utmost dejection as he stood with it agin the wall.

'Well!' said Our Missis, with dilated nostrils. 'Take a fresh crisp long crusty penny loaf made of the whitest and best flour. Cut it longwise through the middle. Insert a fair and nicely fitting slice of ham. Tie a smart piece of ribbon round the middle of the whole to bind it together. Add at one end a neat wrapper of clean white paper by which to hold it. And the universal French Refreshment sangwich busts on your disgusted vision.'

A cry of 'Shame!' from all—except Sniff, which drawed up his leg with a sort of relish, and rubbed his stomach with a soothing hand.

'I need not,' said Our Missis, 'explain to this assembly, the usual formation and fitting of the British Refreshment Room?'

No, no, and laughter. Sniff agin shaking his head in low spirits agin the wall.

'Well,' said Our Missis, 'what would you say to a general decoration of everythink, to hangings (sometimes elegant), to easy velvet furniture, to abundance of little tables, to abundance of little seats, to brisk bright waiters, to great convenience, to a pervading cleanliness and tastefulness positively addressing the public and making the Beast thinking itself worth the pains?'

Contemptous fury on the part of all the ladies. Mrs. Sniff looking as if she wanted somebody to hold her, and everybody else looking as if they'd rayther not. †

'On my experience south of Paris,' said Our Missis, in a deep tone, 'I will not expatiate. Too loathsome were the task! But fancy this. Fancy a guard coming round, with the train at full speed, to inquire how many for dinner. Fancy his telegraphing forward, the number of diners. Fancy every one expected, and the table elegantly laid for the complete party. Fancy a charming dinner, in a charming room, and the head-cook, concerned for the honour of every dish, superintending in his clean white jacket and cap. Fancy the Beast travelling six hundred miles on end, very fast, and with great punctuality, yet being taught to expect all this to be done for it!

'Putting everything together,' said Our Missis, 'French Refreshmenting comes to this, and O it comes to a nice total! First: eatable things to eat, and drinkable things to drink.'

A groan from the young ladies, kep' up by me.

'Second: convenience, and even elegance.'

Another groan from the young ladies, kep' up by me.

'Third: moderate charges.'

This time a groan from me, kep' up by the young ladies.

'Fourth—and here,' says Our Missis, 'I claim your angriest sympathy—attention, common civility, nay, even politeness!'

Me and the young ladies regularly raging mad all together.

'And I cannot in conclusion,' says Our Missis, with her spitefullest sneer, 'give you a completer pictur of that despicable nation (after what I have related), than assuring you that they wouldn't bear our constitutional ways and noble independence, for a single month, and that they would turn us to the right-about and put another system in our places, as soon as look at us; perhaps sooner, for I do not believe they have the good taste to care to look at us twice.'

The swelling tumult was arrested in its rise. Sniff, bore away by his servile disposition, had drored up his leg with a higher and a higher relish, and was now discovered to be waving his corkscrew over his head. It was at this moment that Mrs. Sniff, who had kep' her eye upon him like the fabled obelisk, descended on her victim. Our Missis followed them both out, and cries was heard from the sawdust department.

You come into the Down Refreshment Room, at the Junction, making believe you don't know me, and I'll pint you out with my right thumb over my shoulder which is Our Missis, and which is Miss Whiff, and which is Miss Piff, and which is Mrs. Sniff. But you won't get a chance to see Sniff, because he disappeared that night. Whether he perished, tore to pieces, I cannot say; but his corkscrew alone remains, to bear witness to the servility of his disposition.

THE SIGNALMAN

CHARLES Kent, reviewing *Mugby Junction* in the *Sun* (7 December 1866), had found Dickens's tale 'The Signalman' much the best of his contributions— another example of 'his mastery of the terrible. . . . It is, surely, the finest Tale of Presentiment that has ever been told.' Dickens doubtless devised his Reading of it at the same time as the other two *Mugby Junction* items, but he did very little with it. The *All Year the Round* text is hardly altered at all, beyond the omission of phrases like 'I said' and 'he rejoined', and some passages describing the participants' appearance or manner (such as 'speaking in a tone but a little above a whisper'). His privately-printed copy contains no further deletions or revisions by Dickens—indeed, not a mark or word of his writing—and the Reading was never performed.

It is worth remarking that Mr. Emlyn Williams has lately had some success in reading this eerie little story. For his version, which is much more succinct than Dickens's, see his *Readings from Dickens* (1954), pp. 35–40.

All italics and small capitals in the privately printed edition are as in the *All the Year Round* text. There are no omissions lengthy enough to justify an asterisk.

The Signalman

'HALLOA! Below there!'

When he heard a voice thus calling to him, he was standing at the door of his box, with a flag in his hand, furled round its short pole. One would have thought, considering the nature of the ground, that he could not have doubted from what quarter the voice came; but, instead of looking up to where I stood on the top of the steep cutting nearly over his head, he turned himself about and looked down the Line. There was something remarkable in his manner of doing so, though I could not have said, for my life, what. But, I know it was remarkable enough to attract my notice, even though his figure was foreshortened and shadowed, down in the deep trench, and mine was high above him, so steeped in the glow of an angry sunset, that I had shaded my eyes with my hand before I saw him at all.

'Halloa! Below!'

From looking down the Line, he turned himself about again, and, raising his eyes, saw my figure high above him.

'Is there any path by which I can come down and speak to you?'

He looked up at me without replying, and I looked down at him without pressing him too soon with a repetition of my idle question. Just then, there came a vague vibration in the earth and air, quickly changing into a violent pulsation, and an oncoming rush that caused me to start back, as though it had force to draw me down. When such vapour as rose to my height from this rapid train, had passed me and was skimming away over the landscape, I looked down again, and saw him re-furling the flag he had shown while the train went by.

I repeated my inquiry. After a pause, during which he seemed to regard me with fixed attention, he motioned with his rolled-up flag towards a point on my level, some two or three hundred yards distant. I called down to him, 'All right!' and made for that point. There, by dint of looking closely about me, I found a rough zig-zag descending path notched out: which I followed.

The cutting was extremely deep, and unusually precipitate. It was made through a clammy stone that became oozier and wetter as I went down. For these reasons, I found the way long enough to give me time to recal a singular air of reluctance or compulsion with which he had pointed out the path.

When I came down low enough upon the zig-zag descent, to see him again, I saw that he was standing between the rails on the way by which the train had lately passed, in an attitude as if he were waiting for me to appear. He had his left hand at his chin, and that left elbow rested on his right hand crossed over his breast. His attitude was one of such expectation and watchfulness, that I stopped a moment, wondering at it.

I resumed my downward way, and, stepping out upon the level of the railroad and drawing nearer to him, saw that he was a dark sallow man, with a dark beard and rather heavy eyebrows. His post was in as solitary and dismal a place as ever I saw. On either side, a dripping-wet wall of jagged stone, excluding all view but a strip of sky; the perspective one way, only a crooked prolongation of this great dungeon; the shorter perspective in the other direction, terminating in a gloomy red light, and the gloomier entrance to a black tunnel, in whose massive architecture there was a barbarous, depressing, and forbidding air. So little sunlight ever found its way to this spot, that it had an earthy deadly smell; and so much cold wind rushed through it, that it struck chill to me, as if I had left the natural world.

Before he stirred, I was near enough to him to have touched him. Not even then removing his eyes from mine, he stepped back one step, and lifted his hand.

This was a lonesome post to occupy (I said), and it had riveted my attention when I looked down from up yonder. A visitor was a rarity, I should suppose; not an unwelcome rarity, I hoped? In me, he merely saw a man who had been shut up within narrow limits all his life, and who, being at last set free, had a newly-awakened interest in these great works. To such purpose I spoke to him; but I am far from sure of the terms I used, for, besides that I am not happy in opening any conversation, there was something in the man that daunted me.

He directed a most curious look towards the red light near the tunnel's mouth, and looked all about it, as if something were missing from it, and then looked at me.

That light was part of his charge? Was it not?

He answered in a low voice: 'Don't you know it is?'

The monstrous thought came into my mind as I perused the fixed eyes and the saturnine face, that this was a spirit, not a man. I have speculated since, whether there may have been infection in his mind.

In my turn, I stepped back. But in making the action, I detected in his eyes some latent fear of me. This put the monstrous thought to flight.

'You look at me,' I said, forcing a smile, 'as if you had a dread of me.'

'I was doubtful whether I had seen you before.'

'Where?'

He pointed to the red light he had looked at.

'There?'

Intently watchful of me, he replied (but without sound), Yes.

'My good fellow, what should I do there? However, be that as it may, I never was there, you may swear.'

'I think I may. Yes. I am sure I may.'

His manner cleared, like my own. He replied to my remarks with readiness, and in well-chosen words. Had he much to do there? Yes; that was to say, he had enough responsibility to bear; but exactness and watchfulness were what was required of him, and of actual work—manual labour —he had next to none. To change that signal, to trim those lights, and to turn this iron handle now and then, was all he had to do under that head. Regarding those many long and lonely hours of which I seemed to make so much, he could only say that the routine of his life had shaped itself into that form, and he had grown used to it. He had taught himself a language down here—if only to know it by sight, and to have formed his own crude ideas of its pronunciation, could be called learning it. He had also worked at fractions and decimals, and tried a little algebra; but he was, and had been as a boy, a poor hand at figures. Was it necessary for him when on duty, always to remain in that channel of damp air, and could he never rise into the sunshine from between those high stone walls? Why, that depended upon times and circumstances. Under some conditions there would be less upon the Line than under others, and the same held good as to certain hours of the day and night. In bright weather, he did choose occasions for getting a little above these lower shadows; but, being at all times liable to be called by his electric bell, and at such times listening for it with redoubled anxiety, the relief was less than I would suppose.

He took me into his box, where there was a fire, a desk for an official book in which he had to make certain entries, a telegraphic instrument with its dial face and needles, and the little bell of which he had spoken. On my trusting that he would excuse the remark that he had been well educated, and (I hoped I might say without offence), perhaps educated above that station, he observed that instances of slight incongruity in such-wise would rarely be found wanting among large bodies of men; that he had heard it was so in workhouses, in the police force, even in that last desperate resource, the army; and that he knew it was so, more or less, in any great railway staff. He had been, when young (if I could believe it, sitting in that hut; he scarcely could), a student of natural philosophy, and had attended lectures; but he had run wild, misused his opportunities, gone down, and never risen again. He had no complaint to offer about that. He had made his bed, and he lay upon it. It was far too late to make another.

All that I have here condensed, he said in a quiet manner, with his grave dark regards divided between me and the fire. He threw in the word 'Sir,' from time to time, and especially when he referred to his youth: as though to request me to understand that he claimed to be nothing but what I found him. He was several times interrupted by the little bell, and had to read off messages, and send replies. Once, he had to stand without the door, and display a flag as a train passed, and make some verbal communication to the driver. In the discharge of his duties I observed him to be remarkably exact and vigilant, breaking off his discourse at a syllable, and remaining silent until what he had to do was done.

In a word, I should have set this man down as one of the safest of men to be employed in that capacity, but for the circumstance that while he was speaking to me he twice broke off with a fallen colour, turned his face towards the little bell when it did NOT ring, opened the door of the hut (which was kept shut to exclude the unhealthy damp), and looked out towards the red light near the mouth of the tunnel. On both of those occasions he came back to the fire with the inexplicable air upon him which I had remarked, without being able to define, when we were so far asunder.

Said I, when I rose to leave him: 'You almost make me think that I have met with a contented man.'

(I am afraid I must acknowledge that I said it to lead him on.)

'Well! I believe I used to be so,' he rejoined, in the low voice in which he had first spoken; 'but I am troubled, sir, I am troubled.'

'With what? What is your trouble?'

'It is very difficult to impart, sir. It is very, very difficult to speak of. If ever you make me another visit, I will try to tell you.'

'But I expressly intend to make you another visit. Say, when shall it be?'

'I go off early in the morning, and I shall be on again at ten to-morrow night, sir.'

'I will come at eleven.'

He thanked me, and went out at the door with me. 'I'll show my white light, sir, till you have found the way up. When you have found it, don't call out! And when you are at the top, don't call out!'

His manner seemed to make the place strike colder to me, but I said no more than 'Very well.'

'And when you come down to-morrow night, don't call out! Let me ask you a parting question. What made you cry "Halloa! Below there!" to-night?'

'Heaven knows! I cried something to that effect——'

'Not to that effect, sir. Those were the very words. I know them well.'

'Admit those were the very words. I said them, no doubt, because I saw you below.'

'For no other reason?'

'What other reason could I possibly have?'

'You had no feeling that they were conveyed to you in any supernatural way?'

'No.'

He wished me good night, and held up his light. I walked by the side of the down Line of rails (with a very disagreeable sensation of a train coming behind me), until I found the path. It was easier to mount than to descend, and I got back to my inn without any adventure.

Punctual to my appointment, I placed my foot on the first notch of the zig-zag next night, as the distant clocks were striking eleven. He was waiting for me at the bottom, with his white light on. 'I have not called out,' I said, when we came close together; 'may I speak now?' 'By all means, sir.' 'Good night then, and here's my hand.' 'Good night, sir, and here's mine.' With that, we walked side by side to his box, entered it, closed the door, and sat down by the fire.

'I have made up my mind, sir,' he began, bending forward as soon as we were seated, 'that you shall not have to ask me twice what troubles me. I took you for some one else yesterday evening. That troubles me.'

'That mistake?'

'No. That some one else.'

'Who is it?'

'I don't know.'

'Like me?'

'I don't know. I never saw the face. The left arm is across the face, and the right arm is waved. Violently waved. This way.'

I followed his action with my eyes, and it was the action of an arm gesticulating with the utmost passion and vehemence: 'For God's sake clear the way!'

'One moonlight night, I was sitting here, when I heard a voice cry "Halloa! Below there!" I started up, looked from that door, and saw this Some one else standing by the red light near the tunnel, waving as I just now showed you. The voice seemed hoarse with shouting, and it cried, "Look out! Look out!" And then again, "Halloa! Below there! Look out!" I caught up my lamp, turned it on red, and ran towards the figure, calling, "What's wrong? What has happened? Where?" It stood just outside the blackness of the tunnel. I advanced so close upon it that I wondered at its keeping the sleeve across its eyes. I ran right up at it, and had my hand stretched out to pull the sleeve away, when it was gone.'

'Into the tunnel.'

'No. I ran on into the tunnel, five hundred yards. I stopped, and held my lamp above my head, and saw the figures of the measured distance, and saw the wet stains stealing down the walls and trickling through the arch. I ran out again, faster than I had run in (for I had a mortal abhorrence of the place upon me), and I looked all round the red light with my own red light, and I went up the iron ladder to the gallery atop of it, and I came down again, and ran back here. I telegraphed both ways: "An alarm has been given. Is anything wrong?" The answer came back, both ways: "All well."'

Resisting the slow touch of a frozen finger tracing out my spine, I showed him how that this figure must be a deception of his sense of sight, and how that figures, originating in disease of the delicate nerves that minister to the functions of the eye, were known to have often troubled patients, some of whom had become conscious of the nature of their affliction, and had even proved it by experiments upon themselves. 'As to an imaginary cry,' said I, 'do but listen for a moment to the wind in this unnatural valley while we speak so low, and to the wild harp it makes of the telegraph wires!'

That was all very well, he returned, after we had sat listening for a while, and he ought to know something of the wind and the wires, he who so often passed long winter nights there, alone and watching. But he would beg to remark that he had not finished.

I asked his pardon, and he slowly added these words, touching my arm:

'Within six hours after the Appearance, the memorable accident on this Line happened, and within ten hours the dead and wounded were brought along through the tunnel over the spot where the figure had stood.'

A disagreeable shudder crept over me, but I did my best against it. It was not to be denied, I rejoined, that this was a remarkable coincidence, calculated deeply to impress his mind. But, it was unquestionable that remarkable coincidences did continually occur, and they must be taken into account in dealing with such a subject. Though to be sure I must admit, I added (for I thought I saw that he was going to bring the objection to bear upon me), men of common sense did not allow much for coincidences in making the ordinary calculations of life.

He again begged to remark that he had not finished.

I again begged his pardon for being betrayed into interruptions.

'This,' he said, again laying his hand upon my arm, and glancing over his shoulder with hollow eyes, 'was just a year ago. Six or seven months passed, and I had recovered from the surprise and shock, when one morning, as the day was breaking, I, standing at that door, looked towards the red light, and saw the spectre again.' He stopped, with a fixed look at me.

'Did it cry out?'

'No. It was silent.'

'Did it wave its arm?'

'No. It leaned against the shaft of the light, with both hands before the face. Like this.'

It was an action of mourning. I have seen such an attitude in stone figures on tombs.

'Did you go up to it?'

'I came in and sat down, partly to collect my thoughts, partly because it had turned me faint. When I went to the door again, daylight was above me, and the ghost was gone.'

'But nothing followed? Nothing came of this?'

He touched me on the arm with his forefinger twice or thrice, giving a ghastly nod each time:

'That very day, as a train came out of the tunnel, I noticed, at a carriage window on my side, what looked like a confusion of hands and heads, and something waved. I saw it, just in time to signal the driver, Stop! He shut off, and put his brake on, but the train drifted past here a hundred and fifty yards or more. I ran after it, and, as I went along, heard terrible screams and cries. A beautiful young lady had died instantaneously in one of the compartments, and was brought in here, and laid down on this floor between us.'

Involuntarily, I pushed my chair back, as I looked from the boards at which he pointed, to himself.

'True, sir. True. Precisely as it happened, so I tell it you.'

I could think of nothing to say, to any purpose, and my mouth was very dry. The wind and the wires took up the story with a long lamenting wail.

'Now, sir, mark this, and judge how my mind is troubled. The spectre came back, a week ago. Ever since, it has been there, now and again, by fits and starts.'

'At the light?'

'At the Danger-light.'

'What does it seem to do?'

He repeated, if possible with increased passion and vehemence, that former gesticulation of 'For God's sake clear the way!'

'I have no peace or rest for it. It calls to me, for many minutes together, in an agonized manner, "Below there! Look out! Look out!" It stands waving to me. It rings my little bell——'

'Did it ring your bell yesterday evening when I was here, and you went to the door?'

'Twice.'

'Why, see how your imagination misleads you. My eyes were on the bell, and my ears were open to the bell, and if I am a living man, it did NOT ring at those times. No, nor at any other time, except when it was rung in the natural course of physical things by the station communicating with you.'

He shook his head. 'I have never made a mistake as to that, yet, sir. I have never confused the spectre's ring with the man's. The ghost's ring is a strange vibration in the bell that it derives from nothing else, and I have not asserted that the bell stirs to the eye. I don't wonder that you failed to hear it. But *I* heard it.'

'And did the spectre seem to be there, when you looked out?'

'It WAS there.'

'Both times?'

'Both times.'

'Will you come to the door with me, and look for it now?'

He bit his under-lip as though he were somewhat unwilling, but arose. I opened the door, and stood on the step, while he stood in the doorway. There, was the Danger-light. There, was the dismal mouth of the tunnel. There, were the high wet stone walls of the cutting. There, were the stars above them.

'Do you see it?'

'No. It is not there.'

'Agreed.'

We went in again, shut the door, and resumed our seats. I was thinking how best to improve this advantage, if it might be called one, when he took up the conversation in such a matter of course way, so assuming that there could be no serious question of fact between us, that I felt myself placed in the weakest of positions.

'By this time you will fully understand, sir, that what troubles me so dreadfully, is the question, What does the spectre mean? What is its warning against? What is the danger? Where is the danger? There is danger overhanging, somewhere on the Line. Some dreadful calamity will happen. It is not to be doubted this third time, after what has gone before. But surely this is a cruel haunting of *me*. What can *I* do!'

He pulled out his handkerchief, and wiped the drops from his heated forehead.

'If I telegraph Danger, on either side of me, or on both, I can give no reason for it,' he went on, wiping the palms of his hands. 'I should get into trouble, and do no good. They would think I was mad. This is the way it would work:—Message: "Danger! Take care!" Answer: "What Danger? Where?" Message: "Don't know. But for God's sake take care!" They would displace me. What else could they do?'

His pain of mind was most pitiable to see. It was the mental torture of a conscientious man, oppressed beyond endurance by an unintelligible responsibility involving life.

'When it first stood under the Danger-light, why not tell me where that accident was to happen—if it must happen? Why not tell me how it could be averted—if it could have been averted? When on its second coming it hid its face, why not tell me instead: "She is going to die. Let them keep her at home?" If it came, on those two occasions, only to show me that its warnings were true, and so to prepare me for the third, why not warn me plainly now? And I, Lord help me! A mere poor signalman on this solitary station! Why not go to somebody with credit to be believed, and power to act!'

When I saw him in this state, I saw that for the poor man's sake, as well as for the public safety, what I had to do for the time was, to compose his mind. Therefore, setting aside all question of reality or unreality between us, I represented to him that whoever thoroughly discharged his duty, must do well, and that at least it was his comfort that he understood his duty, though he did not understand these confounding Appearances. In this effort I succeeded far better than in the attempts to reason him out of his conviction. He became calm; the occupations incidental to his post as the night advanced, began to make larger demands on his attention; and I left him at two in the morning. I had offered to stay through the night, but he would not hear of it.

That I more than once looked back at the red light as I ascended the pathway, that I did not like the red light, and that I should have slept but poorly if my bed had been under it, I see no reason to conceal. Nor, did I like the two sequences of the accident and the dead girl. I see no reason to conceal that, either.

But, what ran most in my thoughts was the consideration how ought I to act, having become the recipient of this disclosure? I had proved the man to be intelligent, vigilant, painstaking, and exact; but how long might he remain so, in his state of mind? Though in a subordinate position, still he held a most important trust, and would I (for instance) like to stake my own life on the chances of his continuing to execute it with precision?

Unable to overcome a feeling that there would be something treacherous in my communicating what he had told me, to his superiors in the Company, without first being plain with himself and proposing a middle course to him, I ultimately resolved to offer to accompany him (otherwise keeping his secret for the present) to the wisest medical practitioner we could hear of in those parts, and to take his opinion. A change in his time of duty would come round next night, he had apprized me, and he would be off an hour or two after sunrise, and on again soon after sunset. I had appointed to return accordingly.

Next evening was a lovely evening, and I walked out early to enjoy it. The sun was not yet quite down when I traversed the field-path near the top of the deep cutting. I would extend my walk for an hour, I said to myself, half an hour on and half an hour back, and it would then be time to go to my signalman's box.

Before pursuing my stroll, I stepped to the brink, and mechanically looked down, from the point from which I had first seen him. I cannot describe the thrill that seized upon me, when, close at the mouth of the tunnel, I saw the appearance of a man, with his left sleeve across his eyes, passionately waving his right arm.

The nameless horror that oppressed me passed in a moment, for in a moment I saw that this appearance of a man was a man indeed, and that there was a little group of other men standing at a short distance, to whom he seemed to be rehearsing the gesture he made. The Danger-light was not yet lighted. Against its shaft, a little low hut, entirely new to me, had been made of some wooden supports and tarpaulin. It looked no bigger than a bed.

With an irresistible sense that something was wrong—with a flashing self-reproachful fear that fatal mischief had come of my leaving the man there, and causing no one to be sent to overlook or correct what he did—I descended the notched path with all the speed I could make.

'What is the matter?'

'Signalman killed this morning, sir.'

'Not the man belonging to that box?'

'Yes, sir.'

'Not the man I know?'

'You will recognize him, sir, if you knew him,' said the man who spoke for the others, solemnly uncovering his own head and raising an end of the tarpaulin, 'for his face is quite composed.'

'O! how did this happen? How did this happen?'

'He was cut down by an engine, sir. No man in England knew his work better. But somehow he was not clear of the outer rail. It was just at broad day. He had struck the light, and had the lamp in his hand. As the engine came out of the tunnel, his back was towards her, and she cut him down. That man drove her, and was showing how it happened. Show the gentleman, Tom.'

The man, who wore a rough dark dress, stepped back to his former place at the mouth of the tunnel:

'Coming round the curve in the tunnel, sir, I saw him at the end, like as if I saw him down a perspective-glass. There was no time to check speed, and I knew him to be very careful. As he didn't seem to take heed of the whistle, I shut it off when we were running down upon him, and called to him as loud as I could call.'

'What did you say?'

'I said, Below there! Look out! Look out! For God's sake clear the way!'

I started.

'Ah! it was a dreadful time, sir. I never left off calling to him. I put this arm before my eyes, not to see, and I waved this arm to the last; but it was no use.'

I may point out the coincidence that the warning of the Engine-Driver included, not only the words which the unfortunate Signalman had repeated to me as haunting him, but also the words which I myself—not he —had attached, and that only in my own mind, to the gesticulation he had imitated.

THE END

SIKES AND NANCY

'I have been trying, alone by myself, the Oliver Twist murder,' Dickens told a friend in 1863, 'but have got something so horrible out of it that I am afraid to try it in public' (*N*, iii. 353). Five years later, when preparing for his Farewell tour, he revived the notion, partly (he maintained) because a new attraction was necessary to ensure that his impresarios, Messrs. Chappell, would not lose on their liberal payment of £80 a performance, but also because, as he told Forster, 'I wanted to leave behind me the recollection of something very passionate and dramatic, done with simple means, if the art would justify the theme' (*N*, iii. 679). None of his items except the storm-scene in *Copperfield* had enabled him to display his talent for 'very passionate' acting. So *Sikes and Nancy* was devised, in the early autumn of 1868. 'When you come to see me on Monday,' he wrote to George Dolby on 29 September, 'you shall look through the Murder as I have arranged it. It is very horrible, but very dramatic. If I decide on doing it at all, we will strike boldly for London' (MS Huntington).

His uncertainty about whether performing it was advisable (evident back in 1863) and whether 'the art would justify the theme' appears in various letters and conversations during the next few weeks. From 6 October until Christmas, when he was giving his Farewell readings, *Sikes* was still not introduced into the repertoire. Instead he decided to give a special trial performance before an invited audience who could 'advise' him. This took place in St. James's Hall on 14 November; for accounts of it, see Kent, pp. 253–6, and Dolby, pp. 349–53. It was a very full-dress effort, with printed tickets, a distinguished audience of about a hundred, a feast laid on to assist them in their advisory functions—and some members of the press. The *Times* critic, like everyone else, was enormously impressed: 'Mr. Dickens displayed a degree of force to which nothing that he has hitherto done can be compared. He has always trembled on the boundary line that separates the reader from the actor; in this case he clears it by a leap' (17 November 1868). Edmund Yates recorded that when

... gradually warming with excitement, he flung aside his book and acted the scene of the murder, shrieked the terrified pleadings of the girl, growled the brutal savagery of the murderer, brought looks, tones, gestures simultaneously into play to illustrate his meaning, there was not one, not even of those who had known him best or who believed in him most, but was astonished at the power and the versatility of his genius. ('Mr. Charles Dickens's New Reading', *Tinsley's Magazine*, iv (1869), 62)

Dickens noted, with unconcealed glee, that at the end all his guests were 'unmistakably pale, and had horror-stricken faces', and he was similarly exultant when William Harness (the Shakespearean scholar) wrote to him, the day after,

... and saying it was 'a most amazing and terrific thing', added, 'but I am bound to tell you that I had an almost irresistible impulse upon me to *scream*, and that, if anyone had cried out, I am certain I should have followed.' He had no idea that, on the night, Priestley, the great ladies' doctor, had taken me aside and said: 'My dear Dickens, you may rely upon it that if one woman cries out when you murder the girl, there will be a contagion of hysteria all over this place.' It is impossible to soften it without spoiling it, and you may suppose that I am rather anxious to discover how it goes on the Fifth of January!!! . . . I asked Mrs. Keeley, the famous actress, who was at the experiment: 'What do *you* say? Do it or not?' 'Why, of course, do it,' she replied. 'Having got at such an effect as that, it must be done. But,' rolling her large black eyes very slowly, and speaking very distinctly, 'the public have been looking out for a sensation these last fifty years or so, and by Heaven they have got it!' With which words, and a long breath and a long stare, she became speechless. Again, you may suppose that I am a little anxious! (*N*, iii. 687)

Ninety out of the hundred present urged him to include this sensational piece in his repertoire, but the opponents included two formidable friends, Forster and Dolby (both of whom had tried from the start to dissuade him from the notion), and also his eldest son Charley. 'The finest thing I ever heard, but don't do it' was Charley's verdict earlier, after hearing a rehearsal, and now, after the 'trial performance', though pronouncing it 'finer even than I expected', he reiterated his advice—and, to Dickens's 'intense amazement', even the hard-boiled vulgarian Edmund Yates joined in with 'I agree with Charley, Sir' ('Reminiscences of my Father', *Windsor Magazine*, Christmas Supplement 1934, pp. 28–9). But Dickens was by now in no mood to be dissuaded. The trial performance was intended (I surmise) less as an occasion for seriously listening to advice than as a triumphal demonstration which would both silence Forster and the other doubters and remove his own private reservations. As George Dolby had already found, and was often to find later, 'he would listen to no remonstrance in respect of it' (Dolby, p. 344).

Dickens's worry—at least explicitly—had been mainly whether this horrific reading would disturb his relationship with his public: 'I have no doubt that I could petrify an audience . . . But whether the impression would not be so horrible as to keep them away another time, is what I cannot satisfy myself upon' (*N*, iii. 674). It is significant—and both endearing and humiliating—that his apprehensions were thus limited to whether he would please his public and whether Messrs. Chappell's profits might suffer. Dolby's and Charley's concern was (very justly, as it proved) for his health, already precarious and likely to be further undermined by a reading so exhausting both physically and emotionally. Forster's objection was partly the same, but partly an aesthetic distaste for the platform exploitation of this sensational subject. It may be remarked that dramatizations of *Oliver Twist* were among the tiny number of plays currently banned by the Lord Chamberlain, precisely because of the violence of audiences' reaction to the murder scene—and British readers may recall that the television version of this episode, in 1962, led to questions being asked in the House of Commons and the BBC's being reprimanded. Probably no episode in Victorian fiction has had such a stormy theatrical history.

After the trial reading, however, advice of a quite different tenor came from two other friends, Charles Kent and Wilkie Collins, who both urged—independently, it would seem—that the Reading should not end, as it then did, with Sikes's leaving the room where he had murdered Nancy, but should continue with his attempts to escape from his conscience and from the authorities, and should culminate in his death. 'My dear fellow,' he wrote to Kent on 16 November, 'believe me, no audience on earth could be held for ten minutes after the girl's death. Give them time, and they would be revengeful for having had such a strain put upon them. Trust me to be right. I stand there, and I know' (*N*, iii. 678). Three weeks later, however, he had changed his mind and was telling Collins that he had devised just such an extension, and was 'trying it daily with the object of rising from that blank state of horror into a fierce and passionate rush for the end. As yet I cannot make a certain effect of it; but when I shall have gone over it as many score of times as over the rest of that reading, perhaps I may strike one out' (*N*, iii. 681). Several critics, however, including Edmund Yates in the article cited above, regretted that the Reading continued as far as it did; it should have ended, they thought, with the murder of Nancy.

The original text was privately printed in or about September 1868 with *The Chimes*, as was noted in the headnote to that item. This prompt-copy, now in the Berg Collection, is entitled *Sikes and Nancy*: | *A Reading | from | Oliver Twist*. | *By Charles Dickens*. | (printed by William Clowes and Sons; text paginated 79–112). The narrative is divided into three chapters. Chapters I and II are taken from chs. 45 and 46 of the novel, and begin and end as they had done. Thus, Chapter I shows Fagin setting Bolter on to 'dodge' Nancy; Chapter II is the scene at London Bridge in which Nancy—with Bolter eavesdropping—agrees to help Mr. Brownlow and Rose Maylie (but a few phrases from Nancy's earlier encounter with Rose in ch. 40 are interpolated). Chapter III is mostly taken from ch. 47 (Sikes, incensed by Fagin, murders Nancy), but it ends with the opening page of ch. 48 (dawn breaks, and Sikes leaves the house). The text of the novel was abridged, but not very severely; subsequent manuscript deletions reduced its length by about one-sixth. One other form of revision may be noted: Sikes loses his oaths. 'Damme!' becomes 'Hallo!', and 'Hell's Fire!' and another 'Damme!' are deleted. Many more stage-directions are inscribed in the margin than Dickens usually employed at this stage of his career.

The extra narrative devised on the suggestion of Kent and Collins is written in at the end of the *Berg* copy—three manuscript pages, equivalent to about three-and-a-half printed pages. This is a brilliantly condensed version of parts of chs. 48 and 50, concluding with the death of Sikes and his dog (the end of ch. 50). The text here contains rewriting more interesting than in any of the other Readings. Events are seen through Sikes's eyes which had not been presented that way in the novel. A good example is the moment when he is taking refuge at Folly Ditch. 'But what man ever escaped the men who are after you?' exclaims the unnamed fellow-thief (a speech not to be found in the novel), and the Reading continues: 'Hark! A great sound coming on like a rushing fire! What! Tracked so soon? The hunt was up already? Lights gleaming below, voices in loud and earnest talk, . . .' The ejaculated words from 'Hark!' to 'up already?'—obviously Sikes's terrified view of the situation—have no equivalent in the novel, the text of which resumes with 'There were lights gleaming below . . .' (and the Reading text is shorter and sharper, omitting 'There were' and substituting 'talk' for the more cumbersome 'conversation').

This revised text was what Dickens performed in public, and he had a new edition of the Reading privately printed, incorporating the extension to the narrative: *Sikes and Nancy*: | *A Reading*. | *By Charles Dickens*. (printed by C. Whiting; text paginated 3–47). It is a sign of the particular significance which he attached to this item that he both went to all this trouble of giving an elaborate trial performance, and adding a substantial episode to the narrative, and also had a new edition printed. As has been seen, he was generally frugal over such printings, and would make do with a much amended prompt-copy He must then have made a new prompt-copy of *Sikes and Nancy*, writing his stage-directions, etc., in a copy of the Whiting edition; but its present whereabouts—if it has survived—are unknown. Charles Kent does not seem to have seen it (for the copy he describes is *Berg*), nor has its existence ever been recorded. Fortunately, however, a copy of this edition survives into which its first owner (Adeline Billington) had transcribed Dickens's underlinings, stage-directions, etc. She was an actress whom he knew and admired; he must both have given her this copy, and lent her his own prompt-copy so that she could transcribe his markings. They differ considerably from those in *Berg*, but there are enough agreements—particularly in the stage-directions—to make it certain that this is indeed a careful transcription of his performance-signs and textual emendations. A notable feature of this copy is the elaboration of its performance-signs—much heavier than in *Berg*, though that too was thoroughly sign-posted. Underlinings are not merely single or double, but treble or even quadruple. Significant pauses are indicated by the insertion of extra dashes (making the printed dash resemble a large 'equals' sign), and emphatic climaxes are marked by the insertion of as many as four exclamation-marks. In the text below, the 'equals' is represented by a long (2-em) dash. For further particulars, see my article in *TLS*, 11 June 1971, pp. 681–2.

Adeline Billington later gave this copy to the theatrical manager John Hollingshead, who in 1883 gave it to Henry Irving. It is now in the Suzannet Collection. Representing the latest state of Dickens's text, it (*Suzannet*) is used as the copy-text for the present edition; but the footnotes record some variants in *Berg*.

A limited edition of *Sikes and Nancy* (only 250 copies for sale) was published in 1921 by Henry Sotheran, with a useful Introduction by John Harrison Stonehouse. This is a facsimile of a proof-copy of the Whiting edition (without any marks or writing by Dickens). It differs from *Suzannet* in a few details of spelling and punctuation.

The first public performance of *Sikes and Nancy* was given in St. James's Hall on 5 January 1869, when Dickens resumed his farewell series after a Christmas holiday. It received what would now be called rave reviews; a number of these were collected in a pamphlet—*Mr. Charles Dickens's Farewell Readings* (undated; printed by J. Mallett, London). There is a copy, very rare or perhaps unique, in Dickens House. Critics then and during the provincial tour which immediately followed concurred in describing this as Dickens's most remarkable platform feat—a performance which 'our greatest histrionic artists might deem it the height of their ambition to produce' (*Daily Telegraph*, 6 January 1869). 'Never, probably, through the force of mere reading was a vast concourse held so completely within the grasp of one man . . . Every personage in the tale is played with a distinctness that belongs to the highest order of acting' (*The Times*, 8 January 1869). As the earlier *Times* report had indicated, Dickens here abandoned the convention of the public-reader who acknowledges the presence of his audience and only half-acts his personages. One forgot that it was Dickens who was reading, said another critic: 'Fagin with his mingled fiendish glee and terror and inhuman cunning seems actually before us' (*Glasgow Daily Herald*, 23 February 1869). The characterization of Fagin was generally reckoned the most remarkable achievement. It was said to be quite unlike the conventional 'Stage-Jew' of the period:

... he is sordid, mean, avaricious, and revengeful; and Mr. Dickens shows him to you in every phase. You read it in his rounded shoulders, in his sunken chin, in his puckered cheeks and hanging brow, in his gleaming eyes, and quivering, clutching hands, in the lithe shiftiness of his movements, and the intense earnestness of his attitudes. (Edmund Yates, loc. cit.)

Many reports noted how Dickens thus took on the physical shape, as well as the voice, of the Jew.

For some critics, including Charles Kent (whose chapter on the Reading is of great interest), Nancy was an even finer impersonation. Particularly in her final appeal to Sikes, she was found very moving, and this is the more surprising because her long speeches are difficult and (one would have thought) theatrically unrewarding to deliver: but, as one critic usefully noted, 'Here the acting of Mr. Dickens is much beyond his writing, which strikes us as fantastic and unreal'; indeed, 'no language we think will praise too highly the passionate power with which he delivered the appeal to Sikes' (*Bath Chronicle*, 4 February 1869). Nothing in the previous Readings, wrote another critic, could compare with this moment and her 'burning words' to Mr. Brownlow—

There was an amount of natural and genuine acting which we had not expected to see now-a-days. Without the accessories of the stage, it was more truthful and effective than anything of the kind we have ever seen on the stage. It was a masterpiece of reading, quite unparalleled in its way; and it is with no small pride one feels it can honestly be said that Mr. Dickens is the greatest reader of the greatest writer of the age. (*Freeman's Journal* (Dublin), 14 January 1869)

At least one critic, however, judged Nancy the one character who fell below the high level of vivid realism present elsewhere in the Reading: but he added, 'Instead of being surprised at this, however, it is a matter of wonder how Mr. Dickens should be able to throw such dramatic intensity into the simple reading of a narrative' (*Yorkshire Post*, 17 April 1869).

Adverse criticism of this Reading is very scanty. A surprising one comes from Dickens's young colleague Percy Fitzgerald, who was usually sycophantic in his admiration of the Chief: 'Boz had persuaded himself that this was one of his most powerful and effective efforts for the Readings. But this was not the general opinion. It was a gruesome thing enough, but somewhat overstrained and melodramatic ... The Dublin audience showed little appreciation' (*Memories of Charles Dickens* (Bristol 1913), p. 61). Fitzgerald certainly seems wrong about 'the general opinion', however: and even that Dublin performance, which had not satisfied Dickens either, elicited the ecstatic notice quoted above.

The tribute which pleased Dickens most was Macready's, which he enjoyed quoting. He had insisted on touring into Cheltenham, so that the great actor (living there in his retirement) could hear this item, and the result was gratifying. Macready gasped out: ' ... "In my—er—best times—er—you remember them, my dear boy—er—gone, gone!—no," with great emphasis again,—"it comes to this—er—TWO MACBETHS!" with extraordinary energy' (*N*, iii. 704). The tribute to its effect most often cited by biographers, however, is unfortunately based on a misreading of Forster—the famous occasion when, during a performance at Clifton, 'we had from a dozen to twenty ladies borne out, stiff and rigid, at various times' (*N*, iii. 702). This episode is often quoted as evidence of the power of *Sikes and Nancy*, but a more careful reading of Forster (who quotes this letter in *Life*, p. 801) and a study of the local newspapers show that this 'contagion of fainting' occurred during a performance of *Copperfield* and *The Trial*. One cannot but regret, however, having to spoil a story so *ben trovato*.[1]

The effect of the Reading upon Dickens himself was remarkable, and is indisputable. His desire to repeat it became a fierce obsession. There are the extraordinary stories of his sudden fury when Dolby, seeing how badly it was affecting his health, tried to reduce the number of scheduled performances, and of how, having 'worked himself up to a pitch of excitement' over the murder, this mood 'invariably recurred later on in the evening after the audience had left, either in the form of great hilarity or a desire to be once more on the platform, or in a craving to do the work over again' (Dolby, pp. 379–88). Clearly his attachment to this piece went far beyond the understandable satisfaction of a professional performer in being able to create such an impression and win such acclaim for his talents. Recent biographers have speculated about the more arcane motivation behind this choice of subject and obsession with performing it, despite his friends' persuasions and the clear evidence of its effect upon his health.

The Readings' ill effects upon him must have been increased by his practice of never (except once) ending a performance with this item. He had an endearing desire to send his audience away feeling cheerful, so *Sikes* almost always appeared in a triple-bill, preceded by *Boots* and followed by *Mrs. Gamp* or *Bob Sawyer*. (Occasionally he read *Sikes* first, and followed it by the *Carol*.) At the end of *Sikes* his pulse-rate, normally 72, would be as high as 124, and he would often have to lie on a sofa, quite unable to speak a word, for an interval of ten minutes before gathering his strength and staggering back to the platform to read another item. (His doctor's records of his pulse-rates during the anxious final season of 1870 are printed in *Dickens to his Oldest Friend*, ed. Walter Dexter (1932), pp. 253–4.) If I might cite some personal experience here: I have performed *Sikes and Nancy*, in a slightly abbreviated and doubtless much less energetic form, and while younger and in better health than Dickens then was, and I always put it at the end of a programme, for I would certainly find intolerable the strain of then proceeding to another lengthy item. But Dickens was often doing this four times a week during a tour when he was eventually 'extremely giddy, extremely uncertain of my footing . . . and extremely indisposed to raise my hands to my head' (*N*, iii. 720). No wonder that many of

---

[1] In '*Sikes and Nancy*: Dickens's Last Reading' (*TLS*, 11 June 1971, pp. 681–2) I also show that another often cited story about this Reading—that Dickens performed it as many as ten times a week—is based on a mistranscription of a letter (*N*, iii. 708). He never read it more than four times a week. In this essay I also argue that his decision to give this Reading may have been affected by two factors: increasing competition among recitalists in the late 1860s, which led to their trying to devise new sensations, and the great popularity among recitalists (Henry Irving being a conspicuous instance) of Thomas Hood's poem about a murderer, 'The Dream of Eugene Aram'. Hood's poem may indeed also have influenced the writing of this part of *Oliver Twist*.

his friends thought, as did Wilkie Collins, that this Reading 'did more to kill Dickens than all his work put together' (Kenneth Robinson, *Wilkie Collins* (1951), p. 243).

On his way to the platform, the last time he performed *Sikes and Nancy*, he whispered to Charles Kent: 'I shall tear myself to pieces' (Kent, p. 87). But he knew that this effort had been foolish, maybe even suicidal; several weeks earlier he had acknowledged, in a letter, what he around this time said to the faithful Dolby, that he had torn himself to pieces too often in this way—'he confessed to me at this time that it was madness ever to have given the "Murder" Reading, under the conditions of a travelling life, and worse than madness to have given it with such frequency' (Dolby, p. 442; cf. *N*, iii. 761). Nevertheless no item was performed more often in the 1870 Farewells, and though the final performance was devoted to the old favourites, the *Carol* and *Trial*, *Sikes* was the *pièce de résistance* in his penultimate appearance on 8 March 1870. It is reported, moreover, that a day or two before his death he was discovered in the grounds at Gad's Hill re-enacting the murder of Nancy (John Hollingshead, *According to my Lights* (1900), p. 19).

Sikes and Nancy

CHAPTER I

FAGIN the receiver of stolen goods was up, betimes, one morning, and waited impatiently for the appearance of his new associate, Noah Claypole, otherwise Morris Bolter; who at length presented himself, and, cutting a monstrous slice of bread, commenced a voracious assault on the breakfast.[1]

'Bolter, *Bolter*.'

'Well, here I am. What's the matter? Don't yer ask me to do anything till I have done eating. That's a great fault in this place. Yer never get time enough over yer meals.'

'You can talk as you eat, can't you?'

'Oh yes, I can talk. I get on better when I talk. *Talk away*. Yer won't interrupt me.'

There seemed, indeed, no great fear of anything interrupting him, as he had evidently sat down with a determination to do a deal of business. *

'I want you, Bolter,' *leaning over the table*, 'to do a piece of work for me, my dear, that needs great care and caution.'

'I say, don't yer go a-shoving me into danger, yer know. That don't suit me, that don't; and so I tell yer.'

'There's not the smallest danger in it—not the very smallest; it's only to *dodge a woman*.'[2]

'An old woman?'[3]

'A young one.'

'I can do that pretty well. I was a regular sneak when I was at school. What am I to dodge her for? Not to——'

'Not to do anything, but tell me where she goes, who she sees, and, if possible, what she says; to remember the street, if it is a street, or the house, if it is a house; and to bring me back all the information you can.'

'What'll yer give me?'

'If you do it well, a pound, my dear. One pound. And that's what I never gave yet, for any job of work where there wasn't valuable consideration to be got.'

'Who is she?'

---

[1] On the character of 'the half-knowing, half-stupid Claypole, . . . a light is thrown by the "reading" that is scarcely to be found in the book'. This opening scene 'caused now and then a little mirth' (*The Times*, 8 January 1869).

[2] *woman* doubly underlined.

[3] Question-mark (as in the novel and in *Berg*) editorially supplied.

'One of us.'

'Oh Lor! Yer doubtful of her, are yer?'

'She has found out some new friends, my dear, and I must know who they are.'

'I see. Ha! ha! ha! I'm your man. Where is she? Where am I to wait for her? Where am I to go?'

'All that, my dear, you shall hear from me. I'll point her out at the proper time. You keep ready, in the clothes I have got here for you, and leave the rest to me.'

That night, and the next, and the next again, the spy sat booted and equipped in the disguise of a carter: ready to turn out at a word from Fagin. Six nights passed, and on each, Fagin came home with a disappointed face, and briefly intimated that it was not yet time. On the seventh he returned exultant. It was Sunday Night.

'She goes abroad to-night,' said Fagin, 'and on the right errand, I'm sure; for she has been alone all day, and the man she is afraid of will not be back much before daybreak. Come with me! Quick!'

They left the house, and, stealing through a labyrinth of streets, arrived at length before a public-house. It was past eleven o'clock, and the door was closed; but it opened softly as Fagin gave a low whistle. They entered, without noise.

Scarcely venturing to whisper, but substituting dumb show for words, Fagin pointed out a pane of glass high in the wall to Noah, and signed to him to climb up, on a piece of furniture below it, and observe the person in the adjoining room.

'Is that the woman?'

Fagin nodded 'yes'.

'I can't see her face well. She is looking down, and the candle is behind her.'

'Stay there.' He signed to the lad, who had opened the house-door to them; who withdrew—entered the room adjoining, and, under pretence of snuffing the candle, moved it in the required position; then he spoke to the girl, causing her to raise her face.

'I see her now!'

'Plainly?'

'I should know her among a thousand.'[1]

The spy descended, the room-door opened, and the girl came out. Fagin drew him behind a small partition, and they held their breath as she passed within a few feet of their place of concealment, and emerged by the door at which they had entered.

'*After her!!* To the *left*. Take the left hand, and keep on the other side. *After her!!*'[2]

---

[1] Marginal stage-direction *Beckon down.*

[2] All underlinings double in this paragraph: also for *She looked nervously round*, below.

The spy darted off; and, by the light of the street lamps, saw the girl's retreating figure, already at some distance before him. He advanced as near as he considered prudent, and kept on the opposite side of the street. *She looked nervously round.* She seemed to gather courage as she advanced, and to walk with a steadier and firmer step. The spy preserved the same relative distance between them, and followed.

CHAPTER II

THE churches chimed three quarters past eleven, as the two figures emerged on London Bridge. The young woman advanced with a swift and rapid step, and looked about her as though in quest of some expected object; the young man, who slunk along in the deepest shadow he could find, and, at some distance, accommodated his pace to hers: stopping when she stopped: and as she moved again, creeping stealthily on: but never allowing himself, in the ardour of his pursuit, to gain upon her. Thus, they crossed the bridge, from the Middlesex to the Surrey shore, when the woman, disappointed in her anxious scrutiny of the foot-passengers, turned back. The movement was sudden; but the man was not thrown off his guard by it; for, shrinking into one of the recesses which surmount the piers of the bridge, and leaning over the parapet the better to conceal his figure, he suffered her to pass. When she was about the same distance in advance as she had been before, he slipped quietly down, and followed her again. At nearly the centre of the bridge she stopped. He stopped.

It was a very dark night. The day had been unfavourable, and at that hour and place there were few people stirring. Such as there were, hurried past: possibly without seeing, certainly without noticing, either the woman, or the man. Their appearance was not attractive of such of London's destitute population, as chanced to take their way over the bridge that night; and they stood there in silence: neither speaking nor spoken to.[1]

The girl had taken a few turns to and fro—closely watched by her hidden observer—*when the heavy bell of St. Paul's tolled for the death of another day. Midnight had come upon the crowded city. Upon the palace, the night-cellar, the jail, the madhouse: the chambers of birth and death, of health and sickness, upon the rigid face of the corpse and the calm sleep of the child.*

A young lady, accompanied by a grey-haired gentleman, alighted from a hackney-carriage. They had scarcely set foot upon the pavement of the bridge, when the girl started, and joined them.

'*Not here*!! I am afraid to speak to you here. Come away—out of the public road—down the steps yonder!'[2]

[1] *Berg* here included the next paragraph in the novel ('A mist hung over the river . . .'), until Dickens deleted it.   [2] Marginal stage-direction *Point R[ight]*.

~~his fury~~ and he beat it twice ~~████████████~~
~~████████~~ upon the upturned face that almost
touched his own.

She staggered and fell ~~████████████████~~

but raising herself on her knees,

she

~~knees~~ drew from her bosom a white handkerchief—
Rose Maylie's ~~████~~—and holding it up ~~████~~
~~████████ as high~~ towards Heaven ~~as her feeble~~
~~████████████~~, breathed one prayer for
mercy to her Maker.

It was a ghastly figure to look upon. The murderer staggering backward to the wall, and shutting
out the sight with his hand, seized a heavy club
and struck her down.

mystery

~~Of all bad deeds that,~~ under cover of the darkness,
had been committed within wide London's bounds
since night hung over it, that was the worst. Of
all the horrors that rose with an ill scent upon the
~~morning air, that was the foulest and most cruel.~~

The ~~████ the~~ bright sun ~~████████████████~~

light alone but new life, and hope, and freshness to
man, burst upon the crowded city in clear and
radiant glory. Through costly-coloured glass and
paper-mended window, through cathedral dome and
rotten crevice, it shed its equal ray. It lighted up
the room where the murdered woman lay. It did.
He tried to shut it out, but it would stream in. If
the sight had been a ghastly one in the dull morning, what was it, now, in all that brilliant light!

Terra

To

The End

He had not moved; he had been afraid to stir.
There had been a moan and motion of the hand;
and, with terror added to rage, he had struck and
struck again. Once he threw a rug over it; but it
was worse to fancy the eyes, and imagine them
moving towards him, than to see them glaring upward, as if watching the reflection of the pool of
gore that quivered and danced in the sunlight on
the ceiling. He had plucked it off again. And
there was the body—mere flesh and blood, no more
—but such flesh, and so much blood!

He struck a light, kindled the fire, and thrust the
club into it. There was hair upon the end, which

From the *Sikes and Nancy* prompt-copy (*Berg*). Shows 'double-interrupted' as well
as continuous underlining. The apparent underlining of 'been afraid to stir' and the
apparent deletion after 'He struck a' are blots from the opposite page

The steps to which she pointed, were those which, on the Surrey bank, and on the same side of the bridge as Saint Saviour's Church, form a landing-stairs from the river. To this spot the spy hastened unobserved; and after a moment's survey of the place, he began to descend.

These stairs are a part of the bridge; they consist of three flights. Just below the end of the second, going down, the stone wall on the left terminates in an ornamental pilaster facing towards the Thames.[1] At this point the lower steps widen: so that a person turning that angle of the wall, is necessarily unseen by any others on the stairs who chance to be above, if only a step. The spy looked hastily round, when he reached this point; and as there seemed no better place of concealment, and as the tide being out there was plenty of room, he slipped aside, with his back to the pilaster, and there waited: pretty certain that they would come no lower down.

So tardily went the time in this lonely place, and so eager was the spy, that he was on the point of emerging from his hiding-place, and regaining the road above, when he heard the sound of footsteps, and directly afterwards of voices almost close at his ear.

He drew himself straight upright against the wall, and listened attentively.

'This is far enough,' *said a voice, which was evidently that of the gentleman.* 'I will not suffer the young lady to go any further. Many people would have distrusted you too much to have come even so far, but you see I am willing to humour you.'

'To humour me!' *cried the voice of the girl* whom he had followed.[2] 'You're considerate, indeed, sir. To humour me! Well, well, it's no matter.'

'Why, for what purpose can you have brought us to this strange place? Why not have let me speak to you, above there, where it is light, and there is something stirring, instead of bringing us to this dark and dismal hole?'

'I told you before, that I was afraid to speak to you there. I don't know why it is,' *said the girl shuddering,*[3] 'but I have such a fear and dread upon me to-night that I can hardly stand.'

'A fear of what?'

'I scarcely know of what—I wish I did. Horrible thoughts of *death*— and *shrouds* with *blood*[4] upon them—and a fear that has made me burn as if I was on fire—have been upon me all day. I was reading a book to-night, to while the time away, and the same things came into the print.'

---

[1] Sir Frederick Pollock noted how graphically Dickens conjured up this London Bridge scene by gestures and voice: 'What an actor he would have made! what a success he must have had if he had gone to the bar!' (*Personal Remembrances* (1887), ii. 199).

[2] The underlining should probably have continued to the end of this sentence, as in *Berg*.

[3] Marginal stage-direction *Shudder*.

[4] *blood* doubly underlined.

'Imagination!'

'No imagination. I swear I saw "*coffin*"[1] written in every page of the book in large black letters,—aye, and they carried one close to me, in the streets to-night.'

'There is nothing unusual in that. They have passed me often.'

'*Real ones.*[2] This was not.'

'Pray speak to her kindly,' said the young lady to the grey-haired gentleman. 'Poor creature! She seems to need it.'

'Bless you, miss, for that! Your haughty religious people would have held their heads up to see me as I am to-night, and would have preached of flames and vengeance. Oh,[3] dear lady, why ar'n't those who claim to be God's own folks, as gentle and as kind to us poor wretches as you!'[4]

—'You were not here last Sunday night, girl, as you appointed.'

'I couldn't come. I was kept by force.'

'By whom?'

'*Bill——Sikes*[5]—him that I told the young lady of before.'

'You were not suspected of holding any communication with anybody on the subject which has brought us here to-night, I hope?'

'No,' replied the girl, shaking her head.[6] 'It's not very easy for me to leave him unless he knows why; I couldn't have seen the lady when I did, but that I gave him a drink of *laudanum* before I came away.'

'Did he awake before you returned?'

'No; and neither he nor any of them suspect me.'

'Good. Now listen to me. I am Mr. Brownlow, this young lady's friend. I wish you, in this young lady's interest, and for her sake, to deliver up Fagin.'

'Fagin! I will not do it! I will never do it! Devil that he is, and worse than devil as he has been to me, as my Teacher in all Devilry, I will never do it.'

'Why?'

'For the reason that, bad life as he has led, I have led a bad life too; for the reason that there are many of us who have kept the same courses together, and I'll not turn upon them, who might—any of them—have turned upon me, but didn't, bad as they are. Last, for the reason—(*how*

---

[1] *coffin* doubly underlined, and enclosed in double quotation-marks.

[2] Italic in the novel, and in *Berg* and *Suzannet*, where it is also doubly underlined.

[3] *Oh* in the novel, altered to *Ah* in *Berg*.

[4] In *Berg*, Mr. Brownlow's speech here about 'the Mussulman' was printed, amended, and finally deleted.

[5] Double dash after *Bill*, and *Sikes* is doubly underlined.

[6] In *Berg*, the phrase 'replied the girl, shaking her head' is underlined. There are other such occasions where underlining is used in *Berg*, more often than in *Suzannet*, simply to isolate a narrative phrase inside a dialogue; they will not be mentioned hereafter.

can I say it with the young lady here!)[1]—that, among them, there is one—
this Bill—this Sikes—the most desperate of all—*that I can't leave.*[2] *
Whether it is God's wrath for the wrong I have done, I don't know, but I
am drawn back to him through everything, and I should be, I believe, if I
knew that I was to *die* by his hand!'

'But, put one man—not him—not one of the gang—the one man Monks
into my hands, and leave him to me to deal with.'

'What if he turns against the others?'

'I promise you that, in that case, there the matter shall rest; they shall
go scot free.'

'Have I the lady's promise for that?'

'You have,' replied Rose Maylie, the young lady.

'I have been a liar, and among liars from a little child, but I will take
your words.'

After receiving an assurance from both, that she might safely do so,
she proceeded in a voice so low that it was often difficult for the listener
to discover even the purport of what she said, to describe the means by
which this one man Monks might be found and taken. * But nothing
would have induced her to compromise one of her own companions;
little reason though she had, poor wretch! to spare them.

'Now,' said the gentleman, when she had finished, 'you have given us
most valuable assistance, young woman, and I wish you to be the better
for it. What can I do to serve you?'

'Nothing.'

'You will not persist in saying that; think now; take time. Tell me.'

'Nothing, sir. You can do nothing to help me. I am past all hope.'

'You put yourself beyond the pale of hope. The past has been a dreary
waste with you, of youthful energies mis-spent, and such treasures
lavished, as the Creator bestows but once and never grants again, but, *for
the future, you may hope!*[3] [I do not say that it is in our power to offer
you peace of heart and mind, for that must come as you seek it; but a
quiet asylum, either in England, or, if you fear to remain here, in some
foreign country, it is not only within the compass of our ability but our
most anxious wish to secure you. Before the dawn of morning, before this
river wakes to the first glimpse of daylight, you shall be placed as entirely
beyond the reach of your former associates, and leave as complete an
absence of all trace behind you, as if you were to disappear from the earth
this moment.] Come! I would not have you go back to exchange one word

---

[1] Double vertical lines in the margin against the bracketed interjection. The following
sentences are taken from ch. 40.

[2] *that I can't leave*, and *die* below, doubly underlined.

[3] *future* doubly underlined. A pencilled footnote (not, it would seem, in the handwriting of either Adeline Billington or John Hollingshead) reads: 'The passage in square
brackets deleted'. The passage is deleted, in the same ink as the rest of the manuscript
underlinings and words.

with any old companion, or take one look at any old haunt. Quit them all, while there is time and opportunity!'

'She will be persuaded now,' cried the young lady.

'I fear not, my dear.'

'*No, sir—no, miss*.[1] I am chained to my old life. I *loathe* and *hate* it, but I cannot *leave* it.—When ladies as young and good, as happy and beautiful as you, miss, give away your hearts, love will carry even you all lengths.[2] When such as I, who have no certain roof but the coffin-lid, and no friend in sickness or death but the hospital-nurse, set our rotten hearts on any man, who can hope to cure us![3]—This fear comes over me again. I must go home. Let us part. I shall be watched or seen.[4] *Go! Go!* If I have done you any service, all I ask is, leave me, and let me go my way alone.'

'Take this purse,' cried the young lady.[5] 'Take it for my sake, that you may have some resource in an hour of need and trouble.'

'*No!* I have not done this for *money*. *Let me have that to think of*.[6] And yet——give me something that you have worn—I should like to have something—*no, no,* not a *ring*, they'd rob me of that—your *gloves* or *handkerchief*—anything that I can keep, as having belonged to you. There. *Bless you! God bless you!! Good-night, good-night!*'

The agitation of the girl, and the apprehension of some discovery which would subject her to violence, seemed to determine the gentleman to leave her. The sound of retreating footsteps followed, and the voices ceased. *

After a time Nancy ascended to the street.[7] The spy remained on his post for some minutes, and then, *after peeping out*, to make sure that he was unobserved, darted away, and made for Fagin's house as fast as his legs would carry him.

---

[1] *No, sir* and *miss* doubly underlined. The novel does not contain 'no, miss'. This insertion, like other differences between the novel and the Reading texts, enlarges Rose Maylie's prominence in this encounter.

[2] In *Berg* a marginal stage-direction is written against the next sentence—*Start coming.* The 'Start' presumably came at 'This fear comes over me . . .'

[3] In *Berg,* the next sentence from ch. 40 is here inserted in Dickens's handwriting, and subsequently deleted: 'Pity us, Lady! pity us, for having only one feeling of the woman left, and for having that turned—by a heavy judgment—from a comfort and a pride, into a new means of suffering.—'

[4] Marginal stage-direction *Look Round with Terror.* The following *Go! Go!* is doubly underlined.

[5] Marginal stage-direction *Action.*

[6] In the remainder of this paragraph, there is a double dash after 'And yet'; *ring* is trebly underlined; *handkerchief* and *God bless you!! Good-night, good-night!* are doubly underlined. The dash after 'they'd rob me of that' (a manuscript insertion) is editorially supplied.

[7] In the margin there is a vertical line against the remainder of this paragraph.

CHAPTER III

It was nearly two hours before daybreak; that time which in the autumn of the year, may be truly called the dead of night; when the streets are silent and deserted; when even sound appears to slumber, and profligacy and riot have staggered home to dream; it was at this still and silent hour, that Fagin sat in his old lair. Stretched upon a mattress on the floor, lay Noah Claypole, otherwise *Morris Bolter*, fast asleep. Towards him the old man sometimes directed his eyes for an instant, and then brought them back again to the wasting candle. *

He sat without changing his attitude, or appearing to take the smallest heed of time, until the door-bell rang. He crept up-stairs, and presently returned accompanied by a man muffled to the chin, who carried a bundle under one arm. Throwing back his outer coat, the man displayed the *burly frame of Sikes, the housebreaker.*[1]

'*There!*' laying the bundle on the table. 'Take care of that, and do the most you can with it. It's been trouble enough to get. I thought I should have been here three hours ago.'

Fagin laid his hand upon the bundle, and locked it in the cupboard.[2] But he did not take *his eyes off the robber, for an instant.*

'Wot now?' cried Sikes. 'Wot do you look at a man, like that, for?'

Fagin raised his right hand,[3] and shook his trembling forefinger in the air.

'Hallo!' *feeling in his breast.* 'He's gone mad. I must look to myself here.'

'No, no, it's not—you're not the person, Bill. I've no—no fault to find with you.'

'Oh! you haven't, haven't you?' *passing a pistol into a more convenient pocket.*[4] 'That's lucky—for one of us. Which one that is, don't matter.'

'I've got that to tell you, Bill, will make you worse than me.'

'Aye? Tell away! Look sharp, or Nance will think I'm lost.'

'*Lost!* She has pretty well settled that, in her own mind, already.'

He looked, perplexed, into the old man's face, and reading no satisfactory explanation of the riddle there, clenched his coat collar in his huge hand and shook him soundly.

'Speak, will you? Or if you don't, it shall be for want of breath. Open

---

[1] *Sikes* doubly underlined.

[2] Marginal stage-direction *Cupboard action.* Just below, *an instant* is doubly underlined.

[3] Marginal stage-direction *Action.* In *Berg*, this paragraph has double vertical lines against it in the margin. According to Kent (p. 261), 'Not a word of it was said. It was simply *done.*' And similarly about the next *Action*: 'Not a word was said about the pistol —the marginal direction was simply attended to.'

[4] Marginal stage-direction *Action.*

your mouth and say wot you've got to say. Out with it, you *thundering, blundering, wondering* old *cur*,[1] out with it!'

[2]'Suppose that lad that's lying there———' Fagin began.

Sikes turned round to where Noah was sleeping, as if he had not previously observed him. 'Well?'

'Suppose that lad was to peach—to blow upon us all. Suppose that lad was to do it, of his own fancy—not grabbed, tried, earwigged by the parson and brought to it on bread and water,—but of his own fancy; to please his own taste; stealing out at nights to do it. Do you hear me? Suppose he did all this, what then?'

'What then? If he was left alive till I came, I'd grind his skull under the iron heel of my boot into as many grains as there are hairs upon his head.'

'What if *I*[3] did it! *I*, that know so much, and could hang so many besides myself!'

'I don't know. I'd do something in the jail that 'ud get me put in irons; and, if I was tried along with you, I'd fall upon you with them in the open court, and beat your brains out afore the people. I'd smash your head as if a loaded waggon had gone over it.'

Fagin looked hard at the robber; and, motioning him to be silent,[4] stooped over the bed upon the floor, and shook the sleeper to rouse him.

'Bolter! Bolter! *Poor lad!*'[5] said Fagin, looking up with an expression of devilish anticipation, and speaking slowly and with marked emphasis. '*He's tired*—tired with watching for *her*[6] so long—watching for *her*, Bill.'

'Wot d'ye mean?'

Fagin made no answer, but bending over the sleeper again, hauled him into a sitting posture. When his assumed name had been repeated several times, Noah rubbed his eyes, and, giving a heavy yawn, looked sleepily about him.

'Tell me that again—once again, just for him to hear,' said the Jew, *pointing to Sikes* as he spoke.[7]

'Tell yer what?' *asked the sleepy Noah, shaking himself pettishly.*

'That about———NANCY!!'[8] You followed her?'

'Yes.'

---

[1] Underlining in crescendo: once for *thundering*, twice for *blundering*, thrice for *wondering*.

[2] Marginal stage-direction (*Points to Bed*). In *Berg*, this is *Bed Action*.

[3] Like the *I* in the next sentence, this is italic in the novel and in both Readings texts.

[4] Marginal stage-direction *Bed Stooping Action.*

[5] Doubly underlined.

[6] *her . . . her* italic in the novel and in the Readings texts; also, in both cases, doubly underlined.

[7] Marginal stage-direction *Pointing Action*. In *Berg*, which here has *Point Action*, there is a rough sketch of a hand with pointing forefinger.

[8] NANCY is in capitals thus in the novel and the Readings texts; in *Suzannet* it is doubly underlined.

'To London Bridge?'

'Yes.'

'Where she met two people?'

'So she did.'

'A gentleman and a lady that she had gone to of her own accord before, who asked her to give up all her pals, and Monks first, which *she did*— and to describe him, which *she did*—and to tell her what house it was that we meet at, and go to, which *she did*—and where it could be best watched from, which *she did*—and what time the people went there, which *she did*. *She did all this*.[1] She told it *all*, every word, without a threat, without a murmur—*she did*—*did she not?*'

'All right,' *replied Noah, scratching his head*.[2] 'That's just what it was!'

'What did they say about last Sunday?'

'About last Sunday! Why, I told yer that before.'

'Again. *Tell it again*!'

'They asked her,' as he grew more wakeful, and seemed to have a dawning perception who Sikes was, 'they asked her why she didn't come, last Sunday, as she promised. She said she couldn't.'

'*Why?* Tell *him that*.'[3]

'Because she was forcibly kept at home by Bill—Sikes——the man that she had told them of before.'

'What more of him? What more of Bill—Sikes—the man she had told them of before? Tell him that, *tell him that*.'

'Why, that she couldn't very easily get out of doors unless he knew where she was going to, and so the first time she went to see the lady, she —ha! ha! ha![4] it made me *laugh* when she said it, *that* did—she gave him, a drink *of laudanum*!! ha! ha! ha!'[5]

Sikes rushed from the room, and darted up the stairs.

'Bill, *Bill*!'[6] cried Fagin, following him, hastily. 'A word. Only a word.'

'Let me out. Don't *speak* to me! it's not *safe. Let me out*.'

'Hear me speak a word,' rejoined Fagin, *laying his hand upon the lock*.[7] 'You won't be——you won't be——*too—violent*, Bill?'

The day was breaking, and there was light enough for the men to see

---

[1] *She did all this* doubly underlined; so, below, are *all* and *she did—did*.

[2] Marginal stage-direction *Sleepy Action*.

[3] *Why* and *him* doubly underlined. After 'Tell *him that*' there is a manuscript insertion, deleted, of a repeated 'Tell *him* that'.

[4] Doubly underlined; so, below, are *that* and *laudanum*.

[5] Dickens wrote to Georgina Hogarth on 7 March 1869: 'As always happens now— and did not at first—they [the Manchester audience] were unanimously taken by Noah Claypole's laugh' (*N*, iii. 710). The concluding 'ha! ha! ha!' is added in handwriting in *Suzannet*.

[6] Doubly underlined.

[7] Marginal stage-direction *Action*.

each other's faces. They exchanged a brief glance; there was the same fire in the eyes of both.[1]

'I mean, not too——*violent*——for——for——*safety*. Be *crafty*, Bill, and not too *bold*.'[2]

The robber dashed into the silent streets.

Without one pause, or moment's consideration; without once turning his head to the right or left; without once raising his eyes to the sky, or lowering them to the ground, but looking straight before him with savage resolution: he muttered not a word, nor relaxed a muscle, until he reached his own house-door.——He opened it, *softly*,[3] with a key; strode lightly up the stairs; and entering his own room, *double-locked the door, and drew back the curtain of the bed*.[4]

The girl was lying, half-dressed, upon the bed. He had roused her from her sleep, for she raised herself with a hurried and startled look.

'Get up!'

'It *is*[5] you, Bill!'

'*Get up*!!!'[6]

There was a candle burning, but he drew it from the candlestick, and hurled it under the grate. Seeing the faint light of early day without, the girl rose to undraw the curtain.

'*Let it be*. There's light enough for wot I've got to do.'——[7]

'*Bill, why do you look like that at me?*'[8]

The robber regarded her, for a few seconds, with dilated nostrils[9] *and heaving breast; then, grasping her by the head and throat, dragged her into the middle of the room, and placed his heavy hand upon her mouth.*

'You were watched to-night, *you she-devil; every word you said was heard*.'[1]

'Then if every word I said was heard, it was heard that I spared you. Bill, *dear Bill*, you cannot have the heart to kill me. Oh! think of all I have given up, only this one night, for *you*. Bill, *Bill*![2] For dear God's sake, for your own, for mine, stop before you *spill my blood*!!! I have

---

[1] In *Berg*, the whole paragraph is underlined, and 'there was the same fire in the eyes of both' doubly underlined.

[2] *safety* and *bold* doubly underlined.

[3] *softly* doubly underlined. *Suzannet* has here the marginal stage-direction *Murder coming*; in *Berg* it occurs, more plausibly, at the end of this paragraph.

[4] Marginal stage-direction *Action*.

[5] *is* italic in the novel and in both Readings texts; doubly underlined in *Suzannet*.

[6] Trebly underlined.

[7] *Let it be* doubly underlined. After '. . . got to do', a very long dash, followed by (*Pause*), trebly underlined.

[8] Whole speech has double interrupted underlining.

[9] *dilated nostrils* doubly underlined.

[1] *devil* trebly underlined; *she-* and *word* and *heard* doubly underlined.

[2] *Bill* and, below, *upon my guilty soul I have*, doubly underlined.

been *true* to you, *upon my guilty soul I have*!!! The gentleman and that dear lady told me to-night of a home in some foreign country where I could end my days in solitude and peace.[1] Let me see them again, and beg them, on my knees, to show the same mercy to you; and let us both leave this dreadful place, and far apart lead better lives, and forget how we have lived, except in prayers, and never see each other more. It is never too late to repent. They told me so—I feel it now. But we must have *time*—we must have a *little, little time*!'[2]

The housebreaker freed one arm, and grasped his pistol. The certainty of immediate detection if he fired, flashed across his mind; and he beat it *twice* upon the upturned face *that almost touched his own*.[3]

She staggered and fell, but raising herself on her knees, *she drew from her bosom a white handkerchief—Rose Maylie's*[4]*—and holding it up towards Heaven, breathed one prayer, for mercy to her Maker.*

It was a ghastly figure to look upon. The murderer staggering backward to the wall, and shutting out the sight with his hand, seized a heavy club, and struck her down!!![5]

The bright sun burst upon the crowded city in clear and radiant glory. *Through costly-coloured glass and paper-mended window, through cathedral dome and rotten crevice*, it shed *its equal ray*. It lighted up *the room* where *the murdered woman* lay.[6] It did. He tried to shut it out, but *it would stream in*. If the sight had been a *ghastly* one in the *dull morning*, what was it, *now*, in all that *brilliant light*!!![7]

He had not moved; he had been afraid to stir. There had been a moan and motion of the hand; and, with terror added to rage, he had struck and

[1] The speech to which this refers is the square-bracketed (optional?) deletion: see above, p. 477, note 3.

[2] Doubly underlined. 'It is [in the murder-scene], of course, that the excitement of the audience is wrought to its highest pitch, and that the acme of the actor's art is reached. The raised hand, the bent-back head, are good; but shut your eyes, and the illusion is more complete. Then the cries for mercy, the "Bill! dear Bill! for dear God's sake!" uttered in tones in which the agony of fear prevails over the earnestness of the prayer, the dead, dull voice as hope departs, are intensely real. When the pleading ceases, you open your eyes with relief, in time to see the impersonation of the murderer seizing a heavy club, and striking his victim to the ground' (Edmund Yates, op. cit., p. 63).

[3] *twice* doubly underlined.

[4] *Rose Maylie's* doubly underlined.

[5] *struck her* underlined doubly. Marginal stage-direction *Action*. Dickens wrote on 9 April 1869: 'I don't think a hand moved while I was doing [the murder] last night, or an eye looked away. And there was a fixed expression of horror of me, all over the theatre, which could not have been surpassed if I had been going to be hanged to that red velvet table' (*N*, iii. 718–19).—This ends ch. 47; *Berg* continues with the first paragraph of ch. 48, subsequently deleted by Dickens, and has against it the marginal stage-direction *Mystery*. (In *Suzannet* this is placed half-way down the paragraph.) In both texts, most of the underlining here is of the double interrupted kind.

[6] *the room*, and *now* below, doubly underlined.

[7] Marginal stage-direction *Terror to the End*; in *Berg*, this is emphatically capitalized— *Terror To The End*.

struck again. Once he threw a rug over it; but it was worse to *fancy* the *eyes*,[1] and imagine them moving towards him, than to see them glaring upward, as if *watching the reflection of the pool of gore that quivered and danced in the sunlight on the ceiling*. He had plucked it off again. And there was the body—mere flesh and blood, no more—but *such* flesh, *and so much blood*!!!

He struck a light, kindled a fire, and thrust the club into it. There was hair upon the end, which shrunk into a light cinder, and whirled up the chimney. Even that frightened him; but he held the weapon till it broke, and then piled it on the coals to burn away, and smoulder into ashes. He washed himself, and rubbed his clothes; there were spots upon them that would not be removed, but he cut the pieces out, and burnt them. *How those stains were dispersed about the room! The very feet of his dog were bloody*!!!![2]

All this time he had, *never once*, turned his *back* upon the *corpse*. He now moved, *backward*, towards the door: dragging the dog with him, shut the door softly, locked it, took the key, and left the house.[3]

As he gradually left the town behind him all that day, and plunged that night into the solitude and darkness of the country, he was *haunted by that ghastly figure following at his heels*. He could hear its garments rustle in the leaves; and every breath of wind came laden with that last low cry. If *he* stopped, *it* stopped.[4] If *he* ran, *it* followed; not running too—that would have been a relief—but borne on one slow melancholy air that never rose or fell.

At times, he turned to beat this phantom off, though it should look him dead; but the hair rose on his head, and his blood stood still, for it had turned with him, and was behind him then.[5] He leaned his back against a bank, and felt that it stood above him, visibly out against the cold night sky. He threw himself on his back upon the road. *At his head it stood, silent, erect, and still : a human gravestone with its epitaph in Blood*!![6] *

Suddenly, towards daybreak, he took the desperate resolution of going back to London. 'There's somebody to speak to there, at all events. A hiding-place, too, in our gang's old house in Jacob's Island.—I'll risk it.'

Choosing the least frequented roads for his journey back, he resolved

---

[1] *fancy* and *eyes*, and *so much blood* below, doubly underlined.

[2] *The very feet of his dog were bloody* trebly underlined. Vertical lines in the margin, against this sentence.

[3] Here the printed text of *Berg* (the version performed at the Trial Reading) ends. The extra narrative resumes at a point several pages later in ch. 48.

[4] The *he . . . it . . . he . . . it* were underlined in the *Berg* manuscript, and printed as italic in *Suzannet*, where they are all underlined; *ran* and *followed* are doubly underlined.

[5] In *Berg*, the words from 'but the hair' to 'behind him then' are underlined.

[6] *Blood* underlined doubly.

to lie concealed within a short distance of the city until it was dark night again, and then proceed to his destination. * He did this, and limped in among three affrighted fellow-thieves, the ghost of himself—blanched face, sunken eyes, hollow cheeks—*his dog at his heels covered with mud, lame, half blind, crawling as if those stains had poisoned him*!!¹

All three men shrank away. Not one of them spake.

'You that keep this house.—Do you mean to sell me, or to let me lie here 'till the hunt is over?'

'You may stop if you think it safe.² * But what man ever escaped the men who are after you!'

Hark!!!!³ A great sound coming on like a rushing fire! What? *Tracked so soon?* The hunt was up already? Lights gleaming below, voices in loud and earnest talk, hurried tramp of footsteps on the wooden bridges over Folly Ditch, * a beating on the heavy door and window-shutters of the house, * a waving crowd in the outer darkness like a field of corn moved by an angry storm!

'The tide was in, as I come up. Give me a rope. I may drop from the top of the house, at the back into the Folly Ditch, and clear off that way, or be stifled. *Give me a rope*!'

No one stirred. They pointed to where they kept such things, and the murderer hurried with a strong cord to the housetop. *Of all the terrific yells that ever fell on mortal ears, none could exceed the furious cry when he was seen.*⁴ Some shouted to those who were nearest, to set the house on fire; others adjured the officers to shoot him dead; others, with execrations, clutched and tore at him in the empty air; some called for ladders, some for sledge-hammers; some ran with torches to and fro, to seek them. * '*I promise Fifty Pounds*,' cried Mr. *Brownlow*⁵ from the nearest bridge, 'to *the man who takes that murderer alive*!' *

He set his foot against the stack of chimneys, fastened one end of the rope firmly round it, and with the other made a strong running noose by the aid of his hands and teeth. With the cord round his back, he could let himself down to within a less distance of the ground than his own height, and had his knife ready in his hand to cut the cord, and drop.

At the instant that he brought the loop over his head before slipping it beneath his arm-pits, *looking behind him* on the *roof* he *threw up his arms, and yelled*, '*The eyes again*!'⁶ Staggering as if struck by lightning, he lost his balance and tumbled over the parapet. The noose was at his neck;

---

¹ Doubly underlined from *lame* to *poisoned him*. The final phrase ('crawling as if...') does not appear in the novel.
² On the textual differences from the novel, in the following sentences, see the head-note.
³ *Hark* trebly underlined. Marginal stage-direction *Action*.
⁴ *he was seen* doubly underlined.
⁵ *Brownlow* doubly underlined.
⁶ *yelled* and *again* trebly underlined; *eyes* underlined four times.

it ran up with his weight; tight as a bowstring, and swift as the arrow it speeds. He fell five-and-thirty feet, and hung with his open *knife clenched in his stiffening hand*!!!

The *dog* which had lain concealed 'till now, ran backwards and forwards on the parapet with a dismal howl, and, collecting himself for a spring, jumped for the *dead man's shoulders*. Missing his aim, he fell into the ditch, turning over as he went, and striking against a stone, *dashed out his brains*!![1]

THE END OF THE READING

[1] *dashed out his brains* underlined doubly.